ANALYSIS

OF

M. ORTOLAN'S

INSTITUTES OF JUSTINIAN,

INCLUDING THE

HISTORY AND GENERALIZATION

OF

ROMAN LAW.

BY

T. LAMBERT MEARS, M.A., LL.D. (LOND.),

OF THE INNER TEMPLE, BARRISTER-AT-LAW.

Published with the late M. Ortolan's permission.

THE LAWBOOK EXCHANGE, LTD.
Clark, New Jersey

ISBN: 9781584777571 (hardcover)
ISBN: 9781616190835 (paperback)

Lawbook Exchange edition 2010

The quality of this reprint is equivalent to the quality of the original work.

THE LAWBOOK EXCHANGE, LTD.
33 Terminal Avenue
Clark, New Jersey 07066-1321

*Please see our website for a selection of our other publications
and fine facsimile reprints of classic works of legal history:*
www.lawbookexchange.com

Library of Congress Cataloging-in-Publication Data

Mears, T. Lambert (Thomas Lambert), 1839-1918.
  Analysis of M. Ortolan's Institutes of Justinian, including the
history and generalization of Roman Law / by T. Lambert Mears.
    p. cm.
  Originally published: London : Stevens and Sons, 1876.
  Includes index.
  ISBN-13: 978-1-58477-757-1 (cloth : alk. paper)
  ISBN-10: 1-58477-757-5 (cloth : alk. paper)
  1. Roman law--Sources. 2. Roman law--History. I. Ortolan, J.-L.
-E. (Joseph-Louis-Elzéar), 1802-1873. Explication historique des
Instituts de l'empereur Justinien. II. Ortolan, J.-L.-E.
(Joseph-Louis-Elzéar), 1802-1873. Histoire de la législation
romaine et généralisation du droit. III. Title.
  KJA190.M43 2007
  340.5'4--dc22
                              2007048368

Printed in the United States of America on acid-free paper

ANALYSIS

OF

M. ORTOLAN'S

INSTITUTES OF JUSTINIAN,

INCLUDING THE

HISTORY AND GENERALIZATION

OF

ROMAN LAW.

BY

T. LAMBERT MEARS, M.A., LL.D. (LOND.),
OF THE INNER TEMPLE, BARRISTER-AT-LAW.

Published with the late M. Ortolan's permission.

LONDON:
STEVENS AND SONS, 119, CHANCERY LANE.
1876.

PREFACE.

M. ORTOLAN'S *Explication Historique des Instituts de Justinien* has been long recognised in this country as the standard text-book on Roman Law, and, by the regulations of the University of London, the study of the entire work is made compulsory on all candidates for its Law Degrees.

The commentary was first published in 1827. Between that time and M. Ortolan's lamented death, in 1873, seven new editions appeared; and, as each embodied the latest researches of this laborious and talented writer, the work grew into three bulky volumes.

The difficulty experienced by English students in attempting, without assistance, to master so exhaustive and lengthy a French commentary on a Latin work, has compelled many to resort to English authors, whose works, though of a much less comprehensive character, are mainly based upon M. Ortolan's labours.

The original work consists of three parts, viz.:—

(1). The History of Roman Law;

(2). The Generalisation of Roman Law;

(3). The Commentary on the Institutes of the Emperor Justinian.

The analysis is divided in the same way as, and embodies the whole of the information contained in, the original work; but to make the compendium of practical utility to the student, pains have been taken to collect, condense, transpose, and occasionally interpolate additional matter; whilst repetition has been avoided by references in one part to the corresponding portions of the other two parts.

As the third part practically includes also a commentary on the elementary treatise which served as the basis of the Imperial compilation, a student who is provided with the text of the *Institutes of Gaius* will find himself able to dispense with any special commentary on that author.

The review of the epochs in the history of Roman Law, and M. Ortolan's masterly summaries of the contents of the four books of the Institutes, have been retained in a very condensed form, so as to give the student an opportunity of testing his knowledge as he proceeds; and the paragraphs are numbered as in the original work, in order that the index to the present volume may be used to supply that deficiency in the French text. For the convenience of the English student, the dates are given throughout the analysis according to the Christian era, instead of being referred to the foundation of the city of Rome.

T. L. M.

9, *King's Bench Walk, Temple,*
1st August, 1876.

CONTENTS.

Part I.—History of Roman Legislation.

FIRST EPOCH.—The Kings.

B.C.		PAR.
	Introduction	1
	Mythical origin of Rome	2
	Indigenous population of Italy	8
	Conjectures of Niebuhr	12
	Civil and political Institutions—Patricians, plebeians, slaves	15
	Patrons, clients, *gentes*	16
	Tribes, *Curiæ*	21
	Comitia Curiata	27
	Senate	33
	King	36
753.	*Romulus*, Elements of private law	37
715.	*Numa Pompilius*—Sacred law	38
	Calendar, *Dies fasti*	41
	Lex Regia	45
	Feciales	46
640.	*Ancus Martius*—Separate plebean population	47
617.	*Tarquinius Priscus*—Alteration in the gens and the senate	47
578.	*Servius Tullius*	47
	Census	55
	Centuriæ	56
	Equites	61
	Comitia Centuriata—Local tribes	66
534.	*Tarquinius Superbus*—**Lex Papiria**	76
510.	Expulsion of the Kings	77
	Review of the preceding period—	
	Foreign policy	78
	Sacred law	84
	Private law	85
	Manners and customs	86

SECOND EPOCH.—The Republic.

§ 1. *To the Laws of the Twelve Tables.*

B.C.		PAR.
	New government—consuls—senate	93
508.	**Leges Valeriæ**—*Quæstores parricidii*	94
501.	*Dictator—Magister Equitum*	98
494.	**Leges Sacræ**—Secession of the Plebs, *Tribuni plebis*	103
489.	*Comitia Tributa*—**Plebiscita**	106
	Ædiles Plebeii	108
452.	*Decemviri—Ten* Tables, origin and character	109
451.	**Twelve Tables**—Fragments of	112
	Legis actiones	140

§ 2. *From the Twelve Tables to the submission of all Italy.*

		PAR.
449.	**Lex Valeria Horatia**	149
445.	**Lex Canuleia**	150
	Tribuni militum	151
443.	*Censores*	152
396.	*Stipendium*—Rome burnt by the Gauls, Plebeians admitted to the Consulate	157
367.	*Prætor Urbanus*	160
	Ædiles Curules	161
	Judex, Arbiter, Recuperatores	162
	Centumviri	166
326.	**Lex Petillia Papiria**	175
303.	**Jus Flavianum**	176
286.	**Lex Hortensia**	178
272.	Fall of Tarentum	180
266.	Submission of all Italy	
	Review of the preceding period—	
	Foreign policy	181
	Public law	198
	Sacred law	210
	Private law	212
	Manners and customs	219

§ 3. *From the submission of all Italy to the Empire.*

		PAR.
247.	*Prætor Peregrinus*	222
	Provinces	225
	Provincial Prætors	227
	Pro-consuls, Pro-prætors	228
	Responsa Prudentium	233
244.	**Lex Silia**, *condictio certæ pecuniæ*	242
234.	**Lex Calpurnia**, *condictio de omni certa re*	242
202.	**Jus Ælianum**	239

B.C.		PAR.
171.	**Lex Æbutia**	244
	Formulæ, ordinaria, and *extraordinaria judicia* ...	247
	Influence of Stoicism	263
	Leges Agrariæ. The Gracchi	265
	Quæstiones perpetuæ	272
	Leges Judiciariæ...	283
	Senatus-Consulta	287
	Jus Honorarium	290
91.	The Social War	298
87.	Civil Wars of Marius and Sylla	300
73.	Servile War	301
53.	Death of Crassus	302
48.	Cisalpine Gaul receives citizen rights, *Ædiles Cereales* ...	302
44.	Death of Cæsar	302
43.	Death of Cicero	302
	Review of the preceding period—	
	Foreign policy	308
	Public law	315
	Sacred law	327
	Private law	329
	Manners and customs	336

THIRD EPOCH.—The Emperors.

§ 1. *From the Establishment of the Empire to Constantine.*

31.	*Augustus* Emperor	337
	Imperial magistracies	338
	Constitutiones Principum	350
	Jus publice respondendi	355
	Proculeiani and *Sabiniani*	362
18 (and A.D. 9).	**Leges Julia et Papia**	369
	Fidei-Commissa, codicilli	378
A.D.		
4.	**Lex Ælia Sentia**	378
8.	**Lex Furia Caninia**	378
14.	*Tiberius*	381
19.	**Lex Junia Norbana**	382
117.	*Hadrian:* Institution of Appeal—*Consistorium* and *Auditorium principis*	385
138.	*Antoninus Pius*	392
161.	*Divi Fratres* (Marcus *Aurelius* and Lucius *Verus*) ...	393
	Papirius, Scævola, Marcellus, and *Gaius*	393
193.	*Septimius Severus, Papinian*	395
211.	*Caracalla.* Modification of *Leges Julia et Papia.* Citizenship conceded to all subjects of the Empire ...	396
	Ulpian, Paul, Modestinus	419

viii   CONTENTS.

A.D.		PAR.
222.	*Alexander Severus*—Decline of letters and law ...	420
	Introduction of Christianity. Irruption of the Barbarians	422
284.	*Diocletian*. Division of the Empire between two Augusti and two Cæsars. Decay of the system of *formulæ*. *Judicia Extraordinaria*	427
	Review of the preceding period—	
	External situation	434
	Public law	435
	Sacred law	445
	Private law	446

§ 2. *From Constantine to Justinian.*

313.	*Constantine* Emperor	456
321.	Constitution invalidating notes of *Paul* and *Ulpian* ...	456
327.	Writings of *Paul* invested with authority	456
	Gregorian and *Hermogenian codes*	459
325.	Christianity the religion of the Empire. Council of *Nicæa*	467
	Foundation of *Constantinople*	469
	Magistracies created by Constantine	471
	Innovations in private law	479
	Agricolæ (*Coloni*)	488
339.	*Constantine II*, partial abolition of *formulæ* ...	493
342.	*Constantius*, suppression of *formulæ*	493
360.	*Præfectus urbi* at Constantinople	494
361.	*Julianus*, revival of Polytheism	495
363.	*Jovianus*, restoration of Christianity	495
379.	*Valens, Valentinian* and *Theodosius—Defensores Civitatum*	496
395.	Division of the Empire	497
425.	*Theodosius II*. Public schools at Constantinople ...	498
426.	**Lex de responsis prudentum**	499
438.	**Codex Theodosianus**	502
	Fragmenta Vaticana—Mosaïc. et Roman. leg. collatio—Consultatio veteris cujusd. juris-consulti ...	511
476.	Fall of the Western Empire	526
506.	**Lex Romana Visigothorum—Lex Romana Burgundiorum—Edictum Theodorici**	529
527.	*Justinian* Emperor...	533
529.	*Codex Vetus*	539
533.	*Digesta*	544
	Institutiones	548
534.	*Codex Repetitæ prælectionis*	550
	Novellæ Constitutiones	552
	Tribonian	565

CONTENTS. ix

A.D.		PAR.
	Theophilus	566
	Schools of law	570
	Review of the preceding period—	
	External situation	576
	Public law	577
	Sacred law	581
	Private law	582

Roman Law after Justinian.

§ 1. *Destiny in the East.*

	Greek jurists of the sixth century	590
	Codes of Byzantine Emperors	592
	Greek jurists subsequent to the Basilicæ ...	594
1453.	Fall of the Eastern Empire	594
	Byzantine law after the sixteenth century ...	595

§ 2. *Destiny in the West.*

Cause of the maintenance of Justinian's laws	...	596
The School of Bologna	...	611
The *Scribentes* and *Humanistes* ...	...	629
Roman law as an element of French law	...	633

Periods in the History of Roman Law.

Part II.—Generalisation of Roman Law.

Introduction	..	1

§ 1. *Law and causes producing it.*

Idea of law	...	8
Consequences of law	...	15
Elements producing law	...	17

Persons.
Definition of persona	...	21
Composition of status	..	24
Libertas—servitus—civitas	...	26

x   CONTENTS.

	PAR.
Familia—potestas—manus—mancipium	40
Justum matrimonium	58
Cognatio	62
Agnatio	64
Gens	65
Affinitas	67
Existimatio	74
Rank	77
Religion	79
Domicile	80
Sex	84
Age	86
Infirmities	93
Tutela—cura	95
Juridical persons	99

Things.
Meaning of the word	105
Classification in respect of creation	109
,, ,, religion	111
,, ,, State	113
,, ,, owner	131
,, ,, physical nature	134
,, ,, divisibility	138
,, ,, genus and species ...	139
,, ,, aggregation	143

Facts, Events, or Acts.
Facts	145
Legal forms	150
Acts of the jus gentium	161
Consensus, Dolus	164
Non-juridical facts	167
Time and place	169
Proof	172
Presumptions	176
Doubt	181
Fictions	182

§ 2. *Of Rights and of Actions.*

Rights.
General classifications	187
Personal rights (obligations), creation	196
,, ,, transfer	210
,, ,, extinction	211
Real rights	217
,, Dominium	219
,, Possessio	221
,, kinds of ownership	226

CONTENTS. xi

	PAR.
Real rights, mode of acquisition	229
,, abstractions	235
,, successions	236

Actions.
Necessity of law and procedure	239
Meaning of actio	241
Jus-judicium	247
Public administration of justice	255
Systems of procedure—legis actiones	256
,, ,, formulæ	266
,, ,, extraordinaria judicia	291

Part III.—Commentary on Justinian's Institutes.

Argument and Preface ... 1

BOOK I.
TIT.
i. Of justice and of law	9
ii. Of natural law—jus gentium—civil law	19
iii. Of the law of persons	40
iv. Of the freeborn	50
v. Of freed persons	54
Modes of manumission	57
vi. By whom and for what reasons manumissions cannot be made	70
vii. Of the abrogation of the lex Fusia Caninia	78
Actions relating to liberty, &c.	82
viii. Of those who are their own masters, and of those under the power of others	83
Power over slaves	89
ix. Of paternal power	92
x. Of marriage	97
Effects of marriage	118
Dissolution of marriage	120
Concubinage	122
Legitimation	123

TIT.		PAR.
xi. Of adoption		129
Marital power		150
Power over the freeman acquired by mancipation		153
xii. By what means potestas is dissolved		155
Mode of dissolving the mancipium		166
Actions relating to family law		175
xiii. Of tutorship		180
xiv. Who could be appointed tutors under a will		185
xv. Of the legitimate tutorship of agnates		193
xvi. Of the loss or diminution of caput		197
xvii. Of the legitimate tutorship of patrons		218
xviii. Of the legitimate tutorship of ascendants		219
xix. Of fiduciary tutorship		221
xx. Of the Atilian and Juliotitian tutor		224
Of the administration of tutors		231
xxi. Of the authorisation of tutors		241
xxii. Of the extinction of the tutorship		250
Of the tutelage of women		254
xxiii. Of curators		263
The administration and termination of the cura		274
xxiv. Of the security given by tutors and curators		275
xxv. Of exemptions from tutorships and curatorships		280
Actions relating to the tutela and cura		284
xxvi. Of suspected tutors or curators		287

Abstract of Book I.

BOOK II.

i. Of the division of things		289
Things and ownership at the time of the Twelve Tables		292
,, ,, Gaius and Ulpian		302
,, ,, Justinian		322
Possession		346
Means of acquiring possession and ownership		354
Loss of possession and ownership		425
Actions relating to possession and ownership		431
ii. Of corporeal and incorporeal things		434
iii. Of prædial servitudes		444
iv. Of usufruct		471
v. Of usage and habitation		497
Slave labour		505
Actions relating to servitudes		507

CONTENTS. xiii

TIT.		PAR.
	Other real rights than ownership and servitudes	510
vi.	Of usucapion and possession of long standing	514
	Actions relating to usucapion and prescription	540
vii.	Of donations	541
	Gifts in view of death	548
	Gifts during lifetime	565
	Gifts between husband and wife	577
	Dowry and gifts on account of marriage	582
	Actions relating to donations	591
viii.	Of the power of alienation	595
ix.	Through whom property can be acquired	608
	Acquisitions by the filius familias	611
	Acquisitions by slaves	616
	Acquisitions by a stranger	630
	Acquisition by universality	637
	Inheritances	639
x.	Of the formalities of wills	648
xi.	Of the wills of soldiers	669
	Wills where the ordinary forms were dispensed with	680
xii.	Of persons incapacitated from making a will	681
xiii.	Of the disinheriting of children	692
xiv.	Of the constitution of heirs	715
	Who may be instituted	718
	Division of the inheritance	725
	Conditions affecting the inheritance	735
xv.	Of common substitution	742
xvi.	Of pupillary substitution	749
	Substitutions made by soldiers	771
xvii.	By what means wills may become invalid	773
xviii.	Of inofficious wills	788
xix.	Of the quality and differences of heirs	804
	Actions relating to testamentary inheritances	830
xx.	Of legacies	833
	Dies cedit and dies venit	850
	Catonian rule	857
	Things which may be left by legacy	865
	Accrual between co-legatees	868
	Things which may be left by legacy (continued)	885
	Loss, accruals, or diminutions of legacies	895
	Legacies of part of the inheritance	904
	Persons capable of receiving legacies	906
	Who may be charged with a legacy	921
	Conditions affecting legacies	924
xxi.	Of the revocation and transference of legacies	936
xxii.	Of the lex Falcidia	940
xxiii.	Of fidei-commissary inheritances	949
xxiv.	Of fidei-commissa of particular objects	971

CONTENTS.

TIT.		PAR.
xxv.	Of codicils	973
	Of the opening and preservation of wills	982
	Actions relating to legacies and fidei-commissa	988
	Abstract of Book II.	

BOOK III.

		PAR.
i.	Of intestate succession	994
	Law of the Twelve Tables	999
	Prætorian law	1008
	Imperial constitutions	1013
	Justinian's legislation	1014
ii.	Of agnate succession	1018
	Law of the Twelve Tables	1018
	Intermediate legislation	1021
	Prætorian law	1022
	Imperial constitutions	1023
	Justinian's legislation	1024
	The succession of the Gentiles	1032
iii.	Of the senatus-consultum Tertullianum	1054
iv.	Of the senatus-consultum Orphitianum	1065
v.	Of cognate succession	1070
vi.	Of the degrees of cognation	1075
vii.	Of the succession to freedmen	1081
	Law of the Twelve Tables	1082
	Prætorian law	1084
	Lex Papia Poppæa	1087
	Justinian's legislation	1088
viii.	Of the assignment of freedmen	1096
ix.	Of possessio bonorum	1099
	Collatio bonorum	1127
	Accrual between co-heirs	1132
	Transmission of the inheritance	1134
	Of those deprived for unworthiness	1138
	Actions relating to inheritances ab intestato, and to the possessio bonorum	1141
	Novels of Justinian as to succession	1143
x.	Of acquisition by adrogation	1145
xi.	Of the addictio of property in order to preserve gifts of freedom	1154
xii.	Of the abolished successions resulting from a venditio bonorum, or from the s. c. Claudianúm	1161
xiii.	Of obligations	1176
	General notions and kinds of obligations	1176
	Effects of obligations	1182
	Sources of obligations	1185
	Meaning of term conventio	1200

TIT.	PAR.
xiv. Of the modes of contracting obligations re	... 1205
Actions arising from contracts re	... 1230
xv. Of obligations verbis	... 1235
Actions resulting from stipulations	... 1260
xvi. Of co-stipulators and co-promissors	... 1264
xvii. Of the stipulations of slaves	... 1280
Stipulations of sons or daughters	... 1298
xviii. Of the division of stipulations	... 1304
xix. Of useless stipulations	... 1324
Adstipulators	... 1377
Sponsores and fide-promissores	... 1384
xx. Of fide-jussors	... 1392
Actions relating to adstipulatio and adpromissio	... 1401
S. C. Velleianum	... 1411
xxi. Of obligations litteris	... 1414
Chirographæ, syngraphæ, cautiones	... 1429
The exceptio non numeratæ pecuniæ	... 1435
xxii. Of consensual obligations	... 1442
xxiii. Of the contract of sale	... 1444
The form of the contract	... 1447
The object of the obligations in the contract	... 1450
The effects of the contract	... 1457
Accessory pacts	... 1481
Rescission	... 1486
Actions relating to the contract	... 1489
xxiv. Of letting on hire	... 1492
Emphyteusis	... 1501
Superficies	... 1511
Effects of the contract of hiring	... 1512
Extinction of the contract	... 1515
Actions relating to the contract	... 1520
xxv. Of partnership	... 1523
Actions relating to partnership	... 1544
xxvi. Of mandates	... 1550
Actions relating to mandates	... 1577
Civil law pacts	... 1580
Prætorian pacts	... 1611
Imperial law pacts	... 1618
Pactum nudum	... 1619
Prohibited agreements	... 1620
xxvii. Of obligations quasi ex contractu	... 1622
Culpa	... 1633
Mora	... 1655
Usuræ	... 1658
xxviii. Through whom obligations are acquired	... 1665
Transference of obligations	... 1669
xxix. Of the modes in which obligations are dissolved	... 1672

Abstract of Book III.

BOOK IV.

TIT.		PAR.
i.	Of obligations arising from delicts	1715
	Actions relating to theft	1726
ii.	Of the action for robbery with violence	1738
iii.	Of the lex Aquilia	1746
iv.	Of injuria	1764
v.	Of obligations quasi ex delicto	1781
	Natural obligations	1793
	Alternative and joint and several obligations	1809
vi.	Of actions	1829
	Legis actiones	1833
	Formulæ	1909
	Extraordinaria judicia	2055
vii.	Of contracts made with persons in the power of others	2201
viii.	Of noxal actions	2219
ix.	Of damage caused by animals	2227
x.	Of the power of representation	2228
xi.	Of security	2237
xii.	Of perpetual and temporary actions, and of those for and against heirs	2242
xiii.	Of exceptions	2248
xiv.	Of replications	2283
xv.	Of interdicts	2288
xvi.	Of the penalties on rash litigation	2335
xvii.	Of the office of judge	2342
xviii.	Of public accusations	2348

Abstract of Book IV.

PART I.

HISTORY OF ROMAN LEGISLATION.

1. The **Historical Method** is adopted and legal history traced through political history. Hence the subject is discussed under three divisions corresponding with the three epochs: (1) The Kings; (2) The Republic; (3) The Emperors.

FIRST EPOCH.—The Kings.

2. The **Origin of Rome** is shrouded in doubtful tradition. From the 6th century (Perizonius, 1685; Vico, 1725; De Beaufort, 1738; Niebuhr died 1831), attempts have been made to build up the real history of Rome and discard the myths of Roman historians.

6. The tendency of the poetry of Rome was to ignore the true ancestors of the people, the ancient inhabitants of Italy, and ascribe the origin of the city to the Greek legends of "The return of Hercules from his Iberian Expedition"; "The voyage of the Argonauts"; "The wanderings of Ulysses and Æneas after the fall of Troy"; and the legends of the wandering race known as the Pelasgians.

7. But the primitive source of the institutions, the religion, and the habits of the Romans (*e.g.*, religious rites, the magistracies—exterior signs, as *fasces, lictors, curule chairs*, etc.), is to be found in the early inhabitants of the country, and the discoveries of comparative philology point to a common origin in remote times of the whole of the tribes then scattered over Europe.

8. Of the so-called indigenous population of Italy three races formed the elements: (1) The Iberian; (2) The Celtic; and (3) The Ionian: but in the later period, immediately preceding the foundation of Rome, three smaller nationalities formed the germ of the Roman people, viz.: (1) The Latins; (2) The Sabines; (3) The Etruscans.

9. *Quirites* was the sacred name of the Sabines (derived from the goddess *Curis*, and hence their town *Cures*), from which came the

name *Quirinus*, applied to Romulus, the Quirinal hill, the name *Populus Romanus Quiritium*, and the symbol of the *lance* (*Hastæ Sabinæ* were called *cures*, indicating power).

10. *Luceres* was probably derived from *lucumo*, an *Etruscan* title (as suggested by Niebuhr), borne by Cælius Vibennus, the Etruscan chief; and hence indicates the Etruscan element in the origin of Rome.

12. Niebuhr accounts for the three national elements in the composition of the state by assuming that Rome was a little fortified town, on the *Palatine* hill, deriving its origin from remote Pelasgian times, and uniting to itself, in the course of time, the villages on the neighbouring hills, then a *Sabine* town on the Quirinal, and an *Etruscan* town on the Cælian hill; but these assertions are purely conjectural.

14. The present attempt to present a view of the external history of Roman law is based as far as possible on written sources furnished by the Romans themselves, and follows the course of events under the heads of—(1) Public Law, which prescribes the constitution of the State, determines the mode of making laws, of rendering justice, appointing officers, making peace and war. (2) Sacred Law, which, with the Romans, was intimately connected with political law, and governed the ceremonies of religion, and the nomination and authority of the Pontiffs. (3) Private Law, including customs, which together regulate the interests of individuals in their mutual relations, as in marriage, contract, property, succession.

Civil and Political Institutions.

15. The earliest historical evidences of Rome exhibit a state of society common to all the Italian cities at that time, and the inhabitants are divided into two great classes—*aristocracy* and *slavery*—the latter consisting of two sub-divisions.

The **Patres-Patricii** were a superior and dominant caste, consisting of a number of noble families (*gentes*), with distinct rites of marriage, peculiar laws, and a monopoly of priestly functions, both political and judicial. *Patres* and *patricii*, both from *pater*, indicate the kind of absolute power of primitive times (though Roman writers differ as to the etymology), and *pater familias* meant simply chief of the family; for he might have been without children or himself an infant, and only possessed of goods or slaves; hence *pater* expressed power, not tenderness, and possibly *patricii* may have meant, in early times, the descendants of *patres*.

The **Plebs-Plebeii** were an intermediate class, consisting of an inferior and oppressed caste, unable to unite in marriage with the former, not admitted to their rites or to their laws, distributed by families under their protection (*patroni-clientes*), and excluded from public functions.

The **Servi-Mancipia** were a third portion of the population, without rights of any kind, living like animals, and standing towards the head of the family as a thing, an object of property.

FIRST EPOCH.—THE KINGS.

16. **Patroni-Clientes.**—The reciprocal duties of patrons (*Patronus* diminutive of *Pater*) and clients (? *colientes*, *i.e.*, cultivators of the patrician estates) were, on the part of the *patrons*—protection and assistance, inform clients of the law, take care of their interests, and carry on their affairs in their absence as well as presence, act as plaintiffs or defendants for them in civil actions—on the part of the *Clients*—contribution towards the marriage portion of their patrons' daughters, ransom their patrons or their sons, pay costs of actions or penalties, and assist towards the costs of magistracy, and other public expenses. Between the two—mutual good faith, impossibility of being accuser, or witness, or of giving a vote for, or of passing into the ranks of the opposite side, under penalty of being regarded as a traitor, and liability to be sacrificed to the gods (*sacer esto*) or killed by anyone with impunity.

The analogy between this and the later *feudal* system is obvious.

The **Gens** may be defined thus : To constitute it no ancestor must ever have been in slavery or subjection of any kind (*Quorum majorum nemo servitutem servivit*—Cicero. *Patricii—Qui patrem ciere possent, id est nihil ultra quam ingenuos. Plebs—In qua gentes civium patriciæ non insunt*) ; and to this idea of pure blood still clings the modern gentilhomme—gentiluomo—gentleman.

Ingenuus signified primitively the fact of being a member of a *gens*, *i.e.*, of ancestors having never been enslaved, etc.

The *gens* had reversionary rights of guardianship, and succession to clients and freedmen.

20. **Populus Romanus** meant the Roman people composed of *both patricians and plebeians* (not, as Niebuhr assumes, ignoring the latter altogether).

21. **Tribus Curiæ.**—Probably from the same three races mentioned above (par. 8) sprang the division from the earliest times of the people into *three tribes* : viz. (1) *Ramnenses* (from Romulus, chief of the Latins); (2) *Tatienses* (Tatius, chief of the Sabines); and (3) *Luceres* (Lucumon, chief of the Etruscans) ; and this was not only *personal* but also territorial, the *Ager Romanus* being divided into three portions. Each tribe was divided into ten *curies*, making thirty *curiæ* in all.

23. Members of the same tribe, *tribules*, and *curia*, *curiales*, were bound together by various ties, *e.g.*, religious (*curionia sacra, curiales flamines*, etc.) ; social (common annual feast, etc.) ; military (each curia furnished 1000 men for a legion) ; and political (grouped by curiæ for voting).

27. **Comitia Curiata.**—This meeting of the thirty *curiæ* in the *Comitium* was the most ancient assembly. Its business consisted (1) In appointing to those *priestly offices*, the election to which rested with the people ; (2) In selecting magistrates (including the king) ; (3) In making the *lex curiata* (the *lex regia*, under the emperors), by which the *imperium* (or right to command) was conferred on magistrates (including the king) after their election ; (4) In deciding as to the composition of families ; and (5) As to testamentary successions.

28. The power of the *Comitia curiata* was restrained by the following means: (1) It must be convoked by the magistrates for one matter at a time; (2) The magistrates were patricians and acted under the orders of the Senate; (3) The Augurs were patricians, and necessary parties; (4) Yes or no, the only possible decision; (5) An Augur, declaring the auspices unfavourable, dissolved the assembly; (6) The subsequent assent of the senate necessary (*potestas in populo, auctoritas in senatu sit*).

29. Each *curia* had *one* vote (their order decided by lot); so that when sixteen *curiæ* had voted in the same way, the rest were not consulted. According to Niebuhr, the members of each *curia* were arranged in their respective gentes, and each *gens* had *one* vote in deciding the vote of the *curia*, so that the *plebeian* element in the population was effectually excluded from any political power.

31. In later times, for certain matters connected with religion—for investing the *imperium* by the *lex curiata*, etc.—the vote was given by thirty *lictors* representing the thirty *curiæ*.

33. **Senatus.**—If each *curia* was divided into *ten gentes*, probably one representative from each formed the *Senate* of 300 in the time of Tarquinius Priscus, which number continued down to the Republic.

The *Patres majorum gentium* probably were those and their descendants existing before Tarquin (or belonging to the two senior tribes, Ramnenses and Tatienses?). *Patres minorum gentium*, those subsequently enrolled (or belonging to the third tribe?). The *plebeian* senators admitted at a later period were called *conscripti* (or *adlecti*); hence the expression *patres conscripti*. Probably the senators were chosen by the king. The senate deliberated on public matters and discussed the propositions to be submitted to the *comitia curiata*. Its *auctoritas* was required even by the king.

36. **Rex.**—The king, nominated by the *curiæ*, and (after confirmation of the election by the *auctoritas* of the *senate*) invested with power by the *lex curiata*, was—(1) The general; (2) The high priest; and (3) A judicial magistrate.

37. **Jus Privatum.**—The elements of *private* law are ascribed to *Romulus* (B.C. 753); but they probably have their origin in the manners of the age which made the Romans regard their possessions, including wives and children as so much booty, over which they had entire control, extending even to life and death; hence the early views as to the *marital* and *paternal* power of the *pater familias*.

38. **Sacra Publica. Sacra Privata.**—To *Numa Pompilius* (B.C. 715) is ascribed the foundation of the sacred law, which formed an important element in Roman affairs. Human sacrifices were originally common, and led to the phrase "*sacer esto*." The religious practices were chiefly derived from the Etruscans, and *Labeo* wrote a commentary on them (lost).

Sacerdotal functions were a privilege of the Patrician caste, and borne by them like any other public duty, so that the individual was not debarred from marrying or aspiring to other dignities. The king was the head of the priests' colleges. The Augurs were consulted, and victims immolated on all important public occasions, and the validity of an act or its suspension often depended on the decisions of the priests after observation of the entrails of victims, flight of birds, etc.

The *sacra publica* were performed in the name and at the expense of the city.

40. The *sacra privata* were transmitted in families as part of the inheritance, and all important acts assumed a religious character: hence the sanctity of the oath, respect for things sacred, veneration for tombs, worship of their lares, etc.

41. **Dies-Fasti, Nefasti, Intercisi.**—The *Calendar* is said to have been improved by *Numa*, who, to the *Alban lunar* year of ten months added two more months; but this being still too short, the Pontiffs were charged with the necessary intercalations: hence their great power as to *dies fasti* and *nefasti*, for, besides the duration of magistracies, public and private fête days, etc., thus resting with them, no *sacramental* suit nor any of the acts of individuals done in imitation of these suits, such as constituting or extinguishing servitudes, freeing, emancipating, or adopting, etc., could be performed on *nefasti* days, and magistrates could only sit in the middle of the day on *intercisi* days; *i.e.*, days which were *nefasti* in the morning and evening.

43. Each year was marked by a *nail* fastened into the wall of the temple of Jupiter by the chief magistrate of Rome.

45. **Lex Regia** (see ante, par. 27, 31, and post, par. 350).

46. **Feciales.**—This college was devoted to *international* law, and to its twenty priests, drawn from the first Patrician families, were referred the arrangement of treaties, questions of peace, of war, of truces, of embassies, and as to the declaration of war. Sacramental formulæ accompanied each phase of the negotiation. Hurling a javelin across the frontier by the Fecial herald was the symbolic mode of commencing hostilities. In later times the ceremony was performed in a small field near the temple of Bellona, set apart for the purpose, and called the "enemy's field".

47. **Reforms of Servius Tullius.**—Under *Ancus Martius* (B.C. 640) the defeated people brought into the city, and admitted to its rights, were not made clients of the patrician *gentes*, and hence a new class of plebeians, who disturbed the existing divisions based on the three tribes and the thirty *curiæ*, and led to the attempts at an alteration made by *Tarquinius Priscus* (B.C. 617), carried out by his successor *Servius Tullius* (B.C. 578), who substituted an aristocracy of *money* for that of *race*, and instituted—(1) The census; (2) The *comitia centuriata*; (3) A new order of knights; (4) New *local* tribes.

55. The **Census** (*lustrum, populum lustrare*) took place every *five* years in connection with a review of the people and religious purification. A chapter (*caput*) was opened for each head of a family,

and his sons, wives, slaves, and property were detailed after *his name*. Hence the simple method, adopted in later times, of *freeing* a slave by inscribing his *name* in the register.

56. **Classes, Centuriæ.**—The details as to *property* ascertained by means of the census, led to the distribution of the citizens into classes and centuries for the purposes of—(1) Taxation; (2) Military service; and (3) Voting.

For *taxation*, the division was into *five* classes, all called *assidui*; *i.e.*, *assem dare*, taxed. The mass of the people, possessing less than the amount fixed for the lowest class (11,000 *as.*), were free from taxes (*proletarii*), and hence the popularity of the measure.

For *military service* (infantry) the same classes decided the nature and expense of the weapons, to be provided at the cost of the individual, but the liability to serve was carried below the lowest taxed class, though without expense to the individual. The mass of the Proletarii were for this purpose divided into three classes: (1) *Accensi* (or *Velati*), whose property exceeded 1500 *asses*, and who followed the army, taking the arms and place of those who fell. (2) *Proletarii*, or those possessing over 375 *asses*, and never called out except in extreme urgency, whilst the remainder (*capite censi*) were excluded from the army until the time of Marius.

61. **Equites.**—The division into classes was confined to the infantry. The *cavalry* held the place of honour, and consisted of *eighteen centuries*. Of these, six took precedence of the rest, because formed by doubling the three old patrician bodies of one hundred knights each, which, together constituted the guard (*celeres*) of Romulus, and were drawn from the three tribes. The remaining twelve centuries were made up by Tullius from the richest and best families in Rome.

63. The necessities of military service compelled distinctions *of age*: hence the infantry classes were divided into Centuries:—

(1) *Juniorum*, from sixteen upwards, for service abroad.

(2) *Seniorum*, from forty-five upwards, for defence at home, and additional centuries were composed of skilled soldiers (engineers), bandsmen, and supernumeraries.

64. In *Voting*, the aim of the arrangement was most apparent, for the internal division of classes into centuries was so arranged that the higher the class the greater the number of centuries composing it; hence, as each century had *one* vote, the rich, though inferior in number, balanced the poor, the whole mass of the *proletarii* having only one vote; the old balanced the young, etc.: and, on the whole, *wealth* had the majority, and therefore the power. The mode of voting further secured this result.

66. The **Comitia Centuriata** were held outside the walls, on the Field of Mars. They were convoked by trumpet, and attended by the people under arms; the votes were given in the order of the classes; the order of the centuries in the classes being decided by lot (those first entitled being called *prærogativa—præ-rogare*): hence, practically the lower classes were never consulted, for a

majority of votes stopped the proceedings. In course of time, the powers of this comitia were—(1) To make laws; (2) To decide on criminal accusations; (3) To create magistrates; and the powers of the *comitia curiata* were curtailed accordingly, until they became a shadow: but the six restraints (par. 28) were the same, until in B.C. 340, *Q. Publilius Philo,* a Plebeian Dictator, by the *Lex Publilia* (*Ut legum quæ comitiis centuriatis ferrentur, ante initum suffragium, Patres auctores fierent*—Livy), made the *auctoritas* of the senate to be given beforehand.

70. The precedence accorded to the knights (*Equites*) ultimately led to their placing themselves between the senate and the plebeians. The State defrayed the cost of the horses (*æs equestre*), and of their provender (*æs hordiarium*).

71. The three ancient tribes (*ex generibus*) gave place to the new tribes of Servius Tullius (*ex locis*):—

(1) Four *Urban* tribes, included the three ancient city tribes.

(2) *Rural* tribes, to an uncertain number (according to Livy, the total of urban and rural reached thirty-five), contained the district round Rome, and these rural tribes were increased as the frontier extended.

76. Jus civile Papirianum (B.C. 534).—*Pomponius* states that in the reign of the next and last king (Tarquinius Superbus), the Pontiff, *Sextus Papirius,* collected the *leges curiatæ* (or *regiæ*) passed by Romulus and his successors into one book; but this *lex papiria* is lost to us, and the laws themselves, on the expulsion of the kings, were all abolished by the *Lex Tribunicia.*

77. In B.C. 510, a revolution drove out the Tarquins, and a consular republic was established two and a half centuries after the building of Rome.

REVIEW OF THE PRECEDING PERIOD.

78. The policy of Rome was encroachment. At first the vanquished inhabitants of neighbouring towns are transported to Rome, and become citizens; then *colonies* of Roman citizens are sent to occupy conquered cities; and *dediticii* (or prisoners of war who surrendered to escape a worse alternative) come into existence. Those cities strong enough to resist the efforts of Rome, become at length *allies,* and originate the term *latini* (vetus Latium).

81. Three political bodies exist: (1) The people; (2) The senate; (3) The king: and these three exercise the *legislative* power—the king initiates a project, the senate discusses it, and refers it to the Comitia. The decision of the people is confirmed by the auctoritas of the senate; the *executive* power rests with the king, subject to the advice of the senate, and peace or war requires the assent of the people; the *judicial* power is in the king, who determines private matters himself; but *criminal* accusations, involving the life of a citizen, are referred to the people; the *electoral* power for high magistracies (including the king) rests with the *Comitia curiata.*

84. *Sacred Law* has an important influence through *three* institutions:—

(1) The *College of Pontiffs*, composed of *four patrician* members elected for life by their own body, the chief being the "*Pontifex maximus*", charged with adoptions, burials, private worship, etc., and keeping the annual *album* or record of events.

(2) The *College of Augurs*, of four members, who, when the auspices are unfavourable, can dissolve an assembly, stop a general about to fight, etc.

(3) The *College of Feciales*, or priests charged with matters concerning international law, alliances, and wars.

85. In *Private Law*, documents relating to the period are wanting, and the existence of laws made by the kings, as to marriage, *potestas*, debtors, etc., is disputed.

86. The *Manners* and *Customs* of this epoch must be looked at to discover those fixed *customary* rules which constituted the civil law of the period, and preceded *written* law.

The *jus Quiritium* confined the *connubium* (legal capacity to marry) and *commercium* (legal capacity to contract) to Roman citizens. Intermarriage was not permitted between patricians and plebeians: hence a tendency for the patrician *gentes* to die out.

88. *Manus, mancipium* (*manu capere*). The hand, the symbol of power, is the basis of all the Roman ideas as to property, slaves, children, wives, and freedmen; and the *lance*, the original means of acquiring everything, continues the symbolic mode of transacting business.

89. Although money (*pecunia*) existed in very early times in Italian cities, the method of weighing copper is retained in the ceremony *per æs et libram*, called *nexum* (later *mancipatio*), used in all dealings between the citizens, and adopted in plebeian marriages as one method of acquiring a wife (the religious ceremony, *confarreatio*, being exclusively patrician). The same symbolic mode of transfer was used by plebeians in *wills*, the patrician method being virtually a *lex curiata*.

91. The *Pater familias* is the only member of the family possessing a complete *persona* in private law; *i.e.*, capable of having, and being subject to rights; for he is absolute proprietor of the lives and property of all those under him, and from this spring six important heads, viz.:—

(1) Slavery—assimilating one class of men to things.

(2) Paternal power—rendering the son subject to the father all his life.

(3) The marital power.

(4) The power over free men, whether over adopted children or debtors: the latter, of two kinds, over those sentenced by law to work out their debt (*addicti*), and those voluntarily doing so (*nexi*).

(5) The power over the freed man.

(6) The power over the client, by which the old plebeian inhabitants were distributed amongst the patrician *gentes*, but which decayed with the latter.

SECOND EPOCH.—THE REPUBLIC.

92. The *Ager Romanus* at this time meant the actual Roman territory. It was successively extended by the kings, and distributed amongst the citizens, but *remained fixed* from the time of *Servius Tullius* (the present "*agro romano*").

The *Ager Publicus* was the land in the hands of the State, belonging to the people collectively, and either cultivated for the public profit or let out to private holders. This is the land of which the patrician *gentes* acquired possession without paying the rents due to the state, and hence the frequent demands made by the plebeians for their share. It *extended* with the arms of Rome, and embraced, before redistribution to private persons, the known world.

SECOND EPOCH.—The Republic.

§ 1. *To the laws of the twelve tables.*

93. The patricians and plebeians had united and overthrown the kings. They now commenced a struggle, which terminated only in both being subject to an imperial despotism.

The duties of the king passed to *two* annual *patrician consuls* elected by the people. The effect of this change was greatly to increase the power of the *Senate*, for the consuls acted under the direction of the latter.

Among the more important enactments of the period were the—

94. **Leges Valeriæ** passed in the *comitia centuriata* (B.C. 508), at the instance of the consul *Valerius Publicola*, and enacting that which probably existed as unwritten law previously, viz.:—

(1) The right of appeal (*provocatio ad populum*) should always lie against the decision of the magistrate whenever a *citizen's* life, liberty, or civic rights were involved in the sentence.

(2) *Quæstores parricidii* (*paris-cidium*, murder of one's like, homicide) should be appointed to preside at criminal trials (*qui capitalibus rebus præessent*), directing the mode of procedure and giving judgment in the name of the people.

These laws did not apply to strangers or slaves or extend beyond a mile from the city, nor did they interfere with the *patria patestas*.

97. To the same consul is attributed the separation of a part of the consular duties by the nomination of *two Questors* of the public treasure. At first the office was reserved to patricians, and subsequently became the preliminary step towards the dignities of the State.

98. The patricians evaded these *Leges Valeriæ* by providing (B.C. 501) for the nomination by the consuls of a *Dictator*, who should hold his irresponsible office in times of danger for six months. His deputy was called *magister equitum*, and both were patricians.

103. The contest between patricians and plebeians ended in the *secession of the Plebs*, and the appointment (B.C. 494) from their body

of two *Tribuni plebis*, who were invested with the *veto* or power of opposing (*intercessio*) the acts of the consuls, magistrates, and senate. Their persons were sacred (*sacrosancta*), as were also the laws by which they were appointed (*leges sacræ*), and the Aventine, on which the plebeians had encamped, became the *mons sacer*.

106. These magistrates were increased to five, and subsequently to ten. They convoked the *Plebs* in B.C. 489, with the assent of the senate, for the judgment of a patrician (Cariolanus), and from this dates the origin of the *Comitia Tributa*, or assembly of the Plebeians by tribes which subsequently acquired legislative power, the laws passed by it being called *plebis-scita*—ordinances of the plebeians. The unit for voting was the tribe, and each citizen in the tribe had an equal right. Hence the preponderance of caste in the *curiata*, and of wealth in the *centuriata*, was now overpowered by the local arrangements upon which the *tributa* depended.

108. In analogy to the position of the *Questors* towards the *consuls*, the plebeians created *two Ædiles Plebeii*, who acted under the Tribunes, and were entrusted with *Police* and other municipal duties.

109. The struggle made by the plebeians for an equality of rights, led at length to the appointment of the *Decemviri*, or ten annual absolute magistrates, whose exactions and despotism, culminating in the Virginia incident, brought about their speedy overthrow and the re-establishment of consuls and tribunes. But the special object for which these magistrates had been created, viz., the publication of the law, was attained, the Decemvirs first appointed having drawn up a code of *ten* tables, which was sanctioned by the *comitia centuriata*. Their successors (B.C. 451) added two more, making the *twelve tables* (*lex, leges XII Tabularum, lex decemviralis*), the foundation of Roman law.

Whether an embassy was sent to Greece for information as to their laws, is disputed; but though Attic legislation would appear not to have been unknown to the compilers of the twelve tables (see table vii (2)), they bear internal evidence of being a written enunciation of existing local customs; details are presumed known; and only principles are stated, except as to funerals, neighbours, and debtors. In these tables are to be found the germ of a number of institutions developed in the law of a later period, and hence the Romans always viewed them as the basis of their civil law. Many of the regulations are barbarous, and the style is abrupt and imperative. Their consideration reveals the actual habits of the nation and its degree of civilization.

112. From the "Republic" of Cicero, from the fragments found in the Digest, of the six books, written by Gaius, on the twelve tables, and from the Institutes of Gaius and other authors, an attempt may be made to partially reconstruct these tables, which formed the model for subsequent legislation (*e.g.*, the Edict of the Prætors, the Code of Theodosius, the Code and Digest of Justinian).

The fragments of the Twelve Tables.

The first three tables give the opening, the course, and the issue of the trial to execution. The titles of the tables are conjectural.

i. *De in jus vocando.*—Of summoning before the magistrate:—
(1) If after summons the defendant fail to appear, he may be seized in the presence of witnesses. (2) If attempting flight he may be detained by force. (3) But a conveyance must be provided if he be ill or infirm. (4) The surety for a taxpayer must also be a taxpayer; (5) The case may be settled by mutual agreement. (6) Otherwise it is to be brought on in open court before noon in the presence of both parties. (7) After mid-day, judgment by default against the absent party. (8) No further steps to be taken in the suit after sunset. (9) But recognisances to be entered into for re-appearance.

ii. *De judiciis.*—Of judicial proceedings:—
(1) Regulations as to the sums to be deposited in court as security for costs. (The sum staked by the loser went towards the expenses of public worship, and the amount was fixed at 500 *asses* for objects exceeding 1000 *asses* in value, and 50 *asses* for those of less value, as well as where the freedom of a citizen was involved, so as not to endanger his liberty by exposing him to any difficulty in obtaining security. Gai. Inst. iv. § 14.) (2) Illness or one of the parties being an alien, are good grounds for an adjournment. (3) Witnesses to be summoned by verbal notice at their domicile, twenty-seven days previous to the trial. (4) Theft may be the subject of compromise.

iii. *De ære confesso rebusque jure judicatis.* Of execution after confession or condemnation:—The dispositions referred to in this table, viz., the preliminary delay, the presence of the magistrate, the surety, limitation as to weight of chains, the food ordered, the production of the debtor during the second delay, combined with table viii. (18), as to the limitation of interest, point to the concessions wrung from the patricians by the plebeians.

(1) Thirty days allowed for payment. (2) After that time, the debtor to be brought before the magistrate (action of *manus injectio*.) (3) And in default of payment or satisfactory security, the debtor to be adjudged to the creditor, who may load him with chains not exceeding fifteen pounds in weight. (4) The debtor may provide his own sustenance, otherwise one pound of meal at least per day to be given him. (5) In default of a settlement of the claim, the debtor to be kept chained for sixty days, proclamation of the sum due being made on three market days in the presence of the *prætor* and the debtor. (6) After this delay, the debtor may be put to death or sold beyond the Tiber, or if more than one creditor, the debtor's body may be divided between them. (This literal meaning is disputed, and *partes secanto* held by some to refer to the debtor's goods.)

iv. *De jure patrio.* Of the paternal power. This and the next table are concerned with the civil rights, such as inheritance, tutorship, and curatorship, growing out of the Roman family system, *i.e.*, the Roman *civil* family bound together by the *patria potestas*, and involving the rules as to *agnatio* and *gens*:—

(1) Malformed infants to be immediately destroyed. (2) Absolute power over children extending to life and death. (3) After three sales by the father the son to be free. *Si pater filium ter venumduit, filius a patre liber esto.* Gai. Inst. 1 § 132. (4) The extreme term of gestation fixed at ten months.

v. *De hæreditatibus et tutelis.* Of inheritance and tutelage:—

(1) Regulations as to the perpetual tutelage of women. Vestals released from this tutelage and also from paternal power. (This table points to the social subjection of women at this period.) (2) *Res mancipi* of women in agnate tutelage cannot be acquired by *usucapion* unless alienated by the ward with the authority of her tutor. (Hence the distinction between *res mancipi* and *nec mancipi* existed at this period. (3) The dispositions made by a deceased person as to his property and the guardianship of his substance are to be binding. *Uti legassit super pecunia tutela ve suæ rei, ita jus esto.* (Hence the Plebeian has a legal right to make a will, and the form of words used in the Testament refers to this law, "*Quo tu jure testamentum facere possis secundum legem publicam.*" Gai. Inst. 29, § 104.) (4) On intestacy and in default of a *suus hæres*, the nearest agnate to succeed. (5) And in default of an agnate, the *gens*. (The succession, as fixed by the twelve tables, is α, the *hæredes sui, i.e.*, the co-proprietors, consisting of the children in power, including the wife if in *manu*. β, the nearest agnate. γ, the nearest member of the *gens*, hence no distinction as to sex, and no privilege of primogeniture. In early times and in respect of one another the terms *agnate* and *gens* would as to the *Patricians* be synonymous, and the distinction therefore superfluous, but not so in respect of the succession to their clients or enfranchised slaves, for these would not be their agnates, but having taken their name and adopted their religious rites, they would fall into the civil *gens* of the particular Patrician household they belonged to, and the same may be said of the enfranchised slaves of those *plebeian* families who never having been clients were *ingenui*.) (6) In default of testamentary guardians, the agnates become tutors by the operation of law. (7) The care of the person and property of an imbecile not provided with a curator falls to his agnates and in default to the *gens*. (8) In default of a *suus hæres*, the patron succeeds to his freedman's property. (9) Debts due to the estate are in the eye of the law divided between the heirs. (10) Regulations as to the action *familiæ erciscundæ* (partition suit.) (11) The slave freed by testament, on condition of giving a sum to the heir, may, if parted with by the heir, acquire his freedom by paying this sum to the alienee.

vi. *De dominio et possessione.* Of ownership and possession. All the regulations in this and the following table, relating to rights and obligations in connection with property, are coloured by that *citizenship* which was the characteristic of a Roman. The modes of acquiring *quiritarian* ownership indicated are: *mancipatio* (*i.e.*, alienation by the solemn form *per æs et libram* of things, which could not be parted with by mere *traditio*, but required a mancipa-

SECOND EPOCH.—THE REPUBLIC.

tion—viz., Roman land, with the house on it, and the rural servitudes attaching to it, freemen under power, slaves and beasts of burden), *lex* (*i.e.*, a testamentary declaration), *usus auctoritas* or *usucapio* (*i.e.*, continuous possession during a fixed period), in *jure cessio*, *addictio*, and *adjudicatio* (*i.e.*, the judgments of a court of law). The theory of obligations is but imperfectly developed, and the mode of *contracting* referred to is the *nexum*—*i.e.*, the same solemn form *per æs et libram*, and in this manner deposits and pledges are made, and the debtor transfers his personal services to his creditor, but other and simpler forms must have existed, for table iii. (6) refers to a sale to an alien, and the property in vi. (10) would seem not to have been parted with by mancipation. The effects of an obligation are also shown in the rules as to *noxa* (see table viii.), and in the case of co-succession, legacies, tutorship, and neighbours.

(1) The legal effect of a contract or conveyance is to be determined by the verbal statement *(nuncupatio.)* (2) Penalty of double for denying the declarations so made. (3) The prescriptive guarantee against eviction *(usus auctoritas)* is acquired after two years' possession for realty, and one year for other kinds of property. (4) Marital power is acquired after one year's possession. Absence each year for three consecutive nights defeats it. (The means of acquiring the *manus* by which the wife fell into the position of the daughter of her husband is all that is referred to here, not the marriage itself.) (5) An alien cannot acquire a title by possession to a Roman citizen's property. (6) After the preliminary inquiry as to the right to property *(manuum consertio)*, the magistrate may use his discretion to whom interim possession is given, but always in favour of liberty. (The disregard of the latter part of this rule by Appius Claudius, in respect of the custody of the person of Virginia, is referred to in Dig. 1, 2, 2, 24.) (7) The owner of timbers, built into a house, or forming supports for vines, cannot remove them. (8) But he has a right of action for double the value. (9) But if such materials become detached, the owner may claim them. (10) The property in a thing sold and delivered does not pass to the vendee until the vendor is paid. (11) Regulations as to *in jure cessio* and *mancipatio*.

vii. *De jure ædium et agrorum.* Of real property law:—

(1) A space of two and a half feet to be left between buildings. (2 and 3) Conditions as to distances, etc., between neighbouring plantations, constructions, and excavations. (The extract from Gaius in Dig. 10, 1, 13, shows that these details were taken from Solon's Athenian code.) (4) A space of five feet, incapable of being acquired by usucapion, must be left between fields for the purposes of access and the use of the plough. (This indicates the existence of a class of servitùdes, the most important of which was *via* or the right of way. (5) For the settlement of boundary questions, three arbitrators to be appointed by the magistrate. (This refers to the action *judicis postulatio*.) (6) A road must be eight feet broad in the straight and sixteen feet in the bends. (7) If the road is impassable, the charioteer may diverge. (8) The owner of property, prejudiced by

the construction of an aqueduct or rain-water channels, may demand security against damage. (The result of a complaint of this sort would be the appointment of an arbitrator, *aquæ pluviæ arcendæ*, Dig. 39, 3, 23, 2.) (9) The branches, below fifteen feet, of a tree, extending over adjoining property, must be lopped. (10) The owner of fruit, fallen on a neighbour's ground, may collect it.

viii. *De delictis*. Of wrongs or torts: The subject of wrongs, as here treated, exhibits the usual characteristics of early criminal legislation, the individual interest predominates over the social; the penalty, a sort of ransom or pecuniary compensation, has rather a private than a public character, and the further prosecution of the suit may be compromised. When inflicted in the name of the public, the penalty assumes the character of torture (*e.g.*, retaliation, sacrifice to Ceres, hurled from the Tarpeian rock, burning, etc.), or is tainted with superstition, as in the punishment of death for magic arts. The ancient name for wrong was *noxa*, indicating the source of the obligation resulting from injury done to another, whether designedly or not, if wrongfully. The twelve tables refer to three varieties— theft, damage, injury.

(1) Penalty of death for publishing libels and public defamations. (2) Retaliation in the case of limbs fractured and the injured party not indemnified. (3) For broken teeth, if a freeman, 300 *asses*; if a slave, 150 *asses*. (4) For other injuries 25 *asses*. (5) Accidental damage must be repaired. (6) The damage caused by an animal must be repaired or the animal forfeited. (7) Action for pasturing flocks on another's ground. (8) As to punishment on him who shall by magic arts destroy crops or remove them from one field to another. (9) The penalty for cutting or pasturing off crops at night to be death, but if the culprit is under age he is to be scourged and fined double the amount of damage. (10) The intentional firing of a house or barn to be punished by scourging and burning. If the act the result of negligence, the damage to be repaired, but if too poor, moderate chastisement. (11) Penalty 25 *asses*, for unlawfully felling another's tree. (12) A nocturnal robber may be killed with impunity. (13) But in the day time, only if he defend himself with weapons. (14) A free man taken in the act of thieving is to be scourged and delivered over to the party aggrieved; if under age, he is to be scourged and compelled to repair the damage. A slave is to be scourged and then hurled from the Tarpeian rock. (15) The penalty to be the same for property stolen and discovered in the thief's possession after search, wearing a girdle only and holding a plate (*lance licioque conceptum*, a proceeding turned into ridicule in Gai. Inst. iii, § 192), but for thefts discovered without this prescribed method (*conceptum*), or for the clandestine deposit of the stolen property on the premises of another (*oblatum*), the penalty to be three times the value of the property. (16) For thefts not falling under the above heads (*nec manifestum*), the penalty to be double the value. (17) Prescription (*usucapio*) does not run in respect of stolen property. (18) Penalty of quadruple

for exceeding the legal interest fixed at one-twelfth of the principal (*unciarum fœnus*), *i.e.*, about eight and one-third *per* cent. *per* year of twelve months. (19) Penalty of double against a fraudulent bailee. (20) Any one may bring an action for the removal of a suspected tutor, and the latter is to be fined in double the value of any of the pupils' property abstracted. (21) The patron abusing his position towards his client to be sacrificed to the gods. (Hence the position of clients is recognised by the twelve tables.) (22) The witness or scale-bearer refusing to give evidence incurs the penalties of infamy. (23) False witnesses are to be hurled down the Tarpeian rock. (24) Capital punishment for homicide. (25) The same penalty for affecting anyone with magic arts or administering poison. (26) The same penalty for seditious meetings by night. (27) Corporate bodies may make their own rules, if not inconsistent with the law.

ix. *De jure publico.* Of public law. The only reference to the political constitution of the State is contained in the first four heads of this table and table xii. (5), but the divisions of the people, the powers of the three *comitia*, of the senate, and of the consuls, are not legally determined here, because these tables are only an embodiment of customs presumed to be known, and in active operation.

(1) No law shall be passed affecting an individual only. (2) The *comitia centuriata* alone have the power of legislating, so as to affect life, liberty, or civic rights. (3) The arbitrator or judge guilty of receiving a bribe, to be put to death. (4) Regulations affecting the court for the punishment of homicide (*Quæstores Parricidii*), and as to the right of appeal to the people. (5) Penalty of death for inciting an enemy to make war, or for giving up a citizen to them.

x. *De jure sacro.* Of sacred law:—
(1) Dead bodies are not to be interred or burnt within the city. (2 to 9.) In funerals, undue pomp and unnecessary indications of grief forbidden. (10) In the absence of consent, a funeral pile or sepulchre cannot be placed within sixty feet of another man's house. (11) Usucapion cannot affect the ownership of a sepulchre.

xi. This supplemental table prohibited marriage between patricians and plebeians, and hence an equality of rights was not effected by the twelve tables.

xii. This second supplemental table embraced miscellaneous heads. (1) A creditor was entitled to seize the property of a debtor, who had omitted to pay the price of a victim or the hire of a beast of burden, when the amount of the hire was to be devoted to sacrificial purposes. (This is the *legis actio* called *pignoris capio*, referred to in Gai. Inst. iv. § 28.) (2) A noxal action lies against the master of a slave who is guilty of theft or other injury. (3) Penalty of double the fruits against anyone convicted by three arbitrators, appointed by the *prætor*, of wrongfully acquiring *interim* possession. (Hence the characteristic distinction in Roman law is here recognised between *jus* as involving the *jurisdictio* and *imperium* of the magistrate, and *judicium* as involving the duties of the *judex* or *arbiter*

(4) Penalty of double for consecrating the subject of litigation. (5) Subsequent legislation causes the repeal of previous enactments inconsistent therewith.

Legis actiones.

140. Forms of procedure were in existence before the twelve tables, and the four actions of the law are mentioned in them; but it is probable that the settlement of the practical details necessary to bring these actions into harmony (*legum verbis accommodatæ*, Gai. Inst., iv, § 11), with the abstract rules of law now promulgated, was referred to the pontiffs, and hence these actions (two of which are for the conduct and decision of the dispute, and two for peculiar modes of execution) date from this period, the word *actio* being used generically to denote the form of procedure in its entirety. The lance (*vindicta*) and the fictitious combat (*manuum consertio*, table vi, (6)), point to the simulation of the acts of violence of a more barbarous age. The sacred character of the words pronounced is shown in the loss of the action consequent on the use of a wrong term (*vites* for *arbores*, Gai. Inst., iv, § 11-30), and the use to which the *sacramentum* is put, and the original object of the *Pignoris capio* (table xii, 1), indicate the strength of the sacerdotal system.

(1) *Actio Sacramenti*.—The oldest form, and used with variations of detail, for enforcing obligations or trying real rights. The peculiarity was the *sacramentum*, as to which see table ii, (1). Originally used for the *vindicatio* of a thing or a real right, this action had come to be employed for enforcing obligations, and also assumed a fictitious character in the process called *in jure cessio* (confirmed by table vi, 11), or the collusive recovery in a court of law of property sought to be conveyed. By this latter means, the enfranchisement of slaves (*manumissio vindicta*), the emancipation and adoption of a *filius familiæ*, the change of guardians of women, etc., was effected.

(2) *Judicis postulatio*.—A simplification of the foregoing, dispensing with the *sacramentum*, and summed up in the formula J. A. V. P. U. D. (*judicem arbitrum ve postulo uti des*), see table vii, (5), where it would be used with a view to the settlement of boundaries.

(3) *Manus injectio*.—Seizure of the body of the debtor in order that he might be *addicti*, *i. e.*, adjudged to the creditor by the *prætor* (see table iii, (2)).

(4) *Pignoris capio*.—Seizure of the property of the debtor. This last, unlike the three former, did not take place before the magistrate (*in jure*), hence the doubt whether it was a *legis actio* (Gai. Inst., iv, § 29).

In spite, however, of the promulgation of the twelve tables and the settlement of these forms, the Patricians contrived to maintain their ascendancy by keeping secret the rules as to the *dies fasti* (see par. 41), as well as the method of adapting the process of the law to the precise wants of the particular case.

SECOND EPOCH.—THE REPUBLIC.

§ 2.—*From the Twelve Tables to the Submission of all Italy.*

The perpetual dissensions between the patricians and plebeians led to the latter obtaining a portion of the political power.

149. **Lex Valeria Horatia** *de Plebiscitis* (B.C. 449).—In the consulship of Valerius and Horatius, this law was voted in the *Centuriata*, and by it the *plebiscita* of the *Comitia Tributa* were made obligatory on all (*post*, par. 178).

150. **Lex Canuleia** *de Connubio patrum et plebis* (B.C. 445). This *plebiscitum*, proposed by the tribune Canuleius, repealed the 11th table.

151. **Tribuni Militum.** The struggle made by the plebeians to gain access to the consulate was defeated by the substitution for that office of *three* military tribunes, elected by the *comitia centuriata*. For some time, tribunes and consuls alternately replaced one another, according as the patrician or plebeian element was in the ascendancy, but it was not until after the increase of these tribunes to *six*, that the plebeians secured the election of some of their own number.

152. **Censores** (B.C. 443). In order to counteract the influence of the plebeian military tribunes, the duty of numbering the people every fifth year, formerly performed by the consuls, was given to *two* censors elected for five years (afterwards every fifth year for one and a half years) by the *comitia centuriata* from the members of the *senate*. The power thus given to these officers enabled them to determine the status of every citizen for the term of five years, and, if both were agreed, a citizen could be degraded by transferring his name to the list of non-voters (*Ceritum tabulæ*, so called because the town of Ceres had no vote).

157. At this period, the ten years siege of Veii took place, and during it (B.C. 396), the Roman soldiers for the first time received pay from the public treasury (*stipendium*). Six years later (B.C. 390) Rome was burnt by the Gauls. After the recovery of the city from this disaster, the plebeians succeeded in obtaining admission to the consulate, and the senate thereupon withdrew a portion of the consular duties and conferred them upon patrician magistrates, then created and called the Prætor and the Curule Ædiles.

160. **Prætor.** (B.C. 367). The name, derived from *præ ire*, had been early used as a synonym for consul (see table xii. 3), but it now designated a *patrician* magistrate, nominated by the *centuriata*, a colleague of the consuls, and sometimes called by their title because, in the absence of the consuls with the army, he convoked and presided over the senate, assembled the *comitia*, and proposed the laws. His legitimate functions were, however, purely magisterial, and as these were limited to Rome, he was styled the *prætor urbanus*.

161. **Ædiles Curules.** The establishment of these *two patrician* magistrates, with analogous but higher functions, reduced the two *ædiles plebeii* (par. 108), to a subordinate position, and hence these

c

superior officers were also called *ædiles majores*. They had a separate tribunal and jurisdiction, and their duties comprised the maintenance of roads, bridges, temples, and amphitheatres, the provisioning of the city, and securing its tranquillity. They were also charged with the direction of the public games, and were expected to give at their own expense one exhibition at least during their administration, a costly duty readily incurred, as being a sure means of obtaining votes. The dates of the origin of the following offices is uncertain, but they may be usefully enumerated here.

162. **Judex.** This judicial office, for which at first only senators could be selected, approached in character the functions of the modern jury. The *magistrate*, whether king, consul, or prætor, before whom the summons *in jure* was made, the solemn rites of the actions of the law performed, and who had the power of declaring the law *(jus dicere)*, of regulating the conduct of the case, and (if he did not terminate it himself) of directing a judge to examine into it and pass sentence, was created and elected by the city, but the *judge* was agreed upon by the parties themselves or determined by lot, and, after taking an oath, was invested by the magistrate with his powers for the settlement of the particular case. By this ingenious division of juridical and judicial functions, a few magistrates sufficed for the administration of justice.

The **Arbiter** appears to have been a *judex* with wider powers, and table vii. (5) and xii. (3) contemplate as many as three arbitrators, although there was usually but one *judex*.

The **Recuperatores** were a later institution, and had no connection with the *legis actiones*. They did not supersede the *judex* or *arbiter*. They were usually three or five in number, and as they might be taken indiscriminately from any of the citizens on the spot, the plebeians through them obtained some share in judicial functions. They were probably employed in matters beyond the scope of the Roman law, where the interests of an alien were involved, and their use became more frequent after the establishment of the *prætor peregrinus* (par. 222). This view of their duties is confirmed by the fact that we find *reciperatores* or *recuperatores* in the provinces, whilst the *judex* is confined to Rome, and that from early times they were employed in virtue of international treaties, to settle questions arising between Rome and other cities. Another class of judges, taken from amongst the citizens, consisted of the

166. **Centumviri.** The origin of the centumvirate tribunal is involved in obscurity, but probably *four* citizens from each *tribe* were taken to form it at the time (about B.C. 366) when the tribes numbered *twenty-five*, though subsequently its members were increased, and Pliny mentions as many as one hundred and eighty. It was a *permanent* tribunal, and probably plebeians were eligible for election by the *comitia tributa* to serve as its annual members. It was divided into *four* sections *(consilia tribunalia)*, and causes were heard before two sections at a time *(duplicia judicia, duæ*

hastæ) or before all four united, but voting separately *(quadruplex judicium)*. The lance *(hasta)* was planted before it in the *forum* (later in the Basilica Julia), and it was presided over by the *questors* or by the *prætor*, and under Octavius by special magistrates, the *decemviri in litibus judicandis*.

Probably this tribunal could be selected by the parties interested, and it had some competence in criminal matters, but it did not possess any magisterial powers *(jurisdictio)*, and could only determine the cases sent down to it. It declined with the disuse of the *legis actiones* because the *actio sacramenti* was the only form of procedure which could be applied to the three classes of questions which fell within its cognizance—viz., (1) *status*. (2) Quiritarian *ownership*. (3) *successions* (testamentary and intestate), and its duties in relation to the last head are noticed in the Digest and Code of Justinian.

By the year B.C. 338, the Gauls had been driven back and Latium subdued. The plebeians, who had already attained to the consulship, the censorship (through the latter the senate), and the prætorship, now obtained some further important advantages.

175. **Lex Petillia Papiria** *de nexis* (B.C. 326). This law originated in the indignation of the plebeians at the position of the mass of their fellow citizens, who, unable to meet their debts, had voluntarily sold their services to their patrician creditors. After this date, debtors might pledge their *goods per æs et libram*, but not their *persons*, though the provisions of the statute did not affect the position of those *addicti* or taken in execution as the result of the action *manus injectio*.

176. **Jus civile Flavianum.** (B.C. 303). According to the popular account *Cnæus Flavius*, the grandson of a freedman, and the secretary of the jurisconsult, Appius Claudius Cæcus, published a work disclosing the rules as to the *dies fasti* and the *formulæ* of the *legis actiones*. The consequence was a loss of power in the pontiffs and patrician jurisconsults, and an advance in the position of the plebeians for three years later, the college of *pontiffs* (par. 84) was increased to eight members and four plebeians admitted, and the college of *augurs* to nine members with five plebeians.

178. **Lex Hortensia** *de plebiscitis*. (B.C. 286). This law was wrung from the dictator *Hortensius* by the secession of the plebs to the Janiculum. It gave binding force to the *plebiscita* of the *comitia tributa*, and probably this, the third of the so-called *leges publiliæ*, finally settled the question as to the non-necessity of the *auctoritas* of the Senate. (See par. 66 and 149).

180. The fall of Tarentum in B.C. 272 hastened the subjugation of the rest of Italy, and when this was completed in B.C. 266 a great change occurred in the position and in the manners and mode of life of the Romans.

REVIEW OF THE PRECEDING PERIOD.

Foreign Policy.
181. The consideration of the position of the allies and vanquished enemies of Rome is, at this time, one of infinite detail, for it depended on the strength and disposition of each particular state, whether it should be debarred altogether or admitted to the whole *(optimum jus)*, or any portion of the five principal privileges which citizens enjoyed by virtue of the *jus Quiritium (jus civitatis, jus civile)*.

185. *Private* law included three of these privileges, viz. (1) *Connubium*, or the legal capacity to marry, involving the paternal power, agnation, etc. (2) *Commercium*, or the legal capacity to contract, involving the power of becoming quiritarian owner of land. (3) *Testamenti factio*, or the legal power of receiving or bequeathing by testament (a right usually resulting from the *commercium* after the adoption of the *mancipatio* fiction for wills). The remaining rights were *political*, viz. (4) *Jus honorum*, or the capacity to hold office. (5) *Jus suffragii*, or the right of voting in the *comitia*.

186. In respect of the enjoyment of these rights there are six distinctions to be enumerated.

(1) The sovereign *city of Rome*, of which the inhabitants *(cives)* alone at first possessed full civil and political rights. The title of citizen was afterwards imposed on the conquered, but is now guarded with jealously, and only accorded as a mark of favour.

(2) *Coloniæ Romanæ* (or *togatæ*). About thirty of these Roman colonies existed at this period. A *lex* (or a *senatus-consultum*) was necessary for the formation of each, and by it *triumviri* or *quinqueviri* were authorised to enrol freedmen, convey them to the conquered city, and there distribute amongst them the whole or part, as policy dictated, of the lands belonging to the former inhabitants. The constitution adopted resembled that of the mother city, and included a senate *(curia)* with two consuls *(duumviri)*, and a patrician and plebeian order. Probably the citizens *(Romani coloni)* had no political rights *(civitas absque suffragio)*, but they enjoyed the three privileges of private law (par. 185), and hence held their *land* as proprietors *ex jure Quiritium*, so that it was assimilated to the *ager Romanus* (par. 92), and distinct from conquered territories which were held by the occupiers at an annual rent *(vectigal)* paid to the state as owner.

187. (3) *Civitates liberæ* (or *fœderatæ*). Of these there were two classes.

(a) The cities of *Latium* which had the *commercium*, and could hold their land *ex jure Quiritium*, but had not the *connubium*, and probably only possessed the *testamenti factio* in the limited form, afterwards bestowed on a class of freedmen called by analogy *Latini juniani* (see part iii. par. 65), though the inability of the latter to *make* a will did not affect the true Latins. The more ancient towns of Latium *(Latini veteres)* appear to have had the *connubium*, and their citizens enjoyed the privilege when at Rome of voting in the *comitia*, their temporary place in a tribe being determined by lot. The full rights of citizenship could also be acquired by the inhabitants *(Latini* or *Socii Latini)* of all these cities by the performance of certain acts *(e.g.*, holding an annual magistracy, removing to Rome, leaving a child behind, bringing a public accusation, and procuring the conviction of a citizen for extortion), and the possession of this last important privilege mainly distinguished the towns of Latium from,

(β) The free *Italian* cities in alliance with Rome, which possessed, with this exception, nearly equal rights. In addition to these, there were cities in and out of Italy called *civitates fundanæ* (or *populi fundi)*, which had of their own accord adopted Roman law, and thereby facilitated the acquisition of a share of the rights of Roman citizens.

188. (4) *Latinæ* (or *latini nominis) coloniæ*. These were colonies enjoying the *jus Latii*, and the inhabitants (*Latini coloni)* consisted of Latins or other people established, where policy dictated, by generals and consuls in conquered territories. Any Roman enrolled in the colony thereby lost a portion of his Quiritarian rights.

The *jus Latii* (or *Latinitatis)* when thus conferred on towns in Spain, Gaul, and other countries, ceased to have a local meaning, and originated the so-called *Jus Italicum*, a concession, the import of which was subsequently narrowed, so as to refer only to the distinction between Italian and provincial *soil*.

191. (5) *Municipia*. This class of towns enjoyed greater privileges than any other, and the title refers not to origin or geographical position, but to the nature of the constitution, which closely resembled that of Rome. They were allowed full liberty as to interior administration *(legibus suis utunto)* so only that nothing conflicted with the interests of the dominant city or with the *plebiscitum* (*lex* or *formula)*, which conferred upon each town more or less of the rights of citizenship. Sometimes these rights only amounted to the *jus Latii*, in other cases they embraced the entire aggregate, so that the *municeps* became a citizen of Rome without being a Roman. *Ceres* was the first town erected into a *municipium* of this kind (B.C. 389), but its inhabitants had not the *jus suffragii (ante*, par. 152).

195 (6) *Præfecturæ*. Under this class would fall any of the above towns to which a *prefect* was sent from Rome, probably as a temporary measure, and for the purpose of securing order.

197. Outside the classes of citizens came the *peregrinus, hostis* and *barbarus*. The first was the alien friend, settled in Rome, or the resident in a conquered country to which citizen rights had not yet been granted; the second *(hostis* which at first included *peregrinus)* was an alien enemy, or the inhabitant of a country not yet overcome, whilst the term *barbarus* was perpetually receding, as it only included those beyond the pale of Roman civilization and geography.

Public Law.

198. Three political bodies now exist (exclusive of the *knights*, whose influence is increasing), viz.

(1) The *people, i.e.,* all the citizens without reference to rank or fortune. (2) The *senate,* consisting of those whose names have been inscribed by the censors on the senatorial list. (3) The *plebeians,* for these are no longer excluded from political rights or dignities.

Many of the powers of these political bodies are transferred to magistrates whose tenure of office (except the censors) is annual. Royalty has given place to two consuls, some of whose duties has again been transferred to censors, prætors, and curule ædiles. The plebeians have their own tribunes, questors, and ædiles. The higher are distinguished from the subordinate magistrates *(magistratus pedarii)* by the right conferred on the holders of the former of being carried in a chair of state *(sella curulis),* and of bequeathing to their families their images *(imagines majorum)* to be exhibited on important occasions.

200. *Legislative power.* The three sources of *written* law existing are—

(1) *Leges* passed by the *comitia centuriata* (the *curiata* hardly existing, except for the investiture of the *imperium* after some elections, and the determination of a few family rights). The senate discuss the bill, a senatorial magistrate convokes the *comitia* and proposes the law; each citizen in passing the scrutineer declares aloud "yes" or "no," unfavourable auspices dissolve the assembly, *(Jove tonante cum populo agere nefas),* the *auctoritas* of the senate is given beforehand.

(2) *Plebiscita* emanate from the *comitia tributa* or plebeian assembly, convoked in the forum or capitol. The tribunes take the initiative, and introduce the bills *(rogationes),* the votes are given aloud. Neither the sanction of the senate or the vote of the *centuriata* are necessary to make these decrees binding on all.

(3) *Senatus consulta* are the result of the deliberations of the senate as to matters of government and administration, and probably did not refer to private law. If the decision of the senate was stopped by the veto of a tribune, the *senatus consultum* was called *senatus auctoritas.*

201. The sources of *customary* law are mainly (1) the *interpretatio* of the *jurisconsults (post,* par. 236); (2) the *disputatio fori,* resulting from the discussion of precedents by the bar; (3) the *mores majorum* or ancient usages, the whole falling under the technical term *jus civile,* and completing the modes of legislation of this epoch.

202. *Executive power.* The senate exercised this power through the following magistrates: two consuls who rule at Rome and command the army; two *urban prætors,* who, in addition to their judicial duties, can be supplied by, or supply the place at Rome of, the consuls; two *censors* for classing the citizens at the census and fixing their taxes; two *major ædiles,* who superintend the police; two *questors* of the public treasure, and finally the plebeian *questors*

and *ædiles*, whose duties, strictly speaking, are confined to their class.

204. The ten plebeian *tribunes (ante* par. 106) do not possess the *imperium* or *jurisdictio* of executive magistrates, but only the *auxilium* or power of interference, which assumes an active form in the *intercessio* or individual opposition to the decrees of the senate and the acts of magistrates (an obstacle sometimes overcome by securing the sympathy of the other tribunes). This *potestas* or *vis tribunicia* was first developed to its full importance when, in B.C. 432, the senate invoked its aid to prevent the appointment of a dictator by the consuls, and the tribunes now show their power by summoning before them magistrates and even consuls, who during their term of office have been hostile to the plebeians.

205. *Electoral power.* The people assembled in the *comitia centuriata* elect the consuls, censors, prætors, and major ædiles. The plebeians in the *comitia tributa* elect their own questors, ædiles, and tribunes, and select for life from the college of pontiffs the *pontifex maximus*, but as the election to the two latter offices formerly rested with the *comitia curiata*, the fiction of a *lex curiata* is carried out by the thirty electors representing the thirty *curiæ* (*ante* par. 31), ratifying the decision of the tribes.

206. *Judicial power.* In respect of—

Criminal matters the *comitia centuriata* could alone condemn to death, the sentence of the *comitia tributa*, being restricted to a fine or exile usually for political offences. Less grave or private wrongs are referred to a *quæstor parricidii* (*ante* par. 94), and trivial matters or the punishment of aliens and slaves are left to the *prætor*. The senate and the consuls have some powers, but the extent of the criminal jurisdiction of the *centumvirs* is uncertain.

In *civil* matters the action is commenced and all the formalities of the *legis actiones* performed in the presence of the *prætor (in jure)*, who, by virtue of the *jurisdictio* and *imperium* vested in him, organises the suit, and either decides the matter himself by declaring the law, or refers it to the *centumvirs* (when relating to status, Quiritarian ownership, or succession), to a *judex* or arbitrator (when relating to obligation or possession), or to *recuperatores* (when an alien is involved, so that the *legis actio* is not applicable).

208. The dual system of magistracies, with ill-defined powers and no well-marked gradations, combined with the personal independence of each magistrate and his irresponsibility in his own sphere during his term of office, would have been found inconvenient in practice, but for (as shown by M. Laboulaye) the maintenance of equilibrium by the right vested in each magistrate to veto the acts of a colleague or inferior, and in the case of the tribunes of all other magistrates and the senate. Procuring this opposition on the part of a tribune or colleague was called *tribunum appellare, collegam* or *magistratum appellare,* and this (combined with the *provocatio ad populum*) is the origin of the *appellatio* (or *provocatio*) under the emperors, and of the modern "appeal," except that the word now refers to the demand for the interference of a *superior* judge.

Sacred Law.

210. After the admission of plebeians to the college of the pontiffs and to that of the augurs *(ante,* par. 84, 176), a change occurred in the effect of the influence exerted by sacred law and matters connected with religion, formerly decided by the king, are now referred to the tribunal of the *pontifex maximus* (ante para. 205) to whom also is entrusted the duty of keeping the *annales maximi,* or record of historical events.

Private Law.

212. In respect of *persons,* the characteristic distinctions relate to: *sui juris,* or heads of families; *alieni juris,* or those in the power of another; *potestas,* whether paternal or over slaves; *manus* or the marital power; *mancipium,* or the rights over the freeman purchased, or over the person of him who is *addictus* by the magistrate for the payment of a debt, or in reparation of some damage *(nexi* no longer exist, *ante,* par. 175), *agnatio,* or the civil family tie, against which *cognatio* or blood relationship avails nothing; *gentilitas* or the agnation of *ingenui* families giving rights over clients and freedmen; and lastly, the perpetual *tutelage* of women.

213. In respect of *things,* the two classes of *res mancipi* and *nec mancipi* exist, the ownership of the former being indestructible, except by the Quiritarian methods of alienation *(mancipatio, in jure cessio, addictio, adjudicatio, usucapio, lex),* so that the subject matter may be recovered again if the required formalities have not been complied with. *Res nec mancipi* pass by the *traditio* of the *jus gentium.*

214. As to *wills.* The *testamentum calatis comitiis,* by which formerly the head of the family disposed of all his property, including that acquired by other members of the family, is now replaced by the solemn form of sale of the inheritance *(testamentum per æs et libram, per mancipationem).*

215. As to *succession,* the right to inherit is determined solely by the rules of *agnatio* and *gentilitas,* hence the son out of the family has no claim, the mother cannot succeed to her child, nor the child to the mother.

216. As to *contracts,* the first simplification of the *nexum* is coming into use in the form of the contract *verbis (sponsio, stipulatio)* where the ceremony *per æs et libram* is dispensed with, and the *nuncupatio* (the *lex mancipii)* is couched in the technical words restricted to Roman citizens *spondes ne? spondeo.* No other form of contract is binding unless rendered so by part performance.

217. As to *actions.* The consecrated formulæ and symbolic acts of the four *legis actiones* must be scrupulously observed, any omission is fatal to the further progress of the suit.

Manners and customs.

219. The earlier customs of the city have been for the most part transformed into laws. The antipathy to luxury and the simple habits which formerly characterised the inhabitants, are giving way

before the accumulation of wealth and extension of dominion, consequent on the successes of the Roman arms. The patriciate is declining, and, with the rise of the plebeians, the system of clientage has been disturbed, and, in lieu of individuals, powerful patrons now make clients of entire cities and provinces.

§ 3.—*From the submission of all Italy to the Empire.*

The remaining life of the republic may be divided into two parts—in the first, which terminated with the destruction of Carthage, Numantia, and Corinth, there were wars without, but no internal dissensions, for the plebeians had triumphed ; in the second part there were no important wars, but the state was torn by internal discord, arising from the struggles for power of generals, consuls, and dictators, and ending in the triumph of one—*i.e.*, in the empire.

222. **Prætor Peregrinus.** (B.C. 247). The subjugation of all Italy necessarily extended the commercial relations of Rome. Crowds of strangers flocked into the city, where occupation was offered to those willing to engage in crafts despised by the Romans. For the settlement, by the rules of the *jus gentium*, of the disputes of this class of persons, whether as between themselves or in their dealings with Roman citizens, a new magistracy was created, inferior in rank to that of the *prætor urbanus*, but the two prætors could supply each other's place.

According to Pomponius, the following officers were created subsequently to the *prætor peregrinus*, viz., the *tribuni ærarii*, public accountants under the questors, the *triumviri monetales*, officers of the Mint, the *triumviri capitales*, prison superintendents, and the *quinqueviri*, magistrates on duty at night.

The great extension of the Roman dominion during the period of more than a century (B.C. 264-146) comprised by the three Punic wars, led to many important changes in legal and political institutions.

225. **Provinces.** The political relations of some of the new countries acquired were determined by treaties, but the greater number were reduced to the condition of *provinces (e.g.,* Sicily, Sardinia, Cisalpine Gaul, Illyria, Spain, and Carthage), placed under the direct surveillance of Rome, and governed by Roman magistrates, according to the terms of the *lex plebiscitum*, or *senatus-consultum*, which established them, and regulated the greater or less amount of privileges enjoyed. The *soil* of the province belonged by right of conquest to the Roman people, the actual holders paying a tax *(vectigal)* for its use, and as these holders were *subjects* or *tributaries*, not citizens, they also paid tribute in the form of a *personal* tax.

Within the provinces, *colonies, municipia, præfecturæ*, etc., were established free from both the personal and land tax, and possessing more or less of the rights of citizenship, according to the constitution of each (see *ante*, par. 186-195).

227. **Provincial Prætors.** At first, the *comitia* at Rome specially

appointed magistrates for the provinces, but after four such provincial prætors had been created, the system was adopted of sending the consuls and prætors, on the expiration of their duties at Rome, as governors to the provinces under the title *pro-consuls* or *pro-prætors* (see below), and the four provincial prætors remained the first year at Rome without special jurisdiction, but assisting their colleagues.

228. **Pro-consuls, Pro-prætors.** When the term of office of a consul at the head of an army in the field had expired, he was frequently retained at his post by a *lex curiata*, which made him a representative of the consul *(pro-consule)* nominally for a year, though usually prolonged through the influence of party intrigue. In this way originated the provincial *governors*, to whom the civil administration was also confided, and who bore the title of *pro-consuls*, if they were military commanders, otherwise *pro-prætors*. They were assisted by *legati pronconsulis* (deputies whose number only was determined by the senate), and *questors* of the public treasure sent direct from Rome. The judicial functions were performed by *recuperatores*. The taxes were collected by the vicious system of farming, and for a time the knights claimed the exclusive privilege of being selected as *publicani*.

233. **Responsa Prudentium.**—At first only the patricians were acquainted with the mysteries of the civil law. Seated in his *atrium*, the jurisconsult delivered his opinion, like an oracle, to those who consulted him, confining himself to the precise point to be determined, and not divulging or teaching the law. After the publication of the twelve tables and of the *dies fasti*, the patricians could no longer succeed in maintaining a monopoly, and the plebeians entered the profession. It then assumed a more liberal character, and became a means of acquiring popularity, and so attaining the honours of the state.

The first plebeian pontifex maximus, *Tiberius Coruncanius* (died B.C. 245), not only advised suitors but publicly taught law, and *Caius Scipio Nasica* (Consul in B.C. 191) had a house erected for him in the Via Sacra by the senate at the public expense, in order that he might be the more readily consulted; but the terms *publice respondere, publice profiteri*, merely refer to the public nature of the profession which any one who felt himself competent might practise, and not to any office in, or salary paid by, the state.

235. Cicero sums up the duties of a jurist in four words. *Respondere*, to advise generally; *cavere*, to point out the proper forms to pursue; *agere*, to appear in the Forum; *scribere*, to publish legal treatises. Pomponius (Dig. 1, 2, 35, etc.) gives a biographical summary of writers on law, and ascribes the origin of the practice to *Papirius* (*ante*, par. 76), who was followed by *Appius Claudius Cæcus*, censor in B.C. 307, with a work, *de Usurpationibus*, now lost, and *Sextus Ælius* (*post*, par. 239), but he does not mention *Flavius* (*ante*, par. 176), probably because he was not a professional jurist. Other distinguished names were *Cato* and his

eldest son, and the pontifex maximus, *Publius Mucius Scævola*, and his son and successor, *Quintus M.S.* (Consul B.C. 96), the tutor of Cicero, and the first to publish a manual of the entire civil law.

236. The education of lawyers consisted in learning the twelve tables by heart, and in noting down the answers of the *juris-consulti* (or *periti* or *prudentes*), whose consultations they attended. The mass of unassorted decisions thus collected, formed the *Responsa prudentium* or *juris interpretatio*, which became part of the *unwritten* law, deriving its authority from the reputation of its authors, and as being logical deductions, applications, and expositions of the law, it fell under the term *jurisprudentia* in its strict sense.

237. The defect in this method of creating law was its great bulk, and the necessity of reducing into order the mass of matter thus accumulated, induced *Cicero* to undertake a work, *De jure civili in artem redigendo*, and with the same view, *Julius Cæsar* is said to have contemplated a codification of the existing law.

239. **Jus Ælianum** (or *Tripertita*, B.C. 202).—The jurisconsult *Sextus Ælius*, who filled the offices of curule ædile, consul, and censor, published a work called *Tripertita*, from its division into three parts, comprising—(1) The twelve tables; (2) their interpretation; (3) the *legis actiones*. But the story is probably unfounded that this last part amounted to a second divulging of *new formulæ* invented by the patricians and concealed under abbreviations (*per siglas expressæ*); though the appearance of this work, combined with the previous public profession of the law, deprived the *legis actiones* of their mysterious character, and paved the way for the decay of these forms which, from their sacerdotal, symbolic, and perilous sacramental characters, had become unsuited to the age.

242. **Condictio,** *certæ pecuniæ* (? B.C. 244), *de omni certa re* (? B.C. 234). Even before the twelve tables, the *actio sacramenti* had been simplified by the use in some cases of the *judicis postulatio* (*ante*, par. 140); and a further simplification now took place through the introduction by the *Lex Silia* of a fifth *legis actio*, the *condictio* for a certain sum, extended by the *Lex Calpurnia* to anything certain. The action received its name from the fact that the defendant was called upon by the plaintiff (*denuntiabat, condicebat*) to appear before a magistrate in thirty days for the appointment of a judge.

244. **Lex Æbutia** (? B.C. 171). This law effected the partial suppression of the *legis actiones*, and its date is fixed by reference to the *Leges Silia* and *Calpurnia*, the *jus Ælianum*: all three mentioned above, and the *Lex Furia Testamentaria* (part iii, par. 940). Gaius attributes the suppression to the *lex Æbutia* and the two *leges Juliæ;* but the latter probably belong to a later date, and are thought to be the laws passed by Augustus in ? B.C. 26, regulating the procedure in private and criminal matters (*Lex Julia Judiciaria privatorum* and *publicorum*); or, instead of the latter, the reference may be to the *Lex Julia Judiciaria* of Julius Cæsar, ? B.C. 46.

In two cases, the procedure of the *legis actiones* was retained. (1) When the case was to be heard by the centumvirs, and (2), in cases of an application for an injunction against threatened damage (*propter damnum infectum*), but this mode of proceeding fell into disuse when the edict of the prætor furnished a more speedy remedy.

247. **Formulæ.**—The introduction of the system of formulæ transferred the administration of justice from the domination of the patricians into the realm of science. The process of development was gradual, and the key to the system lies in the study of the parts composing the *formula*, by which term is now meant, not the symbolic acts of the old procedure, but the *written instruction* which the magistrate, after having heard the outline of the case (*in jure*), delivered to the parties, and by which they were empowered to proceed with the suit.

249. The *Formula* always commences with the appointment of the judge, *Judex esto*, and may consist of four clauses (see part ii, par. 269; part iii, par. 1909; and Gai. Inst., iv, § 39, etc.)

(1) The *demonstratio* (e. g., *Quod Aulus Agerius Numerio Negidio hominem vendidit*), or statement of the plaintiff's case. This is sometimes omitted (*e. g.*, when there is a simple assertion of ownership, *ex Jure Quiritium*, to be proved by evidence or the question is one of fact and not of law), as being contained in

(2) The *intentio* (*Si paret*, etc.), or precise statement of the legal right asserted by the plaintiff, *i. e.*, the *juris contentio* (Gai. Inst., iv, § 60), and always present when a civil right was involved.

(3) The *condemnatio* (...*condemnato, si non paret absolvito*), or authority to condemn or acquit, according to the evidence. This is sometimes omitted, *e. g.*, where a decision is only required as to the fact of paternity, patronage, amount of dowry, etc. The peculiarity is that the judge can only condemn in a *pecuniary* penalty, and to avoid this inconvenience and protect real rights, ingenious expedients were resorted to.

(4) The *adjudicatio* (*e. g.*, *quantum adjudicare oportet, judex Titio adjudicato*), or power to assign, in the proportions the judge thought fit, the ownership of the property in litigation. If used, this clause would come in before (3), but it only occurred in the formulæ of three actions. 1. *familiæ erciscundæ* (suits for the partition of an inheritance); 2. *communi dividundo* (partition suits between co-owners); 2. *finium regundorum* (settlement of boundaries.)

250. The word *actio* now means the right conferred by the magistrate to carry the suit before the judge (*nihil aliud est actio, quam jus quod sibi debeatur judicio* (before a judge), *persequendi,—Celsus*), or the *formula* itself by which this right was declared, or the *judicium, i. e.*, the suit itself as organised by the formula; hence, *actio, formula*, and *judicium*, are often used synonymously.

251. The magistrate has no powers beyond those included in the *formula*, and the system is, in fact, an ingenious method of constituting a *jury* in civil matters. The preparation of the *formula* is the essential part, and to this juridical science devotes all its powers. The terms employed are not sacramental, and therefore may be adapted to the peculiarities of the case.

General *formulæ* are drawn up and exposed to public view upon the album. The plaintiff before the magistrate (*in jure*) points out the one he requires, the precise terms are then discussed between the parties, and the formula so suited to the actual case is delivered by the prætor (*postulatio, impetratio, formula vel actionis, vel judicii*). Then the judge, confining himself within the limits of the *formula*, hears the evidence, and determines the fact or point of law in dispute by giving his sentence (*sententia*).

252. It is not probable that the system of *formulæ* existed in the *legis actiones*, and that the whole change consisted in dropping the symbolic acts before the magistrate. The reasonable inference is that the system resulted from the wants of the *peregrini*, and was developed by the appointment of the *prætor peregrinus*, for the *legis actiones*, the civil law, the ordinary judge, and the centumvirs, could not be employed for *peregrini*, and hence, as soon as it was admitted that this class of the inhabitants had a right to apply to the legal tribunals, it became necessary for the *prætor*, with the aid of the *imperium* and *jurisdictio* vested in him, to create the judge, the procedure, and the law itself. In this way originated the *formulæ*, which consisted of the *demonstratio* and the *condemnatio*, or the instruction to the *recuperatores* of the point to decide, according to the rules of the *jus gentium*, and the sentence to pass.

When the citizens perceived the simplicity and ready flexibility of this mode of action, they employed it in preference to the *legis actiones*. The *prætors* then endeavoured to amplify the parts of the *formulæ* so as to adapt it to questions of civil law (the process of development is traced in part iii, par. 1829, etc.), and in assimilating the formulæ to the terms of the old sacramental action, they substituted the *demonstratio*, or simple statement, for the first part of the symbolic acts of the *sacramenti actio*, and the direction of the *prætor* in the *intentio* (e. g., *si paret hominem ex jure Quiritium Auli Agerii esse*) will be found to be nearly identical with the words of the plaintiff when placing the lance (*vindicta*) on the subject of litigation (e. g., *Hunc ego hominem ex jure Quiritium meum esse aio*).

258. In this state of affairs, the *Lex Æbutia* simply legalised a method already sanctioned by custom, and in the result, the actions, *judicis postulatio* and *condictio* disappeared, and the procedure for citizens and *peregrini* was assimilated. Hence,

(1) *Recuperatores* (a name for all judges in the provinces), and the *unus judex* and *arbiter* (both at Rome still taken from the senatorial list), came to be employed by citizens as well as *peregrini*.

(2) The college of *centumviri* gradually decayed, the use of the

actio sacramenti with them dwindling to trials as to the validity of testaments.

261. *Extra ordinem cognitio.*—If the magistrate decided the case himself, the method of procedure was called *extra ordinem cognoscere*, hence the term *extraordinaria judicia*, as opposed to the procedure by *formulæ*, which was the *ordinaria judicia*.

263. **Influence of Stoicism.**—According to Suetonius, a deputy from Greece between the second and third Punic war, who had broken his leg, employed the period of his convalescence in publicly teaching philosophy. This led to the foundation of Stoic and Epicurean schools, in spite of the efforts of the senate to put down such innovations.

Stoicism was adapted to the Roman mind, and was, therefore, rapidly imbibed. It took firm root, penetrating deeply Roman jurisprudence, and leading to the settlement of the principles of law according to reason, rather than, as hitherto, resting them on arbitrary power. The new philosophy powerfully tended to the decay of Quiritarian law, by substituting for it a scientifically created system.

265. **Leges Agrariæ.**—The *ager publicus* (*ante*, par. 92), or conquered lands reserved as public property, had increased enormously in extent, and, in accordance with the Agrarian law of *Servius Tullius*, (B.C. 577), a portion of it ought to have been distributed amongst the poorer classes, and the rest let out for the profit of the state; but, under one pretence or another, the whole had accumulated in the hands of patricians and the richer plebeians, who cultivated it with the aid of gangs of slaves furnished by the wars. The ownership of the land being in the state, the tenants only had possession, but by transmitting the property to their heirs, and by freeing it in course of time from the rent *(vectigal)* due to the state, they had suceeeded in acquiring such a title as enabled them to raise a cry of spoliation whenever an attempt was made to oust them.

This was the misunderstood origin of those *leges agrariæ*, whose introduction was usually attended by an insurrection, as aiming at a re-distribution of the public land.

268. The *lex Licinia de modo agrorum*, passed by *C. Licinius Stolo* in B.C. 367, declared that no one should hold more than 500 *jugera* of land, but the tribune violated his own law, and was fined 10,000 *asses* for holding 1,000 *jugera*. Subsequently, the law became obsolete, and all Italy and the provinces having fallen into the hands of the Romans, the evil became worse than ever. Hence the endeavours of the tribune *Tiberius Sempronius Gracchus* to re-model the *lex Licinia*, by passing the *plebiscitum* called the—

269. *Lex Sempronia agraria* (B.C. 133), by which no one was to have more than 500 *jugera* of the *ager publicus* for his own share, and 250 *jugera* for each of his sons. All the rest and all future acquisitions

were to be divided among the poorer citizens at an annual rent, to be paid to the state. But Tiberius was murdered and his brother *Caius Gracchus*, after vainly attempting to carry out the law, was forced to commit suicide. Similar results attended all efforts at legislation on the subject, and in B.C. 107 the *lex Thoria agraria* was passed, which was in the nature of a re-action in favour of the holders of public land. This led to seven successive enactments to counteract its effects, but it was only the last which succeeded in partially remedying the injustice, as by the *lex Julia agraria*, passed by Julius Cæsar when consul in B.C. 59, the public lands of Campania were distributed amongst poor citizens having three or more children.

271. In analogy to the agrarian laws were the *leges frumentariæ*, providing for the distribution of corn gratuitously, or at a low price. The first of these was the *lex Sempronia frumentaria* (B.C. 123), passed by *Caius Gracchus*.

272. **Quæstiones Perpetuæ.** The jurisdiction in *criminal* matters is not clearly defined in Roman law. It was originally vested in the kings with a right of appeal *(provocatio)* to the people; then capital punishment was reserved to the *comitia centuriata*, whilst the *comitia tributa* acquired a repressive power of a political rather than of a judicial nature (*ante*, par. 206). The undefined jurisdiction of the *senate* was usually directed to matters concerning the provinces or strangers, and a number of inferior crimes were left, as private wrongs, to be remedied by action at law. But the regular tribunals had, from early times, been in the habit either of summoning the criminal before themselves, or of referring the inquiry *(quæstio)* to special commissioners *(quæstores)*, *appointed for the particular case*. In this way, the *king* delegated such investigations to patricians; the *comitia* to the senate or to *quæstores*, the *senate* to consuls, prætors, or governors of provinces.

But sometimes these *quæstiones* assumed a more general character, as where a *quæstio* was appointed for a particular class of public offences (*e.g.*, B.C. 186, the *quæstio de clandestinis conjurationibus*, and B.C. 184, the *quæstio de veneficiis* (poisoning) and the *quæstio de homicidiis*), and in this way, with the increase of population and crime, originated the *quæstiones perpetuæ*, the first of which dates from the *lex Calpurnia de repetundis*, passed in B.C. 149, and establishing a permanent commission for the conduct of investigations into complaints of extortions practised on provincials. This was followed, in B.C. 119, by the *lex Maria de ambitu*, for cases of bribery in candidates for magistracies, and the *quæstio peculatus* was also created for misappropriation of public money. In (?) B.C. 106 came the *lex Servilia repetundarum*. In B.C. 102 the *lex Apuleia majestatis* for cases of high treason, and the *lex Luctatia de vi*. In B.C. 95 the *lex Licinia Mucia de civitate*, and in B.C. 89 the *lex Fabia de plagio*, and under Sulla, two *quæstiones* were appointed for crimes against individuals—the one by the *lex Cornelia de falsis* or *testamentaria* (part iii, par. 691), and the other by the *lex Cornelia de Sicariis* (part iii, par. 1775).

From this period, a *plebiscitum* determined precisely the crime, its penalty, the procedure, and the organisation of the particular *quæstio perpetua*, which should have jurisdiction over that class of crime. The expression *perpetual* applies to the tribunal, for it was *annual* in respect of its members, and it was usually presided over by one of the prætors with no special jurisdiction. Hence the sentence was not passed by permanent judges, but by jurymen, whose numbers varied from 32 to 50, 70 or 100, the prosecutor usually selecting double the required number, and the accused rejecting one half. Any citizen could prosecute. He pointed out the accused, named the law he relied upon, and stated the facts in support of the case, took an oath that the charge was not slanderous, became a party to the cause, and was obliged to prove it. The judges were limited to a verdict of guilty, not guilty, or not proven *(condemno, absolvo, non liquet)*, according to the law appealed to, and could not vary the punishment provided, but, in capital cases, the accused could retire into voluntary exile, his property being confiscated.

281. *Cognitiones extraordinariæ (criminal)*. Those crimes not specially provided for were left, as before, to be tried by special *Quæstores*, nominated by the *comitia* or the senate, and this was called *extra-ordinem cognoscere* in *criminal* matters *(ante,* par. 261).

283. **Leges Judiciariæ.** Up to the tribuneship of the second Gracchus, the *senators* had retained the right of being *judges*, probably in both civil and criminal matters, but that tribune succeeded in passing a *plebiscitum* (B.C. 122, *lex Sempronia judiciaria)* transferring the right to the *knights*, and then a series of conflicting laws were enacted according to the temporary ascendancy of the senators or the knights. In B.C. 106, the *lex prima Servilia* divided the right between the two orders; B.C. 100, the *lex secunda Servilia* to the knights; B.C. 91, *lex Livia* between the two orders: B.C. 82, *lex Cornelia* (of Sulla) to the senators, B.C. 70, *lex Aurelia* and B.C. 55 *lex Pompeia* (both under Pompey) between the two orders.

It was the duty of the *prætor urbanus*, after taking an oath to adhere to the prescribed number and class of citizens, to prepare the *annual* lists of *judices selecti* (or *in albo relati)* exhibited in the forum. By the *lex Aurelia*, the lists were to be in three decuries. (1) Senators; (2) knights; (3) tribunes of the treasury. Under Augustus there were four, and under Caligula five lists with particular names, and the number of judges gradually rose from the original 300 to about 4,000.

287. **Senatus Consulta.** *Theophilus*, in his paraphrase of Justinian's institutes, asserts that the *lex Hortensia (ante,* par. 178) effected a compromise, and gave the senate's decrees binding force, at the same time that *plebiscita* were finally made compulsory on all classes, *Cicero*, when including the *senatus consulta* under the sources of law, employs nearly the same expressions as used by *Gaius* and *Justinian (post,* inst. i. 2 § 3), and *Pomponius* assumes their authority to have

arisen from the necessity of the case. It seems probable that no legislative enactment ever gave *senatus consulta* the force of law, but that after the passing of the *lex Hortensia* the senate only directly interfered on extraordinary occasions, and that the right of such intervention was tacitly admitted. In republican times and in relation to *private* law the number of their decrees is small, the more important being one in B.C. 177, requiring magistrates to administer an oath as to the genuine object of the *manumissio vindicta*, another, in existence previous to B.C. 100, preventing *freemen* recovering their liberty after a fraudulent sale, and a decree subsequent to Cicero's time conferring the right of bequeathing the *usufruct* of the entire patrimony. But it was a recognised principle that the senate could not repeal any existing law, and in later times (*post*, par. 350) their decrees assumed rather the form of direct orders to magistrates, as in the case of the *senatus consultum Velleianum*, and that of *Macedonianum* (part iii, par. 1411 and 2217).

290. **Jus Honorarium.** Roman magistrates, such as consuls, prætors, curule ædiles, censors, and plebeian tribunes, had always necessarily exercised the right of publishing orders and notices respecting the matters within their jurisdiction. This was called *edicere,* a term derived from the sacramental words *do, dico, addico.* Certain of these magistrates and the governors of provinces had also in various ways publicly to state the law, and hence the expressions :

Jus dicere, to declare the law or organise the formula.
Addicere, to assign ownership by a declaration of law.
Edicere, to declare the law beforehand.
Inter-dicere, to make a law between the parties to a suit.

The result of this system was the existence of part of Roman law in the shape of edicts.

Prætoris edictum, composed by the *prætor urbanus,* who had to supply defects in the law, and the *prætor peregrinus,* who had to introduce an entirely new law, the *jus gentium.*

Edictum Ædilium (or *Ædilitium edictum*), made by the ædiles in the course of regulating the games, streets, police, markets, etc.

Edictum provinciale, built up by the governors of provinces in the effort to fuse Roman law with the law of the conquered country.

Hence, not by design but from necessity *(propter utilitatem publicam)*, these edicts not only laid down rules, but supplied the wants and corrected the defects of the civil law *(adjuvandi, vel supplendi vel corrigendi juris civilis gratia.*—Papinian).

In course of time the publication of edicts became regularised by precedent and by the *lex Cornelia de edictis* (B.C. 66); the edict must be (1) published on taking office, and (2) the magistrate issuing it is to be bound by it; but this law only confirmed a usage, for the second head was taken by Cicero as a point in his oration against Verres, delivered before the passing of the act in question.

The obligatory force of the edict *(lex annua)* ceased at the end of the year of office of its author. His successor appropriated, altered, or annulled it as he thought proper ; but except as to additions or modifications in details *(edictum novum)*, the edict as a whole naturally passed from one magistrate to the next *(edictum tralatitium)*, and thus, becoming part of the *customary* law, the power of annulling any important portion of it ultimately ceased.

Edicts for the whole year were called *edicta perpetua* (for the subsequent change of meaning in the word *perpetuum* see *post*, par. 384), to distinguish them from *edicta repentina*, made to serve temporary ends, and the term *interdictum (edictum inter duos)* referred to orders in respect of two particular parties. The law thus introduced through the medium of magistrates was called *jus honorarium*. It was divided into *jus prætorium* and jus *ædilium*, the former being the more important portion, and as this law embodied the teachings of science and philosophy, it moulded itself according to the principles of equity and nature adopted by an advancing civilisation. Hence it gradually overlaid the Quiritarian law, and Cicero complained that the twelve tables were no longer studied, being replaced by the Prætorian edict.

298. *The Social War* (B.C. 91). The cities of Italy had been long put off with promises of receiving more complete rights, and they at length broke out into open insurrection, which was only quelled by inscribing as citizens those who had not taken part in the war, and finally those still fighting (B.C. 90 *lex Julia*, and B.C. 89 *lex Plautia de civitate*). Thus within two years nearly the whole of Italy acquired the full rights of citizenship, including the suffrage, and the soil of Italy became assimilated to the *ager Romanus*. After this period, the distinction as to inhabitants and land was confined to the provinces outside Italy.

300. *The Civil Wars* (B.C. 87). The struggles for power between *Marius* and *Sulla* ended in the supremacy of the latter, and he was made perpetual *dictator*, an office which had not existed for nearly a century, as the senate in times of danger had temporarily increased the powers of the consuls under the formula, *caveant consules ne quid detrimenti respublica capiat*. Sulla, in his endeavours to revive the ancient republic, restored the position of the senators, invested the *comitia centuriata* with full powers, whilst he dissolved the *tributa*, and degraded the *knights*, together with the *plebeians* and their *tribunes*. The laws passed by him as to judges, testaments, and murder are noticed *ante*, par. 272, 283.

301. *The Servile War* (B.C. 73). The war of the slaves and of the gladiators severely tried the power of Rome and was only extinguished after hard fighting by the destruction of *Spartacus* and his followers.

302. In B.C. 70 the *civil wars* broke out again, and *Pompey*, when in the ascendant, undid the work of *Sulla*, by restoring to the *plebeians* their *assembly*, to the *tribunes* their privileges, to the *knights* their *judicial* powers (*ante*, par. 283). Then came the first triumvi-

rate of Pompey, Cæsar, and Crassus. In B.C. 53 Crassus was killed, and five years later, after Pompey's assassination, Cæsar was appointed dictator. In the same year (B.C. 48) all *Cisalpine Gaul* received citizen rights, and the two *ædiles cereales* were created *(qui frumento præessent)*. Then followed the wars consequent on the assassination of Cæsar, B.C. 44. The second triumvirate (Antony, Lepidus, and Octavius), was disgraced by the proscriptions in which Octavius sacrificed Cicero (B.C. 43) to the vengeance of Antony, and finally *Octavianus*, the adopted son of Cæsar, remained master of Rome.

REVIEW OF THE PRECEDING PERIOD.

308. *Foreign Policy*. The armies of Rome have succeeded in conquering the known world. More than one king has by will instituted the Roman people his heirs, and other kings have applied to be decorated with the title of *civis*.

Italy, both as to soil and inhabitants, enjoys the Roman law, hence the greater or less concessions included under the terms Latin allies, Italian allies, colonists, and municipes, refer only to the provinces.

In Africa, Asia, Spain, and Gaul, *colonies* have been planted, some *Roman* some *Latin (i.e.*, with the *jus Latinitatis)*, and a new description or *military* colony has been created by distributing a portion of the conquered territory as a reward to the soldiery.

In the provinces, the expression *subjecti* includes all the inhabitants not enjoying special rights. These, besides the rent *(vectigal)* for their land and the personal tax, groan under indirect contributions of all sorts levied by the pro-consuls, quæstors, and publicani, who calculate the sum they can sacrifice to secure their election by the amount they can subsequently extract from the province.

315. *Public Law*. The people, the senate (the knights), and the plebeians are still the political bodies, but only nominally, for all are under the despotism of the ambitious and the tyranny of the army.

The *legislative* power rests with the *comitia centuriata* and *tributa*, the senate and certain magistrates, whose edicts constitute annual laws. The difference between the ancient standards of fortune and those now existing has caused an alteration in the composition of the *comitia centuriata*, the details of which are uncertain, but one important change is the secrecy of the ballot, and this is regulated (according to Cicero) by four *leges tabellariæ* (B.C. 140, *lex Gabinia*, as to the appointment of magistrates; B.C. 138, *lex Cassia* as to criminal sentences; B.C. 108, a *lex* of *Papirius Cælius Caldus*, as to high treason; B.C. 92 a *lex* of *Papirius Carbo* as to voting for laws). Each citizen has two tickets *(tabellæ)*, one bearing the letters U.R. *(uti rogas)*, the other A. *(antiquo)*, the tribes or centuries are collected in pens *(septa, ovilia)*, and the individual voters pass one by one over narrow bridges dropping the ticket into a long wicker basket. Endless artifices are employed to secure votes, whether for an election, a criminal judgment, or for the adoption of laws.

318. The sources of *written* law are :—

(1) *Leges*, now rare and almost replaced by (2) *plebiscita*, and (3) *senatus consulta*, which will soon replace both the former. For *unwritten* law the sources are :—

(1) *Edicts* of the magistrates, which although written *in albo*, are not statute laws, each edict being only a *lex annua*, but they are becoming *customary* law, and are removing the austerities of the *jus Quiritium*, and bringing it into harmony with natural equity. (2) *Responsa prudentum*, by which legal principles are evolved.

319. The *executive* and *electoral* power remain, in principle, as before, the *elections* with the people and the plebeians, the *administration* with the senate and some magistrates, the command of the armies with the consuls or (through a *lex curiata*) with the proconsuls and pro-prætors, but in reality force, money, and intrigue regulate affairs. The plebeian *tribunes* have long claimed the right of convoking the senate *(senatus habendi)*, and the *lex Atinia*, a *plebiscitum* passed in B.C. 129, gave them senatorial dignity, and consequently admission into the senate. Their power of *intercessio* has increased (though temporarily suspended by Sulla, *ante*, par. 300, 302), but they and other magistrates are not now allowed to exercise it in respect of *senatus consulta*.

322. The *judicial* power is exercised by sixteen prætors, acting as magistrates, whilst the centumvirs, decemvirs, judices (or arbitri), and the recuperatores perform the functions of a jury. The ædiles have also a tribunal and jurisdiction.

323. In *criminal* law the establishment of *quæstiones perpetuæ* has improved the administration in respect of the crimes falling within their cognizance, for no one can be brought before these tribunals except by virtue of a *lex, plebiscitum*, or *senatus-consultum*, approved by the tribunes.

324. In *civil* matters the *legis actiones* have almost disappeared, and the centumvirs and decemvirs (of whose duties little is known) are seldom called upon to act, but the system of *formulæ* still maintains the distinction between the *jurisdictio* of the magistrate and the *judicium* of the judex, arbiter, or recuperatores.

326. *Taxation.* Previous to Servius Tullius, each citizen paid an arbitrary capitation tax *(viritim)*. After the establishment of the classes (*ante*, par. 56) taxes varied according to fortune, the *proletarii* being exempt; and subsequently unmarried men and women, orphans under age, and all those falling under the term *ærarii (i.e.*, not inscribed in a tribe), were subjected to a poll tax fixed by the censor, and applied towards the pay of the soldiery, but from the battle of Pydna (B.C. 168), resulting in the conquest of Macedon by Æmilius Paulus, and until the reign of Augustus, *no direct* taxes were paid by Roman citizens. The *public revenue* was derived from the public lands, booty, tribute of provinces, mines, the monopoly in the sale of salt, customs dues, and a duty of one-twentieth on the sale or enfranchisement of slaves. The *public expenditure* was

mainly for the pay of the troops, and the conduct of distant wars, for public buildings, roads, and aqueducts, and especially for the gratuitous distribution of corn to certain classes of the citizens. Magistrates were not yet salaried, but governors of provinces and their subordinates enriched themselves at the expense of the provincials.

327. *Sacred Law* is still connected with political administration, but its influence in civil law is partly gone. The Augurs are regularly consulted. Their number, since the time of Sulla, has been increased to fifteen, and they, like the pontiffs, are appointed by the *comitia*. The gods multiply indefinitely as each successful Roman general in a set form of prayer undertakes to erect altars, and establish games in honour of those tutelary divinities, who will abandon conquered cities and transfer their protection to Rome.

329. *Private Law*. In respect of *persons*, the *potestas* over slaves is the same, but their position has improved, the *patria potestas* is softened, the *manus* has nearly disappeared, and of the three modes of acquiring it (1) *co-emptio (ante*, par. 89), is rarely employed; (2) *confarreatio* is restricted to the pontiffs, and (3) *usus (ante*, twelve tables vi. 4) has fallen into disuse. The *mancipium* over the free man only takes place fictitiously or in a modified form, *gentilitas* is nearly extinct, *cognatio* begins to affect the position of relations. The perpetual tutelage of women is nearly abolished, the guardian only interferes in important acts, and cannot refuse to give his *auctoritas* unless he is an agnate, in which case his opposition can be got rid of by the *co-emptio* (see above) or fictitious sale *per æs et libram*, by which the woman feigns to pass *in manu* of the purchaser, and so defeats agnate rights, including tutorship (this is an example of using the ancient law, in order to evade it).

330. As to *things*, the distinction of *mancipi* and *nec mancipi* still exists, but the word *dominium*, recognising the idea of the co-proprietorship of the children in the property (*in domo*), has taken the place of the expression *mancipium*, indicative of the arbitrary and absolute rights of the head of the family, and a new kind of ownership "*in bonis*" (the *dominium bonitarium* of the commentators) has arisen.

331. As to *wills*, the absolute powers of the paterfamilias are curtailed, and, as a result of the idea of the children's co-ownership, he must now, if he wish to exclude them, formally disinherit them (*exhæredatio*), and a just motive is necessary, or the testament may be attacked before the centumvirs as *inofficiosum* (part iii, par. 788), *i.e.*, under the fiction of insanity, and thus a cause of nullity, unknown to the old law, is brought in under one known.

332. In the rules as to *succession*, the claims of natural ties are recognised, and the prætor has evaded the law by means of the change of a word. Under the title of *bonorum possessor*, an emancipated child, or one given in adoption, may be protected in his

practical ownership of the property, and the nearest *cognate* is now preferred to the *fiscus*.

333. The number of *contracts* has increased. The *nexum* has been transformèd, and produced four binding agreements contracted *re*, *i.e.*, by the delivery of the thing, viz., *mutuum*, *commodatum*, *depositum*, *pignus* (part iii, par. 1205, etc). In the *stipulatio*, the first derivative of the *nexum*, the words *spondes*, *spondeo* are still exclusively for citizens, but strangers may use the words *promittis promitto*, and another derivative, the contract *litteris* (part iii, par. 1414) has been introduced and extended to strangers.

The *jus gentium* has given rise to four contracts, depending on consent alone, viz., *emptio-venditio*, *locatio-conductio*, *societas*, and *mandatum* (part iii, par. 1444, 1492, 1523, 1550); and some agreements *(pacta)* producing no bond and no action at law, unless accompanied by a stipulation, have been enforced by the prætor, and so acquired the name *Prætorian pact*.

Jurisprudence has also, in addition to the delicts classed under the civil law, recognised other wrongs *(e.g.*, deceit and violence) as the source of obligations, and hence *civil*, *prætorian*, and *natural* obligations now exist.

334. *Actions*. Owing to the disappearance of the *legis actiones* (*ante*, par. 324), the word *actio* now means the right to sue, given by civil or prætorian law. In cases where equity seems to demand it, and the civil law affords no remedy, the prætor gives a prætorian action *(honoraria actio)*, and on the other hand, where the civil law gives an inequitable action, the ꞌprætor does not abolish it, but renders it useless by means of an *exception*, *i.e.*, a restriction in the *formulæ* on the power to condemn.

Roman law commenced to flourish at this period. Advancing civilization, bringing in its train ideas as to equity and natural law, has caused the practical disappearance of the *jus Quiritium*, and though the legaľ machinery contains two conflicting elements (civil and prætorian law), the ingenuity of the jurisconsult has been so successfully applied to their nice adjustment that they now work together with tolerable harmony.

336. *Manners and customs*. Two peculiarities may be noticed:—
(1) Consuls and other principal magistrates of the city appear before the civil and criminal tribunals to plead the cause of citizens, a practice probably due to the notoriety acquired by delivering the discourse in the forum, especially when of a political nature; and (2) the habit of committing suicide, due to the fact that with the defeat of a party, punishment by the proscription follows and escape is impossible.

THIRD EPOCH.—The Emperors.

§ 1. *From the establishment of the Empire to Constantine.*

337. *Augustus, Emperor,* B.C. 31.—The *senate* in B.C. 29, conferred on Octavian the military title of *imperator*, and confirmed all his acts. In B.C. 27 he was styled *Patriæ Pater* (P.P.) and *Augustus* (name for sacred things), the supreme power was vested in him for ten years, the most important provinces (*provinciæ Cæsaris*) were delivered to him, and only the tranquil ones reserved to the people (*provinciæ populi*). Later the *people* bestowed upon him in perpetuity the tribunician, consular, and proconsular power, and the *senate* renewed the absolute power for ten years, after which the people made him sovereign *pontiff*, so that, without apparently destroying the republican magistracies, Augustus accumulated them in his own person, and so acquired absolute power.

Imperial Magistracies.

338. Although the consuls, prætors, etc., were nominally subordinate colleagues of Augustus, the change in the constitution led to their gradual disappearance, and the creation of offices more immediately dependent on the emperor, viz:—

Legati Cæsaris. — *Military* commanders of the *provinciæ Cæsaris*, the proconsuls in the *provinciæ populi* being only *civil* magistrates, but both bearing the general title of *præses provinciæ*.

Procuratores Cæsaris.—Under this title freedmen and private agents of the emperor collected in the *provinciæ Cæsaris* the *tributum*, which went into the *imperial* treasury (*fiscus*); whilst *quæstors*, in the *provinciæ populi* collected the *stipendium*, which went into the *public* treasury (*ærarium*).

Subsequently, these *procuratores* acquired jurisdiction in fiscal matters, and at times replaced the *præses provinciæ*.

Præfectus urbi.—This was the old title of an officer who remained in Rome for its protection when the head of the government was absent with the army. The office was now made *permanent*, and its power so increased as finally to take precedence of the prætors, and to include nearly the whole *criminal* jurisdiction, and some of the functions of the curule ædiles, but limited to a circuit of one hundred miles from Rome.

Præfecti Prætorio.—These were the two commanders of the *Prætorian guards*, said to be derived from the *celeres* (*ante*, par. 61) of Romulus. Subsequently these officers acquired *civil* authority, and when their duties were ultimately restricted to *civil* matters, several illustrious jurisconsults held the office.

Quæstores Candidati Principis.—These officials read the emperor's addresses to the senate.

Præfectus Annonarum.—Prefect of provisions, and subordinate to the urban prefect.

Præfectus Vigilum. — This officer replaced the *quinqueviri* (*ante*, par. 222), and was in charge of the seven cohorts (each commanded by a tribune) which acted as the night guard of the fourteen quarters of Rome. He was also a subordinate magistrate for misdemeanours (*e.g.*, burglary, thefts in the baths, etc.)

The principal magistrates were allowed to select *adsessores* to assist them in the routine portion of their duties, and these officials were paid by the state.

Constitutiones Principum.

350. After the fall of the republic, and in respect of *private* law, *senatus consulta* (*ante*, par. 287) acquired more extension, and *Gaius* (Inst., i, § 4), writing in the time of Marcus Aurelius, speaks of the authority of the senate as indisputably established; but the last *senatus consultum*, of which the date is known with certainty, was passed in the reign of Septimius Severus, A.D. 206. Hence, it may be assumed, that they were gradually superseded by the will of the emperor which ultimately became the only source of law. The *imperial* decrees were of three classes,

(1) *Edicta, i.e.*, general ordinances, or laws for the future.

(2) *Decreta, i.e.*, judgments pronounced in the emperor's tribunal (*cognoscens*), and these might serve as precedents.

(3) *Mandata, Epistola, Rescripta, i.e.*, directions to legati, prætors, etc., on matters of law referred to the emperor, or answers to the petitions of private persons (part iii, par. 136).

All these three classes probably existed in the time of Augustus, though he disguised his power by appearing to consult the people or the senate, and hence the first direct constitution referred to by Justinian dates from Hadrian only (*post*, par. 384 and 550), but the following are earlier examples, *Mandata* or *rescripta*':—Julius Cæsar temporarily authorised informal military testaments; Augustus, Nerva and Trajan gave soldiers the power of bequeathing by will their *peculium castrense;* Augustus ordered the execution of *fideicommissa*. *Edictum :*—Augustus, and afterwards Claudius, forbad wives to charge themselves with the debts of their husbands. *Decretum :*—Tiberius decided a point of law as to one of his slaves (part iii, par. 748).

The origin of the right of issuing constitutions (*jus constituere*) may be traced to the power shared by the emperor, with other superior magistrates, of publishing edicts. This right was conferred upon the emperor by the *lex regia*, a law which was formerly the subject of dispute until the discovery of the Institutes of Gaius and of the Republic of Cicero showed that the *lex curiata* (*vetus regia lex, simul cum urbe nata*—Livy), which gave the king, and the magistrates of the republic, the *imperium* (*ante*, par. 27), was still employed for investing the emperors with their powers (*qua de ejus imperio lata est.*—Just. Inst., i, 1, 6. *Cum ipse imperator per legem imperium accipiat.*—Gai. Inst., i, § 5).

The term *lex regia* is not used by Gaius, *lex imperii* (or *de imperio*) being the later expression for the *lex curiata*, proposed by an *interrex* for the vote of the lictors (*ante*, par. 31). The power given to Sulla by L. Flaccus, the interrex, was *Ut omnia quæcumque ille fecisset, essent rata* (Cicero).

355. **Jus publice respondendi.**—Under the emperors, a privileged class of official jurisconsults arose who were invested with authority (*ut ex auctoritate ejus responderent*) and in proof of it appended their *seal* (*responsa signata*); but the opinions thus delivered were, probably, not in the time of Augustus binding on the judges, nor were the jurisconsults paid by the state, and it is difficult to determine the position of those who still continued to advise on their own responsibility. There is no extant list of these privileged jurisconsults, and, according to Pomponius, *Masurius Sabinus*, in the time of Tiberius, was the first to receive the imperial authority, so that Augustus would appear not to have himself made use of the innovation he introduced. See *post*, par. 384 (7).

361. **Consistorium.**—Following a practice, which had been in use in republican times, of seeking similar assistance, Augustus assembled a number of these selected jurisconsults to form the *consilia semestria*, by whom projects to be laid before the senate were previously discussed, and from this *consilium*, or private council, originated the *consistorium*, which, in the time of Hadrian, became a regular institution; and, because, when hearing legal questions, it sat in the *auditorium*, the council also acquired the latter title, and subsequently the two councils were distinct (*post*, par. 384).

In Just. Inst., ii, 25, Augustus is stated to have called in these jurisconsults respecting codicils; and, according to the Digest (34, 14, 17), Marcus Aurelius and L. Verus consulted them respecting the succession of freedmen. Celsus, Neratius, and Julianus, are known to have formed part of the Council of Hadrian; Mœcianus and Marcellus of that of Antoninus Pius; and, under Alexander Severus, the legal tribunal consisted of at least twenty.

362. **Proculeiani and Sabiniani.**—These two schools of jurisprudents were founded by *M. Antistius Labeo* and *C. Ateius Capito*, the former an independent, incorruptible republican, with liberal views and wide scientific training; the latter a courtier and consul of Augustus, and an opponent of innovation. It is probable that by this time, *teaching the law* (*legum doctores docentes*—Modestinus) had become separated from the practical work of the jurisconsult, for *Sabinus* supported himself by the voluntary fees received from his auditors, and *Labeo* spent six months of the year in town with his students, so that schools (*scholæ*) could be formed with regular students (*studiosi*), who propagated the particular views in matters of detail of their leaders (*præceptores*), and widened the schism (*eas dissensiones auxerunt*). Hence the distinction became more apparent after the schools had been in existence for some time, and this

may account for the sects bearing the names of the early disciples and not of their masters (Proculeians or Pegasians, from *Proculus* and *Pegasus*, followers of *Labeo;* Sabinians or Cassians, from *Sabinus* and *Cassius*, followers of *Capito*).

Pomponius (*post*, par. 392) gives a list of the leaders of the two schools up to his time; viz.:

Sabinians—Capito, Masurius Sabinus, Cassius, Cælius Sabinus, Javolenus, Valens, Fuscianus, Salvius Julianus.

Proculeians — Labeo, Nerva, Proculus, Nerva (son), *Pegasus, Celsus, Celsus* (son), *Neratius Priscus.*

Gaius (Inst., ii, § 195) in the time of Marcus Aurelius, (*post*, par. 393) calls the Sabinians *præceptores nostri*, and the Proculeians *diversæ scholæ auctores*.

Members of opposite schools occasionally adopted the opinions of their opponents on particular points, *e. g., Proculus* of the *Sabinians*, (Dig. 7. 5, 3); and *Javolenus* of the *Proculeians*, (Dig. 28. 5, 11); and after a rivalry of nearly two centuries the schools disappeared, or were united in the person of the "prince of jurisconsults", *Papinian* (*post*, par. 395); but the differences of views of the two schools are found in the Digest of Justinian in spite of the harmony which the editors were directed to introduce.

The existence of a third sect (*Erciscundi* or *Miscelliones*) appears to be a mistake of Cujas.

369. **Leges Julia et Papia** (B.C. 18, and A.D. 9).—Augustus endeavoured to remedy the corruption of manners and exhaustion of the legitimate population by a *plebiscitum* (*lex Julia de Maritandis ordinibus*), which was rejected by the *comitia* in B.C. 28, but adopted ten years later. A second project (*lex Papia Poppæa*), passed twenty-six years afterwards, completed the system.

These laws (called also *Novæ Leges*, or *Leges*) were the most important legislative enactments since the twelve tables, and greatly affected the position of individuals in respect of the private law.

Society was divided by the *lex Julia* into *married* persons and *cœlibes, i. e., unmarried* persons at the moment in question, a *vacatio*, or interval of 2 years after the death of a husband, or 1½ years after divorce, being allowed *women*.

The *lex Papia* made a division into *those persons with children* (*patres, matres*), and *orbi, i. e.*, those not having a living legitimate child; but, in the case of women, fecundity (for a *free* woman 3 births, for a *freed* woman 4 births), whether legitimate or not gave the *jus liberorum*.

By the combination of the two laws, although all had the *testamenti factio* (*ante*, par. 185), yet the *jus capiendi ex testamento* was taken from the *cœlibes* altogether, and from the *orbi* to the extent of one half, unless within 100 days from the *opening of the will*, the first were married, or the second had children.

This distinction between the capability of being named in the will and of actually receiving testamentary bequests became very marked in Roman jurisprudence, and then disappeared.

Legacies lost *(in causa caduci)* by failure to comply with the conditions imposed by these laws were called *caduca*, and as *præmia patrum* went in certain proportions (Gai. Inst., ii, § 206, 286) to those of the heirs or legatees who had legitimate offspring *(qui in eo testamento liberos habent)*, and hence the *jus caduca vindicandi* is referred to as a mode of acquiring ownership *ex lege* (Ulp. Reg. xix, § 17). Failing these *patres*, the lapsed legacy fell into the *ærarium*, a term which, under the emperors, came to be synonymous with *fiscus*—i.e., the procedure with reference to the *caduca* would take place before the prefect of the *ærarium*, and the *fiscus* would take the property (see *ante*, par. 338).

Personæ exceptæ, from age or other impossibility of complying with these laws, could take, as before, the whole legacy (*solidi capaces*.)

Ascendants and descendants of the testator to the third degree enjoyed the ancient law *(jus antiquum intactum eis conservans in caducis)*, and could take lapsed legacies also.

Previous to the discovery of the Institutes of *Gaius*, that is of the writings of a jurisconsult who died previous to Caracalla, the words of *Ulpian* (Reg. xvii, § 2), who lived through the reign of that emperor, could not be understood, "*Hodie ex constitutione imperatoris Antonini omnia caduca fisco vindicantur, sed servato jure antiquo liberis et parentibus,*" for the original destination of the *caduca* was not known. The change referred to by Ulpian resulted from the constitution of *Caracalla (post,* par. 396), preserving the rights of the ascendants and descendants, but shutting out the *patres* and making the *caduca* of *cœlibes* and *orbi* go at once to the *fiscus*. To satisfy public feeling, the successors of Caracalla (? Macrinus or Alexander Severus) probably restored the rights of *patres ;* and the influence of Christianity, which was supposed to reprove second marriages and favour celibacy, caused *Constantine (post,* par. 479) to publish a constitution, A.D. 320, removing the incapacities of the *cœlibes* and *orbi*, though, to avoid undue influence, the caduca laws were allowed to remain in force in respect of gifts between married persons, unless they had a *common* child ; but this source of incapacity was removed by Honorius and Theodosius in A.D. 410.

Justinian represents these laws as having fallen into disuse, and in A.D. 534 (code vi, 51, *de caducis tollendis*), removed the confusion which had arisen in the subject by restoring the *jus antiquum* to all, so that probably the only causes of *caduca* in his time would be those of the old civil law, viz., the legatee's death, refusal to accept, loss of rights of citizenship, or failure to comply with some condition imposed; and Justinian restored the rule as to the death of the testator being the date, not the opening of the will (part iii, par. 875).

378. In the latter part of the reign of Augustus, the wishes of testators couched in the form of *fidei-commissa,* and often embodied in *codicilli*, came to be enforced (part iii, par. 973), and a stop was put on the ostentatious manumission of slaves by the *lex Ælia Sentia* and the *lex Furia Caninia* (part iii, par. 64 and 79).

381. After the accession of *Tiberius*, A.D. 14, the elections were transferred from the people to the *senate*, the emperor nominating some candidates. The cognizance of cases of high treason was referred to the senate, and as the crime was extended to include actions, writings, words, or thoughts against the emperor, it called into existence a numerous class of informers *(delatores)*.

382. The *lex Junia Norbana*, passed in A.D. 19, divided freedmen into two classes (part iii, par. 65), and the incapacities of the *latini juniani*, gave rise to a new application of the laws as to *caduca*.

383. The juriconsults of eminence during the reign were *Masurius Sabinus (ante*, par. 355), *Cassius, Nerva*, the elder, and *Proculus (ante*, par. 362).

384. Under *Claudius* (A.D. 41) two *fidei commissarii prætors* were created, and under *Titus* (A.D. 79), one of them suppressed (part iii, par. 950). In the reign of *Trajan* (A.D. 98) lived the juriconsults *Celsus*, the younger, *Neratius Priscus*, and *Javolenus*.

385. *Hadrian, Emperor*, A.D. 17. This reign is remarkable for :—

(1) The division of Italy into four consular provinces, the consuls being subsequently replaced by *correctores* or *præsides*.

(2) The division of the council of the emperor into the *consistorium* and the *auditorium principis (ante*, par. 361).

(3) The commencement of the *civil* jurisdiction of the *prætorian prefects (ante*, par. 338).

(4) The perfecting of the system of appeal *(appellatio provocatio, ante*, par. 208), condemned persons being allowed to apply to a superior magistrate, and finally to the emperor.

(5) The commencement of imperial constitutions *(ante* par. 350).

(6) The appearance of the *edictum perpetuum* (or *divi Hadriani*). Several juriconsults had endeavoured to reduce the *prætorian* law into a methodical system, particularly (according to Pomponius) *Aulus Ofilius*, a friend of Cæsar; and of the three eminent Sabinian jurists in this reign, *Salvius Julianus, Valens*, and *Africanus*, the first-named, who was a prætor, and who had also been *præfectus urbi* and twice consul, now prepared an edict, intended to embody the whole of that prætorian law, which time had developed to its full proportions. This work of *Julianus* was published by order of the emperor, and sanctioned by a *senatus-consultum*, so that the perpetual edict was no longer merely the *lex annua* of a magistrate *(ante*, par. 290), and though *Gaius* (Inst., i, § 6) speaks of the prætors and ædiles still exercising their right of publishing edicts, it is probable that they were bound to conform to the general rules of the Julian edict.

(7) The *sententiæ* and *opiniones* of certain privileged juriconsults *(quibus permissum est jura condere)* now became part of the *written* law, for by a rescript of Hadrian the judges were to be bound by them if unanimous (Gai. Inst., i, § 7).

392. *Antoninus Pius* succeeded Hadrian in A.D. 138. He founded at the public expense several classes of philosophy, both at Rome

THIRD EPOCH.—THE EMPERORS.

and in the provinces, and forbade cruelty towards slaves (part iii, par. 89). The jurisconsults were *Clemens*, *Mæcianus*, and *Sextus Pomponius*, the last named of whom wrote the abridgment of the *History of law* (Dig. i, 2), from which our information on the subject is mainly derived *ante*, par. 362).

393. The *Divi Fratres*, Marcus *Aurelius* and Lucius *Verus*, succeeded Antonine in A.D. 161, and in A.D. 169 the former reigned alone.

The jurisconsults were *Papirius*, *Q. Cervidius Scævola*, *Marcellus*, and—

Gaius. This is the only name that has survived of this illustrious jurisconsult, who probably lived under Hadrian, Antoninus Pius, and Marcus Aurelius (see use of the word *divus* and *pius* in his Inst., ii, § 195, and their absence in i, § 53, 74, 102, 120, 126). He was a *Sabinian* (*ante*, par. 362); and our knowledge of the points of difference between the two schools is mainly derived from him. The first recognition of the value of his writings is in the *lex de responsis prudentum* (*post*, par. 499); but he published a large number of works, chiefly on the twelve tables, on the three edicts (*urbanum*, *ædilium*, *provinciale*), on the *lex Papia*, on the works of Quintus Mucius *Scævola*, besides *Regulæ*, and seven books of *Rerum quotidianarum*, which received the name *aurearum*. A MS. of 126 leaves, of a date anterior to Justinian, was discovered by Niebuhr, in 1816, at Verona, which proved to be a palimpsest, containing underneath the letters of St. Jerome, the *Institutiones* of Gaius, an elementary work in four commentaries, upon which Justinian's Institutes (*post*, par. 548) were founded, and presenting a synoptical review, under three heads (persons, things, actions), of the jurisprudence of the time of Antoninus Pius and Marcus Aurelius.

395. *Septimius Severus* was proclaimed emperor A.D. 193. He was a pupil of the Prætorian prefect and celebrated jurisconsult— *Æmilius Papinianus*, who wrote the *Quæstionum*, *Responsorum*, *et Definitionum libri*, of which many fragments are found in the Digest. It is said that Caracalla put him to death for refusing to appear before the senate in defence of the murder of Geta. Two centuries later, students whose studies were sufficiently advanced to read Papinian's works were called *Papinianistes* (*post*, par. 570).

396. *Antoninus Caracalla* became sole emperor in A.D. 212. His reign is remarkable for—

(1) *The modification of the leges Julia et Papia*, by which, in order to increase his revenue, he, besides doubling (from $\frac{1}{20}$th to $\frac{1}{10}$th) the tax on inheritances, legacies, and gifts *mortis causa*, made *caduca* fall at once to the *fiscus* (*ante*, par. 369).

(2) *The rights of citizenship conceded to all subjects of the empire.* Under imperial rule, the Roman people generally were deprived of political life; but the *coloniæ* and *municipia*, established in the provinces, continued to enjoy their local administration. The bronze tables of *Malaga* and *Salpensa*, discovered in 1851, have thrown much light on the position of *municipia* in the time of Diocletian,

and Pliny, writing in the time of Titus, has classified with care the differences in the privileges (*ante*, par. 186) conferred upon cities and provinces. These various degrees of concessions varied under the emperors, according to the dictates of policy, affection, or folly (*e.g.*, Claudius, born at Lyons, was favourable to the Gauls, Trajan to Spain; Nero, crowned at the Olympic games, gave Achaia its liberty; Vespasian gave all Spain the *jus Latii*; and Septimius Severus took away citizen rights from Neapolis, in Palestine, for assisting his competitor Niger). These considerations indicate that the *jus Latii* or *jus veteris Latii* (especially after the *Lex Junia Norbana*, creating the class of freedmen called *Latini Juniani*) had acquired, besides its original *local* signification, a *personal* character, that the inhabitants of the empire were classed as *cives, latini*, and *peregrini*. On the other hand, Savigny has shown that after Italy had acquired, as the result of the social war, complete rights, the *jus Italicum* applied as a *territorial* distinction to mark the difference between land assimilated to that of Italy as opposed to *provincial* soil, the advantages to the dwellers on such land being (1) freedom from the *vectigal*, (2) power of holding land *ex jure Quiritium*, involving powers as to *mancipatio, in jure cessio, usucapio*, etc., (3) the right to claim the *jus liberorum* (*post*, par. 479).

Dion Cassius asserts that Caracalla's object in conferring Roman citizenship upon all the inhabitants of the empire was to increase the number of persons liable to the tax on the manumission of slaves, on legacies, and on successions; but there are many difficulties in the way of realising the effect of the change. Probably the word *peregrini* now only referred to those Barbarians who mixed with the subjects of the empire, and that with the exception of these and certain *freed* persons (for it was not until Justinian that all distinctions were suppressed, part iii, par. 63), and those disgraced by a condemnation, the equality of rights was universal, and the terms *quirites* and *gens togata* now applied to all the varieties of the human race constituting the Roman world. Hence the *connubium* or power of contracting *justæ nuptiæ* became common to all, slaves could only now be made of Barbarians beyond the limits of the empire, and all provincials became eligible to serve in the legions.

But Caracalla's constitution did not touch the soil, for the loss of the *vectigal* would not have fallen in with his fiscal views, and therefore, though the *personal jus Latii* rights disappeared, the exclusively *territorial* distinction implied by the terms *solum italicum* and *solum provinciale* continued down to Justinian.

419. Much of the information of the jurisprudence of this period is derived from the writings of—

Domitius Ulpianus of Tyre, and *Julius Paulus* of Padua, who both lived in the time of Papinian, and both became prætorian prefects. Besides other works the former wrote the *liber singularis regularum Ulpiani*, the latter the *Pauli sententiarum receptarum libri* v. Their annotations of the works of *Papinian* were subsequently deprived of authority (*post*, par. 456).

THIRD EPOCH.—THE EMPERORS.

The other jurists of the period, of whose writings fragments appear in the Digest, were *Saturninus, Callistratus, Marcianus, Florentinus, Macer,* and *Modestinus,* but after the next reign that of—

420. *Alexander Severus* (A.D. 222 to 235) the period of the decline of letters, science and law commences. The brilliant professors of law, who had held the highest dignities in the state, die out, and with them the publication of those works which fall under the heads of :—(1) Commentaries on the edicts of prætors and pro-consuls (*ad edictum, ad edictum provinciale*). (2) Treatises on the functions of magistrates (*de officio præfecti urbi, proconsulis,* etc. (3) Works on the whole law *(Digesta Pandectæ)*. (4) Abridgments or elementary lessons in law *(Institutiones, regulæ, sententiæ)*.

422. In the interval between Severus and Diocletian (A.D. 235-284), the pages of history are filled with the struggles of opposing candidates for the throne, during which two important events occurred.

(1) *Introduction of Christianity.* This religion, by separating itself from the existing institutions, attacked a fundamental basis of public law (*ante*, par. 14, 38, 84), and hence the persecutions of Nero, Domitian, Verus, and Gallus, and, as a result, the division of the inhabitants of the empire into Christians and pagans. The juriconsults, imbued with Greek philosophical speculations, were probably at first inimical to the new faith, but it silently innovated upon the existing law, and lent its aid to the futherance of equitable views.

(2) *Irruption of the Barbarians.* The compression produced by the forcing back of numerous barbarous nations, together with the increasing inability of the Roman arms to protect the frontier, produced a reaction, and the bribes distributed amongst the border nations to keep them quiet, only served to whet their appetite and increase their ravages, until they were temporarily put down by the energy of Diocletian.

426. *Diocletian, Emperor.* A.D. 284. This reign is remarkable for (1) the division of the empire between two *Augusti* and two *Cæsars* (the latter being lieutenants and presumptive heirs of the former), and (2) for the decay of the system of *formulæ (judicia ordinaria),* and the substitution for it of the—

427. **Judicia Extraordinaria.** The separation of *jus* and *judicium,* existing in the *legis actiones* (see table xii, 3), was still further developed in the system introduced by the *lex Æbutia* (*ante,* par. 247), and in both systems the *cognitio extraordinaria* or cognizance and decision of the whole case by the magistrate (as where his *jurisdictio* could settle it, or his *imperium* was required, or no suitable, civil, or prætorian action existed), was viewed as an exception, and the proceeding was a *persecutio,* not an *actio.* Under the emperors the omnipotence of the prince, and the delegation at will of his powers to any officer who decided the case on his behalf without observing the ordinary procedure, thus combining the *jus* and *judicium,* had tended, prior to the accession of Diocletian, to the decay of the

distinction, but the legislative abolition of the *ordo judiciorum* dates from the *constitution* of *Diocletian* (A.D. 294), which was specially intended for the provinces, but subsequently applied to the whole empire. By this edict, the Præsides of the provinces were directed to decide all causes and to refer those they could not attend to themselves to inferior judges, who should also decide the whole matter. Hence the term *judex (judices majores)*, now applied to the magistrate, and the *judices pedanei*, who could be rejected by the litigants in favour of arbitrators, and who possibly represented the old *judices selecti*, now became *permanent* inferior magistrates, and were formed by Justinian into a college at Constantinople, with a jurisdiction limited to 300 solidi.

The term *actio* therefore now means the plaintiff's right, resulting from direct legislation, of applying to the competent judicial authority or the act of suing itself; the word *exceptio* (if it has any meaning) refers to the defence set up by the defendant, and *interdicts* are replaced by direct actions, but, as in the case of the *legis actiones*, so now in respect of the system of *formulæ*, the old forms survived for a time, and the demand of the formula *(impetratio actionis, ante*, par. 251) was made up to the time of Theodosius and Valentinian.

REVIEW OF THE PRECEDING PERIOD.

434. *External situation*. The title of *citizen* now belongs to all born *free* within the limits of the empire, but the bearers of the name of *Barbarian* are steadily increasing in strength, and by their incessant inroads tending to the ultimate destruction of the empire.

435. *Public Law*. Jurisprudence had become a science in the hands of the distinguished jurisconsults who flourished under the emperors, but that branch of it devoted to *political* law remained at a standstill after Augustus laid the foundations of despotism. The power in the state had passed from the people, the plebeians, and the knights to—

(1) The *army*, which at first held its power by force, and made and unmade emperors at its pleasure, but under Diocletian returned to nearly its proper functions.

(2) The *senate*, which was composed of members designated by the emperors, and retained only so much power as he chose to leave it.

(3) The *emperor*, who should be nominated by the senate, but a *senatus-consultum* was always ready for him who advanced upon Rome at the head of a victorious army. The magistracies which have replaced the republican system are all held at the will of the emperor.

440. The *legislative, executive*, and *electoral* powers have been gradually absorbed by the emperors, and the edicts of the magistrates are confined to matters of administration. Nominally the senate

designates and confirms the election of the emperor and of certain magistrates, and a council of state *(consistorium)* aids in the management of imperial concerns.

The *judicial* power is exercised by the emperor, the senate, the prætors, the consuls, the præfectus urbi, the prætorian prefect, and the local magistrates of each city. The college of centumvirs has nearly disappeared, and the annual lists of judges are no longer prepared. The council called the *auditorium* is consulted by the emperor as to legal questions submitted for his decision.

441. In *criminal* matters, the list of *crimina extraordinaria (ante,* par. 281) has increased, and these are for the most part brought before the *præfectus urbi*, but the emperor often pronounces judgment himself, and the senate has cognizance of high treason.

442. In *civil* matters, there are eighteen prætors to administer the law at Rome, and the duty is performed in the provinces by the *rector (præses)* or the *vicarius* or other deputy, and appeals are heard by the *prætorian prefect* as representing the emperor *(vice sacra)*, and finally by the sovereign himself. All procedure is *extraordinaria*, but the magistrate *(judex major)* may, in case of multiplicity of business, remit minor matters to the *judices pedanei,* and professional pleaders *(advocati)* now appear before the judges. A *rescript* from the emperor sometimes instructs the judge what to do, and sometimes a *decree* decides the case itself.

444. In *towns*, the inhabitants, from whom the members of the local senate *(curia)* are drawn, form a special order *(curiales)*, their children are ranged in the order *(curialis origo)*, and rich citizens may gain admittance. The curiales who compose the senate are *decuriones*, and are drawn alternately from the whole list *(in albo decurionum describendo)*. The *duumviri* or annual magistrates, who direct the affairs of the city, preside in the *curia*, and they, as well as the other principal magistrates, are taken from the *curiales*, who thus form the first order in the town, and are exempt from some penalties falling on the lower classes, but as they are responsible for the payment of the taxes, and the acceptance of office is compulsory, the onerous nature of the duties has originated the term *curiæ subjecti.*

445. *Sacred Law.* The senate adds the deceased emperor to the list of Roman gods, and hence the use of the epithet *divini*, but Christianity is extending its influence, and the legal protection still afforded to polytheism is its only strength.

446. *Private Law.* The attention of the distinguished jurisconsults of this period being drawn off public law *(ante,* par. 435), and concentrated on private law, may perhaps partly account for the high pitch of perfection the latter has attained, and the universal domination, by infusing general ideas applicable to large masses of people, may also help to account for the softening of the rigours of the ancient law, and the introduction of equitable principles, but the old

E

civil law is still the assumed basis, and this contradiction gives a peculiar character to the Roman jurisprudence.

448. As to *persons, freedmen* are divided into three classes :—(1) *citizens* ; (2) *latini juniani*, with the rights of the ancient *latini coloni* (*ante*, par. 188) ; (3) *dediticii*, assimilated to enemies who have surrendered (*ante*, par. 78). The master has no longer the power of death, and for bad treatment the slave may appeal to the magistrate. The father can generally neither sell nor pledge his children, the son has the exclusive ownership of and power of bequeathing property acquired in war *(peculium castrense)*. Marital power scarcely exists. The claims of *cognatio* continue to be favoured by the prætor. *Gentilitas* is extinct. The perpetual tutelage of women to their agnates has ceased, but since the time of Augustus, the position of legatees not possessing the *jus liberorum* has given rise to a new class of disabilities.

449. As to *things*, the distinction between *res mancipi* and *nec mancipi*, and between immovables in Italy and in the provinces, still continues, but the term *proprietas*, recognising the *individuality* of the members of the family, has superseded the use of the words *mancipium* and *dominium* (*ante*, par. 330).

450. As to *wills*, the prætor has introduced a simpler form, and *codicilli* may be enforced, but the *mancipatio* of the inheritance still exists. Soldiers may dispense with all formality.

451. In *successions*, the claims of natural connection are gaining ground. Children can now succeed to their mother, and in some cases the mother to the children (part iii. par. 1054 and 1065).

452. In *contracts*, the rules as to the four agreements of the *jus gentium*, being obligatory by consent alone, are now fully developed (*ante*, par. 333). The number of *pacts*, as opposed to civil law contracts, has increased, and the formulary system has been replaced by the *extraordinaria judicia*.

§ 2.—*From Constantine to Justinian.*

The struggles of the six emperors, Maximian, Maxentius, Galerius, Maximin, Licinius, and Constantine, resulted in the last two becoming emperors of the east and west, A.D. 313.

456. *Constantine* in A.D. 321 published a constitution inserted in the code of Theodosius, *invalidating the notes of Paul* and *Ulpian* on the writings of *Papinian*, as corrupting the text ; and a subsequent constitution for the same reason condemned the *notes of Marcian* (*post*, par. 499, 544). In A.D. 327, four years after he became sole emperor, Constantine invested with authority the writings of *Paul* himself, particularly his *sententiæ*.

459. **Gregorian and Hermogenian Codes.** *Papirius Justus*, under Marcus Aurelius, and *Paul*, under Caracalla, published summaries of imperial constitutions ; and in the period between Diocletian and Constantine, the two jurisconsults, *Gregorianus* and *Hermogenianus*, collected, chronologically arranged, and annotated

the most important *rescripts* of the emperors, from Septimius Severus to Diocletian and Maximian, A.D. 196 to 296. These collections were without legislative authority, but formed the model for the codes of Theodosius and Justinian *(post,* par. 502, 539), and as rescripts of Valentinian aud Valens are asserted to have found a place in the code of *Hermogenian,* his date ought perhaps to be A.D. 364, but this is doubtful, as also whether the same jurisconsult was the author of the *epitome of law,* arranged in the order of the perpetual edict, of which extracts are found in the Digest (i, 5, 2, etc.).

467. **Christianity the religion of the Empire,** A.D. 325. Licinius in A.D. 314 issued the *edictum Mediolanense* for the protection of Christians. Eleven years after, Constantine proclaimed this religion as that of the state and openly professed it, an example followed by most of his subjects. In the same year, the emperor, with 318 bishops, assisted at the first general council at *Nicæa,* when the opinions of Arius were condemned as heretical. The sacred law of ancient Rome, including the part of political law connected with it, now disappeared. Pontiffs, Flamens and Vestals were replaced by bishops and priests. Christians and Pagans changed places, the former being under the protection of the laws, but the latter, together with heretics, were subjected to various incapacities.

469. Constantine being desirous of a capital in the centre of his dominions, selected *Byzantium* as the most favourably situated, and after rebuilding the city, called it after his own name.

471. **Magistracies created by Constantine.** The change of capital and of religion necessarily led to modifications in the existing magistracies, and to the rise of a new class of functionaries—

(1) *Episcopi.* Christian bishops attained to the first rank amongst the dignitaries of the empire. They were specially entrusted with the *care of the poor,* of *captives,* and of *children* exposed or prostituted by their parents. They were members of the *councils* nominating *tutors* and *curators.* They received the power of *enfranchising slaves* in churches. They also at times replaced the consuls and prætors, and advised the emperor himself.

The Roman judicial organization had always permitted the rejection of a'judge in favour of the arbiter ; and the spirit of Christianity, in its repugnance to legal proceedings, increased the tendency towards arbitration. Constantine therefore invested the bishops with jurisdiction *(episcopalis audientia),* which was compulsory as to certain classes of persons and in respect of matters relating to religion, otherwise the recourse to this tribunal was voluntary.

(2) *Patricii.* Eminent persons in the state who had held high magistracies, and who could serve as privy councillors in case of need, were dignified for life with the honorary title of fathers *(loco patris honorantur),* but the distinction did not carry with it *jurisdictio* or *imperium.*

(3) *Comites consistoriani.* The number of the members of the

consistorium (ante, par. 361) was increased and this became the council of the emperor; whilst a *senate,* similarly organised to that of Rome, became in the new capital the council of the empire. The title of *comes* or companion (comte, count), and of *dux* or duke was also applied to other functionaries.

(4) *Quæstor Sacri Palatii.* This high chancellor probably superseded the quæstor candidatus of Augustus *(ante,* par. 339). His duty was to draw up new constitutions, keep lists of the favours and dignities conferred by the prince, and prepare and forward rescripts.

(5) *Provincial Magistrates.* The empire was divided into four great prætorian prefectures—the Eastern, Illyrian, Italian, and Gallic, each governed by a *prætorian prefect.* The prefectures were divided into several dioceses, thirteen in all, ruled by *vicarii.* The dioceses were subdivided into provinces, 117 in all, with a *rector provinciæ* over each.

(6) *Magistri militum.* Constantine suppressed the prætorian guard, leaving the prefects only *civil* authority, and transferring their military power to commanders of the cavalry and infantry.

(7) *Palatini.* This general title included the crowd of officers of the palace forming the emperor's household, and divided into *cubicularii, castrensiani, ministeriani, silentiarii,* etc.

Out of these dignities arose a new nobility with insignia, honours, and privileges peculiar to each degree, *nobilissimi* included princes of the imperial family, *illustres* the prætorian prefect, the quæstor of the palace, etc., *spectabiles,* some pro-consuls, vicars, counts, dukes, etc., *clarissimi,* consuls, etc., *perfectissimi,* duumvirs, etc., and in the lowest rank came the *egregii.*

479. **Innovations in Private Law.** The following changes, due to the influence of Christianity, may be traced to Constantine.

(1) *Patria potestas* softened in character. The father could only sell his child at the moment of birth or when compelled by extreme misery.

(2) *Peculium quasi-castrense.* Members of the emperor's household, although *filii-familias,* acquired exclusive ownership of any property gained at court, as if they had been with the army.

(3) *Peculium adventitium.* The father was only allowed to have the *usufruct,* not the ownership of the son's property derived from the mother.

(4) *Incapacities of cœlibes and orbi suppressed (ante,* par. 369). After Constantine's legislation, the emperor would still be implored to grant the *jus liberorum* in the case of (1) testamentary bequests where parents had no *common* child, and hence fell under the Lex Papia. (2) On intestacy where a free woman had had less than *three,* or a freed woman less than *four* children born, and so could not avail herself of the *senatus-consultum Tertullianum* (part iii, par. 1054), and yet desired to obtain more than the third allowed by Constantine to the mother of *one* child. (3) Dispensations from guardianship, when desired to be relieved from tutor-

ships or curatorships, although had not *three* children living at Rome, or *four* in Italy, or *five* in the provinces.

488. **Agricolæ (Coloni).** The laws regulating the condition of these persons date from this period, but the origin of a class intermediate between the freeman and the slave was anterior to Constantine.

The term *agricola* or *colonus* at first referred to the cultivation of the soil, and then acquired a technical servile signification in the same way that *inquilinus* came to imply residence on as well as cultivation of land.

All *coloni* were attached in perpetuity to the lands they cultivated, they could not go elsewhere, nor could their masters remove them, and on the sale of land they passed with it. Hence they differed from the *mancipia, villici,* and *coloni,* referred to by *Scævola* (Dig. 37, 7, 20), for the point discussed by him is whether they are to be included in the legacy *cum fundo instructo* (part iii, par. 896), nor are they alluded to by *Paul* (Sent. iii, 6, § 48) in the question as to *coloni* being passed from one property to another, but passages from *Marcian, Ulpian,* and *Paul* (Dig. 30, 1, 112, and 50, 15, 4, 8, Paul Sent. iii, 6, § 70) show that this class was then being introduced. *Salvian,* in the 5th century, in Gaul, speaks of freemen reduced by necessity to become the *coloni* of the rich, thereby losing their liberty and falling into the condition of *inquilini*, and a constitution of *Honorius* (Cod. Theod. 5, 4, 3) provides for the transfer of vanquished barbarians to lands to which they should be attached as *coloni*.

Two classes of *agricolæ* may be distinguished :—

(1) *Servi censiti (adscriptitii, tributarii)*. These had sprung from slavery, and like slaves all their property *(peculium)* belonged to their masters, who in lieu of providing for their maintenance, allowed them and their families to live on the land, paying rent in kind or in money. The term *censitus* implies that they were subject to a capitation tax.

(2) *Inquilini (coloni liberi)*. These had been originally free, but they or their ancestors had accepted the condition of partial slavery for the sake of the land thereby acquired for cultivation. Their property, movable and immovable, belonged to themselves, and for this they were subject to a property tax. The annual rent *(canon, reditus)* in kind or in money paid to their masters could not be increased.

Children followed the condition of their parents, and through the effects of *prescription* a free citizen might be reduced to the condition of a *colonus liber*, if during thirty years he had been deemed such, and had paid the annual rent.

493. **Suppression of Formulæ.** A.D. 342. *Constantius* (Cod. ii, 58) extended to all legal *formulæ*, the partial abolition introduced by *Constantine II*, in A.D. 339, in relation to testaments. The effect of this was to deprive the words or acts themselves of any inherent virtue, or legality, the spirit and intent of the transaction being alone regarded.

494. *Præfectus urbi.* About A.D. 360, *Constantius* established at Constantinople this officer with analogous duties to those attaching to that functionary at Rome *(ante,* par. 338).

495. In the same reign the pagan temples were closed, and death and confiscation decreed against any persons celebrating pagan rites. Heretics, apostates, Jews, and Gentiles were subjected to many incapacities, and aruspices, pontiffs, magicians, and mathematicians (*i.e.*, astrologers, not geometricians) were liable to be burnt; but *Julianus*, who became emperor in A.D. 361, endeavoured to revive the ancient institutions of the Romans and discouraged Christianity in favour of polytheism. His successor, *Jovianus*, however (A.D. 363), restored the Christian religion to its previous position in the state.

496. **Defensores Civitatum.** The constitutions of Valens, Valentinian, and Theodosius, about A.D. 379, refer to the existence of this new class of municipal magistrates. They were nominated in an assembly composed of the bishop, the curiales, and the distinguished men of the city. Their functions lasted five years, and they could not resign before the end of that period. Their principal duty was to act as guardians of the poor, and in addition they were charged with the repression of theft, and had jurisdiction in cases not involving more than 50 solidi; but prior to Justinian the magistracy fell into contempt, and the duties were performed by subordinates (*post*, par. 579).

497. *Division of the Empire*, A.D. 395. On the death of *Theodosius I*, the Roman world was separated into *two distinct Empires*, under his sons *Arcadius* and *Honorius*, the former ruling in the East, the latter in the West.

498. *Public Schools.* *Theodosius II*, in A.D. 425, established, at Constantinople, a school for rhetoric, philosophy, and jurisprudence, similar to one already existing at Rome.

499. **Lex de responsis prudentum**, A.D. 426. To obviate the confusion arising from the multiplicity of the writings of the ancient jurisconsults, *Theodosius II*, in the West, issued a constitution, which was first published in the East under Valentinian III. This "Citation Law" made the writings of the following jurisconsults authoritative, viz.: *Papinian, Paul, Gaius, Ulpian,* and *Modestinus*, including the passages introduced from the works of other jurisconsults, such as *Scævola, Sabinus, Julianus, Marcellus*, etc., but still excluding the notes of Ulpian, Paul, and Marcian on Papinian (*ante*, par. 456). If these writers differed, the majority decided the point; if equal, the views of Papinian were to prevail; but if he were silent, the judge was at liberty to follow either opinion. Justinian abrogated this method of numerical computation in the Digest (*post*, par. 544).

502. **Codex Theodosianus**, A.D. 438. Theodosius II, in A.D. 429, directed a commission, under the presidency of the prætorian prefect *Antiochus*, to collect the imperial constitutions which had appeared subsequent to the Hermogenian and Gregorian codes (*ante*, par. 459).

The work, of which the greater part is now extant, was completed in nine years, and was published simultaneously in the West under the authority of Valentinian III. It was to be the sole source of imperial law (*jus principale*), and was divided into 16 books, and these subdivided into titles, with the imperial constitutions, from Constantine to Theodosius II, chronologically distributed under them. The first five books, arranged in the order of the edict, contained the *jus privatum;* the rest include the different magistracies, military, criminal, fiscal, and ecclesiastical matters, public works and games, etc. In order to maintain the general agreement of the laws of the two empires after the issue of the code, it was arranged that the *novellæ*, or new constitutions (*post*, par. 552), subsequently published, should not acquire binding force until they also appeared in the other empire; but this practice was discontinued after a time, and the projected new *code* of Theodosius never appeared which was to contain, not the constitutions in their entirety, but only such extracts from the Gregorian, Hermogenian, and his own code, and from the works of the jurists, as should represent the actual living law.

511. The precise date of the three following works, which appeared about the beginning of the fifth century, is uncertain.

(1) *Fragmenta Vaticana*. Under this title appeared, in 1828, at Berlin, a collection of materials discovered some years previously in the Vatican library, and apparently belonging to the period immediately preceding the code of Theodosius. The collection appears to have been made preparatory to some other composition, and contains fragments of Paul, Ulpian, and Papinian, and, in the shape of notes, numerous quotations from a large number of other classical jurists. The imperial constitutions cited range from Marcus Aurelius, A.D. 163, to Valentinian I, A.D. 372, and the Gregorian and Hermogenian codes are referred to. The work is important as containing additional information not previously obtainable respecting usufruct, *dos*, and the *lex Cincia*.

(2) *Mosaïcarum et Romanarum legum collatio*. This work, also known as the *Lex Dei*, was first printed at Paris in 1573, and is a comparison of the laws of Moses with extracts from the writings of the five authoritative jurisconsults (*ante*, par. 499), to show that the latter were drawn from the former; and the date A.D. 390 occurring in it proves that the author lived subsequently to that date. It has been attributed to Rufinus, the prætorian prefect of Theodosius I, who died A.D. 395, and, with more probability, to Rufinus, one of the fathers of the church, who died in A.D. 410. The extracts referred to have been of service in reconstructing the *sententiæ* of Paul, the *regulæ* of Ulpian, and the Gregorian and Hermogenian codes.

(3) *Consultatio veteris cujusdam jurisconsulti*. The compiler of this production is unknown, and the work itself was first published by Cujas in 1577. It consists of solutions of legal questions on the principle enunciated by Theodosius II (*ante*, par. 499). The quotations are confined to the sentences of Paul and the Gregorian, Hermogenian, and Theodosian codes.

526. *Fall of the Western Empire*, A.D. 476. The empire of the west gradually succumbed to the steady flow of the barbarian races westward. Alaric (died A.D. 410) led the Goths into Gaul; Attila (died A.D. 453) headed the Huns in their descent into Italy; and Genseric, with the Vandals, sacked Rome in A.D. 455, after conquering Spain and the African provinces.

Gaul became divided into *three* kingdoms, in which the Romans and the ancient inhabitants of the country were mixed with the new comers, but held an inferior position. The conquering nations were: the *Franks*, who, in the *north*, occupied, about A.D. 410, the provinces around the Loire and the Seine; the *Burgundians*, in A.D. 413, settled in the *east*, along the Saone and the Rhone; and the *Visigoths*, about the same date, took possession of the *south*, between the Loire and the Pyrenees; whilst the *Ostrogoths* penetrated further south, and finally conquered Italy A.D. 493, making Ravenna their capital.

529. **Roman Laws published by Germans.** The barbarians settled in Gaul, Spain, Africa, and Italy, did not interfere with the existing Roman law, but the legislation took the peculiar turn of becoming *personal* instead of territorial, *i. e.*, each individual was judged according to the laws and customs of the nation to which he personally belonged; and after a short period, several barbarian kings published collections of Roman laws by the side of the *leges barbarorum*, or national laws and customs, mostly of Germanic origin, peculiar to themselves.

(1) *Lex Romana Visigothorum*, A.D. 506. This compilation, for the use of the Romans in the kingdom of the *Visigoths*, was drawn up by the orders of Alaric II (hence called *Breviarium Alaricianum*), and published at Aire, in Gascony, with the assent of the ecclesiastics and the principal nobles. It was prepared by Roman jurisconsults under *Gojaric*, the Count of the Palace; and all the official copies were signed by the secretary, *Anianus* (hence the work is sometimes called *breviarium Aniani*). It contains *leges*, or constitutions, derived from the code of Theodosius, and subsequent novels down to Severus (A.D. 461), and *jura*, or the law of the jurists, consisting of an epitome of Gaius (omitting the fourth book, etc., as obsolete), and fragments of the sentences of Paul, of the Gregorian and Hermogenian codes, and of the responses of Papinian, and the text is accompanied by a running commentary (*interpretatio*). In the middle ages, the work is cited as the *lex Theodosiana, corpus Theodosianum, liber legum*, or *lex Romana*. Its authority, as the Roman Law of the barbarians, extended the widest, and lasted the longest, and it is important as containing fragments of Roman Law which would otherwise have been lost. It is not to be confounded with the *Codex legis Visigothorum*, published for the Visigoths in Spain one-and-a-half centuries later.

(2) *Lex Romana Burgundiorum*. This code, also known as the *responsa Papiani* (contraction for *Papiniani*), by a mistake of

Cujas, was intended for the Romans dwelling amongst the Burgundians, and was announced in the preface to the second edition of the *lex Gondoboda* (a body of Germanic law published by king Gondobald previous to A.D. 517); but it did not survive the fall of the kingdom and its absorption by the Franks in A.D. 534, as it was then superseded by the source from which it had been derived, viz., the breviary of Alaric and the code of Theodosius.

(3) *Edictum Theodorici.* This general edict, binding on the Ostrogoths in Italy as well as the Romans, was probably published at Rome about A.D. 506. It was drawn up by Cassiodorus and Boetius, but scarcely deals with *private* law, and it was superseded by the code of Justinian on his conquest of the kingdom of the Ostrogoths in A.D. 554.

533. **Justinian,** *Emperor*, A.D. 527-565.—Born A.D. 482 at Taurisium, of Sabatius and Bigleniza, the young Uprauda took the name of Justinian on being adopted by his maternal uncle, Justin, under whose care he was brought up at Bederina. The uncle was a soldier of fortune and successively rose to be military tribune, then prætorian prefect, and finally emperor, A.D. 518. On the uncle's assumption of the imperial dignity, Justinian was sent for from Italy, where he had been left as a hostage with Theodoric, and, after being created Cæsar, was finally associated in the government. Four months later, by the death of Justin, he became sole Emperor of the East at 45 years of age.

In order to ally himself with Theodora, he had induced his uncle to remove the prohibition against senators marrying actresses, and Justinian himself subsequently confirmed the repeal of these laws.

At the time of the accession of Justinian, Africa and Spain were held by the Vandals and Goths; Gaul by the Franks, Burgundians, and Visigoths; Italy by the Ostrogoths; and the empire of Constantinople stood alone, still bearing the title of Roman, though Grecian would have been more appropriate. The topics of the day were religion and the circus. Orthodox Christians, heretics and arians, quarreled amongst themselves, but united against Jews and idolators, and the colours worn by the charioteers in the circus divided the city into four political factions, white, red, blue, and green.

This state of society influenced the conduct of Justinian, and hence his persecutions of heterodox Christians, his massacre of Samaritan Jews, and his espousal of the blue against the green. This last proceeding nearly cost him his life, for, in A.D. 532, the general discontent at the exactions of the prætorian prefect John, and the questor Tribonian (*post*, par. 565), induced the populace to join in a sedition of the green, and Hypatius, a member of the Anastasian family, was proclaimed in the circus; but the opportune arrival of Belisarius dispersed the insurgents, and Hypatius was, by Justinian's order, thrown into the Bosphorus.

Wars. Belisarius, the greatest of Justinian's generals, overthrew the Vandals on the coast of Africa, and made that country a præfecture, A.D. 533; Sicily and Italy followed, and the keys of Rome were sent to Constantinople, A.D. 537. On the disgrace of Belisarius, the conquest of Italy was completed by Narses the eunuch, who was established as exarch at Ravenna, A.D. 554. But in other directions Justinian was less fortunate, and in the end an annual tribute was paid to the Persians, the Huns, and other tribes, either to keep them quiet or secure their services as mercenaries.

Buildings. The tribute paid to frontier tribes could only be met by loading the country with taxes, which were further increased to cover the enormous sums spent in beautifying every city in the empire.

Laws. With the exception of *Charisius* (the author of a work on the office of the prætorian prefect, etc.), and *Hermogenianus* (*ante,* par. 459), it may be said that, since Alexander Severus, the jurists had degenerated into a class who, in their pleadings before the magistrates, or in their lectures in the public schools, simply quoted the *jura* or writings of the classical prudentes, and the *leges* or imperial constitutions; and the law itself, in the course of centuries, had become a chaotic mass, consisting of plebiscita of ancient Rome, senatus-consulta, prætorian edicts, works of the authorised prudentes, the Gregorian, Hermogenian, and Theodosian codes, and the subsequent novellæ of the emperors.

The orderly arrangement and revision of this chaos of legislation was commenced by Justinian shortly after his accession to the throne; and, in six years, he completed the body of laws which bears his name, but he continued to issue supplementary constitutions until his death at the age of 84.

As emperor, Justinian was a warrior, architect, and legislator; of his wars nothing remain, of his architecture some few monuments; but his laws, included under the general term of Corpus Juris *Civilis,* (by way of antithesis to the Corpus Juris *Canonici*), have formed the basis of all modern legislation.

The changes he introduced were simple, equitable, and well adapted to the age in which he lived; his legislation in respect of slaves and freedmen was mild and christian, and, in the result, he entirely eradicated the last traces of the strict civil law (*post,* par. 582). The mutilation of the opinions of the ancient authors is not to be laid to his charge, for he was not presenting his subjects with a picture of ancient jurisprudence, but giving them laws for their guidance.

His innovations were, however, carried to the extreme. The code modifying the Digest and the Institutes, the novels modifying the code introduced the very confusion he sought to remove, and gave colour to the assertion that he participated with Tribonian in the sale of judgments and laws.

539. *Codex Vetus,* A.D. 529. This was a collection in 12 books of the imperial constitutions and was called a *code,* as that name had

become consecrated by usage to such compilations. Its object was to unite in a single work the Gregorian, Hermogenian, and Theodosian codes (*ante*, pars. 459 and 502), and the novels of the emperors subsequent to Theodosius. Ten jurists were engaged in the task, including the ex-consul John, Tribonian, and Theophilus (*post*, pars. 565, 566). The editors were permitted to add, or expunge, or modify, in order to render the sense clear, but the chronological order was preserved.

The work was completed in one year, when the whole of the contents received the force of law (see *post*, par. 550), and the citing of any other constitutions was forbidden, except those concerning particular interests specified in the code.

540. *Quinquaginta decisiones.* Shortly after the publication of the code, a series of constitutions appeared, particularly in A.D. 529-30, settling controverted points in ancient law, and hence called the 50 decisions. These were probably all subsequently embodied in the new code (*post*, par. 550), as well as a number of separate constitutions also issued at this time.

544. *Digesta or Pandectæ*, A.D. 533. Treatises on the whole law are called by the ancient writers Digests or Pandects (*ante*, par. 420), and Justinian, by a constitution addressed to Tribonian, ordered the composition of a work of this nature which should embody all that was valuable in the scattered volumes of those jurists whose writings were deemed authoritative. The work to be in 50 books, the titles in the order of the code or edict, the opinion of the majority of authorised jurists (*ante*, par. 499) need not be adopted; the *notes* of *Paul, Ulpian*, and *Marcian* on *Papinian* not to be rejected (*ante*, par. 456) if found useful. Corrections might be made, and misplaced, obsolete and superfluous matter expunged. There were to be no contradictions (antinomies), no repetitions, and no constitutions inserted that already existed in the code.

Sixteen professors and advocates assisted Tribonian, and a constitution in Latin, with a paraphrase in Greek, gave the Digest the force of law on its completion in three years, a period too short for the execution of a task of that magnitude, and hence repetitions and antinomies do exist. The work is like a mosaic of fragments extracted from the writings of 39 of the most illustrious jurists, but, owing to the corrections permitted by the emperor, the quotations are not always accurate, and these falsifications are now known as *tribonianisms*.

From a careful examination of these fragments, Blume has inferred that the commission was divided into three sections corresponding with the three years' course of study (*post*, par. 570), and that the professors in each section revised those works which they were in the habit of using as text-books, viz.: (1) works forming a commentary on the writings of Sabinus, etc.; (2) commentaries on the urban and provincial edict; (3) works of Papinian and others.

548. *Institutiones*, A.D. 533. Under the term *Institutes* were included in Roman jurisprudence treatises devoted to the exposi-

tion, in a simple and methodical manner, of the general principles and elements of law. Prior to Justinian, the institutes whose existence is known in modern times, all date in the seventy years between Antoninus Pius and Alexander Severus (A.D. 138 to 222) viz.: The Institutes of *Gaius* in 4 books, of *Florentinus* in 12 books, of *Callistratus* in 3 books, of *Paul* and of *Ulpian* each in 2 books, and of *Marcian* in 16 books. Three centuries later came the Institutes of *Justinian*, but only the first and last have been preserved, the rest being known by scattered fragments in the Pandects.

The Digest was in progress when Justinian confided to *Tribonian, Theophilus*, and *Dorotheus* (professor of law at school of Berytus), the task of preparing an elementary work drawn from the ancient Institutes, but especially from that of Gaius (*ante*, par. 393). The distribution of the subject matter is the same as in Gaius, and many passages are identical, but with obsolete portions cut out and new theories introduced by the editors. Although the work was intended as an elementary text-book in the public schools, it received the force of law by a constitution which serves as an introduction (see part iii, par. 1).

550. *Codex Repetitæ prælectionis*, A.D. 534. Justinian, in a constitution addressed to the senate of Constantinople, informed them that he had directed Tribonian, Dorotheus, Menas, Constantine, and John, to prepare a *second edition*, also in 12 books, of the code (*ante*, par. 539), corrected up to that time, and containing the 50 decisions and new constitutions which had appeared since the former edition. On the publication of this work, the old code was forbidden to be cited, and was probably destroyed; hence, some references in the Institutes are incorrect, as they relate to constitutions existing in the first edition, but suppressed in the second. The earliest constitution dates from the time of Hadrian (*ante*, par. 350).

552. *Novellæ Constitutiones*. The abbreviated term *novellæ* had been given to the edicts issued by Theodosius and his successors (*ante*, par. 502); and Justinian, who reigned thirty years after the publication of the second edition of the code, modified the Digest, the Institutes, and the Code, by a series of novels to the number of at least 152, of which 30 relate to ecclesiastical matters, 58 to public and criminal law, and 64 to private law. Tribonian must have been the indirect author of the larger number, as only 21 were issued after his death. Our knowledge of these *novellæ* is mainly derived from four sources. (1) Extracts from the novels bearing on ecclesiastical law, included in a work (Νομοκανων) on the Canon Law composed by *John of Antioch*, who was nominated by Justinian patriarch of Constantinople A.D. 564. (2) A Latin abridgment of 125 of the novels, subsequently used as a text-book in the schools, and called the *Epitome Novellarum*. It was prepared by *Julianus*, a professor of law, and successor of Theophilus, at Constantinople A.D. 570. (3) A Greek collection of unknown origin, possibly containing the actual text of 152 novels of Justinian, together with some published by his successors. (4) A Latin ver-

sion, by an unknown author, called the *Versio vulgata Novellarum* or *Corpus Authenticum*, and the 134 novels contained in it are called *Authenticæ*, to distinguish them from Julian's abridgments.

565. *Tribonian* (or *Tribunian*) died A.D. 543. This eminent statesman and jurist, by his exactions, caused a sedition of the people (*ante*, par. 533), which compelled Justinian to banish him for a time, but he was subsequently completely restored in the imperial confidence. He was the principal editor of the whole of the Corpus Juris, and the merits and defects of that great work are mainly to be attributed to him.

566. *Theophilus* enjoyed the title of *illustris* as being a public professor of law (*antecessor*) at Constantinople and a member of the *consistorium* (*ante*, par. 471). He was engaged in preparing the first Code, the Digest, and the Institutes, and made a Greek paraphrase of the last.

570. *Schools of Law.* The private method of educating lawyers described in pars. 236 and 362 had developed, by the time of Cicero, into a regular system combining theoretical with practical instruction, and subsequently professorial chairs in connection with the public delivery of lectures were created (*ante*, par. 498) at Rome and Constantinople.

On the same day that the Digest was completed (A.D. 533), Justinian addressed a constitution to Theophilus, Dorotheus, Anatolius, Cratinus, and four other professors of law, on the course of study to be pursued at the schools of law existing at *Rome* (at this time in the hands of the Ostrogoths), *Constantinople*, and *Berytus*. The subjects of instruction were to be as follows:—

1st year. The Institutes and the preliminary portion of the Digest, *i. e.*, bks. i, ii, iii, iv. The students were to be called *Justiniani novi* in lieu of *Dupondii*; and this course was substituted for the Institutes of Gaius and parts of four special books dealing with res uxoria, tutelage, wills, and legacies.

2nd year. Either the 7 books *De judiciis*, or the 8 books *De rebus*, and four other books of the Digest—viz., one of the three upon *dos*, one of the two upon tutelage and curatorship, one of the two upon wills, and one of the seven upon legacies and fideicommissa. The students were to be called, as before, *Edictales*, the subjects of study being principally those formerly discussed in the Edict.

3rd year. Either *de rebus* or *de judiciis*, according to which subject had been studied in the 2nd year, together with the special subjects—pledges and mortgages, interest, the edict of the ædiles, the actio redhibitoria, evictions, double stipulations, and the works of Papinian. The students were to be called, as before, *Papianistes* (*ante*, par. 395).

4th year. The remaining ten books of the fourteen on special subjects studied in the 2nd year. This made 36 books in all perused in class, and the remainder of the Digest (parts vi and vii, 14 books) the student was expected to get up in private; and this course was in lieu of a review of the previous subjects and the study of a portion of the works of *Paulus*. The students were called *Licentiates*.

5th year. The Constitutions in the Code. The students were called *Prolytæ*.

REVIEW OF THE PRECEDING PERIOD.

576. *External situation*. Constantine had migrated to a new capital, the Roman world had divided into two empires, the western empire had disappeared. Under Justinian, Italy, Sicily, and the seaboard of Africa have been temporarily reconquered. The republic of Rome is the Exarchate of Ravenna. The Bulgarians, Persians, and Thracians are pressing on the eastern empire, and are only kept off by tribute.

577. *Public Law*. The *legislative, judicial*, and *executive* power is in the hands of the Emperor. The number of prætors is reduced to three, and their position is inferior to the urban and prætorian prefect.

578. In *criminal matters*, the denunciation is brought before one of the superior officers of Constantinople; and in the provinces before the rector, the president, or the provincial prætorian prefect. These magistrates take cognisance of the suit themselves, and decide it. Sometimes the Senate, or the Emperor himself, determines a case of importance.

579. In *civil matters*, since the constitutions of Diocletian, Constantius, Theodosius, and Valentinian, solemn judicial formulæ, even by way of fiction, have been dispensed with, and all trials are *extra-ordinem*. The action commences with the plaintiff's statement of his claim (*editio*); after a certain delay comes the order for compulsory appearance (*in jus vocare*), then the pleadings of the advocates, after which judgment is pronounced and execution follows; so that the judge now unites *jurisdictio, imperium*, and *judicium*.

Outside the capital, the towns have their *decuriones*, and other municipal magistrates; and Justinian has endeavoured to restore the position of the discredited *defensores* of the city (*ante*, par. 496), to whose tribunal inferior matters are referred.

581. *Sacred Law*. Pagans and heterodox Christians are subject to severe penalties. The bishops, elected by the vote of the faithful, unite very extensive *civil* powers to their spiritual functions. The wealth of the church is increasing, convents and nunneries multiply, councils meet in vain to settle the theological controversies perpetually arising.

582. *Private Law*. At the period of the submission of all Italy, the primitive *jus civile* had yielded to the prætorian law of nature

and equity, and at the fall of the republic it only existed by fiction. Turned into a science by a brilliant series of jurisconsults, imperial constitutions, aided by the change of capital, tended to destroy its character, and inharmonious institutions gradually disappeared until Justinian's body of jurisprudence left no trace of primitive legislation except its most salient feature, the civil composition and consequent rights of the family, and this the 127th novel finally eradicated.

583. As to *persons*, enfranchisement is favoured by the laws, and there is no difference between the *freed* and the *ingenui*, but a new system of bondage, serfdom, has sprung up. The *patria potestas* differs little from the natural power of the father, and the son can hold several kinds of property.

584. As to *things*, the distinctions as to *mancipi* and *nec mancipi*, and Italian and *provincial* property, have disappeared, and therefore there is no mancipation or other solemn formality required for the transference of ownership.

585. As to *wills*, simpler formalities have been substituted, for the fiction of the sale of the inheritance. The *filiusfamilias* has the power of bequeathing by will several kinds of property. There are no restrictions on *cœlibes* and *orbi*.

586. As to *successions*, the distinction between agnation and cognation is abolished, and the order of intestate succession established by a novel of Justinian is based entirely on blood relationship.

587. As to *contracts*, the prætorian conventions not sanctioned by the civil law have been embodied in Justinian's system of jurisprudence, and in stipulations, the fact of the interrogation and response being in accord is sufficient. As to the meaning the word *actio* has now acquired, and as to the formal method of conducting litigation (see *ante*, pars. 427 and 579).

ROMAN LAW AFTER JUSTINIAN.

§ 1. *Destiny in the East.*

590. **Greek Jurists of the Sixth Century.** The legislative works of Justinian preserved a nominal authority for five centuries after his death, but the empire was in fact Byzantine, and when the successors of Justinian became the guardians of the Greek church, ecclesiastical law tended practically to absorb secular jurisprudence.

The process was gradual, and the first phase commenced in the lifetime of Justinian himself, continuing for about fifty years subsequently, viz., the appearance in the *Greek* language, with his permission, of translations, summaries, and concordances; and, in spite of his prohibition, of commentaries and abridgments on his works. The greater part of these are only known by the quotations made from them in imperial compilations of the ninth century, particularly in the *Basilicæ* (*post*, par. 592), and their authors are collectively known as the *antiqui*. The more important of these works were:—

On the Institutes. The paraphrase of Theophilus (*ante*, par. 566) and commentaries by Dorotheus and Stephanus, the latter a professor of law at Berytus, A.D. 555.

On the Digest. Commentaries by Theophilus, Dorotheus, Isodorus, Stephanus, Cyrill, Theodorus of Hermopolis, Gobidas (Cubidius), and Anastasius.

On the Code. A translation and short commentary by Anatolius; commentaries by Isodorus, Thalleleo and Phocas; abridgments by Stephanus and Theodorus of Hermopolis.

On the Novels. In addition to the four collections enumerated in par. 552, there were three abridgments; one by an anonymous writer (probably the same Julianus who made the *Latin* epitome), one by Athanasius of Antioch in Syria, and another by Theodorus of Hermopolis, the two latter being extant in a nearly complete form. Besides these, there were commentaries by Philoxenes and Symbatius.

This period of activity was followed by nearly two centuries and a half of torpor, during which the Latin text was gradually superseded by these translations and abridgments, and for upwards of a century, from about A.D. 717 to 866, the school of law at Constantinople was closed.

592. Manuals or Codes of Byzantine Emperors. The second phase in the transformation which Justinian's jurisprudence underwent, was due to the official nature of the works founded on the Greek text of his laws, and published with the imperial authority, viz.:—

(1) The *Ecloga legum* (or *Enchiridium*) of Leo the Isaurian, published in conjunction with his son, Constantine Copronymus, in A.D. 740. This manual of Isaurian law consists of a preface and 18 titles, and was edited by the two Nicetas and Marinus. Annotated editions are known as *Ecloga Privatæ*, and the copy in the Paris library (probably of the middle of the ninth century) has, in addition to the Greek versions of the text of Justinian, an appendix containing extracts from the Rhodian, or military and maritime laws, and from the Georgian or rural laws.

(2) The *Prochiron* of Basil the Macedonian, appeared in A.D. 870, by order of Basil and his sons, Constantine and Leo. This manual condemns and abrogates the work of Leo (surnamed the Iconoclast), and is also known as the Constitution of Basil, or of the three Emperors. It consists of a preamble and 40 titles, containing fragments from the Greek translations of Justinian's works, from the Ecloga of Leo, and from some imperial constitutions. It was followed between A.D. 879 and 886, by a second edition, published by Basil, in conjunction with his sons Leo and Alexander, under the title of *Epanagoge* (*repetita prælectio legis*), and intended as an introduction to an entire revision of the ancient law which was carried out in the—

THIRD EPOCH.—THE EMPERORS.

(3) *Basilicæ* (or *Repurgatio veterum legum*) of Leo the philosopher, published in conjunction with his brother Alexander and his son Constantine Porphyrogenitus, between A.D. 906 and 911.

The name Basilicæ was subsequently given to this work either in memory of its projector Basil or from the Greek βασιλικαὶ διατάξεις (*imperatoriæ constitutiones*). The work was prepared by a commission, probably under the presidency of Symbatius, and is only known now in a fragmentary state. It was divided into 6 volumes and 60 books, with subdivisions under titles, and is composed of extracts from the works of the jurists of the 6th century—*i.e.*, from the Greek paraphrases, commentaries, and abridgments of Justinian's body of laws, which were intended to bring it into harmony with subsequent legislation.

The preamble condemns, as embarrassing, the fourfold division adopted by Justinian (Institutes, Digest, Code, and Novels), and proposes to unite the whole subject in one work, but it treats Justinian's legislation as the main source of law to be followed where not overruled by subsequent provisions, and it was not until the latter part of the 11th century that the Basilicæ definitively replaced the corpus juris of Justinian.

594. **Greek jurists subsequent to the Basilicæ.** The impulse given by the legislative labours of Basil and his sons led to the issue from that period, with occasional intervals down to the fall of the empire, of a number of private works by way of commentary on these Greek versions of Justinian's laws; and an examination of the annotation (*scholia*) which accompanies the text (*capitula*) of the Basilicæ, shows that a portion of these notes (*antiqua*) are drawn from the juriconsults of the 6th century, but that the remainder (called *scholia* in the restricted sense) are the work of the *scholiasts*, living subsequent to its promulgation, and at times contradict the text where subsequent legislation had modified the law. Only five of these scholiasts of the 11th and 12th centuries are known—viz., John Nomophylax, Calocyrus Sextus, Constantine of Nicæa, Gregory Doxapater, and Hagiotheodoritus.

An unknown jurist of the middle of the 10th century made a useful abridgment of the Basilicæ in the form of an alphabetical concordance, and called the *Synopsis Basilicorum*. It was revised from time to time, and continued to be used to the end of the empire.

About 1072 Michael Attaliota brought out the ποίημα, or methodical abridgment of the Basilicæ, and a jurist of the 13th century published a short alphabetical manual founded on these two works, and called the μικρόν, or *synopsis minor*.

The *Epitome legum*, in 50 titles, and drawn from the works of Justinian and from Basil's Epanagoge, appeared about A.D. 920, and obtained the name *Epitome ad Prochiron mutata*, because a reissue appeared towards the end of the same century edited in the same order as the Prochiron. After this appeared the *Ecloga ad*

F

Prochiron mutata, a compilation including the Ecloga, the Prochiron, and the Epitome, with corrections.

The *Epanagoge aucta*, a correction, with additions, of Basil's Epanagoge, is probably of the 11th century, and the *Prochiron auctum*, a revision greatly enlarged of the Prochiron, dates from the beginning of the 13th century.

To these may be added the following works: the πειρα or *Experentia Romani*, which appeared in the 11th century; a collection of cases drawn from the writings of Eustathius Romanus, and about the same period the *Synopsis legum*, written in verse by Psellus, and dedicated to his pupil the Emperor Ducas. In 1335 appeared the manual of civil and canon law of the monk Matthew Blastares, and ten years later the *Hexabiblus* or *Promptuarium* of Constantine Harmenopulus, judge at Thessalonica. The six books of the latter are made up of the Prochiron, the Synopsis Basilicorum major, the Synopsis minor, and the πειρα, adapted to subsequent legislation, and the work maintained its authority amongst the Greeks even after the Turkish domination.

As additional monuments of Græco-Roman law must be mentioned the Novels, mostly relating to political or religious matters, published by the successors of Justinian, and the works of those jurists who treated of ecclesiastical law. Amongst these latter were the writings of *Psellus*, *Doxapater*, and *Blastares*, jurists already referred to in connection with their secular works, a revision of the nomocanon of John of Antioch (*ante*, par. 552), published by *Photius*, under Basil the Macedonian in A.D. 883, and works by *Zonoras*, of the 12th and *Balsamon* of the beginning of the 13th century.

Fall of the Eastern Empire. In 1453 the last Emperor, Constantine Palæologus, perished in the attempt to defend Constantinople against Mahomet II, and the Koran then replaced the Prochiron and the Basilicæ, but these laws remained peculiar to the conquered race, and so continued until 1834, when a series of codes, in analogy to those introduced in France, were promulgated in Greece, and are now used, modified by subsequent additions and alterations, in harmony with the traditional laws of the country and local customs.

595. **Byzantine law after the 16th Century.** Amongst the Greeks who expatriated themselves on the fall of Constantinople were Constantine and John *Lascaris*, both of whom brought with them valuable Byzantine legal documents, and John was entrusted by Francis I with the formation of his library at Fontainebleau. Through their influence is to be attributed the revival of the study of Greek literature in the West; and the knowledge of Græco-Roman law, thus disseminated in France, Germany, and England, led to the publication at Basle, in 1534, of the Greek paraphrase of the Institutes by Theophilus, and of the Promptuarium of Harmenopulus at Paris in 1540. The activity in this department of

legal literature passed to Germany at the beginning of the present century, and the Græco-Roman MSS. have been laboriously studied by the jurists of that nation (*e.g.*, Puhl, Haubold, Biener, Heimbach, Witte, Bekk, Zacharia), but the information to be thus derived has now rather an historical than a practical interest.

§ 2.—*Destiny in the West.*

596. Cause of the maintenance of Justinian's laws. On the re-conquest of *Italy*, in A.D. 554, the edict of Theodoric (*ante*, par. 529) was supplanted by the laws of Justinian, and official copies of the Institutes, Digest, Code, and Novels were deposited by Narses at Rome; but according to Odofredus, who was a contemporary of Accursius, and died in 1265, the school of law at Rome, with its official library, was subsequently, on account of the wars, transferred to Ravenna, the seat of the exarchate, and from thence to Bologna. In A.D. 568 a portion of the country was conquered by the Lombards, and by the 8th century Italy was divided into Frankish, Pontifical, and Lombardian, but the power of the Byzantine emperors was maintained in parts for upwards of 300 years, and Justinian's body of laws remained the foundation of private law, unaffected by the subsequent fortunes of his laws in the East, for the interference of the successors of Justinian related rather to public or political matters, and the final merger of the text of Justinian in the Basilicæ took place after the domination of the Eastern Empire had ceased in Italy.

600. The foundation of the States of the Church in A.D. 774 further tended to maintain the force of the laws of Justinian throughout Italy, for the pontifical court placed Roman law next in order to the canonical rules, and extracts from the corpus juris civilis are common in those canonical texts used by the clergy in the 9th, 10th, and 11th centuries, before the publication in 1151 of the *Decretum Gratiana*, which formed the first part of the *corpus juris canonici*.

604. The principle of the *personality* of laws, which became very marked after the overthrow by the Barbarians of the Western Empire (*ante*, par. 529) also tended in the same direction, and the edict of Theodoric, though general, did not affect the principle, as it scarcely dealt with private law. A constitution of the Emperor Lothaire I, at the end of the 9th century, directed that the inhabitants of Rome should be individually questioned as to the law they would adopt, and it may be concluded that the ecclesiastics and the mass of the people selected the Roman law—*i.e.*, in this part of Italy, the corpus juris of Justinian. This principle of personality would tend to die out as the distinctive nationalities in the same commonwealth disappeared, and a combination of Roman and Barbarian law, applicable to all, would result, but in this process the canon and the civil law would be likely not only to survive but to absorb the Barbarian laws, owing to the religious authority on which the first was based, and the scientific unity which characterised the second.

607. In *France* the constitution of Clotaire I, of about A.D. 560, shows the principle of personality in full force, but during the subsequent period of three centuries, and prior to the publication in A.D. 864 by Charles the bald of the "édit sur la paix du royaume," a change occurred, and the distinction became *territorial* in lieu of personal, in other words, the individuality of the inhabitants in respect of the law to govern them disappeared, and the southern portion of the country was ruled according to the *lex Romana*—*i.e.*, the ante-Justinian law embodied in the Breviarium Aliricianum *(ante*, par. 529), for, according to Laferrière, no portion of Justinian laws, except the Julian epitome of the novels, was current in the country until the end of the 11th century.

But in France, as in Italy, the influence of the clergy tended to the introduction and maintenance of the laws of Justinian; and St. Ives, of Beauvais, Bishop of Chartres, who was born about 1035, and died in 1115, made in A.D. 1092 the collections of canonical texts known as the *Pannormia* and (?) the *Decretum*, in which the Institutes, Digest, and Code of Justinian are freely used, besides the Breviarium and the Epitome of Julian. It is probable that St. Ives availed himself of the collections of the same kind already in use in Italy, and with which he would be acquainted, for he and St. Anselm of Aosta, afterwards Archbishop of Canterbury, were fellow pupils of Lanfranc, who commenced his legal studies in his native city, Pavia, but subsequently opened the celebrated school at the Benedictine abbey of Bec, in Normandy, and was transferred to the see of Canterbury by William the Conqueror.

611. **The School of Bologna.** Although the Lombardian law was enforced in the north of Italy, it may be assumed that the study of Justinian had not altogether ceased, for St. Damian (born A.D. 988, died 1072), Bishop of Ostia, refers to discussions in his native city, Ravenna, on the differences in the civil and canonical laws, in respect of relationship, in which the authority of the Institutes of Justinian was invoked, but the enthusiastic revival of the study is due to the chief of the Glossators, *Irnerius* (Werner), the successor of Pepo, and the founder of the famous school of Bologna. Irnerius passed into the service of the Emperor Henry V in 1116, and his lectures ceased in 1118, so that the statement that the revival of the study was due to the discovery of the MS. of the pandects at the sacking of Amalfi by the people of Pisa in 1137, may be treated as without foundation, the only truth in the story probably being that a valuable MS. of great antiquity, now known as the *Pandectæ Florentinæ* existed at Pisa, and was transferred in 1406 to Florence, on the former town falling under the domination of the latter. This Florentine copy of the Pandects is the only one now existing, anterior to the time of the Glossators; but they were in possession of other ancient MSS., and it is by a comparison of these with the Florentine text that the Glossators produced the work in three volumes, known as the *littera Bononiensis*, or the *Vulgate*. The object of

dividing this work into three parts (*Digestum vetus, Infortiatum, Digestum novum*) has never been clearly ascertained, and the division disappeared in the editions published subsequent to the 17th century.

618. Irnerius may possibly be the author of a brief summary of Roman law, which appeared, according to Savigny, in Italy about the commencement of the 12th century, and now known as the *Brachylogus totius juris civilis*. It is constructed on the model of the Institutes of Justinian, and divided into four books, with extracts also from the Pandects, the Code, and Julian's epitome of the novels. About the same period, according to Laferrière, another work of a similar character, called the *Petri exceptiones legum Romanorum*, was published by an unknown jurist of Valence in Dauphiné, and dedicated to Odilo, the vicar of the Emperor of Germany in the kingdom of Arles, but, unlike the former work, the extracts of Roman law in the latter are modified by the canon law and local customs.

The term **glossator** refers to the practice of explaining difficult passages and abstruse terms in the text by marginal notes (*glossa* or *glosa*), but, in addition to this, their characteristic work, and to their incessant labours in the way of tabular references to comparisons, parallelisms, concordances, and contradictions in the text of the corpus juris, the professors of law of this period supplemented their oral teaching by the publication of *apparatus*, or continuous notes, serving as a complete commentary on a title or larger portion of the Digest ; *summæ*, or preliminary reviews of the subject matter for study ; *casus*, or examples illustrating difficult points of law ; *brocarda*, or general rules, evolved from a consideration of the details given in the text.

Amongst the successors of Irnerius were : the four doctors of Bologna (*Bulgarus*, died 1166 ; *Martinus Gosia*, who died shortly before that date ; *Jacobus*, died 1178 ; and *Ugo*, who died between 1166 and 1171), *Placentinus*, who was born about 1120 at Placentia, founded the school of Montpellier in 1180 and died 1192. *Vacarius*, who was a Lombard, and accompanied Theobald, Archbishop of Canterbury, from Bologna to England in 1144. He extracted and glossed parts of the laws of Justinian for the use of the students who attended the school of law he founded at Oxford, and from the title of the book, *Liber ex universo enucleato jure exceptus et pauperibus præsertim destinatus*, it is said the name *pauperistes* was applied to students at Oxford.

The enthusiasm generated by the work of the glossators was felt in France, and a large number of manuscript translations of the Digest, the Code, and the Institutes, in the old French of the 13th century, show the ardour with which the study was prosecuted ; and as the canon law fell into neglect, three councils held in the 12th century forbad the study of Roman law by ecclesiastics under pain of excommunication. In 1220 the prohibition was particularly directed to the University of Paris, and in spite of the protest of Dumoulin 300 years after, and of the exceptional parliamentary decree of 1576 in favour of Cujas and others, the prohibition was not finally removed until 1679. The effect of this hindrance to the study in Paris was to increase the number of students at Montpellier, and to lead to the establishment of the schools of Toulouse, 1228, and of Orleans, 1236.

626. The list of eminent glossators closed with *Accursius*, who was a pupil of *Azo*, celebrated for his apparatus, summæ, and brocarda (see above). Accursius was born about 1182, near Florence, and died 1260. He was professor of law in the University of Bologna, and subsequently completed in retirement, with some aid from his son Cervottus, the annotated corpus juris known as the "great gloss," and containing a selection from the notes of the glossators during the 160 years of their labours.

629. **The Scribentes and the Humanistes.** For a period of 80 years after the death of Accursius, his gloss practically superseded the text, but fell into contempt on the rise of the school of the so-called *scribentes*, headed by *Bartolus*, who was born in 1314 at Sasso Ferrato, in Umbria, and died 1357. He became professor of law in the University of Pisa in 1339, and of Perugia in 1343, and wrote commentaries on the Digest and Code, as well as *consilia*, *questiones*, and *tractatus*, which were greatly used in Italy, France, Spain, and Portugal, and substituted rules founded on references to the text for the servile submission to the works of the glossators.

630. Three names in particular (Budé, Zazius, and Alciat) are connected with the rise in the 16th century of the third school called by Pasquier the *Humanistes*, because their studies were not confined as hitherto to Justinian's compilations, but embraced the earlier and later monuments of law, combined with the auxiliary information to be gleaned from historians, prose writers, and poets.

Budé, of Paris, who was secretary to Louis XII, Master of Requests under Francis I, and a friend of the librarian, John Lascaris (*ante*, par. 595), published his annotations upon the Pandects in 1508, but he and the German *Zazius*, the author of several annotations of ante-Justinian works, were rather scholars than jurists, like André *Alciat* (born at Milan 1492, died 1550), who published in 1518 commentaries on the three last books of the code, and became professor of law in the University of Avignon 1522, in that of Bourges, 1529, and subsequently taught at Pavia, Bologna, and Ferrara. He was succeeded by the most illustrious of the humanists, James *Cujas* (born at Toulouse in 1522, died 1590), who produced his notes on Ulpian in the same year (1554) that he became professor of law at Cahors, and by his writings and teaching gave a great impulse to the philosophic study of Roman law.

633. **Roman law as an element of French law.** The study in the south of France (*ante*, par. 607, 618), without legislative authority, of the corpus juris of Justinian, caused it in the course of the 12th and 13th centuries gradually to supersede the ante-Justinian

law, on the ground that it was only a more accurate expression of the same law, and this district from being known as that of the lex Romana, came to be called the *pays de droit écrit*—*i.e.*, the part of the country where the body of laws of Justinian served as the basis, modified by local customs; and even in the north, in the *pays de coutume*, evidences of the legislation of Justinian may be traced from the reign of St. Louis in the old law books, although Roman law was only accepted there as a supplement to the local customs, and to serve as a scientific model for the instruction of the jurist. Matters thus continued until the end of the last century, when the new system of codes appeared, producing a uniform legislation in harmony with the social condition.

The history of Roman law may usefully serve as an introduction to the history of French law, but Roman law is only one of many elements producing the law of France, the other elements are to be sought in barbarian, feudal, customary, and canon rules, and in the monarchical ordinances.

PERIODS IN THE HISTORY OF ROMAN LAW.

The epochs in the history of Roman law, adopted with slight variations by, Hugo, Gibbon, Mackeldey, Giraud, Warnkœnig, and Blondeau, are based on internal considerations without regard to the course of external history, and may be summarised thus :—

(1) *Infancy.* From the foundation of Rome to the twelve tables, B.C. 753 to B.C. 451. In this period the effect of the *written* code as regards *private* rights, is to place patricians and plebeians on the same footing. Information as to this epoch is derived from the fragments of the twelve tables themselves, and the most celebrated jurisconsult of the age was *Papirius*.

(2) *Youth.* From the twelve tables to Cicero, B.C. 451 to B.C. 100. During this period the law divides into *jus civile* and *jus honorarium*, and the greater part of the inhabitants of Italy acquire citizen rights. The works of *Cicero* are the principal source of information, and the leading jurists were *Appius Claudius, Flavius, Coruncanius, Ælius,* and *Cato.*

(3) *Manhood.* From Cicero to Alexander Severus, B.C. 100 to A.D. 250. The empire has become vast in extent, jurisprudence has attained a high pitch of perfection as a science, and nearly all the subjects of the empire are assimilated to Roman citizens. Information as to this period is derived from the extant works of the jurisconsults on the laws which emanated in the form of plebiscita, senatus-consulta, and imperial constitutions. The leading jurists

were *Scævola, Servius Sulpicius, Labeo, Sabinus, Julian, Gaius, Papinian, Paul, Ulpian, Modestinus.*

(4) *Old age.* From Alexander Severus to Justinian, A.D. 250 to A.D. 550. During this period the provinces were devastated, and the empire itself threatened at all points. The science of law degenerated into the quotation of the writings of the ancient prudentes supplemented by imperial constitutions. Information as to this epoch is obtained from the constitutions themselves, and the leading jurists were *Hermogenianus, Gregorianus, Tribonian,* and *Theophilus.*

PART II.

GENERALIZATION OF ROMAN LAW.

1. IN this portion of the work the rules of the Roman law are presented in the form of general principles, so as to afford the student a comprehensive view of the whole subject, apart from details and from the constitutions and fragments in which they lie imbedded.

5. *Arrangement of subject matter.* The principal monuments of Roman law (such as the twelve tables, of which the order is only known by conjecture, the prætors' edict, the sentences of Paul, the Theodosian code, and the Justinian Digest and Code) do not present a methodical arrangement. The nearest approach to a scientific division is that found in the Institutes of *Gaius*, followed (nearly) in the regulæ of *Ulpian*, and adopted in the Institutes of *Justinian* (part i, par. 548), according to which law is treated under the heads of *persons, things, actions,* but the arrangement is not carried out in details, and the modern *German* school, to whom the law is *living*, is therefore divided into two sects, one adhering to the above division, the other adopting a more philosophic system in which the first part is reserved for the exposition of general principles, and the second part devoted to the special subjects falling under the heads of real rights, obligations, family rights, and successions.

But in countries where Roman law is treated as the legislation of the past, it should be studied historically and according to its own classifications, though in this generalization some latitude may be permitted, because the idea of a philosophical survey of the general principles of law is itself a modern creation.

§ 1.—*Law and the causes producing it.*

Idea of Law.

8. In the infancy of Rome the word law *(jus)* suggested the idea of the imperative and harsh order *(jussum)*, the technical and rigorous formula which was a patrician mystery and an aristocratic weapon, but in the course of time, and with the progress of civilisation and science, it acquired a totally different charac-

ter, so that on the completion of the system its foundation was no longer based on *authority* but upon *reason,* and the science of law reposed upon that of philosophy *(Non ergo a prætoris edicto neque a xii tabulis sed penitus ex intima philosophia hauriendam juris disciplinam putas*—Cicero), and imperial constitutions adopt the principle of reason over-riding positive rules *(Placuit in omnibus rebus præcipuam esse justitiæ æquitatisque quam stricti juris rationem.* Code 3, 1, 8.) From this philosophical point of view the Roman jurisprudents used the expression law in an abstract and general sense to mean *"that which is always good and equitable" (quod semper æquum ac bonum est jus dicitur ut est jus naturale,* Paul), or in a collective sense as a body of precepts or doctrines, it was *"the art of that which is good and equitable" (jus est ars boni et æqui,* Celsus), and so employed for the whole body of law *(jus publicum, civile, gentium.)* These definitions are wanting in precision, for what is *bonum* and what is *æquum ?* but they indicate the change of ideas, and Cicero alludes to the true principle when he says that the explanation of the nature of law must be sought in the nature itself of man *(Natura enim juris nobis explicanda est, eaque ab hominis repetenda natura...Nos ad justitiam esse natos neque opinione sed natura constitutum esse jus*—Cicero, *de legibus*), for law is nothing but a metaphysical conception, deduced by reason from the relations of man to man, in consequence of which one man acquires the power of exacting action or inaction from another. This law is rational if the necessity of action or inaction is deduced from reasoning alone, but it is positive if, rightly or wrongly, the necessity results from authority.

15. The *immediate consequences of law* are the powers and the advantages it confers. The word *jus* or rather *jura,* rights, is still used, but now indicates, not the objective *cause,* but the subjective *effect*—*i.e.,* the power of doing, omitting or requiring something.

17. The *elements producing law* are three, viz. :—

(1) *Persons, i.e.,* beings, whether men or legal abstractions, capable of being the active or passive *subjects* of rights.

(2) *Things, i.e.,* corporeal or legal abstractions, capable of being the *objects* of rights. These two the Roman lawyers recognised, but they omitted—

(3) *Events,* facts, acts of man, *i.e.,* the efficient cause and comprehending the idea of time, place, intention, form.

These three elements combine to engender, transmit, modify, and extinguish rights, but the idea of the share of the last mentioned is the work of modern analysis.

Of Persons.

21. The word *persona* has two meanings.

(1) Every being capable of having and being subject to rights, *i.e.,* of being the subject, active or passive, of rights, and therefore consisting of two divisions—(α) natural or physical persons, the *singularis persona* of Ulpian ; (β) moral, abstract, fictitious,

civil, juridical persons, *i.e.*, pure legal creations, and hence a *slave* being only the object of rights, had strictly no *persona*, but from the earliest times the fact of the slave's existence as a living being, in relation with other men, compelled their classification amongst *persons*.

(2) Each character sustained by the same man, in virtue of which he had rights or obligations, as father, son, husband, tutor ; and hence the expression *sustinere personam, hereditas personam defuncti sustinet*, *i.e.*, sustains the *mask* (the *persona*) of the deceased.

24. *Status* was composed of three elements—(1) *libertas*, (2) *civitas*, (3) *familia*, and their union constituted the *caput* or *persona* of the Roman civil law, but both status and caput are also used by Roman jurists in a more general sense (part iii, par. 197).

26. *Libertas* is opposed to *servitus*, and hence the first division of men into free *(liberi)* and slaves *(servi)*. The influence of stoic philosophy led to liberty being considered the *natural* state and slavery as *against nature*, but established by the custom of nations. Christianity came later, and by introducing the dogma of equality, tended to abolish the institution, and hence in connection with the subject there were three periods in the history of the growth of ideas. A new class, that of the *agricolæ* or *coloni*, arose with the fall in the value of land, and the admission of barbarian hordes within the limits of the empire (see part i, par. 488, 583), and these prepared the way for the modern serfs and domestic servants.

29. The *manumissio* was at first a political act, and on account of the importance of making a new citizen, required the intervention of the city, but it was gradually abandoned to private law. The effects of enfranchisement were to divide men into two classes :—

(1) *Ingenui*, *i.e.*, those born free.

(2) *Libertini*, *i.e.*, those freed, the *liberti* of their patrons.

31. In primitive law there existed but one class of *libertini*, and they were Roman citizens, though of an inferior condition. Under *Augustus* and *Tiberius* two new classes sprang up without city rights, viz., the freed *latini juniani* and the *dediticii*, but Justinian made them all citizens, and under his last novels the only distinction from *ingenui* was the bond and rights of the patron.

32. *Civitas*. The whole life of the Roman was tinged with the fact of citizenship, and without it he had no *status*, *i.e.*, no power of exercising civil rights. Opposed to the *civis* was the *peregrinus*, the *hostis*, and the *barbarus*, all three terms equivalent as regards the civil law, to whom it had no application; but *peregrini*, in a restricted sense, applied to those strangers at Rome who ultimately exceeded the citizens in number and for whom the *prætor peregrinus* was established (see part i, par. 197, 222, 396). The intermediate class, whether of individuals or of whole communities, which subsequently sprang up between the *civis* and the *peregrinus*, possessed only a portion of the rights (greater or less, according to the particular concession) arising out of the components of the *jus civitatis* (viz., the *connubium* and the *commercium*, the latter usually

including the *testamenti factio*), hence the distinctions (part i, par. 186, 187, 188, 448) as to the *romani coloni, socii latini, latini colonarii, latini juniani, dediticii*, and the class of freedmen assimilated to the last.

Under *Caracalla* all the subjects of the empire became Roman citizens, and under *Justinian* the two inferior classes of freedmen (*latini juniani* and *dediticii*) were suppressed.

As the title of citizen extended, so the character of the civil law altered and approximated to the *jus gentium*, until under Justinian the characteristic peculiarities of the former disappeared.

40. *Familia.* Under the word "family" may be included:—

(1) The paterfamilias and his wife and children in power.

(2) The reunion of all the agnates under the common chief, if he were alive (the real civil law family).

(3) All the slaves, and those *in mancipio*, although only classed as things, without any family tie.

(4) All the property, the patrimony of the chief.

The last head is the sense in which the word is used in the twelve tables, v, (4), *adgnatus proximus familiam habeto* (5) *gentilis familiam nancitor*, for the type of the Roman family was an aggregation, bound together in three ways.

Politically. The patrician family dominated, and had within it the plebeian families, united by the bond of clientage (part i, par. 15). Any alteration in the constitution of the family involved the aid of the comitia.

Religiously. The family was united by particular acts of sacrifice (*e.g.*, the *sacrificia piacularia gentis Horatiæ*, founded by the Horatii for the murder of their sister), and the pontiff's interference was necessitated in case of any alteration (part i, par. 40).

Privately. The property, obligations, and inheritance centred in the persona of the deceased, and the transference of these rights, or the faculty of representing in the city this persona, required the aid of the comitia.

The foundation of the family is due to marriage (with the Romans the *civil* marriage), but legally the *potestas* is the basis, for this civil law bond marks the limits of the family, not the ties of blood or marriage.

46. *Potestas.* The chief of the household is the only independent individual. He is proprietor of all the others and of all the goods of the family, and hence another division of persons arises, viz. :—

(1) *Sui juris* or independent persons (*paterfamilias* or *materfamilias*) of any age, and whether married or not, and whether with or without children.

(2) *Alieni juris* or those subject to the *potestas* of another (*alieno juri subjectus*).

The second class was only the representative, the instrument of the first, and had no individual persona, *except in public law*, according to which, if free and a citizen, the members of this class were independent, and could vote and hold office, though it is

OF PERSONS.

uncertain how they could vote in the *comitia centuriata* (part i, par. 56, 66), for the citizens were there classified according to fortune, and only the *sui juris* had property. The *potestas* was of three kinds :—

(1) *Potestas* proper, *i.e.*, the power of the master over the slave *(potestas dominorum)* and that of the father over the child *(patria potestas)*, the latter acquired by *justæ nuptiæ, adrogatio* or *adoptio*.

(2) *Manus*. The power of the husband over the wife, by which she became a daughter, and due to *justæ nuptiæ* (*post*, par. 58), resulting from *confarreatio* for patricians, *co-emptio* or *usus* for plebeians (see part i, par. 88, 89, 329).

(3) *Mancipium, i.e.*, the power over the freeman, acquired by the solemn alienation or civil sale (*mancipatio*). In this way the chief could sell his children or wife in power, or by the same method abandon them, to avoid repairing damage caused by them (*noxali causa mancipatio*). The effects of the power were in general to assimilate the person so sold to a slave in the family *(servorum loco constituuntur)*, whilst free in public law, and every five years at the census all those *in mancipio* for fictitious rather than serious causes recovered their freedom. (Gai. Inst. i, § 140.)

The old expression was *nexus (nexu vinctus)*, that is, the position of the *paterfamilias* debtor, who gave himself as security to his creditor by the sale *(nexum, mancipatio, alienatio per æs et libram)* of his person, and hence that of his family and patrimony. This kind of alienation was prohibited in B.C. 326 (part i, par. 175), and probably never was irrevocable, being put an end to by the payment of the debt, when the released debtor was called *solutus*. The same power was acquired by a person being *addictus* by the magistrate, either because he was a defaulter in respect of the payment of a debt or on account of the commission of an offence, such as *furtum manifestum*, and *adjudicatus* was the position of the person sentenced *(judicatus)* by the judge, after which the creditor proceeded to get him *addictus*. Gaius (Inst. i, § 141) scarcely alludes to the *nexum* or the *addictio*, though he details the *mancipium*, which had, however, softened in character and was chiefly used fictitiously.

58. The *justum matrimonium (justæ nuptiæ)* was an exclusive privilege of citizens or of those having the *connubium*. A public solemnity was not essential to marriage, consent and tradition sufficing, but *farreum, co-emptio,* or *usus*, was required to give the husband the *manus* over the wife (*ante*, par. 46). The *lex Canuleia* (*ante*, par. 150) gave the *connubium* between *patricians* and *plebeians*. The *lex Papia Poppea* gave it between *ingenui* and *libertini*, and the constitutions of *Justinian* allowed *senators* to ally themselves with the *freed* or with those of low birth.

Sponsalia lead to, and *repudium, divorcium*, dissolve the marriage.

Other unions were—(1) *Concubinatus, i.e.*, licit intercourse without marriage, the children were *naturales liberi*, having a recognised father, but *legitimation* was required to produce the *patria potestas*. (2) *Stuprum, i.e.*, illicit connection, the children were *spurii, vulgo quæsiti*, and *incestus* or *adulterium* made the issue *incestuosi* or *adulterini*. (3) *Contubernium, i.e.,* the natural union of slaves producing no civil effects, but the laws contained dispositions in respect of the position of children born through the union of slaves and free persons (Gai. Inst. i, § 84, 85).

62. *Cognatio* was the bond between persons united by blood, or (as in the case of adopted persons) that which the law reputed as such *(cognati; quasi una communiter nati)*. The direct line is *linea recta*, and is *superior* when ascending, *inferior* when descending, collateral lines are *transversa (obliqua, ex transverso, a latere)*, and each generation is one degree. Civil law took little notice of cognation, except as to prohibitions of marriage (see part iii, par. 106).

64. *Agnatio* was the *civil law* bond uniting cognate members of the same family *(qui ex eadem familia sunt)*, and of which the paternal or marital *potestas* was the efficient cause, so that persons not under the *potestas* did not belong to the family, that is to say, those would be excluded who would not be of the family if the most distant ascendant were still alive (see part iii, par. 1018).

65. *Gens* was an ancient civil bond, the nature of which it is difficult to trace (see part i, par. 16; twelve tables, v. (5); part iii, par. 1032), probably it was originally *patrician agnation*, but it also implied privileges in respect of the relations of patron and client, and in the absence of agnates it gave the inheritance and tutorship. It was rare in the time of *Cicero*, and had disappeared prior to *Gaius* (Inst. iii, § 17).

67. *Affinitas* was alliance by marriage. It affected the position of the contracted parties, and of their cognates, but it did not confer any civil rights. The degrees of relationship arising from this bond were assimilated to those arising from cognation.

The *gens* disappeared first, then the *nexum* and the *addictio* of the free man. After these the *manus* and the *mancipium* (except as fictions to elude the civil law, see part i, par. 329). The *filius familias* acquired a separate entity as to person and goods. The prætor sided with cognates; and finally, under Justinian, of the four family ties—(1) *political*; (2) *religious*; (3) *private civil law*, and (4) *natural*, only the last remained.

70. *Loss or change of status.* Of the three elements (*ante*, par. 24) of *status* or *caput*, if—

(1) *Liberty* was lost it entailed the other two.

(2) *Citizenship* lost entailed the family, and therefore both entailed the loss of civil status (*status amittitur*).

(3) *Family* lost did not affect the others *(salvo statu)*, but the status was modified (*status mutatur*), for the individual changed familia, property, and persona.

The first event was styled *maxima*, the second *media*, and the third *minima capitis diminutio* (see part iii, par. 197).

74. *Existimatio.* Independent of *status*, other considerations, political and physical, affected the position of a citizen. For civil rights his honour must be intact, *Existimatio est dignitatis illæsæ*

OF PERSONS.

status legibus ac moribus comprobatus, and this *existimatio* might be lost (*aut consumitur*) or diminished (*aut minuitur*). The alterations were three—

(1) *Infamia*, entailing legal incapacities, and attaching to *famosi, qui notantur infamia*, or simply *notati, i.e.*, those marked by the censor, on account of following certain professions, or of having been guilty of certain acts, *e.g.*, bankruptcy or condemnation in particular actions (see part iii, par. 287, 2335).

(2) *Turpitudo*. This resulted from course of life (see part iii, par. 790), and gave rise to similar legal incapacities, though only due to *opinion*, and not caused by *written* law.

(3) *Levis nota*, attaching to freed persons and to the children of actors (*qui artem ludicram faciunt*). The regulation incapacitating such persons from marrying senators or their children was suppressed by Justinian.

Although the expressions *personæ turpes, viles personæ*, etc., were very indiscriminately applied, the distinctions were well marked, but the senate, the emperor, or the magistrate could remove the brand of disgrace, and time also tended to obliterate its effects.

77. *Rank.* The legislation of Rome tended to perpetuate strong *caste* divisions, and society also drew distinctions as to occupation or profession. In respect of immunity from many of the rules of law, *soldiers* were the most favoured, and certain privileges attached to the liberal professions (*liberalia studia*).

79. *Religion.* The differences in the rights of persons, according to their religion, commenced with christianity. At first, the penalties of the law were directed against christians, but afterwards in their favour, and hence two classes—(1) *Christians, i.e.*, the faithful or orthodox catholics (*orthodoxi catholici*), recognising the dogmas of œcumenical councils. (2) *Heretics* (*hæretici*), divided into apostates and Jews. Only *orthodox christians* enjoyed the plenitude of rights, the *Jews* being in the worst position, not having the *connubium* with, or the capability of being *witnesses* against, christians, nor could they hold any magistracy. The Codes of *Theodosius* and of *Justinian* contain many regulations on this subject.

80. *Domicilium.* The domicile of a person is where he is assumed to be in the eye of the law (*ubi quis larem rerumque et fortunarum suarum summam constituit; unde non discessurus, si nihil avocet; unde cum profectus est peregrinari videtur; quod si rediit, peregrinari jam destitit*—Code 10, 39, 7); and this assumed place of residence may vary according to the rights to be exercised, *e.g.*, for the contract of marriage, or in respect of real rights, or in relation to electoral privileges. It is not the *legal relation* existing between a person and the place where he exercises his rights; nor is it *the place* where he has his principal establishment, but it is *at the place*. It gives the quality of *incola*, in relation to public duties, magistracies, and particular jurisdictions. Conjointly with this, by origin, adoption, or manumission, the individual may belong to the local city, which makes him a citizen, with greater or less rights (*civis, municeps*).

After the constitution of *Caracalla* (part i, par. 396), *Rome* became the common country; but the question was still of importance, on account of differences in the *soil*, which continued until the time of Justinian: hence three political conditions might be involved, viz.:—(1) Rome, the common country. (2) The local city. (3) The domicile; but the subject of *absence* in respect of the distinction between the actual place of residence and the assumed domicile, was not clearly defined or understood in the modern sense.

84. *Sex* has been a ground of exclusion from *public* law in both ancient and modern times, but in private law the condition of women has tended to improve with the progress of civilization. In primitive law the woman was under the *potestas* of her father or the *manus* of her husband, and if she became *sui juris* (*materfamilias*), she was placed under the perpetual tutelage of her *agnates* and deprived of power over her children; hence the expression *mulier autem familiæ suæ et caput et finis est*. But, through the aid of fictions, the rigours of the civil law had been undermined even during the Republic, and under Justinian the character of the ancient system disappeared, though legal distinctions between men and women continued to exist; for women arrived at puberty earlier, and the law was sometimes less and sometimes more favourable to them. The *hermaphroditus* was held to belong to that sex which predominated in the individual.

86. *Age.* The *primitive* law took account of two physical phenomena—the power of speech and that of procreation; the former for the sacramental words, which could not be pronounced by another, and the latter in relation to marriage. The tendency of *Prætorian* law was to look to the intellectual development, and hence the following divisions:—

(1) *Infancy*, or the period of about two years, during which the individual *fari non potest*, according to *primitive* law, or has *nullum intellectum*, according to later jurisprudence.

(2) *Infancy to puberty, i.e.*, from the time that the infant can pronounce the sacramental words, until the necessity ceases for a tutor to augment or fill up (*augere*) his *persona*, in order to enable him to perform a civil law act. Philosophical jurisprudence here made a *moral* division. (a) *Infanti proximus*, terminating at seven years, owing to the ancient medical ideas as to the changes in the bodily organization, but still the infant was allowed by a favourable interpretation (*propter utilitatem*), even at this period, to act as soon as he could pronounce words, in those cases where his own presence was necessary (Gai. Inst., iii, § 109). (β) *Pubertati proximus*, commencing at seven years, when the child was considered to have some intellect (*aliquem intellectum habet*) though no judgment, and hence the pupil could act even without his tutor in matters not requiring *judicium*. A constitution of Theodosius (see Just. Cod., vi, 30, 18) seems to assimilate the minor under seven years to the *infans*, without reference to the exact age when he acquired the power of speech (*sive maturius,*

sive tardius, filius fandi sumat auspicia), and hence *infans* came to imply less than seven years, and was therefore equivalent to the term *infanti proximus*. As to the duties of the tutor in relation to these periods in the age of the pupil, see part iii, par. 234.

(3) *Puberty* was fixed for women at twelve years, but it was not until the time of Justinian that the age of fourteen was also arbitrarily established for men as the term when the *impubes* became *pubes*. After puberty *justæ nuptiæ* could be contracted, and the tutelage for men ceased as, according to the civil law, the *persona* of a Roman citizen was complete, and according to the theory of jurisprudence, the individual possessed intelligence and judgment.

(4) *Majority* was attained at twenty-five years, after which, under ordinary circumstances, the prætor would no longer interfere for the protection of the interests of the individual (part iii, par. 263).

(5) *Old Age* (*senectus*), as a ground for exemption from public duties, commenced at seventy years.

The terms *major* and *minor* were only comparative, but if used alone they usually meant above or below twenty-five years of age.

93. *Infirmities, bodily and mental.* Legal incapacities and exemptions might arise in the case of *spadones, castrati*, deaf persons, dumb persons, the deaf and dumb, and those afflicted with incurable maladies.

The theory of *curators* originated from the consideration of *mental* infirmities, but the Roman law was not very precise in its distinction. The *furiosi* were those who had lost their intelligence, the *menti capti* or *dementes* were idiots or those wanting in intelligence, and as to the *prodigus* see part iii, par. 263.

95. *Tutela-Cura.* To persons *sui juris*, but incapacitated from general causes (impuberty, and, formerly, sex), the *civil law* gave a *tutor* to *complete the persona;* and for accidental incapacities, due to the particular individual, a *curator* was appointed to *take care of the property*, the idea of protecting the individual belonging to an advanced period of prætorian jurisprudence.

99. *Juridical Persons.* The people (*populus*), the state (*respublica*), or later the emperor (*i. e.*, in his public capacity), the magistracies, the *municipia* and other cities, the *curiæ* of the towns, the *ærarium* of the people (finally absorbed in the *fiscus* of the emperor), the inheritance not yet acquired (*hæreditas jacens*), the *peculium*, the pagan temples, and colleges of Pontiffs, and the christian churches and different orders of the clergy which replaced them, the convents, hospitals, and charitable foundations, universities, and corporations, were all abstract persons, and might be the active or passive subject of rights; but every corporation had to be specially authorised by a law, or senatus consultum, or an imperial constitution; and at least three persons must join to found, though not necessarily to continue, the existence of such corporate bodies.

102. *Extinction of persons.* Death, physical or legal (as in the

case of loss of liberty) terminated the existence of the individual, either actually or in the eye of the law, but the *persona* by death was merely shifted to the new bearer.

Of Things.

105. The word *res* denotes everything which *may be the object of a right*, hence it includes slaves and abstractions, though the earlier jurists probably only included corporeal objects useful to man.

108. *Classification of things*. The Roman jurisconsults did not arrive at any very methodical arrangement.

109. In respect of their *creation*, things were divided into—

(1) *Corporales*, *i.e.*, *quæ tangi possunt*, or physical bodies, as *fundus, homo, vestis*, etc.

(2) *Incorporales*, *i.e.*, *quæ tangi non possunt*, or juridical objects, as the inheritance, a servitude, usufruct, obligation, etc.

111. In respect of *religion*, and according to *Gaius* (see part iii, par. 302), the principal division of things was into (1) *Divini juris* and (2) *humani juris*, the former on account of the sacerdotal character of primitive law, being again subdivided into—

(α) *Sacræ*, or consecrated to the gods; (β) *Religiosæ*, or abandoned to the lower gods, as tombs, etc., but the tomb of *an enemy* was not religious, though that of a slave was, and a divine thing in the power of an enemy was profane, and its divine character only restored by re-conquest, by a sort of *jus postliminii*; (γ) *Sanctæ*, or things assimilated to those divine for the sake of protection, as walls, gates of city, etc. And under this head are included the sacred things of each family or gens *(sacra familiæ, sacra gentis)*.

113. In respect of the *state* and of *private* law, through the rules as to *commercium*, a territorial distinction affected *immoveables*, according as they were situated on the—

(1) *Ager Romanus*, or soil of the civil law (part i, par. 92).

(2) *Italicum solum*, or Italian soil, assimilated to the *ager romanus*, and from which sprang the *jus italicum*, accorded to cities and countries beyond the confines of Italy.

(3) *Solum provinciale*, or land not enjoying the rights of the civil law.

The constitution of *Caracalla*, in so far as it affected these differences, was *personal* only, but *Justinian* (code 7, 25, and 31) abolished all distinctions. See part i, par. 396 (2).

121. *Mancipi and nec mancipi*. This distinction existed at the time of the *twelve tables*. See part i, tables v (2) and vi. The *res mancipi* were not synonymous with things of the *civil law*, although everything outside the civil law was *nec mancipi*, but they required a juridical and sacramental act, the *mancipium* (later *mancipatio*) to transfer them *(mancipi vero res (sunt) quæ per mancipationem ad alium transferuntur unde...mancipi res sunt dictæ*. Gai. Inst. 2, § 22), whilst simple tradition sufficed for *res nec mancipi*; and *mancipi* things could not be alienated in all cases where *nec mancipi* things could be, for even when the authority of the tutor

had become a fiction, certain tutors to woman could not be compelled to authorize three acts, viz. :—(1) Her testament; (2) obligations incurred by her, and (3) the alienation of things *mancipi*, and without this authorization *usucapion* would not give possession.

Ulpian (Reg. 19, § 1) gives a list of *res mancipi*, viz. :—(1) *prædia in italico solo, tam rustica, qualis est fundus, quam urbana qualis domus*; (2) *jura prædiorum rusticorum, velut via, iter, actus, aquæ ductus* (*i.e.*, only on the soil of Italy, and no *urban* servitudes for the isolation of Roman houses *(insulæ)* rendered urban servitudes rarer and later in coming into existence; (3) *servi et* (4) *quadrupedes quæ dorso collove domantur, velut boves, muli, equi, aseni.*

Hence all *incorporeal* things (except *rural servitudes*, which were identified with the soil) and the *whole patrimony (familia pecuniaque),* sold by a fictitious mancipation, were *res nec mancipi.*

Res mancipi therefore originally consisted of the important objects of a man's household, *i.e.*, those things identified with himself, as his land, the house on it (*mancipi*, because attached to soil, not otherwise), his wife, children, slaves, and beasts of burden, and this list never increased, though instruments of cultivation *(instrumenta)*, if incorporated for perpetual use with the land, were held to be *mancipi*, otherwise not. But *res nec mancipi* were not necessarily outside the civil law (*i.e.*, except mancipation, every other Roman method of acquisition applied to them), for otherwise there would always have been two kinds of ownership, one *Roman*, the other not, but according to *Gaius* (Inst. ii, § 40) there was at first but one ownership, that according to civil law *(aut enim ex jure quiritium unus quisque dominus erat, aut non intelligebatur dominus)*. Before the time of Justinian the distinction between *mancipi* and *nec mancipi* had practically disappeared, and he formally destroyed it. (Code vii, 31.)

131. In respect of the *owner*, things were divided into—

(1) *Res communes omnium, e.g.*, the air, running water, the sea and its shores, etc., which all may use but not acquire.

(2) *Res publicæ*, (α) common to all, as public roads, rivers, harbours; (β) in the hands of the state, as public land, revenue, slaves *(in pecunia, in bonis, in patrimonio populi).*

(3) *Res universitatis*, in the hands of corporations.

(4) *Res privatæ* (or *singulorum*), in the hands of private persons.

(5) *Res nullius* (under which some include *res divini juris* and *res communes, res publicæ, res universitatis*, because they belong to no one in particular), either having no owner, as wild animals, etc., or abandoned *(pro derelicto)*, or ownership has ceased, and no new owner has yet succeeded (as in the case of an inheritance not yet acquired).

All these may be included under the general expressions—

(1) *Res nullius*, or *extra nostrum patrimonium*, and (2) *res alicujus*, or *in nostro patrimonio* (called *bona, pecunia).*

133. The *ager publicus* was opposed to the *ager privatus*, and meant land reserved as the property of the state (part i, par. 92,

265), and of which the actual holders only had possession, not ownership. It was susceptible of the following subdivisions:—

(1) *Agri quæstorii*, or conquered territory to be sold in lots by auction.

(2) *Assignati*, to be gratuitously distributed in lots to the plebeians, and later exclusively to veteran soldiers. After sale or distribution both (1) and (2) would become *ager privatus*.

(3) *Occupatorii*, open to any citizen to occupy and clear, sometimes gratuitously, at other times at a small rent.

(4) *Vectigales*, when strictly a rent was due to the public treasury. This land was given to farm, or in emphyteusis, or abandoned to indefinite possession, or seized by patrician and powerful families and made hereditary.

(5) *Subcisivi*, *i.e.*, the land remaining to the public after the distribution of the rest.

In the time of the emperors a distinction also existed between—

(1) *Provinciæ populi Romani (prædia stipendiaria)* or provinces of the senate, and (2) *Provinciæ Cæsaris (prædia tributoria)* (see part i, par. 338).

134. In respect of *physical* nature, distinctions were incidentally noticed in Roman law, *e.g.*—

1. *Res mobiles*, or *se moventes*, or simply *moventes*.

2. *Res immobiles*, or *quæ soli sunt*, or *res soli*, or *quæ immobiles sunt vel esse intelliguntur*, but usually designated by particular expressions as *prædia*, *fundi*, *ædes*. *Res mobiles*, when *vincta*, *fixa*, or *perpetui usus causa*, might become a part of and share the fate of *res immobiles*, and *incorporeal* things might (as in the case of *servitudes*) become attached to and form part of *immobiles*.

The consequences resulting from these distinctions were important, *e.g.*—

(1) As to the civil law applying to the territory where the immoveable situated; (2) As to the soldiers' acquisitions of moveable booty only; (3) As to the difference of time fixed for the *usucapion* of moveables and immoveables; (4) As to the presence of and the quantity of things which could be the subject of a mancipation (part iii, par. 312); (5) As to the *deductio* or solemnity in addition for immoveables in the *actio sacramenti* (part iii, par. 1864); (6) As to the later law of dowry in respect of immoveables (part iii, par. 582); (7) As to *furtum* not being applicable to immoveables; (8) As to the interdict *utrubi* for moveables and *uti possedetis* for immoveables; (9) As to real servitudes, necessarily only existing for immoveables; (10) As to the cases where moveables allowed to be sold before immoveables, as in pledges; (11) As to what went with immoveable things sold or left by legacy; (12) As to what was included in a legacy of moveables.

138. Other divisions were—

(1) Things *divisible*, *i.e.*, either physically or in a juridical sense, and (2) things *indivisible*, *i.e.*, in law no part held distinct from the whole.

(1) *Res principales* and (2) *accessiones, i.e.*, dependent or subordinate things.

139. The following distinction was of practical importance—
(1) *Genus, i.e.*, kind, as some wine, oil, wheat, money (see part iii, par. 1209).
(2) *Species, i.e.*, the particular individual thing, as the wine, the oil contained in such a vase, the money in such a coffer.

As the first were usually determined by their number, weight, etc., the Romans called them things *quæ pondere, numero, mensurave constant*, for the only question would be whether equivalents were *in eadem qualitate et quantitate*, but according to the intention of the parties the same thing might be considered either in *genere* or in *specie*. From this distinction of things, capable of being or of not being replaced by others, came the barbarisms, *res fungibiles* or *non fungibiles*, the former referring to things which could be replaced by one another *(quarum una vice alterius fungitur)*, and the same distinction led to a further division of things—

(1) *Quæ ipso usu consumuntur (quæ in abusu continentur)*. These things were usually in *genere*, but the contract of the parties might determine otherwise.
(2) *Quarum salva substantia utendifruendi potest esse facultas, i.e.*, things which could be used without destroying them.

143. In respect of *compositiou* or *aggregation, Pomponius* draws the following distinctions:—
(1) *Res singulares*, individual things, *i.e.*, contained in a single being *(uno spiritu)*, as a man, a tree, a stone.
(2) *Rerum universitas*, and of two kinds (α) *ex contingentibus, i.e.*, several bodies bound together, as a building, a ship ; (β) *ex distantibus (uni nomini subjecta)*, different distinct bodies united under one name, and composing one whole, as a drove of oxen, or of horses, or of slaves, and so the comic poets speak of their staff of actors as *grex noster*, and *taberna* means a shop furnished with merchandise, *fundus instructus*, a farm with its instruments of cultivation. In the same way legal aggregations may exist, as the *peculium*, the *dos*, or the *hæreditas*, and to these the term *universitas* eminently applies, and the commentators call them *universitates juris*, as opposed to those *facti*.

Of Facts, Events, or Acts.

145. The Roman jurisconsults excelled in recognising the notion of facts or acts, but they did not include them in their classifications of the subjects and objects of rights, although they are the efficient cause, the generating element of all rights, and are present in every part of the law.

Factum, from *facere*, to do, implies an action of man, but the expression is generally understood in a larger sense, for facts may be caused either (1) without the intervention of man ; (2) by his direct or indirect intervention ; (3) by the immediate effect of his will ; and they may consist in negation, *i.e.*, in an event not happening, as where a man refuses or omits to do, or the fact may be an abstract creation really not existing.

Facts may affect man himself (*e.g.*, his birth producing filiation, and so as to paternity, marriage, illness, death), or things (*e.g.*, their creation, composition, alteration), or both combined (*e.g.*, possession or loss of possession of a thing by a man).

150. *Juridical acts*, or facts, are intended to create legal relations between different parties, hence regulations are laid down beforehand as to the *forms* of proceeding, as to the witnesses to be present, as to the necessity or not of the intervention of the state ; in some cases the validity of the act depending on the form imposed, in others not, *e.g.*, in the manumission of slaves, the emancipation of children, marriage, adoption, wills, contracts, etc. As civilization advances, the tendency is to look more and more to the mental attitude of the parties, but in primitive times the attention is fixed on the outward form, and according to the spirit and ideas of the particular nation, so do the nature of the juridical acts vary which are employed by way of pantomimic representation of the actual life of a still earlier period, hence the method *per æs et libram* indicates a time when money was actually weighed, after which the symbol was employed in an executory contract of sale, and also in fictitious alienations, as in the emancipation of children, and in wills, etc.; so the lance *(hasta)*, the weapon with which property is originally forcibly acquired, becomes the wand *(festuca)* used in the fictitious combat *(manuum consertio)* commencing an action involving a real right, so again the piece of turf *(gleba)*, or a tile *(tegula)*, produced in court, dispenses with the visit of the magistrate to the place itself, and in the same way thirty lictors represent the actual assembly of the thirty *curiæ*.

The absence of writing also involves the necessity of impressing the memory by means of solemn forms of question and answer in the national language—a practice retained in some cases in modern times, as in the contract of marriage. After the introduction of writing, its use is at first usually an accessory precaution only, but finally public registration is made at times indispensable.

The spiritualising tendency may be traced in the laws of most nations, but the history of Roman jurisprudence illustrates the march of ideas in a very remarkable way. Gaius (Inst. iv, § 30) asserts that in the sixth century of Rome the symbolic acts of the law had become the object of popular hatred, and that therefore the lex Æbutia and the lex Julia had nearly suppressed them. Cicero turned them into ridicule, and in the time of Augustus the favourable reception of modifications in respect of wills led to the introduction of fidei commissa and codicils. The labours of the prætor were also incessantly directed to remedy the abuses arising from a slavish adherence to forms. Constantine II, Constantius, and Constans deprived legal formulæ of their sacramental character, on the ground that they were merely snares to entrap, and finally Justinian reduced juridical acts to their utmost simplicity.

OF FACTS, EVENTS, OR ACTS. 87

161. *Acts of the jus gentium.* According to the strict civil law, one person could not supply the place of another, except in the case of the head of the household, who might be represented by his children, slaves, and others in his power (as where a paterfamilias being an infant and unable to speak, benefited by acts done for him by one of his slaves), but expediency early suggested that as acts of the *jus gentium* were common to all men, whether citizens or strangers, they might be performed through the instrumentality of others (see part iii, par. 234, etc).

164. *Consensus.* This implies the accord of two or more persons to the same act, as opposed to those acts performed by the will *(voluntas)* of one only, and it involves questions as to *ignorantia*, or want of knowledge, and *error*, or false knowledge, both of which vary in their effects, according as they relate to law or fact. So also the rights of parties may be affected by—

Dolus, i.e., every alteration of the truth of facts, or words intentionally employed to induce another erroneously to be influenced in his will or acts, and divided into—

Dolus bonus, or licit deceit employed in self defence, and

Dolus malus, or illicit deceit, used with the intention of injuring another *(omnis calliditas, fallacia, machinatio, ad circumveniendum, decipiendum, alterum adhibita*—Ulpian).

In strict law *error, dolus,* and *vis (i.e.,* violence, the menace of which inspires fear, and so constrains the will) did not affect the legality of the act performed, provided consent had been given, but prætorian law neutralised and evaded this inequitable rule (see *post,* par. 280).

167. *Non-juridical facts.* These entail legal consequences, according to *Ulpian's* laconic maxim, *Alterum non lædere, suum cuique tribuere, i.e.,* every one must repair the damage occasioned by his own fault, and no one ought to enrich himself at the expense of the right of another; to which may be added the maxim of *Paul, secundum naturam est, commoda cujusque rei eum sequi quem sequuntur incommoda, i.e.,* each person incurs the responsibilities for good or for evil attaching to the things or the rights claimed by him.

169. *Time and place.* These are two inseparable elements of facts and *dies*, or time relates either to the moment from which rights commence *(dies a quo, a die, ex die)*, or when they expire *(dies ad quem, ad diem)*, or again *dies* may refer to the term itself, and under this head are included the rules relating to *dies fasti* and *nefasti*, and the method of reckoning time by the number of useful days *(tempus utile, dies utiles)*, or simply the number without distinction *(tempus continuum, dies continui)*.

172. *Proof.* In order to deduce a right arising from a fact, the existence of the fact must be ascertained, and *probatio* consists in an operation of reasoning, by which, from certain known facts, the existence of an unknown fact is inferred. Means of proof more or less conclusive, are (1) *testes*, or the declarations of witnesses; (2) *monumenta,* or writings, marks, signs, or vestiges of any kind; (3)

confessio, and (4) *jusjurandum*, or the oath, all of which in Roman law fall under the general term *instrumenta*, and may be *publica*, *privata*, or *domestica* ; but in a more restricted sense *instrumenta* denote *scripta*, or *scriptura*, terms alluding to the writing itself; *tabulæ, codices, codicilli, ceræ* (on wax), *membranæ* (on parchment), *chartæ* (on paper), terms all referring to the material used ; *chirographum*, indicative of the act of writing ; *syngraphæ* (signed copies given to each) ; *apocha* (receipt), *antapocha* (declaration of having received receipt), and the very general word *cautio (cavere)*, because writing as a means of proof is a security, but the collection at the time the act is performed of proofs intended to establish its existence, is not to be confounded with the solemnities, *i.e.*, the acts themselves.

The general principle governing the *burden of proof*, is that he who appeals to a fact as having created, modified, or extinguished some right, is bound to prove the existence of the fact *(ei incumbit probatio qui dicit, non qui negat*—Paul), otherwise things are assumed to remain in *statu quo*.

176. *Presumptions.* These are the result of the same kind of intellectual operation as in the case of proof, but the conclusion from a known fact in respect of an unknown fact is drawn by the *law* itself, by way of an induction from the general to the particular. A *presumptio (præ* and *sumere)* is not inferior to *probatio*, but takes precedence of it, and sometimes excludes it. When the induction is made irrevocably, it is a—

(1) *Præsumptio juris et de jure*, *e.g.*, *res judicata pro veritate accipitur* (Dig. 50, 17, 207). The child born ten months after death of husband not legitimate (twelve tables iv, 4). The *exceptio non numeratæ pecuniæ* (part iii, par. 1435). When the presumption is made by a general induction, and contrary *proof* is admitted, but thrown on the person against whom it exists, it is a

(2) *Præsumptio juris tantum*, *e.g.*, *pater is est quem nuptiæ demonstrant* (Dig. 2, 4, 5), *Credendum est eum qui ex justis nuptiis septimo mense natus est justum esse* (Dig. 1, 5, 12).

Both these expressions originated with the commentators, and do not belong to Roman law, but the subject was treated with care by the jurisconsults.

181. A *doubt*, difficult of satisfactory solution, may envelop the facts, and yet a decision must be come to. In such a case the law, on the ground of expediency, lays down general rules for the settlement of the question, *e.g.*, that the strongest survived longest where both died in the same catastrophe (Dig. 34, 5, 9, 4).

182. *Fictions.* Purely imaginary facts abound in both the civil and the prætorian law. Their object was usually to adapt the rude and inflexible primitive civil law to a more equitable and philosophic system, and they amount to the laconic formula, "the right will be determined, as if such a fact had existed," (see for example the class of *fictitiæ actiones*, part iii, par. 1979).

OF RIGHTS.

§ 2.—*Of Rights and of Actions.*

Of Rights.
187. The Roman lawyers made no general classification of rights, but from their partial attempts, and by analogy, a primary division has been deduced of all *rights* into—

(1) *Personal*, or those which give the faculty of compelling *some person* to do or not to do something.

(2) *Real*, or those which give the faculty of deriving an advantage, more or less extended, from some thing; in both cases putting aside the obligation on the rest of the world to abstain from hindering the exercise of the right.

The expressions *absolute* and *relative* are more philosophical, but tend to mislead, and therefore the terms *personal* and *real* are employed, although they are not absolutely correct, for every right is *personal* as regards the active and passive subject, *i.e.*, no right can exist except in relation to persons, and every right is *real* as regards the object, *i.e.*, the thing; but the expressions are preferable to the barbarisms of the middle ages, *jus in re* for real rights, and *jus ad rem* for personal rights, which appeared in the Brachylogus (part i, par. 618), and passed into secular jurisprudence from the canon law. The terms *jus in rem* for real rights, and *jus in personam* for personal rights, are equally foreign to Roman law, though taken from analogous expressions, *e.g.*, the division of actions into those *in rem* and those *in personam*, but here they were in harmony with the procedure and correct in their use *(post*, par. 275).

196. *Personal rights (obligations).* These always imply another person, who is individually the passive subject of the right; and this idea of a relation of dependence is conveyed in the expressions *obligare, obligatio, vinculum juris, ad-stringere, contrahere, contractus*, and hence also the use of the terms *solvere* and *solutio* with reference to the destruction of the bond *(post*, par. 211).

From the active point of view, *i.e.*, in relation to the subject enjoying the right, the term used to express this personal right is *nomen*, less often *creditum*, and the active subject is the *creditor*. From the passive point of view the personal right is *obligatio*, and the passive subject is the *debitor*.

The Roman jurisconsults appreciated the fact that the object of the obligation was secondary to the obligation itself, *i.e.*, in the words of *Paul* (Dig. 44, 7, 3), *Obligationum substantia non in eo consistit, ut aliquod corpus nostrum, aut servitutem nostram faciat, sed ut alium nobis adstringat ad dandum aliquid, vel faciendum, vel præstandum*, and the general expressions, *dare, facere, præstare*, embraced in Roman law the object of every possible obligation, and either of the two last might include all three.

199. Justinian's definition of an obligation, viz., *Juris vinculum quo necessitate adstringimur alicujus solvendæ rei, secundum nostræ civitatis jura* (see part iii, par. 1176), applies to the obligation proper

of Roman law, *i.e.*, to the *civilis obligatio*, giving the right to a *civil* action, and hence Roman jurisconsults marshalled *obligatio* and *actio* together as correlatives, and in strict civil law only a few rigorously determined obligations were recognised, so that a person was bound according to the civil law or not at all, and if he was so bound it was immaterial whether natural equity approved or condemned; but in the course of time the prætor introduced *prætoriæ (vel honorariæ) obligationes*, giving rise to prætorian, *i.e.*, *utiles*, or special actions, and the rules deduced from the *jus gentium* and from natural reason led to the class of *naturales obligationes*, through which a creditor might acquire legal rights, though usually only by way of defence (see part iii, par. 1793).

201. *Sources of obligations.* Philosophical reasoning tends to group facts generating obligations under four heads, viz. :—

(1) Mutual consent; for natural reason indicates this as a fact sufficing to create the obligation when neither the object nor the motive is contrary to morality, or public order, or physically impossible, and the consent is given by a person having the capacity, and is free from *error, dolus,* or *vis*.

(2) One person injured by the voluntary or involuntary fault of another.

(3) One person enriched, whether voluntarily or not, by the property of another.

(4) Family and social relations. These were generally classed by Roman jurisconsults under obligations *quasi ex contractu*, but their existence does not always require a personal and particular act of the obligor, but may result from the nature of the relation.

The most general word for obligations resulting from mutual consent was *conventio (pactum conventum)*, the word *contractus* being reserved for conventions specially recognised as obligatory, and provided with an action under the ancient civil law, though *Labeo* (see Dig. 50, 16, 19) also uses the word with reference to *bilateral* contracts.

Historically the gradation of ideas is traced through the—

(1) *Nexum (i.e., quodcumque per æs et libram geritur)*, at which five Roman citizens, together with the *libripens*, were present as witnesses, and after the requisite formalities had been gone through, the *vinculum juris* was formed on the utterance of the solemn words, see part i, twelve tables vi (1); and hence there came to be two parts, (1) the fictitious sale *per æs et libram*, and (2) the *nuncupatio*, or statement in solemn form. Subsequently the proceeding would be gone through with a view to the obligation only thereby contracted, and not for the purpose of effecting a conveyance. In this way were entered into the contract of loan *(mutuum)*, of pledge *(pignus)*, of deposit *(depositum)*, though in later times simple tradition sufficed to engender the civil obligation, and to form the contract *re* (see part i, par. 333).

(2) *Verbis.* Here the symbolic acts have disappeared. The solemn words only remained, and these were reduced to the

question *(stipulatio)*, and the answer *(responsio, promissio)*. From the words used, *spondes? spondeo*, came the term *sponsio*, and the peculiarity consisted in the interrogation coming from the promisee (*i.e.*, the stipulator), and the result being a unilateral obligation binding on the promissor (see part iii, par. 1235).

(3) *Litteris*. This form only applied to the payment of a sum of money, and it also assumed the operation *per æs et libram* accomplished. The amount of the debt (*nomen*) was entered with the debtor's consent in the creditor's ledger, as if weighed and given (*expensilatio*), and hence the contract was called *nomen transcriptitium*, but it gradually fell into disuse, and by the time of Justinian only had the value of a *cautio* or written proof (see part iii, par. 1414).

(4) *Consensu*. The contracts formed by simple consent (*emptio-venditio, locatio-conductio, societas, mandatum*) were derived from the *jus gentium*, and produced mutual obligations (*ultro citroque*). Their effects were determined by equitable rules *(ex æquo et bono)*.

A fifth form might be added, that of the *emphyteusis*, but some held this to be a sale, others a letting, until Zeno finally made it a distinct kind of convention.

According to the strict civil law, any agreement outside the four contracts *re, verbis, litteris, consensu*, produced no obligation but prætorian, and imperial legislation and the circumstances of the case might give them juridical effects.

208. *Noxa*. Obligations not arising from consent were thus at first called (see part i, twelve tables, viii), and subsequently *maleficium* or *delictum*. The ancient civil law determined a certain number, and prætorian equity made some additions. There were therefore two sources of obligations *ex contractu* and *ex delicto*. To these jurisprudence assimilated others as being varied figures of them (*variæ causarum figuræ*, Dig. 44, 7, 1 Gaius), and when the obligation arose, as if from a contract, it was called *quasi ex contractu*, and when, as if from a delict, *quasi ex delicto*. Hence four sources of obligations—(1) *ex contractu* ; (2) *quasi ex contractu* ; (3) *ex maleficio* ; (4) *quasi ex maleficio*.

210. *Transference of obligations*. A personal right could not be transferred from one person to another, and it was only by procurations that analogous results were indirectly arrived at (see part iii, par. 1550).

211. *Extinction of obligations*. The general term for the liberation of the debtor was *solutio*, and it was a general principle that civil law bonds could only be destroyed by civil law rules *(ipso jure)*, though equity furnished means of defence *(exceptionis ope)* against the effects of the bond still nominally existing.

(1) *Performance* was obviously the first method of extinguishing an obligation, and to this, in a restricted sense, the term *solutio* particularly applied.

(2) *Novation* dissolved any kind of obligation by substituting

another for it, but the new one must have been formed either *verbis* or *litteris*.

(3) *Release*. In order to free the debtor altogether the *civil* law fell back on symbol and formula, and required an *imaginaria solutio*, either the (1) *solutio per æs et libram* or the (2) *solutio verbis (acceptilatio)*, couched in the form *quod ego tibi promisi, habes ne acceptum? habeo*, or the result, might be attained by the (3) *solutio litteris, i.e.*, an entry in the ledger that the sum was held to be received, but in some cases mutual consent sufficed, so that the same gradations may be traced in the forms employed to release as to bind the debtor, the *solutio per æs et libram* for obligations so contracted, the *acceptilatio* for stipulations, the *solutio litteris* for inscribed debts, and simple consent for obligations so formed; but the *acceptilatio, i.e.*, the *solutio verbis* was generalized and used for effecting a novation, and then dissolving all kinds of obligations (see part iii, par. 1687).

217. *Real rights*. There being no intermediate person or a passive subject, a real right consists in the faculty of disposing of the thing in a manner more or less extended, and in the possible varieties of disposition consists the variety of real rights.

219. *Dominium*. The three terms successively employed to express complete ownership indicate the gradual change of ideas on the subject. The earliest expression used was *mancipium*, which meant the juridical act of mancipation, or the right of property produced by the act, and sometimes the thing subject to the right (part i, par. 88). The term *dominium* referred to the *domus* (see part i, par. 330), and in the time of Neratius the word in use was *proprietas*, as to which see part i, par. 449.

This is the most absolute real right *(plenam in re potestatem)*, and includes—

Usus, or the use of the thing; *fructus*, or the produce of the thing: *abusus*, or the power of destroying the thing, whether by alienation or consumption, and with no other limit than the general interest.

221. *Possession*. Physical detention only, as in the case of a tenant or bailee, was *nuda detentio*, but if coupled with the intention of holding as own then there was true *possessio civilis*. The Roman jurisconsults were at variance whether this was a *fact* or a *right*, but though it essentially consists in the fact, yet when considered in respect of the protection afforded to it by the law, a *right* of possession may be asserted. Possession and ownership are quite distinct, but the former, in the absence of proof to the contrary, presumes the latter.

226. *Kinds of dominium*. Owing to the primitive civil law rules as to the *commercium*, there could be but one kind of ownership, viz., the *dominium ex jure Quiritium*, and therefore land not enjoying the *jus italicum* was susceptible of *possession* only, which could not ripen through prescription into ownership; but subsequently a

qualified kind of ownership, due to the *jus gentium*, was introduced, viz., that *in bonis habere*, called by Theophilus, in his paraphrase of the Institutes, δεσπότης βονιτάριος, and translated by the commentators *dominium bonitarium*. The prætor protected the holder under this title against the civil law owner, but prior to Justinian the distinctions lost their value, and the names were therefore suppressed by him (see *ante*, par. 121, and part iii, par. 342).

229. *Modes of acquisition.* Throughout the history of Roman law, contracts produced *obligations*, *i.e.*, personal, not *real* rights. The contract bound the parties between themselves, and the personal right so engendered might compel a transference *(dare)* of the property, but it did *not* transfer the ownership. For the acquisition of property in individual objects the Romans required some outward and public act, *i.e.*, a fact of a different nature from the mere contract, *e.g.* :

(1) *Occupatio*, or the taking possession of a thing belonging to an enemy, or to no one.

(2) *Traditio*, or the delivery of the possession. This required no solemnity, and could take place with aliens, for both *occupatio* and *traditio* belonged to the *jus gentium*, though they were recognised by the civil law. It only applied to corporeal things, *nec mancipi*, and must have been made by the true owner, *ex justa causa*, and in conformity to law (Gai. Inst. ii, § 19, 20).

(3) *Nexum*, or *mancipium*, or *mancipatio*. This form was employed for both contracts and conveyances (see *ante*, par. 201), but did not transfer the possession without *traditio*.

(4) *Usucapio*, one year for movables, two years for immovables.

(5) *In jure cessio*, or the collusive action, in which the defendant not disputing the plaintiff's claim, the magistrate (*addicens*) made *addictio* of the thing, by declaring it the property, *ex jure Quiritium*, of the alienee. See part i, par. 140 (1).

(6) *Adjudicatio.* Here the judge *(judicans)* adjudged the thing to one of several persons, as in the actions *finium regundorum*, *familiæ erciscundæ*, *communi dividundo*.

(7) *Sub-corona*, *sub-hasta.* Public sales by the questors *ærarii* of prisoners of war or of booty.

(8) *Lex.* For examples of this class see part iii, par. 312.

Under Justinian the *mancipatio* and the *in jure cessio*, and the distinction between *mancipi* and *nec mancipi*, did not exist, and *traditio* applied to all corporeal things.

233. Besides *proprietas* and *possessio*, other real rights constituting fractional parts, more or less restricted, of the ownership, might be enjoyed, as in the case of the real rights involved in the *usus*, the *usus fructus*, the *emphyteusis*, and the *superficies*, but the Roman jurists regarded *locatio-conductio* and *commodatum* only in the light of contracts, and the *pignus* and *hypotheca* were viewed simply as securities and not as any dismemberment of the right of ownership, although the first certainly affected the possession. This sort of *real* right might be created by simple consent, and some real rights,

as in the analogous case of natural *obligations (ante,* par. 199), were only protected by *exceptions,* not by actions.

235. *Abstractions* constituted a large body of *real* rights, *e.g.,* the quality of father, son, free, freed, patron, citizen, etc.

236. *Successions,* or acquisitions *per universitatem,* included both *real* and *personal* rights, for the aggregate of rights (except those expiring with him) of a deceased (and sometimes of a living) person, were detached and transferred to another, a proceeding involving the intervention of the state, or at least of a magistrate, though ultimately the rules governing this subject passed from the *public* into *private* law. Under this head fall the *hereditas ex testamento* or *ab intestato,* the *bonorum possessio,* the *fidei-commissaria hereditas,* the *arrogatio,* and *legacies* in certain respects, particularly under Justinian.

Of Actions.

239. Rights in themselves are inert abstractions. To make them realities three things are required, viz. : (1) Law ; (2) the organization of judicial authority, and (3) procedure.

241. The word *actio (agere)* etymologically means putting the law in action, but figuratively it refers to the right of appealing to the authority of the law, and in a third sense it is used to denote the means, *i.e.,* the form prescribed for so doing. *Historically* the meaning of the word changed with the growth of ideas.

247. *Jus and judicium.* The key to the Roman system lies in the distinction between *jus, i.e.,* the law, and *judicium, i.e.,* the organised law suit. To be *in jure* was to be before the magistrate. To be *in judicio* was to be before the judge.

The *magistrate* was appointed by the state, and invested during his term of office with the *juris-dictio,* or power of declaring the law, and with the *imperium,* or power of enforcing it. He was the organ of the law, deciding every case where a declaration of the law sufficed, otherwise conferring the power of judging on another person.

The *judge* was only a citizen selected for the decision of the particular case, but as he filled a public office, he was taken from such classes of the citizens as the political constitution of the city determined. He could not refuse to perform this public duty without a legitimate excuse, but whether the matter was important, as the status, the *existimatio,* of a citizen, or trifling, as in a small pecuniary matter, the choice of the judge usually rested with the plaintiff *(judicem ferre),* or resulted from the agreement of the parties *(judicem sumere),* unless the one proposed by the magistrate was accepted, though the litigants had the right of rejecting him *(judicem ejurare, rejicere, recusare),* without stating motives, but if they could not agree, the selection was arrived at by elimination from a fixed number, or by lot (see part i, par. 272). After selection he was appointed by the magistrate *(judicem addicere),* and after examining the particular point in dispute between the parties, settled it by a sentence, the execution of which was part of the magistrate's duty. Hence the separation of *jus* and *judicium* corresponds nearly with the distinction which has been much extended in modern times between questions of *law* and *fact*, though the office of the judge was not limited to a simple question of *fact*, for, according to the nature of the case, and the extent of the powers conferred on him, the *law* (as is often the case in the verdict of a modern jury) was more or less determined by his judgment.

255. *Justice was administered publicly.* The magistrate and the judge sat in the *forum*, the one on the raised *tribunal*, the other on the *subsellium*, but the magistrate could, in case of need, remove his court elsewhere (*tribunal ponere*), and the judge might be directed to take cognizance of the affair on the spot where the cause of action arose. In later times special buildings (*prætoria*) for the administration of justice were erected, but the publicity remained, except that when the magistrate was deliberating with his assistants a curtain (*velum*) could be drawn across the *secretum* or reserved place.

256. *Systems of procedure.* Three systems were successively developed in Roman law.

(1) *Legis actiones.* This was the primitive and characteristic system of the *jus Quiritium*, and was in use down to the lex Æbutia, B.C. 171. It consisted in ingenious methods of accommodating simulated acts of violence to legal inquiries. The distinction between *jus* and *judicium* existed (see part i, table xii, 3), but the subject is obscure as to when the magistrate should decide the case himself, and when and to which of the three classes of judges he should refer the matter. The *magistrates* were, at *Rome*, the kings, then the consuls, the prætor, and for certain cases, the ædiles (sales of slaves and animals in the public markets, and as to weights and measures, etc); in the *municipia*, the decemvirs; in the *provinces* (commencing only at the end of this time), the proprætors or proconsuls. The *judges* were the judex or arbiter, the recuperatores, and the centumvirs (see part i, par. 162, 166).

257. The word *actio* here refers to the five forms of procedure, viz., the four enumerated in part i, par. 140, together with the *condictio*, which was not introduced until B.C. 244, and was concerned with obligations only (see part i, par. 242).

263. The *actio sacramenti*, applicable to laying claim to a thing or to a real right (*vindicatio*), was also employed fictitiously (as in the collusive action called *in jure cessio*, *ante*, par. 229) to arrive at results not contemplated by the primitive law, and hence transactions of this nature were sometimes called actions of the law (*idque legis actio vocatur*, Gai. Inst. ii, § 24).

265. The *decline* of the *legis actiones* was due to their patrician and perilous character (see part i, par. 217, 239), and to the vestiges they bore of plebeian slavery. They were at first abandoned in practice, and then legislatively suppressed (see part i, par. 244, 258), and finally only employed fictitiously in the *in jure cessio* and its derivatives.

266. (2) *Formulæ (ordinaria judicia)*. This is the most important system for study, and lasted to the reign of Diocletian (see part i, par. 247). Through it the law became humanitarian, and was extended to strangers. The separation of *jus* and *judicium* was complete, the proceedings being *extraordinaria* when otherwise. The *magistrates* were, at *Rome*, the prætors, the ædiles, the prefect of the city, and the prætorian prefect; in the *provinces* the proconsuls, pro-prætors, legati, presidents, and prefects, who held occasional assizes (*conventus*) in the principal towns; and the appeal lay finally to the emperor in person. The *judges* were the judex or arbiter, the recuperatores, and the court of the centumvirs, but the monopoly of the patricians in respect of judicial functions was partially destroyed after B.C. 122 (see part i, par. 283).

269. The magistrates charged with organizing the *judicium* delivered the *formula* to the litigants (see part i, par. 247, 250, 251), and the word *actio* in its widest extent now embraced every kind of attack and defence (actions, exceptions, interdicts, etc.) involving the aid of a court of law, and in this sense the jurisconsults used it when dividing the matter of law under the heads of persons, things, actions.

275. *Actions in rem and in personam*. This division arose from the fact that in the action *in personam* a debtor figures in the *intentio* as the passive subject of the right, in addition to the active subject, and the thing, the object of the right (*e.g.*, *si paret Numerium Negidium Aulo Agerio dare facere, præstare, oportere*), as occurs in all cases where we assert that a person is bound to give, do, or furnish something; whereas in the action *in rem*, a thing or a right is asserted to be ours, and hence only the claimant and the thing, the object of the right, appears in the *intentio* (*e.g.*, *si paret hominem ex jure Quiritium Auli Agerii esse*). But these expressions were not exclusively applied to actions, for the term *in personam* was used with reference to dispositions relating specially to persons, and *in rem* for general dispositions; so that in this sense they were used with reference to the edict of the prætor, to pacts, and to exceptions, and the expressions have descended to modern times, though the idea of *mixed* actions (*i.e.*, *in rem* and *in personam*) was an impossibility under the formulary procedure, and must have arisen after the decay of that system. Actions *in rem* were called *vindicationes*, and actions *in personam*, actions properly so called, but sometimes *condictiones*, an expression, however, in a technical sense, usually reserved for particular kinds of personal actions (see part i, par. 242).

280. *Adjectiones*. Besides the principal parts of the formula (part i, par. 249) there might be accessory clauses, viz.:

The *exceptio* inserted usually in the *intentio*, but sometimes in the *condemnatio* (see part iii, par. 1945), and setting out some equitable plea, tending to defeat the plaintiff's strict right, as where the defendant averred that his promise had been obtained by fraud or violence. The *magistrate* decided if, in *law*, there were grounds for granting or refusing the action, or for allowing or disallowing the exception without discussing the merits, the *judge* ascertained if the pleas were justified or not, and an exception, if proved, settled the matter finally.

The *replicatio* was the plaintiff's exception to the defendant's plea, and so as to the *duplicatio*, the *triplicatio*, etc. The prætor's powerful use of the exception, to mitigate the rigour of the civil law, affected legislation, and some statutes, senatus-consulta and imperial constitutions, introduced laws under the form of exceptions.

The *præscriptio*, placed at the head of the formula, had approximately the object of an exception, and it ultimately disappeared, or was transferred into the latter (see part iii, par. 1939).

285. The *interdict* (part i, par. 290) was a decree made by a magistrate of the people (the prætor at Rome or the pro-consul in the provinces) at the request of a person who asserted the existence of some impediment to his rights, and it imperatively ordered or forbad something (*vim fieri veto, exhibeas, restituas*). The term was used generally to cover both classes (Just. Inst. iv, 15, 1), but specially it applied to *prohibitory* orders of the prætors, the word *decretum* being used when the prætor directed something to be done (Gai. Inst. iv, § 140). Interdicts were principally employed for matters not regulated by general laws, but coming under the surveillance of the public authority, *e.g.*, temples, tombs, navigable rivers, public roads, etc. They were also granted in respect of private interests, when a breach of the peace was imminent, as in disputes about possession, and the system continued even after the gaps in the legislation had been filled up. *Savigny*, following up Niebuhr's conjectures, and perhaps drawn away by the fact of writing on the special subject of possession, traces the origin of interdicts to the time when the patricians, farming the public lands, were obliged to have recourse to the intervention of the prætor each time their possession was threatened, as they had not the *dominium ex jure Quiritium*, and were consequently unable to avail themselves of the civil law actions. Possibly from the *interdictum*, or special law, providing for an unforseen and particular case, originated the prætor's power in respect of the issue of the *edictum* or general law for all.

If the person against whom it was directed submitted to the terms of the interdict, the affair was at an end, but, if he refused, the magistrate referred the matter to a judge or to the recuperatores (Gai. Inst. iv, § 141), *i.e.*, the prætor would draw up a *formula*, of which the *intentio* would be conceived in the terms of the interdict; but this power arose from the magistrate's right to publish an edict, and not from the *jurisdictio*, which gave him the right to prepare the formula, and the interdict was not a substitute for an action, but served as the basis of it, provided the case went so far (see part iii, par. 2288).

288. When the magistrate himself decided the civil or criminal case, the judgment was called a *decretum*, and the procedure was *extra ordinem*. This course was always followed in cases of *restitutio in integrum*, of *missio in possessionem bonorum* (see part iii, par. 2015),

or in disputes as to *fidei-commissa*, for which a special magistrate was created, the *prætor fidei-commissarius* (part iii, par. 950); and by the side of the procedure *per formulam* and *extraordinem*, the employment of the *legis actio* was retained in a few cases (see part i, par. 244, 258).

291. (3) *Extraordinaria judicia*. This third system, from being the exceptional form of procedure, became the rule, first in the provinces, and then throughout the empire (see part i, par. 427), and has been adopted in nearly all modern Europe. Under it the functions of the magistrate and the judge were united, and the separation of *jus* and *judicium* only occurred as an exception.

The superior *magistrates* were the rector and his deputy, the vicarius, and, on appeal, the prætorian prefect and the emperor (see part i, par. 442 '. Inferior matters were disposed of under the limited and subordinate jurisdiction of the local magistrates of each city (see as to the *judices pedanei* and the *defensores civitatum*, part i, par. 427, 496, 579). Rome, Constantinople, and Alexandria, had each separate judicial organizations. Fiscal matters were confided by the emperor to special agents, the military administration was completely severed from the civil power, and the ecclesiastical jurisdiction of the bishops was compulsory on the clergy, but voluntary in the case of other citizens.

The word *actio* now acquired the meaning given in part i, par. 427; and to the other meanings referred to in part i, par. 140, 250, 334, and *ante* 269, may be added that it was applied also to the general conduct of the case by the counsel employed.

PART III.

COMMENTARY ON JUSTINIAN'S INSTITUTES.

1. **Argument.** The subject matter of the Institutes is divided as follows :—
Preface, containing the sanction, the character, and the object of the work.
Book i. General notions of justice and of law, and treats of *persons*.
Book ii. *Things*, means of acquiring particular objects, testamentary inheritances, legacies and fidei-commissa.
Book iii. Inheritances *ab intestato* and other universal successions, obligations arising *ex contractu* and *quasi ex contractu*.
Book iv. Obligations arising *ex delicto* and *quasi ex delicto*, and of *actions*.
Hence there is an equal division of the bulk rather than of the matter, and on the whole the classification appears to be *persons, things, actions* (see part i, par. 548; part ii, par. 5).

The **Procemium** or preface, consisting of the Constitution, giving the force of law to the work, and dated at Constantinople 22nd November, A.D. 533, commences with a list of Justinian's titles, in which the epithets *Africanus, Vandalicus, Gothicus*, etc., appear, on account of the then recent successes of Belisarius (see part i, par. 533).

§ ii refers to the completion of the first code (A.D. 529), and of the Digest, the confirmation of which latter did not take place until a month after the Institutes (see part i, par. 539, 544).

§ iii announces the appointment of the editors *Tribonian, Theophilus*, and *Dorotheus* (see part i, par. 548, 565, 566).

§ iv states that the Institutes are mainly based on the commentaries and *res quotidianæ* of *Gaius* (see part ii, par. 393).

BOOK I.

Tit. i. De justitia et jure.

9. *Jus.* The French term *droit* is derived from the figurative allusion to a straight line, and *règle* from the rule or instrument with which it is drawn, but the Latin word *jus* is a contraction of *jussum*, and acquired the various shades of meaning given in part ii, par. 8, and which may be summed up thus :—

(1) A positive order or prescribed rule, emanating from power.

(2) The collection of rules determining what is good and equitable.

(3) The effects of the law, viz., rights *(jura)*.

(4) The place where it was applied *(in jus vocare)*, but the second and third meanings were the most usual.

12. *Justitia* is defined as the *constans et perpetua voluntas, jus suum cuique tribuendi*, and

13. (§ i) *Jurisprudentia* as the *divinarum atque humanarum rerum notitia, justi atque injusti scientia*, the terms divine and human being used in their general, not their technical sense (part ii, par. 111). Hence *jus* is the law, *justitia* the wish to observe the law, *jurisprudentia* the knowledge of the law.

16. (§ iii) *Jurispræcepta* (maxims of the law) are (1) *honeste vivere*, *i.e.*, to live in accordance with those moral rules made imperative laws *(e.g.*, marriage prohibitions, etc.) ; (2) *alterum non lædere*, and (3) *suum cuique tribuere*, as to both which see part ii, par. 167.

17. (§ iv) The study of the law is divided into two parts, viz. :—

(1) *Publicum jus*, or that portion of the law which relates *ad statum rei romanæ, i.e.*, the law determining the reciprocal rights and obligations between a nation and its members, and including the *jus sacrum (publicum jus in sacris, in sacerdotibus, in magistratibus consistit*, Dig. 1, 1, 1, 2, Ulpian), but without reference to *international* law (or that existing between nations), which was only recognised in a rudimentary form by the Romans (see part i, par. 46).

(2) *Privatum*, or the law relating *ad singulorum utilitatem, i.e.*, the law between private persons (see part i, par. 14), and consisting of precepts drawn from (1) the law of nature, as to which see *post*, par. 20 ; (2) the *jus gentium ;* and (3) the civil law.

At the time of the Institutes, *public* law had passed into the will of the emperor, but as to the condition of *private* law, with which only the Institutes are concerned, see part i, par. 446, 582.

Tit. ii. De jure naturali gentium et civili.

19. *Jus naturale* is defined as that which *natura omnia animalia docuit, i.e*, the law of animated beings, *e.g.*, as to marriage, or the union of male and female, the procreation and education of children, etc.

20. (§ i) *Jus gentium* is that which *naturalis ratio inter omnes homines constituit—apud omnes populos peræque custoditur*, *i.e.*, the law of men, strangers as well as citizens, *e.g.*, the rules regulating the contracts of *emptio-venditio, locatio-conductio, societas*, etc.

The *jus civile* is that which *quisque populus ipse sibi constituit*, the *jus proprium ipsius civitatis*, *i.e.*, the law of the citizen, *e.g.*, the laws of Draco or Solon were the civil law of Athens, the *jus Quiritium*, that of Rome ; but this threefold division, derived from Ulpian, and probably due to the fact of slavery being recognised by the *jus gentium*, but held contrary to the laws of nature (see *post*, par. 41), is made no further use of in the Institutes, and is foreign to any system of jurisprudence, for *law* can only exist between man and man, and *Gaius* (Inst. I, § 1) divides law into the *jus gentium* (including *natural* law) and the *jus civile* only.

The term *civil* law is now used in the sense of *private* law, but in the early days of Rome it meant the *city* law, of which strangers could not avail themselves, and when with the creation of the office of the *prætor peregrinus* (part i, par. 222), the *jus gentium* was introduced ; this term referred to the parts of the law which strangers also could use, not necessarily that a neighbouring nation used it, and most Roman jurists included the *jus naturale* under it, and often used the terms synonymously.

24. (§ iii) *Private* law, as to *form*, was divided into *written* and *unwritten*.

Scriptum jus consists of—

(1) *Lex*, a term here used in a restricted sense, and equivalent to the *populi-scitum*, or law passed on the proposition of a magistrate senator (*e.g.*, consul, or prætor, or dictator) by *all* the citizens, *i.e.*, plebeians, patricians, and senators.

(2) *Plebiscitum*, *i.e.*, a law passed on the proposition of a tribune by those citizens who were not patricians or senators, and became equal to the *lex*, and the terms used indifferently after the passing of the *lex Hortensia* (part i, par. 178). The last plebiscita were probably published under Tiberius, *e.g*, the *lex Junia Norbana* (*post*, par. 65), and the *lex Visellia de juribus libertinorum* (A.D. 24).

(3) *Senatus-consultum*. The decrees of the senate had the force of law from an uncertain date up to A.D. 206 (see part i, par. 287, 350), and were called after the names of consuls or emperors, *e.g.*, the *s.c. Claudianum* from *Claudius* (*post*, par. 1175), the *s.c. Trebellianum* from *Trebellius*, consul under Nero (*post*, par. 959), but as to the title of the *s.c. Macedonianum* see *post*, par. 2217.

(4) *Constitutiones principum* or *principum placita* (see part i, par. 350).

(5) *Magistratuum edicta*. As to the edict of the prætors (now reduced to three) and of the ædiles see part i, par. 290. These magistrates were styled *magistratus populi romani* (M.P.R.), to distinguish them from those of particular cities.

(6) *Prudentum responsa* (see part i, par. 233). As to those

jurisconsults, *quibus a Cæsare jus respondendi datum est*, and as to whose opinions *judici recedere non 'liceret*, see part i, par. 355, 384 (7), and 499. Theophilus draws a distinction between the *sententiæ* and the *opiniones*, the former being positive decisions, the latter expressions of opinion.

These six heads constituted the sources whence the body of written Roman law was derived, but in the time of Justinian his will alone was the actual source of law.

32. (§ ix) *Jus non scriptum* was that which *usus comprobavit, i.e.*, the *jus moribus constitutum*, for it was held immaterial whether the legislature (*i.e.*, the people constituting the state) expressed itself by words or by acts, provided the latter had been sufficiently long in use to become customary.

This distinction between written and unwritten law is traced by Justinian (§ x) to the customs of the Athenians and the Lacedæmonians, the former of whom wrote their laws, whilst the latter confided them to memory; but it really arose with the natural growth of civilization. Hence the *written* law was that established by the express will of the legislature, and divided into civil and prætorian law, whilst *unwritten* law was introduced by usage, and through the tacit consent of the legislator.

34. (§ xi) The *civil* law was liable to change, either by the tacit consent of the people or by express statutory abrogation (*receptum est ut leges non solum suffragio legislatoris, sed etiam tacito consensu omnium per desuetudinem abrogentur*, Dig. 1, 3, 32, 1 Julian); but *natural* law, in the sense of the *jus gentium* (*ante*, par. 20), is unalterable, because based on the unchangeable nature of man.

35. (§ xii) *Private* law, as to its *objects*, is concerned with *persons*, *things*, and *actions* (see *ante*, par. 1).

Tit. iii.   De jure personarum.

40. (§ i) As to the meanings of the word *persona* see part ii, par. 21. The first division of persons is into *freemen* and *slaves*.

Libertas is defined as the *naturalis facultas ejus quod cuique facere libet, nisi quod vi aut jure prohibetur*, but as to *vis* the impediment interposed by force may be removed on application to the interference of the law.

41. (§ ii) *Servitus* is a *constitutio juris gentium qua quis dominio alieno contra naturam subjicitur*. This definition is taken from the Institutes of *Florentinus* (Dig. 1, 5, 4, 1), and points to the philosophical mode of viewing the subject (see *ante*, par. 20, and part ii, par. 26).

42. (§ iii) The term *servus* is derived by Justinian from the fact that the generals, instead of putting prisoners of war to death, used to keep (*servare*) them for sale, but the want of persons to till the soil, labour at the humble mechanical arts, and minister to the luxury of the rich, probably originated the class, and led to its enormous increase in the latter days of the republic.

44. (§ iv) *Slaves* became so :—

BOOK I—TIT. IV. 103

(1) *By captivity*, according to the rules of the *jus gentium*, and applied to the combatants on both sides, but see as to the *jus postliminii, post*, par. 163.

(2) *Born so, i.e.*, the children of slaves, and called *vernæ*, in respect of the master of their mother when born in his house.

(3) *Made so* by the rules of the civil law, as where a man (1) avoided military duty, or being inscribed in the census; (2), was guilty of *furtum manifestum*; (3) unable to pay creditors; or (4) in the case of illicit intercourse by a *free* woman with a slave; (5) condemnation to the mines; (6) a freedman guilty of ingratitude towards his patron; and (7) the fraud was so punished of the *freeman* who sold himself as a slave, for the sake of sharing the price of his sale (if over twenty years of age, knowing himself to be free, intending to share the price, the price really paid, the purchaser ignorant of the fraud), and then endeavoured to recover his freedom by the method *ad libertatem proclamare*, grounded on the rule that liberty was inalienable (if subsequently freed, the man who had been so punished would be a *libertus*). (1), (2), and (3) had ceased to exist, and (4) and (5) were suppressed by Justinian (see *post*, par. 160, 1175).

47. (§ v) *Liberi* were either *ingenui* or *libertini*, but there was no difference in respect of the condition of slaves, though the ordinary slaves *(servi, mancipia)* are to be distinguished from the *servi populi romani*, or the *servi pœnæ (post*, par. 160), or again from the *coloni censiti* and the *inquilini* (part i, par. 488), and the kind of work they performed caused various distinctions, dependent on the will of their master, as the teacher of the children *(educator)*, the steward *(actor)*, the overseer *(dispensator)*, the actor *(comœdus)*, the chained slave *(compeditus)*, and those *(vicarii)* who were placed in the service of other slaves.

Tit. iv. De ingenuis.

50. He is *ingenuus* who *statim ut nascitur liber est*, hence the term had lost all reference to the *gens* (part i, par. 16), and turns only on the question of liberty.

51. (§ i) The birthright of freedom could not be destroyed by facts not contemplated by the civil law, *e.g.*, if pirates carried off and sold a child into slavery, the child, if eventually freed, would be a freeman as before.

The rules as to the condition of a child were as follows :—

(1) The issue of a legal marriage between persons having the *connubium*, followed the condition of the *father* from the time of conception.

(2) If born out of wedlock, or the issue of a marriage between persons not having the *connubium*, the child followed the condition of the *mother* from *birth*, though by the *lex Mensia* (? the same as the *lex Ælia Sentia* of Gai. Inst. 1, § 80), a child born of a female citizen and a *peregrinus* was a *peregrinus*, but see *post*, par. 123. Gaius (Inst. i, § 67 to 97), on account of the different classes of

citizens then existing, devotes considerable space to this subject, but *Caracalla's* law (part i, par. 396 (2) existed in Justinian's time, and the opinion of *Marcellus*, a contemporary of Gaius, *in favour of liberty*, is inserted in the Institutes, so that if at any time during gestation the mother had been free, the child was free.

Tit. v. De libertinis.

54. *Libertini* were those who *ex justa* (actual, bona fide) *servitute manumissi sunt, i.e.*, those who *desierant esse servi*. The freedman had no civil family at the moment of freedom, and he took the name of his master, and usually attached himself to his house. He could work at occupations considered derogatory to the *ingenuus* (*e.g.*, attend to a shop). He could not marry a patrician or aspire to certain dignities, nor wear the gold ring *(jus aureorum annulorum)*, which at first was the distinctive mark of knights, but afterwards became common to all *ingenui*, and subsequently, as a mark of imperial favour, was at times conferred upon freedmen who by this *jus regenerationis* were ranged amongst the *ingenui*.

57. *Public* methods of enfranchisement were :—

(1) *Censu.* Introduced shortly after Servius (part i, par. 55), but fell into disuse under the empire; and for nearly two hundred years, from Vespasian to Decius, no census was taken, and then (A.D. 249) the last was taken, hence, not being abolished, some jurisconsults speak of it as still existing (Gai. Inst. i, § 17), others as not existing, because in disuse (Ulp. Reg. 1, § 8).

(2) *Vindicta.* As the census only took place once in five years, a fictitious employment of the *causa liberalis* came into vogue. In this suit, a person interested applied to the consul, and claimed the liberty *(in libertatem proclamare)* of a free man unjustly detained in servitude, and hence by analogy, a friend or the lictor *(assertor libertatis)* claimed the liberty of the slave, and the master not disputing it the magistrate declared him free. This was a particular application of the *in jure cessio* process, which was also employed for the transference of property, for adoptions, etc. (see part i, par. 140 (1), and the name came from the *festuca* (or *vindicta)*, a kind of wand used, and which represented the lance of ancient times. Under the emperors the solemn words and formalities fell into disuse, and it might take place (§ 2) anywhere before the magistrate without the presence of lictors.

(3) *Testamento.* This method at first required the aid of the *comitia*, because a new citizen was made, but gradually the formalities became less rigorous, and a few witnesses sufficed. Liberty might be given, either (1) *directly (e.g., servus meus Cratinus liber esto)*, or (2) by *fidei-commissum (e.g., Heres meus, rogo te ut Saccùm vicini mei servum, manumittas)*. In the first case the slave must be the testator's own, he was free from the moment there was an heir, and was the freedman of the deceased *(libertus orcinus)*, and the latter's family had the patronage. In the second case the slave might belong to another, the heir must buy him and free

him. The slave was not free until made so by the person charged with the duty, and that person was the patron. Liberty could be given on a condition *(sub conditione)*, or from a certain day *(a die)*, but *not* to a certain day *(ad diem)*.

(4) *In sacrosanctis ecclesiis.* There are two constitutions, A.D. 316 and 321, of Constantine, inserted in the Code (i, 13) on this subject, and this method was probably introduced by him when he began to protect Christians. The ceremony was usually performed by the bishop, and the deed was signed by him in presence of the people on some festival.

Anciently, only the first three public methods were known, and the master must have possessed the slave, *ex jure Quiritium*, otherwise the slave only lived in liberty *(in libertate morabatur)*, and was freed from the pain of serving *(tantum serviendi metu liberatur)*, but he was not free. After the *lex Junia*, the public methods made citizens, and other methods only gave irrevocable liberty, *i.e.*, the prætor would not allow slaves freed privately to be reduced again into slavery, but on the death of the slave his master took, as owner, all he left. Under Justinian the distinction between public and private methods disappeared, and all produced the same effect.

61. *Private* modes of manumission were :—

(1) *Per epistolam* ; (2) *inter amicos* ; (3) *per codicillum*. This last form is alluded to under the words "*per quamlibet aliam ultimam voluntatem*," and in all three cases the signatures of five witnesses were required.

62. Amongst other modes mentioned in a constitution of Justinian (Code 7, 6, 1, § 3 to 12) were :—

(4) Abandoning a slave dangerously ill, or prostituting a slave sold not to be so treated, the slave became free without a patron ; (5) bearing cap of liberty at funeral (to prevent simulated generosity) ; (6) payment by a third person of the price fixed for a man adjudged to be the slave of another ; (7) marrying a female slave to a free man, and giving a dowry with her ; (8) in some public way calling a slave a son (see *post*, par. 148) ; (9) returning or destroying before five witnesses the title deeds of slavery ; but the method of making the slave sit at his master's table (*per convivium, per mensam, inter epulas*) was not sanctioned by Justinian.

63. (§ iii) There were anciently no distinctions in the condition of *libertini* (see part ii, par. 31), but at the commencement of the empire three classes existed, viz. :—

(1) The *freed citizen*, with full rights (except in respect of *ingenui*), if the three essentials for enfranchisement existed which were required by the *Lex Ælia Sentia* (A.D. 4, see part i, par. 378).

(1) Ownership, *ex jure Quiritium*.
(2) Ceremony public (*vindicta, censu,* or *testamento*).
(3) Slave thirty years old, but if under thirty the ceremony must be performed by *vindicta*, after approval by the *consilium*, *i.e.*, in Rome, five senators and five knights, in the provinces, twenty recuperatores, who met on the last day of the assizes.

If slaves had been branded for a crime, or if they had been given for circus combats, the same law placed them on footing of—

64. (2) *Dediticii* (see part i, par. 78). This class could only acquire property by means available to peregrini. They could not make a will or live within 100 miles of Rome under penalty of being publicly sold. They could not improve their condition, and at death their master took their property by *right of succession*, if they had been publicly freed with the required conditions, but otherwise by *right of peculium* (Gai. Inst. iii, § 74, 75, 76).

65. (3) *Latini Juniani*. Those slaves whose enfranchisement was imperfect did not, under the *Lex Ælia Sentia*, count as freed, but were in the position of those *qui in libertate morabantur* (see *ante*, par. 57), and were formed into a third class by the *lex Junia Norbana* (see part i, par. 382), and called *latins*, on account of their position (part i, par. 187), and *Junians* on account of the law (Gai. Inst. iii, § 56). It is probable that *Gaius* and *Ulpian* refer to the *lex Junia Norbana* as earlier than the *lex Ælia Sentia*, because both laws existed prior to the date of these two jurists, and the effect of the later law was to place the class constituted by it in a superior position to the *dediticii*. These *latini juniani* in *public* law had no vote or aptitude for office; in *private* law they had the *commercium* (including *mancipatio*, Ulp. Reg. xix, § 4) and the *testamenti factio*, so far as to enable them to assist in the *per æs et libram* will as *emptor familiæ*, *libripens*, or *testis*, but they could not make their own will or be named as testamentary tutors, nor had they the *jus capiendi ex testamento* in respect of inheritance or legacies directly left them, unless at the death of the testator, or during the subsequent delay *(cretio)*, they became Roman citizens (Ulp. Reg. xxii, § 3), but they could take by *fidei-commissum*. At death their property fell to their master, and hence the words of Justinian (Inst. iii, 7, § 4), *In ipso ultimo spiritu, simul animam atque libertatem amittebant.* But the members of this class could become citizens in various ways, *e.g.*, (1) *beneficio principali*, *i.e.*, by rescript of the emperor; (2) *liberis*, after going through the form *per causam probare* (see *post*, par. 123); (3) *iteratione*, *i.e.*, by being freed over again and fulfilling all conditions; (4) *militia, i.e*, by military service for a certain term in the Roman guards; (5) *nave*, *i.e.*, by building a ship and carrying corn for six years; (6) *ædificio*, *i.e.*, by erecting a building; (7) *pistrino*, *i.e.*, by establishing a bakehouse.

67. In the time of Justinian *dediticii* had ceased to exist, and *Latini juniani* were rare. He effaced (Code 7, Tit. 5 and 6) the distinctions between *freed* persons by giving them all citizen rights, without reference to the age of the slave or the public mode of manumission, and he also removed (Nov. 78, c. 1) all differences between *ingenui* and *libertini*, leaving only the *rights of patronage*, viz. :—

(1) *Obsequia* or the duty of respect and gratitude towards the patron. The Digest (37, 15, 9) treats of the duties of children and freed persons as the same, *e.g.*, could not summon patron *in*

jus without the permission of the prætor, nor bring an action entailing infamy, nor exact from him more than he could pay. The freedman was also bound to support his patron, and he might be punished or re-enslaved for insulting him, or otherwise injuring him.

(2) *Operæ* or services usually stipulated for beforehand, as they were not necessarily due, *e.g.*, to work as a domestic *(in ministerio)* or as a workman *(in artificio)*.

(3) *Jura in bonis*, or rights of succession, as to which see *post*, par. 1088.

Tit. vi. Qui, et quibus ex causis, manumittere non possunt.

70. Both the *lex Ælia Sentia* and the *lex Furia Caninia* (tit. vii) were designed by Augustus to check manumission (part i, par. 378), but in the time of Justinian the value of the citizenship had so far diminished that his laws were conceived with the view of favouring enfranchisement. This title is concerned with two additional provisions of the *lex Ælia Sentia*, viz. :—

(1) Freedoms in fraud of creditors void: a rule extended by a *senatus consultum* under Hadrian, to include *peregrini* debtors. (Gai. Inst. i, § 47.)

(2) Master under twenty could only free by *vindicta*, and after proving a cause satisfactory to the council.

The term *creditor* included any one to whom any thing was due, but it was necessary that the debtor should have acted in bad faith and that he was aware of the loss he was inflicting, *i.e.*, Justinian (§ iii) decided in favour of the opinion which held that *intention* must be an ingredient in the fraud *(Fraudis interpretatio semper in jure civili non ex eventu duntaxit sed ex consilio quoque desideratur*, Dig. 50, 17, 79, Papinian), and the result would be that after the manumission the slave was at liberty, but the creditors had the power of proving the fraud, and so showing that the freedman was still a slave. Hence the slave was in the position of a *statu liber (nam dum incertum est an creditor jure suo utatur interim statu-liberi sunt*, Dig. 40, 5, 1, 1), *i.e.*, of a freed slave whose liberty was not to take place for a time or until a given event. In the interval, the slave was in the same condition as others in the inheritance, and his children were slaves; but, on the expiration of the time or on performance of the condition, he became free, although he might have been parted with by sale or gift. In the case of the freedom in fraud of creditors the slave was free until the creditors attacked the manumission, and in the case of freedom by *fidei commissum* the slave could not be sold, and he could compel the *fidei commissarius* to free him.

The master could not avail himself of his own fraud, and therefore liberty was absolutely acquired on payment by the master or by a third person of the sum due; and so where the *fiscus* was concerned, if it did not make a claim within ten years; and the rule only applied to the last sales of slaves actually producing the insolvency.

73 (§ i). But when there was *no other* heir, and to avoid the disgrace of insolvency attaching to his name (part ii, par. 74), the master might appoint his slave heir (if several named, it only applied to the first), who would be answerable for the debts, and in whose name the creditors could sell the goods (see *post*, par. 1161). The slave became *free, citizen* and *heir*, and it being compulsory, he was called *solus et necessarius heres* (*post*, par. 804). The fact of naming the slave *heir* made him *free* also, according to Justinian, who decided (Code 6, 27, 5) the point against the argument of Ulpian requiring the freedom to be expressly given.

77 (§ v). As to the second head, in respect of enfranchisement *inter vivos, justæ causæ* would be, *e.g.*, to free father or mother, son or daughter, teacher, nurse, etc., or to make the slave a procurator (if over 17, as under that age, he could not appear before a judge in defence of his patron), or to marry a female slave (within six months, otherwise not free, unless master died or became senator, or otherwise incapacitated from complying with condition), and (§ vi) the motive once approved by the council could not be retracted.

78 (§ vii). As the master under twenty could only enfranchise in this prescribed way, he could not do so *by will*, but Justinian, in the Institutes, allowed the master over the age of seventeen to free by will, and eight years subsequently (Nov. 119, c. 2) reduced the age to fourteen, being that at which, by the old law, he was able to make a will at all.

Tit. vii. De lege Fusia (or Furia) Caninia tollenda.

78. This law, passed A.D. 8 in the consulate of *Furius* Camillus and *Caninius* Gallus, and repealed by *Justinian* (*ante*, par. 70), was enacted for the purpose of restraining posthumous pride, and limited the power of enfranchisement by *will* thus:—If had *two* slaves, *both* might be freed, from two to 10, ½; from 10 to 30, ⅓; from 30 to 100, ¼; from 100 to 500, ⅕; but never more than 100. The slaves must be *named*, and the first names taken; if in a circle *none*. (Gai. Inst. i, § 46).

82. *Actions* to procure liberty, *ante*, par. 57 (2), or to declare *ingenuus*, belonged to the *præjudicial* class (*post*, par. 2112), and took place before the superior judges, *e.g.*, rectors, præses, prætors, and consuls.

Tit. viii. De his qui sui, vel alieni juris sunt.

83. As to the division of persons into those *sui juris* and those *alieni juris* see part ii, par. 46. *Gaius* (Inst. i, § 49) classifies the *alieni juris* under three heads (*earum personarum quæ aliæno juri subjectæ sunt, aliæ in potestate, aliæ in manu, aliæ in mancipio sunt*); but, owing to the disappearance of the *manus, Justinian* has only two divisions, viz., those falling under the *patria* and the *dominica potestas*.

89 (§ i). *Dominica potestas.* This power of the master over the slave in respect of his—

(1) *Person*, extended, up to the end of the republic, to life and death; but even before the introduction of christianity the extreme rigour of the law had been modified, and a *lex Petronia*, probably under Augustus (A.D. 11), did not permit slaves to be forced to fight with wild beasts. *Hadrian* (A.D. 117) enacted that they could not be put to death except after condemnation by a magistrate. *Antonine* (part i, par. 392) punished as homicide the death of a slave by the master's hand. *Constantine* only permitted moderate castigation, and *Justinian* confirmed the rescript of Antonine, rendering the master liable to death or deportation who killed his slave *sine causa legibus cognita*, such as adultery with wife or daughter, or in self defence. Slaves who fled for protection to temples or statues were to be sold by the *præsides* of the provinces, and the masters were not allowed to attach unfair conditions to the sale, as that the slave should be employed at hard work or kept chained.

(2) *Property*. Everything the slave earned, received, or found, belonged to his master, but *custom* tended to prevent the master depriving him of his *peculium*, *i.e.*, his private savings.

Tit. ix. De Patria Potestate.

92. The *dominica potestas* was derived from the *jus gentium*, but only a Roman citizen could have the *patria potestas*, because it was due to the *civil* law, and was supposed by *Gaius* (Inst. i, § 55) to be peculiar to the Romans, except the Galatæ, though it is probably an institution suited to the infancy of civilization. It was acquired by *justæ nuptiæ, legitimation*, or *adoption*, and extended over the—

(1) *Person* of sons and daughters and the descendants of male children, even to life and death; involving the right to sell them; abandon them in reparation, part ii, par. 46 (3); or expose them; but time modified these rights. *Gaius* (Inst. i, § 117, 118; iv, § 75, etc.) refers to *mancipatio*, chiefly as a mode of fictitiously freeing from power. Only sons, not daughters, could be abandoned, and the practice then fell into disuse. Exposure was prohibited, and *Justinian* confirmed Constantine's legislation, as to the sale of children. See part i, par. 479 (1).

(2) *Property*. Originally the child in power was in the same position as a slave, but for the effects of legislation in respect of the *castrense peculium, quasi castrense peculium*, and the property of the mother, see *post*, par. 611.

Tit. x. De nuptiis.

97. The terms *nuptiæ, matrimonium*, refer to union by marriage in general, but *justæ nuptiæ, justum matrimonium*, to the Roman civil law marriage giving the *potestas, agnatio* and *familia* rights (part ii, par. 58).

98. Although placed under the protection of paganism, and subsequently of christianity, marriage was a *civil* contract without public solemnity, but involving *consent* and *tradition*, *i.e.*, it must be classed

amongst the real contracts perfected by delivery (*re contrahebatur*); hence the absent wife could not be married by letter or messenger, though the husband could be so married if the wife were taken to his house (*si in domum ejus deduceretur*—Paul), because that was equivalent to tradition, and the expressions *uxorem ducere, uxor duci*, convey this idea, which is literally carried out in the bridal array and procession to the husband's house; but, as in other cases (*e.g.*, things of great weight or size), the consent to the delivery in the presence of the thing sufficed (*si in re præsenti consenserint—sed oculis et affectu*), and so the wife might be put (or if *sui juris* place herself) in possession. Hence it is that if the husband and wife are present, consent alone (*solus affectus*) is spoken of as constituting the marriage, and hence the wife was frequently not led home until after the marriage, or she might be in the house some days before the marriage, in which case delivery would not be complete until the consent was given, and hence the concubine only differed from the wife by the fact of consent.

100. Sometimes a deed was drawn up either as to the settlement of the property (*instrumenta dotalia*) or in the shape of marriage articles (*instrumentum ad probationem matrimonii*), but these only served to prove the marriage, which might also be done by the evidence of friends and neighbours, and consummation by cohabitation was not necessary.

101. *Justinian* suppressed the ancient rule as to the necessity of a dowry contract between persons of unequal condition, though the novels (74, c. 4) enacted that (1) persons holding high rank must have a dowry contract, and (2) that others, with the exception of the very poor, should declare their marriage in church in the presence of three or four witnesses, but this appears to have been repealed by novel 117, c. 4.

102. The term *sponsalia* (*sponsio et repromissio nuptiarum futurarum*) for betrothals was derived from the primitive *spondes ne, spondeo*. They could be entered into by the consent of the heads of the families, and of the affianced if over the age of seven, though the marriage itself would not be lawful before puberty. There was no action to compel the marriage, and a notification (*conditione tua non utor*) broke off the engagement, but the *arrhæ*, usually given to the bride elect, were liable to be forfeited.

104. For *justæ nuptiæ* three conditions were indispensable, viz., puberty, consent, and connubium.

(1) *Puberty*, see part ii, par. 86 (3).

105. (2) *Consent*. This applied to the parties themselves, and to the heads of their families. The latter could not force it from the former, and a knowledge of the nature of the contract was acquired, hence an idiot could not marry. As the question of the consent turned on the *patria potestas*, neither that of the mother nor of the natural father (in the case of an adopted child) was required, nor of any one in the case of a child, *sui juris*, though a constitution of Valens and of Valentinian (Code 5, 4, 18, and 20) required an

emancipated daughter under twenty-five to get her father's consent, and if he were dead, that of the mother, and nearest relations. Grandsons (not granddaughters) had to get the consent of their father and of their ancestor also, for the latter's consent alone would have made the father's agnates more numerous, and it was only in the power of the ancestor to diminish, not increase his son's family (see analogous case of adoptions, *post*, par. 138). After a constitution of Severus and Antonine, the præsides of the provinces could compel consent if it was unreasonably refused, and if the consent of the paterfamilias was given subsequently, the marriage from that date was lawful, but it had no retrospective effect. If the consent was prevented by insanity, the *daughter* could always marry, and Justinian finally decided in favour of the son also, if the ceremony was performed in the presence of the curator, and of the relations of the father, and the terms of the dowry and nuptial gift were settled before a magistrate. The captivity or disappearance of the father enabled the children to marry after three years, but the *potestas* was restored on the father's return (*post*, par. 163).

According to primitive law, the paterfamilias could send the *repudium* (*post*, par. 120), and separate the husband and wife against their will, but the words of Paul—*sed contracta non solvuntur* (Sent. ii, xix, § 2) refer to a constitution of Marcus Aurelius, forbidding such a divorce, except for weighty reasons.

For marriage it was further necessary that the parties should be free, *i.e.*, not already married, and that the husband should not be in holy orders, and not castrate unless the wife consented.

106. (3) *Connubium* is defined (Ulp. Reg. v, § 3) as the *uxoris jure ducendæ facultas*, *i.e.*, the ability in general to take a lawful wife, but in the proper restricted sense it was the *relative capacity* to marry each other, *i.e.*, it was a civil right, exclusively reserved for Roman citizens, and for those on whom, prior to Caracalla's legislation (part i, par. 396), the privilege was specially conferred, but though without *connubium* the marriage would be according to the *jus gentium*, and the parties would be *cœlibes*, in respect of the lex Julia (part i, par. 369), still the nullity was confined to civil law rights, and the bond was recognised, for the wife (*uxor injusta*) might be guilty of adultery.

107. *Impediments to marriage.* These might arise from the ties of cognation, agnation, affinity, and natural and political considerations, *e.g.*, marriage was forbidden between :—

(1) Direct ascendants and descendants ad infinitum.

(2) Uncle and niece, great niece, etc., ad infinitum, and so in respect of aunt and nephew, great nephew, etc. (when Claudius wished to marry his niece Agrippina, the daughter of his brother Germanicus, a law was passed, making marriage between an uncle and his brother's daughter lawful, but this was repealed by Constantine).

(3) Brother and sister.

The *cognate* ties of blood could never cease, but *agnate* relations could marry after the bond had been severed, as where the adopted person or the person to marry the adopted was emancipated, but although thus sent out of the family, the father could never marry his adopted daughter, granddaughter, etc. The tie resulting from *affinitas* (part ii, par. 67) prevented marriage between the father-in-law *(socer)* and his deceased son's wife *(nurus)*, or his wife's daughter *(privigna)*, granddaughter, etc., and between the son-in-law *(gener)*, grandson, etc., and his wife's mother *(socrus)*, or father's wife *(noverca)*, but in the collateral line the prohibition only extended to the brother and sister-in-law, and that only from the time of Constantine, who forbad marriage with the brother's wife or two sisters (Code v, 5, 5).

The *contubernium* and *concubinatus* (*post*, par. 122), although not recognised in law, produced impediments to marriage from *natural* ties.

116. (§ xi) *Political* considerations, varying at different periods, also interposed barriers, *e.g.*—

By the twelve tables there was no *connubium* between patricians and plebeians, repealed six years later (see part ii, par. 58).

The *leges Julia et Papia* (part i, par. 369) permitted *ingenui* to marry *libertini*, but forbad senators and *ingenui* to marry actresses and other inferior classes of women—a prohibition extended by Constantine to all *humiles abjectæve personæ*, but Justin altered this if the woman abandoned her profession, and Justinian (Nov. 117, c. 6), on account of Theodora, repealed the law altogether (part i, par. 533).

Neither the tutor nor the curator, or their son, could marry the adult ward unless she had been affianced by her father, or was over twenty-five years of age. A magistrate could not marry a woman of the province during his tenure of office, nor the ravisher the person ravished, nor the adulterer his accomplice, nor the Jew a Christian.

117. (§ xii) *Nullity of marriage.* If the conditions necessary for *justæ nuptiæ* were not fulfilled, the union would come under the general head of *stuprum*, and the children would be *spurii*, the dowry and marriage gift were liable to confiscation, and bigamy and incest entailed punishment.

118. *Effects of justæ nuptiæ.* The husband (*vir*) was bound to protect and maintain his wife (*uxor*), and she shared his honours and dignities, owed him respect and obedience, and had no other domicile than his. The children born during the marriage were presumed legitimate, and so if born within ten months of the husband's death (part ii, par. 176), and the *patria potestas* resulted from the marriage. As to the *dos* brought by the wife and the *donatio propter nuptias* given by the husband see *post*, par. 562. Marriage being an indivisible union, the wife always followed the son, emancipated or given in adoption, but children born or conceived before that time were left in the power of the paterfamilias.

120. *Dissolution of marriage.* As marriage was a contract formed by consent and tradition, it was capable of dissolution, according to

the rule *quod ligatum est etiam dissolvi potest* (Nov. 22, c. 3), and hence the *divortium* dates from the origin of Rome, though it was not abused until the last years of the republic, after which period the *leges Julia et Papia* and imperial constitutions endeavoured to restrain it. Divorce might result from the—

(1) Consent of both (*bona gratia*), when the terms regulating it were left to be settled by the parties themselves.

(2) Will of one, when motives were fixed by Theodosius and Valentinian, and extended in the novels of Justinian.

The intervention of a magistrate was not necessary, but seven witnesses were required, and a deed of separation (*repudium*) must be sent, containing the words—*Tuas res tibi habeto; tuas res tibi agito.*

121. Second marriages were favoured by the *leges Julia et Papia*, though the widow could not re-marry until after the year of mourning, but later legislation, confirmed by Justinian, tended to restrain re-marriage if there were children of the first bed, otherwise there was no impediment.

122. The *concubinatus* (part ii, par. 58) was permitted by the customs of the Romans, as between a man and one woman, and was distinguished from the *stuprum*. No penalty attached to it, but it was not an honourable state for the woman, and she was usually a freed person or of low extraction, or a prostitute. If she was free-born and virtuous, the presumption was in favour of her being the wife, unless she had become a concubine by a formal act, for otherwise the intercourse would fall under the head of *stuprum*, and such a woman, consenting to become a concubine, lost her title of *mater-familias* or *matrona*.

No formalities were required for entering into or dissolving the connection, and in this it resembled marriage, but the social status before the connection, and the position of the woman in the house afterwards, showed her rank, *e.g.*, a woman domiciled in the province must be the concubine of the magistrate. It gave none of the rights of marriage, but there was no difference in respect of the mother, whether the children were *legitimate, naturales,* or *spurii* (see *post*, par. 1054), though, as the father of the second class was recognised, these children, as opposed to the *spurii*, could be legitimated, and *Justinian* (Nov. 18, c. 5) gave them some rights in the succession to property. Leo the philosopher, Emperor of the East, repealed the laws permitting concubinage, in A.D. 887, as contrary to religion and natural decency.

123. (§ xiii) *Legitimation* was under the republic acquired as an accessory to the rights of citizenship accorded to aliens, and the *lex Ælia Sentia* and the *lex Junia* (*ante*, par. 63, 65) had some special provisions on the subject detailed by *Gaius* (Inst. i, § 29, 66, 67), viz. :—

(1) *Per causam probare.* The freed Latin who had taken a wife for the purpose of having children (*liberorum quærendorum causa*), and had a child a year old (*anniculus factus*), was allowed on

proof of these facts before the prætor or præses to become a Roman citizen, and acquire *potestas* over the child, who was at the same time legitimated.

(2) *Per causam erroris probare.* The Roman citizen, who by mistake had married a freed Latin or an alien (or vice versa), and had children, was allowed to prove this, and the union became *justæ nuptiæ* with its consequences.

But these methods fell into disuse, and Constantine introduced the two following means:—

(1) *Per subsequens matrimonium.* The conditions of this were that—(1) at the time of the conception of the child, marriage between the father and the mother was not forbidden by any law; (2) a deed of settlement or marriage articles must be prepared; (3) the children must consent to be legitimated, or at least must not refuse. The result of complying with these rules would be that the natural children and those subsequently born would be legitimate, and Justinian, in spite of the first rule, enacted (Nov. 78, c. 4), that the children of a slave, freed and married by her master, should become free and legitimate.

(2) *Per oblationem curiæ.* This method originated with Theodosius and Valentinian (A.D. 442), and was confirmed by Justinian. It was confined to the rich, and its object was to induce citizens to become *curiales* (part i, par. 444), and to confer a favour on those already members. Children could not be compelled to belong to the *curia*, but if they consented, they became legitimate, acquired the fortune of their father and rights *ab intestato*. They also fell under the *potestas* of their father, but with this peculiarity, that the child was in the family, only as against the father, and not as against cognates and agnates.

Justinian, by novel 74, c. 2, further introduced :—

(3) *Per rescriptum principis.* Granted if there was no legitimate child, and it was impossible to marry the mother.

(4) *Per testamentum.* If the father had expressed the wish in his will, the emperor would grant the legitimation by rescript, and the children thus became heirs.

128. The method of *adoption* for legitimating natural children was introduced by Anastasius, but repealed by Justin and Justinian.

Tit. xi. De adoptionibus.

129. This subject is only referred to by Gaius and Ulpian, and in these Institutes, as producing the *patria potestas*. According to primitive law, the adoptee became a stranger to his natural family, and on entering the family of the adoptor he acquired rights of succession, agnation, and cognation *(qui in adoptionem datur, his, quibus, agnascitur, et cognatus fit.* Dig. 1, 7, 23). He also shared the *lares* and *res sacra* (*in sacra transibat*), and took the name of the adoptor, retaining that of his own house as an adjective, with the termination *ianus*, hence adoptions entailed the right of succeeding to (1) name; (2) property; (3) domestic gods (*hereditas nominis, pecuniæ, sacrorum, secutæ sunt.*—Cicero).

BOOK I—TIT. XI. 115

132. There were two kinds of adoption :—

(1) *Adrogation*, by which a *paterfamilias*, *i.e.*, a person *sui juris*, with all his property and all those in his power, passed under the potestas of another (*e.g.*, Germanicus, having been previously adopted by Tiberius, became the grandson of Augustus, when the latter adopted, *i.e.*, arrogated Tiberius, though in adoption proper this does not occur, as the adoptee, being only a *filius-familias*, he and his children are in the power of their ancestor). The house of the adoptee merges in that of the adoptor, involving the loss of the family *sacra (quid? sacra Clodiæ gentis, cur intereunt quod in te est?*—Cicero), hence the necessity for a *lex curiata* (afterwards reduced to a formality, see part i, par. 31), and the origin of the name of this form of adoption, for the adoptor and adoptee were asked if they were willing, the people if they ordered it, and the College of Pontiffs if they had any opposition to offer.

(2) *Adoption.* Persons *alieni juris* were adopted by a fictitious employment of the *mancipatio (post*, par. 153). After the process had been repeated three times for a son, *i.e.*, a male of the first degree, the *patria potestas* of the father was destroyed, according to the terms of the twelve tables (iv, 3), but the child was then in *mancipio* to the purchaser, and had to be claimed by him as a son by means of the *in jure cessio* process, gone through in the presence of the prætor, consul, or præses, by whom the child was *addictus* to the fictitious father, whose adopted son he thus became.

In the time of Gaius and Ulpian, these forms were outwardly the same, but they had degenerated into mere fictions, and a custom had grown up from the last years of the republic of adopting by testament (*e.g.*, Julius Cæsar so adopted Octavius), but ratification by a *plebiscitum* was necessary.

136. (§ i) Under Justinian-the methods were :—

(1) *Principali rescripto* for the *arrogation* of a person *sui juris*, and granted on satisfactory proof *(causa cognita)* of the following facts, viz. :—That the adoptor was over sixty years of age, and therefore despaired of children of his own, and that he was at least eighteen years older than the adoptee (a rule applying to adoptions also), and that he had no other natural or adopted children. Justinian allowed *women* to be arrogated, but no law to that effect existed at the time of Gaius (Inst. i, § 101) or Ulpian (Reg. viii, § 5), though the passage in the Digest (i, 7, 21), *nam et feminæ ex rescripto principis adrogari possunt*, is attributed to Gaius by a *tribonianism* (part i, par. 544). Antoninus Pius allowed *impuberes* also to be arrogated if security was given, and a verbal covenant entered into before a *tabularius (i.e.*, a public officer, formerly a public *slave*, but after Arcadius and Honorius a *freeman)* in respect of the following conditions—(1) that the arrogation was honourable and advantageous to the ward ; (2) that if the ward died before puberty, all his property should be restored to his relations ; (3) if emancipated or disinherited, all the ward's property to be restored to him, including (if there was

no proper motive) a fourth (*quarta antonina*) of the adoptor's goods; (4) that if the ward, on attaining puberty, proved the arrogation unfavourable, he could claim his property and emancipation.

(2) *Imperio magistratus.* For the adoption of persons *alieni juris* Justinian suppressed the *mancipatio* and *in jure cessio* processes, substituting a deed drawn up before a superior magistrate, in the presence, and with the consent, of the adoptor, and of the person giving up the adoptee, and after the non-refusal of the latter, though he or she might be an infant unable to speak.

138. (§ ii) Under Justinian's legislation, *arrogation* always produced the *patria potestas*, and all the property and children passed into the new family; but in the case of *adoption*, if the *adoptor* was—

(1) *Extraneus, i.e.,* not an ascendant, the adoptee retained all his rights in his own family, and did not acquire any in the new family he entered, except the right of succession *ab intestato*, so that an adopted child, in the event of intestacy, acquired *one additional* right over children left in the family.

(2) *Non extraneus, i.e.,* if the adoptor was an ascendant, he acquired full rights over the child, and the person giving him up lost all his rights, for both being naturally related to the child, he was not likely to suffer; *e.g.,* a *maternal* ancestor must adopt the children of his daughter, for they would not otherwise be in his power; so a child born after the emancipation of the son would not be in the power of its grandfather, and an emancipated son, to get his own child in power, must adopt it from its grandfather.

142. (§ v) The adoptee could rank in the new family as a son or grandson, etc., and so differently affect the rights of succession and of marriage prohibitions. If not placed under any one in particular, he was *quasi incerto natus*, but if placed as a grandson under a son (*quasi ex filio*) living, that son's consent was required *(ne ei invito suus hæres agnascatur)*, for this would increase the number of the son's heirs on the death of the father.

145. (§ ix) Castrates could not adopt children, but impotent persons might, and so, by a constitution of Diocletian and Maximian, could *women* who had lost their children, but no *patria potestas* was in their case acquired.

148. (§ xii) A *freedman* could only be adopted by his patron, otherwise the rights of patronage would be disturbed, and a *slave* adopted thereby acquired his freedom, *ante*, par. 62, (8), but not the rights of a son.

149. The *dissolution* of the tie of adoption would follow from the—

(1) Emancipation of the adoptee.

(2) Adoption of the adoptee by a third person, not a stranger, and the bond could not be renewed, the result being that the child was no longer either an agnate or cognate of the former, though marriage prohibitions might still continue to affect him.

150. *Manus.* The three methods employed to acquire the marital power were distinct altogether from the marriage.

(1) *Usus.* This was fixed by the twelve tables (vi, 4), in analogy to the year's possession *(usucapio)* of moveables, but could be defeated by three nights' absence *(usurpatum ire trinoctio.)* The remaining two methods produced the manus *immediately.*

(2) *Farreo (confarreatio)* or the sacrifice of the corn cake with sacramental formalities in the presence of ten witnesses. The issue of the marriage were eligible to various sacerdotal functions, and hence this method was reserved to patricians.

(3) *Co-emptio.* The husband was the purchaser (*co-emptionator*) of the wife by the *mancipatio* process, but the same words were not used, and hence the wife was never *in mancipio, i.e.,* in the position of a slave.

The effect of these three methods was to take the wife out of her own family and make her an agnate of her own children, with the rank and rights of a daughter in her husband's family.

According to *Gaius* (Inst. i, § 108, etc.) the *manus* acquired by *usus* had been partly destroyed by law, and partly fallen into disuse. *Confarreatio* was practised by the great flamins, *i.e.,* the priests of Jupiter, Mars, and Quirinus, and this method is mentioned also by *Ulpian* (Reg. ix), but disappeared with Paganism under Constantine. *Co-emptio* still took place, and was also employed fictitiously to elude the law (part i, par. 329). The passage in Gaius is illegible, but probably the *manus* could be dissolved by—(1) emancipation; (2) deed of divorce (*repudium*) sent to husband by wife.

In the time of Justinian all these three methods had disappeared, and *manus* is not mentioned in the Institutes. The wife did not enter the family of her husband, but was only allied to it, and remained in the father's family, retaining all her agnate rights, and *senatus-consulta* had established rights of inheritance between mother and children.

153. *Mancipium,* see part ii, par. 46 (3). As slaves, children in power and wife *in manu* were *res mancipi,* a *mancipatio* was required to transfer the *dominium ex jure Quiritium.* After the sale had been gone through in the presence of five Roman citizens, (*puberes*) and the *libripens,* the person was *in mancipio* to the purchaser, but did not lose the quality of a *free* man, and therefore would be *ingenuus,* as well as *sui juris,* if subsequently *freed* by the methods applicable to those in the position of slaves, viz., *vindicta, censu,* or *testamento (ante,* par. 57), but still the *manumissor extraneus* would be *per similitudinem patroni,* and therefore have a patron's rights as to succession and tutorship *(post,* par. 166 and 1109). In the time of *Gaius,* the process was only used fictitiously for freeing children from power *(post,* par. 166), and though seriously for *noxal* abandonments this also fell into disuse *(post,* par. 2226), and the *mancipium* is therefore not described in the Institutes.

Tit. xii. Quibus modis jus potestatis solvitur.

155. The power over the slave *(dominica potestas)* was destroyed by enfranchisement *(ante,* par. 57, 61), though the death of the master, or his slavery, etc., only transferred the property in the slave to another.

156. The *patria potestas* was dissolved by children becoming *sui juris* by the death of the father or the loss of liberty, citizenship, or captivity to an enemy of father *(post,* par. 163) or child, but this would only apply to grandsons, etc., if no intermediate ancestor became *sui juris* by the event, as otherwise they would fall under his power.

159. *Relegation, i.e.,* perpetual or temporary exile to a fixed place, did not affect the *patria potestas* or any city rights, but *interdiction* from fire and water, or *deportation* (see *post,* par. 205), degraded the citizen into a *peregrinus,* and therefore, if *sui juris,* his *potestas* was gone, and if *alieni juris* he was freed from power. He could recover these rights as to the future through the favour of the emperor, but if the *restitutio* was not *in integrum,* it only freed him from punishment, and permitted him to return as a citizen to his country.

160. (§ iii) *Servi pœnæ.* Justinian, in a novel (22 c. 8) five years subsequent to the Institutes, abolished the slavery and consequent loss of potestas, etc., due to condemnation to the mines, or to wild beasts, but the result of slavery in general was necessarily to reduce the individual to the position of a thing, and consequently to deprive him of *potestas* and other citizen rights.

162. (§ iv) The priests of Jupiter and the Vestal virgins, on entering upon their respective offices, were freed from the *patria potestas,* without suffering *minima capitis deminutio (post,* par. 197), by an altogether exceptional rule, applying to their peculiar position, but both these classes disappeared with Paganism. Justinian accorded the privilege to *Patricii* (part i, par. 471), and subsequently to bishops, consuls, and to all those dignitaries whose rank freed them from the *curia (ante,* par. 123), *e.g.,* the prætorian prefect, the questor of the palace, the master of the cavalry or infantry. These persons, however, lost none of their rights, they continued to be agnates in the family, and on the death of the head they became his heirs, and acquired power over their own children.

163. (§ v) The *jus postliminii* affected the patria potestas by holding it in suspense. *Postliminium* was of two kinds :—

(1) As to certain things, which, if taken by the enemy and retaken, reverted to the original owner, *e.g.,* immoveables, as slaves, houses, ships, but never arms *quod turpiter amittantur.*

(2) As to free persons. A citizen taken by the enemy became their slave, but in his own country his condition was in suspense, depending on his return. If he returned, he regained all his rights, past and future ; but if he died in captivity, according to the strict law he was held to have lost all his rights from the moment he was made a slave ; though by the *lex Cornelia Testamentaria* (part i, par. 272), his testament was construed as if he had lost his rights by

death, and not by slavery, and therefore the directions contained in it as to the inheritance, tutorship, etc., would be valid.

Hence, according to *Ulpian* (Dig. 49, 15, 16), the *jus postliminii* came to be :—

(1) If returned from captivity, the citizen was considered never to have ceased to be such.

(2) If he did not return, he was held to be dead from the moment of captivity, and this is what is called by the commentators the *fiction of the lex Cornelia*, but according to *Gaius* (Inst. i, § 129), the question was doubtful whether this rule applied to the *patria potestas*, a point, however, settled by Justinian, who confirmed the opinion in favour of the children, stated by *Tryphoninus* and Ulpian thirty years after the doubts expressed by Gaius.

A son returning fell under the *potestas* again and recovered all his rights, and as to the children marrying in the interval see *ante*, par. 105.

The position of a citizen *during captivity* may be summed up thus :—

(1) *Enjoyment of rights*, all in suspense, *e.g.*, *dominica* and *patria potestas*, acquisitions of children and slaves. If instituted heir, the institution is in suspense, and so as to the rights of tutorship and succession.

(2) *Exercise of rights*, withdrawn, *e.g.*, cannot contract *justæ nuptiæ*, adopt, stipulate, or make a will.

(3) *Everything consisting in facts*, lost, *e.g.*, usucapion interrupted, marriage broken, and, if wife in captivity also, the legitimacy of the children is in suspense.

(4) *In virtue of the lex Cornelia*, the will made before captivity is valid.

166. (§ vi) *Emancipation*. Primitive law did not provide any direct means for freeing a child from the *patria potestas*, but by a forced construction of the terms of the twelve tables, iv (3), the object was indirectly attained, and the *patria potestas* was exhausted on the fictitious *third* sale in respect of a son, for the word *filius* was held not to apply to daughters or grand-children, so that *one* sale sufficed for them. But the result of the process was to give the *manumissor extraneus* rights of patronage, tutorship, and succession *(ante*, par. 153), to obviate which a *contracta fiducia* was entered into, obliging the purchaser to remancipate the child back again to the father, by which means the child became *in mancipio* (not *in potestate*) to the father, who could now free him, and so acquire the patron's rights, or the same *contracta fiducia* might compel the purchaser to free the child. As to the position of the offspring of the person so emancipated, it was held that the child conceived in the interval between the sales, and before the last, was in the power of the paterfamilias, because his *patria potestas* had not been finally extinguished, and *Labeo* maintained that the child conceived during the third mancipation was in the power of the master of his father; but *Gaius* (Inst. i, § 135), in whose time the process was nearly always fictitious,

inclined to the opinion that the children were *sui juris* if the father died *in mancipio*, and under his power if he were freed. The emancipation called *Anastasian* by the commentators, because introduced by that emperor, simplified the matter by reducing it to obtaining an imperial rescript authorising the emancipation, and *Justinian* merely required the ascendants to present themselves before the superior magistrates, and if their descendants did not object, they became free, and the ascendants acquired all rights of patronage, including tutorship, etc.

169. The emancipation was not irrevocable, but could be rescinded if the child treated his father badly or otherwise injured him.

172. Children, whether natural or adopted, could not compel their ascendants to emancipate them, except in cases of—
   (1) Prostitution of daughter.
   (2) Exposure.
   (3) Contracting an incestuous marriage, and see also *ante*, par. 136 (4).

175. *Actions* relating to family law. Among the more important of these were :—
   (1) *De partu agnoscendo*, for the wife against the husband during marriage or after divorce, to compel him to acknowledge her child, or within thirty days after divorce to obtain a declaration that she was pregnant by him, and the husband could dispute his liability, as well as appoint guardians to prevent fraud *(custodes mittere)*.
   (2) For father against child, or vice versa, to be recognised as such, but not available in respect of children *vulgo concepti*.
   (3) For the father to claim or reject the *patria potestas*, or for the son to assert himself to be or not *sui juris*.

All these actions were *prejudicial (post*, par. 2112), but to reclaim a son from a stranger, anciently the father proceeded by the *vindicatio*, with *adjecta causa*, that claimed him as *filium suum ex jure Quiritium*, but prætorian law subsequently introduced a more summary process *(post*, par. 2301).

Tit. xiii. De tutelis.

180. (§ i) Justinian adopts Servius' definition of the *tutela*, cited by Paul (Dig. 26, 1, 1), viz.:—

Vis ac potestas (a pleonasm for *vis* implies the force of authority, see Gai. Inst. i, § 192, where, in reference to a class of tutors over women, the expression occurs—*legitimæ tutelæ vim aliquem habere intelliguntur*).

— *in capite libero (i.e.*, in respect of those free from power and *sui juris*).

— *ad tuendum eum qui propter ætatem se defendere nequit* (for under Justinian, tutorship only existed over *impuberes*, that due to *sex* having disappeared, see part ii, par. 84, 95).

—*jure civili* (for created *legibus, senatus-consultis,* and *moribus,* not by the prætor or through the *jus gentium*).

— *data ac permissa* (also a pleonasm, though *data* may be held to refer to the right given by law to agnates, etc., and *permissa* to the power allowed by law to testators).

182. *Testamentaria tutela.* This was the most important tutorship, and other kinds were only instituted in default of it. The *testamentarii tutores (tutor=tuitor, i.e., defensor)* were also called *tutores dativi* when specially named in the will (though the expression was extended by the commentators to include those given by the magistrate, *post,* par. 224). The right of the *paterfamilias* was expressly recognised by the twelve tables (v. 3), but he alone could appoint this kind of tutor, and that in virtue of his *patria potestas,* so that he could disinherit and yet appoint a tutor. It could only refer to those who were in his power, and who at his death would be *impuberes* and *sui juris,* hence such a tutor could not be given to a grandson whilst an unemancipated son was living, for the child would fall under his own father's power on the death of the ancestor, but he could at the same time disinherit and appoint a tutor to the *posthumous* child who, conceived before death, would have been one of the *hæredes sui* if he had been born at death. This innovation, modifying the old law *(ac ne hæres quidem potest institui postumus alienus, est enim incerta persona,* Gai. Inst. ii, § 242) in the single case of the death of a *paterfamilias* putting a child only conceived in the position of heir, is copied in the Institutes from *Gaius* (Inst. i, § 147), and under this rule the position of a posthumous child would be—(1) that to protect his interests he was considered as already born, but (2) as against a person dead before his birth, he was only considered as already born, relatively to the chief whose heir he would be. Under Justinian's legislation, posthumous children could receive gifts by testament from any one, and in respect of their rights they were deemed already born as against all the world (*post,* par. 697, 907).

184. If the father appointed a tutor by will to a child, in respect of whom he had not strictly the power, the appointment would be confirmed by the magistrate without inquiry, and the term *liberi* (but not *filii*) was held to include posthumous children.

Tit. xiv. Qui testamento tutores dari possunt.

185. The tutor must be a person *cum quo testamenti factio est* (part i, par. 185 (3). *Women* could not be tutors, except in the case of their own children by the emperor's special permission, for it was a *public* office, and hence a *slave* could not hold it, though if the testator appointed one of his own slaves he thereby became *free* and *tutor,* and ultimately the opinion of *Paul* was confirmed, and *libertatis et pupillorum favore* the slave of another appointed tutor was to be *freed* for the purpose by the heir by *fidei-commissum.*

Soldiers or uncertain persons could not be appointed, but an *insane* person or a *minor* under twenty-five years could hold the tutorship *after* the first became sane or the second attained full age.

191. The appointment was valid, whether given simply *(pure)*, or to a certain time *(ad certum tempus, ad diem)*, or from a certain time *(ex certo tempore, a die)*, or under a condition *(sub conditione)*; hence, in respect of tutorships, a deceased person could be partly testate and partly not—a condition never allowed in respect of the succession to an inheritance, and the opinion of *Labeo* and *Proculus* was confirmed by Justinian, that the appointment might even be before the institution of the heir *(post,* par. 715), but the tutorship could not, in any case, according to Justinian, be restricted to a special thing or affair, although several tutors might be appointed, and the management of the property divided between them, as where parts were separated by long distances.

Tit. xv.   De legitima agnatorum tutela.

193. In default of a *testamentary* tutor, the *law, i.e.,* in particular the twelve tables (v. 6), made the nearest *agnate* the *legitimus* tutor, rather as a family right depending on *agnatio* and *gens*, and accorded to the nearest relatives, in consequence of their interest in the property in the event of the pupil's death, than as a means of protecting the infant ward. There might be several agnate tutors, if they were all of the same degree, and hence the rules were similar to those in succession *(ubi emolumentum successionis, ibi et onus tutelæ)*, but the tutor and the presumptive heir were not necessarily the same person, for an agnate heir, if impubes, deaf and dumb, or a woman, etc., could not be tutor, and the nearest agnate might be tutor, and yet not be presumptive heir, as where the testator named an heir to his *impubes* son *(post,* par. 749).

Agnates, i.e., those related through the male sex by reason of marriage, legitimation, or adoption, and *in* the family (part ii, par. 64), became tutors when—

(1) The paterfamilias died *intestate* or *without* appointing a tutor by will.

(2) The tutor named died before the testator.

(3) The testamentary tutor died or lost the rights of citizenship before the puberty of the pupil.

(4) The time of the testamentary tutor expired or the condition was not fulfilled.

Tit. xvi.   De capitis deminutione.

197. This subject is introduced here in order to show its effect on agnation and cognation.

Capitis deminutio is defined as *prioris status mutatio*, and *capitis deminutio* is a more ancient expression than *status permutatio*, though both mean the same thing, viz., a change due to the loss of one of the three elements of citizenship, see part. ii, par. 24, 70.

204. (§ i) *Maxima capitis deminutio* resulted from condemnations such as—

(1) *Servi pœnæ (ante,* par. 160).

(2) For ingratitude to patron, *ante,* par. 67 (1).

BOOK I—TIT. XVI.

(3) For fraudulent sale *ad pretium participandum, ante,* par. 44 (7).

205. (§ ii) *Media c.d.* resulted from—

(1) *Interdiction* of fire and water, see *ante*, par. 159. This mode of punishment indirectly attained the end, by compelling self-banishment at a time when a citizen could not be deprived of his liberty or civitas against his will (part i, par. 272), but this method was replaced by

(2) *Deportation*, confining the condemned person to a fixed place, which he could not leave under pain of death.

As he who was deprived of either liberty or citizenship lost his civil law *persona*, and hence ceased to be inscribed in the *census*, the expression *capitales*, in respect of accusations, included not only those entailing loss of life, but also those menacing these two rights, and on this account both *maxima* and *media c.d.* are compared to death.

206. (§ iii) The *minima c.d.* resulted from—

(1) *Arrogation (ante,* par. 132, 136), whereby a person *paterfamilias* and *sui juris* became *alieni juris*, and all those at the time in the power of the arrogated person also suffered the *minima c.d.*

(2) *Adoption*, which under the ancient method *(ante,* par. 132, 2) entailed a *minima c.d.* at each mancipation.

(3) *Emancipation*, whereby a *filius-familias* became *sui juris*, and the *capitis deminutio* also took place here at each mancipation under the primitive method, *ante*, par. 166.

(4) *Mancipium* of free man *(ante,* par. 153), which did not exist in the time of Justinian, nor did any of the—

(5) Modes of passing a woman *in manu viri, ante,* par. 150.

208. Except in the case of *flamines diales* and *vestals (ante,* par. 162) every *family* change caused a *minima capitis deminutio*, for a *new persona* arose extinguishing the former; and the effect of leaving the family or losing the rights attaching to it may be divided under the heads of—

(1) *Sacred law.* Loss of the *sacra privata*, and their extinguishment in the case of a *paterfamilias* being the only representative of a house, *ante,* par. 132 (1).

(2) *Private law.* Change of *persona* and rights of inheritance, loss of agnation and *gens* (though the *cognate* ties of blood, apart from the civil rights attaching to them, subsisted), loss of patronage, either by the *c. d.* of freedman or patron, testament *irritum (post,* par. 677), property and debts due gone, usufruct and other personal rights extinct, creditors ceased to have a debtor, and civil obligations became natural, though the rights attaching to the natural person subsisted (as *e.g.,* the obligation arising from a delict, or the necessity of providing an ascendant with food), but as to the method of obviating these inconveniences introduced by the prætor, see *post,* par. 1145, etc.

(3) *Public law.* The person suffering *c. d.* passed into another chapter of the *census*, and therefore possibly into another class

(part i, par. 55, 56), and it is in relation to this transference of a person from one *caput* of the *census* to another, that *Niebuhr*, followed by *Savigny*, uses the word *deminutio*.

214. (§ iv) A *slave* on being freed did not suffer *c. d.*, because in a legal sense he had no *caput (Servile caput nullum jus habet, ideo nec minui potest*, Dig. 4, 5, 3, 1, Paul).

215. (§ v) *Dignities* acquired or lost *(e.g.*, a senator excluded from the senate) did not affect the *status*, and therefore no *c. d.* resulted.

216. (§ vi) All *three c.d.* destroyed *agnation* and the rights attaching to it, and *maxima* and *media c.d.* destroyed the rights of *cognation*, hence a person enslaved lost all agnate and cognate rights, and never recovered them, for on being freed he commenced a new *persona* and entered a new family, and the same effect resulted from *deportation*, unless restored *in integrum (ante*, par. 159).

Tit. xvii. De legitima patronorum tutela.

218. A slave freed under the age of puberty could not have a testamentary tutor, for he would not be in the testator's power, and he had no agnate, but as the twelve tables (v, 8) gave the patron, and then his children, the rights of inheritance, on the ground that they were the only members of a civil family that the freedman possessed, therefore by *analogy* the tutorship was given to the same persons, and hence called *legal*.

Tit. xviii. De legitima parentum tutela.

219. *Tutelæ fiduciariæ* were so called because they resulted from the *contracta fiducia (ante*, par. 166), by which, after the simulated mancipation, the fictitious purchaser was compelled either himself to free the child under the age of puberty or to remancipate him to the father for the same purpose. Hence the *tutela* might fall to either—

(1) The fictitious purchaser, who in execution of the *fiducia* had himself freed the child,

(2) The father emancipator (or, after his death, his children, see tit. xix), when the child had been remancipated to him.

Under Justinian, the first did not exist, and as to the second class, in order that the *father* or ancestor might not have less honour than a patron (whom now the father resembled), he was always called *legitimus* instead of *fiduciarius tutor*, so that the latter title was finally only retained by the *children* of the father emancipator.

Tit. xix. De fiduciaria tutela.

221. When the father (or ancestor) emancipator *(ante*, par. 219, 2) died, those of his children who were over twenty-five became as the agnate relations of the emancipated child, *fiduciarii tutores, e.g.*, if a grandfather emancipated his grandson and died, the son became the *fiduciarius tutor* of his own child.

222. *Legitimi tutores (post*, par. 230). If the term is used in its extended sense, it included all the classes called by law, and to hold

such a *legitima tutela*, the rules were more strict than in the case of the *testamentary* tutor *(ante,* par. 185), for the person must be over twenty-five years of age, and not insane, deaf, or dumb, otherwise he was passed over in favour of the next *legal* tutor. This system existed at the time of the Institutes, but when Justinian in A.D. 544 (Novel 118, c. 5, *post*, par. 1143) introduced a new order of succession, determined by the degree of relationship, without distinguishing agnates from cognates, the same change was effected in the subject of tutorships, though *women*, except the mother or ancestress *(ante,* par. 185), were still excluded.

Tit. xx. De Atiliano tutore, et eo qui ex lege Julia et Titia dabatur.

224. *Tutela a magistratibus data.* It was not within the general powers of a magistrate to appoint tutors, but under the *lex Atilia* (probably in existence prior to B.C. 196) at *Rome*, the prætors and a majority of the tribunes *(i.e.,* at least six out of ten), and under the *lex Julia et Titia* (? B.C. 30) in the *provinces,* the præsides received special authority in this matter.

225. The *Atilianus* or *Juliotitianus* tutor would be given when—
  (1) There was no tutor at all.
  (2) Testamentary tutorship suspended or interrupted *(ante,* par. 191), or during the captivity of such tutor, or his term of office expired, or
  (3) Declined or deprived of the office.

226. (§ iii) Under *Claudius,* the power of appointing tutors was given to the consuls, but under *Antoninus Pius,* transferred to the prætors. Under *Justinian,* at Constantinople, the city præfect or the prætor undertook the duty, according as the position of the ward brought him under the jurisdiction of the one or the other. In the provinces, the duty was performed after inquiry *(ex inquisitione)* by the præsides, but if the fortune of the ward did not exceed 500 solidi, *i.e.,* about £480, the *defensores civitatum* (part i, par. 579), together with the bishop and the magistrates or judge of Alexandria, were able to appoint tutors and curators *(post,* par. 267) without inquiry, but with security.

230. (§ vi) The theory of the tutorship is said to be derived from *natural* law (Gai. Inst. i, § 189), but with the Romans it (like the *justæ nuptiæ)* was restricted to citizens, and depended on the rules of the civil law. The Institutes appear to divide the *tutela* into four kinds, viz :—
  (1) *Testamentaria (ante,* par. 182).
  (2) *Legitima (ante,* par. 222), *i.e.* (1) agnates ; (2) gentiles ; (3) patron and his children, and by courtesy only ; (4) the father emancipator.
  (3) *Fiduciaria (ante,* par. 221).
  (4) *Magistratibus data* (ante, par. 224).

231. *The administration of tutors.* Except in urgent cases, the formalities before taking office were—

(1) To find security, unless dispensed with *(post*, par. 275).

(2) To make an inventory, unless dispensed with by testator.

After this was done, the tutor must proceed to administer the estate, and was responsible for the consequences of any delay *(post*, par. 288).

232. When there were several tutors, the tutorship was given to—

(1) The tutor who voluntarily offered to give security when not compelled to do so *(post*, par. 275), and the other tutors were then obliged either to accept him or to place themselves on an equality by giving security also, or to

(2) The tutor named by the testator to act, or to

(3) The tutor named by a majority of themselves (in which case the rest were as *honorarii tutores*, only responsible to the extent of watching the conduct of the acting tutor), or to

(4) *All* the tutors in common, when they would not agree to the one appointed by the magistrate (in which case the act of each, in the absence of fraud, was valid, but the responsibility was common), or the tutorship was

(5) *Divided between them* by the desire of the testator or the act of the magistrate, each tutor taking a part or a district, and the responsibility was also divided.

233. *Duties of the tutor.* In respect of the *person* of the pupil, the tutor was bound to see to his education and maintenance, in accordance with his rank and fortune. In respect of the *property*, he was bound to use *quantum in rebus suis diligentia*, and was responsible for fraud and fault. Animals and things liable to spoil must be sold, debts collected (including his own, if any due to the father), and creditors (including himself if so) paid, he must receive all the rents, place money out at interest, otherwise he himself would be liable for the customary rate, and if he used any of the pupil's money for his own profit, he was debited with the highest legal rate of interest *(centesimæ usuræ, i.e.*, 12 per cent). He must also act as plaintiff or defendant in any action brought by or against the pupil.

234. *Nature of the tutor's powers.* The tutor did not represent the *persona* of the pupil; he either acted in his own name, without the pupil as a *manager (negotia gerere)*, or he joined himself to the pupil, who acted himself *(auctoritatem interponere)*.

In early times, all those acts of the *civil* law requiring prescribed words and solemnities could *not* be performed at all whilst the pupil was *infans* (part ii, par. 86), but *after* that age the pupil pronounced the words, and the tutor did what else was requisite. Acts of this class would be—(1) those performed in the *comitia* (arrogation, testament); (2) *legis actiones*; (3) fictitious actions *(in jure cessio*, manumission, adoption); (4) mancipation and emancipation; (5) testament *per æs et libram*; (6) stipulation and acceptilation; (7) *cretio*; (8) *aditio hereditatis* (but see below).

In respect of contracts and acts of the *jus gentium* (part ii, par. 161), agents were early employed (though they contracted in their own names, and were themselves bound as well as their principal), and the tutor, therefore, could act as agent by himself or authorise the pupil to do so. Subsequently, when under the formulary procedure, the employment of an agent was permitted, the tutor could conduct the cause in his own name (*suscipere judicium*) or in that of his pupil, and also make the *aditio hereditatis* whilst the pupil was *infans*.

Tit. xxi. De auctoritate tutorum.

241. The word *auctor* was employed from very early times in various ways, *e.g.*, *auctor*, the vendor, promissor, etc., *auctor secundus*, the fidejussor, *auctoritas*, the guarantee against eviction, the action given for the purpose and the right itself, the decision of the senate, the power of the magistrate, etc., and the terms *auctor fieri*, *auctoritatem præstare* were technically used from the date of the twelve tables to indicate the intervention of the tutor in the way of filling up the *persona* of the pupil.

244. The pupil could, *without* the *auctoritas* of the tutor, render his condition better but not worse, and therefore he could bind others towards himself, and stipulate but not promise, these rules being based on the principle that *aliquem intellectum* sufficed for the first, whilst *animi judicium* was required for the second. Hence, in *reciprocal* obligations, such as *emptio-venditio, locatio-conductio, mandatum*, and *depositum*, the other contracting party was bound, but not the pupil, except to the extent he had been actually benefited, and if the tutor vindicated a thing so parted with, he would have to refund all monies paid, which had not been squandered or otherwise turned to bad account by the pupil.

246. (§ i) The pupil could *not*, in any event, without the *auctoritas* of the tutor, perform the following acts :—

(1) *Adire hereditatem.*
(2) *Petere bonorum possessionem.*
(3) *Hereditatem ex fidei-commisso suscipere—*

for he would be compelled to pay the debts of the deceased, and be put under an obligation, and it was immaterial that the act was clearly advantageous, because (1) *animi judicium* was required to discern this, and (2) the transaction was incapable of decomposition into two parts (as in the case of reciprocal obligations), viz., (α) that part requiring judgment which would be void, and (β) that part only requiring intelligence, and therefore valid.

247. (§ ii) The *auctoritas* of the tutor must be given at the time, simply and without any condition, approbation beforehand, or ratification afterwards, were alike of no avail. The formula used in early times was *auctor ne fis* ? *auctor fio*, but subsequently assistance and approval sufficed.

248. (§ iii) Pending an action between pupil and tutor, it was the custom to appoint another tutor (*tutor prætorius, prætorianus*), but Justinian substituted a *curator* to conduct the pupil's affairs during the existence of the suit.

Tit. xxii. Quibus modis tutela finitur.

250. The tutelage entirely ceased on the—

(1) Death or *puberty* of pupil. *Gaius* (Inst i, § 196) records the difference of opinion between the Proculeians and the Sabinians on the subject of the puberty of men, the former inclining to assume a fixed age, as had been always done in the case of women, and the latter viewing the question as one of fact. *Justinian* (Code 5, 60, 3) finally settled the point by deciding that men at fourteen and women at twelve years of age should be *freed from tutelage*, and be able to marry and make a will, see part ii, par. 86 (3).

(2) *Maxima, med.* or *min. c.d.* of pupil, whether resulting from arrogation or deportation (which latter was possible above the age of seven years, because the child being then *pubertati proximus* could be *doli capax*), or slavery (*e. g.*, for ingratitude towards patron), or captivity. The causes terminating the tutelage in respect of the *tutor* only would be

(1) Death of tutor.

(2) *Max.* or *med. c. d.* and in the case of the *legitimi tutores*, derived directly or indirectly from the twelve tables, the *minima c. d.* also, because family and *potestas* rights were thereby destroyed.

(3) Captivity, during which the tutorship really only suspended.

(4) The term of the testamentary tutor ended, or the condition fulfilled.

(5) Removal on suspicion, or released on legitimate excuse.

254. *The perpetual tutelage of women* was a result of the political constitution of the family and of the rights of agnation, and *Gaius* (Inst. i, § 190), from whom the information on the subject is mainly derived, remarks on the irrationality of the system and on the absurdity of assuming its existence to be *propter animi levitatem*.

A tutor could be appointed to a woman *sui juris* (part ii, par. 84) by—

(1) *Testament* (*ante*, par. 182) by the *paterfamilias* to his daughter or granddaughter, by the father-in-law to the wife placed *in manu filii* (as to a granddaughter), by the husband to the wife he had *in manu* (as a daughter), and in this case the wife might have the right (*tutoris optio*) of choosing the tutor herself (*Titiæ uxori meæ tutoris optionem do*, Gai. Inst. i, § 150), and hence this kind of tutor was called *tutor optivus*.

(2) *Law.* Owing to the perpetual and therefore onerous nature of the tutelage, *legitimi* tutors (*ante*, par. 193) could transfer their duties to others by the *in jure cessio* process before a magistrate, and the new tutor was called *cessicius tutor*, but the tutorship ceased on the death of the former, and if the latter died, the *legitimi* became tutors again. It was a doubtful question whether this privilege existed in the case of the *fiduciarius* tutor (*ante*, par. 219). The children of the patron of a *freed* woman were *legitimi* tutores, although they were under the age of puberty, and therefore could not give the *auctoritas* (Gai. Inst. i, § 1, 79).

(3) The *magistrate*. See the *lex Atilia*, ante, par. 224.

The *termination* of the tutelage might result from loss of liberty, citizenship, or from the woman becoming *alieni juris* (*e. g.*, passing *in manu*); and *vestal* virgins were altogether free from tutelage by the twelve tables (v. i).

The rigorous nature of the system softened even under the Republic, tutors were only required to give their *auctoritas* as a matter of form, and, if refused, it could be compelled by the prætor; but *legitimi tutores* (agnates, gentiles, patrons, and ascendant emancipators) retained their powers, and in some cases (as for the preservation of property) their *auctoritas* was indispensable; hence the introduction of the method of destroying the tutor's rights by the fictitious sale (*co-emptionem facere*, part i, par. 329) of the woman, with the consent of the *tutor legitimus*, to a third person, who freed her or resold her back to the tutor for the same purpose; in either case the person who ultimately freed her becoming a powerless and nominal (*fiduciarius*) tutor.

The *Lex Papia Poppæa* (part i, par. 369) to reward fecundity freed the *ingenua* with three children from even the *legitima tutela*, and the *libertina* under the same circumstances from the other kinds of tutelage, so that at that period there were some women free from all authority. The effect of the *lex Claudia* (? a *senatus consultum*) under Claudius, A.D. 45, was to leave only the tutorships of ascendants and patrons existing, in which state the law stood in the time of *Gaius* (Inst. i, § 157) and *Ulpian* (reg. xi, § 8), after which the perpetual tutelage of women fell into disuse, and had ceased to exist prior to the time of Constantine.

Tit. xxiii. De Curatoribus.

263. *Curators* were given to those who from particular and accidental causes were incapacitated from exercising their rights (part ii, par. 93, 95), and they gave their *consensus* to the acts of the adult, or carried on his affairs for him as agents. They may be classed as—

(1) *Legitimi*, resulting from the twelve tables (v, § 7), by which the *furiosus* (*i. e.*, a madman) and the *prodigus* (*i. e.*, a dissipator of the paternal goods descended *ab intestato*) were placed under the curatorship of their agnates or gentiles.

(2) *Honorarii*, or those resulting from the prætor's legislation, under which the urban præfect, the prætor, and the presidents, practically overrode the agnate curatorship, and gave curators, after inquiry, to the *prodigus* (a term extended to include also the dissipator of property descended *ex testamento*), to the freedman, the insane, the imbecile, the deaf and dumb, and those with perpetual infirmities.

265. The growth of the idea of protecting the interests of the minor may be traced thus :—

(1) The *lex Plætoria* (*Lætoria, Lectoria*), a *plebiscitum* in the second Punic war, alluded to by Plautus as the *lex Quinavicennaria*, (α) allowed any one to prosecute a person who had deceived a minor under twenty-five; (β) probably appointed curators in

cases of licentiousness or want of intelligence, and (γ) led to the special exception under the formulary system, *pro minore viginti-quinque annis circumscripto*.

(2) The *prætor* introduced the *restitutio in integrum* (*post*, par. 285).

(3). A constitution of *Marcus Aurelius* directed the appointment of curators, simply on the ground of the minor being under twenty-five years of age.

(4) A *senatus-consultum* under *Septimius Severus* prohibited, without special permission, the alienation or mortgage of the rural or suburban immovables of minors under twenty-five, even with the authority of their tutors or curators.

There were three periods during which (after the perpetual tutelage of women had ceased) a *curator* might be appointed to men or women—

(1) During tutorship for *impuberes* (*post*, par. 268, 272).
(2) From puberty to twenty-five years.
(3) Above twenty-five in the case of lunatics, prodigals, etc.

267. (§ i) Curators could not be appointed by will, but such an appointment would be confirmed by the prætor or the præses, and the same magistrates who were entrusted with the appointment of *tutors* also appointed curators (*ante*, par. 226).

268. (§ ii) A tutor, an adversary, or a debtor, had the power of compelling an adult against his will to apply for a curator, by refusing to settle with him unless he did so, in the case of—

(1) The accounts of the tutor.
(2) A lawsuit.
(3) Payment of a debt.

The retiring tutor was responsible if he did not recommend a curator to be taken, and on the application of the pupil a curator was then appointed, who remained with him until the age of twenty-five, but after twenty in the case of men, and eighteen in the case of women, a dispensation might be obtained from the emperor (*ætatis venia*) when the minor was treated as if he or she had attained twenty-five, but rule 4, par. 265 still applied.

271. (§ iv) Justinian decided (Code 5, 70, 6) that during lucid intervals the aid of the curator was not necessary, but that his office continued to exist in case of need.

272. (§ v) Curators might be appointed during the interval a tutor was excused, or to assist unskilful tutors and those unsuited to the duties required.

If the tutor was incapacitated by illness or other similar cause from carrying on the tutorship, and the pupil was absent or an infant, the prætor or the præses would appoint an agent (*actor*, not to be confounded with the *curator*) at the risk of the tutor, but if the pupil were present, or over the age of *infans*, he could appoint one himself with the aid of the *auctoritas* of the tutor.

274. The *cura* terminated with the cause for which it was established, viz. :—

(1) At puberty when given in tutelage.
(2) In the case of adults at twenty-five, or after the *venia ætatis*.
(3) In the case of lunatics when cured.
(4) In the case of prodigals, when the interdict was withdrawn.
(5) On the conclusion of a special matter.

Tit. xxiv. De satisdatione tutorum vel curatorum.

275. Testamentary tutors and those appointed after inquiry were not obliged to give security *(ante,* par. 231), nor was it usual to exact it from the patron or father, but both *tutors and curators* falling under the class of the *legitimi* and those appointed by the inferior magistrates of cities were obliged to give *satisdatio* by *fidejussores (post,* par. 1392). The form of the stipulation belonging to the class *communes (post,* par. 1313) would be *Promittis-ne rem pupilli salvam fore?* and the question would be put (1) by the pupil or adult himself if present and able to speak, otherwise by (2) one of his slaves, or by (3) a public slave or person designated by the prætor. The tutor answered *promitto,* and then one or more of the guarantors replied to the question : *Fidejubes-ne rem pupilli salvam fore? fidejubeo.*

277. If the *satisdatio* were not forthcoming, recourse could be had to the property of the tutor or curator, over the whole of which a tacit *mortgage* was held to exist.

278. As a last resource *(ultimum subsidium),* an action *(subsidiaria actio)* lay against the *magistrates* (and in the event of gross negligence on their part, against their *heirs* also) who had neglected to compel the giving of *satisdatio,* or had accepted insufficient ; but the superior magistrates, such as the urban prefect, the prætor, and the præses, were not liable to be thus sued, because it was the duty of the inferior magistrates not only to see to the nature of the security offered, but to inquire into the fitness of the person they *proposed (nominare* as opposed to *dare)* to the præses for appointment as tutor or curator.

Tit. xxv. De excusationibus tutorum vel curatorum.

280. The *tutela* and *cura* were public burdens, in the sense that every citizen (except a soldier or a minor under twenty-five) was liable to serve, but dispensations could be obtained if applied for to the magistrate of lowest jurisdiction (from whose decision an appeal lay to a higher court) within a period varying with the distance, and amounting to 50 days for 400 miles or less, and one day for every 20 miles over.

The excuses admissible by law were :—

(1) By the *lex Papia Poppæa* three children living at Rome, four in Italy, and five in the provinces. (This is so stated in the Institutes, though at that time Rome and Italy were in the hands of the Ostrogoths, part i, par. 369, 479, 526). Children were counted who had died in battle, and those adopted were reckoned in favour of the natural father.

(2) That engaged in the administration of the *fiscus*.

(3) That absent in the service of the state (when a curator was temporarily appointed), and though bound to re-assume the burden immediately on return, an exemption for the space of one year could be claimed in respect of new guardianships.

(4) That invested with some public charge.

(5) That a suit was pending between the parties in respect of the whole inheritance, and Justinian, subsequently to the Institutes, by Novel 72, c. 1, decided that the fact of being a debtor or creditor of the ward sufficed.

(6) Three unsought guardianships.

(7) That poverty great, or health too bad, or not able to write, but the acceptance of the last excuse was discretionary with the magistrate.

(8) That the person who made the appointment by testament did it out of enmity to impose a burden, but this excuse was not admissible if the person charged had promised the testator to undertake it, and that the person was unknown to the testator was not a valid excuse.

(9) Deadly hatred *(inimicitiæ capitales)* between the father of the pupil and the person appointed.

(10) That the father of the pupil had disputed the status of the person charged, *e.g.*, brought an action to prove him to be a slave.

(11) That 70 years of age.

(12) That was at Rome a grammarian, rhetorician, or physician, or that elsewhere was included in the fixed number exempted.

282. A *freedman* could not excuse himself from the *tutela* or *cura* of his patron's children; but persons who had acted as tutors could not be compelled to act as curators to the same wards, and as the husband could not, for fear of undue influence, be the curator to his wife, so the curator of a woman could not marry her.

A false excuse, though accepted, did not release the person from the burden, and hence in favour of pupils an exception was made to the rule *res judicata pro veritate accipitur*.

The method of claiming exemption by pointing out a more fit person to the magistrate *(tutorem potiorem nominare)* had fallen into disuse prior to Justinian.

284. *Actions in respect of the tutela and cura.* On the expiration of the tutorship there were three actions available, of which one of the two first (not both) was open to the ward, viz.:—

(1) *Actio directa tutelæ* (or *judicium, arbitrium*) given to the pupil or his heirs against the tutor or his heirs for an account including frauds, mistakes, and negligence.

(2) *Actio de distrahendis rationibus* for the pupil against the tutor (only) in respect of some abstraction from the trust estate. Both these actions entailed the penalties of *infamy*, though only in the first if *fraud* was proved.

(3) *Actio contraria tutela* for the tutor against the pupil to obtain an indemnity for advances and obligations incurred.

The word *contraria* here refers to the accessory action resulting from the particular circumstances, as opposed to *directa, i.e.*, the principal action resulting directly from the contract or fact.

285. In respect of the *cura* the actions were :—

(1) *Actio utilis negotiorum gestorum*, which could be brought at any time by the ward against the *curator*, to compel him to render an account.

(2) *Actio contraria utilis negotiorum gestorum*, for the curator to recover advances made on behalf of his ward.

Here the word *utilis* implies an action introduced by prætorian equity in analogy to a *directa, i.e.*, a civil law action, and the action was utilis, because the position of the curator somewhat differed from that to which the *actio directa negotiorum gestorum* applied, for the latter action only lay against him who had *voluntarily* and *without the knowledge* of the owner undertaken his affairs.

The *restitutio in integrum* was applicable to both the *tutela* and *cura*, and when the loss was sufficiently great it was given after inquiry by the prætor against the strict law to the minor under twenty-five, who, with or without the *auctoritas* of the tutor or the *consensus* of the curator, had suffered loss.

286. Other actions were :—

(1) *Ex stipulatu* against those acting as guarantors of tutors or curators, *ante*, par. 275.

(2) *Subsidiaria, ante*, par. 278.

(3) *Suspecti cognitio, post*, par. 287.

Tit. xxvi. De suspectis tutoribus vel curatoribus.

287. The *cognitio* or proceeding by way of accusation for the removal of all suspected tutors or curators, whether they had given *satisdatio* or not, was derived from the twelve tables (viii, 20). It could only be preferred before or during the existence of the *tutela* or *cura*, and, being intended to protect the private interests of the ward, it belonged to the *civil* jurisdiction of the prætor at Rome, and the præses or *legatus pro-consulis* in the provinces, thóugh it approached in its nature a *criminal* trial, because it was not preceded by the demand for a judge, and could be brought by any one, including *women* (if nearly related or obviously impelled by affection), and hence called *quasi publica*.

Impuberes could not accuse their tutors, though adults, with the advice of their relations, might their curators. *Infamia* resulted if removed for *fraud*, though not for fault, and if the action was brought against an ascendant or patron, his reputation could not be attacked *(famæ parcendum)*, though he might be removed or a curator associated with him.

During the inquiry, the administration was stopped, and if in the meanwhile the tutor or curator died, or the *tutela* or *cura* expired, the accusation fell to the ground.

288. The allowance for the support of the ward might be fixed by testament or by the magistrate, but if not, and the tutor wilfully absented himself, the pupil could bring this accusation, have possession of the property given him, a curator appointed, the amount of the deterioration of any goods ascertained by sale, and the tutor charged with the liability. The urban prefect, as a *criminal* judge, punished the tutor who made false statements as to the poverty of the pupil, or the tutor who had purchased the duty by bribing the prætor's officials, as also the freedman, who, as tutor, fraudulently managed the affairs of his patron's children; and bad moral conduct was ground for the removal of a tutor or curator, though mere poverty was not.

ABSTRACT OF BOOK I.

Of Law and Justice.

Jus, from *jussum* in its primitive conception, is the *præceptum commune* or rule generally and rigorously prescribed, but this material idea was subsequently spiritualised, and the law was said to be the *ars boni et æqui*, though this definition, besides confounding positive law and morality, does not explain the meaning of *æquum*. Theoretically, law is a conception of human reasoning, deduced from the relations of man to man, through which one has the power of requiring action or inaction from another.

Justitia was defined by the Romans as the will always to observe the law, *Jurisprudentia* as the knowledge of the law, and the *Jurispræcepta* were *honeste vivere, alterum non lædere, suum cuique tribuere*.

Divisions of Law.

Law is divided into (1) *international*; (2) *public*; (3) *private*, and the latter—

(1) As to *origin* into (α) *jus naturale*; (β) *jus gentium*; (γ) *jus civile*, but α in its improper sense is excluded from the domain of law, and in its proper sense is included in β.

(2) As to *form* into (α) *scriptum, i.e.*, introduced by the express will of the legislator whether as *jus civile* (*lex, plebiscitum, senatusconsultum, constitutiones principum*) or *jus prætorium* (*edicta magistratuum, responsa prudentium*); (β) *non scriptum, i.e.*, resulting from usage and tacit consent of legislator.

(3) As to *objects*, private law is concerned with *persons, things, actions*.

Of persons.

The term *persona* (mask) may include—

(1) Every being capable of having or being subject to rights, or in a narrower sense—

(2) Each quality, in virtue of which a person has certain rights and obligations.

The remainder of the first book is concerned with a review of *persons* in their different relations—

(1) In respect of *society* generally, as to which an individual stood in the position of (α) *free* or *slave*; (β) *citizen* or *alien*; (γ) *freeborn* or *freed*.

(2) In respect of *family*, in which he might be (α) *sui juris;* (β) *alieni juris*.

(3) In respect of *capacity* or *incapacity*, involving as to those *sui juris* the rules relating to (α) tutelage; (β) curatorship.

In respect of Society. The definitions of *libertas* and *servitus* show that the *freeman* has the right to do everything except what the law forbids, the *slave* nothing but what the law allows.

Slaves are so (1) by the *jus gentium (ex captivitate);* (2) by *birth (ex ancillis nostris);* (3) by *law (punishment)*.

The *ingenuus* is he who has been free from birth, the *libertinus* he who has ceased to be a slave.

Subject to exceptions, the status of a child—

(1) In legal marriage follows condition of father at conception of child.

(2) Out of legal marriage, according to condition of mother at birth of child, but ultimately, in favour of liberty, the child is free if the mother were so at any time during gestation.

Under *Justinian* it is immaterial whether a slave is freed—

(1) Publicly *(vindicta, testamento, in ecclesia)*, or

(2) Privately *(inter amicos,* by letter, by codicil, etc.)

Under *Augustus* and *Tiberius*, laws were passed limiting the power of enfranchisement, viz. :

(1) *Lex Ælia Sentia,* by which (α) enfranchisement of a slave under thirty is forbidden, except by *vindicta,* with approbation of council; (β) the class of *dediticii* created; (γ) freedom in fraud of creditors prohibited; (δ) master under twenty unable to free slave, except by *vindicta,* with approval of council. *Justinian* repealed (α) and (β), but as to (δ) the age of the master at which he was able to free, *ex testamento,* was finally reduced to fourteen.

(2) *Lex Furia Caninia,* limiting the number freed by will, but repealed by Justinian.

(3) *Lex Junia Norbana,* establishing a third class of freedmen, the *latini juniani,* but the effect of *Justinian's* legislation was to repeal this law, and leave no distinction between the *ingenui* and the *libertini,* except the rights of patronage (α) *obsequia*; (β) *operæ*; (γ) *succession*.

The *statu-liber* was a freed slave whose liberty was suspended for a term or subject to a condition.

In respect of family. The word itself either means in a narrow sense a single house, *i.e.*, the head and all the persons under him, or in a wider sense it includes the several houses having a common origin, and descending from a common head.

The *paterfamilias* and the *materfamilias* are the only persons *sui juris*, but the latter has no *potestas*. Persons *alieni juris* were (1) *in potestate*; (2) *in manu*; (3) *in mancipio*, but (2) and (3) had ceased to exist prior to Justinian.

The *potestas* means the power of the head of the household over—

(1) *Slaves*, in respect of whose (α) *persons*, their position being that of things, they may be sold, given away, or left as a legacy, but the power of life and death was gradually reduced to reasonable limits, and as to whose (β) *property*, although altogether the master's, yet custom gave rights as to the *peculium*.

(2) *Children*, as to whose (α) *persons* the power of life and death and exposure was withdrawn, the right of simple domestic correction only being reserved, but the parent could sell his child at birth and in cases of great distress. As to (β) *property*, various kinds of *peculia* were gradually admitted.

The *patria potestas* was acquired by (1) lawful marriage; (2) legitimation of natural children; (3) adoption.

By *nuptiæ* was understood the union of the man and the woman, entailing the obligation of living together, *justæ nuptiæ* meant the marriage prescribed by the law, producing paternal power over sons and daughters and descendants of males. The requisites for this *justum matrimonium* were (1) *puberty*, fixed at twelve for women, fourteen for men; (2) *consent* of both and of paterfamilias, and in the case of a grandson, of the father also; (3) *connubium*, or the relative capacity to unite in marriage, the obstacles to which were (1) the fact of being an alien, and (2) relationship, whether arising from (α) *cognatio*, or natural ties; (β) *agnatio*, or civil ties, or (γ) affinity, *i.e.*, the bond established by marriage between the cognates of each side.

The *marriage* required no formality, *consent*, and *traditio* of the woman sufficing. The parties might be betrothed, but the marriage could not be enforced. The *dissolution* of the marriage might arise through (1) death; (2) loss of liberty or citizenship; (3) captivity; (4) divorce. The marriage contrary to law was null and void, the children *spurii*, the *dos* confiscated, and the law punished incest or bigamy.

The *concubinatus* was permitted, and opposed to unlawful intercourse called *stuprum*, whilst the term *contubernium* referred to the natural union of slaves.

Legitimation, with the consent (or non-opposition) of the children, drew after it the *patria potestas*, and might result from—

(1) Subsequent marriage of parents.

(2) Oblation to the *curiæ*, but the child did not enter the family, as he only acquired rights in respect of the father.

(3) Rescript of emperor.

(4) Testament, the last two methods were introduced by novels of *Justinian*.

Adoptions might result from—

(1) *Adrogation, principali rescripto*. The paterfamilias *sui juris*, with all his property and children, passed into the power of the arrogator. After *Antonine, impuberes* might, under certain conditions, be arrogated, and under *Justinian, women* also.

(2) *Adoption, imperio magistratus* of persons *alieni juris*. Under *Justinian*, if the adoptor was an *ascendant*, the *patria potestas* resulted, otherwise, the adoptee only acquired rights of succession *ab intestato*. If the person was adopted as a grandson with son living, the latter's consent required, and relationship, marriage, and family rights thereby affected.

It was an essential condition that the difference of age between the adoptor and adoptee should be equal to full puberty, and permission was difficult to obtain if adoptor less than sixty or had children.

Emancipation, or giving in adoption to another, dissolved the bond, which could not be renewed.

The *mancipium* was not in use, and the *manus* had ceased to exist under *Justinian*.

The *potestas* was dissolved in the case of a *slave* by enfranchisement, and in the case of a *son* by

(1) *Accidental events*, as the death of head of house, loss of liberty or citizenship by father or child, and if either in power of enemy, the *jus postliminii* suspended all rights.

(2) *Solemn acts*, as emancipation, and adoption also (in certain cases).

(3) *Attainment of dignities*, formerly reserved to *flamins* and *vestals*, but Justinian accorded the right to *patricii*, and to all whose rank freed them from the *curia*.

In respect of capacity or incapacity. The *tutela* and *cura* only concerned persons *sui juris*, and under *Justinian* the former only applied to *impuberes*.

Testamentaria tutela. The rules as to this were :—

(1) Given by will in virtue of the *patria potestas* of the *paterfamilias*.

(2) Applied to children *impuberes* and becoming *sui juris* by the testator's decease, including *postumi* in certain cases, and emancipated children if the appointment was confirmed by the magistrate.

(3) Only citizens having *factio testamenti* with the testator could be tutors, excluding women, slaves, insane, minors under twenty-five, but the three latter capable when free, sane, or over twenty-five.

(4) Appointment may be before or after institution of heir, and be pure and simple, or under a term or a condition. There may

be several tutors, but it cannot fall on an uncertain person or be for a special object.

Legitima tutela. This was given when the first was wanting or had ceased, and the term implied *generally* that it was given by *law*, but *specially* that it resulted from the twelve tables directly *(propalam)*, as in the case of *agnate* tutorship, or deduced therefrom *(per consequentiam)*, as in the case of the patron, the gentiles, and the manumittor of the person *in mancipio*.

(1) *Agnates.* These were called by the twelve tables, provided they were capable of holding it, and in the same order as in the case of succession. If several of the same degree, they held in common. In relation to this subject, the Institutes examine into the causes of the loss of *agnation* and *cognation*. The *status* of a Roman citizen consisted of (α) *libertas*; (β) *civitas*; (γ) *familia*; and these rights might be more or less affected by the three kinds of *deminutio capitis*. *Agnatio*, together with all rights attached to it, was destroyed by any *c.d.*, but not *cognatio*, as to which, however, the civil rights were destroyed by *maxima and media c.d.*

(2) *Patrons.* These and their children were indirectly called by the twelve tables on account of their rights of succession.

(3) *Fiduciary.* These were by analogy to the patron's rights, given in the case of emancipated children as the result of the *contracta fiducia*, but the father emancipator was out of respect called *legitimus*, and fictitious emancipation having ceased to exist prior to Justinian, the only tutorships under this head were those of the children of the father emancipator.

(4) *A magistratibus data.* These resulted from the *lex Atilia* and the *lex Julia* and *Titia*, and were given when there was no testamentary or legal tutor, or he was excused or deprived, or the tutorship was suspended or interrupted.

As to the *administration* of the tutor, he was bound, before entering on his duties, to give security, and to make an inventory. If there were several tutors, the duties may be given to one, to all in common, or divided between them.

The *auctoritas* of the tutor implied his active participation in the act, in order to complete the imperfect *persona* of the pupil, and it could not be given before or after. If the pupil was

(1) *Infans*, *i.e.*, unable to speak, the tutor acted in his own name as agent.

(2) *Infanti proximus*, *i.e.*, up to seven. The child having *nullum intellectum*, the tutor acted mostly as agent, but as the child could pronounce the solemn words, he might with or without the *auctoritas* of the tutor, according to circumstances, do acts eminently for his benefit, as in the case of the *stipulatio*, the *cretio*, the *aditio haereditatis*.

(3) *Pubertati proximus*, *i.e.*, over seven. The child having some intelligence but no judgment could only improve his condition, but not render it worse, and the tutor ought generally to make the pupil act with his *auctoritas*.

The *tutela* terminated with the puberty or any of the three *c.d.* of pupil, in respect of the tutor only by his death or *maxima or med. c.d.* (of legal tutors), or captivity (really only suspended), or the term or condition arrived, or on account of exemption or deprivation.

The *tutelage of women* was softened even under the republic. The *lex Papia Poppæa* freed women from it in certain cases. The *lex Claudia* freed them entirely from agnate tutorship, and though it existed in the time of *Gaius* and *Ulpian* there was no trace of it under the Eastern empire.

The *cura* might take place—

(1) During tutorship for *impuberes*.

(2) Between puberty and twenty-five for adults, but not against their will, except in the case of the tutor's accounts, an action or a payment.

(3) Above twenty-five in the case of the insane, idiots, prodigals, etc.

(1) and (3) were *legitimæ* and belonged of right to the *agnates*, or formerly, in default, to the *gentiles*. The other curators were given by the same magistrates as appointed the tutors. The curator was appointed to the *property* not to the person. He gave his *consensus* to the acts of the adult, or in case of necessity transacted the affairs as agent, and his office terminated with the cause for which it was established.

Security was given by tutors (except those appointed by will or after inquiry) and curators. The ward has a subsidiary action against the magistrate (and his heirs), if no security, or insufficient, obtained.

Excuses were admissible as grounds for exemption from this public duty, but they must be made to the magistrate within a fixed interval.

Actions arising out of the *tutela* and *cura* were :—

(1) *Tutelæ-directa* against tutor to render account, and *contraria* to enable tutor to recover advances.

(2) *De rationibus distrahendis* against tutor as to abstractions from patrimony.

(3) *Utilis negotiorum gestorum* against curator to obtain accounts, and *contraria* for curator to recover advances.

(4) *Ex stipulatu* against fidejussors, *subsidiaria* against magistrates, and *suspecti cognitio* for the removal of guardians, were all three common to the *tutela* or *cura*.

Minors under twenty-five, prejudiced in respect of a matter, valid according to strict law, could obtain, after *causa cognita*, a *restitutio in integrum*.

BOOK II.

Tit. i. De rerum divisione.

289. *Res.* In Roman law this term, in its original and positive sense, included all corporeal objects considered as under the power of, or at least destined for, man, and in its improper and figurative sense it also included all the rights which the law gives over those objects *(rei appellatione et causæ, et jura continentur.* Dig. 50, 16. 23, Ulpian, see part ii, par. 105 to 138). The jurisconsult studies this subject in order to determine, not the physical nature and properties of things, but the rights that man can have over them, though the latter question is often decided by the former.

292. *Of things at the time of the twelve tables.* It is not known whether the twelve tables contained an express division of things, but from the organisation of the pontiffs, the references in table ten to funeral matters, and the connection of the fable of the death of Remus with city walls, it would seem that the three subdivisions of *res divini juris,* viz., *sacræ, religiosæ,* and *sanctæ,* existed at this time, as also the classification of things into *publicæ* and *communia,* and although the distinction between *movables* and *immovables* never formed the precise basis of a division of things in Roman law, yet table six (3) shows the distinction in force.

293. *Ownership at the time of the twelve tables.* Only one kind of *dominium* existed, viz., that known subsequently as *ex jure Quiritium.* It was exclusively reserved for the citizen who was called *dominus legitimus,* see part ii, par. 121, 226.

294. *Manner of acquiring and transmitting ownership.* Though only one kind of ownership existed at the time of the twelve tables, this *dominium* could be acquired by *natural* as well as civil methods, for the *occupatio* of booty or slaves taken from an enemy gave ownership *ex jure Quiritium.* See in part i, the head note to table vi, and part ii, par. 229.

302. *Of things at the time of Gaius and Ulpian.* Gaius (Inst. ii, § 2) makes a preliminary division, derived from the twelve tables, of things into *divini* and *humani juris,* the former comprehending *res sacræ, religiosæ,* and *sanctæ,* the latter *res publicæ* and *privatæ.* The soil is also distinguished into *Italian* and *provincial.* Of the latter, some belongs to the *provinciæ populi Romani,* and some to the *provinciæ Cæsaris,* and *dominium* cannot be acquired of this provincial soil except through the concession of the *jus Italicum.*

The second divison is into *corporeal* and *incorporeal,* and the third into *mancipi* and *nec mancipi,* as to which latter see *Ulpian's* list, given in part ii, par. 121.

307. *Ownership at the time of Gaius and Ulpian.* Gaius (Inst. ii, § 40) states that in the case of strangers, as formerly with the

Romans, only one kind of ownership existed, but that a second kind, *in bonis habere*, had been introduced. The date when this mode of holding property came into use is uncertain, but it probably resulted from the employment of the rules of the *jus gentium* after the conquest of Italy, see part ii, par. 226. The effect of this distinction was that the holder *in bonis* would be able to use the thing, take the produce, and by the lapse of time acquire the *dominium ex jure Quiritium*, but in the interval the power of disposing of it or of vindicating it would be in him who held *ex jure Quiritium, e.g.*, if a master held a slave both *ex jure Quiritium* and *in bonis* he had (1) *dominica potestas*, and he could (2) free him, but if he held him only *in bonis* he had the *dominica potestas*, but could not free him except as a Latin. On the other hand, if he held him *only ex jure Quiritium*, he had neither the *dominica potestas* nor the power of freeing him, and the holder *in bonis* could defeat the attempt of the owner *ex jure Quiritium* to vindicate the slave, by the insertion in the formula of an equitable plea, as in the case cited in the Digest (21, 3) of a person who, not having had the ownership at the time, sells and delivers a thing without transferring the ownership (see *post*, par. 1444, etc.), and subsequently wishing to vindicate it, is met by the *exceptio rei venditæ et traditæ*.

312. *Manner of acquiring and transmitting ownership in time of Gaius and Ulpian.* If (1) a thing *mancipi* were received by mancipation (or by the other civil methods given below), or if (2) a thing *nec mancipi* were received by tradition, occupation, accession, or other natural but legal means, the *dominium ex jure Quiritium* would be acquired, but though formerly no effect would be produced at all, it now results from the existing legislation that if the first kind were transferred by a natural mode of acquisition *(e.g., traditio)* the property would be *in bonis* of the recipient.

The *civil* methods were, according to *Ulpian* (Reg. xix, § 2), five in number, viz. :—

(1) *Mancipatio* for *res mancipi* only, and restricted to Roman citizens, Latin colonists, Latin junians, and such aliens as possessed the *commercium* (see part i, par. 185). The solemn words were pronounced in the presence of the *libri pens*, and five witnesses (citizens and *puberes*). *Movables* must be brought into court, and only so much could be emancipated as could be seized with the hand, but *immovables* need not be produced, and several could be mancipated at one time. Although no legal effect beyond that involved in the *traditio* part of the transaction resulted, yet it is probable that the *mancipatio* process was sometimes gone through in respect of *res nec mancipi* (as in Pliny's example of rare pearls) for the sake of the advantage of the presence of witnesses and the additional solemnity.

(2) *Usucapio* (*capio usu*, acquisition by use, *i.e.*, possession) is the *usus auctoritas* of the twelve tables (vi, 3), and is defined by *Ulpian* as the *dominii adeptio per continuationem possessionis anni* (for movables) *vel biennii* (for immovables).

If (a) a thing *mancipi* or *nec mancipi* were received *bona fide* from a person, not the owner, or if (β) a thing *mancipi* were received by tradition, without the intervention of a legal method, the effect of *usucapio* would be to turn the mere possession in the one case, and the property *in bonis* in the second case, into *dominium ex jure Quiritium.* As *immovables* in the *provinces* did not enjoy civil rights, *usucapio* did not apply to them, but the edicts of the president gave prescriptive rights after a lapse of ten or twenty years, see *post*, par. 514.

Usureceptio, or recovering the ownership of property by *usus*, occurred when a thing had been handed over by the *mancipatio* or *in jure cessio* process, with *fiducia*, *i.e.*, an agreement as to its return, and the thing had again come into the possession of the owner for *one* year.

(3) *In jure cessio.* This process simulated a *vindicatio* action (part ii, par. 229), and applied to both *mancipi* and *nec mancipi* things. It required the presence of three persons, the owner or alienor *(in jure cedens)* the alienee or vindicator *(vindicans)*, the prætor or præses declaring the ownership *(addicens)*. The process was *in jure*, because there being no dispute the parties were not sent *in judicio*, and it was employed for *incorporeal* things, for which (except rural servitudes) *traditio* and *mancipatio* were inapplicable, *e.g.*, in the cases of usufruct, inheritance, legal tutorship, and liberty, so that the enfranchisement by *vindicta* was really this *in jure cessio* process, but *debts* could not be transferred by the *in jure cessio*, *traditio*, or *mancipatio* methods, as a *stipulatio* was required to effect novation (Gai. Inst. ii, § 38).

(4) *Adjudicatio.* This applied to both *mancipi* and *nec mancipi* things, and took place *in judicio* in the three cases of apportioning an inheritance, dividing common property and determining boundaries.

(5) *Lex.* As examples of this mode of acquisition, whether of *mancipi* or *nec mancipi* things, Ulpian cites the *legacy per vindicationem*, resulting from the twelve tables (v, 3), the *caducum* or legacy taken away by the lex *Papia Poppæa* from the legatee who was unmarried or without children and given to those with children (part i, par. 369), the *ereptorium* or the testamentary gift taken away on account of unworthiness and given by the law to another or to the fiscus.

322. *Of things according to the Institutes of Justinian.* The principal division of things is into those :—

(1) *Extra nostrum patrimonium*, and

(2) *In nostro patrimonio, i.e., res privatæ, res singulorum.*

As to the second class, see *post*, par. 342. The first class was subdivided into—

(1) *Res publicæ*, in the sense of things belonging to *no one in particular*, *i.e.*, not private, and including—

(a) *Res communes*, under which was included the *sea shore* (see part ii, par. 131), meaning that portion of land covered by the highest waves, and therefore the limit beyond which the territory of the empire did not extend. The *use* of the shore was free to all, as *e.g.*, to dry nets, etc. Fragments of the shore might be appropriated, and the constructions thrown out on piles into the sea belonged to those who raised them, but a decree of the prætor was required, and this was not given if public or private interests would be thereby prejudiced ; and if the construction was raised without permission, anybody thereby sustaining loss might claim an *utilis* interdict from the prætor, though the penalty might assume the form of damages or an annual rent, as, unless absolutely necessary, it was contrary to public policy to demolish such erections.

The property in the fragment of the *common* thing so appropriated ceased on the return of the thing to its original condition.

(β) *Res publicæ*, in the restricted or proper sense, included those things the *property* in which belonged to the people, but the *use* of which was common to all, and hence in respect of, *e.g.*, rivers and harbours, public roads, places, fields, lakes, ponds, etc., the prætor interdicted any impediment to navigation, embarkation, or debarkation, or any attempt to change the course of the water, and any constructions required the authority of the emperor, and must not prejudice the rights of others. In a different sense the term included those things in the hands of the state as slaves *populi Romani*, mines, the *ærarium*, and the *fiscus*.

The *banks* of a river belonged to the riparian proprietors, and they therefore had the right to take the fruits, cut the rushes, and fell trees, but not so as to prejudice the use of the river by the public. The public had the right to repose, etc., on the banks, but they would not be the owners of anything constructed there.

(γ) *Res universitatis*. *Universitas* meant any union of persons forming a corporation, a sort of legal person (see part ii, par. 99), and the property owned by such bodies consisted of two kinds (1) that which, although owned in common, was not placed at the disposition of each member, *e.g.*, money, debts, slaves ; (2) that which was for the common use of the members, and at times of strangers also, *e.g.*, racecourses, theatres, public baths.

(2) *Res nullius*, *i.e.*, things belonging to no one, and differing from *res communes*, in that they could become private property. They included—

(1) Those not in the power of man, or abandoned by him, *e.g.*, wild animals and their young, shell fish, seaweed, islands in the sea.

(2) Those withdrawn from man and called *res divini juris*, and subdivided (see part ii. par. 111) into :—

(*a*) *Sacræ*, which, previous to Constantine, were consecrated to the gods by pagan priests, and after that date to God, with Christian ceremonies. In either case, *private* consecration had no effect, and the dedication of the place or the building required in early times the authorization of the people, then of the senate, as representing them, and finally of the emperor. If the original building was destroyed, nothing else could be built upon the spot, because once consecrated it always remained so, and *res sacræ* could not have a value put upon them, or be sold, pledged, acquired by use, or be the subject of a stipulation. Sacrilege was severely punished, and might lead to condemnation to wild beasts, the mines, or deportation, and an interdict of the prætor protected the place from damage *(In loco sacro facere, inve eum immittere quid veto.* Dig. 43, 6, 1). Justinian prohibited the alienation of church property in the shape of *immovables* altogether, and of church plate, vestments, and other *movables*, except for the ransom of captives, or to provide food for the poor in the case of famine, or (in respect of superfluous plate) to pay the debts owing by the church. The bishop or other custodian could reclaim such property wherever found, as well as the remains of it, or its price if melted.

(β) *Religiosæ.* These could be made so by private individuals. In pagan times they were things abandoned to the *manes*, but under Justinian the term indicated the actual spot occupied by the body or ashes of a deceased person, so that the rules would not apply to an empty monument. A person must be the owner of the land he attempts to make *religiosus* by interment, otherwise the consent at the time or subsequently is necessary of the co-owner, usufructuary, or person having the usus or servitude, and the co-owner could compel the removal of the body by an *actio in factum*, but the co-owner would be liable to the *injuriarum actio* if he exhumed the bones without a pontifical decree or imperial authorization. The interdict of the prætor could be invoked, or the *actio in factum* used in aid of the rights of families and their heirs to bury or to be buried in family sepulchres. The remains could not be exhumed or the spot changed, even by the owner, without authorisation, and if so removed the place ceased to be religious, but whilst so occupied the place could not be sold, given away, or acquired by use. *Profanation* was punished (1) *civilly,* by the *(popularis) actio sepulchri violati* which could be brought by the person interested or in default by any citizen; the action entailed infamy and damages, the latter being fixed in the case of a person not interested in the tomb at 100 solidi; (2) *criminally,* by an accusation which might result in death, deportation, relegation, or the mines.

(γ) *Sanctæ.* These things were protected by an interdict of the prætor, and among them were included *laws* and *ambassadors*, whose persons had to be respected under penalty of being made a slave to the people they represented; and death was entailed by damaging, getting over, or putting ladders against walls, circumvallations, and gates.

342. *Of ownership in the time of Justinian.* The expression *dominium ex jure Quiritium* was abolished by Justinian (Code 7,

25, Const. Justin.) as having lost its distinctive signification, and the imperfect natural ownership, called *in bonis habere*, also vanished, so that one undivided kind of property was left, viz., *proprietas*, of which the rights are usually included under four heads (see part ii, par. 219), *e.g.*, the owner of a house had the right to live in it *(jus utendi)*, to let it and receive the rent *(jus fruendi)*, to sell it, give it away, demolish it *(jus abutendi)*, and as the sanction of the rest he had the right to reclaim it from a person unlawfully detaining it *(jus vindicandi)*. The *jus abutendi* is the essential element of ownership, as the others may only imply the right of using the property of another.

346. *Of possession.* *Physical* possession *(naturalis* or *corporalis possessio)* is a fact only, and consists in the actual detention or occupation of the thing, but is not without its influence on law, though independent of it. The *possessio* in the eye of the law *(civiliter possidere)* is not only a fact but a right *(possessio non tantum corporis sed juris est.*—Dig. 41, 2, 49, § 1, Papinian), and *intention* is of its essence, hence it consists of two elements :—

(1) The *fact*, not necessarily consisting in actual corporeal detention *(non est enim corpore et tactu necesse apprehendere possessionem, sed etiam oculis et affectu.*—Dig. 41, 1, 21, Paul), *e.g.*, handing over the keys of the warehouse containing the goods (to be done, however, near it, *apud horreum*), giving over an estate, a sack of money or other object, in the presence of it, and so possession by a tenant, mandatory, son, or slave, is in the eye of the law possession by the landlord, father, master, etc., *i.e.*, the fact of the thing being at the free disposition of the possessor, constitutes the first element of *legal* possession.

(2) The *intention*, *i.e.*, the will to hold as owner, the *animus dominii*, involving the *intellectus præsidendi*, so that a tenant, a borrower, a mandatory, a lunatic, a child, or a person asleep, may have *physical* possession, but, the *intention* being absent, there is not *legal* possession, though the intention is independent of good or bad faith.

He being the *possessor* in whose name others hold, there is but one kind of legal possession, and *Savigny's* threefold division (viz., possession (α) *natural, i.e.*, where no intention of holding as own exists ; (β) *prætorian, i.e.*, protected by recourse *ad interdicta* ; (γ) *civil, i.e.*, leading by *usucapio* to ownership), though useful for expressing with brevity these differences, is not a correct representation of Roman law, in which no such distinctions were expressly made.

The advantages to be derived from possession may be detached from one another, *e.g.*, the owner possesses legally the thing pledged, but he cannot get it back again without paying the debt, and of the rights of possession he only has that of acquiring by *usucapio*, the other rights having passed to the pledgee, to whom actions are available to protect his share of these rights. Possession involves :—

(1) The right to detain the thing until another is proved owner *(post,* par. 2306).
(2) The right to sue to preserve.
(3) The right to acquire the ownership of things *nullius,* or of things the owner wishes to part with.
(4) In certain cases to acquire the produce consumed, and at the end of a 'fixed period, the ownership of another's property.

Quasi possessio was introduced by equitable jurisprudence in respect of *incorporeal* objects, and consists in (1) the fact of having the power of exercising the right, and (2) the intention of exercising the right as owner.

354. *Of the means of acquiring possession and ownership under Justinian.* The Institutes (§§ xii to xviii) discuss the *natural* means of acquisition first, as being more ancient than the *civil* law methods.

Occupatio. Things belonging to no one are acquired by him who first gets them *(quod autem nullius est, naturali ratione occupanti conceditur),* a rule based on the fact of work done, and the right of property thus springs from possession. Two points only require determination.

(1) Did the thing capable of coming into the possession of man belong to no one? *i.e.,* fall under the head of *res nullius,* e.g., wild animals, deer, birds, and nests (and including peacocks and pigeons, but not farm chickens and geese), fishes, bees and their honey. All *movables* (not immovables) of an enemy that could be personally acquired, but the booty which was collected by a detached band would belong in common to all the army engaged. Things found in the sea or on the shore, *e.g.,* shells, pearls, precious stones, coral and islands springing up in the sea (not in rivers). Objects purposely abandoned by the owner, etc.

(2) *Has possession been acquired,* involving the *intention* and the *fact,* the latter depending on the nature of the case? It was immaterial whether force, cunning, education, or want, had brought the thing under the power of the possessor, *e.g.,* the lion in a cage, the fish in a tank, the bird with wings cut, the tame stag, taught to go and come back, the bees returning to hive, the pigeons to dove cot. The *place* also was immaterial for the chase, and the rights of fishing were free to all (the *injuriarum actio* lying for any impediment to these two rights in a public place), even on the land of another person, for the owner of the land was not owner of the animal, though the better opinion was that the owner of the land might forbid persons to come on his land, and could bring an action against trespassers who persisted in entering.

But the ownership only lasts with the possession, *i.e.,* the thing ceases to be possessed when it has returned to its natural state, and the bond was held to be severed when, though possibly still in sight, the pursuit was difficult, *e.g.,* if the lion broke his bars and escaped, the bird's wings grew and it flew away, the stag lost its tame habits and did not return, the bees left their hive, or the pigeons their cot;

and so the enemy who escaped ceased to be possessed after he had succeeded in returning to his own people; and stones, shells, etc., dropped in the sea, were gone, though, if they had fallen unperceived on the way, they still remained the property of the possessor. During the continuance of the possession, an *actio furti* lay to recover the thing stolen, but Justinian confirmed the opinion cited by *Gaius* (Dig. 41, 1, 5, 1) against Trebatius, that a wounded animal did not belong to the hunter until seized by him, so that another person obtaining possession of it would not be guilty of theft.

361. *Accessio.* This general term (including the special varieties falling under the heads of *alluvio, specificatio, adjunctio, confusio, commixtio,* etc.) was given by the commentators, followed by Italian, German, and French jurists, to another natural mode of acquisition, and refers to the property acquired in an accessory thing by the owner of the principal thing to which it is attached. As an expression covering a ruling principle, *accessio* does not belong to Roman law, any more than do the distinctions of *natural, artificial,* and *mixed* accession, according as nature, art, or both, had united the accessory to the principal; but this cause of acquisition existed in Roman law, and must be recognised in all systems, and the Roman jurisconsults collected different cases to which the principle applied.

The term is also used to indicate, not the fact of the union, but the accessory itself united as a subordinate thing to the principal, whether corporeal or incorporeal, *e.g.*, pledges, mortgages, fidejussors, etc., are referred to as *accessiones* to the principal obligation.

The laconic maxim of Ulpian, *accessio cedat principali,* indicates the rule which came to be universally applied in every disposition, in order to ascertain what objects were comprised in it, and the accessory was always included, unless expressly excepted, so that revocation as to the principal thing applied also to the accessory, and generally if the principal perished the disposition or rights as to the accessory vanished also, *e.g.*, as to legacies, *Quæ accessionum locum obtinent extinguuntur cum principales res peremptæ fuerint* (Dig. 33, 8, 2, Gaius), and as to the extinction of obligations, *In omnibus speciebus liberationum etiam accessiones liberantur, puta adpromissores hypothecæ, pignora* (Dig. 46, 3, 43, Ulpian).

The various examples given in §§ 29 to 34 of the application of the maxim may be summed up in the rules—*Necesse est ei rei cedi, quod sine illa esse non potest—Quærumque aliis juncta sive adjecta accessionis loco cedunt, ea quamdiu cohærent, dominus vindicare non potest* (Dig. 6, 1, 23, 3 and 5).

The *jus accessionis* is in some cases a result of the right of ownership, as where the accessory attaches itself indissolubly; in other cases it may result from the will of the legislature dictated by expediency. It produces a sort of *occupatio,* resulting from possession, often without the knowledge or against the inclination of the possessor, and it may occur as to three different kinds of property—

(1) *Res nullius.* Here, as no one else is deprived, the rule of

law need not be very stringent in requiring absolute indissoluble connection, *e.g.*, the possessor of tame pigeons or bees becomes owner, even without his knowledge, of wild pigeons or bees attracted to the dove cot or hive, and to remove them would be theft.

(2) *Originally the property of another*, but undistinguishable, and hence also no one deprived, *e.g.*, fallen leaves mixed with mine, ooze deposited by inundation, etc.

(3) *Belonging to another.* Here three positions are involved— (α) incorporation, irremediable absorption, *e.g.*, the case of a dog eating the bread taken from a baker, or a thief eating the stolen bread, in both which examples the accessory thing has ceased to be what it formerly was; (β) a separation possible, but the balance of utility against it, and therefore in both these cases the question of indemnity arises; (γ) return to former condition possible. In this case, he who has lost the thing is entitled to have it back.

In any case, the right of ownership reasserts itself in the absence of agreement to the contrary, or considerations of public utility, if the thing returns to its primitive state; but, in some cases, the legislature may have to determine which is the principal and which the accessory thing, and if this cannot be done, to decide what are the rights of the interested parties.

378. (§ xix) *Produce of animals.* The young of animals belong to the owner of the female, the owner of the male being paid for the hire of it (see *post*, § 37).

379. (§ xx) *Alluvio.* The alluvion insensibly deposited belongs to the owner of the bank, but not in the case of *agri limitati*, *i.e.*, in the time of Justinian fields definitely limited by boundaries, as a wall or a ditch separating them from the river, or public lands assigned *per modum*, as opposed to fields termed *arcifinales*, *i.e.*, not having fixed but only natural boundaries, as mountains, rivers, etc.

In the case of fragments of land carried off bodily by an inundation or other cause and deposited against a neighbour's ground, the owner would have the right to vindicate them, but not after a sufficient lapse of time had united them; and the roots of trees extending from the one land to the other would serve as a proof of the juncture.

An island may be formed in a river :—

(1) By the river cutting off and surrounding a piece of land, in which case it belongs to the owner of the land.

(2) By uncovering a portion of its bed and flowing round it.

(3) By gradual deposits raising an island. In these two cases, the usage of the river being public, and, so long as the river flowed over it, the bed being *res nullius*, on being uncovered, it is attributed, if in the middle of the stream proportionally, to the riparian owners *ratio vicinitatis*, but if on one side to that side only, unless the fields lining the bank were *agri limitati*, in which case the island would belong to the first occupant.

(4) A floating island would be public property, like the river which carried it.

If a river abandoned its bed, the bed belonged to the owners of the adjoining lands, and if the river abandoned the *new* bed, the adjoining owners could claim it, so that, though the case is unlikely, and equitable principles would be invoked, if the new bed had been an entire property the owner would lose it altogether; but these rules did not apply to an inundation, as the real owner had the right to recover his land on the waters retiring.

384. (§ xxv) *Specificatio*. This term was introduced by the commentators to include cases of the *production of a new thing (species)* out of given materials, and they classed it among the natural modes of acquisition, some viewing it as a kind of *occupatio*, and others as a particular case of accession, the material being, according to circumstances, considered the principal, and the new form the accessory, or vice versa; but there is here an altogether peculiar reason for the attribution of ownership, viz., the creation of a thing which did not previously exist. According to a passage from Gaius in the Digest (41, 1, 7, 7) the *Proculeians* attributed the new thing to its creator, *quia quod factum est, antea nullius fuerat*, the *Sabinians* to the owner of the materials, *quia sine materia nulla species effici possit*, but *Justinian* finally decided that in the case of a material no longer existing in its original form *(suam speciem pristinam non continet)*, and incapable of being restored to its former condition, the creator of the new object is the owner of it, *i.e.*, he who made it or ordered it to be made, not the workman employed upon it, and the consent of the owner of the materials must not have been given (otherwise it would be a case of the intention of the parties). This rule is independent of good or bad faith, so that the stealer of grapes or of wool is the owner of the wine or of the cloth with which the materials are made, for the new object was held to belong to no one, and the owner of the materials could not therefore vindicate the thing, but had the :—

(1) *Actio furti*, a penal action for quadruple or double the value, according to circumstances *(post*, par. 1726), and the

(2) *Condictio furtiva* or the *actio ad exhibendum* (not both), for an indemnity.

The owner of the new object had a *rei vindicatio* to recover it, but on the ground that no one may enrich himself at the expense of others, he would have to give an indemnity for the material employed or the labour expended.

If the materials remained, though changed in form (*e.g.*, ears of corn beaten and the grain detached), the owner could vindicate them by asserting the material to be his.

According to the better opinion, if the new object was formed partly out of his own materials, the maker of the new object having given his industry, in addition to part of the materials, the object was undoubtedly his.

389. (§ xxvi) *Adjunctio* is the term used by the commentators to indicate the joining of an accessory to a principal thing, *e.g.*, if a person worked purple belonging to another into the cloth of his own

clothes, the purple, although more valuable, was held to be an accessory, because employed to ornament the dress *(cum quærimus, quid cui cedat, illud spectamus, quid cujus rei ornandæ causa adhibetur.* Dig. 34, 2, 19, 13, Ulpian). If the accessory thing was capable of separation, the owner might vindicate it (but see par. 391) after first bringing an action *ad exhibendum*, to get it detached. If stolen, the *actio furti* lay and the *condictio* (*ante*, par. 384), the latter extending to the successors of the thief.

391. *Ferruminatio* implied the absorbing of something as an accessory of the principal object, on account of the unity of the whole, though not necessarily incapable of removal (*e.g.*, a foot or arm added to a statue), and if removed, it still belonged to the owner of the principal thing, on the ground of utility, and only an *actio in factum* lay to enable the real owner to obtain an indemnity.

392. (§ xxvii) *Confusio.* The union of liquid things or things reduced to a liquid state may take place :—

(1) By the will of the owners, in which case, whether separation is impossible or not, the result is common to both.

(2) If the union resulted from chance, and separation was impossible, the same result.

(3) By the act of a third person, when, if a new species created, the thing is his, otherwise, the result is common to all.

In any of these cases, a division may be arrived at by the action *communi dividundo*.

393. (§ xxviii) *Commixtio.* This term refers to the mixture of objects not liquids, and the particles of which do not blend, so that each continues to exist separately. If the mixture results from the consent of the owners, it is common to all, and the action *communi dividundo* lies to acquire separate shares. If the mixture is accidental, or the act of one, separate ownership continues to exist, and a *rei vindicatio* lies. In the case of a mixed flock of sheep, there would be no difficulty, but in the case of corn of different quantities and qualities mixed together, the arbitration of a judge would be required.

394. (§ xxix) *Constructio.* According to the rules *omne quod inædificatur solo cedit* and *superficies solo cedit*, a building became, as an accessory, the property of the owner of the land on which it was erected, but the separate movable pieces, as abstracted from the mass, still remained in the eyes of the law the property of the original owner, so that if the building was destroyed, they could be acquired by the *vindicatio* or *ad exhibendum* action (unless the builder had acted in good faith, see below), a principle applying generally to all *accessio* cases.

The twelve tables (vi, 7, 8, 9), to prevent a waste of property *(ne ruinis urbs deformetur)*, forbad the destruction of buildings or of the trellises in vineyards, although the materials of another had been employed in the construction, and the rules with regard to indemnity were :—

(1) If the materials had been employed in *good* faith, only the

action *de tigno juncto* lay, and if the penalty of double the value resulted from the action, there was no further remedy.

(2) If in *bad* faith the owner could choose between the *de tigno juncto* and the *ad exhibendum actio*, and it being impossible to produce the materials, for he would not be required to demolish the buildings, the user of the materials would necessarily be condemned.

(3) If the act was that of a thief, the *actio furti* and the *condictio* (or *ad exhibendum*) both lay, or, if preferred, the *de tigno juncto* could be brought at once; and if the building was subsequently destroyed, the owner of the materials could still vindicate them, the double value already paid being regarded as a penalty for the theft.

If the building had been erected on the ground of another, with a knowledge of that fact, the Institutes held that the owner of the material had voluntarily alienated them; but the general rules were—

(1) If the construction was made in *good* faith, and the owner of the materials in possession, he had against the owner of the soil vindicating the building as an accessory to his land the *exceptio doli mali* for the cost of the materials and the workmanship; but if he was not in possession, he could only vindicate the materials after demolition.

(2) If in *bad* faith, strictly and according to the Institutes the constructor had no action or exception open to him, but the more favourable opinion gave him an indemnity for necessary or useful expenses; and a constitution of Antonine allowed him, when the building was destroyed, to vindicate the materials if he had not intended giving them to the owner of the land (*si non donandi animo ædificia alieno solo imposita sint*, Code 3, 32, 2); hence a farmer erecting buildings on his landlord's ground, had a right to an indemnity (Dig. 19, 2, 55, 1, *Paul*).

398. (§ xxxi) *Plantatio.* According to the rule *plantæ quæ terræ coalescunt solo cedunt*, whether the plant of another is put into own ground or own plant into the ground of another, the owner of the ground is, in the opinion of *Gaius* (Dig. 41, 1, 7, 13) and of these Institutes, the owner of the plant, after it has taken root, a tree with roots in both fields being *common*; but, according to *Pomponius* (Dig. 47, 7, 6, 2), if the plant were on the border, and the roots struck into the neighbour's ground, the plant would still belong to the original owner. After its fall, the tree cannot be vindicated, because, as an organic body, it has changed its substance.

(§ xxxii) The same rules apply to *seed sown* (but an *exceptio doli* lay to recover expenses, if the field of another had been sown in good faith); and (§ xxxiii) the *writing* belongs to the owner of the parchment (*litteræ quoque, licet aureæ sint, chartis, membranisve cedunt*); but if the parchment was in the hands of the writer in good faith, an *exceptio doli* lay for expenses, and the rule applied to the actual writing, not to the property in the literary composition.

(§ xxxiv) In the case of *pictures*, opposite opinions are inserted in the Digest. *Paul* held that the picture was accessory to the canvas, but *Gaius*, in whose favour *Justinian* decided, held that the picture should govern the canvas, though, if painted on the walls of a building, the necessity of the case would probably incline opinion to favour Paul's view.

If the owner of the canvas was in possession of the picture, the painter attempting to vindicate it without paying for the canvas could be met by the *exceptio doli mali*. If the painter was in possession in good faith (for otherwise if canvas stolen the owner had an *actio furti*), the owner of the canvas could not strictly have a *vindicatio*, because the owner of the painting would be owner of both; and, if he brought a *utilis actio*, it could be stopped by the painter paying for the canvas, and, if proceeded with, and no offer to pay for the painting, an *exceptio doli mali* could be opposed.

400. The four following sections (35, 36, 37, 38) are outside the present subject (viz., the *natural* modes of acquiring property), and are not found in the Institutes of *Gaius*. They are probably inserted here to show the exceptional cases where *produce*, instead of belonging to the owner, may be acquired by others.

(§ xxxv) A person *knowingly* possessing the property of another is responsible for the estate, the produce, and the *produce consumed;* but a person having received the estate in good faith, by sale, donation, or other *justa causa*, whether *lucrativa* or not, from another person whom he believed to be the owner, had two advantages in respect of the *produce*, if the real owner attempted to vindicate the property, viz.:

(1) The possessor in good faith is considered as an owner having all rights, including the *rei vindicatio* action, over produce from the time of *separation* by any means from the soil; *i.e.*, Paul's opinion on this point prevailed against Pomponius, and all the produce collected, whether the result of labour or not, was held to be his as a reward for *cultura et cura*, and hence his rights are similar to those of an *emphyteutor*.

(2) The possessor in good faith was *not* liable to account for produce consumed.

Hence the real owner claiming the estate *cum sua causa (accessiones) et fructibus* (produce) could be opposed by an *exceptio doli mali*, which would lead to an adjustment by the judge of the respective rights.

After the *litis contestatio*, all the produce belongs to the real owner, and so as to all the produce existing before that time, but subject to deductions for expenses, improvements, etc., and the produce consumed remains for the benefit of the possessor; so that, if the possessor in good faith has not been personally benefited, he was entitled to an allowance where the price of the produce consumed had been spent in paying off a mortgage, or in improvements, etc.

(§ xxxvi) The rights of the *usufructuary* (*post*, tit. iv) only arise with the actual collection of the produce, so that if he dies, the produce, though ripe and even accidentally detached, belongs to the owner of the estate, because not actually gathered in; and the rights of the *colonus* are similarly limited, except that, on his decease, his lease, and therefore his rights, are transmitted to his heirs.

(§ xxxvii) The young, the milk, the hair, and the wool of animals, are all counted as produce in favour of the usufructuary (though he is bound to replace dead cattle, trees, vines, etc., out of the produce), but an exception was made on the ground of the dignity of man, and the child of a female slave was held to belong to the owner.

410. (§ 39) *Treasure trove.* *Thesaurus est vetus quædam depositio pecuniæ* (used in general sense), *cujus non extat memoria, ut jam dominum non habeat* (Dig. 41, 1, 31, 1, *Paul*). Hence two essentials, (1) that there should be an ancient deposition of the thing, (2) with all remembrance as to the ownership gone, and therefore this is not the case of *occupatio* or *accessio* of a thing strictly *nullius*, but assimilated to it by analogy.

Justinian, adopting Hadrian's legislation, laid down the following rules, grounded on the principles of natural equity, though the ideas on the subject of *chance* were due to lingering superstition in relation to criminal sacrifices and other artifices.

(1) If found on *own property*, it belonged to the owner.

(2) If found by chance on sacred or religious ground, to the finder.

(3) If found by chance on another's property, half to finder, remainder to the owner of the ground, whether a private individual or the Emperor, the fiscus, the city, etc.; but if not found by chance, then the whole to the owner.

411. (§ 40) *Traditio.* An intimate relation exists between *traditio* and *possessio*, for the former is the handing over of the possession (*possessionis translatio*). In the *occupatio* of a *res nullius*, the possession immediately gives ownership, but in *traditio* the will of the owner must concur; hence *nuda traditio*, *i.e.*, physical possession will not transfer ownership, *legal* possession being required to make the possessor also owner, *i.e.*, the *fact* and the *intention* must be combined, hence, for *traditio*—

(1) The thing must be placed in some way at the disposition of the receiver.

(2) It must be so placed and received with the intention of the immediate transference of the ownership.

(3) The person making the delivery must have the capacity to alienate.

The expression *justa causa*, (see *post*, par. 529 (2), as applied to *traditio* (*Nunquam nuda traditio transfert dominium, sed ita si venditio, aut aliqua justa causa præcesserit propter quam traditio sequeretur*—Dig. 41, 1, 31, Paul), meant that a contract or other fact had entailed, as a consequence, a wish to transfer the property, and for this purpose to make *traditio ;* hence delivery by a child or insane person, or if made for the purpose of lending, letting, depositing, etc., produced no ownership, only *physical* possession ; but a sale or payment, exchange, legacy, donation, etc., involved the requisite intention (though, as to the peculiarity in respect of the *payment of the price* in the case of a sale, see *post,* par. 1475), but it was immaterial whether the will resulting from the *fact* of the contract was due to the *dolus* of one of the parties or to a misunderstanding, the alienation of the thing was perfected, and personal actions only resulted.

The *traditio* may be made by *another* person with the will of the owner, and hence by him who has a general order to administer, at least where sales are required by the circumstances, as in the case of produce and other things likely to deteriorate.

The will alone may suffice to transfer the ownership, where *physical* detention is already acquired, and the will of the owner alone is wanting to give *legal* possession, *i.e.,* alienation may take place without *traditio*—

(1) By an agreement that the thing lent, let, deposited, etc., shall belong to the person in whose possession it already is.

(2) By agreement that the thing sold or given shall be retained in usufruct, or as let, pledged, etc., in which case, without corporeal tradition, legal possession is acquired by the vendee, and the vendor immediately begins to possess for the vendee.

(3) When legal possession acquired by purchase, gift, or legacy from a person who was not owner. Here, when the will of the real owner to alienate is added, immediate ownership is acquired, though there is no tranference of the possession, for the property is already in the hands of the alienee, and so in the cases given *ante,* par. 346 (1).

The will alone may also transfer the ownership to an uncertain recipient, as in the case of money thrown to the people by prætors and consuls.

A *quasi traditio* was introduced by analogy in the case of *incorporeal* things, and consisted in delivering over or permitting the exercise of a right.

425. *Of the loss of possession and of ownership.* *Legal* possession being composed of the fact and of the intention, ceases to exist if one of those elements is wanting ; *i.e.,* in the words of *Papinian*—*possessionem amitti vel animo, vel etiam corpore,* in opposition to the dictum of *Paul*—*quemadmodum nulla possessio adquiri nisi animo et corpore potest ; ita nulla amittitur nisi in qua utrumque in contrarium actum est* (Dig. 41, 2, 44, 2, and 8).

Hence legal possession is lost—

(1) By the *fact* (*corpore, facto*), *i.e.,* when the thing is no longer at the free disposition of the possessor, but this does not include absence for *animo retinetur possessio ;* and *Papinian* (Dig. 41, 2,

46) lays down that if, during absence, possession is taken of an estate, the possession is not lost so long as the original possessor is ignorant that his rights are contested or ignored. In respect of (a) *movables*, this rule applies when they are abstracted or carried off by violence, or absolutely lost, so as not to know where they are, and so in the case of stones submerged in the Tiber, or a wild animal which has regained its liberty. (β) As to *immovables*, the rule applies where the possessor is violently expelled from the estate, or in the case of a river or the sea occupying the land.

(2) By the *intention* (*animo*), as where a person no longer wishes to possess, although he still holds the thing, *e.g.*, retaining it by hiring or borrowing the thing sold (*igitur amitti et animo solo potest quamvis adquiri non potest*); hence a pupil or an insane person, not having legal will, cannot in this way lose possession by themselves.

Ownership is necessarily lost if—

(1) The owner is incapable of holding, as in the case of death or slavery.

(2) The thing is destroyed, or leaves the patrimony of man as where it becomes *sacra* or *religiosa;* or, in the case of a wild animal, it recovers its liberty.

(3) The thing transferred to another.

(4) Abandoned by the owner as being no longer wanted (*pro derelicto*), in which case, after the owner has lost all property in it, the thing becomes *res nullius*, and the next possessor can then immediately acquire the ownership; hence the intention to abandon being of the essence, things thrown overboard to lighten the ship are as if dropped unperceived from a carriage, and he who carries them off from the shore, or from the bottom of the sea, commits a theft.

431. *Actions relating to Possession and Ownership.*—Possession and *quasi possession* were specially protected by four classes of interdicts which were subsequently transformed into actions for the same ends (*post*, par. 2302).

(1) *Adipiscendæ possessionis causa*, to acquire possession not already obtained.

(2) *Retinendæ*, to maintain a disputed possession.

(3) *Recuperandæ*, to recover possession of which deprived.

(4) *Double interdicts*, to acquire and to recover.

Ownership was principally protected by real actions (*actiones in rem*) called generically *vindicationes*, whether founded on the prætorian or civil law. By these, the owner asserted his right to possess a corporeal or incorporeal thing (as a servitude, status, or family right). The *rei vindicatio* was a special example of this class, and by it the owner followed his property into the hands of any possessor, in order to be acknowledged the proprietor and to obtain restitution.

Tit. ii. De rebus corporalibus et incorporalibus.

434. As to the division of things into *corporeal* and *incorporeal*, see part ii, par. 109. An important class of *incorporeal* things were—

Servitudes, so-called because they constituted a sort of bondage over the thing subject to them, and divisible into—

(1) *Servitutes personarum*, for the special benefit of the person to whom they belonged, as the right given to one of gathering the produce of another's field.

(2) *Servitutes rerum* (or *prædiorum*), *i.e.*, rights attached to the ownership of another thing, and therefore passing with that thing to every possessor, as a right of way over one field in favour of the owner of a neighbouring field; hence, fixity and relation by neighbourhood or situation is indispensable, and the right can only exist in respect of *immovables*.

Principles common to both kinds are :—

(1) Being fragments of ownership, they are *real* rights.

(2) The owner cannot have a servitude over his own property (*nulli res sua servit*), and hence, an *owner* of the property, and a *holder* of the servitude, must always exist.

(3) No servitude can compel the owner of the property to do anything, otherwise it would be an *obligation*, *i.e.*, a servitude is positive, and consists in suffering something to be done, or is negative in abstaining from doing something. (*Servitutum non ea est natura ut aliquid faciat quis, sed ut aliquid patiatur, vel non faciat.* Dig. 8, 1, 15, 1, Pomponius.)

(4) There cannot be a servitude upon a servitude, for the holder of the servitude burdening it would alter the rights of the owner of the property, though agreements or legacies may give rise to obligations of this nature.

(5) Only positive servitudes admit of quasi possession.

Tit iii. De servitutibus prædiorum.

444. *Prædial* servitudes are so called because they cannot be created without estates (*prædia*). They probably existed at the time of the twelve tables, but the subject was not developed until the time of Cicero.

They may affect the *jus utendi* or the *jus fruendi*, but they always more or less affect the *jus abutendi* of the owner of the property by negatively paralysing this right, as in the case of not planting, not building, not raising higher, or of not consuming, not destroying or modifying, the property, so as to affect the servitude; and they are *indivisible*, *i.e.*, they cannot be acquired, exercised, vindicated, lost in part only, or subjected to a term or condition, though they may be limited in their use as to time, place, or manner; and, where the estates are separated, they may be separately acquired or extinguished, and, in certain cases, part retained.

The servitude must be of some utility or profit to the dominant estate; hence, one estate cannot have a right of way over another if separated by a piece of land that cannot be traversed. It must also have a perpetual cause, *i.e.*, it must not be made artificially so as to compel the servient tenement to do something, as in the case of a pond kept filled by slave labour, but it must depend rather on the laws of nature, the cause perpetually existing though not always acting.

446. *Rural and urban servitudes.* The distinction between *servitutes prædiorum*, (1) *rusticorum* and (2) *urbanorum*, depends on whether the soil or the buildings erected on it are regarded, *i.e.*, whether they are *in solo* (*e. g.*, a right of way, of water, of pasturage), or *in superficie* (*e.g.*, right of light, of view, of gutter), and hence the nature of the servitude decides the class it belongs to, as in the case of the right of leading water which, if over land, would be *rural*, if over a building, *urban;* and therefore, an *urban* servitude may exist without any building or other estate; *e. g.*, a negative right of servitude in favour of one plot of ground that nothing shall be built on the next plot.

According to the ancient law, *rural* servitudes were *res mancipi* (part ii, par. 121), and subsequently *rural* servitudes could be pledged or mortgaged, but *urban* not, and other important legal differences arise from the distinction, as in the case of quasi possession, loss, and non-usage, for *urban* servitudes are necessarily continuous (*e.g.*, in the case of a beam against a wall, a gutter over land, a window overlooking a court), but *rural* usually not so (*e. g.*, right of way); though the case of aqueducts and of not drawing water from a well in order not to diminish that in the well of a neighbour, are examples of *rural* servitudes in conflict with the rule.

451. The more important *rural* servitudes were:—

(1) *Iter*, *i.e.*, the right to pass along (*eundi gratia*) on foot, in a litter, on horseback, etc.

(2) *Actus*, *i.e.*, the right to lead along (*agendi gratia*). It includes *iter*, and applies to animals and carriages.

(3) *Via*, *i. e.*, the right to make use of the road without damaging the plants or produce. It includes *actus* and *iter*, and the width of the road was fixed by the twelve tables (vii, 6) at eight feet and sixteen feet in the bends. The law did not fix the breadth of *iter* and *actus*, but if done by agreement, or if the breadth of the *via* were made more or less, the consequent rights may be affected. The servitude *navigandi*, *i. e.*, the right of traversing a lake or pond, etc., in order to reach an estate, was an analogous right to the *via*.

(4) *Aquæductus*, *i. e.*, the right of leading water through another's estate. To these other examples may be added, as (5) *aquæ haustus*, or the right to draw water; (6) *pecoris ad aquam adpulsus*, to water a flock; (7) *jus pascendi*, pasture a flock; (8) *calcis coquendæ*, burn lime; (9) *arenæ fodiendæ*, extracting sand, etc.

453. Amongst *urban* servitudes, or those *quæ ædificiis inhærent*, were:—

(1) *Oneris ferendi*, *i. e.*, that the neighbour's pillar or wall

(*columna vel paries*) should support the weight of the dominant tenement. As this involved keeping the wall in repair, and was, therefore, an exception to the rule that servitudes never consist in *doing* anything, it was advisable, according to the better opinion, to add a condition necessitating repair, *e.g.*, that the sustaining wall remain always as it is (*paries oneri ferendo, uti nunc est, ita sit*).

(2) *Tigni immittendi*, *e.g.*, the right of inserting a beam in the neighbour's wall, but not involving any repair.

(3) *Stillicidii vel fluminis recipiendi*, *i.e.*, the right of replenishing cisterns, etc., from the water naturally running off a neighbour's roof, or collected or poured from a gutter. The contrary servitude to this, *i.e.*, *non recipiendi*, seldom occurred, but probably referred to the right specially accorded in a particular case of not receiving this water where the local arrangements otherwise entailed a common obligation.

(4) *Altius non tollendi*, *i.e.*, of not erecting a building above a given height; and the contrary servitude, *altius tollendi*, probably referred to the right of contravening local statutes on this subject.

(5) *Ne luminibus officiat.* In respect of light two kinds of servitude may exist; (a) the *jus luminum*, or right to have windows in a neighbour's or our own wall, so that the neighbour must let the openings exist; and the larger right (β) *ne luminibus officiatur*, *i.e.*, the power of preventing a neighbour impeding the access of light by plantations, constructions, or any other works.

In addition to these, there existed servitudes of a similar class, falling under the heads of *jus prospectus, ne prospectui officiatur, projiciendi, protegendi, fumi immittendi*, etc.

461. *Establishment of servitudes.* A servitude might be created according to the rules of the *civil* law, or only subsist by the prætor's protection, and the distinction was important between the establishment of a servitude as a *real* right in the first instance, and the creation of an obligation giving a right of action against the owner to compel him to establish the servitude, though the expression, *jus constituere*, is used by *Gaius* indifferently in either sense.

Predial servitudes might be established by :—

(1) *Mancipatio* and *in jure cessio* (in *ante-*Justinian law); the former for *rural*, the latter for both *rural* and *urban* servitudes.

(2) *Pacts and stipulations.* The expression *pactis et stipulationibus*, as used by *Gaius* (Inst. ii, § 31), refers to the methods of establishing quasi-servitudes on *provincial* soil where true ownership did not exist, but the distinction had disappeared under Justinian. The *pact* settled the nature and conditions of the servitude, and the *stipulation*, fixing a penalty in default, created the legal bond. Occasionally a simple agreement resulted in a servitude, *e.g.*, an agreement to purchase a right of way, and then the *actio venditi, empti*, or *condictio incerti*, could be brought into play, but the better opinion was that *security* should be given for

the purpose of compelling the owner of the servient tenement to submit to the servitude, or a difficulty would exist in enforcing it.

Commentators are divided in opinion whether pacts and stipulations could of themselves create servitudes, and probably *quasi-traditio* was necessary, though this was impracticable in the case of negative servitudes; but, at least in Justinian's time, pacts could establish a servitude as a *real* right, *e.g.*, the owner of two immovables, delivers one to a person with the pact accompanying the delivery that his tenement shall be liable to a servitude in favour of the one retained, or vice versa.

(3) By *testament*, either by condemning the heir to suffer them, or leaving the servitude to a neighbour as a direct legacy, in either case, under Justinian, creating a real right, though formerly the legacy *per damnationem*, as opposed to that *per vindicationem*, would only have created an obligation binding on the heir. So a legatee's estate might be burdened with a servitude in favour of other estates.

(4) *Usucapion.* The creation of servitudes by this method appears to have been suppressed by a *lex Scribonia* (? B.C. 33), and jurisconsults subsequent to that date lay down that neither urban nor rural servitudes are susceptible of usucapion, but the prætors and the præses gave *utiles* actions and *interdicts* to protect servitudes long enjoyed, a distinction, however, being made, viz., *discontinuous (i.e.,* rural or *in solo*) servitudes could not be acquired by usucapion, though an exception existed in favour of a right of drawing water, etc., see *Interdicts, post,* par. 507 ; *continuous (i.e., in superficie)* servitudes could be acquired by usucapion, so only that the possession had been obtained *nec vi, nec clam, nec precario*. The time depended on circumstances, and was not definitely fixed, a law relating to aqueducts speaks of usage extending beyond the memory of man. It is disputed whether the term of ten years as between present, and twenty years as between absent persons applied to prescription over immovables before the time of Justinian in respect of prædial servitudes, but at any rate the prescriptive rules were enforced, viz., besides usage there must be good faith resting on a *justa causa* mode of acquisition.

(5) *Adjudicatio.* The judge, when by his sentence, assigning shares in a common property, established the servitude as a real right over one estate for the benefit of another.

It may be laid down that, under *Justinian, pacts* accompanying the *traditio* of one estate, or *legacies*, or *long usage*, or *adjudicatio*, established servitudes as *real* rights, immediately, before any exercise, or any *quasi-traditio*, though in the case of *pacts* and *stipulations*, as the contract only gave birth to an obligation, the servitude could not exist as a *real* right until after the *quasi-traditio*, and this being impossible for *negative* servitudes, the latter could not in the later Roman law be created by agreement, though anciently it could be effected by the *in jure cessio* process.

467. *Extinction of servitudes.* This may arise from—

(1) Loss or destruction of the dominant or servient tenement, *e.g.*, the edifice thrown down, the land carried away or flooded; but by an equitable interpretation differing from the case of *usufruct*, see *post*, par. 488 (6), if the edifice was rebuilt the servitude revived.

(2) By *confusion, i.e.*, the same person becoming entire owner of both estates.

(3) By *remission, i.e.*, when the owner of the dominant tenement allowed the owner of the *servient* to do something preventing the exercise of the servitude. When the *cessio in jure* process existed it would, if employed for the purpose, have extinguished it at once, but a *pact* would only give rise to an *exceptio* in favour of the owner of the servient tenement.

(4) *Non usage.* The *lex Scribonia, ante,* par. 461 (4) applied only to the establishment not to the extinction of servitudes, and therefore, according to the civil law, the period of *two* years extinguished all servitudes (and so stated in the Digest, A.D. 533, but see below) and a servitude not used according to the condition (*e.g.*, if water to be drawn at night was drawn in the daytime) was equally lost at the end of two years, for the *usucapion* of two years did not apply to the creation of servitudes. If *force* had been used, strictly, the right was lost, but the prætor would aid the dispossessed party, and a distinction existed, viz., the rule applied as to *rural* or discontinuous servitudes, if not used for the utility of the estate by the owner, farmer, or other person interested; but for *urban* or continuous servitudes it was further necessary that the owner of the *servient* tenement should obtain his liberation *(libertatem usucapere)* by doing some contrary act, as *e.g.*, turning off the gutters.

In A.D. 531, a constitution of *Justinian* (Code 3, 34, 13) substituted the prætorian *prescription* which had been previously in use on *provincial* soil for the *civil usucapion*, and then predial servitudes were only lost by non-usage after ten years between present and twenty years between absent persons, but it is incorrect to assume that Justinian required in *all cases* some *contrary* act to be done, *i.e.*, that the action in vindication of the servitude (applying if true to the *usufruct* as well) would only be *actually* extinguished by time after thirty years, independent of presence or absence, good faith or *justa causa.*

Tit. iv. De usufructu.

471. *Personal* servitudes existed for the special advantage of the person, and were introduced long subsequently to the twelve tables, some of them *(e.g.*, the *quasi-usufruct)* not being in force in the time of Cicero. They applied to both movables and immovables, and only consisted in suffering something to be done. They were not all *indivisible*, as, *e.g.*, a part may be acquired or lost of the rights of usufruct connected with gathering the produce.

472. *Ususfructus* is the most important of these survitudes, and is treated at great length in the Digest, and by Gaius, Ulpian, and Paul,

as well as in the Fragmenta Vaticana. It is defined as the *jus alienis rebus utendi fruendi salva rerum substantia*, *i.e.*, it is the right of using and enjoying the property of another *without altering* the substance.

474. The usufructuary rights and obligations are :—

(1) *Jus utendi*, *i.e.*, the right to draw from the thing all the utility that it is capable of furnishing, short of taking any produce or altering the substance, *e.g.*, the right to inhabit the house, and dwell on the rural estate, make use of the servitudes of simple usage due to it, and employ oxen and horses at their proper work, ships for navigation, etc.

(2) *Jus fruendi*, *i.e.*, the right of gathering all the fruits that the thing was designed to produce, viz., those things which form the periodical revenue, and hence excluding accidental accessories (*e.g.*, alluvion, treasure trove, a legacy made to a slave, the child of a slave), as well as objects which are rather a part of the thing than its ordinary produce (*e.g.*, wood not intended to be cut, trees dying or torn up by the violence of the wind), and hence it follows that the decomposition of ownership into the *jus utendi, fruendi*, and *abutendi* is not strictly accurate, for the owner has still left in him, besides the *jus abutendi*, the right to those accessories which are not produce, but the revenue of cut wood *(sylva cædua)*, as far as is required for domestic wants or the repairs of the building, falls to the usufructuary.

476. The usufructuary could give up gratis or sell or let his rights in whole or in part, in which case the rent was called *civil* produce, but if it represented *natural* produce, (*i.e.*, not the work of a slave, the rent of a house, etc.), it was only due to the usufructuary if the harvest was made in his lifetime ; for the usufructuary was not *owner* of the produce, but only had the exclusive right to *gather* it, or have it gathered, and so differed from the possessor in good faith *(ante*, par. 400), who, in respect of third parties, was held to be the owner from the time the thing was detached. Fruit, therefore, which had naturally fallen, and had not been gathered, or which had been taken by others than his representatives, did not belong to him ; hence against a thief he would only have the *actio furti*, not the *rei vindicatio* or the *condictio furtiva ;* and fruit not gathered at the time of his death would not go to his heirs, but remain to the owner, though he had the right to gather produce hanging at the commencement of the usufruct ; and no action lay against him or his heirs for gathering fruit before it was ripe, if there was no fraud, and it was done as a good paterfamilias, as in the case of plucking unripe oranges in order to export them.

The usufructuary must use the property as a *bonus paterfamilias*, and not degrade it from its intended purpose, *e.g.*, a house must not be turned into an hotel or bath house ; a slave who is a musician must not be made a baker ; nor must the substance of the thing be altered, *i.e.*, the essential character of it, as by building on the land, making a pleasure into a kitchen garden, etc. He must also replace vines and fruit trees that have perished, and dead head of cattle by

M

their young. He has to bear the expenses of repairing *(modica refectio)*, and pay the taxes and other burdens on the produce. The prætorian law also called upon him to give security that he would use the property as a good paterfamilias, and restore what remained at the end of the time.

481. (§ i) *Modes of constituting the usufruct.* The usufruct may be detached by giving it *(dare)*, *i.e.*, transferring the usufruct and retaining the *nuda proprietas*, or by deducting it *(deducere usufructum)*, *i.e.*, giving the *nuda proprietas*, and retaining the usufruct.

It was the better opinion that usage or quasi-possession never established a right of usufruct, but it might be accomplished by :—

(1) *Legacy.* This was the most usual and the most favourably construed. By it under Justinian the usufruct was transferred as a *real* right, without *quasi traditio*, the right of enjoyment vested at once, there being no interval between the *dies cedit (i.e.*, the moment, generally the day of death, when the eventual right to the legacy was fixed for the benefit of the legatee, and therefore of his heirs), and the *dies venit (i.e.*, when, generally at the *aditio hereditatis*, it could be claimed). If one legatee was to have the *usufruct* and another the *nuda proprietas*, the estate must be given to the latter *deducto usufructu*, or he would share the usufruct with the first, and a legacy of the *fructus* was held to mean the *ususfructus*.

(2) *Pacts and stipulations*, see *ante*, par. 461 (2). Under Justinian, when accompanying a tradition, they invariably gave a real right, otherwise they only created an obligation, and the real right was not acquired until after *quasi traditio.*

(3) *Adjudicatio* in the cases of *familiæ erciscundæ* and *communi dividundo.*

(4) *Lex*, *e.g.*, in the case of the usufruct given to the father over certain property of the children.

487. (§ ii) *Quasi-usufruct.* Strictly the usufruct was confined to things which were not consumed by the use, but a *quasi usufruct* (somewhat analogous to the *mutuum)* was introduced, probably in the first instance in the case of legacies only, by a *senatus-consultum* under Augustus or Tiberius, of things consumed by using, as, *e.g.*, wine, oil, corn, clothes, coin ; and security was then given to the heir that the value would be made good at the end of the usufruct.

488. (§ iii) *Extinction of usufruct.* This might arise from :—

(1) *Death,* in the case of a city or corporation after one hundred years.

(2) *Capitis deminutio.* To obviate this, legacies were given for each year, or each month, or each day *(in singulos annos vel menses, vel dies)*, by which means a succession of new rights arose, and so the effects of the *c.d.* or *non-usage* were defeated. Anciently the *minima c.d.* caused an extinction of the usufruct, as in adrogation the former *persona* was gone, but under Justinian only the *maxima* and *media c.d.* effected this, and then only in the case of a paterfamilias ; and if a son had acquired the usufruct for the

father, it was transferred to him on the death or *c.d.* of the father.

(3) *Non-usage, i.e., non utendo per modum* (according to the condition, as, *e.g.*, had the right to gather all the grapes, and had gathered all the corn) *et tempus, i.e.*, during the time fixed. Formerly the time of non-usage was like *usucapion*, one year for movables and two years for immovables; but Justinian made it three years for *movables* and for *immovables*, the same as for loss of ownership or predial servitudes, viz., ten years present, twenty years absent.

(4) *Cession.* This can only be done to the owner, for though the *exercise* of the right may be *permitted*, it cannot be *transferred* to a third person. The expression *domino cedatur*, in the text of Justinian, is mutilated from Gaius (Inst. ii, § 30), where it applies to the *in jure cessio* process, which could take place only with the owner, as otherwise it had no effect, though *Pomponius* (Dig. 23, 3, 66) asserts that, if done with a third person, the act was not altogether a nullity, for the usufructuary would thereby lose his rights, and the usufruct would return to the owner.

(5) *Consolidation.* As where the usufructuary acquired the ownership.

(6) *Loss or change* of the thing. It was not necessary that the thing should be completely destroyed, if only its essential character disappeared; hence if an edifice were burnt, overthrown by an earthquake, or by faulty construction, the right was not resuscitated when the house was rebuilt (compare *ante*, par. 467, 1), and so as to a flock reduced to one head or the carcase of a dead horse.

(7) The *term* or the *condition* fulfilled.

496. When the *totus ususfructus* is extinguished, the *dominus* of the *nuda proprietas* acquires again *plenam in re potestatem*, but, not being indivisible, part only might return to the owner; *e.g.*, if Titius has the usufruct of half a house and Seius the other half, and Titius dies, though if the usufruct of the whole house were left to both Titius and Seius, and Titius died, Seius would get the share of Titius by right of accretion as a co-legatee, and this as against the heirs, even after the legacy has become due, and after the exercise of the right.

Tit. v. De usu et habitatione.

497. The *use* of a thing, the right of gathering the *produce* and the *nuda proprietas*, might belong to three different persons, and *nudus usus* was the term used to express the right of the person who could simply use the thing, see *ante*, par. 474 (1), without gathering the produce. This right was established and extinguished like the usufruct, and, according to strict law, it was restricted to the bare use, and being considered indivisible, it was confined to the person himself, but modifications subsequently crept in, so that the person enjoying the right could take vegetables, fruit, flowers, hay, straw, and wood for daily use; though the jurisconsults differed as to the extent of this user, *Ulpian* making it depend on the quantity produced by the estate and the rank of the person. The person enjoy-

ing the right could also live on the premises, walk or be carried about, use the oil or wine cellars, and prevent the owner of the premises or his agents from coming on the estate, except to cultivate it; but he could not let, sell, or give his rights gratis to another, for that would be drawing civil produce (*ante*, par. 476), though he might have his family with him, and a guest or even a tenant, if he himself occupied part *(et si pensionem percipiat, dum ipse quoque inhabitat, non erit ei invidendum*, Dig. 7, 8, 4, Ulpian). Strictly the use of a flock only extended to manuring the ground, but Ulpian favours the view that it included the right of taking a little milk, and Hadrian decided that a legacy of the *use* of cut wood, or of things which are consumed by use, was equivalent to the *usufruct* of them.

504. (§ v) *Habitatio*. The extent of this right, whether granted by legacy or otherwise, was a fruitful source of controversy, and *Justinian* finally confirmed the opinion of *Marcellus* by treating it as a peculiar right, giving the donee the privilege not only of living in the house himself but also of letting it, and the right lasted for his life, without being affected by non-usage or *minima c.d.*

505. *Slave labour*. The legacy *operarum servi* was still further removed than the *habitatio* from the nature of a true personal servitude. It was not extinguished by *minima c.d.* or *non-usage*, and the right to the services and labour of the slave passed to the *heirs* of the legatee during the lifetime of the slave, though *usucapion* of the slave destroyed the right to his labour.

507. *Actions relating to servitudes*. For the protection of the *quasi-possessio* of incorporeal rights like servitudes, *utiles*, analogous to possessory, *interdicts* were introduced *(interdicta veluti possessoria)*, *i.e.*, the interdicts, *e.g.*, *uti possidetis* for immovables, or *utrubi* for movables, or *unde vi*, where force had been used, were adapted (by introducing the necessary changes in the formula) to personal and real servitudes. In addition to these there were also special interdicts used for some rural servitudes, *e.g.*, three to protect a right of way or the right of drawing water and watering cattle for those who during the year had used the right *nec vi, nec clam, nec precario,* viz., (1) *de itinere actuque privato ;* (2) *de aqua quotidiana et œstiva ;* (3) *de fonte ;* and two others existed with reference to any impediment to the right of repairing the conduits of water *(de ripis)* and drains *(de cloacis)*.

For the vindication of either real or personal servitudes there were two *real* actions, viz. :—

(1) *Actio in rem confessoria*, for the owner of the servitude to assert his right to the quasi-possession, after he had been disturbed by the owner.

(2) *Actio in rem negatoria,* for the owner of the property to assert the non-existence of the servitude, and a peculiarity was

that either action could be brought by the person in possession (*post*, par. 2069).

For rights of servitude inserted in the deed of sale, or in a stipulation with a penal clause, the personal actions *empti*, or *venditi*, or *ex stipulatu*, could be brought.

510. *Other real rights than ownership and servitudes.* Three important fragments or modifications of ownership grew up in the later Roman law, viz. :—

(1) *Emphyteusis.* This real right, indirectly derived from the *civil* law, came into existence shortly before the time of *Justinian*, and is therefore but slightly discussed by him, see *post*, par. 1501.

(2) *Superficies.* A prætorian real right, analogous to the above, but not alluded to by Justinian, see *post*, par. 1511.

(3) *Pignus* (or *hypotheca*). This real right, originated by and owing its sanction to prætorian law, is only referred to by Justinian, in respect of the action to which it gives rise, see *post*, par. 1225 and 2087.

Tit. vi. De usucapionibus et longi temporis possessionibus.

514. The text of the Institutes proceeds to examine the modes of acquisition of particular objects, according to the *civil* law.

Usucapion, see *ante*, par. 312 (2), had two principal effects, for it gave :—

(1) The ownership over property received in good faith, though not from the owner.

(2) The ownership of a thing which, being *mancipi*, and received by tradition, was only *in bonis*.

But *provincial* soil, except that enjoying the *jus Italicum*, was not susceptible of private ownership, and therefore the prætors, by their provincial edicts, confirmed by Imperial constitutions, introduced for *immovables* the *præscriptio longi temporis* after ten years of possession as between present, and twenty years as between absent persons, see *ante*, par. 461 (4). The distinctions between *usucapion* and prescription were :—

(1) *Usucapion*, after one year for movables and two years for immovables, gave the ownership and the right to vindicate the thing, but *præscriptio* was only a *means of repelling* the vindicating action of the owner (or the holder of provincial soil) after the expiration of the time, and hence was equivalent to an *exceptio* (*post*, par. 1939), the words in this sense being used indifferently by Paul and Ulpian, but under Justinian *prescription* gave the same vindicating action against every possessor, as in the case of usucapion.

(2) *Usucapion* gave the ownership, but burdened with any existing charge; whereas if persons having rights of servitude, usufruct, mortgage, etc., allowed the property to be possessed as free, their rights were extinguished, for the effect of non-usage during the same time was to deprive them of their rights, and

hence prescription could be opposed not only to the owner, but to any creditor who had not exercised his rights.

(3) *Usucapion* went on after the action had commenced, up to the day of sentence, so that it might complete itself in the interim, but *prescription* was interrupted if not complete before the action was brought, *i.e.*, before the *litis contestatio*.

Under *Justinian* the distinctions of soil did not exist, and the effect of his legislation was to merge usucapion and prescription into one; the former term being usually employed in his system to designate the period of three years for *movables*, and the latter in respect of the periods for immovables, though the general expression *acquisition by possession* included both.

519. (§ 1) Amongst things that could not be acquired in this way were a freeman, a sacred or religious thing, and a fugitive slave. The twelve tables and the *lex Atinia* (? B.C. 197) prohibited the usucapion of *stolen* things, and the *lex Plautia* (B.C. 59) *et Julia* (? B.C. 7) things taken by *violence*. In these two cases the thing cannot be acquired because possession began in *bad* faith, and the third party, into whose hands it comes, does not thereby acquire a better title; but the vice may be purged if the thing return to the real owner, or the latter has sold the thing to the thief or to the possessor, or consented to its being in other hands; and as in order to constitute theft, a *guilty intention* is necessary, third parties may acquire by usucapion, although the thing has not been received from the owner, as, *e.g.*, an heir by mistake giving in sale, donation, or dowry, a thing lent, let, or deposited with the deceased; a usufructuary selling the child of a slave, thinking it belonged to him; a person in good faith believing himself heir, selling part of the inheritance; and so as to the possessor of an object which he believed the owner had abandoned, etc. Theft was also inapplicable to *immovables*, because it was held to impart the idea of abstraction and displacement, and third parties might acquire by possession from one whose possession did *not* begin by *violence*, even though in bad faith; but a novel (119, c. 7) subsequent to the Institutes made thirty years necessary in such a case (unless the real owner knew of his rights and did not attempt to enforce them), see *post*, par. 539. Things belonging to the *fiscus* were also not susceptible of acquisition in this way, but *bona vacantia (i.e.*, property comprising an escheated succession) were not held to be part of the fiscus until they were claimed, and therefore, previous to that, they might be acquired. To the above list may be added ecclesiastical immovables, the property of pupils or minors under twenty-five, the property composing a dowry (unless prescription had begun to run before the marriage), and generally inalienable things, or things tainted with any *vitium*.

529. *Conditions necessary for acquisition by use.* These were:—

(1) *Possession*, *i.e.*, legal possession, founded on

(2) *Justa causa*, *i.e.*, preceded by some contract or other act conformable to law, and constituting a *justus titulus*, and through which possession has been received or taken, with a view of

acquiring ownership; but owing to some vice in the donor *(e.g.,* not the owner), or the donee *(e.g.,* had no right to the delivery), or the thing itself *(e.g.,* thing not capable of being acquired by possession only), the acquisition of the ownership required the aid of prescription.

As examples of *justa causa* leading to title by prescription, may be cited *pro emptore, i.e.,* as a purchaser; *pro donato,* as a gift; *pro dote,* as dowry; *pro soluto,* as payment; *pro derelicto,* as a thing abandoned; *pro legato,* as, *e.g.,* when a testator gives the legatee something not his own, or the legacy is revoked by an unknown codicil, or a wrong name is inserted, in which two last cases the legatee had no right, and therefore the ownership was not acquired at once; *pro suo,* specially applying to the possession of produce gathered in good faith, as also in respect of *res nullius,* as alluvion, wild animals, etc.; *pro herede, i.e.,* in the quality of heir, and *pro possessore, i.e.,* in the quality of possessor.

(3) *Acquired in good faith, i.e.,* the possessor must be ignorant of the vice of his acquisition as to *facts (e.g.,* ignorant that the vendor was not the owner, that he was *impubes,* that the legacy revoked), not as to *law (juris ignorantiam in usucapione negatur prodesse, facti vero ignorantiam prodesse constat.* Dig. 22, 6, 4, Pomponius), nor must the ignorance have arisen from gross mistake or from the neglect to procure the necessary information; but it was only required at the *commencement of possession,* because it is from that moment that the person would have been owner, if the vice, of which he is ignorant, had not existed, and this applied to the case of gratuitous acquisitions; though in the case of sales the ignorance was required at the time of tradition also; and it was held that there must be both *justa causa* and *good faith* combined, so that one would not do in proof of the other, though probably this was only a general rule; for if there was *apparent justa causa,* as in the case of one person giving another that which he thought he owed him, and the other receiving it, thinking it was owed, the cause of the tradition would be false, but if the error was excusable, acquisition might be made by usucapion.

(4) *Continued during the stipulated time, i.e.,* under Justinian for *movables* three years, and for *immovables* ten years, between persons present *(i.e.,* when possessor and owner both had their domicile in the same province, irrespective of the place of the thing), and twenty years between absent persons *(i.e.,* when both not domiciled as above). If part of the time present and part absent, a novel (119, c. 8) made two days' absence equal to one day of presence.

535. *Tacking in the case of possession.* As the universal heir, whether by civil or prætorian law *(i.e., pro herede* or *pro possessore),* continues the *persona* of the deceased, therefore, in respect of the mass of objects constituting the inheritance, he acquires by usucapion and prescription, or does not so acquire, according as the deceased held in good or bad faith, independent of his own views,

and hence the meaning of the expression that possession *pro herede* or *pro possessore* cannot serve as a foundation for usucapion in respect of particular objects. But the possessor *pro emptore, pro donato*, etc., commences a new possession; and if the possession of the vendor, donor, etc., was also in good faith, and *ex justa causa*, then the two are united *(conjungi tempora)*, and this is called *accessio possessionum*.

538. *Usurpatio* was the name for the interruption of usucapion or prescription. It might occur:—

(1) Naturally by any event through which possession was lost, *e.g.*, violently expelled from immovable, movable object taken away by owner or other person, land invaded by the sea or public river changing bed, the possessor falling into the power of the enemy; for the rules as to the suspension of rights by the *jus postliminii* do not apply to things like possession consisting in facts.

(2) By the true owner holding it by some right, as by having bought it, received it in pledge or lease.

(3) By legal interruption, dating from the commencement of the action of the owner, and not from the *litis contestatio*, which did not really exist under the procedure of Justinian, and when the possessor was absent the mode of interrupting the prescription was by presenting a *libellum* to the præses, bishop, or defensor of the city.

539. *Longissimi temporis præscriptio*. This from being merely a method of repelling actions *(post,* par. 1939), became under Justinian a true means of acquisition. The periods were:—

Thirty years when no *justa causa*, or the thing stolen or taken *vi*, etc., *ante*, par. 519.

Forty years for ecclesiastical property.

Things bought from the *fiscus* were held to have a good title, but four years was allowed within which an action might be brought by those claiming as owners, mortgagees, etc., and the same rule applied to things received from the emperor or empress.

540. *Actions relating to usucapion and prescription*. Two positions are involved, viz.:—

(1) During the time that the usucapion or prescription was *running*, the holder being in legal possession, all interdicts destined to protect that possession were applicable, but if *interrupted*, strictly there was no remedy, the party grieved being neither possessor nor owner, and hence the origin of the *Publiciana in rem actio*, introduced by the prætor *Publicius* to enable the thing to be fictitiously reclaimed, *as if* it had been already acquired by use when the possession had been begun in good faith, *ex justa causa*, and then lost; and as there was no necessity to prove the title of the claimant's predecessors, this action was often used by true owners instead of the *vindicatio*.

(2) When the time *expired*, the possessor having become owner,

Tit. vii. De donationibus.

541. *Donatio* in primitive law meant the gratuitous transfer of property. It was not a particular kind of acquisition, for the acquisition itself was made in the ordinary forms, but it was a means of acquisition founded upon a particular motive; and hence, in a larger sense, it came to include any means of gratuitously incurring an obligation or releasing a debtor.

544. *Classification of Donations.* These gifts may be (1) *mortis causa*, or (2) *non mortis causa;* and Julian divides donations generally into three kinds:—

(1) *Donation proper*, *i.e.*, the donee received the gift absolutely.

(2) *Conditional gift*, *i.e.*, the donee was only to acquire the ownership on the accomplishment of a certain condition, *e.g.*, a sum of money given to Titius to be his when Seius was named consul. Under Justinian, in spite of the tradition, the ownership did not pass, and the donee could not avail himself of the *vindicatio* until the condition was fulfilled.

(3) *Gift determinable on a condition*, *i.e.*, the donee acquired the immediate ownership; but it reverted to the donor on a given event, *i.e.*, on the performance of the condition the donor had a personal action *(condictio)* to compel the re-transference; though this strict view was controverted in *Ulpian's* time, for that jurisconsult held that the ownership was re-transferred *ipso jure*, and forty years later (A.D. 259) Valerianus and Gallienus laid down that the donor had not only the *condictio*, but also a *vindicatio utilis*.

548. (§ i) *Mortis causa donatio.* The essential character of this form of gift consisted in that it was not only given *propter mortis suspicionem*, *i.e.*, in view of death, but also *subject to the condition* 'of the death of either the donor or a third person, and in view of death generally, or more frequently in view of death from some particular event, and might be given either—

(1) *Conditionally; ut si mors contigisset, tunc haberet cui donatum est*, or—

(1) *Determinable on a condition; ut jam nunc haberet, redderet si convaluisset, vel de prælio, vel peregre rediisset.*

557. Besides these *mortis causa* translations of ownership, gifts in the form of *obligations*, *releases* of debtor, etc., might be made on the same ground by way of *stipulation, delegation, ex promissio* (a form of the contract *verbis*) *acceptilatio*, delivery of *chirographa*, etc.

As *decease* was the only irrevocable manner of confirming these gifts, a change of intention could revoke them, and a *rei vindicatio* could be employed in the case of the conditional gift, for the donor had never ceased to be owner, or a *condictio* (and by a favourable interpretation a *rei vindicatio utilis*), in the case of the gift determinable on a condition, would effect the revocation just as if the event had not occurred or the donee had died first.

559. *Application of legacy rules.* The Roman jurisconsults had been struck by the analogy between the *donatio mortis causa* and gifts *inter vivos* on the one hand, and legacies on the other, and opinions were divided as to the classification. *Justinian* decided to number them with *legacies* in nearly everything, but where they differed the rules applying to them were similar to those in the case of the *donatio inter vivos*. Hence, in respect of the *donatio mortis causa* :—

(1) It could be made *by all* who could make a will or codicil.

(2) *To all* who could receive testamentary bequests.

(3) The *leges Julia et Papia* and the *lex Falcidia* applied to it, though not the *lex Cincia* (*post*, par. 566).

(4) It was affected by the rights of the patron to the succession of the freedman.

(5) It was affected by the insolvency of the donor at his decease, and by his capital condemnation, including *maxima* and *media c.d.*

(6) If only irregularly affected the case would be governed by the rules as to *fidei-commissa*.

561. The more important *differences* between the *donatio mortis causa* and legacies were :—

(1) The gift operated through the accord of two present persons (*præsens præsenti dat*), i.e., the donor and the donee.

(2) It was independent of the testament, and therefore valid; although the will was null, revoked, useless, or the heir refused the inheritance; and hence, the person who failed in attacking the will as null, or *inofficiosum*, lost the *legacies*, but not the *donatio mortis causa*.

(3) It was irrevocably realised by the *death*, without waiting for the *aditio hereditatis*.

(4) The *cat. reg.* (*post*, par. 857) did not apply, as the capacity of the donee to receive was only determined at the time of the decease of the donor; and it was only necessary at the time of making the disposition that the donee should be capable of the mancipation, tradition, stipulation, or other act operating the gift.

(5) If consisting of a stipulation of an annuity, it was treated according to the stipulation, not the legacy rules.

562. *Form of donatio mortis causa.* In strictness the *dominium* existed, or it did not; but terms and conditions came to be admitted which controlled otherwise absolute transferences, as in the case of things being given in dowry on the condition *ut tunc ejus efficiantur cum nupserit* (Dig. 23, 3, 7, 3, Paul). Hence these donations were in ancient times effected by *traditio* for *res nec mancipi*, or *mancipatio*, or *in jure cessio* for *res mancipi*, and the result was modified by the condition attached. The *Vaticana fragmenta*, § xlix, lay down that "*nulla legis actio prodita est de futuro*"; and that, therefore, no such mode could be employed for a gift conditional on death; but *Marcellus* (Dig. 40, 1, 15) gives an example of a manumission *vin-*

dicta mortis causa, which would be giving, by the *in jure cessio* process, liberty to a slave conditioned in the donor's death, *i.e.*, the slave would, on that event happening, become free. *Justinian* finally decided (Code 8, 57, 4) that the disposition could take place between husband and wife (*post*, par. 577), that it should produce the same effect as a legacy, and should be valid without the necessity of writing or the presence of a public officer or registration, if made *verbally*, or in *writing*, before *five witnesses*. Hence, after *Justinian's* legislation, the gift without *traditio*, itself transferred the ownership at the moment of death, just as a legacy (without distinction as to whether *per vindicationem* or *per damnationem*), or a *fidei commissum*.

564. *Mortis causa capio.* This expression for acquisitions on account of death, included in a general sense the *donatio mortis causa*, legacies, fidei-commissa, successions, etc.; but it was technically reserved for other than specially named acquisitions, *e.g.*, for that which a father gave to the poor on the death of his son, or for that which a slave freed by testament, or a legatee, paid, as the condition imposed by the testator.

565. (§ ii) *Donatio inter vivos.* In early times a promise, verbal or in writing, to give something to another, not being one of the recognised forms of contract, was only a manifestation of a liberal intention, and as a mere pact was not obligatory in itself; but, with the course of time, legislation effected changes in the subject.

566. *Lex Cincia* (B.C. 23). The practice of freedmen, at fixed periods of the year, or on certain occasions, making gifts to their patrons, became a custom of society, and the gifts received in early times by orators from their clients, ultimately degenerated into exactions extorted by the patricians from the plebeians. Hence the origin of the plebiscitum of the tribune *Cincius*, which applied especially to donations *inter vivos*, and was followed by the *leges Furia*, *Voconia*, and *Falcidia*. By the *lex Cincia*—

(1) Orators were forbidden to receive gifts for their pleading *(ob causam orandam)*.

(2) A certain unknown limit *(certum modum, legitimum modum)* was fixed, which donations were not to exceed, though certain persons (*post*, par. 571) united by cognation, potestas, or affection, were excepted from this provision.

But this *lex Cincia* was an example of an *imperfect* law, inasmuch as it did not pronounce the gift a nullity, although it exceeded the amount, and therefore it could only be used by way of an *exceptio* to a demand. This difficulty was, however, got over by calling in the aid of the interdict *utrubi*, when possession of a *movable* had not been parted with for more than six months, and in the case of *obligations* by the use of the personal action *condictio indebiti*. Probably, also, at a later period, the *actio rescissoria* could be used for the amount exceeding the limit, as this action was held to be open to him who, to a demand, could oppose a *perpetual* exception, and the *exceptio legis Cinciæ* fell within this class, and passed to the heirs of the donor; but, after the reign of Alexander Severus, the gift was held, on the death of the donor, to be irrevocable if he had shewn no intention of reclaiming it.

571. *Form of gift inter vivos.* Antoninus Pius made the *donatio inter parentes et liberos* (who, as *exceptæ personæ*, were not included under the *lex Cincia*) valid by *consent* alone, without tradition or mancipation, provided there was no question about the intention of the parties. *Constantius Chlorus*, and after him Constantine, made special provisions as to registration in respect of *all* donations; and, finally, *Justinian* generalised the special enactment of *Antoninus Pius*, so that the donation became an obligatory pact, a legitimate pact, giving a right of action against the donor for the purpose of enforcing it; but *tradition* was required to render the donee owner, and therefore the pact was only a cause, not a mode of acquisition. Gifts exceeding 500 *solidi* had to be registered, otherwise the excess above that sum was void; except in the case of gifts made by or to the emperor, or for the ransom of captives, or the reconstruction of buildings damaged by fire or otherwise.

574. *Revocation of the donatio inter vivos.* In certain cases personal to the donor, revocation was permitted; *e.g.*, for serious injuries or violence to the person of the donor; for *dolus* involving losses of fortune; for attempts against life; for non-execution of conditions; for ingratitude; and on account of the birth of a subsequent child in the case of a patron who, when childless, had given his property to a freedman.

577. *Donatio inter virum et uxorem.* When a wife was *in manu viri* no question of gift could arise between them; and previous to *Caracalla* the settled rule was, that all gifts between married people after they actually became *vir* and *uxor* were absolutely void, except those not impoverishing the one to enrich the other; as in the case of the gift of a place of sepulture, or of a slave to free, or in order to attain to a dignity, or to restore a building, or for divorce. But after a *senatus-consultum*, passed in the reign of that emperor, the rigour of the law was modified, and though the donor could always revoke, yet if he died without so doing, the gift became valid, and hence the same rule applied as in the case of *legacies* and *fidei-commissa, ut sit ambulatoria voluntas ejus, usque ad vitæ supremum exitum.*

582. (§ iii) *Of dowry and gifts on account of marriage.* The *dos* (or *res uxoria*) made its appearance early in Roman society, and is defined as all that which the wife brings to bear the burdens of the marriage *(ad ferenda matrimonii opera).* At first the husband acquired the property before the marriage by a *datio*, made by the *mancipatio* or *in jure cessio* for *res mancipi*, and by *traditio* for *res nec mancipi* (Gai. Inst., ii, § 63); and when the wife fell *in manu* she was absorbed in the personality of her husband, and therefore all the property became irrevocably and universally at his absolute

disposal. When the *dos* was not given immediately, the *stipulatio* was employed, and a special form was introduced (restricted to the wife and the paternal ascendants) for solemnly declaring what should constitute the *dos;* but it is disputed whether the husband replied, and whether this *dictio dotis* was to be considered as a contract, and it disappeared prior to Justinian.

Augmenting or settling the *dos* during the marriage was early permitted, as it was held different from a *donatio inter vivos*; and, finally, an agreement of any kind was considered obligatory, though, if made *before* marriage, a tacit condition was implied that the marriage should take place. The laws of Augustus, with a view to encourage marriage, favoured the subject of dowry, and actions were available to daughters to compel the father or paternal ancestor to give them a dowry; and the restoration of the *dos* at the dissolution of the marriage was enforced by the *rei uxoriæ actio*.

587. *Kinds of dos*. In respect of the persons who gave it, the dowry was—

(1) *Profectitia*, when given by the father or paternal ancestor, and it returned to him if the daughter died during the marriage.

(2) *Adventitia*, if from any other source, *e.g.*, the wife's own property, or from a third person; in which case it remained to the husband surviving, unless it was—

(3) *Receptitia, i.e.*, its return stipulated for by the third person.

If the marriage was dissolved during the wife's lifetime, the dowry, whether *profectitia* or *adventitia*, returned to her and her heirs, and *Justinian* made the *adventitia* on the death of the wife during marriage return to her heirs. Other property of the wife, not comprised in the *dos*, was called *parapherna*, of which the wife had the ownership, and the husband only such rights as she yielded to him (code 5, 14).

588. *Dowry immovables*. A *plebiscitum* of Augustus, the *lex Julia de adulteriis et de fundo dotali*, prohibited on *Italian* soil *mortgages* of the dowry estate of the wife, even with her consent, and its *alienation* without her consent. *Justinian* made dowry *immovables* everywhere *inalienable*, even with the consent of the wife, and practically the husband was no longer the owner of the *dos*.

589. *Donatio ante (or propter) nuptias*. This form of gift was of much later origin, but is mentioned by Theodosius and Valentinian as then already established. It was given by the husband to the wife *before* the marriage, as a provision for his family, and to guarantee the *dos;* hence the rules as to the wife by way of punishment, incurring the loss of the dowry, applied in respect of the husband and this donatio; and if an agreement was entered into in respect of survivorship, the amounts to be reserved out of the dowry by the wife and out of the donatio by the husband were, according to Justinian (Nov. 97, c. 1), to be equal.

The *donatio* was protected from creditors, so that on the husband actually becoming insolvent, the wife had a *personal* and *hypothecary* action to compel its delivery, and even a *real* action to vindicate it, if fraudulently alienated, and she enjoyed it throughout the marriage, after which it was restored to the husband.

In order to assimilate it to the rules affecting the *dos*, *Justinian* allowed the *donatio* to be augmented or even settled *during* marriage, and therefore he altered the name to *donatio propter nuptias*.

590. (§ iv) *Enfranchisement by a co-proprietor.* According to the old civil law, if a slave owned in common was freed *vindicta* or *testamento* by one owner, so that he would have become a freed Roman citizen, he fell altogether into the power of the other by right of accrual. This method of acquisition was destroyed by Justinian, and the slave was to become really free, and the price to be paid the remaining owner was fixed by a constitution (Code 7, 7, 1, 5), according to a scale, varying with the employment of the slave.

591. *Actions relating to donations.* For gifts *mortis causa*, if they were—

(1) *Conditional on decease,* the donor remained owner, and had a real *vindicatio actio;* if the condition was fulfilled, the *donee* acquired the right to the *vindicatio*, and in either case, under Justinian, independent of tradition.

(2) *Immediate,* but revoked by survivorship. In this case, as the donee immediately received the thing, he became owner, and had a *vindicatio*, but the donation being determinable if (α) the donor repented of his gift, a *condictio* or a *utilis rei vindicatio* was open to him to compel the donee to restore, and (β) if the donor survived, the event provided for not having occurred, he had the *condictio quasi re non secuta*, by which he could also obtain the value of the thing if it had been alienated, and only the value if, being a slave, he had been freed. The donor had also, by a favourable construction, an action *in rem*, but not both, and, according to some jurisconsults only the one; according to others, the other.

594. In the case of gifts *inter vivos*, if followed by tradition, the property was transferred, and a real action was open to the donee, but since, under Justinian, the *donor* was bound, independent of *traditio*, he could be sued by the *condictio certi* or *ex stipulatu*, according as the promise was in respect of an ascertained or indeterminate subject; otherwise a *condictio ex lege* was available, *i.e.*, a personal action founded on the particular law, making a simple non-obligatory pact binding, but, in the absence of a special promise or *dolus*, the donor was not liable for eviction, or for more than it was in his power to do.

Tit. viii. Quibus alienare licet vel non.

595. The text examines the exceptions to the two rules, that (1) it is necessary to be the owner in order to transfer property, *i.e.*,

rem alienam facere, and that (2) being owner, the power of alienating follows. An example of an exception to the second rule would be the position of the husband as to his wife's dowry *immovables (ante,* par. 588), and in respect of the first, the powers of the agent and curator over property of a lunatic, or of the tutor over that of a pupil (although the magistrate's permission was generally requisite for the transference of rural immovables), and the creditor in possession of the thing pledged could alienate the property, even against the pact *ne vendere liceat,* for this only compelled him to give notice of the intended sale.

602. (§ ii) The pupil of either sex could not transfer property without the authorisation of the tutor ; a rule founded on the principle that he or she might improve their condition, but not make it worse, hence if the pupil—

(1) Lent, without authorisation, a sum of money, *i.e.*, entered into the contract *mutuum,* involving the return of things of the same quality, weight, number, or measure, and giving the lender the right to the *condictio certi,* he really made no contract at all ; and if the things were not consumed, he had a *rei vindicatio* action to compel their return or the *condictio certi* for an equivalent. If they had been consumed in bad faith, the *actio ad exhibendum* lay, entailing damages ; and the same rules apply to a *payment* by the pupil without authorisation.

(2) Received a payment from a debtor, the pupil could acquire the ownership, but the debtor was not released, *i.e.*, the *auctoritas* of the tutor was in this case necessary for the debtor's, not the pupil's protection, and without it the debtor was unable to vindicate, and could only use the *exceptio doli* if the pupil re-demanded the thing and had not consumed it, on the principle that no one can enrich himself at the expense of another ; but if the amount was paid to the tutor with the permission of the judge, the debtor had, under Justinian, *plenissima securitas, i.e.*, he was not liable in respect of the pupil's right to *restitutio in integrum,* if the tutor did not hand over the sum, or became insolvent.

Tit. ix. Per quas personas nobis acquiritur.

608. The text examines the consequences of the rules (1) that the identification of the person subject to *potestas* with the *persona* of the paterfamilias, enables the former to represent the latter ; and (2) that the *persona* of a Roman citizen could not be represented by another.

611. (§ i) *Acquisitions by the filius-familias.* On the principle that persons *in potestate, in manu,* or *in mancipio,* could have nothing of their own, any one in this position receiving anything acquired it for the *paterfamilias* (Ulp. Reg. xix, § 18), though in respect of *possession,* it was a disputed point whether persons *in manu* and *in mancipio* were to be assimilated to those *in potestate* (Gai. Inst. ii, § 90).

Prior to *Justinian* the *manus* and *mancipium* disappeared, and custom allowed sons and slaves to enjoy their *peculium*. Under Augustus, Nerva, and Trajan, the view became established of regarding the *filius-familias* as a *paterfamilias*, in respect of his acquisitions on military service, and hence the assertion of an independent *persona* as to the disposition by testament or *inter vivos* of the *castrense peculium*. By analogy to this, a *quasi castrense peculium* was recognised as early as the time of Ulpian. *Constantine* allowed it in respect of property saved, or the result of gifts obtained whilst employed in the palace. *Theodosius* and *Valentinian* included advocates and other professional persons. Leo extended it to bishops, presbyters, and deacons; and Justinian included in it everything received by imperial favour.

Constantine established a third kind, called by the commentators *peculium adventitium*, being property received from the mother, either *ex testamento* or *ab intestato*, but extended by Justinian to include everything acquired by any means except through the father. Hence, under Justinian, the son had the—

(1) *Peculium* proper, called by the commentators *profectitium, i.e.*, property coming from the father and belonging in strictness to him.

(2) *Peculium castrense* and *quasi-castrense*, over which the father had no rights.

(3) *Peculium adventitium, i.e.*, property belonging to the son, but which he could not dispose of either *inter vivos* or by testament, and of which the father had the *usufruct*, though he might be deprived of this if a legacy was only left to the son on that condition.

Prior to Justinian a father, on emancipating a son, had the right to *retain* one-third of the property itself, over which he had had the *usufruct*, whilst the son was *in potestate*, but after that emperor he could only claim the *usufruct* of half the same property.

616. (§ iii) *Acquisitions by slaves.* The position of the slave in respect of his actual master falls under four heads :—

(1) The *owner* always possessed, in the eye of the law, the slave's *peculium*, and everything acquired by the slave in any way was acquired for the master without the latter's knowledge, and even against his will, except that as the *aditio hereditatis* implied burdens as well as acquisitions, the slave could not accept without the master's consent; but on that being given, the acquisition was made for the master from the moment of the *aditio ;* and as a *legacy* did not involve any succession to the debts or obligations of the deceased, it was acquired immediately from the death of the testator for the master, unless some condition was attached.

The advantage of leaving the *aditio* or the *legatum* to the slave instead of to the master, who really became heir or acquired the legacy, was that the position of the slave might alter in the interim, for he might change masters, become free, or die, and the result would vary accordingly. The value of a slave with such a right hanging over him was also greater, and the indemnity due to the master would be larger in the event of his being killed.

In respect of the two elements of *possession*, the *fact* could be accomplished in the person of the slave, but the *intention* must depend on the master *(animo nostro, corpore etiam alieno, possidemus*, Dig. 41, 2, 3, 12, Paul), hence, unlike ownership, it could not be acquired *ignorantibus et invitis*, though an exception was made in respect of things relating to the *peculium* of slaves or sons, on the ground, according to Papinian, of utility, and to prevent an incessant inquiry into details.

If the same slave was owned by several persons, each acquired proportionally to his share.

(2) The *usufructuary* only acquired the ownership or possession of that which resulted from the labour of the slave or his labour for others, or from the usufructuary's property *(ante,* par. 474).

(3) He who had the *use* of a slave acquired only that which resulted from such use, and he could not make him work for others, and claim the wages, for that would-be *produce (ante,* par. 497).

(4) The possessor in good faith of a free man or the slave of another, would acquire through the freeman or the slave, as indicated with reference to produce, etc., in par. 400, and by *usucapion* he might become owner of the slave of another, and thereby acquire an owner's rights over all that the slave had acquired, but in the case of the freeman, this would be subject to his rights on asserting his freedom.

636. (§ v) *Acquisitions by a stranger.* From the principle that the *persona* of a Roman citizen could not be represented by another came the rule, *per extraneam personam nihil adquiri posse* (Gai. Inst. ii, § 95), but a distinction was gradually introduced, and for acts of the *jus gentium* agents were admitted (see part II, par. 161); hence, though *ownership* in pure civil law could not be acquired for another by a stranger, yet *possession* could be acquired by a third person, not only in respect of the fact, but also as to the *intention*, so that, if the order was given beforehand, then possession was immediately acquired, but if without our knowledge, then it was acquired as soon as it came to our knowledge. As a consequence of this *possession* for another by an agent, the *ownership* might also be so acquired (*si procurator rem mihi emerit ex mandato meo, eique sit tradita meo nomine ; dominium mihi, id est proprietas, adquiritur etiam ignoranti*, Dig. 41, 1, 13, Neratius) ; but in order that *usucapion* or the *præscriptio longi temporis* might commence to run for us, it was necessary that we should know of it, because it required not only intention, but also *good faith*.

637. *Acquisitions by universality.* The text of the Institutes passes from the consideration of the means of acquisition of particular objects to *Universal successions*, whether *ex testamento* or *ab intestato*.

N

Per universitatem successio was the acquisition of the entire patrimony of a person, including all corporeal and incorporeal property, and all active and passive rights except those necessarily extinguished. This succession might be to a deceased or to a living person; but under Justinian the latter kinds were nearly all suppressed.

639. *Inheritances.* Originally, if a person *alieni juris* died, he occasioned no alteration in the *persona*, for he had none individually; but, on the death of a *paterfamilias*, his juridical *persona* being immortal, immediately fell on others; for, as it was a creature of the civil law, it could only be extinguished by a juridical, not a natural, cause; hence, being a matter of sacred and public law, the intervention of the *comitia calata* was necessary, and a testament was, therefore, in fact, a law. If the comitia was interrupted, it had to begin again; and to this is to be attributed the origin of the necessity for the testament being *uno contextu*; and hence, also, the heir must have had the rights of the city and have been in existence at the time of the making of the testament. But the plebeians were excluded from the *comitia* (part I, par. 27, 28, 29), and hence originated the fiction of the sale of the *familia pecuniaque*, *i.e.*, the will *per mancipationem* (*per æs et libram*), the right to make which was formally recognised by the twelve tables (v, 3); and, as the words were interpreted in their largest sense as the right *legare, legem dicere, legem condere*, the *curiæ* could not now reject a will, but only receive it and affirm it (*teste populo*).

644. The word *hereditas* has two senses :—
(1) The succession, the fact of succeeding universally to the property and rights of the deceased citizen (*nihil est aliud hereditas quam successio in universum jus quod defunctus habuit*, Dig. 50, 16, 24, Gaius).

(2) The universality itself, *i.e.*, the deceased's patrimony, as a whole, whether beneficial or onerous, and called anciently the *familia*, whence came the name *heres*, to indicate the person who acquired it, for the term *herus* was formerly applied to the *paterfamilias* (*Veteres enim heredes pro dominis appellabant*, Just. Inst., ii, 19, § 7).

As the *hereditas*, until acquired, represented the *persona* of the deceased (*hereditas enim non heredis personam sed defuncti sustinet*, Dig. 41, 1, 34, Ulpian), the condition of slaves and their rights as to legacies and stipulations would be affected by the position of the deceased, and not by that of his successor, who might in some cases be a *peregrinus*; but, after the *aditio*, the title of the heir was referred back, according to *Cassius* and *Florentinus* (Dig. 45, 3, 28, § 4, and 29, 2, § 54), to the moment of the testator's death.

646. The *hereditas* was bestowed either
(1) By *testament*, when, if the testamentary dispositions were valid in part, they would extend to the whole, or
(2) By *law, i.e. ab intestato*, when the deceased could enjoin nothing on his successor.

Tit. x. De testamentis ordinandis.

648. (§ i) According to *Modestinus* (Dig. 28, 1, 1), the *testamentum* may be defined as *voluntatis nostræ justa sententia de eo quod quis post mortem suam fieri vult*, and in this title the Institutes briefly review the history of wills, treating of five kinds.

(1) *Calatis comitiis* (see part I, par. 27, and *ante* par. 639). The comitia might be convoked (*calare*=vocare=καλεῖν) for special business, as for the purpose of solemn witnessing in religious matters (*sacrorum detestatio*), and twice in the year for wills (*quæ comitia bis in anno testamentis faciendis destinata erant*, Gai. Inst., ii, § 101.)

(2) *In procinctu.* When a soldier was about to enter on or was already engaged in a campaign, and could not, therefore, wait for the meeting of the calata comitia, he was allowed after a religious ceremony (Cicero) to declare his will formally in the presence of the army.

(3) *Per æs et libram.* Although after the death of the paterfamilias the patrimony as an incorporeal thing was held to be *res nec mancipi*, yet during his life it was viewed by a pure fiction as *res mancipi*, and, therefore, could be sold *per mancipationem* (see part II, par. 121, and *ante*, par. 312, 1) the heir receiving at the same time verbal or written directions as to the wishes of the testator after his death.

The first kind of will had, previous to the time of Gaius and Ulpian, fallen into disuse, and the second had been replaced by the informal military testament (see Tit. xi). The third kind had undergone important modifications, and the inconvenience attending the fact of the heir being absolutely entitled and known beforehand obviated by employing a fictitious *familiæ emptor*—so that, according to Ulpian (Reg. xx, § 9), the transaction was divided into two distinct formalities, viz.:—

(α) *Imaginaria familiæ mancipatio;*
(β) *Testamenti nuncupatio;*

And the second part tended with time to become merely a verbal declaration of having made written dispositions (*hæc uti in his tabulis ceris-que scripta sunt ita do ita lego, ita testor; itaque vos Quirites, testimonium mihi perhibitote*, Gai. Inst. ii, § 104).

(4) *Prætorian Testament.* The *familiæ emptor* and the *libripens* were reduced to the rank of witnesses, thus making seven in all, and these appended their seals to the document; but, as this will rested only on the Prætorian edict, the heir acquired simply the *bonorum possessio*, not the civil hereditas.

(5) *Testamentum Tripertitum.* The commentators invented this term to indicate the threefold derivation (Civil law, Prætorian edict, Imperial Constitutions) of this kind of will, which was introduced by Valentinian III in the East, and partially by Theodosius II in the West (though in the latter Empire the Prætorian will and that *per æs et libram* were used down to the middle ages).

This will was confirmed by Justinian, and it was essential for its validity that it should be—

(α) *Uno contextu* (Civil law rule, *ante*, par. 639), *i.e.*, irrespective of the writing or dictation of the will, the ceremony must be gone through without interruption in the presence of the witnesses.

(β) *Sealed* (Prætorian edict) by and in the presence of the seven witnesses, who, if previously together for some other purpose, must be warned that required as witnesses.

(γ) *Signed* (Imperial Constitutions) by the witnesses and by the testator also (unless the whole will was in his handwriting), or by an eighth witness if he could not write, or in the case of a secret will, where the document was rolled up and only the end (*reliqua parte*) exposed for signature (a method perpetuated in the French will called *mystique*, code, art. 976, etc.) All might use the same seal, for a *superscriptio* (which was independent of the *subscriptio* or attestation signature) in the handwriting of each was placed at side, stating by whom and on whose will the seal was placed.

According to the Institutes (§ iv), the name of the heir had to be in the handwriting of the testator or of a witness; but a novel (119, 9) subsequently suppressed this formality.

659. (§ vi) The *witnesses* were required to be such *cum quibus testamenti factio est*, a rule derived from the old law as to the *mancipatio* process necessitating the possession of the *commercium* (part I, par. 185); hence excluding women, persons under the age of puberty, slaves, madmen, mutes, deaf persons, interdicted prodigals, and those declared by law to be *improbi intestabilesque* (*post*, par. 687, 5); but *testamenti factio* in respect of witnesses was ultimately extended so as to include all who possessed the capability of benefiting by a testamentary disposition, although incapable of making a will themselves (*post*, par. 681, and 804, 3); and it was only required at the time of making the will. The heir himself might be included under any one of the above classes; for under Justinian he was not required in the preparation of the will, and the distinction had ceased to exist between being called to take and the power of taking (part I, par. 369); and Hadrian decided that the attestation of a witness who was, in fact, a slave, but presumed at the time to be free, did not invalidate the will.

663. On the ground that, according to the civil law, the members of a family formed, in respect of the property, but one collective being, the witnesses could not be in the same *civil* family as the testator or the heir (though there was no impediment after the tie was broken); and the opinion of *Gaius* (Inst. ii, § 106) is adopted by Justinian, that the rule applied to the witnesses whom a *filius familias* employed after his return from the army, in order to make a will in respect of his *castrense peculium* (see *ante*, par. 611), though the contrary opinion of Marcellus and Ulpian (grounded on the fact

of the son's exclusive ownership of this particular kind of property) is also inserted in the Digest (28, 1, 20, § ii).

665. As soon as the law permitted the *familiæ emptor* to be a stranger, the heir or any of his family might be witnesses, though the jurisconsults thought it desirable that they should not so act (Gai. Inst., ii, § 108); and Justinian restored the old law, making them inadmissible, though the restriction did not apply to legatees or recipients by fidei commissa, as they were not deemed to be legal successors.

667. It was immaterial on what the will was written, and, to guard against accidents, several might be made, all with the same formalities.

668. The right which always existed of making a *verbal* (or, as called by the commentators, *nuncupative*) testament, by stating wishes in presence of seven witnesses, was confirmed by Justinian; and, although this form of will rested on the civil law, the prætor protected it by giving the *bonorum possessio*.

Tit. xi. De militari testamento.

669. Julius Cæsar originated the privilege referred to under this title as a temporary concession (part I, par. 350). Titus and Domitian confirmed it, Nerva and Trajan generalised it, and the right was finally recognised as a special exceptional law. Justinian grounds the privilege on the unskilfulness of the soldier in such matters; but, since at other times than when on duty he was bound to comply with every formality, it may be assumed that the right arose from the necessities of the situation.

In respect of form a soldier's will was valid, made, whilst in actual service, in any way, as if, when dying, written with his blood on his breast-plate or scabbard, or traced in the sand with the point of his sword (Code vi, 21, 1), or made verbally in the presence of two witnesses, who, however, according to a rescript of Trajan, though not specially summoned for the purpose, must have been informed that they were to act as such. The will was also held valid made by a deaf or dumb soldier while still in the ranks, and before he was invalided from service; but a military testament could not be made before the soldier, though enrolled, had joined the army, nor after his discharge; or, if not in camp, though on service; and, in any case, it was only good for *one year* after his return, and not at all if he had been discharged for misconduct, or, in the case of the superior officers, if superseded in the command; but it was held that, if the soldier died within the year, the will was valid, although, in consequence of a condition imposed on the heir, the testamentary inheritance would not have devolved on him until after that time.

675. (§ iv) A previous and informal will, subsequently ratified in any way whilst on service, became valid as a *soldier's* testament.

677. (§ v) *In respect of the capacity of the testator*, the right accorded to the *filius familius* to will away his *castrense peculium* was originally a purely military privilege; and, as to the capacity of the *re-*

cipients, it was not necessary that they should have *factio testamenti* with him; and, therefore, he could institute as heirs or leave legacies to *peregrini, deportati*, and those not possessing the *jus capiendi, e.g., latini juniani, cœlibes, orbi*, etc.

In respect of freedom from the ordinary restraints, the soldier need not formally disinherit children (*post*, par. 711), his silence being held sufficient evidence of his intention; and, therefore, his will would not be set aside as *inofficiosum*. He could leave more than three-fourths in legacies, be partly testate and partly not, have several wills, and dispose of the inheritance by codicils. The will did not become void (*irritum, post*, par. 773, 2) by the soldier's undergoing any of the three kinds of *capitis deminutio* (*ante*, par. 208, 2), provided the alteration of status caused by the two first resulted from some military penalty; but, if a *paterfamilias* soldier were arrogated, his will would only apply to the *peculium castrense*; and, on the other hand, on the emancipation of a *filiusfamilius*, a will originally applying only to the *peculium castrense* would now include his whole estate.

680. By analogy to the military testament, the wills of *sailors in the fleet*, and of those who died whilst with the army, though not actually soldiers, were similarly privileged. The *actual presence* of witnesses of wills of persons attacked with contagious disorders was dispensed with, and, owing to the difficulty of procuring sufficient and competent witnesses of wills made in the country, the number might be reduced to five, and the rules were relaxed as to the necessity for the subscription of the testator and witnesses (Code vi, 23, 31).

Tit. xii. Quibus non est permissum facere testamentum.

681. *Factio testamenti* at the time of Justinian referred either to—

(1) The legal capacity to make a will, or to

(2) The capacity of being called to the inheritance (see *post*, par. 718), or to the benefit of a legacy for self or another.

682. As to (1) the right resulted from *public* law, and belonged to every *paterfamilias* who was a Roman citizen, though he might be unable to exercise it, as if he were insane (without lucid intervals during which the act would be valid), or under age, or an interdicted prodigal, or deaf, or dumb; but, in respect of the two last, special regulations (Code vi, 22) enabled them to make a will, if not altogether physically incapable. Subsequent capacity would not make the will valid, if incapacity existed at the time; hence the right and the capacity to exercise must concur at the time of making the will, though subsequent incapacity to exercise it would not affect the will if the right continued to exist uninterruptedly up to the time of decease (see *post*, par. 773, 2).

687. The following did not possess the right to make a will:—

(1) Slaves, including those who had suffered *maxima c.d.;* but, according to Ulpian (Reg. xx, 16), the *servus publicus populi romani* could dispose by will of one-half his estate.

(2) *Peregrini, i.e.*, those not possessing the *commercium*, and therefore including those under *media*, c. d. (*ante*, par. 197, 205), but excluding the peregrini of those cities whose municipal law gave them the right.

(3) *De statu suo dubitantes, i.e.*, those of uncertain status, as the slave freed by will, but ignorant of the death of his master, and of the *aditio*.

(4) *Freedmen* prior to the twelve tables, but subsequently reduced to the *latini Juniani* and the *dediticii*. Under Justinian these latter distinctions did not exist.

(5) *Intestabiles, i.e.*, persons who could neither make nor witness a will because they had been condemned for slander, bribery, adultery, or for refusing to recognise their signatures on the opening of a will (*post*, par. 982).

(6) *Filii-familias*, for they had no property of their own, and the right even of willing their *castrense peculium* had to be especially accorded by imperial favour (part i, p. 350), and if not exercised, the property was likened to the *peculium* and returned to the paterfamilias, so that by a sort of *postliminium* any acts of the father affecting it prior to the death of his son would be valid, *i.e.*, if (at the time of Justinian) there were no children or brothers surviving, for otherwise these had claims to the *ab-intestato peculium* (*post*, par. 1023). It was not until the time of Justinian that the power of willing, according to the regular forms, their *quasi castrense peculium* was given to all without distinction who held that class of property.

As to the *peculium adventitium*, see *ante*, par. 611 (3).

690. (§ iv) Justinian's uncle Justin compelled *blind* persons to have a *Tabellarius*, or an eighth witness present, to whom the will was dictated, or by whom it was read aloud.

691. (§ 5) In respect of the *captive*, the effect of the *Jus post-liminii* (*ante*, par. 163) would be, that a will made—

(1) *during* captivity was *invalid* in any case.

(2) *before* captivity was *valid*, for if he returned the *Jus postliminii* would apply, and if he did not return it was valid *ex lege Cornelia*, the *lex Cornelia de falsis*, or *testamentaria* (B.C. 81) providing the penalty of deportation for falsifying wills, including this one, which would have been unnecessary if it had not been intended to make valid a will which in strictness was void as that of a slave.

Tit. xiii. De exheredatione liberorum.

692. The twelve tables (v. 3) imposed no restriction on the power of disposition of the *paterfamilias*, but the idea existing at the time of Cicero of the co-proprietorship of the children in the property (part i, par. 330, 331), favoured the view that the testator was bound to formally declare which member of the family he intended to exclude; but as this only applied to those called to the succession by *law*, it turned upon who would be *heredes sui ab in-*

testato, and as these varied according to primitive, prætorian, or imperial law, these three systems are severally considered in this title, see also *post*, par. 773.

697. According to the *Civil law*—

(1) *Sons in power* must be excluded *by name* (*nominatim exheredare, e.g., Titius filius meus exheres esto*, or if no other, *filius meus*, etc.), or the will would be invalid *ab initio*, even if the son died first, according to the opinion of Gaius (Inst. ii, § 123); and the Sabinians adopted by Justinian, in opposition to the Proculians, and without reference to the equitable views which appear to have existed in the time of Papinian.

(2) *Daughters in power* and other descendants who would be *sui heredes* on death of testator, *collectively* (*inter ceteros exheredare, e.g., et ceteri exheredes sunto*), and if they were simply omitted the will was not invalid, but they would have a fixed share (the *jus adcrescendi ad certam portionem*), *i.e.*, if the instituted heirs were *sui*, they would take an equal share with them, but if strangers, the omitted descendants would get one half the property, and if *sui* and *extranei* were instituted heirs together, the omitted descendants would take an equal share with the *sui*, and deprive the *extranei* of half.

(3) *Posthumous* children could not, according to the old law, be instituted heirs or receive legacies, being regarded as *incertæ personæ*; but, as they might at birth be *sui heredes*, and therefore, whether sons or daughters, render the will invalid, the testator was permitted to institute them or exclude them, if *males* individually (*Quicumque mihi filius genitus fuerit, exheres esto* or by alluding to the mother, *qui ex Seia nascetur*); if *females* collectively, but with some legacy to show that they were not forgotten (*ille mihi heres esto ceteri exheredes sunto postumi vero meæ si quâ nascitur centum solidos do lego*). *Postumi* originally referred only to the child born after the death of the *parent*, but came to include three classes, (1) *postumus suus, i.e.*, the child who when born would be a *suus heres* of the testator; (2) *postumus alienus, i.e.*, the child who when born, though a member of the family, would not be a *suus heres* in respect of the testator, but as the death of his parent in the lifetime of the testator might make him when born a *suus heres, Aquilius Gallus* composed the form given in Dig. 28, 2, 29, to cover this contingency; (3) *quasi-postumus Veleianus, i.e.*, according to the provisions of the *lex Junia* (or *Julia*), *Velleia* passed under Augustus A.D. 10, the child who born (α) before or (β) after the making of the will became a *suus heres*, by so-called *quasi-agnatio*, resulting from his father dying, or otherwise leaving the family in the lifetime of the testator.

708. (§ iii) According to *Prætorian* law, children emancipated, or in any other way not under power, had equal rights *ab intestato* with those of the same degree still in power; and, therefore, if the testator had not either instituted or excluded all males by name

and females collectively, who would have been *sui heredes* if they had remained in the family, the Prætor would give them the *contra tabulas testamenti bonorum possessionem unde liberi* (*post*, par. 1109), so that until Antonine (Gai. Inst. ii, § 126) restricted their rights also to the *jus adcrescendi* (*ante*, par. 697) women under the Prætor's rules, had an advantage over those coming in under the civil law, for the testament was set aside altogether in their favour instead of their merely acquiring a right to a fixed share. By the same method, the Prætor compelled the natural father to institute or exclude a child *adopted* by another, and subsequently emancipated, and who, therefore, according to the civil law, would have no claim on either the adopted or natural father.

711. (§ v) Under *Justinian*, all the distinctions of sex as to sons or daughters, or as to sex in respect of *postumi*, were abolished, and the Prætorian law in respect of emancipated children confirmed, so that as to—

(1) *The mode*, the institution or exclusion must be by name, *i.e.*, they must be referred to specially.

(2) *The result*, the omission involved the nullity of the will *ab initio*, although in respect of *posthumous* children, or those classed with them, the nullity only arose at their birth or quasi-agnation. The *extraneus* adoptor (*ante*, par. 138, 1) was, however, not obliged either to institute or exclude the adopted child, and the same rule applied to the mother or maternal ancestor, for there was no idea of co-proprietorship in respect of the property, the remedy open to their children unjustly excluded being the *querela inofficiosi testamenti* (*post*, par. 788).

Tit. xiv. De Heredibus instituendis.

715. The *institution* was the designation by the testator of the heir or heirs, and this was held to be the principal object of and to constitute the testament; so that prior to Justinian it could only be preceded by an exheredation or a tutorship (*ante*, par. 191), and up to the time of Constantine II (A.D. 339) a set form of words must have been used, as, *e.g.*, *Titius heres esto* (Gai. Inst. ii, § 117).

718. The *persons instituted* could only be those *qui testamenti factionem cum testatore habent* (*ante*, par. 681), hence, according to primitive laws, were debarred :—

(1) Persons not enjoying *civil* rights, as *peregrini*, *deportati*, and *dediticii*.

(2) *Women* by the *lex Voconia* (*post*, par. 940) in respect of inheritances inscribed in the first class as exceeding 100,000 *asses*. As to legacies, see *post*, par. 940; and as to the subsequent extension of the provisions of this law, so that women were excluded *ab intestato* also, see *post*, par. 1021.

(3) *Uncertain persons*, as, *e.g.*, he who shall first come to my funeral, and including municipalities and colleges (unless instituted by their freedmen), the gods (*i.e.*, the temples, but except-

ing a certain number specially privileged), and posthumous strangers (*ante*, par. 697).

Amongst those who could be instituted, but were deprived of the *jus capiendi ex testamento*, were :—

(1) *Latini Juniani*, unless they became Roman citizens within the *cretio* of one hundred days from the death of the testator (see *ante*, par. 65).

(2) *Cœlibes* altogether, and *orbi* to the extent of one-half; but the former, and probably the latter also, could remove the disability by complying within one hundred days from the opening of the testament with the rules of the *lex Papia* (see part i, par. 369).

(3) Women of bad character, by Domitian.

720. Under Justinian, the distinction between *testamenti factio* and the *jus capiendi* no longer existed; the classes of *dediticii, latini juniani, cœlibes*, and *orbi*, the worship of the heathen gods, and the provisions of the *lex Voconia*, had disappeared. *Women* could be instituted and acquire legacies, and *uncertain* persons also (if sufficiently in the testator's mind, *post*, par. 906), including municipalities and their colleges, and other legally established corporations, besides all classes of *postumi* (*ante*, par. 697, 3), together with churches; and, if God or Jesus Christ were instituted, the gift was held to go to the church of the testator's domicile.

Hence all Roman citizens (and their slaves for them) had *factio testamenti*, except :—

(1) *Peregrini* and *deportati*.

(2) *Filii perduellium*, *i.e.*, sons of persons condemned for high treason.

(3) Apostates and heretics.

(4) Parents guilty of, and the offspring resulting from, incest; the second husband or wife, as against the children of the first marriage; and natural, as against existing legitimate children.

722. (§ i) *Position of the slave heir*. Under Justinian, the slave made *heir* by his own master became therefore *free* (*ante*, par. 73); and the same result followed if the master had only the *nuda proprietas* of him; but in this case (instead of, as formerly, remaining a slave without a master) he continued to serve the beneficial owner until the end of the usufruct. If the slave of another was made heir, he acquired for his master, provided the latter had *testamenti factio* with the testator. A woman accused of adultery with her own slave could not institute him heir until sentence of absolution pronounced. The institution followed the slave in his different conditions (*ambulat cum dominio*); and if he became free, the inheritance was his; and if he died, the right vanished (see *ante*, par. 616).

When a master instituted his own slave :—

(1) If the slave remained in the same condition, then, as the institution depended on the express or tacit freedom, if the freedom was in fraud of creditors, or void from any other cause, as

where freed on a condition which failed, the institution was also *void*; but if the freedom was valid, then at the death of the testator, or on the accomplishment of the condition, he was immediately *free* and *heres necessarius*.

(2) If he changed his condition prior to the decease of the testator, whether by having been freed or by alienation, then, as *liberty* was regarded as a legacy which may be *tacitly* revoked (as opposed to the *institution*, which required formal revocation), the effect of the institution was the same as if the slave belonged to another person; and the inheritance would at the *aditio* be acquired for himself if then free, or for his master if he were still a slave; and, as the inheritance prior to the *aditio* represents the *persona* of the deceased, and *factio testamenti* exists with the slave of an inheritance (*hereditarius servus*), the testator could institute the slave of a deceased master heir without the necessity of *factio testamenti* existing with the future heir.

(3) If the ownership was shared by other masters, then, whether the slave was to be *free* and heir, and the other master indemnified, or the inheritance to be acquired by them as co-owners, would be determined by the evidence as to *intention* (see *ante*, par. 590), the presumption being in favour of freedom; but where the slave of several masters, of which the testator was not one, was made heir, he acquired for those of them who ordered him to make the *aditio* proportionately to their interest in him.

725. (§ iv) *Division of the inheritance.* Except in the case of military testaments, a testator could not die partly testate and partly not. Therefore, if only one heir were appointed, and for a portion of the property, he would acquire the whole; and if one person were instituted in respect of a particular thing (*ex re certa*), and another generally, the latter would be held to be the heir, and the former a legatee; and where several persons were named heirs *ex re certa*, they would be co-heirs for the whole, with a special right in each to the particular object bequeathed him.

In the case of co-heirs to whom the whole inheritance was bequeathed, but in unequal shares, and no number of total parts specified, the rule was to add the whole number of shares together, and distribute proportionally; *e.g.*, to Titius, three parts; Cornelius, five; Stichus, two; Gaius, four; total, fourteen: then Titius would have three-fourteenths of the whole inheritance, and so on; and, if some of the co-heirs had no shares assigned, the inheritance was assumed to consist of an *as* divided into twelve ounces, unless the testator had stated the arbitrary number of parts he intended the *as* to contain, or the total parts specially bequeathed exceeded twelve, when the division was assumed to be into twenty-four *uncia* (*dupondius*); or, if exceeding that number, then thirty-six *uncia* (*tripondius*), and so on.

If two or more were taken conjointly, they only counted as one; *e.g.*, *Titius heres esto; Seius et Mævius heredes sunto;* in which case

Titius would have half the inheritance, and Seius and Mævius the other half. If a vacant share was left, it accrued proportionally to all the heirs, as in the case of the remaining one-fourth where three heirs received by bequest one-fourth each; and, if too many shares were given, each heir lost a proportionate part, as where four heirs were to receive one-third each.

735. (§ ix) *Modes and conditions in respect of the inheritance.* The institution may be simple (*pure*) or conditional (*sub-conditione*); in the first case, the right commencing from the death of the testator; in the second, only from the accomplishment of the condition, the inheritance supporting the *persona* of the deceased in the interval (*ante*, par. 644). The institution would be extinguished if in the first case the heir died before the testator, or in the second if he died before the accomplishment of the condition; and as (except in the case of military testaments) the property could not go for a time to the *ab intestato* heirs (*semel heres semper heres*), the institution *from* a certain time (*ex certo tempore*), or *to* a certain time (*ad certum tempus*), was held to be *simple*, the restrictions being looked upon as superfluous (*pro supervacuo*); and, in the same way, *illegal* or *impossible* conditions were treated as unwritten in respect of *institutions, legacies,* and *fidei commissa;* though in obligations (see *post*, book iii, tit. xix) impossible conditions rendered the whole void, the opinion of the Sabinians in favour of supporting the will having prevailed; but *Gaius* (Inst. iii, § 98) questions the possibility of giving a reason for the distinction.

An *uncertain* time was held equivalent to a *condition*, and valid accordingly; *e.g.*, when Titius dies, would be read: I institute Stichus, if Titius dies before him. (See *post*, par. 924, 3). If *several* conditions were jointly imposed (*e.g., si illud et illud facta erint*), they must all be accomplished; but, if separate (*e.g., si illud aut illud factum erit*), one sufficed.

Tit. xv. De vulgari substitutione.

742. *Substitutions* were of three kinds—(1) *vulgaris*, (2) *pupillaris*, (3) *quasi pupillaris;* and all three were, in fact, only *conditional* institutions of a particular kind to provide against the contingency of dying intestate, a risk much increased by the operation of the *caduca* laws, the formal abrogation of which by Justinian was subsequent to the Institutes (see part i, par. 369).

The *vulgaris* substitution was so called because it was the most common. The form *si ille heres non erit, ille heres esto* (which was held to include refusal, incapacity, etc.), might conclude *(novissimo loco)* with the appointment of a slave *(heres necessarius);* and if the slave were substituted in any other than the last place by an insolvent testator (*ante*, par. 73), he would still only come in in the event of all the other substitutions failing. *Several* heirs might be substituted for *one* or one for several; and a third substituted to a second was held to be so also to the first; and so a third was held substituted to both when substituted to one who was co-heir and substitute to another according to rule *substitutus substituto censetur substitutus instituto.* If the instituted were substituted to one another—*i.e.*, if the rest might take in case any of those instituted failed—then the portion so accruing would come to them by right of substitution; and as their acceptance of these shares that had lapsed would be a voluntary act involving a formal *aditio*, they would be liable to any burdens attached to them by the testator *(cum onere)*, instead of being discharged from liability *(sine onere)*, as was the case with vacant shares until the extension by the jurisprudents to the latter of the rescript of the Emperor Severus, charging the substitution with the *fidei commissa* of the original institution.

748. In some cases, if the intention of the testator in respect of a condition was obviously defeated, the substituted went shares with the instituted heir; *e.g.*, if a testator instituted a stranger slave heir, thinking him to be a paterfamilias, and to him substituted Mœvius; then since the actual owner of the slave would otherwise get the whole inheritance, he and Mœvius (according to a decretum of Tiberius) would take half each.

Tit xvi. De pupillari substitutione.

749. A *paterfamilias* was allowed at the time of, or subsequent to the making of his own will, to institute an heir to his *impubes* son or other descendant *in his power* both at the time of making the will (or appointing the substitute) and at his death, conditionally on his surviving him and dying before the age of puberty. This privilege was accorded the father in order to guard against the contingency of the son whilst *impubes* dying necessarily intestate; as, after the decease of the father, he might have the right to make a will, being *sui juris*, but be incapacitated by age from exercising it. Being only an accessory to the principal the institution failed if the will of the father failed, unless the provisions were carried out, though the will upset, as in the case of *possessio bonorum*, given by Prætorian law *contra tabulas;* and as the principal does not share the fate of the accessory, the son's will proving a nullity did not invalidate the former one; and it might be secretly made by arranging that that portion of the father's will should not be opened whilst the son was alive and *impubes*. The power was extended to cover the case of *posthumous* or *disinherited* children, as in the analogous case of tutorships (*ante*, par. 182), and the son need not be instituted heir; but if he was so named, and a substitute appointed in the event of his death, then *vulgaris* substitution was involved, an arrangement stated by Cicero (*De orat.*, i, §§ 39, 57) to have entailed much discussion amongst jurisconsults; but a constitution of Marcus Aurelius decided that, unless the testator directed the contrary, *pupillaris* substitution should always imply the *vulgaris*. A rescript of the Emperor would enable a father to make the will of his son who, though *puber*, was incapable of exercising the right himself, as if, *e.g.*, deaf and dumb.

753. (§ i) The term *quasi pupillaris substitutio* was introduced by

the commentators to mean the analogous kind of substitution (but not resting on the paternal power) introduced by Justinian *(ad exemplum pupillaris substitutionis)* to enable *any ascendant* (? the nearest related) to appoint an heir to his or her *puber*, but insane descendant, conditionally on the non-recovery of reason. The heir so appointed must also, if such existed, be a descendant, or, in default, a brother of the lunatic, otherwise the choice was free. The substitution might be to each *impubes* or to the last so dying, and the heir might be substituted by name *(e.g., Titius heres esto)* or generally *(e.g., quisquis mihi heres erit)*, when it would refer to those who *actually* became heirs to the father; and it was *personal;* so that the substitution, like the institution (*ante*, par. 616) would follow a slave made heir in his various positions. On the accomplishment of the condition, the substituted heir succeeded to all the property, as the child could not die partly testate and partly not.

767. The substitution might fail from the general causes applying to all institutions; and, in addition, it ceased :—

(1) At puberty—*i.e.*, fourteen for males, twelve for females; and though it could not exceed this limit, the term might be shorter, *e.g., si filius meus intra decimum annum decesserit*.

(2) If the child died actually or civilly (*e.g.*, taken prisoner and not returning) before testator.

(3) If the child no longer under power.

(4) If, after the testator's death, the child was arrogated, though the substituted heir would get the security which the arrogator was obliged to give to meet the event of the arrogatee dying *impubes* (*ante*, par. 136).

(5) If the substituted heir neglected to ask for the appointment of a tutor to the *impubes* within the year.

771. The *substitutions made by soldiers* were valid, though they had not made their own will, and though no one made *aditio* of their own inheritance, and in respect of property transmitted by themselves, they could make substitution to a son, though puber or emancipated, and even to strangers.

Tit. xvii. Quibus modis testamenta infirmantur.

773. A will perfectly valid in its inception might become :—

(1) *Ruptum, i.e.*, revoked in two cases; viz., by—

(a) The making of a subsequent will if legally valid, even though it failed in its operation; but the original will, in the absence of a second, would not be avoided by the mere wish of the testator, unless ten years had elapsed prior to the testator's decease, and satisfactory evidence could be produced, either in writing or by the testimony of three witnesses, but the destruction or other obliteration would be proof of voluntary revocation—*i.e.*, of the intention to die intestate.

(β) The agnation of a *suus heres* who had not been instituted or legally excluded, as in the case of (1) subsequent birth of son or daughter to testator; (2) grandson becoming immediately under power through the death or emancipation of son; (3) *quasi* agnation of a *suus heres* through adoption or arrogation, and under the old law; (4) wife passing *in manu;* (5) son refalling under power after first or second emancipation; (6) children proving (in the lifetime of the father, or after his death if excluded) that the marriage of the father with a *peregrina* or a *latina* was made in good faith, believing her to be a Roman citizen. In these cases, the revocation could be avoided (under Justinian) by instituting them by anticipation; but they could not be so excluded; for that would be to deprive them of a right before they had it, though *postumi* and *quasi postumi* could be so excluded (*ante*, par. 697); and a will, though *ruptum* in strict law, might still be supported by the Prætor, and the *possessio bonorum* given, as he looked to only two periods, viz., the time of making the will and the death of the testator, disregarding events which occurred in the interval, *e.g.*, the birth of a child which died before the testator; so a second will revokes a first, though it appoints an heir to certain property only; but if the testator adds a clause in the second will that the dispositions in the first shall hold good, the second heir will be looked upon as a trustee, and compelled to restrict himself to the named objects (or the *quarta Falcidia* under the *s. c. Pegasianum, post*, par. 959, 2), restoring the remainder of the heir under the first will. The fact of the Emperor being the heir would not prevent the successful prosecution of a suit to upset a will in which he had been instituted for the purpose of making him an interested party.

(2) *Irritum*, *i.e.*, useless, ineffectual, as by the testator (not being a soldier, *ante*, par. 677) suffering *capitis deminutio*, in which case the will by strict law could not revive, but the Prætor would give the instituted heir the *possessio bonorum secundum tabulas*, if the testator at death had become again a Roman citizen and *sui juris*.

(3) *Destitutum* (or *desertum*), *i.e.*, abandoned, as when the heir refused to make, or was incapacitated from making, the *aditio*, or obtained *restitutio in integrum* against the *aditio* already made.

Tit. xviii.   De inofficioso testamento.

788. *Officium pietatis* was the term used to imply the duty owed to a near relation; and, about the fifth or sixth century of Rome, the custom mentioned by Cicero (in Verr., 142) became established of regarding a will as *inofficiosum, i.e.*, contrary to the dictates of natural affection (*inofficiosum dicitur testamentum quod non ex officio pietatis videtur esse conscriptum*, Paul, Sent., 4, 5, 1), which, without sufficient motive, *excluded* (in the case of the *paterfamilias* and in respect of children in his power), or *omitted* (in the case of other ascendants in respect of descendants, or *vice versâ*, *not* in power), children or other relations having *ab intestato* claims.

The action, brought before the centumvirs, was fictitiously grounded on an assumed unsoundness of mind in the testator (see part I, par.

331), and, if successful, the will was declared null and void, and the *ab intestato* heirs succeeded to the estate. Up to the time of the Institutes, the reasonableness of the grounds for exclusion or omission was left to the discretion of the judges; but, in a subsequent *novel* (115 c, 3 and 4), Justinian required the motives to be *stated* in the will, and fixed what were *justa causa*. For ascendants against descendants there were fourteen; viz.: (1) Son guilty of *injuria gravis* towards father, or (2) struck him, or (3) attempted his life, or (4) through his instrumentality caused him injury, or (5) associated with evil-doers, or (6) tried to prevent the father making his will, or (7) abandoned him when of unsound mind, or (8) not ransomed him from captivity, or (9) fallen into heresy, rejecting the four first œcumenical councils, or (10) accused his father of some capital crime, except high treason, or (11) had intercourse with his mother-in-law or his father's concubine, or (12) joined a company of actors against his father's wish, or (13) refused to become security to release his father when imprisoned for debt, or (14), in the case of a daughter who refused to marry and receive a dowry, having become a paid prostitute. For descendants against ascendants there were eight *justa causa* specified; viz., the reverse of 10, 3, 11, 6, 8, 7, 9, and (8) if the father had wished to poison their mother, or *vice versâ*. By another novel (22 c, 47), in the case of collaterals, three *justa causa* were enumerated; viz., 3, 10, and (3) great damage caused to fortune.

The will of Ascendants could be attacked by Descendants, and *vice versâ*, in respect of any person instituted; but in the case of collaterals, up to the time of Justinian, only *agnate brothers and sisters* could attack the will, and then only if a *turpis persona* (*i.e.*, a person wanting in *existimatio*, see part II, par. 74) had been instituted. The privilege was extended by Justinian (Cod. iii, 28, 27) to *consanguineous* brothers and sisters, whether still agnates or not, so that finally only *uterine* brothers and sisters were debarred from the right.

794. (§ iii) The action only lay as a last resource in the absence of any other mode of obtaining a recognition of their claim, and when the testator had not left them anything; for, if he had, then the *ab intestato* heirs had been neither excluded nor omitted, and must sue by the *actio in supplementum legitimi* (*post*, par. 830) for the balance to make up the "*légitime*" (*portio legitima*) or fourth part of their share *ab intestato*, and to which they were held entitled by analogy to, or by an extension of the provisions of, the *lex Falcidia* (*post*, par. 940).

796. (§ iv) A *tutor* accepting a legacy for his *pupil* did not thereby exclude himself from bringing the *de inofficioso* action; nor, if he failed in such an action brought by him on behalf of his pupil, did he thereby lose any legacy to himself contained in the testament, as he would do if the action had been brought by himself, the legacy in such cases lapsing and going to the *fiscus*.

798. (§ vi) To *bar* the action *de inofficioso testamento*, it was,

therefore necessary that the heir *ab intestato* should have received the fourth of his share (*quarta legitima*) whether as heir, or legatee, or in the form of *fidei-commissa* or donations *mortis causa*, but in respect of gifts *inter vivos* the cases were fixed by Justinian, *e.g.*, given expressly to be included in the 4th due *ab intestato*, or for the purchase of an office or military grade (*ad militiam emendam*), and so previous constitutions included the *dos* and the *donatio propter nuptias*. The share was calculated on the whole estate of the testator at the moment of death, *ex*cluding funeral expenses, debts, and freedoms, but *in*cluding legacies and donations *mortis causa* (see the analogous case of the *lex Falcidia, post*, par. 940).

802. Justinian, in subsequent Novels (18, c. 4, 115, c. 3 and 4), made important modifications in the above rules. He augmented the *portio* so that, instead of the whole of the claimants taking one fourth of the inheritance to be divided proportionately between them, *one half* went to the *legitimi* if they exceeded four in number, otherwise *one third*. Descendants and ascendants were necessarily heirs, even though only in respect of a particular object; and if the action was successfully brought, the will was only held void as regarded the institution of the heir, all legacies, *fidei-commissa*, freedoms, and nominations of tutors remaining valid.

803. The action *de inofficioso testamento* was a real action, and extinguished by

(1) Compromise with the heirs subsequent to the testator's death.

(2) Desisting from the action.

(3) Recognising in any way the validity of the will (*e.g.*, by taking a legacy).

(4) The limiting period elapsing (at first two, afterwards five, years from the date of the *aditio*, but the instituted heir must in this case make the *aditio* within six months of the testator's death, or one year if not domiciled in the same province).

(5) Decease without attempting to bring the action, otherwise the heirs could go on with it.

Of the above, (3), (4), and (5) did not extinguish the action to complete the *portio legitima*.

Tit. xix. De heredum qualitate et differentia.

804. The difference between the three classes of heirs consists essentially in the mode of acquiring or power of repudiating the inheritance.

(1) *Necessarius heres* (*ante*, par. 722). The slave at the death of his master was free and compulsorily heir, even though *impubes*, or *infans*, of sound or unsound mind; but if a condition attached either as to the liberty or the heirship, then he did not become heir until both were fulfilled. By way of compensation, the slave had (α) his liberty and (β) the *beneficium separationis, i.e.*, a right so called by the commentators, and introduced by the Prætor, of demanding from him (provided the slave had not

o

touched the inheritance) a decree for the separation of so much property as was owed him by the testator, or acquired since his death.

(2) *Suus et necessarius heres.* This was the heir instituted by the testator, and at the same time the successor in his own right to the estate (for those in the power of the deceased as constituting the family had in a collective sense the patrimony in common with him), and might be a son or daughter, grandson (if the father, by death or otherwise, not in the family, for if the father was alive, the son named heir to the grandfather would merely take for his father), or granddaughter, etc., and independently of will, so that immaterial whether *impubes* or insane, and the authorisation of the tutor not necessary; but though thus heirs by strict law, the Prætor allowed them the *beneficium abstinendi, i.e.,* without any active demand of the privilege (though practically some indication of their intention would be given); and if they had not or did not intermeddle with the inheritance, they could not be sued by the creditors, though in name they still continued heirs, and before the sale of the goods by the creditors they could, within a period fixed by Justinian at three years (Cod. vi, 31, 6), withdraw their refusal and take the inheritance.

As the acquisition in respect of the above two classes of heirs took place by law, no voluntary act was necessary, and hence there was no *aditio;* but in the case of *heredes sui,* though there was no *aditio,* there was *immixtio,* an act involving a renunciation of the right of abstaining and giving the creditors the power of suing, hence if *impubes* or insane the act of *immixtio* would not defeat the right to abstain.

(3) *Extraneus heres* (called also *voluntary* heirs by commentators), *i.e.,* any one (whether own child or not) who was not in the power of the testator, *e.g.,* an emancipated child, a child instituted by mother, or a slave instituted heir, but freed subsequent to the making of the will.

The death of the testator or the accomplishment of the condition gave them the *right* to the inheritance, but it was not itself *acquired* until the *aditio, i.e.,* their voluntary acceptance of it, and *testamenti factio* was required at three periods, viz., (a) *testamenti quidem, i.e.,* at the time of making the will (see *post,* par. 857), otherwise the latter would be void *ab initio,* according to the old principles governing wills made *calatis comitiis* (*ante,* par. 639) and *per æs et libram,* (β) *Mortis vero testatoris* for the rights of the instituted heir then commence, though if a condition had been imposed, its accomplishment, and not the death of the testator, would be the period looked to, (γ) *et cum adit hereditatem,* for then the heir acquired the inheritance, and therefore, in strict law, if he died before making the *aditio,* no rights would pass to his heirs.

In the interval between (α) and (β), a change of status, if recovered, made no difference, but if between (β) and (γ), the right was lost. In analogy to the civil law rule as to the *cretio* fixed by the testator (*post*, par. 821), the Prætor gave a right of deliberation (*deliberandi potestas an heres sit*) during a period of not less than one hundred days nor more than nine months (one year by permission of the Emperor), after which the heir was held to have *refused* the inheritance as against the claims of a *substitute*, or the heirs *ab intestato* or *accepted*, with liability to *all* the debts as against creditors and legatees. This *jus deliberandi* was extended to the *heredes sui*, entailing a postponement of the power of sale by creditors, and it was also, by a constitution of Justinian (Cod. vi, 30, 19), extended to the heir of the instituted heir if the latter died within the period.

816. (§ vi) Except in the case of a minor under twenty-five, and to whom the Prætor would give the *restitutio in integrum* (*ante*, par. 265), if he had imprudently undertaken a burdened inheritance, no repudiation could take place after the *aditio*; but Hadrian first accorded this as a special favour in particular cases, and it was then extended to soldiers, and *Justinian* (Cod. vi, 30, 22) gave all in lieu of, but not in addition to, the above *jus deliberandi*, the right of accepting the inheritance, subject to what the commentators term the *beneficium inventarii*, *i.e.*, the benefit of having an inventory made in the presence of a *tabellio*, and of the creditors, legatees, and other interested parties (or in default three witnesses), and commenced within thirty days of being aware of the existence of the right, and finished in sixty more, or one year if the property distant. The effect of this was that

(1) The heir was not liable for any debt or charge beyond the assets.

(2) The rights of the deceased and of the heir were not mixed, so that the heir could bring any action against the inheritance which he could have brought against the deceased, and *vice versâ*.

(3) The heir could indemnify himself for funeral, inventory, and other necessary expenses, and the creditors and legatees were paid in the order they presented themselves, so that the last comers might not get anything unless they could establish preference claims.

821. (§ vii) The *aditio* (*ad ire hereditatem*) could be made in three ways, viz.:—

(1) By a sacramental declaration, according to which time for deliberation (*cretio*), in respect of *extranei* heirs, was fixed by the testator (*e.g.*, *Heres Titius esto*......*cernitoque in centum diebus proxumis quibus scies poterisque quodni ita creveris, exheres esto*). If the heir accepted (*e.g.*, *quod me Publius Mœvius testamento suo heredem instituit eam hereditatem adeo cernoque*) within the interval, the inheritance fell to him, otherwise not. The usual term (*vulgaris cretio*) was one hundred days from the time that the heir knew of his rights, and was in a position to avail himself of them; but if these words were omitted, the time began to run as soon as the right commenced, hence called *cretio continua*, but not so

usual owing to the harshness of the operation of the rule. This method was in full force in the time of *Gaius* (Inst. ii, § 164) and *Ulpian* (Reg. 22, 27, etc.), but was suppressed in A.D. 407 (Cod. 6, 30, 17, Const., Arcad., Honor., and Theod.), and is not mentioned in Justinian's Institutes.

(2) By some *express* but not sacramental declaration, written or verbal, though, to be binding, this must be after the rights have commenced, either by the death of the testator or the accomplishment of the condition, and after the heir knew of his rights arising either by the will of the testator or *ab intestato*. If the *paterfamilias* had been murdered, the will could not be opened, nor *aditio* made, until the slaves had undergone examination.

(3) By simple manifestation or act (*re*) indicating the intention to be the heir (*per herede gerere, e.g.*, selling, letting, cultivating the land), provided in any case that the heir was not acting in ignorance whilst performing, *e.g.*, the duties of agent.

827. The *repudiation* might in like manner be made by a formal declaration (*verbis*), or by acts (*re*), or other method (*alio quovis indicio*) sufficiently indicating the intention, and the effect was (except in cases of *restitutio in integrum*, or under circumstances similar to the contrary case of the *aditio*) to immediately irrevocably repudiate the estate, though the person so repudiating was not prevented from subsequently accepting the inheritance if it fell to him again through another title, *e.g.*, as substitute or as heir *ab intestato*.

828. As the *acceptance* or *repudiation* of an inheritance were classed amongst those acts requiring to be performed by the person himself, the pupil *infans* and the lunatic were incapacitated, and neither their *tutor* nor their *curator* could assist them; but Theodosius and Valentinian (Cod. 6, 30, 18, § 2) for the first allowed the *tutor* (*ante*, par. 234), and Justinian for the second allowed the *curator*, to demand possession of the goods. The pupil above *infans* could accept or repudiate with the *auctoritas* of his *tutor*, the *prodigus* of his own will, and the deaf and dumb also, provided he had sufficient intelligence to understand his rights. Persons in power could only act with the consent of the *paterfamilias*, but the latter could accept or refuse for the *filius familias infans*.

830. *Actions relating to testamentary inheritances.* Those applying to *all* inheritances were

(1) *Hereditatis petitio*—a real action (though it might entail personal condemnation) to vindicate the hereditary right in whole or in part, for self or others, against anyone detaining, in prejudice to this right, the inheritance or any part of it; hence it could only be brought against those whose holding denied this right, *e.g.*, against those possessing *pro herede* (*i.e.* by law, testament, *fidei-commissum*, or *possessio bonorum*), or *pro possessore*, *i.e.*, by the right of possession only, but *not* against those possessing *pro donato, legato, empto*, etc., for these did not dispute the quality of heir.

(2) *Familiæ erciscundæ*, available after the *aditio* for co-heirs against each other to compel partition of the inheritance, and did not apply to particular objects—the judge awarded the shares—so long as the inheritance was *un*divided the action was imprescriptible; but after a division had in *fact* been made, thirty years (as in the case of 1) extinguished the right to bring the action for a division in *law*.

Special actions were—

(1) *Querela inofficiosi testamenti*, a sort of *petitio hereditatis ab intestato* against those instituted (see *ante*, par. 788).

(2) *In supplementum legitimi*, for the balance of the *legitima* (see *ante*, par. 794).

(3) *Querela inofficiosæ donationis*, to attack gifts against the rights of relations.

Tit. xx. De Legatis.

833. Originally the *institution of the heir* (*i.e.*, the designation of the person to continue the *persona* of the defunct) was totally distinct from the recipient of the whole or any part of the inheritance by *donatio mortis causa*, legacy, *fidei-commissum*, etc., for such a person was merely a creditor on the estate.

834. (§ i) The *legatum* was defined as *donatio quædam a defuncto relicta* (the additional words *ab herede præstanda* being rejected, as though formerly *only* the *heir* could be burdened with legacies, this was not true under Justinian), and it was numbered with the civil methods of acquisition (see *ante*, par. 312 (5) and 541), though it often only created a debt. Its essential character is, that it is a *datio* made *dono*, *i.e.*, a gift of pure liberality, independent of the concurrence of will of donor and donee, for it is only after the death of the donor that the donee will be called upon to indicate his intention. *Imperative* words were formerly necessary, but not so under Justinian; and though originally the deceased could not impose any obligation on the heir *ab intestato*, so that a legacy could only exist by virtue of a testamentary inheritance, after Augustus the legacy might be given by *codicil* attached to an anterior or posterior testament, and practically, under Justinian, a legacy remained valid (if only as a *fidei-commissum*) in an inheritance *ab intestato*.

837. (§ ii) Justinian suppressed the distinctions between the four kinds of legacies according to the terms employed, viz. :—

(1) *Per vindicationem*, in which the formula would run, *e.g.*, *Hominem Stichum do lego*, or *capito, sumito, sibi habeto*, and so called because the legatee could vindicate it, and became owner *ex jure Quiritium* immediately after the *aditio*, and independent of his knowledge of the fact according to Gaius (Inst. ii, § 195), and the Sabinians, and confirmed by Antoninus Pius, though disputed by the Proculians. The testator must have been owner *ex. j. q.* (a) at the making of the will, and (β) at death (though only in the latter case in respect of things *quæ pondere, numero mensurave constant*), hence it was a legacy of ownership.

(2) *Per damnationem* (*Heres meus damnas esto dare,* or *dato, facito, Heredem meum dare jubeo*). This gave the legatee only an action *in personam* to compel the heir, *dare,* or *præstare,* or *facere,* but it applied to any subject-matter which could be the object of an obligation, whether belonging to the testator or to the heir, or to any other person, and hence it was called *optimum jus legati,* and was the legacy of a debt.

(3) *Sinendi modo* (*Heres meus damnas esto sinere Lucium Titium sumere illam rem sibi-que habere*). This condemned the heir to allow something to be taken, and strictly his part was only passive, but practically the *actio in personam* could be brought against him (*quidquid heredem en testamento dare facere oportet.*) It applied only to property of the testator or of the heir, and the legatee did not become owner until after taking possession.

(4) *Per præceptionem* (*Lucius Titius illam rem præcipito*). Properly the legatee here must also be heir in part, for *præcipere* meant to take in addition and above his share. It did not transfer the ownership, but the legatee acquired it through the aid of the partition action (*judicio familiæ erciscundæ*), and hence it could be only in respect of the heir and of the property of the testator (*i.e.,* of the inheritance) according to Gaius (Inst. ii, §§ 217, 218, 219) and the Sabinians, though if made to a stranger according to *Julianus* (applying the *s. c. Neronianum, post,* par. 842) it was valid as a legacy *per damnationem,* and according to the Proculians (? confirmed by Hadrian) in this case the prefix *præ* should be struck out as superfluous, leaving the word *capito,* and making the legacy one *per vindicationem.*

842. The *Senatus-consultum Neronianum* under Nero (? A.D. 64) attempted to avoid the *loss* of the legacy through inapt expressions, by making dispositions inappropriate to the thing or the person equivalent to legacies *per damnationem.* Subsequently (see part 1, par. 493) Constantine II, Constantius, and Constans, in A.D. 339, removed the necessity for using expressions according to formula, whether in the institution of the heir or in legacies, and hence, though the four kinds of legacies remained, the intention, and not the precise words of the testator, was regarded.

844. Under *Justinian* all legacies were made of the same nature, and the ownership was transferred immediately after the *aditio,* without the necessity of *traditio,* for the death of the owner was held to have disseised him, and invested the legatee. The latter could also use personal, real, or hypothecary actions, *i.e.,* as far as the terms and the law were concerned, but the nature of the thing would determine whether the transference of ownership could take place at once, and whether, *e.g.,* an action *in rem* were possible which would not be the case in respect of the legacy of the property of another, or in respect of an indeterminate thing before the selection had been made.

846. (§ iii). Justinian also suppressed the distinctions between legacies and *fidei commissa,* so that dispositions invalid as the first

might be binding as the second, and *vice versâ*; and it was therefore no longer important to ascertain whether the disposition was a legacy or a *fidei commissum*, except in the case of freedom, the giving of tutors, and inheritances bequeathed in trust (see *post*, 969, 972, 973 (2), 977); but a difference was kept up in form, as the consecrated formulæ or *civilia verba* constituted a legacy, whilst precative words (*peto, rogo, volo,* etc.), or even a sign of assent (Ulp. Reg. 25, § 3) sufficed for the *fidei commissum*.

850. The terms *dies cedit* and *dies venit* are general expressions applicable to all acquisitions of rights, especially to obligations, and in respect of *legacies* the—

Dies cedit is the moment when the *eventual* right (for it fails if from any cause the testament fails) establishes itself in favour of the legatee, *i.e.*, in the case of pure and simple legacies at the death of the testator (see as to the temporary alteration of the period by the *leges Julia et Papia*, part i, par. 369), and the same when subject to a fixed term (*e. g.*, I leave 100 solidi, payable on the calends of January, or so many years after *aditio*), but in the case of a condition being imposed, not until its accomplishment.

Dies venit was a term rarely employed for legacies, but meant the time when the gift was demandable, which was necessarily after the *aditio* (except in the case of the *heres necessarius*), or after the fulfilment of a condition.

855. The *dies cedit*, therefore, determined four important points, viz.:—

(1) The persons by whom the legacy will be acquired.

(2) The objects comprising the legacy, and, therefore, of accruals or diminutions in respect of them.

(3) The transmissibility of the right (and *dies cedit* has been incorrectly translated "the right is transmissible"; but a *personal* right cannot be transmitted, though a legacy might be such). If the legatee died before the *dies cedens* he never acquired his rights, but dying after that date he transmitted them to his heirs.

(4) In some cases as to the loss or preservation of the right left by legacy, *e. g.*, after the *dies cedens* the extinction by *maxima c. d.*, or non-usage of legacies of *usufruct, usus,* or *habitatio* (see *ante*, par. 481, 488, 504), but when a testator by his will left his slave his *liberty* and a *legacy*, since the slave could not have any right until free, the *dies cedens* for the legacy (if pure and simple) will be when liberty is acquired (*i. e.*, at the *aditio*), and the rights of *usufruct, usus,* and *habitatio* being exclusively *personal* to the legatee, the *dies cedit* only occurs at the *dies venit* (*i. e.*, the right is only fixed at the moment of maturity), the only possible transmissible rights being that to the *produce already gathered* before the death of the usufructuary, not the usufruct itself.

857. *Catoniana regula.* The general principle of Roman law, that an act originally void cannot become valid by mere lapse of time (*quod initio vitiosum est non potest tractu temporis convalescere*, Dig. 50, 17, 29, *Paul*), applied to the *form* of the will, as well as to

the capacity of the testator, and of the person instituted at the time of the making of the will (*ante*, par. 804, 3, (*a*). Applied to *legacies*, the rule invalidated them *ab initio*, unless at the time of the making of the will the legatee had *factio testamenti*—the thing was in *commercium* (*post*, par. 865)—and the acts imposed on the heir in respect of the legacy were lawful.

But where only *relative invalidities* had occurred affecting the heir, the legatee, or the thing, as *e.g.*, a legacy given purely and simply to own slave, but only *conditional* liberty; or the testator had given his own property to the legatee (but see *post*, par. 886), so that the same legacy would be valid if given to other persons, or to the same persons under different circumstances, the principle proposed by (?) the elder Cato about B.C. 195, became (though much controverted) the established rule, viz.:—*To test the validity of a legacy, the testator must be assumed to have died immediately after the making of the will (Quod si testamenti facti tempore decessissit testator inutile foret, id legatum quandocunque decesserit non valere*, Dig. 34, 7, i, but, adds *Celsus, quæ definitio in quibusdam falsa est*, see *post*, par. 886) *i.e.*, the act ought to be such as could produce its effects if required immediately at the then death of the testator.

The rule did not apply to *conditional* legacies, for there was no *dies cedens* until the condition accomplished, nor to any other legacy for which the *dies cedens* did not take place at death, but only after *aditio* (*e.g.*, in the case of usufruct or a legacy to the slave of the testator), and certain relative vices were exempted from the rule, including vices arising from new laws (*e.g.*, the *leges Julia et Papia*), but (at least in the time of Justinian) the rule was applied to *fideicommissa*.

865. *Things which may be left by legacy*. The property might belong to the testator or to the heir (formerly only in legacies *per damnationem*, or *sinendi modo*), or to a third person (formerly only in the *per damnationem* legacy), in which latter case the heir was bound to purchase it; or if this was impossible, or some equitable reason existed for not buying it, *e.g.*, exorbitant price, to hand over its value, provided that the testator knew that the property belonged to another (the proof of which was on the legatee) and that the thing was a subject of commerce (*commercium*) so that it could be purchased (*e.g.*, not the Campus Martius or a Basilica), and so the heir was bound to pay off a mortgage if the testator knew that the legacy was mortgaged, and did not leave the legatee to redeem it.

If the property of another, left by legacy, was already acquired by the legatee (in the lifetime of the testator, or even after his death, before the legacy had been handed over), he could sue by the action *ex testamento* for its value if he had become possessed of it by *purchase* (or other mode involving sacrifice, as the testator had intended it to be gratuitous), but not if it had come to him as clear gain (*ex causa lucrativa*), or by way of gift, except in the case of master and slave, for the same thing left as a legacy by two testators to the master and the slave will be binding on each heir, and in the case of the same thing left to the same legatee by two testators, if the value is first received from one the legatee can still sue the other for the thing, but not *vice versa*, the general rule in obligations being that he who is debtor *causa lucrativa* in respect of a certain thing is released if the creditor becomes possessed of the thing through that title (*omnes debitores qui speciem in causa lucrativa debent liberantur cum ea species ex causa lucrativa ad creditorem prevenisset*, Dig. 44, 7, 17, Julianus).

A legacy may be made (formerly only *per damnationem*) of a non-existing thing if it will hereafter come into being, *e.g.*, the produce of such a field, or the child of such a slave. See for the continuance of this subject, par. 885, etc.

868. *Accrual between co-legatees—the jus caduca vindicandi of the caduca laws.* Though the will valid, three cases of nullity in respect of the legacy may occur :—

(1) *Pro non scripto*, as when the legacy is void *ab initio* from, *e.g.*, the legatee being already dead or incapacitated.

(2) *Irritum* (or *destitutum*), as when the legacy fails because the legatee refuses to take it, or before the *dies cedens* is incapacitated by death, or *maxima*, or *media, c.d.*

(3) *Ereptitium*, as where the legatee is deprived of the legacy on the ground of unworthiness, when generally falls to the fiscus.

In the two first cases the legatee never had the right, and the legacy therefore lapsed to the heir, unless a co-legatee existed to take the lapsed share by right of accrual.

870. The *leges Junia Norbana, Julia testamentaria*, and *Papia Poppæa*, based on the privileges of paternity, introduced special grounds of incapacity, and so modified the law of *accrual* that the latter only determined the order for applying the *jus caduca vindicandi*.

Co-legatees *(collegatarii)* are classified by *Paul* (Dig. 50, 16, 142) in three ways, viz. :—

(1) *Re*, i.e., in respect of the *thing* only, as where the same thing is left in the same testament, but by different dispositions (*disjunctim*), *e.g., Titio hominem Stichum do lego, Seio Stichum do lego*.

(2) *Re et verbis*, when left by one and the same disposition (*conjunctim*), *e.g., Titio et Seio hominem Stichum do lego*.

(3) *Verbis*, i.e., by the words only, as where the same thing has been left, but with the shares indicated, *e.g., Titio et Seio fundum æquis partibus do lego*. In this case the recipients are not really co-legatees, for the gifts are separate; but still the form of the legacy gave certain privileges in respect of the *leges Julia et Papia Poppæa*. See *post*, par. 875 (1).

871. Historically there are three epochs to consider as to the law of *accrual* in respect of legacies.

(1) *Distinction of legacies into four classes anterior to the leges*

Julia et Papia Poppæa. Here the law of accrual alone affects the legacy, the nature of which is rigorously determined by the terms of the formula:—

(α) *Per vindicationem*. In this case, whether *conjunctim* or *disjunctim*, accrual takes place in respect of co-legatees, for the ownership of the *whole* thing is transferred to each, and a division of the property would result only from their own agreement (*in solidum habuerant concursu res divisa est*); hence, if one fails to take his legacy the other gets the whole, though if *verbis* only, the fate of one part, even undivided, cannot affect the other, and therefore no accrual.

(β) *Per damnationem*. Here, as by the general rule of law debts (*nomina*), due or owing and existing in common, divide by their nature (the action *familiæ erciscundæ* not applying to them, see 12 Tables, v, 9 and 10), the legacy would merely give to each legatee the right of claiming the thing from the heir, and there would be no accrual, whether the legacy was *conjunctim*, *i.e.*, condemning the heir to be liable to an action from each in respect of half of the estate, independent of the other; *e.g.*, *Heres meus, fundum Titio et Seio dare damnes esto*, or *disjunctim*, *e.g.*, *Heres meus hominem Stichum Titio dare damnus esto, Heres meus hominem Stichum Seio dare damnas esto*, *i.e.*, making as many debts as dispositions, so that the heir must hand over to each either Stichus or his value.

(γ) *Sinendi modo* and *per præceptionem;* legacies of this class, and in respect of the law of accrual gave rise to irreconcilable divergences of opinion.

The accrual took place for the benefit of legatees (as also in the case of heirs) discharged of liabilities (*sine onere*, *e.g.*, erect a monument, make such a journey, pay such a sum to the heir, see *post*, par. 924), for they profited by the accrual as a consequence, and in exercise of their right, and not by the will of the testator.

875. The next epoch is that of the

(2) *System introduced by the laws Julia et Papia Poppæa.* Under these laws (see part i, par. 369), heirs and legatees who were *cælibes* or *orbi* became incapacitated *capere ex testamento* (*ante*, par. 718), the *aditio* of the inheritance and the *diei cessio* of legacies (*ante*, par. 850, and *post*, par. 986) were delayed until the opening of the will, and in the result dispositions valid under the civil law often failed, and donees otherwise capable lost their bequests, so that *caducum* became a new word with a special meaning not known to prior writers (*e.g.*, Cicero); and as at the same time the *jus capiendi ex testamento* became separated from *testamenti factio*, the word *capere* also acquired a special sense.

In respect of *accrual* dispositions *pro non scriptis*, *i.e.*, invalid *ab initio*, continued subject to the rules of the ancient law, whilst dispositions valid in their origin but lapsing from ancient civil law causes were withdrawn by the *lex Papia* from the law of accrual, and became *in causa caduci*, *i.e.*, in the *condition* of *caduca*, though not actually *caduca*. As they were treated alike, and the word *caducum* applied indifferently to them, the distinction is immaterial, but arose as above stated, and *not* as *Justinian* (Cod. vi, 51) explains, viz.: that if the gifts valid in principle failed *vivo testatore* they were *caduca*, whilst if *mortuo* they were *in causa caduci*.

By the authority of the *lex Papia Poppæa* (not in execution of the will) gifts which were *caduca* or *in causa caduci* were given to the favoured heirs and legatees (without distinction whether *per vindicationem* or *per damnationem*), not by right of accrual, but as a mode of acquisition *ex lege*, in the following order:—

(1) Legatees *conjunctim* (being *patres*) *re et verbis* and *verbis tantum*, though? why *re tantum* excluded (same anomaly exists in Art. 1044 and 5, Code Napoleon).

(2) In default to *heirs* who were *patres*.

(3) In default to *legatees* who were *patres*.

(4) In default to the public treasury (*ad populum*), though if all the instituted were *cælibes*, the *ærarium* was defeated also, as the will fell to the ground for want of an heir, and the inheritance passed *ab intestato*.

Like *substitutions*, and unlike *accruals* (*ante*, par. 742), the gifts, whether shares of the inheritance, legacies, or *fidei-commissa*, must be taken as the testator had made them, *i.e.*, burdened with any charges, freedoms, legacies, or *fidei-commissa* (*caduca cum suo onere fiunt*), for both (*i.e.*, the substituted heir of the testator and *caduca* holder by the *lex Papia*) are called in place of the defaulter and like substitutions also the *caduca* require vindicating, not being forced on the recipient.

The *personæ exceptæ* (see part i, par. 369) who *solidum capere possunt* were:—

(α) *Impuberes* and those *over age* (*i.e.*, in respect of having children, the ages being fixed for men from twenty-five to sixty, for women from twenty to fifty years).

(β) Women entitled to the *vacatio*.

(γ) *Spadones*.

(δ) Persons absent on business of the state.

(ε) Cognates to the sixth degree and to the seventh degree for the *son* of a cousin german on the mother's side (extended by interpretation to *daughters* also).

(ζ) Persons connected by marriage (*adfinitas*) within certain (unknown) limits? the same as applied to the *lex Cincia*.

All ascendants and descendants of the testator to the third degree enjoyed the *jus antiquum*, including the right of accrual *sine onere*, a privilege not accorded to persons simply classed as *exceptæ*.

The *caduca* laws, therefore, made in respect of:—

Testamentary dispositions, three classes, viz.:—

(α) *Pro non scriptis*.

(β) *Caduca*, proper.

(γ) In *causa caduci;* but the laws only applied to the two last.

Persons, four classes, viz.:—

(α) Those under these laws (*i.e.*, all but those excepted) and liable to be deprived of the *jus capiendi ex testamento*.

(β) Those excepted and possessing the *solidi capacitas*.

(γ) Those able to claim the benefit of these laws, and in default the *fiscus*.

(δ) Those having the *jus antiquum*.

The fate of the testamentary gifts, two distinct rights, viz. :—

(α) The right of *accrual*, according to the ancient rules applying to *all* persons, in respect of gifts *pro non scriptis*, and to any mode of lapsing in respect of persons having the *jus antiquum*.

(β) The *jus caduca vindicandi* of the new rules.

881. In the third epoch or—

(3) *System under Justinian*, the rules as to *accrual* applied to *all* legacies, as between co-legatees, to whom the same thing had been left, but if—

(α) *Re et verbis (conjunctim)*, the accrual is voluntary, but with its liabilities attached.

(β) *Re (disjunctim)* the accrual (or rather non-diminution) is compulsory, but *sine onere*.

(γ.) *Verbis tantum*, then, as not really co-legatees, there is no accrual, and the preference rules of the *leges Juliæ* and *Papia Poppæa* no longer applied. *Ante*, par. 870 (3) and 875 (1).

If the legatee died before the right of accrual arose but after the *dies cedens* in respect of his own legacy, he transmitted the right to his heirs, *i.e.*, it fell to the juridical *persona*, whether that *persona* was sustained by the legatee or his heirs; the expression being incorrect that in this case the right falls not to the *person*, but to the *share;* for the share might have been consumed (*e.g.*, in the case of money), or passed into third hands (*e.g.*, in the case of the share of an estate sold), yet the right would not accrue to the third party, but to the heirs of the legatee.

For the surviving co-legatee's rights against the heirs of the deceased co-legatee in the particular case of *usufruct*, see *ante*, par. 496.

If there were more than two, the accrual took place proportionally, co-legatees *re* and *re et verbis*, having a preference, as an estate left to A., and B. C., and D. E. F., then the division would be into three parts, of which A. had one, B. C. one, and D. E. F. one, and if, *e.g.*, C. failed, B. took his share, and so on.

Justinian endeavoured to efface the very name of *caduca* (see part i, par. 369), but the traces of the ancient law remaining in the Digest have led to much confusion on the part of the commentators.

885. (§ ix) *Things which may be left by legacy* (continued). In the case of the legacy of the estate of another made to a legatee who had purchased the *nuda proprietas*, and to whom the *usufruct* subsequently gratuitously fell, Julianus held that the legatee could bring the action *ex testamento*, to recover the estate, it being in the province of the judge to direct payment of the value, *less the usu-*

fruct, for, as the estate had been left, not the cost of the *nuda proprietas*, the claim would not be faulty on the ground of *plus petitio* (*post*, par. 2154), as the *usufruct* would be regarded as a servitude which was always held to be tacitly deducted, and the plaintiff was entitled to the most favourable interpretation of doubtful words in the *intentio*.

886. (§ x) A legacy of the legatee's *own* property, according to *Ulpian* (Digest 30, 1, 41, § ii) and these Institutes, was *void* (see exception in the case of the *liberatio* of a debt, *post*, par. 889), even if alienated subsequently to the making of the will, for by the *Cat. reg.* (*ante*, par. 857) it was void *ab initio*, though Celsus (*Dig.* 34, 7, 1, § ii) thought this case fell within the exception and not under the rule; but if the testator believed it belonged to the legatee or to another, yet really the testator's own property, the legacy was valid, as the actual facts were held to govern the case.

888. (§ xii) Justinian confirmed the opinion of *Celsus* (which was contrary to the general view, Gai. Inst., ii, § 198) that the alienation by the testator of the whole or part; or mortgaging the estate, did not revoke the legacy unless the *intention* to do so was manifest, and in any case the part not alienated was due. The heir, also, might have an action brought against him to redeem the mortgage.

889. (§ xiii) The legacy of release (*liberatio*) of a debt, although, in fact, giving the debtor his own property (*ante*, par. 886), was valid, and whether in the form "I leave such a debtor his *liberatio*", or "I forbid my heir to claim the sum", or "I leave such a debtor what he owes me", the heir could not sue him, *i.e.*, the debtor could oppose the *exceptio doli* to the heir's suit, though the *liberatio* was not, according to the civil law, a recognised mode of extinguishing obligations, and the debtor could bring an action *ex testamento* to compel the heir to release him by some method known to the civil law, *e.g.*, *acceptilatio* (part ii, par. 211, 3), and if it was only possible to free the debtor by *pact* (as where the legacy of release was made to one of two co-debtors, jointly liable for the whole, when *acceptilatio* with one would destroy the debt due from the other), the pact would take the place of the legacy, and so secure the debtor. The gift to the debtor of the evidence of the debt (*chirographum*) would at least hold as a *fidei-commissum*. The debt might be due to the heir or to a third person, in which latter case the heir must procure a *liberatio* for the debtor, though, if the legacy simply deferred the payment (*ad tempus*), the legatee has only the dilatory *exceptio doli mali* if sued before the expiration of the time.

892. (§ xiv) The legacy of a debt to a creditor by his debtor was invalid, as giving him nothing (though? the *ex testamento* action might be preferable to the action for the debt); but it would be valid if the legacy was simple, whilst the debt was due at a term or on a condition, even if these occurred in the lifetime of the testator, because the legacy was valid originally; and so the legacy to the wife of her dowry was valid because by the *ex testamento* action

she would get it without the delay and possible set off attaching to the restitution of the dowry by means of the action *rei uxoriæ* (hence the expression *dos prælegata*), and according to the rule *falsa demonstratio non nocet* (see *post*, par. 912); though the wife had not brought any dowry, still the legacy was valid if a certain sum or object had been specified in the will.

895. (§ xvi) *Loss, accruals, or diminutions of property left by legacy.* The loss falls on the legatee if the thing perishes without the act of the heir (*sine facto heredis*), though if this happens after the *dies cedit* (*ante*, par. 850), he acquires rights as to *débris* and accessories. So, if the slave of another becomes free, he is no longer a thing in commerce (*ante*, par. 865); but if the slave belonged to the heir and was freed by him or given to another who freed him, the heir is liable whether he knew or not of the legacy.

896. (§ xvii) If the legacy includes several distinct and separate objects the loss of one does not entail the extinction of the legacy in respect of the others, *e.g.*, *propter dignitatem hominum*, the children are still due (as exceptions to the rule of accessories, part ii, par. 361) after the death of the mother in the case of a legacy of a slave and her children, so the legatee is entitled to the *vicarii*, *i.e.*, the assistants of a deceased *ordinarius* slave (*i.e.*, one occupying a special position, as steward, cook, etc., *ante*, par. 47), though included in his *peculium*. But the loss of the *principal* object extinguishes all rights to *accessories*, *e.g.*, the *peculium* of a deceased slave left by legacy is not due, nor the instruments of culture, etc., of an estate subsequently alienated, after being bequeathed, together with the appurtenances, whether for profit and pleasure (*fundus instructus*) or only for culture (*vel cum instrumento*); though, according to *Paul* (Dig. 33, 7, 5), a bequest worded *fundum et instrumentum* would be equivalent to two separate legacies.

897. (§ xviii) Diminutions or accretions after the *dies cedit* of a legacy of a flock (see part ii, par. 143, 2) are the loss or gain of the legatee, so that he can still vindicate his legacy, though reduced to one sheep, and so the fixtures, as columns, marbles, etc., added since the making of the will and the *dies cedit*, are included and the legatee is still entitled to the *land*, though the house is burnt or otherwise destroyed (see as to different rule in the case of *usufruct*, *ante*, par. 488, 6).

898. (§ xx) The *peculium* (*ante*, par. 611, 616), like a flock (*ante*, par. 897), was looked upon as a universality which increases or diminishes, and hence, if it was given as a legacy purely and simply to a stranger, the *dies cedit* was fixed at the death of the testator, and accruals or diminutions in the lifetime of the testator were the loss or the gain of the legatee; but unless they were derived from the *peculium* or were accretions to it, this did not give the legatee the acquisitions made by the *slave* after the death of the testator and before the *aditio*, though the slave himself would get these if, being the testator's own slave, the *peculium* was given him with liberty;

for the *dies cedit* in this case only begins at the *aditio* (*ante*, par. 855, 4). On the other hand, the slave freed by testament had no right to his *peculium*, unless it is given him as a legacy, in which case he is deprived of the right to claim sums advanced to the master out of the *peculium*, but a slave freed *inter vivos* has a right to his *peculium*, unless it is taken from him, and it may be given him indirectly, if, *e.g.*, ordered to be free after making up his accounts.

899. (§ xxi) *Things which may be left by legacy* (continued). As both corporeal and incorporeal things may be given as legacies, the testator may leave what is owing to him (unless he has demanded payment in his lifetime, *post*, par. 936, a), but as the juridical *persona* of the deceased passes to the heir and not to the legatee, the heir is the real creditor in respect of this *legatum nominis*, though he is bound to allow the legatee to use the actions available against the debtor. The heir might also be validly called upon in a legacy to do or not to do acts, provided they were neither impossible nor unlawful, as to rebuild the house or pay the debts of the legatee, and so he might be required to allow the legatee to do.

901. (§ xxii) A legacy of a thing not determined specifically (part ii, par. 139), but generally, is called by commentators a *legatum generis*. It was indispensable that it should be determined within certain limits (*e.g.*, a horse, a slave, whether in the inheritance or not), otherwise the legacy was void on the ground of uncertainty, *e.g.*, an animal, or a plant, or a house, an estate when neither existed in the inheritance.

According to the old law, if the legacy was *per vindicationem* (*ante*, par. 837), then, as the object must have been in the inheritance, the choice would be with the legatee, for, as he had a real action (*rei vindicatio*), this required him to point out the thing claimed, but if it were *per damnationem*, the thing need not be in the inheritance, and the legatee, having only a *personal* action, the heir (as in all cases of obligations) released himself by himself choosing and giving the thing. Under Justinian, as both real and personal actions were available to the legatee, he had always the choice, except that, as only a *personal* action was possible in respect of things not in the inheritance, the heir would in such cases have the choice, unless the testator had directed the contrary, and the choice, whichever side it lay, could not be of the best or worst.

903. (§ xxiii) The *optionis legatum* was not the legacy of a thing, but of a right of *election*; the legatee was at liberty to take the best thing, and had the action *ad exhibendum* to compel the heir to produce the things for choice. Being a *personal* right, it died with the legatee, but Justinian (Cod. vi, 43, 3) extended the right to his heir; and if the *optio* was left to several co-legatees, or there were several heirs of the one legatee, and they could not agree, the election was decided by lot.

904. A *partitio*, *i.e.*, a legacy of part of the whole inheritance (*pars bonorum*) could be left by the testator (*Heres meus cum Titio*

hereditatem meam partito dividito, Ulp., Reg., xxiv, § 25), either as a fixed share, or if not fixed, then held to be half; though, even if the whole of the property were so left, the *legatarius partiarius* was not the successor to the *persona*, *i.e.*, not the heir, but only an acquirer of property by universality, so that the gift was lost if the institution of the heir failed, and hence also the heir must sue and be sued, involving reciprocal stipulations (*stipulationes partis et pro parte*) between the heir and the legatee to adjust the respective shares of gain or loss (Gai. Inst., ii, § 254), but this kind of legacy is not mentioned in Justinian's Institutes, as it had disappeared in the fusion of legacies and *fidei-commissa*:

906. (§ xxv) *Persons capable of receiving legacies*. Originally, testamentary bequests were invalid if in favour of persons not having *testamenti factio*, and *uncertain* persons were also excluded, both in respect of legacies and fidei-commissa, for the testator must have a fixed intention, though a gift to an uncertain person out of a certain number of persons was valid (*e.g. Ex cognatis meis, qui nunc sunt, si quis filiam meam uxorem duxerit ei heres meus illam rem dato*); and in any case of uncertain persons, if the legacy or *fidei-commissum* had been paid over by mistake it could not be recovered back, *i.e.*, the *condictio indebiti* would not lie. The incapacity also extended to—

907. (§ xxvi) *Posthumous strangers*, though they could be instituted heirs provided they were not the issue of the testator and a woman whom he could not marry (*nisi in utero ejus sit quæ jure nostro uxor esse non potest*, § xxviii).

908. (§ xxvii) *Justinian* altered the whole law on this subject in his first code, only a short abstract of which exists in the second (part i, par. 550), and *uncertain* persons (including *postumi* strangers), corporations, and the poor, could receive legacies or *fidei-commissa*; and the privilege was extended to a legacy of *liberty*, though not to the nomination of an uncertain tutor. See *ante*, par. 182, 697 (3), 718, 720.

912. (§ xxix) If the *demonstratio*, *i.e.*, the mode of pointing out the particular person, was incorrect, as an error in the name or characteristics, the legacy or inheritance was not lost (*neque ex falsa demonstratione, neque ex falsa causa legatum infirmatur*, Ulp. Reg. 24, § 19, see *ante*, par. 892), provided it was evident whom the testator meant; otherwise the legacy was held *pro non scripto;* and the same remark applies to the *determination* or *limitation*; *e.g.*, I leave a legacy to the first child born of such a woman, in which case the bequest will only fail if nothing falls within the limitation, and so in respect of (§ xxxi) the *cause* or motive inducing the testator to make the bequest; an erroneous statement would not necessarily render the legacy invalid, it being solely a question of the *intention* of the testator to make the gift, though if put *conditionally* (*e.g.*, *Titio si negotia mea curaverit, fundum do lego*), performance would be requisite.

BOOK II—TIT. XX.   209

916. (§ xxxii.) In strictness an *heir* could not be a *legatee* in the same succession, *i.e.*, at the same time creditor and debtor to himself (though if *several* heirs, one might be, for the charge in respect of the legacy would exist against the others); hence if the heir acquires by virtue of the institution, he cannot also acquire through a person in his power, so that a bequest pure and simple to *his slave* would be under the *cat. reg.* (*ante*, par. 857) *void*; though, as this rule does not apply to *conditional* legacies, and in such cases the slave (or person *alieni juris*) acquires for him, in whose power he is at the *dies cedit* (*ante*, par. 855) if the slave had become free, or fallen under another person's power, the validity of the bequest would be upheld in confirmation of the opinion of *Sabinus* and *Cassius* in respect of *conditional* gifts, as opposed to the *Proculians*, who held all such legacies *in*valid, and Servius Sulpicius, who held them all valid (Gai. Inst. ii, § 244, Ulp. Reg. 24, § 23). On the other hand (§ xxxiii), a legacy to the master of a *slave instituted heir* may be valid, for the slave acquires for the master by whose order he makes *aditio* (*ante*, par. 616), and therefore the moment of the death of the testator fixes the *dies cedens* in respect of the *legacy* for the master, but if the slave becomes *free*, or is *alienated* prior to the *aditio*, he or his new master will acquire the inheritance as distinct from the legacy of the former master, though if the slave remaining in the same condition makes *aditio* by order of the legatee the legacy vanishes (Gai. Inst. ii, § 245).

921. (§ xxxiv) *Who may be charged with, and how a legacy may be left.* Formerly all dispositions preceding the appointment of the *heir* were invalid, and only the *testamentary* heir could be imperatively ordered to hand over legacies (*ante*, par. 191, 646), but under *Justinian* (Cod. vi, 23, 24) the order or *place* in the will was of no importance, and legacies burdening other than the testamentary heir were valid as *fidei-commissa* (*ante*, par. 834).

924. The *conditions* affecting legacies might go to the existence, the extent, or the execution of the bequest:—
(1) A condition (*conditio*) subordinates the legacy to a future and uncertain event. If *impossible* or *unlawful*, the gift was held pure and simple, and the condition struck out (*pro non scripto*, see below (4), and *ante*, par. 735). If consisting in a *negative* fact (*e.g.*, I leave 100 solidi to Titius, *si in capitolium non ascenderit* or *si Stichum non manumiserit*), then, as the condition could not be accomplished before death, the method was introduced by Quintus *Mucius* Scævola of allowing the legatee to receive the bequest on giving the heir security (*Muciana cantio*) for the restitution of the gift in the event of the accomplishment of the condition, and this formula was subsequently applied to heirs similarly instituted. Conditions *inherent*, or implied in the nature of the legacy, whether expressed or not, did not render the gift less pure and simple, *e.g.*, "I leave 10 solidi to Gaius if he survives me,"

P

or, "the stipulation in respect of the dowry shall be void if the marriage does not take place."

(2) The mode (*modus*) of carrying out the intention of the testator did not affect the right of the legatee to immediately demand the gift, but he had to give security to the heir, and the bequest might be reclaimed if the act was not performed, *e.g.*, *Luciis Publiis Corneliis, ad monumentum meum ædificandum mille heres meus dato*.

(3). A term (*dies*) might be annexed to a legacy, whether certain (*dies certus*, *e.g.*, three years after my death) or uncertain (*dies incertus*, *e.g.*, at the death of my heir), and in respect of the latter *Papinian* (Dig. i, 35, 75) lays down *Dies incertus conditionem in testamento facit*, and *Ulpian* (Dig. 30, i, 30, § 4), *Dies incertus appellatur conditio*, the effect of which maxims was that (a) for the *institution of the heir* (*ante*, par. 735) such a term could be made, though, as a general rule, an institution at a date was void, and (β) for a *legacy* the same rules were applied as in respect of *conditional* bequests. It was necessary that the event should be accomplished in the life time of the legatee (*i.e.*, that the *dies cedit* should have been fixed in his favour, *ante*, par. 850), in order to transmit the right to his heirs; but if the term, although uncertain, must necessarily fall in the lifetime of the legatee, there was no condition, as, *e.g.*, I leave Titius when he shall die (*cum ipse legatarius morietur*), when it was held that the uncertain term must arrive, as he lived at the moment he ceased to live, and therefore the heirs could certainly take. Justinian also (§ xxxv) destroyed the subtle distinction between the words *at* the death and *after* the death, and made legacies valid which were to be paid after the death of the heir or legatee, though formerly these were void on the ground that the former could never become a debtor or the latter a creditor in respect of the bequest.

(4) A penalty (*pœnæ nomine*) was only a particular kind of condition (*e.g.*, if my heir does not give his daughter in marriage to Stichus I leave 100 solidi to Titius), and was formerly *void*, as implying a burden on the heir (*quod coercendi heredis causa relinquitur*), as opposed to such a condition imposed on the legatee which would be perfectly valid (*e.g.*, I leave 100 solidi to Titius if he gives his daughter in marriage to Stichus). Justinian (Cod. vi, 41) abolished the distinctive character of this kind of legacy, so that it was only void if the condition was impossible or unlawful, because it was not just to punish the heir by compelling him to pay a legacy for failing to perform a condition so tainted, though in the opposite case a legacy involving an impossible or unlawful condition was held pure and simple, because the legatee ought not to be punished for failing to perform such a condition. The same rule as to a condition *pœnæ nomine* was applied to liberty, the institution of the heir, and to *fidei-commissa*, as also to the revocation and transference of legacies, as, *e.g.*, "I leave 100 solidi to Primus, and if he does not drink the Tiber dry and

does not kill Gaius I transfer the legacy to Secundus, or I revoke it," where the impossible and unlawful condition would render the transference and revocation null.

Tit. xxi. De ademptione et translatione legatorum.

936. A legacy valid in principle may be subsequently annulled by :—

(α) Revocation (*ademptio*) by some contrary disposition in the same testament (formerly contrary words required, *e.g.*, in the legacy *per vindicationem*, *do lego* by *non do, non lego*, otherwise in the eye of the civil law the legacy existed, and the legatee could only be repelled by the *exceptio-doli*), or in codicils, or the revocation might not be expressed but implied, a sufficient manifestation of the will only being requisite, as, *e.g.*, in the case of erasure in the will, or destruction of the thing, or putting it out of commerce, as by freeing a slave (*ante*, par. 895), or by making a thing *sacra* or *religiosa*, or alienating it (when effect depended on circumstances, *ante*, par. 888), or calling in the debt left as a legacy (*ante*, par. 899), or through enmity springing up between the testator and the legatee.

(β) Transference (*translatio*) which may include revocation as regards one together with a gift to another, and results from a change of (1) the *legatee*, *e.g.*, *Hominem Stichum quem Titio legavi, Seio do, lego*, or (2) the *heir* who is to give the legacy, or (3) the *thing* which is to be given, or (4) the *condition*. The legacy so transferred passes with all its accessories, conditions, and liberties (*cum sua çausa*), and the incapacity or refusal of the second will not prevent the revocation in respect of the first legatee, though in the case of the thing only being changed, if the second gift fails the first holds good, as the testator would be held not to have intended the legatee to be deprived altogether.

939. A legacy may be extinguished independently of the will of the testator by :—

(1) The will becoming *ruptum, irritum*, or *destitutum* when from the want of an heir there is no debtor (*ante*, par. 773).

(2) The legatee dying or ceasing to have *testamenti factio* before the *dies cedit*, when from the want of a legatee there is no creditor (*ante*, par. 850).

(3) The thing perishing or ceasing to be in commerce when from the want of the thing the debt could not be discharged (*ante*, par. 895).

(4) The gift being withdrawn from unworthiness (*ereptitium*).

Tit. xxii. De lege Falcidia.

940. The effect of the unlimited power of disposal implied in the words *uti legassit suæ rei ita jus esto* (12, Tables v, 3), was that many persons died intestate, as the heir would not accept the worthless inheritance.

To remedy this the *plebiscitum* called the *lex Furia* (*testamentaria*) was passed (?) B.C. 183, by which, except in the case of certain persons, no one was allowed to take as a legacy, or *mortis causa donatio*, more than 1000 asses; but this plan failed, because the testator could exhaust the inheritance by multiplying the number of legacies of 1000 asses (Gai. Inst. ii, § 225). After this the *plebiscitum* proposed by Cato and known as the

Lex Voconia (*testamentaria*) was passed in (?) B.C. 169, by which, besides the restrictions as to women being heirs, in order to prevent the dispersion of large fortunes (*ante*, par. 718, 2) it was provided that no legatee or donee *mortis causa* should take more than the heir, but this also failed, because the testator could so reduce the legacies by multiplying them, that the heir would get but a small portion (Gai. Inst. ii, § 226).

Finally, a few years before the death of Cicero, fiscal motives due to the loss by the state of the tax on wills, led to the passing of the

Lex Falcidia, B.C. 40, forbidding more than three-fourths of the property to be left away by legacy, so that whether there were one or several heirs, he or they would at least get one-fourth of the property known as the *quarta Falcidia*, or *quarta*, or *Falcidia*.

The provisions of the law were subsequently extended—

(1) By the *s.c. Pegasianum* (*post*, par. 959, 2) to fidei-commissary inheritances, and to fidei-commissa, with which the instituted heir was burdened.

(2) By a rescript of *Antoninus Pius* to *fidei-commissa* imposed on the heir *ab intestato*, so that the original intention of the law was lost sight of (*post*, par. 968).

(3) By a rescript of *Severus* and *Antoninus* to donations *mortis causa*.

(4) By a constitution of Diocletian and Maximian to gifts between husband and wife, and finally gave rise to the theory of the *portio legitima* (*ante*, par. 794); but the *lex Falcidia* did not apply to *military* testaments, nor to some other privileged and exceptional cases, and Justinian (Novel i, c. 2, § 2) gave the testator the right to expressly or tacitly forbid its application.

943. (§ I) The calculation in respect of the *lex Falcidia* was made separately for each, so that if several heirs were differently charged with legacies they each obtained one-fourth of their share, but this right was confined to testamentary or *ab-intestato* heirs, and was not conferred on legatees or *fidei-commissarii* charged with *fidei-commissa*.

944. (§ ii) The calculation as to the value of the inheritance and of the legacies was made as from the date of the death of the testator, and (§ iii) debts, funeral expenses, and the value of slaves freed deducted, after which gains before the *aditio* fell to the heir, irrespective of the one-fourth, but if only three-fourths were left by legacy, though before the *aditio* great losses occurred, the legatees could claim the whole, except that as in this case the heir might refuse to make the *aditio*, the legatees, to avoid the total loss of their legacies, would come to terms with him.

Tit. xxiii. De Fidei-commissariis Hereditatibus.

949. The *fidei-commissaria hereditas*, or *universal* trust, had for its object the inheritance, or a definite share of it, with a trustee substituted by the deceased for the civil heir, as opposed to the *fidei-commissum singulæ rei*, or *particular* trust (see *post*, par. 971), which had any other thing than the inheritance for its object (*e.g.*, a determinate thing in kind, as money, or in species, as a particular slave, or a universality, as a *peculium* or a flock), and in which a trustee of the particular object was substituted for a legatee.

950 (§ i) *Historical origin of fidei-commissa*. If a testator desired to leave anything to persons unable to take directly by way of inheritance or legacy (*e.g.*, provincial *peregrini*, female citizens under the *lex Voconia*, the proscribed by the *lex Cornelia*, posthumous strangers or other uncertain persons, as municipalities or the poor, those falling under the *lex Ælia Sentia*, *Junia Norbana*, *Julia* and *Papia Poppæa*), it was the custom to intrust the bequest to the good faith of those who could validly take under the will. Hence these gifts acquired the name of *fidei-commissa*; and though afterwards regulated by law, yet, as their foundation rested on the wishes of the deceased and not on legal rules, they always received a large and favourable interpretation. Not being binding in law, testators endeavoured to secure their performance by appealing to the religious feelings or conscience of the person entrusted, and hence the introduction on the part of the trustee of the oath by Jupiter, by the Lares, etc., *per salutem, per genium principis*. The use of *fidei-commissa* in this way had, before the time of Cicero, acquired the common assent, and subsequently the Emperor *Augustus* (see part i, par. 350, 378, and *post*, par. 973) yielded to the general opinion at first by special intervention in such cases, as, *e.g.*, where a freedman refused to restore a *fidei-commissum* to his patron in spite of his oath to the deceased (Cic. in Verr. ii, 1, 47), and then (though no civil law action was permitted) by vesting a permanent exceptional jurisdiction in the hands of a special Prætor acting *extra-ordinem* (*Fidei-commissa non per formulam petuntur; ut legata, sed cognitio est Romæ quidem consulum aut prætoris qui fidei-commissarius vocatur; in provinciis vero præsidum provinciarum*, Ulp. Reg. 25, § 12, Gai. Inst. ii, § 278, and see *post*, par. 993). After trusts became thus sanctioned it was found necessary to curtail their effects, and the *s.c. Pegasianum* (*post*, par. 959, 2) brought them within the *leges Julia* and *Papia Poppæa*, so that the heir who carried out a secret trust in favour of persons incapacitated by these laws ran the risk of losing his *quarta Falcidia* on such portions of the inheritance, and a *senatus consultum* under *Hadrian* forbad these trusts in favour of *peregrini*, uncertain persons, and posthumous strangers.

959. An *heir* (the *fiduciarius*) must first be duly appointed (but see *post*, par. 968), and then he must be requested by the testator (the *fidei-committens*) to hand over the inheritance to another (the

fidei-commissarius), whether the whole or in part, purely or on a condition, or at a term; *e.g.*, *Lucius Titius Heres esto. . . Rogo te, Luci Titi ut cum primum possis hereditatem meam adire cum Gaio Seio reddas restituas.*

As the *fiduciarius* after handing over the property still remained heir, the *fidei-commissarius* was at first looked upon as a purchaser *(Olim autem nec heredis loco erat nec legatarii sed potius emptoris,* Gai. Inst. ii, § 252), and a fictitious sale of the whole or part of the inheritance was made, involving the ordinary stipulations between vendor and purchaser *(emptæ et venditæ hereditatis stipulationes)* as to reciprocal obligations for either party to sue or be sued as an agent for the other.

In time the *fidei-commissarius* (in defiance of the principles as to the juridical *persona* of the deceased) came to be viewed sometimes as—

(1) An *heir*, when by the *senatus consultum Trebellianum* (passed in A.D. 62, under Nero, in the consulate of *Trebellius* Maximus and Annæus Senæca, see Dig. 36, 1, 1, § 2) all the actions lying for and against the heir, in respect of the portion or the whole of the inheritance for which he was trustee, were transferred for and against him, *i.e.*, *utiles* were substituted by edict for the *civil* actions of the heir, and though strictly the heir might still be sued, he could plead the *restitutæ hereditatis exceptio*, and the debtors to the estate had an *exceptio* against him if he sued them.

(2) A *legatee* and then the *s.c. Pegasianum* (passed? A.D. 70 to 76, under Vespasian, in the consulate of *Pegasus* and Pusio), besides other provisions (*ante*, par. 950) enacted that the heir might retain one-fourth of the *fidei-commissum (quarta, Falcidia, commodum, beneficium legis Falcidiæ,* and incorrectly called by commentators *quarta Trebelliana)*, whether in respect of the inheritance or of particular objects, in those cases where he would otherwise refuse to make *aditio* on the ground of having to hand over the whole or so much of the inheritance as rendered it not worth his while to be troubled with it, *i.e.*, the *lex Falcidia (ante,* par. 940, 1) was extended to this case, and the *fidei-commissarius* thereby assimilated to the *legatarius partiarius (ante,* par. 904), and being *loco legatarii,* similar stipulations, *partis et pro parte,* were entered into with the heir (Gai. Inst. ii, § 254).

964. (§ vi) Hence, if the heir was *not* required to hand over more than three-fourths of the estate, the *s.c. Trebellianum* applied, otherwise the *s.c. Pegasianum,* and if in the latter case the heir did not exercise his right to retain one-fourth, then he fell back upon the stipulations *emptæ et venditæ hereditatis* (Gai. Inst., ii, § 257), and if the heir suspecting the inheritance to be onerous, refused to interfere, the *s.c. Pegasianum* provided that the *fidei-commissarius* might apply to the prætor to compel the heir to make the *aditio (jussu prætoris adeat),* in which case actions for and against the *fidei-commissarius* would be given as if under the *s.c. Trebellianum.*

966. (§ vii) Papinian considered the dispositions of the *s. c. Pegasianum* as vexatious on account of the risk incurred by the heir or the legatee of the non-fulfilment of the stipulations by the insolvency of one of them, and *Justinian united the two senatus-consulta into one* under the name of the former (*Trebellianum*), the result being that

(1) The heir always had the right to retain one-fourth.

(2) The actions were always transferred to the *fidei-commissarius*, and therefore he was always *loco heredis;* but as to his right to retain the *quarta* see *post,* par. 969.

(3) If the heir had transferred the whole inheritance, he could sue for one-fourth back.

(4) If the heir was to retain or take beforehand an object or a sum of money or any large or small portion of the inheritance equal to one-fourth, this was reckoned as the *quarta*, but viewed in the light of a legacy, and therefore not liable to debts, so that the heir, *as a legatee,* was released from liability and all actions passed to the *fidei-commissarius.*

(5) If the heir was required to hand over the inheritance, reserving to himself one-fourth, then the actions divided proportionately, and the heir would still be looked upon as occupying that capacity, and therefore liable to actions arising in respect of his fourth share.

968. (§ x) Justinian confirmed the extension by *Antoninus Pius* of the provisions of the *s.c. Trebellianum* to *fidei-commissa ab intestato* (see *ante,* par. 940), so that such gifts could now be made by codicils, whether testate or intestate (*post,* par. 973).

969. (§ xi) The *fidei-commissarius* may himself be requested to hand over the thing, in whole or in part, or a different thing to another and that other again, but these persons would not be entitled to the *quarta,* because the only object of the *lex Falcidia* was to insure an heir to the inheritance, and hence a difference still existed between the institution and the fidei-commissary heir, though if the heir had made the *aditio* by order of the prætor, and had not deducted his fourth, the *fidei-commissarius* would be entitled to do so in his place.

970. (§ xii) As opposed to the *institution,* in which correctness as to *form* was essential, the *intention* of the deceased alone controlled the devolution of *fidei-commissa,* and (after Justinian) *legacies* also, so that the requisite formalities (viz., writing or five witnesses) were merely means of proof, and if these were wanting the *fidei-commissarius, after* having himself sworn to his own good faith (*cum prius ipse de calumnia juraverit*), could compel the heir or legatee or other trustee to take an oath that he had not been charged with the trust.

Tit. xxiv. De singulis rebus per fidei-commissum relictis.

971. (§ i) Though a *legatee* could not be charged with a legacy,

either he or the heir might be trustees in respect of a *fidei-commissum* (*ante*, par. 949).

The subject-matter of the trust (as in the case of a legacy *per damnationem*, *ante*, par. 837, 2) might belong to the heir, to the legatee, to the *fidei-commissarius*, or to any other person, in which latter case (under *Justinian*) the trustee was bound to purchase it, or if unable, then to pay over its value, though in the time of *Gaius* (Inst., ii, § 262) some juris-consults held the trust extinguished if the owner refused to sell. Any excess in the value of the object of the trust over the gift in the testament was invalid, it being a general maxim that no one was bound to hand over in the form of a legacy more than he had himself received under the will; but this was qualified by the rule *si quantitas cum quantitate conferatur*, so that if the price of a house or slave of another exceeded the sum the trustee had received, he was not bound to purchase them; though, on the other hand, if he accepted, *e.g.*, a sum of money, he could be compelled to carry out a trust which required him to hand over a house or slave of his *own*, as it was presumed that he had calculated the value of the trust before accepting the testamentary bequest.

972. (§ ii) A distinction, however, still existed between *freedom* by legacy (*i.e.*, directly) and by *fidei-commissum* (see *ante*, par. 57 and 846); for, in the latter case, the heir, legatee or *fidei-commissarius*, might be charged to free the slave of *another*, and that other, if he had taken any bequest from the deceased, would be bound to submit; but otherwise, if he refused to sell the slave, Justinian held, overruling the opinion of *Gaius* (Inst., ii, § 265) and *Ulpian* (Reg., ii, § 11), and confirming the rescript of Alexander (Cod. 7, 4, 6), that the gift of liberty was *not* extinguished, on the ground that no sum could be substituted as the value of the liberty, but that it was only deferred until a better opportunity.

If a testator freed a slave *directly*, who could only be freed *per fidei-commissum*, the disposition would be valid as the latter.

Tit. xxv. De Codicillis.

973. According to strict law, no new disposition, however trivial, could be added to a testament without re-making the whole; but Lucius Cornelius *Lentulus* (consul in B.C. 2), when dying in Africa, charged the Emperor Augustus with certain *fidei-commissa* in *codicils* confirmed by his testament. Augustus carried out these trusts (which are said to have been the origin also of *fidei-commissa*, but see *ante*, par. 950), and subsequently others followed his example; whereupon, on the advice of Trebatius and other juris-consults, their validity was admitted (see part i, par. 378); and, finally, *Labeo* himself having left codicils, their legal force was admitted by all. The name was derived from the smaller form of tablet (*codicillus*), which was used instead of the larger sized *codex* (*tabulæ lignum*), on which the testament was written, and as formerly direc-

tions in *codicilli* only had the force of *fidei-commissa*, they were sometimes called *epistolæ fidei-commissaria*.

Codicils may be made either :—

(1) *Ab intestato*, in which case their validity or nullity depended on themselves. They could only contain *fidei-commissa*, as, according to the civil law, legacies could not be charged on heirs *ab intestato;* but all or any part of the inheritance (Gai. Inst., ii, § 273), as well as particular objects, might be included.

(2) Attached to, and confirmed by, an anterior or posterior testament, and they may then contain not only *fidei-commissa* but legacies, revocations of legacies, direct freedoms, giving of tutors, etc., but the inheritance could not be *directly* given or taken away, nor could exclusions be inserted in them or a condition attached to the institution or the substitution of the heir. The date of the making of the will is calculated for their dispositions, and being viewed as a part of the will itself, they, as an *accessory*, shared the fate of the principal. If not specially confirmed by the will, the dispositions contained in codicils only had the value of *fidei-commissa*, and Papinian had advocated annulling them in such cases; but *Severus* and *Antoninus* held it sufficient if there was no indication of a contrary intention in the subsequent will.

979. (§ iii) *Several* codicils might be made, and no solemnity in respect of form was necessary, though Constantine and Constans, A.D. 326, required five witnesses to codicils not preceded by a testament, and Justinian extended the rule to every expression, whether verbal or in writing, of last wishes (except the testament), requiring also, if in writing, the subscriptions of the witnesses; but these requisitions were only for the purpose of proof, and, if wanting, an oath could be substituted, see *ante*, par. 970.

981. A testament, *informal* from any cause, would not be valid as a codicil, unless the deceased *expressly* (except in military testaments) inserted a clause (termed by the commentators *clausula codicillaris*) in the will to that effect, *e.g., Hoc testamentum volo esse ratum, quacumque ratione poterit* (Dig., 28, 1, 29, Paul); but this would not prevent the nullity of the testament if there was a want of *capacity* in the testator.

982. The *opening, examination,* and *preservation* of wills was considered so important by the Romans, that it assumed something of a public character, and the matter was regulated by an edict of the prætor. According to *Paul* (Sent. iv, 6), if the document was :—

(1) *At Rome* the major part of the witnesses identified their seals, and it was in the province of the prætor to compel the recognition of the seals, which in the case of absent witnesses would be done by sending the will to them for verification. The thread was then broken, and the will read, which should be done, as near as circumstances would admit, within the third or fifth day of the testator's death. A copy having been made, the origi-

nal will received the public seal, and was deposited with the public archives; after which, inspection or a copy could be had by any one, except of those parts (*e.g.*, conditions, pupillary substitutions, etc.) which the testator had forbidden to be unsealed until necessary.

(2) *Elsewhere*, the will was read in the forum or basilica in the presence of the witnesses or honourable men, between the second and tenth hour of the day; and, after a copy had been made, the original will was sealed in the presence of the magistrates before whom it had been opened.

985. To obtain possession of the document three courses were open, viz.:—

(1) The interdict *de tabulis exhibendis*, the terms of which are given in Dig. 43, 5, 1, was specially provided by the prætor to compel the production of the will by a person who denied having it.

(2) The *vindicatio* action was open to the heir who asserted his right to the document as a part of the inheritance.

(3) The *ad exhibendum* action could also be used by the heir who wanted to ascertain if the document was in a given person's possession before vindicating it.

986. From the time of the *lex Papia Poppæa* to the reforms of Justinian (*ante*, par. 875) additional importance was attached to the opening of the will, as the *dies cedit* of legacies was referred to that period, and *aditio* was forbidden *ante apertas tabulas*, except in the case of the heir to the whole inheritance (*i.e.*, *ex asse*), for his failure would not advance the objects of the *caduca* laws, as it would let in the heirs *ab intestato*, not the *fiscus* or the *patres*.

987. A constitution of Theodosius and Valentinian also made the date of the opening of the will important, as by it the 'children instituted by male or female ascendants, and dying before that period, transmitted their rights of inheritance to their children (see *post*, par. 1013).

988. *Actions relating to legacies and fidei-commissa.* Under the Ancient law the *form* of the legacy (see *ante*, par. 837) determined the appropriate action, viz., the:—

(1) *Rei vindicatio* for legacies *per vindicationem*.
(2) *Condictio* for these *per damnationem* or *sinendi modo*.
(3) *Familiæ erciscundæ* for those *per præceptionem*.

Under *Justinian*, legacies, being all of the same nature (*ante*, par. 844), the legatee could avail himself of the:—

(a) *Rei vindicatio* to recover the thing, in whosesoever hands it might be, though the use of this action was only possible where ownership resulted from the legacy, the *actio confessoria* lying for a fraction of this ownership as for a usufruct or servitude, see *ante*, par. 507.

(β) *Actio (condictio) ex testamento (actio legati)* against the heir to compel delivery of that for which he was personally liable.

(γ) *Actio hypothecaria*, resulting from the right of lien or legal mortgage, given by Justinian as a guarantee of the legacy on any hereditary property falling to the person charged with the legacy.

990. If the legacy was not immediately demandable, as where it was *a die* or *sub conditione*, or involved in a pending lawsuit, the prætor gave the legatee a special right of requiring *security* by *fidejussors (legatorum seu fidei-commissorum servandorum causa cautio)* from the person charged with the legacy, and if this security was not forthcoming the legatee might be put in possession of the property of the deceased.

991. The *heir*, on the other hand, to recover the *quarta Falcidia* could make use of the :—

(1) *Exceptio doli moli* against a legatee's action, in respect of so much of the legacy as required to be deducted.

(2) The *rei vindicatio*, or the action *ad exhibendum*, or the *condictio indebiti*, or an action *in factum*, according to circumstances, where the legacy was already in the possession of the legatee ; and if this possession had been improperly acquired by the legatee's own authority, the heir, to compel restitution, could obtain from the prætor the special interdict *quod legatorum* (Dig. 43, 3, 2).

993. In respect of *fidei-commissa*, formerly application could only be made to the special prætor acting *extra-ordinem (ante*, par. 950), but under *Justinian* the *fidei-commissarius* could in respect of:—

(1) Particular objects, avail himself of the same actions as the legatee.

(2) The inheritance, make use of the *fidei-commissaria hereditatis petitio*, or, to obtain a partition, the *utilis familiæ erciscundæ*.

ABSTRACT OF BOOK II.

Division of things.

The word *thing* in Roman law included all corporeal objects, or those of pure juridical creation, considered as under the power of (or at least destined for the wants of) man, and consequently capable of being the objects of rights.

The distinctions as to *res mancipi* and *nec mancipi*, and as to *Italian* and *provincial* land, were suppressed, and the principal division of things in the Digest is into *res divini* and *humani juris*, and in the Institutes into : —

(1) *Extra nostrum patrimonium*, consisting of—

(α) Res *communes*, the property in no one, and the use to everyone, *e.g.*, the air, running water, the sea, and its banks.

(β) Res *publicæ*, ownership in the people and use common, as harbours, prætorian or consular ways, as well as streams, of which the *use* of the *bank* was public, though the *ownership* resided in the riparian proprietors.

(γ) Res *universitatis*, the *ownership* in the corporation, but the *use* free to all its members, as theatres, stadia, etc.

(δ) *Res nullius, i.e.* (1) those things which man has not yet got in his power, or which have escaped him, or which he has entirely abandoned; (2) those withdrawn from commerce (res *divini juris*) and divided into (a) *res sacræ, i.e.*, things, since the establishment of the Christian religion, solemnly consecrated to God by the pontiffs, and for which the authorization of the Emperor was required. *Moveable* objects consecrated to worship may, by a constitution of Justinian, be alienated for the ransom of captives, or for feeding the poor in time of famine. (β) Res *religiosæ, i.e.*, places which have served to receive the remains of the dead. Any person by an interment may render ground religious, provided he is owner, or has the consent of the parties interested. Profanation was punished civilly, and criminally. (γ) *Res sanctæ, i.e.*, those things protected by a penal sanction, as the laws, walls, gates of city, etc.

(2) *In nostro patrimonio.* These are *res privatæ (res singulorum).* The *Institutes* also divide things into :—

(α) *Corporeal, i.e.*, existing physically *(quæ tangi possunt).*

(β) *Incorporeal, i.e.*, only legally existing *(quæ tangi non possunt)* but capable of being the objects of rights, and therefore including everything consisting in rights *(quæ in jure consistunt),* *e.g.*, inheritances, obligations, servitudes, etc.

Ownership and other real rights.

Real rights having for their object material riches included, under *Justinian*, ownership, possession, the servitudes (personal and prædeal), right of emphyteusis, superficies, pledge and mortgage.

Dominium (proprietas). Under the 12 Tables only one kind existed, and that peculiar to Roman citizens, but subsequently ownership was distinguished into *dominium ex jure Quiritium,* and *in bonis habere.* Under *Justinian* this distinction, which had become merely nominal, was suppressed, and one ownership recognised, like that of other nations. The rights given by *proprietas* are summed up in the definition of ownership, viz., *dominium est jus utendi fruendi et abutendi quartenus juris ratio patitur.* He to whom the power of disposition remained was considered as owner, though fragments belonged to different persons.

Possessio. This may be *physical (nuda detentio) i.e.*, consisting in the fact only, or *legal,* the latter involving the *intention* in addition to the *fact.* Possession may give the ownership of *res nullius,* or of things the owner wishes to alienate in our favour. It leads at times to the acquisition of produce consumed, and at the end of a fixed period of the ownership of another's property. It gives the right of detaining a thing until some one proves himself owner, and it enables an action to be brought to preserve or to recover possession.

Quasi-possessio of *incorporeal* objects consists in (1) the fact of having the exercise of the right at free disposition, (2) the *intention* of exercising the right as owner. Both *possessio* and *quasi-possessio* were protected by *interdicta* divided as to possession into (1) *acquirendæ*, (2) *conservandæ*, (3) *recuperandæ*, (4) to acquire and recover, and these on the suppression of the formula procedure became true actions.

The rights of *proprietas* gave rise to *real* actions, of which the *rei vindicatio* was the most remarkable; the plaintiff in these actions asserted that the corporeal or incorporeal thing was his property.

Means of acquiring the ownership of particular objects.

The *jus gentium*, or natural methods, were :—

Occupatio resulting from the first possession of *res nullius*, for which it was necessary (1) that the thing was capable of being in the patrimony of man, and that it belonged to no one, (2) that legal possession was acquired.

Accessio in Roman law only meant the thing united, not the fact of the union; but the commentators imply by it a special mode of acquisition, and it is a true method of acquisition of things belonging to no one, as, *e.g.*, pigeons, bees, or other animals coming to a dovecot or beehive, alluvion, detritus carried by the current and deposited by degrees on land so as to be unrecognisable and to form part of the land, islands springing up in the stream, or the bed abandoned; but these examples are to be distinguished from an *inundation*; or where recognisable land is carried away violently by the force of the waters or other cause.

In exceptional cases the rule applies to the property of another perfectly recognisable by the owner, as in *ferruminatio*, but in most other cases there is absorption, consumption, destruction, remediable or *ir*remediable, of another's property, and only the right of indemnity remains.

In the *confusio* of things belonging to *different* owners, and the production of *new* objects, the distinctions are to be noted between the *creation* and consequent acquisition of the ownership of a new thing, where by the industry of the workman a new kind of thing is formed with the material of another; and *confusio* of liquid things, where no new object is produced, or, if so, is so by chance, and results in co-ownership. The prohibition of the 12 Tables as to destroying buildings through the agency of the *vindicatio* or *ad exhibendum* action gave rise to different results, according as erected on own land with another's materials, or own material on another's land, and the rules of accessio differ as to the *writing* in respect to the parchment, and a *picture* in relation to the canvas.

Produce as a general rule belongs to the owner of the estate, as being the fruit of the thing; but the possessor in good faith was considered as owner in respect of all fruit no longer attached to the soil, and was not liable to account to the owner for fruits consumed.

The general rule as to *Treasure trove* was that one-half went to the finder and one-half to the owner of the land.

Traditio is the transference of possession, either simply, *i.e.*, *physically (nuda traditio)*, or including the intention. The *fact* of corporeal traditio did not transfer ownership unless resulting from *justa causa*, though the fact might result from fraud or mistake, and yet suffice if it involved the will to transfer the ownership; but in order that the ownership be transferred *at the time* it was necessary for the owner to have the power to alienate. The will alone sometimes transfers ownership (1) when the thing was physically in the power of the acquirer, (2) when the parties agreed that the owner who alienated it should retain the thing on loan, usufruct, deposit, etc., (3) when the acquirer had already the legal possession; but in these cases the legal possession either exists already, or the will alone suffices to give it.

There are not several *kinds* of traditio, though there are several ways of effecting the delivery, and by analogy a *quasi traditio* applied to *incorporeal* things.

The *civil law* modes of acquisition of particular objects were:—

Usucapio. This formerly differed from *præscriptio* in that the first resulted from the *civil law* and applied to *moveables* everywhere in one year, to immoveables in Italy only in two years, and was a means of *acquisition*, though the ownership remained burdened with any lien or mortgages, but not interrupted by action, and continued during suit; the second belonged to *prætorian* law, and applied to *immoveables* in the *provinces* (ten years when present, twenty years absent), and was a kind of exception to repel the action of the owner as well as of creditors who had not exercised their rights, but it was interrupted at the *litis contestatio*.

Justinian merged the two, and modified the law respecting them; *moveables* were everywhere acquired after three years, *immoveables* by ten years present, twenty years absent.

Things incapable of acquisition by usage were: free men; things not in commerce, sacred or religious; fugitive slaves; stolen things, immoveables taken by violence, until the vice resulting from the flight, theft, or violence, was purged by the return of the thing into the hands of the owner. Things belonging to the fiscus (except *bona vacantia*, not yet claimed by it), immoveables of churches, property of minors, etc.

The conditions for acquisition by use were:—1. *Civil possession.* 2. *Justa causa.* 3. *Good faith.* 4. *The required time* (counted by days, not by hours). Sometimes the time of the first possessor is tacked to that of his successor, whether in the case of successors continuing the *persona* of the deceased or those receiving by sale, donation, legacy, etc.; but the former acquire when the deceased would have so acquired, and irrespective of their own personal good or bad faith; whilst the latter only acquire if there is also good faith on their part, *i.e.*, the times run together when the author and the successor have both possessed according to law.

Prescription, like usucapion, for moveables and immoveables, produces under Justinian *proprietas*. Rights of servitude or mortgage are extinguished, if the thing has been possessed as free.

Usurpatio was the interruption of acquisition by usage, and occurred (α) *naturally* when some event deprived the holder of possession; (β) *civilly*, under *Justinian*, by the action of the true owner.

The longissimi temporis prescriptio of *thirty*, sometimes *forty*, years, served under Justinian as a means of acquisition.

To guarantee possession before the usucapion or prescription was completed, the possessor had possessory *interdicts;* and even if by some event he lost it, the *publiciana in rem actio* enabled him to vindicate it as if already gained by prescription. After completion of usucapion or prescription, all actions and exceptions resulting from ownership were open.

Legatum. This was a civil mode of acquiring *proprietas* by the effect of the law without the necessity of tradition, and is treated in the Institutes with testamentary inheritances. The *fideicommissum* being assimilated under *Justinian* to legacies, ought also to be included in these civil modes.

Mortis causa donatio was in certain cases, like legacies, under Justinian, a civil mode of transferring ownership without tradition and by the simple effect of the law. Other forms of *donatio*, as those *inter vivos*, the *dos*, and that *propter nuptias*, were not means, but only legitimate causes of acquisition, *i.e.*, they did not by themselves transfer the *proprietas*, but served as a cause for the transference being made.

The word *donatio* expressed in its origin the fact of the translation of ownership by way of liberality, and not the means for effecting or the agreement to give. *Mortis causa* implied being subject to the condition of death, but this decease may be general, *i.e.*, in any way, at any time, or specially determined under particular circumstances, and may be that of a third person. If made *sub conditione*, it only existed at the time when death took place, but if it was a gift *quæ sub conditione solvitur*, it existed at instant made, though dissolved if the death did not take place, *i.e.*, it was immediate, but determined by the condition. It was only the first kind that constituted a true means of acquisition, and even then, before *Justinian*, the proprietas was only transferred at the time of the decease by virtue of the conditional *traditio* or *mancipatio* made previously. The *donatio* must be made, according to *Justinian's* legislation, before five witnesses, with consent of donor and donee. It was revocable, had analogies to, but also differed from, legacies, and is not to be confounded with the *mortis causa capio*, an expression covering other kinds of acquisitions on death not bearing special names.

The *donatio inter vivos* in primitive law, was not a contract, or obligatory agreement—the act was accomplished by one of the ordinary methods of transferring the *proprietas*—and so far, and by the effect of the agreement alone, there was no acquisition or obligation. Justinian made it obligatory like the contract of *sale*, but the proprietas was only transferred by *traditio*, and the donatio *inter vivos*, as thus understood, was not a means of acquisition. It required to be registered (with some exceptions). It was irrevocable (except for ingratitude, and in one case only on account of the subsequent birth of children). It differed in important points from the *mortis causa* donatio.

Dos.—Gifts between married persons during marriage were prohibited, but by a *s.c.* under Caracalla, though they were recoverable at the will of the donor, yet they were confirmed if he died without revoking them. A correlation exists between the donatio *propter nuptias* of the husband and the *dos* of the wife. The settlement of the dos (*i.e.*, all that which is brought by the wife to the husband to sustain the burdens of the marriage) was not at first classed amongst contracts; and it was effected by the immediate translation of the proprietas, or, in default, made obligatory by a *stipulatio* or *dotis dictio*, but Imperial constitutions made it binding by itself, and custom early allowed the dos to be settled *during* the marriage. The husband was the owner of the property representing the dos during marriage, but he was bound to restore it at its dissolution in the same quantity and quality for things *fungibiles*, or those whose value was fixed by the contract. Other things had to be returned in specie. Dowry *immoveables* were not originally inalienable, and the husband could mortgage or alienate them with the consent of the wife; but the *lex Julia* prohibited *mortgage*, and *Justinian* alienation.

The *donatio ante nuptias* was introduced after the *dos*, and could originally only be settled before the marriage. It was made by the husband to the wife, by analogy, and in some sort in compensation for the *dos—i.e.*, it was destined, like the *dos*, to sustain the burdens of the marriage. The property comprising it, like the *dos* property, was placed beyond the claims of creditors; and, like the *dos*, it was restored at the end of the marriage. As the wife did in the case of the *dos*, so the husband might incur the risk of the loss of the *donatio ante nuptias*. Any benefit in respect of survival, as to the *dos* or the *donatio ante nuptias*, was reciprocal; and, after a constitution of Leo, it was to be *proportional*. After *Justinian* there was to be numerical equality. *Justin* allowed the donatio ante nuptias to be increased, and *Justinian* even to be settled during the marriage; hence the name was changed to *donatio propter nuptias*.

For the donatio *mortis causa sub conditione*, a *rei vindicatio* action lay when the condition was accomplished; for, under *Justinian*, the ownership was transferred to the donee by law, and *before* Justinian by the conditional *traditio* or *mancipatio* which had been made. So if the condition failed, or the donor before his decease wished to revoke the gift, being always owner, he could use the *rei vindicatio* action against the donee when the latter was in possession.

In the donatio mortis causa *quæ sub conditione solvitur*, the donor, if he wished to revoke and recover the gift before the event, had, in strict law, a *condictio* to get the ownership returned by the donee, and jurisprudence further gave him a *vindicatio utilis* to reclaim the thing as if not alienated. So, if the event (*i.e.*, the case of his survival) had been accomplished, and therefore the gift dissolved, the donor had, for the purpose of getting the thing back, the *condictio quasi re non secuta*, and by a *utilis* extension, the *rei vindicatio*. Donations *inter vivos* not effected by *traditio* gave the donee, for the purpose of acquiring the objects, the *condictio certi* or the *ex stipulatu* action, if there was a stipulation, and the *condictio ex lege* if only simple agreement.

Jus adcrescendi. Prior to Justinian, a particular kind of acquisition existed in favour of the masters of a slave who, belonging in common to several, was *freed* by one or more of them; so that if by all he would be a Roman citizen, but under that Emperor the slave was to be free and the non-consenting masters indemnified.

Loss of possession, legal possession was lost by the *fact* when the thing ceased to be at our disposition; by the *intention*, when we no longer wished to possess; but absence alone did not entail the loss of possession, because it did not prevent the thing being at our free disposition.

Loss of proprietas occurred when he who had it became incapable of being owner—when the thing perished or left the patrimony of man—when the ownership was transferred to another—and when the owner intentionally abandoned the thing.

Servitudes. These, as regards the holder, are more or less important fractions of the right of ownership. As regards he who has to submit to them, they are modifications or alterations of the *proprietas*. They were called *jura* because they consist in certain rights over the *property* of another, and *servitudes* because the property was as it were enslaved to them. They were divided into *rerum (prædiorum)* and *personales*, according as they tended to augment the utility of a thing or the individual advantage of a person. Several principles are common to both kinds, as that (1) they are all real rights over the property of another, (2) *nemini res sua servit*, (3) are to permit, or not to do, *never to do*, (4) *servitus servitutis esse non potest*, (5) cannot be possessed, but a quasi-possession admitted, for those consisting in suffering.

Prædial servitudes have only *immoveables* for their objects. They may consist in suffering or not doing, are indivisible and classified as *rusticorum*, *i.e.*, those *quæ in solo consistunt (e.g., iter, via)*, and

Q

urbanorum, *i.e.*, those *quæ in superficie consistunt (e.g., oneris ferendi, stillicidii recipiendi)*, and immaterial whether in town or country, as they derive their quality from their own nature, not from the dominant or servient tenement. *Rural* were formerly *res mancipi*, the others, *nec*, but the distinction was suppressed under *Justinian*. *Urban* have a continuous character not generally applying to the others, and leading to differences as to quasi-possession, and loss by non-usage.

In order that a *prædial* servitude may exist, it is necessary that the estate should be sufficiently neighbouring for the exercise of the right; that the servitude should be of some utility or some enjoyment, as when useless it vanished; and in general it must have a perpetual cause.

Under *Justinian's* legislation, servitudes were established as real rights, or at least as an obligation (1) by agreement, *i.e.*, either by pacts and stipulations, or by pacts inserted in a contract of sale or in the traditio; or by the sale itself of the right of servitude; (2) by testament, *i.e.*, either by directly willing it, or condemning the heirs to suffer it; (3) by *usage*. No servitude, at least after the *lex Scribonia*, could be acquired by *usucapion*, but the Prætors and Imperial constitutions gave *utiles* actions and *utiles* interdicts to maintain these rights in favour of those who had enjoyed for a long time certain servitudes, *i.e.*, chiefly urban servitudes and rights as to streams of water. For this acquisition by use no title was required, but the enjoyment must have been *nec vi*, *nec clam*, *nec precario*. The time was not fixed, but should be long and sometimes immemorial, according to the kind of servitude and the nature of the case. It is a question whether Justinian fixed it at ten years present, twenty years absent; (4) by *adjudication*, in the actions *familiæ erciscundæ* and *communi dividundo*.

Servitudes were *extinguished* by (1) loss of one of the tenements; (2) confusion; (3) return, which occurred when the owner of the dominant estate voluntarily allowed something to be done which prevented the existence of the servitude; (4) non-usage, by Justinian ten years present, twenty years absent; but for *urban* servitudes the owner of the servient tenement must have acquired his release by some act contrary to the continuance of the servitude, though (?) Justinian did not require this condition in respect of *rural* servitudes.

Personal servitudes may have *moveables* as well as *immoveables* for their object. They only consist in suffering. They are not all *indivisible* (*usufruct* was considered as *divisible* though *usage* not.)

Usufructus included (1) the *jus utendi*, (2) the *jus fruendi*; the latter giving the right of taking all the produce ranged in the class of fruits whether *natural* or *civil*; for the usufructuary may let, sell, or gratuitously yield the exercise of his right, but he does not become owner of the fruits until he takes them or somebody else does so in his name. *Civil* fruits he acquires day by day, unless they are the representation of natural produce, when they are only acquired after they are gathered.

The *usufructuary* was bound to use the thing as a good paterfamilias, without altering the substance; and he had to give security that he would fulfil his obligations.

The usufruct was established by (1) *pacts* and *stipulations* (see *prædial* servitudes), (2) *legacy*, in which case the *dies cedit* was not distinguished from the *dies venit*, (3) adjudication, (4) the law in certain cases.

In ancient law, usage or possession could never be the means of acquiring a usufruct; but (?) whether Justinian held this effect to be produced by ten years present, twenty years absent.

The *usufruct* was *extinguished* by (1) death of usufructuary; (2) by his *capitis deminutio*, formerly the three kinds, but under Justinian *max.* and *med.* only; (3) non-usage, after *Justinian*, three years for *moveables*, ten or twenty years for *immoveables*, but (?) Justinian did *not* change the *mode* of extinction by non-usage as well as the *time*; and a usufruct in *singulos annos, vel menses, vel dies* was *not* extinguished by this means; (4) cession to the *nudus* owner; (5) consolidation; (6) change in substance of thing and other means.

The extinguished usufruct returned to the *nuda proprietas* if the extinction was total.

The term *quasi usufruct* applied to the usufruct of things capable of consumption. The holder of this right had complete ownership of the thing, but gave security to restore in same quantity and quality at end of usufruct, or, more generally, to hand over the value. Death, or *capitis deminutio*, the term expired, or the condition fulfilled, were the means of extinguishing this kind of usufruct.

Usus is the right to have the use and services of the property of another, without taking any product or altering the substance, and it was *constituted* and *extinguished* like the *usufruct*.

Habitatio was ranged by Justinian in the number of *personal* servitudes, and under that Emperor in its *effects* it approached the usufruct, but it differed by nature in that it was not a distinct right, a dismemberment of the *dominium*, but only a benefit acquired day by day by the legatee, and consequently it did not perish by non-usage or *minima c. d.*

The *jus operarum servi* differed still more from *personal* servitudes, in that it was transmissible to heirs and continued as long as the slave lived.

Actions relating to servitudes. The quasi-possession was protected by the *utiles interdicts, uti possidetis, utrubi,* and *unde vi,* and for certain rural servitudes some special interdicts existed when the quasi possession had not arisen unlawfully, and had lasted for a year.

For personal or prædial servitudes two *real actions* existed, viz., the actions *confessoria* and *negatoria*; the first to recover a servitude, the second to assert its non-existence, and, in some cases, personal actions may be brought respecting servitudes.

Emphyteusis. As a real right this was an extensive and particular fraction of the *proprietas*, giving the holder the power of deriving all the utility or the produce of the property of another, subject to a periodical rent, and the *jus superficiarium* (a real right of prætorian establishment) was analogous in its effects to the *emphyteusis*, but it was only given by the owner of land over any construction raised upon it.

Pignus and Hypotheca were as real rights synonymous terms, and referred to the guarantee over a thing pledged for payment of a debt.

Persons capable or incapable of alienating. In general (1) in order to be able to alienate, a person must be owner, and (2) when a person is owner he can alienate; but the position of the husband in respect of the *dos*, the power of the pledgee in respect of property in his possession, and the nullity of contracts made with a minor, offer exceptions to these two rules.

By what persons one acquires. The acquisition of the *proprietas* for the paterfamilias may be through the *filii-familias* in power, or slaves, or those of whom he has the usufruct or usage, and by another's slave or a free person possessed in good faith; but in respect of the *peculium* of the *filius* familias of which there are four kinds, (1) *castrense*, (2) *quasi castrense*, (3) *adventitium*, (4) *profectitium*, the rights in favour of the son were successively ameliorated by Imperial constitutions and by Justinian.

Possession is acquired for the *paterfamilias* by the same persons and within the same limits, but not without our knowledge or in spite of oneself, for intention is necessary; though, in respect of things entering into a *peculium*, the general intention of profiting by what falls within it suffices, without having a particular knowledge of each thing of which possession is so acquired. *Proprietas* is not acquired through *strangers*, though possession may, and through it, by consequence, the *proprietas*. Knowledge and intention as to the possession taken by them in our name is necessary, though an original mandate suffices in the case of an agent.

Universal successions.

Under the legislation of the Institutes universal successions to *living* persons were suppressed, and, therefore, *inheritances, i.e.,* universal successions *to the dead* only existed.

Testamentary inheritances.

Hereditas means (1) the succession to the universality of rights and property of the deceased person, or (2) the universality itself (formerly called the *familia*). Until acquired, it sustains and continues the persona of the deceased. It is deferred by *will*, or in default by law. These methods of devolution exclude each other absolutely, so that, as a general rule, no one can die partly testate and partly intestate.

Form of wills. The ancient Romans had *two* kinds :—

(1). *Calata comitia.* Made in time of peace at a special meeting of the comitia, and hence called *testamentum calatis comitiis.*

(2). *In procinctu, i.e.,* in presence of the army under arms.

To these a third kind was added, viz., that—

(3). *Per æs et libram,* in which the entire patrimony, as a *res mancipi,* was sold by the testator with the formalities of a *mancipatio* to the *familiæ emptor,* who originally was the future heir himself, but later only a third person introduced *propter veteris juris imitationem,* and then the will came to be composed of two distinct formalities, (α) the *familiæ mancipatio,* and (β) the *nuncupatio testamenti.* Prætorian law suppressed the former, but required the seals of seven witnesses ; the *emperors* added *subscription, i.e.,* the signature of testator and witnesses, and from the fusion under Justinian of *civil, Prætorian,* and Imperial law, arose the

(4) *Testamentum tripartitum,* which required to be *uno contextu,* in presence of seven witnesses specially convoked, and their seals and signatures, and that of the testator appended.

As *witnesses* to the will were excluded—women, impuberes, slaves, idiots, deaf, dumb, interdicted prodigals, persons declared *improbi* and *indigni* of witnessing, members of the family of the testator and of the heir, and the heir himself, though the latter could be according to the civil law, in the will *per æs et libram,* after the *familiæ emptor* came to be any third person.

Legatees, fidei-commissarii and the members of their family could be witnesses, and the capacity of witnesses was only considered *at the time* of the making of the will. In general, no one can have more than *one* will, though it may consist of several original copies, and *writing* was not indispensable, as a simple verbal nuncupation in the presence of the required number of witnesses sufficed.

Soldiers obtained by imperial constitutions important privileges in respect of their *own capacity* to make a will, as well as the capacity of those to whom they left their property. The *form* of the will also was immaterial, provided it was seriously done as their last testament. The extent and *form* of their bequests were also exceptionally favoured, but their privileges only existed whilst in camp, and valid for one year only after dismissal.

Factio testamenti was necessary in order to make a will. It was derived from public law, and originally referred to the power of joining in the making of the will, either as *testator,* as *familiæ emptor,* or as a *witness*; but, at the time of *Gaius* and *Ulpian,* it rather implied the capacity of making a will, or of receiving and of acquiring for self or another, by another's will. *Factio testamenti,* in the person of the testator, consisted of (1) the right to make a will, and (2) the capacity of exercising this right, and as to this, two epochs had to be considered, (α) that of making the will, and (β) that of death, besides the intermediate time. The capacity was only required at (a), but the right at both (a) and (β), though in respect of the intermediate time, Prætorian law softened the strict legal rules.

Slaves, captives, peregrini, those whose status was uncertain, those declared *intestabiles* and filiifamiliâ) did not possess the *factio testamenti*, though as regards the captive with the enemy, his will when made *in* captivity was null in any case, but if made *before* captivity, it might be valid by *postliminium* in case of his return, and by the *lex Cornelia* in case of his death, with the enemy. *Filiifamilii* were also allowed to will their *peculium castrense*, and subsequently the *quasi-castrense*. Impubers, idiots, interdicted prodigals, and the deaf and dumb, were debarred, not only the right of having a will, but also the capacity of making it; and the will of the *blind* was subjected to special formalities by the Emperor Justin.

Exheredations. In spite of the latitude allowed the paterfamilias by primitive law, the result of the rules introduced by the prætors and emperors was to compel him to formally institute or disinherit those who would be his heirs at law. By the *civil* law, only children immediately in the power of the chief need be disinherited, since they only were *heredes sui*, and these, if *males* of the first degree, must be excluded *nominatim*, or the testament would be void *ab initio*; but *female* children and others might be excluded *inter ceteros, i.e.*, collectively, and, in case of omission, they only had a right of concurrence for a certain part with the instituted heirs. *Postumi* being uncertain persons could neither be instituted nor disinherited beforehand, and their birth would necessarily destroy the will; hence the custom was introduced of allowing the paterfamilias to institute or exclude *postumi sui*, *males nominatim, i.e.*, by special designation, *females* collectively under the general disinherison, provided the testator had indicated by leaving them a legacy, however small, that he had had them in contemplation.

The *lex Junia Velleia* extended this permission to children (hence called *quasi postumi Villeiani*) who might be born before the death of the testator, but after the making of the will, and also allowed those to be disinherited beforehand, who, already born at the time of the will, but preceded in the family by their father, were not *sui heredes* at that time, though they might become so subsequently if their father died or left the family. Prætorian law having ranked *emancipated* children as *heredes sui*, it became necessary to institute or exclude them also, otherwise they would have the *possessio bonorum contra tabulas*.

The *adoptor* was only obliged to institute or disinherit adopted children whilst they were in their adopted family, but if *emancipated* by the *adoptor* in the lifetime of the natural father, then, although, according to the civil law, no one was obliged to institute or disinherit them; yet the Prætor, by calling them to the *possessio bonorum* of the natural *father*, imposed the same necessity on the latter as in respect of children emancipated by himself.

Justinian suppressed all distinction between *sons* and *daughters* and *granddaughters*, as well as between *male* and *female postumi*. The disinheriting must be *nominatim* in all cases, and omission always entails the rupture of the will. He also confirmed the Prætorian law with regard to emancipated children; and the rights of *adopted* children fell under a new law with regard to adoption, by which the paternal power of the *natural* father was not destroyed, and only *ab intestato* rights were acquired in respect of the succession to the *adopting father*, unless the latter was an ascendant.

The *Institution of the heir* was the designation of him or them whom the testator wished to be heir. If the institution failed, all the other dispositions failed also; and hence it was the *foundation* as well as the *head* of the will; for at first it had to be placed at the commencement; though, after Justinian's time, the place was unimportant, and Constantine II suppressed the necessity for precise, imperative, and solemn terms.

Those *might be instituted heirs* who had *factio testamenti* with the testator, but the distinction between the faculty of being instituted (*testamenti factio*) and that of receiving testamentary liberalities *(jus capiendi ex testamento)*, did not exist under Justinian, though originally under the first head were excluded dediticii, women (by the *Lex Voconia*), uncertain persons, and therefore postumi, excepting postumi sui; whilst, under the second, were excluded Latini Juniani, cœlibes, and persons without legitimate children.

Under Justinian, peregrini, deportati, apostates, and heretics could not be instituted, and certain incapacities fell upon natural children and those born in incest.

As to *slaves*—the testator's own or those of another can be instituted. In respect of the first, Justinian removed the doubts as to his *liberty* by assuming in law the freedom (though not expressly given) where the *institution* was made. So long as the slave remained in the power of the testator, the validity of his institution depended on the express or tacit freedom joined to it, and on the testator's death he became at once by virtue of the will free and necessary heir; but if he changed his condition, *i.e.*, if freed or alienated in the lifetime of the testator, then his institution was as if made in respect of the slave of another. The latter could be instituted if the testator had *factio testamenti* with the master, even though belonging to a vacant inheritance, because the inheritance, until received, represented the deceased. The inheritance is not acquired of right by slaves thus instituted, but is voluntary, and deferred until the moment of the *aditio*, when it is acquired for themselves if they are free at that time, if not for the master by whose order the aditio is made. If he has several masters, he acquires the inheritance proportionally for each of those for whom the aditio is made.

One or several heirs may be instituted, but it must be for the whole inheritance; hence, if the distribution of parts made by the testator does not complete, or exceeds, the inheritance, the parts will have to be augmented or reduced proportionally, and a *usage* grew up of assuming the division to be into twelve or other number of parts or ounces, and the entire inheritance itself being an *as*, it was distributed as if by weight between the heirs.

The institution could not be from a fixed nor to a fixed term; but might be from an uncertain term, as that would be held equivalent to a condition. Terms or conditions contrary to the laws were held to be struck out, so as to render the institution pure and simple, and the accomplishment of any condition attached did not have a retrospective effect in the sense of considering the right of the conditionally instituted person as open from the day of the testator's decease, but only from the moment of the accomplishment of the condition, and the same period was looked to in respect of his capacity.

Substitutions (sub-instituere). These were all conditional institutions, after a principal institution, for the purpose of avoiding intestacy.

(1) *Vulgar,* so-called because the most common, was a conditional institution, to meet the case of the refusal or incapacity of the heirs first instituted, and might be continued to any desired degrees. Several might be substituted for one, or one for several, or such an one to such another, or the instituted amongst themselves; in which latter case those who are heirs acquire the shares of those who fail to become so, *not* by right of *accrual*, but by right of *substitution*, and by a new and voluntary *aditio*. In the absence of any *contrary* disposition, they have in the substitution the same shares as in the institution, and he who was substituted to a substituted was held to be tacitly so to the instituted himself, without any distinction as to whether the rights of the instituted or of his immediate substitute first lapsed.

(2) *Pupillary* substitution was the institution of an heir, by the paterfamilias, in his own testament, in respect of the inheritance of his son in his power, in case that son surviving him should die under age—*i.e.*, it was the testament of the son made by the chief, as an accessory to his own—the same person may be substituted for the son, both by vulgar and pupillary substitution and in the absence of a contrary declaration, one of these substitutions always entailed the other. Children might be disinherited at the same time, and substitutions could be made to *postumi*, who, if born at the decease of testator, would be in his power without any intermediate person, and so in respect of *quasi-postumi*. The arrogator of an *impubes* must give security to the substituted person to return him the property of the arrogated person, if the latter died before puberty, and the pupillary substitution that the arrogator may have himself made only affected the property that would come from him—the substitution may be made either to each child or to the last one dying *impubes*. The father can make pupillary substitutions in respect of all those whom he can insti-

tute for himself, and this may be done in the same testament as the institution, or in a later and separate testament; but being an accessory to the paternal testament, if the latter fails, it fails also; though, if the least effect be preserved to the testament either by strict or Prætorian law, the substitution will be maintained.

The substitution embraces all the property composing the inheritance of the impubes, and the testator himself could not except a part, but military privileges produced several exceptions to these rules.

Authority might be obtained from the emperor to substitute to a *puber* son, when from being deaf and dumb, an idiot, or other cause, he was unable to make his own will.

(3) *Quasi-pupillary* substitution was introduced by *Justinian*, and was an extension of the above, so that under it any ascendant had the power of appointing a substitute in respect of the inheritance of his insane relative.

Invalidation of testaments. A will was *injustum, non jure factum, imperfectum*, when not made according to the rules required by law; but, though valid originally, it might be:—

Ruptum, i.e., broken or revoked by the subsequent agnation or quasi-agnation of a *suus heres* not provided for according to the rules as to institution and disinheriting. To revoke a will it was not essential that another should be made, as the voluntary destruction of the document itself sufficed.

Irritum, when regular and valid by itself—but useless, owing to the testator having changed his *persona* status and capacity,— all the *c.d.'s* produced this effect, except under the privileges exempting military testaments.

The possessio bonorum secundum tabulas would be given by the Prætor in spite of the will being *ruptum* or *irritum* in strict law, if the invalidity had only existed at the intermediate period between the making of the will and that of the decease of the testator.

Inofficious testaments. These were wills drawn up contrary to the duties of affection between relations; and, although valid in strict law, the usage grew up of pronouncing them null, as not being the result of a reflecting and reasonable mind. The action *de inofficioso* was open (in the case of disinherison or omission without just motives) to children, ascendants and brothers and sisters, in the order in which they would have been called to the inheritance *ab intestato;* though brothers and sisters could only avail themselves of the action when the testator had excluded them in favour of vile persons. The causes justifying disinherison or omission were settled by Justinian.

Portio legitima. If the testator had left to his heir by blood a sufficient part of his property, as a legacy, *fidei-commissum*, or otherwise, the testament could not be deemed inofficious; the amount of this part was not at first determined; but by analogy to the *Lex*

Falcidia, it was fixed at a *fourth*, and called the *legitima, i.e.,* the portion due by law, the amount of which was augmented by *Justinian.*

All that the heir by blood had received as a testamentary disposition or *donatio mortis causa* was counted to make up the *legitima;* but only certain kinds of donations *inter vivos* were so included. If the testator left nothing to the heir-at-law the latter had the action *de inofficioso* to get the whole testament declared null; but if he had left him something, however small, only the action for the completion of the *portio legitima* lay. Under *Justinian,* if the will was declared inofficious, only the institution failed, but legacies, *fideicommissa,* and freeings, still remained intact. The action *de inofficioso* was extinguished by any approval of the testament, directly or indirectly, by prescription (at first two, later five years), and by the death of the heir-at-law, before commencing the action.

Different classes of heirs. There were *three* classes of heirs, with respect to whom the rules as to the acquisition of inheritances essentially differed.

(1) *Necessary heirs, i.e.,* slaves of the testator instituted by him, and who had remained in the same condition. The acquisition of the inheritance was forced upon them by law, and they could not repudiate it; but under the *beneficium separationis* they were only liable to the action of the creditors of the deceased in respect of the property included in the inheritance.

(2) *Sui et necessarii heredes, i. e.,* children in the power of the deceased who became his heirs, either *ab intestato* or by institution. They were called *heredes sui* because, being co-proprietors in the family property, they were in some sort their own heirs; and hence the acquisition was also forced upon them by law, and they could not repudiate; but they might abstain if they had not renounced the right by intermeddling with the inheritance (*immixtio*), the result being that, although they remained heirs in strict law, the creditors could not sue them, and the property of the deceased was sold as if there were no heir.

Hence, in respect of *necessary* heirs and *heredes sui et neccessarii,* there was never any *aditio hereditatis.*

Extranei heirs were free to accept or repudiate, and as to their capacity and the nature of their rights, three epochs were considered: (α) that of the making of the testament when their rights are in expectancy; (β) that of the decease, or of the accomplishment of the condition when the right commences to run in their favour; and (γ) that of the *aditio hereditatis,* when the right is complete, but incapacity existing during the first interval mattered little if they recovered it before the decease of the testator or before the accomplishment of the condition; but after this second epoch, in strict law their capacity should continue without interruption up to the *aditio.*

Aditio could originally only take place in three ways, viz.:—

(1) *Cretio,* a sort of sacramental declaration to be made in the

interval fixed by the testator, but this method ceased to be in use in the fifth century.

(2) *Aditio* proper, *i.e.*, an express though informal declaration of the acceptance of the inheritance, either verbally or in writing.

(3) By acting as heir, as by intermeddling with the affairs of the inheritance and doing acts only possible in the capacity of heir.

Repudiation may also be indicated by express declaration or by acts.

The *civil* law fixed no interval within which the instituted person must accept or repudiate, but a suit by interested persons compelled him to declare, though the Prætor then gave him an interval for deliberation; after which, in default of a declaration as to his intention, he might be held to have *accepted* as against creditors, or renounced as against substitutes or the heirs *ab intestato*.

The *aditio*, when made, entailed liability as to all the charges and debts of the inheritance, and was irrevocable, though minors could have the benefit of the *restitutio in integrum*, a favour also accorded to persons over twenty-five under very exceptional circumstances by imperial rescript. *Gordian* established in favour of *soldiers* the non-liability for debts exceeding the assets, from which, under Justinian, was derived the *beneficium inventarii*. The instituted person could, if preferred, abide by the ancient law, and ask for delay to deliberate; but, if so, at the expiration of the time he was obliged to accept or repudiate purely and simply.

Actions relating to testamentary inheritances. The actions—(1) *petitio hereditatis*, and (2) *familiæ erciscundæ*, applied to all inheritances in general, whilst the (α) *querela inofficiosi testamenti*, (β) *in supplementum legitimi*, and the (γ) *querela inofficiosæ donationis*, were special to testamentary inheritances.

Legacies.

The term is derived from *legare*, *i.e.*, *legem testamenti dicere*, and the transference of the property by way of liberality is the indispensable attribute of a legacy, but it only conferred rights of ownership, of servitude, or other real rights, or rights of obligation, for the instituted heir was the successor to the persona of the deceased, and the legatee rather occupied the place of a creditor.

Strictly, also, the legacy was a *lex* imposed by the testator on the instituted heir, and therefore differing widely from other dispositions, as *fidei-commissa*, confided to the good faith of the successor or other person; but though these principles were rigorously maintained up to the time of the Republic, they were then softened and completely disappeared under Justinian, so that legacies and fidei-commissa became merged, and it is only for the sake of clearness that they are separately discussed in the Institutes, and there even existed cases in which the legatee continued up to a certain point the *persona* of the deceased.

How legacies can be left. Formerly the testator must have first provided an heir before he could impose this *lex* upon him, but after *Augustus* it could be done by *codicil* attached to the will, and under *Justinian* it was immaterial whether it came before or after the institution, and it might arise even in an inheritance *ab intestato*, as it would have the force of a *fidei-commissum*.

Originally without the consecrated *civilia verba* the disposition would not have been a *lex* binding on the heir, and the nature, extent, and effects of the legacy varied according as the formulæ employed made the gift one *per vindicationem*, *per damnationem sinendi modo*, or *per præceptionem*.

These rules were modified by the *s.c. Neronianum;* the constitutions of Constantine II, Constantius, and Constans, abolished sacramental formulæ, and the distinction between the kinds of legacies was entirely suppressed by *Justinian*.

Two fundamental principles govern the subject of legacies, viz. :—

(1) The rules as to the (α) *Dies cedit*, *i.e.*, the period when the eventual right to the legacy is fixed for the benefit of the legatee. For legacies pure and simple, or at a certain term, this occurred at the day of decease (though the time was temporarily changed by the *lex Papia Poppæa* to the opening of the will). For conditional legacies, or those at an uncertain term, which was equivalent to a condition, the *dies cedit* arrived on the accomplishment of the condition. (β) *Dies venit*, *i.e.*, the time when the gift may be claimed. This did not occur until after *aditio*, or if there was a term or a condition, not until the first had arrived or the second accomplished.

Hence the *dies cedit* determined (α) the persons to acquire, (β) the things composing the legacy, (γ) the rights, if any, of transmission, (δ) in some cases as to the loss or preservation of the right in respect of the particular individual, and (ε) in some peculiar cases the *dies cedit* departed from the general rules, as, *e.g.*, in the case of a legacy in favour of the slave of the testator, and in respect of exclusively personal rights, as legacies of *usufruct, usus, habitatio*, etc.

(2) The *Catoniana regula* made it necessary, in order to determine the validity of a legacy, to suppose the testator had died immediately after the making of the testament, and if the legacy would under such circumstances have been null and void, the bequest failed. This rule did not apply to radical nullities derived from the general principles of law, nor to the institution of the heir, and from its nature, could not apply to conditional legacies, nor to those in which the *dies cedit* did not occur at the death of the testator.

By whom, at whose charge, and to whom legacies may be left.

Originally the legacy could only be made *by him* who had *factio testamenti*, and who actually made a will, as it must have been imposed on an instituted heir, but the necessity for this disappeared under Justinian, since the disposition would be valid as a *fidei-commissum*.

The legacy could only be left *to those* with whom the testator had *factio testamenti*, but the innovations of Justinian brought in uncertain persons, postumi, etc. Though a legacy could not go purely and simply to the slave of an instituted master, it might to the master of an instituted slave, and if the legacy was conditional it might in *either* case, owing to the combination of the principles governing the *dies cedit* and the *Catoniana regula*.

Things which may be left by legacy were :—

The property of the testator, of the heir, or of another person; provided in this latter case the testator knew that it belonged to another, and as the testator had not himself got the ownership, the legatee in this case only acquired the rights of a creditor against the heir to compel him by action to furnish the thing or its value.

Things actually existing, or those in the future, provided there was a possibility of their coming into being.

Things corporeal or incorporeal, as well as facts and acts that the heir may be condemned to do, to suffer, or not to do. Amongst *incorporeal* things, legacies of usufruct and servitude, and the legacy *liberationis* and *nominis* are specially to be noted, and the two latter are also affected by the rules as to the non-extinguishment of obligations, except by the legal modes of release or transference.

The things may be determined in specie or only in genere, and in respect of the latter the legacy *generis* is to be distinguished from that *optionis*, the last of which underwent important modifications in the time of *Justinian*.

The legacy called *partitio* consisted of a given part of the inheritance, and strictly the *legatarius partiarius* did not succeed even in this case to any action, active or passive, and he and the heir arrived at a settlement of their respective rights by means of the *stipulationes partis et pro parte*; but under *Justinian* such a legacy was looked upon as if it were a *fidei-commissum* of the inheritance, and all actions, active or passive, divided themselves by law between the heir and the legatee, so that the latter, in respect of his share, succeeded to a certain extent to the *persona* of the deceased.

Cannot be left by legacy :—

Things not in commerce, or entailing unlawful acts, nor things belonging to the legatee, and hence the testator could not leave him that which was already due to him, unless in the form of a legacy it would be more advantageous to him than as a debt.

Loss, increase, or decrease of the thing left by legacy.

The rules as to the *dies cedit* regulated this subject.

If the thing perished in the lifetime of the testator, whether by accident or the act of whoever it may be, the legacy vanished for want of an object, and did not subsist even in respect of débris or accessories; for the loss of the principal object entailed extinction of the legacy, as regarded accessories, but this was not so in respect of objects which had their own individuality, so that one man was never considered as the accessory of another, nor the child of the mother, nor the vicarius of the ordinarius slave.

If the thing perished after the death of the testator, whether by the fault or the mere act of the heir, the latter must indemnify the legatee, but if done independent of the act of the heir, the loss falls on the legatee, though if the loss happened after the *dies cedit* the legatee's rights subsisted over the débris or accessories.

A *universitas*, as a flock, or a peculium, must be taken as it existed at the *dies cedit*, hence objects subsequently added to it were *not* included, unless they were produce or otherwise resulting from the universality, and this subject was of especial importance in the case of the legacy of a *peculium* to the slave of the testator, as opposed to such a legacy to a stranger, as the *dies cedit* in the first case did not take place until the aditio, but in the second at the death of the testator.

Modifications affecting the existence, extent, or execution of legacies.

(1) A *condition* suspended the effect of the dispositions, but the *Muciana cautio* (formulated to meet the case of *negative* conditions which could not be accomplished before death) applied both as to legacies and inheritances.

(2) The *modus* did not defer the right to claim the legacy, but security might be required.

(3) If the *dies* was *uncertain*, the legacy fell under the rule common to legacies and inheritances, viz., *dies incertus conditionem in testamento facit*, and *Justinian* suppressed the distinction between the terms *at* and *after* death, and made such bequests equally valid.

The legacy *pœnæ nomine* imposed a condition on the heir by way of coercion, and was invalid until the reforms of Justinian, by whom it was only made to differ from the ordinary conditional legacy, in that an impossible or unlawful condition *annulled* the legacy, instead of such a condition being held *pro non scripto*.

These modifications are to be distinguished from (α) the *demonstration* for the purpose of better pointing out the legatee or the thing left, and to which the rule applies *falsa demonstratio legatum non perimit*, (β) the *determination* or *limitation*, for marking the terms, the limit within which the legatee or the thing left by legacy was to be restrained, and (γ) the *cause* or the motive inducing the testator to leave the legacy, as to which the general rule applies, *neque ex falsa causa legatum infirmatur*.

Invalidity, revocation, translation of legacies.

Although the testament remains valid—

(1) The legacy may be *void, ab initio*, because some indispensable legal condition was wanting, in respect of the legatee or the thing, whether in point of form or otherwise.

(2) The legacy, valid originally, may fail for want of an object, as if the thing perished.

(3) The testator may revoke the legacy (*ademptio*), or transfer

it to another (*translatio*), and the revocation may be express or implied, as by the bequest being erased or the thing alienated.

(4) The legatee may make default, as by dying or losing *factio testamenti* before the *dies cedit*, or by refusing the legacy.

(5) The legacy may be withdrawn on the ground of unworthiness.

The fate of the legacy also hangs on that of the institution of the heir, and hence if the testament becomes *ruptum, irritum* or *destitutum*, the legacy fails.

The *Leges Julia* and *Papia Poppæa* introduced special causes of incapacity as to *cœlibes* and *orbi*, both in respect of their institution as heir and benefiting by legacies, but *Justinian* suppressed both the cases of failure under these laws *(caduca)*, and the cases assimilated to them *(in causa caduci)*.

Right of accrual between co-legatees.

As a general rule he who was burdened with a legacy benefited by it if it lapsed, but the benefit might be transferred to others under the right of accrual between co-legatees, and the *jus caduca vindicandi* of the *lex Papia Poppæa*.

In general, *co-legatees* are those to whom the same thing has been left by the same testament, whether *conjunctim, i.e.*, in one single disposition, or *disjunctim, i.e.*, by as many separate dispositions as legatees, but under the *lex Papia Poppæa* certain effects resulted where the same thing had been left to several, with the shares of each assigned, and hence the threefold division *re tantum, re et verbis, verbis tantum*, although in the latter case the persons so joined are not really in any way co-legatees.

In respect of the right of accrual between co-legatees :—

(1) Prior to the *lex Papia Poppæa* the question had to be examined, according to the rigorous consequences of the terms of the civil formula by which legacies fell into four classes, but bearing in mind that debts divide by law when given in common.

(2) Under the *leges Julia et Papia Poppæa* the right of accrual had to be distinguished from the *jus caduca vindicandi*, then introduced in respect of caduca, or dispositions assimilated to them.

(3) The suppression by *Justinian* of the four classes of legacies, and of the *caduca* and dispositions *in causa caduci* led to a state of the law in which, together with new rules, traces of the preceding systems appeared.

The *Lex Falcidia*, in order to prevent the failure of testamentary inheritances, forbad legacies to exceed *three-fourths* of the property of the inheritance, so that there would always remain to the heir at least *one-fourth ;* and if several heirs, each must, independent of the others, have one-fourth of his share. The benefit of the law was in course of time successively extended to matters not contemplated by it, viz.: to *fidei-commissaria* inheritances, to particular *fidei-commissa*, and even to *fidei-commissa ab intestato*, to donations *mortis causa*, to donations between married persons, to the *querela inofficiosi testamenti*, and it produced the theory of the *portio legitima*.

Fidei-commissa.

A *fidei-commissum*, in the most general sense, was a disposition of property, in which some condition essential, according to the civil law, was wanting, in order to constitute it a valid institution of the heir, or a legacy, and with which the deceased charged his testamentary or *ab intestato* heir or some other person to whom he left something.

As these dispositions were originally deficient in obligatory character, they could only be confided to the good faith of him on whom they were charged, but under Augustus their execution might be enforced by a procedure *extra ordinem*.

The *Fidei-commissaria hereditas* corresponded in some sort to the institution of the heir, as it had for its object the inheritance, or a part of it; and the *fidei-commissum singulæ rei* resembled a legacy in having for its object any other thing than a given part of the inheritance.

Fidei-commissa were governed in their interpretation by the principle that they rested on the wishes and intentions of the deceased.

To obviate the inconveniences resulting from the *heres fiduciarius* still remaining heir, although charged by *fidei-commissum* to restore the inheritance, in whole or in part, a simulated sale was made of the inheritance, and the *stipulationes emptæ et venditæ hereditatis* entered into, but the *s.c. Trebellianum* made the actions divide between the *heres fiduciarius* and the *fidei-commissarius*, so that the latter ceased to be considered *loco emptoris*, and was viewed as an heir *(loco heredis)*. Subsequently the *s.c. Pegasianum* authorised the heir to deduct from the *fidei-commissaria hereditas* the *falcidia*, and in case this was done the *fidei-commissarius* was assimilated to a legatee *(loco legatarii)*, and then, between him and the heir, with respect to the hereditary debts and credits the same *stipulationes partis et pro parte* were entered into as between the heir and a *legatarius partiarius*.

Justinian united the two senatus consulta into one under the name of the former *(Trebellianum)*, and the heir was always to have the right of retaining the *fourth*, the actions in all cases dividing between him and the *fidei-commissarius*.

Though Justinian assimilated *legacies* and *fidei-commissa*, the institution of the heir and the fidei-commissaria inheritance continued to differ as to *form* in the manner of bestowal, and as to *matter* in respect of the retention of the *quarta*, so also the direct legacy of liberty, and the *fidei-commissum* for the same purpose differed somewhat in their effects.

Codicils.

These are expressions of last wishes, but not testaments. Their origin is intimately connected with the fidei-commissum, for the one is the disposition, the other the expression of it, and their employment was, under Augustus, approved at the same time as fidei-commissa, on the ground of practical utility.

Codicils were either:—

(α) *Ab intestato*, when their dispositions were equivalent to *fidei-commissa*.

(β) *Attached to a testament*, either anterior or posterior, and of which they shared the fate. If confirmed in the testament (which may be *in futurum* or *in præteritum*), they might contain legacies, revocations of legacies, giving of tutors as well as fidei-commissa, but never institutions or revocations of the institution of *heir*, and if not confirmed they could only contain *fidei-commissa*.

The presence of five witnesses required by *Justinian* was not indispensable, as, in case of the denial of the existence of the trust, the persons charged might be put upon their oath.

The *clausula codicillaris* made testaments, otherwise void, valid as codicils.

Opening and preservation of testaments. The testament was opened in presence of the witnesses to it, a copy was taken, and the original will deposited in the archives, where it might be subsequently examined or a copy taken, except of dispositions which were intended to remain secret.

Actions relating to legacies and fidei-commissa. When legacies were classed according to the formulæ used, the legatee had the *rei vindicatio* for legacies *per vindicationem*, the *condictio* for those *per damnationem* or *sinendi modo*, and the *familiæ erciscundæ* action for those *per præceptionem*.

Under *Justinian* a *rei vindicatio* lay, unless the legacy had for its object a thing of which the transference of ownership could not have been effected, or the personal *actio* (or *condictio*) *ex testamento* (*actio legati*) could be brought against the heir, and the *hypothecaria actio* could also be used.

If the execution of the legacy was suspended, the legatee could require *security* for the preservation of his rights; and, on the other hand, if the legatee had put himself in possession of the legacy, the heir had the interdict *Quod legatorum* for its restitution.

Particular fidei-commissa, under *Justinian*, gave the same actions as legacies; and for fidei-commissary inheritances there existed the *fidei-commissaria hereditatis petitio*, and the action *utilis familiæ erciscundæ*.

BOOK III.

Tit. i. De Hereditatibus quæ ab intestato deferuntur.

994. As a general rule, the devolution of the inheritance *by law* took place when the deceased died *absolutely intestate, i.e.*, when no will existed in *fact*, or it was invalid in *law*, or failed for want of an heir to succeed under it *(Intestatus decedit qui aut omnino testamentum non fecit, aut non jure fecit; aut id quod fecerat ruptum irritumve factum est, aut nemo ex eo heres extitit)*. Hence:—

(1) The inheritance *ab intestato* might open at the *death* of the testator if no will had been made, or if it was *invalid ab initio* or *ruptum* or *irritum* before his decease, but otherwise it did not open until it was certain that there would be no testamentary heir.

(2) The existence, capacity, quality, and degree of the *heirs ab intestato*, are to be determined at the date of the opening of the inheritance *ab intestato*, and hence the claimants may, or may not, be different from those who would have taken at the date of the death of the testator; but they must have been born or conceived at the date of death, in order to have any claims whether civil or Prætorian.

998. In respect of the order of succession of the heirs *ab intestato* there are four systems to consider, viz., that of the twelve tables, the Prætorian law, the Imperial constitutions, and the time of Justinian.

By the twelve tables there were two orders (table v, § 4 and 5), viz. :—(1) The *heredes sui;* (2) The *Agnates* (and (3) the *Gentiles* for certain cases and persons).

999. (§ ii) *The Heredes sui, according to the twelve tables*, would be those children first in rank, in power (whether resulting from justæ nuptiæ or adoption, or, in later legislation, from legitimation by oblation to curiæ, or subsequent marriage) at the time of decease (and even a son not *in power* at the time by *jus postliminii)*; and as the succession was the result of the law, their ignorance of the fact or insanity was immaterial, and no authorization of tutor or consent of curator was necessary; but a son might be in power at the time, and yet not succeed, if the father had after death been found guilty of high treason, when, his memory being made infamous, confiscation of goods followed: this being the only criminal suit, according to *Theophilus*, exercisable against the dead.

Sons and daughters took *per capita*, but the descendants of the *sons* (descendants of *daughters* not being in the family) took *per stirpes, i.e.*, the *single* equal share the father would have received was divided between his children.

1008. (§ ix) *Children called to rank with heredes sui, by Prætorian law*. Under the first system, three classes of children were shut out *ab intestato*, viz.—(1) Those emancipated; (2) Those given in adoption; (3) Those who were *descendants* of *daughters*.

The Prætor gave *emancipated* children and their descendants (provided they had the rights of citizens) the *bonorum possessionem unde liberi;* hence, *in fact* and *in possession*, they were on a par with the *heredes sui*, though the latter still remained in *law* and in title the only heirs.

Children given in *adoption*, and those who, after being emancipated had given themselves in arrogation, also acquired the rights of *heredes sui* in the *new* family, though they ceased to have any claim on the *old;* but since, if an adopted child was emancipated out of the *new* family in the lifetime of the *natural* father, he would be deprived altogether, the Prætor gave him the possession *unde liberi*, with the heredes sui of the *natural* father. If, however, when thus emancipated, the *natural* father was already dead, he had no claim, except that he might come in as a cognate or under Justinian's system (*post*, par. 1014).

If these classes of heirs were not regularly instituted or excluded, *Prætorian* law gave them the *bonorum possessio contra tabulas* (*ante*, par. 708).

1013. *Children called to the rank of heredes sui by imperial constitutions prior to Justinian.* A constitution of Valentinian Theodosius and Arcadius (Code Theod., 5, 1, 4) provided that descendants of a *daughter*, who would have been amongst the *sui heredes* if she had not predeceased the opening of the succession *ab intestato*, should represent their mother, and take, *per stirpes*, two-thirds of her share if there were other *heredes sui*, though only one-fourth was deducted in favour of the *agnates* if they only were excluded.

1014. (§ xiv) *Children called to the rank of heredes sui by Justinian.* In respect of adopted children, Justinian introduced a new system by which *adoption* did not destroy their rights in the *natural* family (*ante*, par. 138), their only claim on the *adoptive* father being in the successio *ab intestato*, so that they could not complain if excluded or not mentioned in the will, and their right, when adopted out of three males (? why so) under the *s. c. Sabinianum* (? under Marcus Aurelius A.D. 161), to one-fourth of the adopted father's goods, was also taken away.

As to the descendants of *daughters*, though they were still confined to two-thirds, when there were other *heredes sui*, the deduction of one-fourth for *Agnates* was withdrawn.

Adopted children are now true *heredes sui* of the *natural* father, since they neither leave the *potestas* nor the family, but the other children and descendants called by the Prætor, the Emperors, and Justinian, are not *necessary* heirs, as they do not acquire the succession by strict law.

Tit. ii. De Legitima Agnatorum Successione.

1018. By the *twelve tables* (v, 5), after the *heredes sui* (and those descendants ranged by subsequent legislation with them), came the

Agnates (see part ii, par. 64), and from this class also were *excluded* (1) those emancipated; (2) those given in adoption; and (3) the descendants of females.

1021. (§ iii) An *intermediate legislation*, introduced by the jurisprudents in analogy to the *Lex Voconia*, and therefore subsequent to that date, imposed incapacities on *women* by prohibiting their admission as heirs except to *consanguinei* sisters only, whilst *male* agnates could succeed *ad infinitum* to them.

1022. *Prætorian law*. The harshness of the twelve tables was partially remedied by the Prætor, who, although he did not touch the *civil law* system in respect of the rights of *agnates*, seized every occasion of the failure of *agnates* to let in the *cognates*.

1023. *Imperial constitutions anterior to Justinian*. Anastasius, in A.D. 498, allowed *emancipated* brothers and sisters to take along with *agnate* brothers and sisters, though only one-half shares, and the right was *personal*, only not extending to their descendants (Cod. 5, 30, 4); but see *post*, par. 1024.

1024. By *Justinian's constitutions*, the law of the twelve tables as to *women* was re-established, and they received again equal rights with *males*.

Emancipated brothers and sisters were, by legislation, subsequent to the Institutes, A.D. 534, to have equal shares with *agnates*, and their children to succeed them, but not their grandchildren.

Adoption caused no loss of family rights in respect of brothers, sisters, or other relations, given in adoption.

Uterine brothers and sisters were called, in A.D. 528, to the fraternal succession as if *agnates* or consanguineous brothers and sisters. In A.D. 534 the first degree of their children were admitted to rank with agnate nephews and nieces.

By the twelve tables, the *nearest agnate* (whether one or several) succeeded to the exclusion of all others, and hence there was no division *per stirpes*, as in the case of *sui heredes*. Hence, also, if the first degree failed altogether, and, *e.g.*, one deceased brother had left one child, and another several, these all took equally (*Agnatorum hereditates dividuntur in capita*. Ulp., Reg. 26, 4).

Heredes sui were *necessary* heirs, and the question of devolution could not arise except as to those admitted by an extension of the law, but *agnates* only became heirs at the *aditio;* and therefore, if before that event all the members of the first degree died or refused the inheritance, it passed on to the next order. This the Prætor partially remedied by calling in the *cognates*, and Justinian allowed devolution in the case of agnates, and subsequently extended the right to the *heredes sui* also.

Under the law of the twelve tables, the question of the succession of a male ascendant to a deceased child could not occur, for if *in power* the child had no property, and if *emancipated* the child had nothing to do with the natural family; but, ultimately (Cod. vi, 61, 3), when the son acquired rights in respect of *maternal* property left by gift or legacy, an *ab intestato* succession was introduced in the order of—(1) His children and grandchildren, etc.; (2) brothers and sisters; and (3) the father or other ascendant, but by right of succession, not in virtue of the *patria potestas*. *Justinian* also admitted a succession *ab intestato* (viz.—(1) Children; (2) brothers and sisters; (3) paterfamilias) to *peculium castrense* and *quasi castrense;* but here the ancestor took it *jure communi, i.e.*, by *patria potestas*, and not by succession (see *ante*, par. 687, 6).

The rights of patronage to *emancipated* children were by the aid of the *contracta fiducia* (*ante*, par. 166) early secured to the ascendant emancipator, and under *Justinian* this *contracta fiducia* was always implied, the succession being the same as for the *peculium*, viz.—(1) Children; (2) brothers and sisters; (3) ascendant emancipator.

1032. *The succession of the Gentiles.* The twelve tables (v, 5) called the *Gentiles* after the *agnates*. The *Gentiles* (see part i, par. 16, and part ii, par. 65), according to Cicero's definition (Top. 6), were—(1) Those with the same common name; (2) of ingenuus origin; (3) of whom no ancestor had been in servitude; (4) who have never suffered *capitis deminutio;* but the subject is obscure, and the part of the Institutes of Gaius referred to by himself for explanation is missing. Various opinions have been advanced, all based upon limiting the extent of *agnation* and making all the agnates outside these *Gentiles;* and, according to *Niebuhr*, the *gens* was a political union, or clan, of patrician families without blood relationship or connection through the patria potestas, but with common rites and sacrifices and voting as *one* in the *comitia curiata* (see part i, par. 29). To this patrician association plebeian clients belonged; and though *plebeian gentes* were subsequently formed, these only had internal, not political, rights. This description, however, does not coincide with Cicero's definition, and it would probably be more correct merely to assume that the members of a *gens*, as between themselves, were at once *agnates*, *Gentiles*, and *cognates*, with a separate genealogy, whether natural or civil, and that they were also the *Gentiles* of all the members of the different plebeian *agnations* who had taken their name and sacra, and were attached to them as clients, or derived by freeings from them, so that whilst the terms *familia* and *cognatio* belonged to *all* citizens the *Gentiles* were a separate caste.

The *descendants* of *freed* persons would be *ingenui* in the later acceptation of the word, but they would not be of perpetual ingenuus origin, so that on the failure of their own *heredes sui* and agnates, their property *ab intestato* would pass away altogether to the patrician *gens* to which they belonged, but they would be the patrons of the slaves actually freed by themselves, and subsequently would occupy the place of *gentes* in respect of the *free* families descended from these *liberti, i.e.*, they would be the source *(stirpes)* of these latter. Hence, *Cicero* (De leg. i) traces descent through *agnatio, gens, stirps, cognatio,* and the distinction between *gens* and *stirps* formed the ground of the law-suit before the Centumviri, between the Claudian and the Claudian Marcellian families (Cic. De Orat. i, § 39): the former a patrician and primitive family, claiming the succession to the son of a freedman on the ground of being the gens of the plebeian Marcellian family itself, and from which it acquired its name; the Marcellian family, on the other hand, claiming the succession as the source from which the family of the freedman sprang.

1051. That the eventual rights as to tutorship, curatorship, and succession belonging to the *gens* were of real importance, is shewn by the *gentis enuptio*, or privilege of marrying out of the gens, which Livy (bk. 39, § 19) relates was given by a senatus consultum (after being confirmed by plebiscitum) to the freedwoman Hispala Fecenia, in recompense for denouncing the affair of the Bacchanalians.

Tit. iii. De Senatus-consulto Tertulliano.

1054. It was only in the case of the wife being *in manu viri* (*ante*, par. 150) when she ranked as a consanguineous sister, that any reciprocal rights of *agnation*-succession could exist between the mother and her children (*præterquam si per in manum conventionem consanguinitatis jura inter eos constiterint*, Gai. Inst. iii, § 24), and the Prætor only assisted them in the third order as *cognates*. The Emperor *Claudius* first granted a special exemption in a particular case, and under *Antoninus Pius* the *senatus consultum Tertullianum* (A.D. 158) in the spirit of the *Caduca* laws, rewarded the birth of children by giving the *jus liberorum ab intestato* to *ingenuæ*, with *three* children and *libertinæ* with *four* children; but the right was accorded to the *mother* only, not the ancestress, and the children must have been born alive, though the Emperor could give a special dispensation when the conditions were not all complied with. If the mother were in power, the *aditio* could only be made by order of the paterfamilias. The succession involved devolution, and the order was:—

1. Children of son or daughter deceased.
2. The father, but not the ancestor.
3. Consanguineous brothers.
4. The mother, any consanguineous sisters sharing with her.

1061. (§ iv) Constantine made a further concession in respect of the mother of *one* child (see part i, par. 479), and *Justinian* (Cod. 8, 59, 2) abolished the distinction as to the number of births, giving the *jus liberorum* to all mothers. If any agnate or cognate sisters existed, they took one-half and the mother of the deceased one-half. If brothers and sisters existed as well as the mother, they all took *per capita*, and as the mother's rights were derived from natural (not civil) ties, it was immaterial whether the child was legitimate (*ante*, par. 122), but the mother, if over twenty-five years of age, was excluded from the succession to her *impubes* child if she *neglected* to demand within a year the *nomination of a tutor* or his replacement in the event of his being excluded or excused.

Tit. iv. De Senatus-consulto Orphitiano.

1065. In reciprocation of the rules of the preceding title, the senatus-consultum *Orphitianum* passed in the consulship of *Orphitius* and Rufus, under *Marcus Aurelius* (A.D. 178), gave *children* the right of succession *ab intestato* to their *mother* before consanguinei or agnates or father or mother (decided against the rules of the *s. c.* Tertullianum by imperial constitutions. Cod. Thed. 5, 1, 4, *ante*, par. 1013), and extended to *grand*-children by subsequent constitutions. The right was not lost by *minima, c.d.*, a rule applying to all the successions created by senatus consulta, the Emperors, or the Prætors, because they were grounded on *natural* ties, though succession under the *twelve tables* was lost by *minima* (as well as *maxima* and *media*), *c.d.*, as it entailed leaving the *familia*. It was immaterial whether the children were legitimate, but Justinian refused the rights of succession to the *spurii* (part ii, par. 58) of a woman of the rank of *illustris* if she had other children.

Tit. v. De successione cognatorum.

1070. Instead of letting the inheritance fall to the *ærarium* on the failure of *heredes sui* or agnates, and those ranking as such, the Praetor called in the *cognates*, but as *heirs* could only be created by law, or senatus consulta, or imperial constitutions, he made them *possessors of the property*, the order being:—

1. *Heredes sui*, and those classed as such.
2. *Heredes legitimi, i.e.*, agnates, and those classed as such.
3. *Nearest cognates, i.e.*, those after the above (1) and (2), who may not be such near cognates, and to the sixth degree only, this being the general limit for cognates; but to the seventh degree in the case of children of *second cousins*. This order included the collateral line through women, those emancipated who have *arrogated* themselves, uncertain (*vulgo quæsiti*) children, because as such they had no agnation or consanguinity, and lastly, children of concubinage.

Cognation being a *natural* tie, it included *agnates* who had suffered *c.d.*, but *emancipated brothers and sisters* had a preference, and ranked as *agnates* (see par. 1024) before cognates.

Tit. vi. De Gradibus cognationum.

1075. The Roman law language had *names* up to the sixth degree, and there are in the *direct* line, whether ascending or descending, as many degrees as generations, and the same in the *collateral*, except that generations on each line count always omitting the source (see part ii, par. 62).

1079. (§ x) Relationship between slaves was not recognised by law (part ii, par. 58), but Justinian gave children and others rights (see *post*, par. 1081).

Tit vii. De successione Libertorum.

1081. The *freedman* (at least up to Justinian) could only have a *descending line*, and that subsequent to freedom.

1082. *Succession ab intestato to freedmen by the* 12 *Tables* was :—
1. *Heredes sui, i.e.*, his children, including those adopted, and the wife *in manu*.
2. Patron (occupying the place of *agnates*).
3. *Patrons' children*, but like agnates *per capita*.

The order of succession, *ex testamento*, was free, and the *libertus* could will as he chose, so that the *patron* might be excluded (α) by *heredes sui*, or (β) *testament* of his *libertus*, though the *liberta* had no *heredes sui*, and being in the perpetual tutelage of patron could not make a will.

1084. (§ i) *Succession to freedmen according to Prætorian law.*

The Prætor included under *heredes sui* those added by him in the case of other citizens (*ante*, par. 1008), and hence *emancipated* children, and those *given in adoption*, had the possession *unde liberi*, or *contra tabulas*. But the law of the 12 *Tables*, by which the *patron* could be excluded by the mere will of the freedman (*e.g.*, by (1) adoption of a child, (2) wife *in manu*, or (3) testament) was held unjust, and therefore in the absence of the *heredes sui*, and those classed as such, the Prætor gave the patron *one half the succession*, either by possession *ab intestato* if no will existed, or *contra tabulas* if the freedman had not given the patron one-half by testament; but this necessarily did not apply to freed *women* (*ante*, par. 1082). The patron's *male children* had this new right, but the patroness and the patron's female children, only that of the 12 Tables.

1087. (§ ii) *Succession of freedmen by the lex Papia Poppæa.* In accordance with the principle on which this law was enacted as to favouring the number of children, the patron had claims, testate or intestate, where a freed*man* left 100,000 sesterces and *less* than *three* children to a *virilis pars*, *i.e.*, if there was *one* child the patron had one-half, if *two* children the patron had one-third.

Freed*women* with four children were released from the tutorship of the *Patron*, and therefore they could make a will without his *auctoritas*, but a *virilis pars* was always to belong to the patron. The descendants of the *patroness*, and the *female* descendants of the patron, likewise received the *Prætorian male* descendants' rights if they had a fixed number (two or three) of children. See Gai. Inst. iii, §§ 49 to 53.

1088. (§ iii) *Succession of freedmen according to Justinian.* No difference existed between the patron and patroness, or their male or female children, or between freedmen and freedwomen, and the succession to the freedman *ab intestato* was to be :—

(1) Children, whether born in slavery or not, and whatever the fortune, the patron had no rights.

(2) The patron or patroness, or their children, and like *agnates* taking per *capita*.

(3) Collateral relations of patron or patroness, but to the fifth degree only, and taking the place of *cognates*, of which the freedmen, even under Justinian, had none.

1090. The succession *ex testamento* as *regards children* was the same as other citizens in respect of exclusions, omissions, or the *querela inof. test.* ; but as regards the *Patron,* if the freedman had less than 100 *aurei* (100,000 sestertii) he could make a will as he chose, but if he had more than 100,000 sestertii the *Patron* had a right to one-third, and could claim it (or have the amount made up to it) by possession *contra tabulas, i.e.,* if the freedman had no children, or had justly excluded or omitted them, so that the inheritance *ab intestato* would have come to the Patron. This one-third was free from all charges, the debts only being deducted in the calculation.

1092. (§ iv) All freedmen being *citizens* under Justinian the distinctions as to the succession of freedmen who were *latini Juniani, dediticii,* etc. (see *ante,* par. 64, 65) were unnecessary, though lengthily treated of by *Gaius* (Inst., iii, § 63 to 67, 72, 73), and reference made to certain repealed laws, as the senatus consultum *Largianum,* passed under *Claudius* in the Consulate of Lupus, and *Largus,* A.D. 42, giving the children of a patron of freed Latins hereditary rights, unless excluded by the patron *nominatim* from his own inheritance, and *Trajan's* edict as to *salvo jure patroni,* when a freed Latin had citizen rights given him by the emperor against the will of the Patron.

Tit. viii. De adsignatione Libertorum.

1096. If the *Patron* died *before* the freedman, his children acquired his rights, but a *senatus consultum* under *Claudius,* A.D. 45 (Rufus and Scapula consuls) gave the *patron* the right to assign, by will or otherwise, the freedman or freedwoman to one, or several of his children or grandchildren, who thereby became *sole Patrons* and *sole heirs,* and transmitted their rights to posterity (though if they had no children the old law as to patron's descendants was fallen back upon), and this was only a right of *preference, i.e.,* a right of selecting one of several persons who would be heirs, not a change in the law of inheritance, hence the patron assigned must be capable of succeeding to the freedman, and therefore must be one whom the patron has in his power, and if subsequently emancipated the right vanished.

Tit. ix. De Bonorum possessionibus.

1099. The rules as to the *possession of goods* were a prætorian institution, not being regulated by *law,* but by the magistrate, and they arose in the first instance in execution of the civil law, as where during a dispute it was necessary to maintain the heir at law in possession of the deceased's goods. They then supplied gaps, as when taking natural ties into consideration, and finally they overruled it in correcting its rigour (see part i, par. 290). Hence the *law* made the *heir,* the prætor the *possessor* of *goods* who occupied the place of the heir, and was supported by *fictitious* actions given him, as if he were heir, so that finally the *edict* created a sort of *prætorian* succession by which the *legal* inheritance might be either *confirmed* (in which case the additional advantage was gained of using the *interdict Quorum bonorum*, Gai. Inst., iii, § 34), *amended* or *contradicted*, and this either *ab intestato, secundum*, or *contra* tabulas, the object being in each case to secure, according to nature and equity, successors to the deceased.

1103. The *ex testamento* possession of goods given by the Prætor was of two kinds, viz. ;—

(1) *Contra Tabulas*, given in general to children, passed over in silence, whether *heredes sui* or those classed as such, or natural or adopted children, emancipated or given in adoption, male or female, *ante*, par. 708.

(2) *Secundum tabulas*. When those who could claim *contra tabulas* allowed the delay to expire, or were dead or repudiated their rights, the Prætor carried out in a less rigorous manner the civil law, *e.g.*, accepting the prætorian form of will, considering the capacity in intermediate time not material, permitting postumi strangers to be instituted, and giving possession *pendente conditione*, withdrawing it if the condition was not fulfilled.

1109. In default of a *testament*, or of having demanded possession *contra* or *secundum* tabulas within the permitted delay, the prætor passed to the possessio bonorum *ab intestato*, of which there were *eight* descriptions, viz., four for *ingenui*, and four exclusively for *freedmen*.

The names of these divisions were abbreviated from the phrase *ea pars edicti unde liberi vocantur: unde legitimi vocantur*, etc.

(1) *Unde liberi*, common to ingenui and freed, and given to the *heredes sui* and those classed as such, but it could not apply to the succession of women, as they had no such heirs.

(2) *Unde legitimi* applied to men and women ingenui and freed, and was open to all *legal* heirs of any kind, whether deriving their title from the 12 Tables, or senatus consulta, or constitutions, or the *s.c.* Tertul. and Orphit; or as patron or children, or as heredes sui who had neglected to demand *unde liberi*.

(3) *Unde decem personæ*, i.e., to the *ten* persons of the *natural* family (father and mother, grandfather and grandmother, paternal or maternal, son, daughter, grandsons, granddaughters, brother, sister, consanguineous or uterine) placed by the Prætor before the *manumissor extraneus* (*ante*, par. 166) of a free person freed whilst in mancipio to him, and who therefore, according to the *civil* law, had rights of patronage and succession.

(4) *Unde cognati*, i.e., to those called by the Prætor as a new order of successors not existing in the civil law (*ante*, par. 1070), but it might include as blood relations members of the civil family, *e.g.*, *agnates* who had neglected to demand possession *unde legitimi*.

(5) *Tum quem ex familia*. The expression is derived from the commencement of the edict, which then continues . . . . *patroni proximum oportebit, vocabo*, etc. It applied exclusively to *freed* persons, and under it in default of (1) *unde liberi*, and (2) *unde*

legitimi, the (3) nearest member of the patron's family was called, and it included the patron himself, or his children (if they had neglected or refused the succession *unde legitimi*), and in addition his *agnates*.

(6) *Unde liberi patroni patronæ-que et parentes eorum.* In the succession of *freed*men the right of *patronage* was (α) *unde legitimi*, for patron and children, (β) *tum quem ex familia* for *civil* family of patron or patroness, *i.e.*, principally for their agnates, (γ) the above (No. 6) for *descendants* or *ascendants*, *i.e.*, the *natural* family of the patron or patroness, on the ground of blood relationship, (δ) see below (No. 8) for the *collateral* natural family of the patron or patroness. If the patron or his children (*heredes sui*) failed to take in one of these orders they might come in under any other, just as in the succession of *ingenui*.

(7) *Unde vir et uxor.* Under this, which applied to both ingenui and freed, a gap was supplied in the civil law, and reciprocal rights given where there was *justæ nuptiæ*, and the marriage existed at the time of death, without there being any *in manum conventio*.

(8) *Unde cognati manumissoris.* This applied exclusively to *freed* persons (see above, 6 δ), but with a limit fixed by the *Lex Furia* (Ulp. Reg., 28, 7).

In default the property fell to the people, according to the *Lex Julia (caducaria)*.

As in mancipations it became the rule always to imply the clause *contracta fiducia*, the class *unde decem personæ* was unnecessary, and the succession to the *freed* being the same as to *ingenui* (except as to the fifth degree only, *ante*, par. 1088), the *tum quem*, the *unde liberi patroni*, etc., and the *unde cognati* were also suppressed, so that only the four bonorum possessiones of the *ingenui* were left, viz. :—1, *unde liberi;* 2, *unde legitimi;* 3, *unde cognati;* 4, *unde vir et uxor*.

Finally the edict of the Prætor gave an *extraordinarium auxilium* (independent of the *testament* or succession *ab intestato*) when the *possession* of property was expressly ordered to be given by any *law*, and hence called possession *tum quibus ex legibus*. This was distinct from the *unde legitimi*, because there the law gives the *inheritance*, though if the law gave both the *inheritance* and the *possession* either could be claimed.

1120 (§ viii) The *possession of goods* had to be demanded of the Prætor or the governor of a province, and could be repudiated. The *time* within which it must be demanded was:—

One *year* for children and ascendants, natural or adopted.

One hundred days for all others.

On the expiration of this delay, or on the death of the parties first entitled, or on their repudiation there would be

Accrual, if several persons of the same degree.

Devolution to the next degree, if only one of the former degree or all failed.

Next possession of goods in default of degrees.

But only those days were reckoned during which it was lawful to appear before a magistrate after the demand had become possible; and under *Justinian* no formal demand was necessary, it being sufficient to manifest within the prescribed interval the intention of accepting, for the distinction between the *possessio bonorum* and the inheritance had in reality disappeared (*post*, par. 1123).

1123. A distinction in the *bonorum possessio* existed, which is mentioned by *Gaius* (Inst., ii, § 148, 149), but not noticed by Justinian, viz.:—

1. *Cum re* (*id est cum effectu*), when the possessor was protected from eviction by the civil law heir.

2. *Sine re (sine effectu)*, when the possessor was not guaranteed from the *petitio hereditatis* of the civil law heir.

This could only occur when the rights under the *civil* and *Prætorian* law were not united in the same person, as where, *e.g.*, the heir validly instituted by testament accepted the inheritance, but had not demanded possessio bonorum, the latter passed to those called ab intestato, but *sine re*. In time, as the subtleties of the law disappeared, the possessio bonorum *cum re* became the usual form.

1124. The *possessio bonorum* by *Edict* may be called *Edictalis*, as opposed to the *decretalis bonorum possessio*, resulting from a *decree* of the Prætor in a law-suit, in which case the right commenced from the moment of the decree, and the *dies utiles* of delay were those when the magistrate was seated on the tribunal. In this case the possession of the goods could not be repudiated, though as a general rule the possession was only temporary for the purposes of the suit. Examples of such decrees are:—

(α) Bonorum possessio *ex Carboniano, i.e.*, the temporary possession given in virtue of this *edict* of *Cneus Carbon* to a minor whose status and right of inheritance are both attacked, the lawsuit being deferred until puberty.

(β) Bonorum possessio *ventris nomine, i.e.*, the temporary possession given on behalf of a child not yet born, who, if born, would have a claim *contra tabulas* against the institution made to his prejudice.

1127. *Collatio bonorum*. As emancipated children, had they remained in power, would not have possessed any property of their own, it would have been unjust to the *heredes sui* when the *Prætor* called the emancipated with the latter, not to have compelled the emancipated children to throw their property into the mass of the inheritance for re-division, and by interpretation this rule was extended to the daughters' *dos*, afterwards to the *donatio propter nuptias*, and finally Justinian called upon all *children* without distinction succeeding ab intestato to the property of their *ascendants* to make this *collatio* of things on which the *quarta* was due in the *querela inoff. test.* (see *ante*, par. 798). It applied to *ab intestato* and testamentary successions, but it was only imposed on children who were heirs succeeding to *ascendants*, and as against one another. It was not due from those who abstained from, or repudiated, the inheritance, nor if the testator had dispensed with it.

1132. *Accrual between co-heirs.* If one of the heirs by any cause (except indignity, *post*, par. 1138) makes default, his share by right of *accrual* falls to the *juridical persona* of his co-heirs *sine onere*, whether the inheritance be testamentary, ab intestato, or through possessio bonorum. See as to substitutions, *ante*, par. 742, and in respect of legacies, par. 868, 875.

1134. *The transmission of the inheritance.* Strictly, the heir dying before aditio, or the possessor of goods before demanding it, lost his rights, but to this rule exceptions were introduced, for by a constitution of Theodosius and Valentinian, if children instituted heirs of an ascendant died before the opening of the testament, they transmitted their rights to their successors, and if a minor of seven years died before his father had had time to accept an inheritance for him, he could still acquire it as if the child were living. Finally Justinian accorded transmission of rights, and time for deliberation to the heirs of persons dying within the period for declaring their intention. See *ante*, par. 804 (3).

1138. *Of those deprived of property for unworthiness.*

Generally inheritances, legacies, or fidei-commissa, taken away on the ground of unworthiness *(ereptorium)*, fell to the *fiscus* with all the charges depending on them, and the heir still remained so, though the property was gone. The *Lex Papia Poppæa* in some cases gave them like *caduca* as a privilege of *paternity;* and hence, *Ulpian* (Reg. 19, 17) indicates, as a mode of acquiring Roman dominion *ex lege*, the *caducum*, and the *ereptorium*. The grounds of unworthiness would be, if the heir or legatee had, *e.g.*, caused the death of the deceased or neglected to pursue his murderer, or accused him of crime.

1141. *Actions relating to inheritances ab intestato and to the possessio bonorum.* These were the—

(1) *Hereditatis petitio* and *familiæ erciscundæ*, see *ante*, par. 830.

(2) The *quorum bonorum* interdict for the restitution of possession, see *post*, par. 2302.

(3) *Prætorian hereditatis petitio*, for possession and for partition of possession.

(4) *Utilis familiæ erciscundæ.*

1143. *Novels of Justinian as to successions ab intestato.*

By the Novels 118 and 127 of A.D. 544 and 548, Justinian completely effaced the primitive civil family system of the twelve tables, and the vestiges of the civil law succession referred to in the Institutes, replacing it by an order of intestate succession, based upon the natural family, according to blood relationship. The distinction between the *hereditas* and the *bonorum possessio*, *agnati* and *cognati*, males and females, was abolished, and by the 118th Novel

(c. i) *Descendants* succeeded whether emancipated or not,

natural or adopted, through males or females, and took *per capita* in the first degree, *per stirpes* in the second, but the law as to the usufruct due to parents was maintained (*ante*, par. 611).

(c. ii) In default, the nearest *ascendants* took per *stirpes*, but if there were *brothers or sisters* of the *whole blood*, these collaterals took equally with them *per capita*, and (Novel 127, c. i) children of deceased brothers or sisters represented them. The paternal and maternal line each took half, though the number of persons in each line might be unequal. The usufruct of the child's property was taken away from his father in return for the absolute property in his portion given him by this rule.

(c. iii) In default of ascendants *collaterals* come in, viz., brothers and sisters of the whole blood, and in default those of the half-blood, whether consanguineous or uterine, and children, but not grandchildren, representing their deceased parents. In default the nearest relations succeed, taking per *capita* if more than one.

(c. v) The tutorship-at-law (*ante*, par. 222) went to the nearest male relative or to the mother or grandmother.

Tit. x. De acquisitione per adrogationem.

1145. *Adrogation* was one of the methods of universal succession other than by inheritance, and its effects in ancient law were deduced from (1) the *minima c.d.* of the person arrogated, and (2) the acquisition through the *patria potestas* by the arrogator (see *ante*, par. 206).

The extinction affected only the *private persona* of the person arrogated, not his *public* or *physical* person, and therefore the rights attached to these last remained intact; hence:—

(1) *Rights which perished* completely were agnation, gentilitas, patronage, and the tutorships depending thereon—usufruct, usus (*ante*, par. 250, 488, 1032), certain debts due to the person arrogated, as those, *e.g.*, arising from the services due by the oath of a freedman (*operarum liberti obligationes*, *ante*, par. 67) or those resulting from an adstipulation (*post*, par. 1377); and, finally, debts or obligations of private *civil* law.

(2) *Rights remaining in the person arrogated* were *justæ nuptiæ*, eventual potestas over his own children, cognation, testamentary dativi, and the new legal natural bond tutorships (*ante*, par. 105, 250), *habitatio, operarum servi* (*ante*, par. 504, 505), and the rights as to the *peculium castrense* or *quasi-castrense*, rights attaching to the *natural person*, and the same as to debts or obligations (part ii, par. 199, and *ante*, par. 208).

(3) *Rights passing to the arrogator.* The mass of these formed the *per universitatem successio* of the present title, and included those private law rights not referred to above, *e.g.*, the rights of *patria potestas* over the arrogated person, his wife (*in manu*) and his children (*in potestate*); all rights of ownership, of prædial servitudes, mortgages, and other real rights and credits acquired by a

son for his father in virtue of being in power, but *not debts;* for a son does not bind a father directly by his acts (see *post,* par. 1152).

For Justinian's changes, by which the arrogator and the *natural* father were placed on the same level. See *ante,* par. 611, 1024).

1152. (§ iii) The arrogator's succession being founded on the rights resulting from the *patria postestas* (not on the principles governing the devolution of an inheritance by death) he acquired credits, but was not bound by debts, and hence, after the arrogation creditors, ceased to have a debtor, and the debt vanished, except that the person arrogated was held to be bound naturally. In such cases the Prætor gave a *utilis fictitious action,* on the assumption that *c.d.* had not taken place (Gai. Inst., iv, § 38), to the creditors in perpetuity, and if the arrogator, as being the owner of his property, did not defend the person arrogated, and tender security to the creditors, the Prætor gave the creditors the *possessio bonorum,* including the right to sell the property brought by the person arrogated, but under *Justinian* the process was simplified by the arrogator being sued in the name of the son.

Tit. xi. De eo cui libertatis causa bona addicuntur.

1154. A certain Virginius Valens having left by will liberty to several slaves, and no testamentary or ab intestato heir existing or being willing to accept, one of the freed slaves (Popilius Rufus) obtained a rescript from the Emperor *Marcus Aurelius* authorising the goods to be given him by *addictio (bona sibi addici, i.e.,* by an order of the magistrate as opposed to the *adjudicatio* of a judge.)

The grant was subject to the payment of the creditors, and the liberty left by legacy to the other slaves, and by this means the memory of the defunct was also saved from the ignominy attaching to the sale of his goods.

The rules in respect of this kind of succession were :—

1. He (whether the slave himself, or, according to the Emperor Gordian, a stranger) who obtains *addictio* is bound to give good security to creditors.

2. He will stand in the place of the testamentary heir to the slaves freed by testament, and those freed directly will be *liberti orcini,* but he will have the patronage of those freed by *fideicommissum.*

3. He may claim to have *rights of patronage* over all the slaves to be freed, including the *liberti orcini,* but the slaves must consent to this.

4. If in default the *fiscus* claimed the *addictio* the freedoms were to be maintained.

In order for the *addictio* to be granted it was necessary (α) that the freedoms left by the deceased should be by will (or by an extension of the rescript) by codicil, *i.e.,* a codicil in respect of an *ab intestato* estate, (β) that the succession would escheat for want of *testamentary* or *ab intestato* heirs, though if an *heir ab intestato* abstained, the *addictio* may still be made, and if he, being a minor of twenty-five, demanded the *restitutio in integrum* he would have to be bound by the freedoms already given, because they were held irrevocable, although they would not have existed in the *ab intestato* inheritance.

Justinian extended the constitution to include the case of *addictio* being demanded when the freedoms had been given *inter vivos* or *mortis causa*, and the creditors wished to annul them as fraudulent (*ante*, par. 70), and the same emperor also applied the addictio to meet other cases. See Cod. 7, 2, 15.

Tit. xii. De successionibus sublatis quæ fiebant per bonorum venditionem, et ex s.c. Claudiano.

1161. *Cicero* (Pro Quintio), *Gaius* (Inst., iii, § 78, etc.), and *Theophilus* in his paraphrase, give details of this kind of universal succession by sale of the goods.

It was a Prætorian institution, probably introduced by the Prætor Publius *Rutilius* (? B.C. 100), and could be made against:—

(a) The *living*, *e.g.*, a debtor hiding or absent, and not defended, in the case of cession of goods under the Lex Julia, or judicially condemned and had not satisfied execution in the interval accorded by the 12 Tables (in respect of the *manus injectio*, Table iii, § i) or the edict of the Prætor.

(β) The *dead*, *e.g.*, when it was certain that the deceased had no heir or possessor bonorum, or other legal successor.

Though a softening of the rigour, it was a close imitation of the *personal* execution *(manus injectio)* of the primitive law, and it was a *sale* of the whole *juridical* persona of the debtor.

The process was as follows:—

(1) A *missio in possessionem* answering to the *manus injectio*, was granted by the Prætor to the creditors after the legal interval, but this was only *rei servandæ causa*, and continued for thirty days *(continui)* against living persons and fifteen days against the dead.

(2) *Proscriptio*, or the public notice of the future sale to be made by the creditors, an assignee *(magister)* was then appointed for the sale by a new decree of the Prætor, and subsequently the *lex bonorum vendendorum* or publication of the conditions of sale took place under a third decree of the Prætor.

(3) *Addictio* to the *bonorum emptor*, *i.e.*, to the highest bidder, the time allowed between the appointment of the *magister* and *addictio* being thirty days or sixty days, in all, as in the case of the *manus injectio*.

The *bonorum emptor* was not bound beyond a dividend payable to the creditors in proportion to the amount he had given for the property. He did not have *dominium ex jure quiritium*, but only *in bonis*, and hence he had only *utiles* actions, of which there are two forms, the *actio Rutiliana* and a *fictitious* action, on the supposition of the *bonorum emptor* being the *heir*.

He whose goods were thus sold was struck with *infamy*, and hence insolvent masters used to institute their slave necessary heir (*ante*, par. 73), the infamy then attaching to him (Gai. Inst., ii, § 154), but no such infamy followed a sale after *cessio bonorum*. The effects of infamy in *public* law were the loss of the *jus honorum* (part i, par. 185), and (?) the *jus suffragii* (Savigny), and this applied to *local* honours in the provinces. In *private* law the person so stamped could not *postulate* for another (see *post*, par. 1669, and 2034, 4), and after the *venditio bonorum* the debtor lost his *juridical persona*, which passed to the *bonorum emptor*, but he did *not* suffer *minima capitis deminutio*, for it was only his *past* juridical persona, as regarded his estate, that was transferred, and that only by *Prætorian* (not civil) law, so that he did not lose agnation or *gentilitas* or patronage or any future pecuniary rights, and *civil* actions still existed for and against him, and could only be met by Prætorian means; hence *Gaius* (Inst., ii, § 155) speaks of subsequent sales of the debtor's goods when only a dividend had been obtained by the first sale of his property. The infamy attached *after* the *bonorum venditio*, but was suspensory from the time of the *proscriptio*, just as the exercise of rights was suspended, and the debtor treated as a slave during the sixty days after the *addictio*, in the case of the *manus injectio*, although the debtor was not the actual slave of the creditor until the sale had been made. But this mode of universal succession belonged to the Prætorian *Ordinaria judicia*, and fell into disuse when this was supplanted by the *extraordinaria judicia*, and purchasers became mere owners of that which they respectively bought.

1175. (§ 1) *Justinian suppressed* the kind of *maxima c.d.*, and *universal succession*, arising in virtue of the senatus consultum *Claudianum;* when a *woman (ingenua* and a Roman or Latin citizen) persisted in a union *(contubernium)* with a *slave* against the will and in spite of the warning of the slave's master (*ante*, par. 44), and if she was a *freed* woman, she refell into the slavery of the patron if he was ignorant of it; but if he knew of it, then into the slavery of the owner of the slave.

Tit. xiii. De obligationibus.

1176. For *general* notions as to obligations, for *Justinian's* definition of a personal right, and for the kinds of obligations, see part ii, par. 196, 199.

1182. The principal and peculiar *effect* of obligations is the necessity imposed on the debtor of freeing himself by performance, or in default being compelled to do so by *action*.

1185. The *sources* or *causes* of obligations are *facts*, whether arising from *reciprocal consent* or *independent* of *consent*, or by the *will of one* or *without the will* of either (see part ii, par. 145, 201). For the historical gradation of ideas in Roman law, and for the legal division of obligations, see part ii, par. 201, 208.

s

1200. The terms *Conventio, pactum,* and *pactio* are generic expressions, indicating the concurrence of the will of two or more persons in the same matter, as far as the law is concerned and in respect of creating, modifying, or extinguishing a right *(et est pactio, duorum pluriumve in idem placitum consensus.* Dig. 2, 14, § 2, *Ulpian),* see *post,* par. 1579.

Pollicitatio is the simple promise of one not yet accepted by the other, and only quite exceptionally produced a legal bond.

Tit. xiv. Quibus modis re contrahitur obligatio.

1205. There were four contracts in which the obligation did not arise until the delivery of the thing, viz.: the *mutuum, commodatum, depositum,* and *pignus* (see part i, par. 333), for the essential obligation was to *return,* and this could not be done until received, and hence they are called in French law *real* contracts. The expression *credere* more particularly applied to these four contracts, and *res credita* to the *mutuum;* and, on this account, the Prætor included them all in the edict under the title *De rebus creditis* (Dig. 12, 1, 1). At first these contracts were formed through the *per æs et libram* solemnity, but later, consent and simple *traditio* sufficed.

1209. The *mutuum* applied to things *in genere* (part ii, par. 139), and, as the person receiving became *owner,* the Institutes derive it from *ut ex meo tuum fiat,* but this etymology is doubtful. The power of *alienation* was also attached, otherwise the owner would have the action *rei vindicatio* (see ante, par. 602, and *post,* 2217), whereas it only gave rise to the *condictio certi.* It was in relation to this contract that many of the troubles between the patricians and the plebeians arose, as, under it, the debtor bound himself to pay interest *(fœnus, versura, usuræ),* though this really resulted from a special stipulation added to the mutuum.

1213. *Trajectitia (quæ trans mare vehitur),* or *nautica pecunia,* was the term used to indicate the loan in which the sum lent, or the goods bought with that sum, were destined for *carriage by sea.* As the creditor ran a risk from the departure of the ship until its arrival at its destination, and as these risks might apply to the ship or part of it, or to the cargo pledged for the payment of the debt, the rate of interest *(nauticum fœnus, usuræ maritimæ)* agreed upon by special convention might be higher than in the ordinary *mutuum* (Dig. 22, 2, 4, and Paul, Sent. 2, 14, § 3), and by maritime custom a simple *pact* would suffice to make this interest binding.

1215. In the *commodatum,* the property being *in specie,* the identical thing must be returned; hence, the *commodans* (the lender) can bring the *actio commodati* against the borrower *(qui commodatum accepit),* although he may not be owner, and no ownership or possession is transferred to the borrower. Both moveables and immoveables may be objects of the contract, but *res quæ ipso usu consumuntur* only when they would be used for a purpose that would not destroy them, as, *e.g.,* simply for ostentation. The obligation is to *return after use;* but the loan being *gratuitous,* and *generally* for the sole benefit of the bailee, he is bound to use it *only* for the purpose lent; he is responsible for *dolus, culpa* and want of *diligentia* (see *post*, par. 1633), irresistible accident being the only exception, so that he is liable for theft without violence, and in any case he is responsible if the exposure was due to his fault, as if, *e.g.*, taken on a voyage when it was lent to be used at home, or if, in order to save his own property he left the bailment to perish. In some cases the borrower may be liable only for *dolus* or *culpa lata*, as where the benefit is *joint*, *e. g.*, a common friend invited to supper, and silver plate lent by one of the hosts, or where the benefit is for the bailor only, *e.g.*, apparel lent to the bride to conduct her home (Dig. 13, 6, 18, Gaius; and 5, 10, Ulpian).

1220. In the *depositum* the thing being *in specie*, so that in, *e.g.*, the case of money deposited, the coin itself would have to be returned (see *post*, par. 2200), the depositor *(deponens)* retained the ownership and the possession. The obligation entailed upon the *depositarius* was to restore the property on demand (even though a term had been named), at the place where it happened to be, unless this involved *dolus malus* on the part of the depositor. The benefit being for the depositor, and it being his fault if he did not select a good depositee, the latter was only responsible for *dolus*, though this probably included *culpa gravis;* but if the custodian had been specially charged, or he had undertaken to be the depositee, then he was liable also for *culpa*, as well as for *custodia;* and, as he must not *use* the thing, if he was authorised to do so, the contract changed its character. At the time of the twelve tables the depositee, whether *voluntary* or *necessary*, was condemned in double for *dolus;* but, as in a voluntary deposit, the depositor could select the custodian, the Prætor struck out the penalty in this case and only gave an action for the *double* on public grounds against the unfaithful depositee, in whose hands the property had been placed from *necessity*, as in cases of tumult, fire, shipwreck, etc., the heir of such depositee being only liable for the *simple* penalty, unless he himself had also been guilty of *dolus*.

1224. *Sequestrativ* implied a deposit in the hands of a *sequester* for *re*delivery *on a given event*, on account of third parties interested, as in the case of the preservation of property pending a lawsuit; hence, the depositee accepted a sort of office *(officium)*, from which generally only the Prætor could discharge him (Dig. 16, 3, 5, 2, Ulpian).

1225. The *Pignus* must be looked at from two different points of view, viz.:—

(1) In respect of the *real right* conferred on the creditor over the object pledged. This, in the Institutes, is confounded with the *hypotheca*, *i.e.*, the real right conferred without *traditio* by simple consent. See part ii, par. 233; and *ante*, par. 510 (3).

(2) In respect of the contract or personal bond between the creditor (pledgee) and the debtor. The principal obligation is to *return* after complete satisfaction of the debt, and hence it must be delivered *(re)*. It applied to corporeal and incorporeal things, *moveables*, and by the better opinion, *immoveables* also. The

debtor remained *owner;* but, by way of sanction of his real right, the creditor acquired possessory actions and interdicts, in order to keep the property in his power (*ante*, par. 346). The pledgee was bound, as in a *commodatum*, to *exacta diligentia, i.e.*, he was liable, not only for *dolus*, but also for *culpa*.

1229. In addition to the above specially designated contracts, an infinity of other similar but *unnamed* contracts *re* also existed (see *post*, par. 1590).

1230. *Actions arising from contracts re.*

The *mutuum* had only a general action applicable to other cases, viz., the *stricti juris condictio certi;* but the three other contracts had special *bonæ fidei* actions, viz., the *actiones commodati, depositi* (in the case of *sequestratio*, called the *actio depositi sequestraria*), and *pigneratitia*. Hence the *mutuum*, like all strict civil law contracts, was only *unilateral*, and all equitable considerations were disregarded; so that if the lender were to blame, the borrower had to fall back upon the actions based on *dolus* or on the *Lex Aquilia*, etc.; but, for the three other contracts, the actions were reciprocal, and—

Directa for the bailor, because flowed *directly* from the contract;

Contraria for the bailee, because arose out of *ex post facto* collateral circumstances; and the *actio commodati contraria*, would only lie against the bailor for *dolus, culpa gravis*, or expenses incurred on his account.

Tit. xv. De Verborum obligatione.

1235. This was the first derivation of the *nexum*, see part ii, par. 201; and there were three distinct forms, viz.: (1) *dotis dictio* (*ante*, par. 582), (2) *operarum jurata promissio liberti* (*ante*, par. 67), (3) *stipulatio* and *promissio*. The two first were peculiar to their special uses, and bound the obligor *without* any previous interrogation by the obligee; though, if the promise of the freedman was made while still a slave, it was not binding unless renewed when freed. The third was a general form capable of being used for the first two, and is the only form of obligations *verbis* discussed in the Institutes.

The *Stipulatio* consisted of the (1) interrogation *(stipulatio)* on the part of the *reus stipulandi*, and the answer *(promissio)* made by the *reus promittendi;* and the term is said to be derived from *stips* or *stipula, i.e.*, the stake held in the hand of the contracting parties, and broken by them at the time, so that the fracture might serve as a means of proof.

It was a civil unilateral obligation which, to be reciprocal, must be repeated in the contrary way. No representation was allowed, whether by mandatory or messenger; and the bond was formed by words *(verbis)*, without which consent was useless; and in strictness the contract was binding, though *dolus* existed, see *post*, par. 1370.

The stipulation was not a peculiar convention, but applied to all kinds of contracts, as a mode of attaining greater security, or to insure their binding force. The object of the forms employed was to secure attention to the fact of consent, see part ii, par. 150.

The words *Spondes spondeo*, which remained peculiar to Roman citizens, must have been in Latin, but other words of the *jus gentium* were admitted for strangers (Gai. Inst. iii, § 93). After a constitution of *Leo*, A.D. 469 (Cod. 8, 38, 10), the interrogation and affirmative response might be in any words, in any language, or in different languages; and under *Justinian*, its reduction to writing served as proof (*post*, par. 1359).

1246 (§ ii). A stipulation might be :—

(1) *Pure*, *e.g.*, '*Quinque aureos dare spondes?* in which case an action might be brought immediately, unless the nature of the obligation involved delay.

(2) *In diem* (part ii, par. 169), *e.g.*, *decem aureos primis calendis Martii dare spondes?* in which case the debt is due at once, though it cannot be demanded till the time has expired; hence, if paid by mistake before the time, it cannot be redemanded; but if an action was brought too soon, it would entail *plus petitio (præsens obligatio est, in diem autem dilata solutio,* Dig. 45, 1, 46, Ulpian); and this is so, whether the term is *certus* or *incertus* (see *ante*, par. 735, 850, and 924). Strictly, an unilateral civil law contract could not expire by mere efflux of time, as there must have been a *solutio*, and, therefore, such a stipulation was held to be pure and simple; but the Prætor in such cases allowed the *exceptio doli mali*, or that *pacti conventi*, and see also *temporary* actions, *post*, Bk. iv, tit. 12. Stipulations relating to *past* time *(e.g., Si Titius consul fuit)*, or to the *present* time *(e.g., si Titius vivit)*, would be *invalid* if the facts stated were not true, otherwise they would be pure and simple; for an event, if actually accomplished, though unknown to the parties, cannot suspend an obligation.

(3) *Conditional*, *e.g.*, *si Titius consul fuerit factus, quinque aureos dare spondes?* This must be *future* and *uncertain*; for if the event is already accomplished, or must necessarily happen, the obligation exists immediately; but it may be (1) *casualis, i.e.*, depending on chance; or (2) *potestativa, i.e.*, resulting from the act of one of the parties; or (3) *mixta, i.e.*, including both causes: though if *potestativa* as regards the promissor, and depending only on his simple will, the stipulation would be useless, as no compulsion could be applied; but if *negative, e.g., si in capitolium non ascendero*, this would be a conditional stipulation, payment for which could not be demanded until the death of the promissor (see *ante*, par. 924). As, whilst the condition is in suspense, there is only a hope of the existence of the obligation, a payment made by mistake could be reclaimed by the *condictio indebiti*, as not being due; but this hope renders the obligee in some sort a *creditor*, as it gives him the power to take precautionary measures for the preservation of his eventual rights, and he transmits his right to his heirs *(eamque ipsam spem in heredem transmittimus)* if

he die before the accomplishment of the condition. In the same way, this eventual right is acquired by the slave or filiusfamilias for the master or paterfamilias in whose power he was at the time the stipulation was made; hence, in this respect, a great difference existed between legacies and obligations, and the accomplishment of the condition had a retrospective effect, the rights being determined from the time of the making of the obligation.

(4) Restricted as to *place*, e.g., *Carthagine dare spondes?* this, though *pure*, implies a delay which, in case of dispute, would be fixed by the judge. If the parties being, *e.g.*, at Rome, and the word *hodie* were added to the above, the stipulation, as being impossible, would be void.

1257. Stipulations may be made in respect of the translation of the entire ownership of property or of fragments of such ownership as servitudes, or in respect of *facts* to be done or not to be done, *e.g.*, not to prevent me crossing your estate; and the expressions *dare, facere, praestare*, comprehend the generality of cases.

The object may be *certum*, *e.g.*, the slave Stichus; or *incertum, e.g.*, a slave; and stipulations were always uncertain when they consisted of a *fact*, *i.e.*, to do or not to do; and hence it was advisable to add in such cases a *penal* clause; but as this fixed a determinate sum by way of penalty, it immediately made the stipulation *certain*, and therefore an action of that class was available.

1260. *Actions arising out of stipulations*. In the *mutuum*, the object is always certain; but in the stipulation it may be :—

(1) *Certain,* giving rise to the *condictio* proper (part i, par. 242), and called *certi* when in respect of a fixed sum of money (*certa pecunia*). The *intentio* of the formula indicating a certain object (*certa intentio*), *e.g.* (1), *si paret sestertium millia dare oportere*, (2) *si paret hominem Stichum* (or *fundum Tusculanum*) *dare oportere* (Gai. Inst. iv, § 41); but the *condemnatio* in the case of (1), would be *sestertium millia condemna*; whilst it would be uncertain in (2), as the judge must fix the sum (*Quanti ea res erit*).

(2) *Uncertain,* in which case it gave rise to the *condictio incerti* with the *intentio* general (*Quidquid paret dare facere, oportere*, Gai. Inst. ix, § 51, and 136); and the *condemnatio* at most could only have a *maximum* (*taxatio*) fixed by the Prætor (*Duntaxat X millia condemna si non paret absolve*). The *condictio incerti* having been introduced later than the *certi*, imitated the actions of the *jus gentium* (*commodati, depositi,* etc.) in taking special names for special uses, *e.g., actio ex stipulatu, ex testamento,* etc.

Tit. xvi. De duobus reis stipulandi et promittendi.

1264. There were two ways for several persons to stipulate :—

(1) Several or one could interrogate, *correi stipulandi*, and one or several promise, *correi promittendi*, but the whole transaction, though thus made conjointly with another (*cum alio*), formed one contract *verbis*.

(2) After the principal stipulation was completed, an *accessory* contract *(ad* or *pro alio)* might be made to guarantee the former, either by adding a second creditor *(adstipulator)*, or a second debtor *(adpromissor, sponsor, fidepromissor, fidejussor)*, see *post*, par. 1377, 1392.

In the first case, the thing is due *in solidum to each* co-stipulator when there are several, and *from each* co-promissor when there are several; though, according to Papinian (Dig. 45, 2, 11, §§ 1 and 2), the contract might be so made that the co-promissors would not be joint and several obligees, *i.e.*, there would be no *solidarity*, but each would be liable only for a *virilis pars*, as where the question was put by one person to several *collectively*, and they answered *spondemus*, a kind of contract called by the commentators *obligatio pro rata*; but, in the absence of such an arrangement, there was a *unity* in respect of the object of the obligation, and it was only due *once*; though, as regards the *personal* obligation, there would be so many distinct bonds between the one creditor and several debtors, or several creditors and one debtor. From this, it follows that a cause of nullity or dissolution as to the thing *(in rem)*, as *e.g.*, *solutio, acceptilatio*, or *novatio*, or other equivalent act, would annul or dissolve all the obligations; though, when relating exclusively to a particular person, it would only produce an effect as regarded that person, *e.g.*, exemption of one by *c.d.*, or a pact by one of the co-stipulators in favour of one of the co-promissors, in which cases the obligation of the others still remained.

As *each* of several co-stipulators could sue the common debtor *in solidum*, such an action prevented payment, or a valid offer being made to the others; but, if the creditor sued *one* of several co-promissors *in solidum*, this did not, under *Justinian*, release the others, a right of action being preserved against them for complete satisfaction. Under the *ancient* system, the *novatio* at the *litis contestatio*, in the case of *legitima judicia* actions *in personam*, liberated all the debtors except the defendant in the suit; and in actions not of the *legitimum judicium* character, the *exceptio rei in judicio deductæ* or *rei judicatæ* would probably have been a valid plea available to the rest of the debtors if the creditor attempted to sue any of them after having commenced an action against one (see *post*, par. 2046).

Strictly, the stipulation did not give rights as between the co-stipulators or co-promissors unless there was some relationship between them, *e.g.*, partners, in which case the remaining co-stipulators could sue one who had received the whole amount, and so one co-promissor who had paid the whole could sue the others to bear their share by the action *mandati, socii*, etc., according to the nature of the bond between them. One co-promissor might be bound purely and simply, and another *in diem* or *sub-conditione*, but this would not alter the claim on the first.

Tit. xvii. De stipulatione servorum.

1280. This subject is involved in the general considerations discussed *ante*, par. 616, 722, and *post*, par. 1665.

In respect of *obligations* :—

(1) As *creditor*, the slave could bind others towards his master, and all civil, Prætorian, or natural credits acquired by him fell to his master, though personally the slave might be a creditor in his *natural persona*, as *e.g.*, in respect of accounts between the slave and his master, and (?) when abandoned *pro derelicto* without a master, see *post*, par. 1289 (7).

(2) As *debtor*, in strict law, the slave could not bind his master towards others; but Prætorian law modified this rule (see *post*, par. 2201); and the old civil law gave an action against the master in respect of delicts committed by the slave, but the master could free himself from responsibility by abandoning the slave (see *post*, par. 2219). *Personally*, the *civil* law admitted of his being a *debtor*, for the *noxal* action followed him into new hands, and, if he was freed, it became direct; but, in respect of *contracts*, he could not, according to the civil law, bind himself, though *natural* obligations were subsequently admitted.

1289. A slave could *stipulate* for his master, but *not promise*; and his power of stipulating was derived from the *persona* of his master, the latter acquiring the benefit of the stipulation at the time it was made. The obligation formed depended on the words used, and different results followed, according to the position of the slave, *e.g.* :—

(1) *Slave of one master*. If the master was incapable of benefiting by the stipulation, it was useless, *e.g.*, if made in respect of a prædial servitude and the master had no estate, or if the master was a *captive*, in which case, if he returned, it was good by *postliminium*, but, if he did not return and the stipulation had been made *nominatim*, the heirs could not have the benefit of it. The stipulation may be acquired by the master against his will; and it was immaterial whether the slave stipulated for himself *(sibi)*, or for his co-slave *(conservo suo)*, or without special designation *(impersonaliter)*; for in all cases the *master* acquired, but a stipulation made by the slave for a *stranger* would be useless, because the slave could not acquire for him.

(2) *Slave of the inheritance*. Here, as the right was derived from the *persona* of the inheritance, if a *physical* persona was required, the stipulation would be useless, as in the case of usufruct or usus, though this rule did not apply to a legacy to the slave of such rights, because the *dies cedit* was not at once fixed, and, before it was, the necessary physical persona might come into existence.

The *inheritance* acquired, whether the slave stipulated *sibi* or *impersonaliter*, but he could not make it *personaliter*, as there was no *physical persona* existing, and whether he could do so in favour of a *future heir (futuro heredi nominatim)* was a disputed point; the *Proculians* and *Papinian* being for the negative, on the ground that at the time the stipulation is made the heir is a stranger to the slave; the *Sabinians* for the affirmative, because they held

BOOK III—TIT. XVII. 265

this as a consequence of the principle that, after the *aditio*, the title of the heir was calculated as from the moment of the decease (see *ante*, par. 644, and Dig. 45, 3, 16 *Paul*, 28, 4 *Gaius*).

The benefit of a stipulation of a fact *(factum)* is exclusively restricted to him who makes it *(Quæ facti sunt non transeunt ad dominum*, Dig. 35, 1, 44, *Paul)*, *e.g.*, *ut sibi ire vel agere liceat* would only give the slave the right to go or lead along, though the master had the right of compelling the slave to do it.

(3) The *slave of several masters*.

(4) The *nuda proprietas* of the slave in one master; the *usufruct* or *usus* in others.

(5) The slave of another, or a free man possessed in good faith. For these three cases see *post*, par. 1665.

(6) *A public slave*. According to *Ulpian* (Dig. 45, 3, 3), the stipulation was valid in favour of the municipium or colony the slave belonged to, and from this was deduced the method of stipulating for the benefit of a pupil *infans*, and without slaves; for, on the ground that the minor had a share in the common ownership of the public slave, the *nominatim* stipulation would be acquired for him (see *ante*, par. 136 and 275), but this was a derogation from strict principles, and only gave *utiles* actions.

(7) *No master*, as where the slave had been abandoned and no one else had acquired any rights in him, in which case, having no *persona* from which to draw the capacity, the stipulation would be null and void, but (?) as to the slave himself acquiring naturally the benefit of the stipulation.

1298. *Of Stipulations of filii-* or *filiæ-familias*. Beyond the limits of the *patria potestas*, persons *alieni juris* were *free citizens*, and the introduction of the *peculium* gave them a *persona* (see *ante*, par. 611), hence whilst, just as in the case of slaves, they acquired under ordinary circumstances for the paterfamilias, yet :—

(1) They acquired *civilly* for themselves those things which, from their nature, could not be acquired by the paterfamilias, *e.g.*, in *adstipulation* (*post*, par. 1377).

(2) They were *civilly* bound, not only as in the case of slaves for crimes, but for contracts and all causes of obligation which remained with the son, for they could not bind the father, and yet the obligation was valid, so that the son could be sued, even in the lifetime of the paterfamilias; and, if he had no *peculium* or other separate estate, he was permitted by Justinian (Cod. 7, 71, 7) to compromise with his creditors by making a *cessio bonorum* of future acquired property—but see *post*, par. 2217.

The extent of the power of *women sui juris* during the existence of the doctrines as to perpetual tutelage *(ante*, par. 254) to bind *themselves* is not very clear, and is disputed by Cujas, but the *s.c. Macedonianum* and the above mentioned *cessio bonorum* applied to both sons and daughters.

Tit. xviii. De divisione stipulationum.

1304. The contract *verbis* resulted from the will, *i.e.*, the spontaneous agreement of the parties, but in some cases it was enjoined by law, as for example, under the *legis actiones*, where it was required in the *sacramentum* action from the guarantors of the costs (*prædes sacramenti*), and from the guarantors of the party who had provisional possession (*prædes litis et vindiciarum*). Under the *formula procedure*, the *sponsio* and *restipulatio* was required, in *e.g.*, the *certæ creditæ pecuniæ* action and in some interdicts, and the *stipulatio pro præde litis et vindiciarum* was employed in vindications, and the *stipulatio judicatum solvi* in the *formula petitoria*, and of the same character was the *vadimonium*, or stipulation that the defendant will appear *in jus*. Under the *judicia extraordinaria* a similar system existed, as to which, see *post*, par. 2237.

But besides this class of cases, stipulations might also be imposed by authority, either in the form of a *nuda repromissio* from the obligor, but usually coupled with the *satisdatio* of sureties. The compulsory formulæ of these stipulations were inserted in the edict, and they could be made by a *cognitor* or *procurator* as *representatives*, with a *utilis* actio given for or against the real obligor.

1313. The text, following Pomponius, divides stipulations into four kinds, according to the source whence they were derived, viz.:—

1. *Judiciales*, *i.e.*, made when the parties were *in judicio*, and arising *a mero judicis officio*, and enforced by loss of the suit in default of the promise being made, *e.g.*, the stipulation *de dolo cautio*, which was a *nuda repromissio* given by the possessor, that he had not damaged the thing restored, or that poison had not been administered to the slave restored to the owner. The stipulation *de persequendo servo*, with the penalty attached, *restituendove pretio*, by which the possessor in good faith, who acquired him by the termination of the period of usucapion pending the trial, and who, therefore, alone could institute an action to recover him, was bound to pursue and recover for the rightful owner a slave who had fled and, if he failed, to pay the price.

(2). *Prætoriæ*, *i.e.*, made when the parties were *in jure*, and enforced by handing over the possession of the thing or seizing security, or giving or refusing actions. Examples are—(a) the *cautio damni infecti*, given either by *nuda repromissio* or *satisdatio*, and claimed by a neighbour as a guarantee against apprehended damage, where the adjoining house was in a ruinous condition, as by the civil law, in the absence of such a claim, the owner of the latter could escape all liability by abandoning his house on its fall. If a surety was not forthcoming in the given interval, the claimant could get *possessio* of the building, so threatening him, and if default was still made in respect of the guarantee, and after another interval, and verification of the facts, an order to possess was given under which the proprietor could be expelled, and the holder of the order acquired all the rights of possession with their legal effects, including usucapion, etc. (β) The *legatorum cautio* enabled the legatee to get the interim custody of the thing (see *ante*, par. 990). (γ) Amongst *Ædilitiæ* stipulations which were derived from the edict of the Ædiles, and, included under the Prætorian, is to be noted, the vendor's guarantee by *nuda repromissio* and enforced by the *actio redhibitoria*, against such vices in the object sold as entitled the purchaser to return it.

(3) *Conventionales*. These derive their origin from the agreement of the parties only.

(4) *Communes, i.e.,* those which might be ordered either by the *Prætor* or by the *judge; e.g.*, the stipulation *Rem salvam fore pupillo* (*ante*, par. 275) which might be ordered to be given *in judicio—si aliter hæc res expediri non potest*—as where a tutor before giving security sued a debtor of the pupil, and the debtor demurred that no *satisdatio* had been given, in which case, sentence would be void; and, to prevent the suit being interrupted, the judge would order security to be given. For the *de rato* stipulation, see *post*, par. 2237.

Tit. xix. De inutilibus stipulationibus.

1324. The *stipulation* being the most common form of obligation, the remarks in this title are confined to it; though this subject ought to have been generalised and included in an examination as to the conditions necessary to the validity of *all* contracts.

1328. If a stipulation was clearly *nullius momenti (inutilis)* by the *civil* law, the Prætor was bound to refuse its enforcement by action, and the *datio* was null *ab initio* of things *quæ natura sui, dominio nostro exempta sunt,* as *sacred* or *religious* things, though thought to be profane (good faith forming no part of this contract, the *stipulation* deriving its force from the civil law); and so as to *public* things, *e.g.*, a forum, theatre, etc.; or in respect of a *free man* thought to be a slave, or a thing of which the promissor had not the *commercium*; but this was not true of obligations generally, *i.e.*, the person making the promise might be liable in damages for non-execution (see *post*, par. 1486); or if the thing was the stipulator's own property, though a promise in respect of the value of it might be valid. The fact of the property subsequently becoming capable of sale, etc., did not render the stipulation valid, for *quod initio vitiosum est, non potest tractu temporis convalescere* (*ante*, par. 857); so also the stipulation was *extinguished* if the object became impossible of delivery without the *fault*, or *mora*, (*post*, par. 1655) or the *act* of the promissor, and the better opinion was, that it could not revive (see *post*, par. 1711).

1336 (§ iii). From the general axiom *Res inter alios acta aliis neque nocere neque prodesse potest*, was deduced the rule respecting contracts, that *certissimum est ex alterius contractu neminem obligari* (Cod. 4, 12, 3), and therefore, if in a contract we bind a third party and not ourselves, we neither bind him nor ourselves; as, *e.g.*, if a husband managing the affairs of his wife bought property in the name of his wife. This applies with peculiar force in the *stipulation*, for the contract is here formed *verbis*, and only between those pronouncing the words (*ante*, par. 1235) according to the rule, *alteri stipulari nemo potest*, though if the third party had an interest in it, the promissee could compel the promissor to execute, as *e.g.*, if A was bound to build a house for B, and A stipulated that C should build it for B, then A could compel C; and so a tutor on ceding the administration of the property of his pupil to a co-tutor, could stipulate *rem pupilli salvam fore*, as he still remained liable for the due administration and therefore had an interest; and so, if a penal clause were added, it would render the stipulation valid, for this amounts to inserting a condition, *e.g.*, it would be useless if A said, "Do you B promise to give to C"; but it was made valid if A added, "and if not to give me (A) 100 solidi".

1339. A stipulation that a sum shall be paid *mihi aut Seio* is valid in favour of the *stipulator*, for Seius is only to receive for me (*solutionis causa*); but the payment may be validly made to Seius in spite of me, and though Seius is not compelled to receive, yet if he does do so, I have the *mandati actio* against him to account to me for the *whole*; but if the words were *sibi et alii*, the *Proculians'* opinion was adopted by *Justinian* (over-ruling that of *Gaius*, Inst., iii, § 103, and the Sabinians), and the stipulation was held only valid for half the subject matter of the contract.

1341. The promissor could not bind another, and such a stipulation was therefore useless unless a penal clause had been inserted (*ante*, par. 1336); though if he binds himself to get a third to do such and such a thing the promissor is liable.

1342. The exceptions to the above rules were :—

(1) The promissor or the promissee could include their *heirs*, and this generally followed in law as a matter of course.

(2) The paterfamilias could stipulate for his slave or for his son in power, and he himself acquired, but subject to the rules as to the son's peculium, and as to *personal* acquisitions.

(3) The person in power could stipulate and the paterfamilias acquire (*ante*, par. 616, 1289; and *post*, par. 2201).

(4) In respect of *procuration*, necessity early modified the strict law; as, *e. g.*, in the case of the stipulation made by a public slave, *rem pupilli salvam fore* (*ante* par. 1313, 4). So *Prætorian* stipulations could be made through third parties; and the agents of municipalities (*actores municipum*), the tutor of the pupil, the curator of the lunatic or minor, could act in behalf of their respective principals; but where a procurator was employed in this manner, the action for enforcing the contract was only *utilis*.

1345. (§ v) The *words* of the promise and of the stipulation must agree, otherwise there was no contract; and the opinion of *Gaius* (Inst. iii, § 102) was confirmed by Justinian that, *e. g.*, *si decem aureos a te dari stipuletur, tu quinque promittas, vel contra*, the stipulation was useless, though Ulpian and Paul thought it valid for one-half; but the repetition of the words by the promissor was not necessary, as the simple promise was held to include the terms of the stipulation, though a mere sign of assent without words would not suffice.

1348. (§ vii) Neither the *dumb* nor the absolutely *deaf* person could stipulate; and the stipulation or promise of an insane person was only valid if made in a lucid interval. The *prodigus interdictus* could only stipulate.

1350. (§ ix) It followed as a deduction from the rules given in part ii, par. 86, and *ante* par. 244, that the right to *stipulate* was acquired by a pupil as soon as he could *speak;* and though, in progress of time, the tendency was to look not to the physical power of speech, but to the fact of opening intelligence, which is usually a later development, still the expressions used by *Gaius* (Inst. iii, § 107, 109), repeated by *Justinian* here, and by *Theophilus* in his paraphrase, indicate that the earlier ideas still lingered.

1357. (§ xi) Stipulations, as in the case of all contracts involving an *impossible, illegal,* or *immoral* condition, were null and void (see *ante,* par. 735); but a stipulation with a condition *not to do* a physically impossible condition (*ante,* par. 924) was regarded as pure and simple, and therefore valid; *e.g.*, *si digito cœlum non attigero dare spondes?* unless the condition was not to do something contrary to law or morals, for then it would arise *ex turpi causa* (*Quod turpi ex causa promissum est veluti si quis homicidium vel sacrilegium se facturum promittat non valet*), though it would be *valid*, as being in the nature of a penalty, where a sum was to be paid if the promissor did do an *illicit* or *immoral* act, because this would be *ex bonis moribus concepta,* unless the promisee was concerned in the illicit act; and the case of divorce was excepted for special reasons.

1359. (§ xii) As the *verbal* contract could not, owing to the necessity for the oral assent of both parties, take place between *absent* persons, an *alibi* was a frequent method of denying the existence of the contract where a long interval had elapsed since its formation. To obviate this, and as a method of proof only, *Justinian* directed (A.D. 531, Cod. 8, 38, 14) that a *writing* might be prepared of what had passed (see *post,* par. 1687), signed by the *promissor* or *witnesses ;* and if *only* the *promise* was reduced to writing, the previous interrogation was, in the absence of contrary proof, implied; and this was to have the force of an irrebuttable presumption, unless an alibi for the whole day (*toto eo die*) could be proved by the clearest evidence in *writing* or by irreproachable witnesses.

1361. Justinian made valid stipulations framed so that the actions resulting from the obligation would only arise in favour of or against the *heirs* of the deceased stipulator or promissor, and which, on the ground of inconsistency (*inelegans,* Gai. Inst. iii, § 100), had been regarded as void, *e. g.*, *post mortem meam dari spondes?* or *quum mortuus eris, dari spondes?* though *cum moriar* was always valid, because the obligation began in the lifetime of the contracting parties, see *ante*, par. 924 (3); and (extending to testaments and all contracts what the Emperor Leo had already conceded in the case of the *dos*) he also made valid stipulations *præpostere concepta, i. e.*, in which the date fixed for payment was anterior to the accomplishment of the condition, *e. g.*, *si navis ex Asia venerit, hodie dare spondes?* in which case, though payment could not be demanded until the condition was fulfilled, the stipulator acquired some present rights in respect of the sum due.

1367. (§ xviii) If the promissor replied that he would give *one* of the things mentioned by the stipulator, the stipulation would be valid, but for that one only, *e. g.*, *Stichum Pamphilum et Erotem dare spondes?* the answer *spondeo* would include all, but *Stichum dare spondeo* would only bind the promissor in respect of Stichus; and to *Stichum aut Pamphilum dare spondes?* the answer *Stichum spondeo* would render the stipulation *invalid, ante,* par. 1345.

1370. (§ xxiii) As *error* was a cause of nullity, the axiom *non videntur qui errant consentire* was applied to all contracts, but not to all in the same degree. In the stipulation, *consent* being involved in the pronunciation of the words, the contract was only void if there was a material error as to the individual thing itself (*de re*), as in the example given in the Institutes, *si hominem Stichum a te quis stipulatus fuerit, tu de Pamphilo senseris quem Stichum vocare credideris;* otherwise (except as regards any Prætorian remedies), if agreed about the *thing*, an error as to the substance was immaterial, *e. g.*, copper supposed to be gold; and *dolus malus* (unless met by a Prætorian exception see part ii, par. 164) was strictly no cause of nullity of the stipulation, if it had not occasioned error as to the thing itself; and the same rule applied in respect of *violence,* for the person promising was held to have elected between the evil avoided and the consent given (*Quia quamvis, si liberum esset, noluissem, tamen coactus volui*, Dig. 4, 2, 21, 5, Paul); but Prætorian remedies, including restitution, were available to meet such cases.

1376. Strictly, the *cause* or *motive* leading to the *obligatio verbis* was quite immaterial; and though, if the contract was reduced to writing (*cautio, ante*, par. 1359), it generally began with an exposition of the causes; these were held to be mere recitals, but under Prætorian *equity* the practice was introduced of ascertaining whether the consideration, upon which the contract was asserted to have been made, existed as a fact.

1377. *Adstipulator.* When the strict law was in force as to the absolute exclusion of *procuration*, or, later, when such representation was only admitted with embarrassing formalities, absence or other cause might induce a stipulator to add another to himself, so as to enable the latter to acquire the benefit of the contract, and hence the person so joined filled the double office of *mandatary* to the principal stipulator and *creditor* of the promissor. From this it followed (a) that the adstipulation, though it need not be in precisely the same terms, could only come *after* and as *accessory* to the first stipulation (*ante*, par. 1264, 2), that (β) it must be about the *same* thing, and could not include *more*, though it might include *less*, and that (γ) it was *personal* to the adstipulator, as being a confidence reposed in the particular individual by the principal obligee, so that the resulting right and action could not be transmitted by him to another, even to his heirs. Hence, as a slave could only validly stipulate for his master, he could not be an *adstipulator*, nor, according to the better opinion, a free man *in mancipio*, as being assimilated to a slave; but a *filius-familias* might, though the right would only be exercisable when he became *sui juris*, and provided he had not suffered *capitis deminutio*, and similar rules applied to the *filia-familias* and the wife *in manu* (Gai. Inst., iii, § 110 to 114).

As the adstipulator was a true *creditor*, he had (1) the action arising out of the contract, as well as (2) the right to receive payment (though liable as a mandatary to hand over the proceeds under the *mandati actio*), and even (3) to gratuitously release the debtor (though liable under the second head of the *Lex Aquilia*, *post*, par. 1746), and it was this last danger which led to the *disuse* of the adstipulator, especially after the facilities for acting by procuration increased; so that in the time of *Gaius* (Inst. iii, § 117) the adstipulation was only employed in the case of the stipulation *post mortem suam*, which would otherwise be *invalid* (*ante*, par. 1361); but in consequence of the accessory contract, the heirs could obtain the benefit of it from the adstipulator by the *mandati* action. As under *Justinian* such stipulations were in themselves valid, the name of *ad*stipulator does not occur in the Institutes.

1384. *Sponsores and fidepromissores.* An additional *debtor* (*promissor*) was still more frequently employed, and this *cautio* became general for all kinds of obligations; but the particular terms employed were not in this case indifferent, as they gave rise to different classes of sureties. From the word *spondes*, which was exclusively restricted to Roman citizens, came the (1) *sponsores* (*idem dari spondes?*), whilst the question *fidepromittis?* was admitted as equivalent in the case of *peregrini*, and gave rise to the (2) *fidepromissores* (*idem fidepromittis?*), and a further extension, *fidejubes?* originated the class of (3) *fidejussores* (*post*, par. 1392).

As the *fidepromissio* was only an extension of the *sponsio*, so as to include *peregrini*, the first two classes nearly blend, and they correspond exactly to, and fall under the same rules as, those which apply to the *adstipulator*, so that (α) they could only be used in *verbal* contracts (Gai. Inst., iii, § 119); (β) they were employed to avoid the nullity of the original contract; (γ) the accessory promise must be given immediately after the principal one; (δ) be about the *same* thing; (ε) not include *more*; and (ζ) it was *personal*. The *mandati actio* could be used to compel the *principal* promissor to reimburse his surety that which he had paid.

The position of these sureties was regulated by several *plebiscita*, viz. :—

(1) The *Lex Apuleia* (*de sponsu*) (B.C. 102) created as of right a sort of partnership between *sponsores* and *fidepromissores*, so that one of them could sue the remainder by the *pro socio* action, if he had paid more than his share; and as this law, by making them partners, made it necessary to know who was going to be associated with them, if the creditor did not plainly declare what the object was, and how many *sponsores* or *fidepromissores* he relied upon (Gai., Inst., iii, § 123); the sureties had thirty days within which to show that, as this declaration had not been made, they were discharged from liability.

(2) The *Lex Furia* (*de sponsu*) (? B.C. 95) applied only to Italy, and by it the obligation only endured two years and *divided*, so that, as between those living at the time of the demand (Gai. Inst., iii, § 121), each could be sued only for his share, *i.e.*, *per capita*.

(3) A *Lex Cornelia* was passed by Cornelius Sylla (B.C. 81), probably because *fidejussores* were employed to escape the effect of the *Leges Apuleia* and *Furia*. It applied to *all* sureties, and, excepting only certain special cases, it made any excess over 20,000 sesterces invalid when the same person bound himself for the same debtor, towards the same creditor in the same year (Gai. Inst., iii, § 124, 125).

(4) A *Lex Publilia* (? date) gave *sponsores* (only) a special *actio depensi* against the principal debtor to obtain restitution of so much as had been paid by them for him, and the condemnation was in *double* if the claim was disputed (Gai. Inst., iii, § 127, and Paul Sent., i, 19, § 1).

Tit. xx. De Fidejussoribus.

1392. This class of surety completely supplanted the *sponsores* and *fidepromissores*, as they could be employed in any kind of obligation (even in those arising out of delicts), and for any *person* whether the contract was *civil*, *Prætorian*, or *natural*, so that, *e.g.*, if a slave contracted some obligation towards his master, though only *natural*, with no resulting action, yet the debt could be made binding, as a *fidejussor* and his *heirs* might be made liable in a civil action arising from his promise as surety.

The accessory contract might *precede* (in which case it would be in suspense until the existence of the principal debt), or follow the principal obligation; and when there were several sureties, each was liable in *solidum*, but *Hadrian* (Gai. Inst., iii, § 121, 122) allowed the fidejussores to *demand* the *beneficium divisionis* amongst those *solvent* at the time of the *litis contestatio*, so that up to that time they were answerable for the insolvency of the rest, and they would be liable for the whole if they failed to take advantage of this permission.

As in the case of the *sponsores* and *fidepromissores*, the *fidejussores* could not bind themselves for *more* than the principal debt, whether in respect of *amount, time*, or *condition*, though they might be liable for *less*. The *Lex Cornelia* (*ante*, par. 1384, 3) also applied to them, and they had the *actio mandati* against the principal debtor to recover that which they had been compelled to pay; and if the payment had been made without the knowledge or in the absence of the principal debtor, the action would be *negotiorum gestorum*, but by the better opinion, *no* action would lie if done against his will or out of liberality to the principal debtor (*donandi animo*).

As early as the time of *Ulpian*, the words or the language used were immaterial, and proof in *writing* of an agreement to become fidejussor was presumptive evidence that all the requisite formalities had been observed.

1400. The term *satisdatio* equally applied to the three kinds of sureties, and the expression *satis-accipere* referred to *receiving* this kind of *cautio* by *guarantors*, and *satisdare* denoted *giving* the security.

1401. *Actions relating to the adstipulatio and adpromissio.* In respect of the *adstipulator* there were the—

(1) *Condictio certi* (or *actio ex stipulatu*), which was extinguished at his death and lay against the *promissor*.

(2) *Actio mandati* (or *damni injuriæ* under the *Lex Aquilia*) for the *principal* stipulator against him.

The *sponsores* and *fidepromissores* being connected in three ways (1) with the creditor, (2) with the principal debtor, and (3) between themselves, the following actions lay, viz. :—

(1) *Actio ex stipulatu (condictio certi)*, for the *creditor* against them, subject in Italy to the restrictions of the *Lex Furia* (*ante*, par. 1384, 2).

(2) *Actio mandati*, for them against the principal debtor, and the *sponsor* had also the special action *depensi* by the *Lex Publilia*.

(3) *Actio pro socio*, given by the *Lex Apuleia* between themselves, though this, after the *Lex Furia*, could only arise in the provinces.

In respect of the *fidejussores* the actions were:—

(1) *Ex stipulatu (condictio)*, open to the creditor against them.

(2) *Actio mandati* (or *negotiorum gestorum*), open to them against the principal debtor, and though *no action* lay between themselves (except by special agreement), they had under *Justinian* three remarkable advantages, viz., the *beneficium:*—

(a) *Ordinis* (or *excussionis*), given by a *novel* (No. 4, A.D. 539), under which the fidejussor could insist on the principal debtor being first sued, his liability only extending to any unpaid balance; and, if the principal debtor was absent, a fixed period must intervene before the fidejussor could be sued; whereas, formerly the creditor could sue either the principal debtor or any one out of several fidejussores, though after the *litis contestatio*

T

the others were released prior to a constitution of *Justinian* (A.D. 531), which enacted that the action against one should not release the others. See *post*, par. 1557 (2).

(β) *Divisionis*, given by Hadrian (*ante*, par. 1392).

(γ) *Cedendarum actionum*. If, *instead* of claiming the benefit of division, the fidejussor chose, not to pay the amount, for that would *extinguish* the debt, but to buy up the *whole* (but it must be the whole) debt, he could stand in the place of the creditor, *i.e.*, become a *procurator in rem suam*, for a debt could not be otherwise legally transferred from one to another, and then the stipulator was compelled to give him the right to all his actions, pledges, and mortgages, so that the fidejussor had not only his own proper *actio mandati* (or *negotiorum gestorum*) against the principal debtor, but also those of the original creditor, as well as actions against his own co-fidejussors, and this under *Justinian* even after he (the fidejussor) had been sued and condemned.

1411. *Senatus consultum Velleianum*. After *women* had acquired the power of incurring *obligations*, it became necessary to protect them, and even under *Augustus* edicts had *invalidated* obligations sustained by the *wife* in respect of any debt of her *husband.* Under *Claudius* the *s.c. Velleianum* (A.D. 46, Marcus Silanus and Velleius Tutor consuls), the text of which is given by *Ulpian* (Dig. 16, 1, 2, 1), forbad *women* in any way to bind themselves *for any one (pro aliis reæ fieri)*, *i.e.*, women were not forbidden to bind themselves *to pay at once for another*, but to incur any liability in the future for another. If so bound they could defend themselves by means of the *exceptio* of the *s.c. Velleianum*, or recover the amount back if already paid by the *condictio indebiti*, *i.e.*, the obligation existed under the civil law, but the Prætor refused to grant an action against them unless there was *dolus* or (under *Justinian*, Cod. 4, 29, 22, 23), the woman was over twenty-five and had confirmed the obligation after an interval of two years.

The expression *intercedere* refers to this voluntary binding of oneself for the debt of another, whether by releasing him or remaining bound with him and for him, and the agreement to bind oneself is called *intercessio*, he who thus binds himself being the *intercessor*, these terms being general and including all kinds of suretyship.

Tit. xxi. De litterarum obligatione.

1414. The introduction of writing led to a system of recording family accounts. The items were roughly noted at the time in the *adversaria*, which were destitute of probative force *(Itaque adversaria in judicium protulit nemo: codicem protulit, tabulas recitavit.* Cicero, Pro Q. Roscio Comædo, Orat. 3, § 2), but the entries made from these every month in the *tabulæ* or *codex* were received as evidences of the debt (part ii, par. 172 and 201), though the *traditio of the money* constituted the contract (Gai. Inst., iii, § 131). The *name* of the creditor or debtor being thus inscribed, gave rise to debts being called *nomina* and sometimes *arcaria nomina*, because the sum which they recorded came from the chest or coffer *(arca)*.

In course of time this method of keeping accounts gave rise to the civil contract *litteris*, in which the obligation was drawn down, and the contract formed, the moment the *creditor*, with the *consent* of the debtor, had entered the amount in his ledger, *i.e.*, the contract was based upon the agreement of the two parties, the one to consider the sum weighed and given *(pecunia expensa lata)*, and the other to consider it as weighed and received *(accepta relata)*. The fact of the entry, by the *creditor*, of the transaction in the *codex* in the consecrated formula, was a presumption that for this entry *(expensi-latio)* the *debtor* had given his *order* or at least *consent*, for he might be absent at the time, the entry itself being made from the waste-book *(adversaria)* at the end of the month *(sed absenti expensum ferri potest, etsi verbis obligatio cum absente contrahi non possit.* Gai. Inst., iii, § 138). The usual method was (1) for the *creditor* to enter the sum *expensa lata* with the *consent of the debtor;* and (2) for the *debtor* to enter the same sum in his *codex* as *accepta relata*, but the absence of (2) did not vitiate the contract, as the evidence of the *entry*, and proof that it was made with the *consent* of the *debtor*, sufficed.

The use of the *stipulation* was extended in various ways, but the contract *litteris* remained restricted to ascertained sums of money *(certa pecunia)*. It could *not* be made subject to a condition, and the cause of whatever kind must be anterior, for the supposition of a weighing and of a *mutuum* was implied. If it took place immediately after the transaction that led to it, the two formed but one contract, otherwise the contract *litteris* acted as a *novatio*, and the new contract so effected (called *nomen transcriptitium*) dated from the entry made in the ledger *(codex)* from the waste-book *(adversaria)*. Being *stricti juris*, the consideration was immaterial, though the Prætor might intervene with the *exceptio doli* (see *post*, par. 1435). Like the *mutuum*, the contract gave rise to the *condictio certi*; and from the analogy of the *obligatio litteris* to the *mutuum* and the *stipulatio*, Cicero (Pro Q. Roscio Comædo, Orat. 3, § 4) says that the contract giving rise to a claim of *certa pecunia* in a *stricti juris* action, must necessarily have been *re, verbis*, or *litteris*, *i.e.*, the money must have been *data* or *stipulata* or *expensa-lata*.

According to *Gaius* (Inst., iii, § 129, 130), the *nomen transcriptitium* might be :—

(1) *a re in personam, i.e.*, when I, by your order, debit you in my ledger with what you owe me, as the result of some previous transaction, and—

(2) *a personâ in personam, i. e.*, when I debit you by your order, in the place of Titius, that which the latter owes me; the previous transaction in the first case, and the debt of Titius in the second, being extinguished by *novatio* and replaced by the contract *litteris*.

The practice of recording every act connected with the patrimony in the domestic *tabulæ* was observed with scrupulous exactness up to the time of *Cicero*, but probably only the registration in the ledger of *nomina transcriptitia* was in vogue when *Gaius* lived. Under Theodosius the use of the latter was confined to bankers *(argentarii, mensularii, nummarii)*, and prior to *Justinian* the system had disappeared altogether.

1429. *Chirographa, syngraphæ, cautiones.* Gaius (Inst., iii, § 133) refers to the dispute between the rival schools on the subject of the contract *litteris*, the *Proculians* holding that it was inapplicable to any but Roman citizens, whilst the *Sabinians* argued that *peregrini* could make use of it in the form *a re in personam;* but sometime prior to the existence of these schools, another form of the contract *litteris* had come into use for *peregrini*, viz., that constituted by the *chirographum* (when given by the obligor only) and *syngraphæ* (when copies kept by the debtor and creditor), for these documents contained a declaration of the sum owing or to be owed, and served to effect a *novatio* of any pre-existing agreement, and as such are to be distinguished from the *scriptura, libellus, charta, chartula,* and other writings used merely for the purpose of proof (*Fiunt, ut quod actum est per eas facilius probari possit.* Dig. 22, 4, 4, *Gaius*). The *syngraphæ* were the most ancient and disappeared first, but as the term *cautio* came specially to mean a written promise to pay an ascertained sum of money *(certa pecunia)*, generally resulting from a *mutuum*, and as such was synonymous with *chirographum,* the *cautio* in this restricted sense referred to the *chirographum,* and so represented the ancient contract *litteris* in the time of *Justinian.*

1435. *The exceptio non numeratæ pecuniæ.* The effect of a mere memorandum *(cautio)* handed by a debtor to a creditor was, that if the latter sued by the *actio empti, locati, pro socio, damni injuria,* or other action, according to the case, the *burden of proof* fell on the debtor to disprove the existence of the debt, unless the *cautio* did not sufficiently indicate the exact nature of the obligation *(indiscrete loquitur)*, in which case the *creditor* was compelled to prove his case. If, however, by *novatio* the contract had become a *nomen transcriptitium,* then, as this of itself gave rise to a *condictio,* and was conclusive evidence of liability, the debtor was estopped from pleading, except that, if there was a total absence of consideration, Prætorian equity allowed the debtor to oppose the *exceptio non numeratæ pecuniæ* (*i.e.,* the *exceptio doli mali,* drawn up *in factum post,* par. 2263). This plea, as in all cases of exceptions (*post,* par. 2248), required proof, but, probably because the *chyrographum* in the case of the *mutuum* was often made before the handing over of the money, so that the obligatory force of the contract *litteris* enabled the creditor to commit fraud, a special alteration was made, and the doctrine of the necessity of consideration as the basis of the contract was so far admitted that the creditor was compelled to prove the delivery of the money if the debtor asserted that he had not received it. This rule was found, however, to place the debtor in too favourable a position, and therefore a constitution of *Marcus Aurelius* limited the time to *five* years (reduced by Justinian to *two* years), within which the debtor could (1) oppose the *exceptio doli mali* or (*non numeratæ pecuniæ*) to the *creditors'* action, or (2) bring a *condictio* to recover the *chirographum* itself, or (3) render his exception *perpetual* by formally giving the creditor notice of it in the prescribed manner (Cod. 4, 30, 14). As soon as this interval *(legitimum tempus)* was passed, the *chirographum*, or even the *cautio*, acquired its obligatory force, so that the *onus probandi* was shifted and the *debtor* had to prove the non-receipt of the money (see part ii, par. 176).

Tit. xxii. De consensu obligatione.

1442. The contracts of the civil law previously enumerated, viz., the *mutuum, verbis,* and *litteris*, were unilateral and regulated *stricti juris*, but the four *consensual* contracts of the *jus gentium* were bilateral and enforced by actions *bonæ fidei* (see part i, par. 333; and part ii, par. 201).

Tit. xxiii. De emptione et venditione.

1444. Prior to the introduction of money, *sales* were, in fact, *exchanges*; and after the use of stamped pieces, in lieu of metal weighed each time, the idea was still retained, and the thing exchanged for the money was called *merx*, and the money exchanged for the thing *pretium*; hence, *Sabinus* and *Cassius* urged (Gai. Inst., iii, § 141) that exchange *(permutatio)* should be on the same footing as *emptio-venditio*, though the opinion of *Proculus* prevailed, and *permutatio* was not held to produce any bond unless it was followed by *execution* on at least one side, whereas the *emptio venditio* contract of the *jus gentium* might be *executory*, and its obligatory force resulted from the simple agreement of the parties.

1447. *The form of the contract of sale.* By ante-*Justinian* law, the sale was complete the moment the parties were agreed as to the thing and the price, but after *Justinian*, when the parties had agreed to reduce the contract to writing, only a non-obligatory pact existed *(pœnitentiæ locus est)* until the document had been drawn up either in the hand-writing of the contracting parties or signed by them or formally prepared by a tabellio.

Prior to Justinian *arrha* meant a certain sum or any object, as a ring, given usually by the purchaser to the vendor as evidence of the completion of the contract *(emptio et venditio contrahitur simul atque de pretio convenerit . . . nam quod arrhæ nomine datur argumentum est emptionis et venditionis contractæ*, Gai. Inst., iii, § 139); and, unless there was a special agreement to the contrary, it was held equivalent to an *advance*, so that only the balance remained to be paid; but *Justinian* made the *arrha* a *means of retractation* by enacting that when earnest-money had been given—whether the contract of sale was in writing or not, and although there was no agreement to that effect—the *emptor* by *forfeiting his arrha*, and the *venditor* by restoring *double*, could be off the bargain.

1450. *The object of the obligations in the contract of sale.* There were reciprocal but different obligations entailed on the vendor and purchaser in respect of the two distinct things necessary to constitute the contract, viz. :—

(1) *A thing to be sold.* Except those things incapable of circulating in the ownership of man, this might be anything, including the property of another, provided the vendor had not deceived the purchaser on the point, good faith being involved in the contract, and including also the *rei speratæ emptio* or purchase of future but certain produce, as, *e.g.*, in the case of game bought at so much a head if any was killed, or the *spei emptio*, as, *e.g.*, buying the uncertain contents of a cast of the net.

(2) *A price agreed upon.* This must be certain, or at least *ascertainable*, and *Justinian* confirmed the opinion of *Proculus*, that if it was left to the arbitration of a third person, and he actually fixed a price, the contract was binding, and the Emperor Gordian decided (Cod. 4, 64, 1) that if an object, *e.g.*, a slave, was accepted by a vendor as the price *(pretii nomine)* of, *e.g.*, an estate, this contract would be a *sale* and not an exchange.

1457. *The effects of the contract of sale.* Being a contract of the *jus gentium*, its results were only very gradually determined. It did not transfer the ownership *(qui vendidit necesse non habet fundum emptoris facere: ut cogitur qui fundum stipulanti spopondit,* Dig. 18, 1, 25, Ulpian), but only produced bilateral obligations, which on the part of the *vendor* were restricted to :—

(1) *Rem præstare, i.e. rem tradere,* at the time and place agreed upon. This *traditio* involved putting the purchaser in possession as owner (*ante*, par. 411) by giving him *vacuam possessionem, i.e.*, a possession free from all obstacle, including the right to accessories and implying *rem licere habere, i.e.*, the faculty of having the thing, as lawful owner; but see *post*, par. 1476.

(2) *Evictionis nomine obligatur, i.e.*, the vendor was liable in damages *(in id quod interest)* to the emptor, if the latter was ejected from the whole or part by the real owner. This guarantee against *évictio* was called *auctoritatem præstare* (hence the meaning of *usus-auctoritas,* as applied to usucapion, for it was the guarantee against eviction procured by the requisite time of use), but the purchaser was bound to give the vendor notice of the action of ejectment *(litem denuntiare)* to enable him to defend it.

(3) *Liability for secret faults,* of a nature to diminish or destroy the use of the thing. The vendor was always liable for defects, the absence of which was specially warranted; but in other cases, as the contract was founded on good faith, it depended on their importance and on the knowledge of either party. The conse-

quences might be a right to damages, or to a diminution of the price, or to a rescission of the contract and return of the thing (*redhibitio*).

(4) *Dolum malum abesse præstare.* This was a general obligation, applying to all the *bonæ fidei* contracts of the *jus gentium*, and *after* the sale, but *before* delivery; the vendor was also liable for *culpa*, *i.e.*, he was bound, as custodian of the thing, to use the care of a good paterfamilias, and more than he would do in respect of his own property.

1465. Before the principles of the consensual contract were fully recognised, the purchaser used to stipulate for the *datio* or delivery of the property as well as for *vacua possessio*, and the edict of the *Curule Ædiles* (which regulated with great care the matter of sales —at first only in respect of the sale of slaves (*mancipia*) and beasts of burden (*jumenta*), but subsequently extended to all things) compelled, at least in the case of valuable things and slaves, a stipulation of *double the price* in case of *eviction*, and the *emptor* could sue the *vendor* to make this promise, as it was held to be implied (*Ex enim quæ sunt moris et consuetudinis in bonæ fidei judiciis debent venire.* Dig. 21, 1, 31, 20, Ulpian). The edict also gave the purchaser the same *dupla stipulatio*, in respect of certain secret faults, and two particular actions, viz., either the *actio*—

(1) *Æstimatoria* (or *quanto minoris*), for a reduction in the price, or the—

(2) *Redhibitoria*, for annulling the contract, whence the term *redhibitoria* vices.

1468. The obligations of the *emptor* were:—

(1) To pay the price at the time of the *traditio*, or on the day fixed.

(2) To transfer the *ownership* of the money (*emptor autem nummos venditoris facere cogitur*, Dig. 19, 1, 11, 2, Ulpian), so that if the money was not the property of the purchaser the vendor could *at once* bring an action *ex vendito* against him.

(3) To pay interest from the day of delivery.

(4) To reimburse the vendor for *bonæ fidei* expenses incurred after the conclusion of the sale, and in respect of the thing sold (*in re distracta*).

(5) Liability for *dolus* and also for *culpa*, as if, *e.g.*, neglected to give notice of eviction, etc.

Although before *traditio* the vendor still remained owner, yet, after the sale was *completed* and even before traditio, the resulting *obligation* bound the parties, so that any increase or decrease was the profit or loss of the *purchaser* (*periculum et commodum*), and the *whole* price was due, in spite of any loss, unless the vendor had specially rendered himself responsible for the risks as custodian. These rules, however, only applied to sales *in specie* and *per aversionem* (*i.e.*, in a lump), *uno pretio;* hence, they were inapplicable where the sale was conditional, or in the alternative (*Stichum aut Pamphilum*), or *in genere* (*e.g.*, a horse, a slave), or in respect of things sold *pondere numero mensurave*, as, until the things were ascertained, or weighed, or counted, or measured, the sale was not complete.

1475. After the emptor had paid the price, or obtained credit, or in any other way satisfied the vendor, the *traditio* of the thing by the vendor transferred the ownership; hence, it was a peculiarity in the contract of sale, that not only *traditio*, but also *payment* of, or satisfaction for, the price, was necessary in order that the ownership of goods sold and delivered might pass (see *ante*, par. 411).

1476. The validity of the sale of the property of *another* person rested upon the fact that contracts produced *obligations* only, not transferences of ownership (see part ii, par. 229); hence, if both knew of the defective title, or the vendor sold in good faith, and only the *emptor* knew of it, then, so long as the emptor continued to hold the property without being evicted, he could not come upon the vendor, and if both were ignorant of the fact that the property could not be sold, still the contract was held to exist, and actions could be brought to indemnify both, according to the circumstances of the case; but if the vendor *knowingly* sold the property of another to the emptor ignorant of the fact, then, since in *bonæ fidei* contracts, he was liable for *dolus malus*, the emptor would have at once an *ex empto* action to be indemnified, for as much as it was important to him that the property should have become his, so if the thing was not in commerce, *e.g.*, an article dedicated to *religion*, which the purchaser thought was private property, or a free man sold as a slave, the sale was not null, as in the stipulation (*ante*, par. 1328), but the vendor was liable for as much as it was the interest of the purchaser not to have been deceived.

1481. (§ iv) *Conditions and accessory pacts in the contract of sale.* If a term or condition was inserted, the sale was held to be pure and simple, but subject to a conditional cancellation, *e.g.*, (*suspensory* condition), *si Stichus intra certum diem tibi placuerit erit tibi emptus aureis tot,* or (*cancelling* condition) *ut si displicuerit intra certum diem inempta sit.*

Accessory pacts (leges emptionis venditionis), forming part of, and deriving their force from, the principal agreement, may modify its terms, *e.g.*:—

(1) The *in diem addictio, i.e.*, if, within a certain time, better terms were offered to the vendor, the sale to be annulled.

(2) The *Lex commissoria, i.e.*, if something was done contrary to the terms of the contract, the sale should be annulled, as if, *e.g.*, the price was not paid in time.

(3) The *redemption clause*, by which the vendor or his heir was to be at liberty to recover the thing on paying back the price within a certain time.

1486. *Rescission of the sale.* As to *redhibitoria* vices, see *ante*, par. 1457 and 1465. *Vis dolus*, or *læsio*, were also grounds for rescinding the contract, the last referring to a sale at too low a price (*minus pretium*), and was a subject of controversy with the commentators. It applied when less than half the true value, at the time of the sale, had been given (Cod. 4, 44, 2 and 8), but the purchaser could avoid the rescission by paying what was wanting of the full value (*justum pretium*).

1489. *Actions relating to the contract of sale.* Provided the party suing did not obtain more than was due to him, any or all the following actions existed concurrently, viz. :—

(1) *Empti (ex empto)*, for the purchaser, and *venditi (ex vendito)* for the vendor. These were exclusively applied to the contract of sale, and being *ex equo et bono* (*ex bona fide*) they could be used to cover all the consequences of the contract capable of appreciation by the judge.

(2) *Ex stipulatu* (or *condictio certi*), resulting from particular agreements, or from the Ædilitian Edict in respect of eviction and secret faults (*duplæ stipulatio*), see *ante*, par. 1465.

(3) *Æstimatoria (quanto minoris)* usually limited to one year.

(4) *Redhibitoria*, limited to six months.

(5) *Præscriptis verbis*, in respect of accessory pacts.

Tit. xxiv. De locatione et conductione.

1492. This contract bore a strong analogy to the *emptio venditio*, being *ultro citro-que* and *ex æquo et bono*, and grounded on mutual consent as to the price for hiring the particular object, though the innovation of Justinian (*ante*, par. 1447), as to the effect of an agreement to reduce the sale to writing applied also to this contract. The obligation was not, however, *præstare rem habere licere*, but only to procure the use or enjoyment (*præstare re uti, re frui licere*), or to do certain work. The different varieties were—*locatio-conductio*:—

(1) *Rerum*, *i.e.*, letting the use of a thing.

(2) *Operarum*, *i.e.*, services, as to take charge of a house, cultivate a field, navigate a ship.

(3) *Operis*, *i.e.*, work to execute, as to build a house.

The person who let or gave out the work was called *locator*, the person who hired or performed *conductor*, or *inquillinus* when tenant of a house, or *colonus* when tenant of a rural estate. The price was called *merces*, or *pretium*, and, in the case of *rent*, *pensio* (*reditus*) or *canon*.

The *merces* should be certain, and consist in money, hence if, *e.g.*, clothes are given to a tailor to mend, without fixing the price, the proper action would be *præscriptis verbis*, and so in respect of mutual *exchanges* of things. Justinian also decided that it would be a sale (overruling the opinion of *Cassius*, Gai. Inst. iii, § 147, as to its being a *sale* of the *material*, and a *hiring* of the *labour*), if Titius agreed to give a jeweller ten aurei for some rings to be made of a given weight and form out of gold belonging to the jeweller, though if Titius had provided the gold, and fixed a sum for the fashioning, it would be a hiring.

1501. (§ iii) *Emphyteusis (ante,* par. 510). This term does not appear until the constitutions of the lower Empire, and *Gaius* (Inst. iii, § 145) only speaks of the perpetual hirings of the *ager vectigalis* of municipia, which were classed under *locatio-conductio.* The origin of this form of contract must be traced through the struggles and difficulties arising out of the *ager publicus* of ancient Rome, the *ager vectigalis* of colonies, municipia, etc., and the *patrimoniales fundi, fundi rei privatæ, fundi fiscales,* of the Emperor, until the time when property of this kind in vast quantities *(latifundia)* had passed into the hands of private individuals, but owing to political difficulties, combined with the burden of the taxes, the greater part was left unproductive. At this period, the state, or the corporation, or other holder, finding it impossible by themselves or their mandataries to cultivate the land, let it out on a long term at a fixed rent. The improvements made by the tenant (the *conductor,* later *emphyteuta, emphyteuticarius)* on this *ager vectigalis* (later *prædium emphyteuticarium)* tended to give him a real interest in the land, engrafted (εν φυτευω) upon, but without destroying, the ownership of the *dominus, i.e.,* the state, or the corporation. Hence this contract, which sprang from the *locatio-conductio,* became assimilated to the *emptio-venditio,* and *Zeno* settled the disputes which arose as to its classification with the first or second, by placing it between the two as a particular kind of contract with its own action.

The definition of the contract has been a subject of difficulty owing to its being composed of

(1) The *real* right, for the existence of which, in favour of the *emphyteuta,* under *Justinian, quasi-traditio* was necessary. This fragment of the right of ownership was more extensive than even *usus-fructus,* and included (α) all services and produce of the thing, and, as possessor, this produce was acquired by mere separation from the soil, (β) power of disposing of the substance of the thing, (γ) power of making any modifications not deteriorating the property, (δ) power of alienating the right and transferring it, either *inter vivos* or at death, subject to certain reservations to owner.

(2) The *obligation* binding the parties, the principal part of which related to the due payment at the fixed periods of the *rent,* and this obligation was only destroyed by the *total* loss of the thing. In principle the *rent* was always a part of the *emphyteusis,* and if it existed without, it was usual to impose a nominal sum as the sign of ownership.

In the case of alienation to other than heirs the *consent* of the owner was required, and the custom became transformed into a law (regulated by *Justinian*) of paying for this consent by giving one-fiftieth of the estimated value *(laudemium)* of the *emphyteusis* to the owner at each alienation, and in case of *sale* the owner had a right of pre-emption. In default of alienation the lease descended to the *heirs* testamentary, or *ab intestato*, but the rights of the emphyteuta might be extinguished by various events, as by the agreement of the parties, or the total loss of the thing, or the expiration of the term (if any), or the death of the emphyteuta without any heir.

1511. *Superficies.* This real right (*jus superficiarum*), or fragment of ownership, was closely analogous to the *emphyteusis*, but applied only to the *construction* on the soil. It originated from, and was under the protection of, Prætorian law. The right granted to the *superficiarius* might be gratuitous, or for a lump sum, or for a periodical rent (*solarium, pensio*), and there was no special form for the contract.

1512. *Effects of the contract of hiring.* These consist in the reciprocal obligations entailed, *e.g.*, in the *locatio-conductio rerum*—
(1) The *locator* was bound to hand over the thing for the particular use during the agreed term, *i.e., præstare re uti licere,* or *re frui licere,* which included the guarantee against eviction, and reimbursement *ex æquo et bono* for necessary and useful expenses.
(2) The *conductor* was bound to pay the sum agreed upon, and return the thing at the expiration of the time, but he could claim an abatement *ex æquo et bono* if a fortuitous event or *vis major* had caused, before perception of the produce, the loss of a considerable part (*plusquam tolerabile est*).
The contract never gave any *real* right, as the *conductor* in respect of *possession* even, only held *for* the owner, and as his instrument.
In every kind of *hiring* both parties were responsible for *dolus*, including *culpa*, and were bound to use the care of a *pater-familias diligentissimus*, but the ordinary rules of the contract might be modified by *accessory pacts* (*leges conductionis*) or stipulations, and if anything was omitted it would be regulated by the rules of equity.

1515. *Extinction of the contract of hiring.* This occurred at the expiration of the time agreed upon *(impleto tempore conductionis)*, but the contract was held to be tacitly renewed if the conductor remained in possession with the knowledge of the locator.
The alienation of the thing by the *locator*, without covenanting for the continuance of the lease, terminated the letting, *i.e.*, neither the assignee nor the lessee of the assignor were bound to maintain it, there being no contract existing between them, but if the *conductor* was ejected he had a claim for damages against the *locator* or his heirs. Nonpayment of the rent for two years, or the misuse of the thing, or the owner proving indispensable want of it, or the hirer prevented from deriving the agreed enjoyment of it, were also grounds of rescission, but the death of the *conductor* or of the *locator* did not terminate the contract, for either of the heirs could continue it,

though in the hiring of services *(operarum)*, and of work to be executed *(operis)*, the death of the person who had let out his services, or undertaken the work, necessarily terminated the contract.

1520. *Actions relating to the contract of hiring.* These were :—
(1) *Actio locati* for the *locator*, and *conducti* for the *conductor*. Being *ex æquo et bono*, these actions covered both the contract and the accessory pacts, though actions in respect of any particular stipulations were also open, but the following specially referred to the letting of rural estates and houses, and were given for the purpose of acquiring certain real rights by way of guarantee for the execution of the obligation.

(2) *Serviana actio*, a real action (*in rem*) introduced by the Prætor *Servius*, and by which the locator of a *rural estate* sued the farmer, or any third holder, to recover the property of the farmer *specially pledged* for payment of the rent (see *post*, par. 2087).

(3) *Interdictum Salvianum*, introduced by the Prætor *Salvianus* for the pursuit of the same objects, in order to get *possession* of them when on a *rural* estate, and specially pledged for the rent.

(4) *Quasi-Serviana*, or *hypothecaria actio*, an extension of (2) to cover the case of property brought into a *house* by the *conductor*, and which was held tacitly pledged as a guarantee of the rent.

(5) *Interdict de migrando*, to prevent the *locator* impeding the *conductor* leaving the house with all his belongings, when the latter had fulfilled all his obligations.

(6) *Actio emphyteuticaria*, for either of the contracting parties in the *emphyteusis* to enforce the obligation. In addition to this, and to protect the *real* right of the *emphyteuta*, *utiles* actions were given him (*utilis vindicatio, utilis Publiciana, utilis confessoria, vel negatoria,* etc.) even against the owner, and the same method was adopted for the protection of the *superficiarius*, though these *real* rights never having been exactly defined, it was only by way of assimilation to ownership that they were indirectly protected.

Tit. xxv. De societate.

1523. The fact of *consent* was early recognised by the civil law as the foundation of this contract, and, as the reciprocal obligations were *similar*, both the contracting parties were called *socii*, and one action, viz., that *pro socio*, lay for both. The *societas* might be, according to Gaius (Inst. iii, § 148), either, (α) *universal (totorum bonorum)*, or (β) *particular (unius alicujus negociationis)*, but *Ulpian* (Dig. 17, 2, 5) distinguishes five kinds, viz. :—

(1) *Societas universorum bonorum*, under which all the lawful property of both parties became common, so that immediately, and without tradition, the ownership and real rights were shared.

(2) *Societas universorum quæ ex quæstu veniunt.* This was the kind of partnership always implied when nothing was deter-

mined, and by it inheritances, legacies, and donations were excluded, but all lawful gains or acquisitions (*quæstus*) *resulting* from the *acts or operations* of the partners, became common.

(3) *Societas negotiationis alicujus, i.e.*, a partnership in respect of a particular business, as to buy and sell slaves, oil, wine, or corn.

(4) *Societas vectigalis*, a special form of the last for farming the public revenues (*vectigal*).

(5) *Societas rei unius*, under which one object or some determined objects were in common, but the ordinary rules as to the acquisition of ownership were untouched by this form of partnership.

The respective capital of the partners need not be equal, and might consist of anything not unlawful or immoral. The obligation entailed was to bring the promised capital, or work, or industry, and, in the absence of special agreement to the contrary, *equal* shares of profit and loss were presumed, whatever the nature or amount of the capital respectively advanced, and the opinion of *Servius Sulpitius* (in opposition to that of *Quintus Mutius*) prevailed, that the parties might agree to unequal shares of *profit or loss*, and that one might share any *profit* on the whole business without sharing the *loss*, but an agreement excluding one from *all profit* (*leonina societas*) would be null and void. If the *profit* was to be shared in certain proportions, the same rule was implied as to the *loss*, and *vice versâ*, and a settlement of the shares might be referred to the arbitration of a third party.

1534. As a *tacit* authorization for one to carry on the common interests for the other was implied, the principles relating to the *mandatum* were involved, and:—

(1) *As between the partners themselves*, each one had claims on the others for expenses, obligations, and personal losses incurred by him in respect of the partnership; and he was liable to the others for their respective shares of profit, as well as for interest on so much as he had employed for his own profit. They were also liable to each other for *dolus*, but the personal diligence expected did not exceed that which a man employs about his *own* affairs, and therefore the amount of responsibility for *culpa* (*desidia, negligentia*) was restricted to gross negligence.

(2) *As regards third parties*, strictly, only the partner who contracted with the stranger had rights and actions against him, and *vice versâ;* but, as in other cases of a similar nature, *utiles* or prætorian actions were available, *e.g.*, if the interest of the remaining partners could only be maintained by themselves suing the third person, or the third person could sue if the thing had turned to the profit of the partners, or if the acting partner could be considered as the overseer or collector (*institor, exercitor*) of the others.

1537. The contract only existed between those who formed it; and therefore if a third person was substituted or associated with one partner this was held to be a private arrangement between the two, independent of the partnership (*socii mei socius meus socius non est*, Dig. 17, 2, 20, Ulpian); but the partnership might be variously modified, so as to be subject to a *condition*, as in the example given by Justinian (Cod. 4, 37, 6), *si ille consul fuerit*, or instead of being without limitation, *i.e.*, for life, it might be in force *to* or *from* a certain time; but there was no *eternal* partnership, as a partner could not be compelled to remain against his will (*In communione vel societate nemo compellitur invitus detineri*, Cod. 3, 37, 5), and therefore a contrary clause was null and void. Hence any of the partners might dissolve the partnership, but he would be liable to the others if the act was fraudulent, or any loss resulted from the dissolution, so that if in the *totorum bonorum societas* he retired because he had acquired an inheritance, he would be compelled to share it, on the ground that the act was done *callide (dolo malo)*; and so if the withdrawal was *intempestive, i.e.*, at an unseasonable moment, in which case, although his partners would be freed towards him, he did not release himself towards them *(Socium a se, non se a socio liberat*, Dig. 17, 2, 65, 3, *Paul*).

1539. The causes of *dissolution* are summed up by *Ulpian* (Dig. 17, 2, 63, 10) as follows:—

(1) *Ex personis*, as where one partner was dead, or so reputed, from having suffered *maxima* or *media c.d.*, or from other cause, as, *e.g.* (a), *publicatio, i.e.*, confiscation of his property with the fiscus for his successor; (β) *sectio bonorum, i.e.*, a sale for the profit of the public treasury, in consequence of being criminally condemned *(damnatus et proscriptus)*; or (γ) *emptio bonorum, i.e.*, the same kind of sale, but for the benefit of private individuals (see *ante*, par. 1161); (δ) *cessio bonorum, i.e.*, an assignment of his estate for the benefit of creditors, but *Justinian* only speaks of the *publicatio*, and the *cessio bonorum*, as universal sales, involving a new succession to the juridical *persona*, were not in use, and the dissolution only resulted from the fact of the partner being deprived of his property; hence the partnership could be renewed with the partner after the forfeiture of his property or his bankruptcy, for he could contribute his labour; and, as the contract of partnership belonged to the *jus gentium*, it could be formed with strangers (Gai. Inst. iii, § 153, 154), and therefore *media c.d.* would not impede its renewal. The partnership could also go on if there was a special agreement that the death of one should not dissolve the partnership of the remainder, for this was in fact equal to a new partnership, but the partners could not agree to continue the partnership with the *heirs* of a deceased partner, for they were uncertain persons, and only succeeded to the active and passive rights in the partnership at the moment of the death of the deceased partner; but in the case of the *societas vectigalis* (a) his *heirs* did participate in the profit and loss after the death of the partner, and (β) an agreement might be made beforehand to continue the partnership with the heirs.

(2) *Ex rebus, i.e.*, when the thing perished, or ceased to be in commerce, or the purpose of the partnership was accomplished or failed.

(3) *Ex voluntate, i.e.*, when one partner withdrew from the partnership by due notification (*renuntiatio*).

(4) *Ex actione, i.e.*, when by a stipulation or a suit to dissolve the partnership *novation* was effected.

(5) *Ex tempore, i.e.*, when the term had expired, as then each partner was free to withdraw.

1544. (§ ix) *Actions relating to partnership.* These were the actions:—

(1) *Pro socio*. This *bonæ fidei* action sprang directly from the partnership agreement, and was open to each partner in his own name for every kind of breach of the partnership duties, whether included in the contract or under accessory pacts, against his co-partners individually, according to their share; but as the bond was looked upon in the light of a *fraternity (quum societas jus quodammodo fraternitatis in se habeat)*, one partner could not be condemned towards another beyond the amount of his means (*in quantum facere potest*), though the Prætor's edict made a partner *infamous* who was condemned in this action (see *post*, par. 2336).

(2) *Communi dividundo*, in order to compel by a judicial decision the respective *shares* being handed over to each partner. So only that a partner did not obtain the same thing twice over this action might be used concurrently with the action *pro socio*, for the latter was to get the contract of partnership executed, whilst the *communi dividundo* was to cause the communion to cease as far as the thing divided was concerned, and therefore might be either *during*, or at the *end* of, the partnership.

(3) *Furti, vi bonorum raptorum, legis Aquiliæ, ex stipulatu*, etc. These actions would also lie for acts giving rise to them, so only that a partner did not obtain the same thing twice over.

Tit. xxvi. De Mandato.

1550. The expression *Mandatum (manu-datum)* had its origin in the sacredness and good offices of friendship. It then passed into the civil law as an agreement of the *jus gentium*, resting on simple, even tacit consent, and importing obligations *ex æquo et bono*.

The *mandatarius* was a *procurator* (*curare pro*) who acted, not as representative of, but as agent in his own name for, the *mandator* (*mandans*), and the contract involved *three* essentials, viz.:—

(1) It must be gratuitous.

(2) The care of the most diligent paterfamilias was required, at least on the part of the *mandator* (see as to the *mandatarius, post*, par. 1633); *e.g.*, if the mandatarius was ordered to buy a slave who had been guilty of theft, and he thieves from the mandatarius, the mandator was liable, although ignorant of the

vice; for, if he had used the prudence of a very diligent paterfamilias, he would have discovered the bad character of the slave.

(3) Infamy resulted from condemnation in the *actio mandati*.

Strictly, the contract only gave rise to an *unilateral* obligation on the part of the *mandatarius* to fulfil his mission with the greatest care, render an account, and hand over all the property and rights acquired; but the execution of the mandate would render the *mandator* liable to reimburse with interest the expenses incurred, and to release the agent from all obligation, as well as to indemnify him for injuries resulting from the *dolus* or *culpa* of the mandator; so that this contract is included under those termed imperfectly sunallagmatic.

1552. In all consensual contracts, an agreement could be come to through the medium of a messenger (*nuntius*) or letter (*ante*, par. 98); but in the case of the *mandatum*, as the *mandatarius* contracted in his own name, strictly it was he and the third party who were reciprocally bound towards one another; but in process of time this became purely nominal, and by indirect means the liability, and even the acquisition or alienation of possession or ownership, were brought home to the person for whom another had acted (see *ante*, par. 234, 608, 630, 1336, and *post*, par. 1669, 2201, 2228); so that, in imitation of the *institoria actio*, the third party acquired *utiles* actions against the *mandator*, e.g., the *condictio utilis*, for a *mutuum* or *stipulatio*, the *actio utilis empti* or *venditi*, in respect of a purchase or sale, and similar *utiles* actions, were given to the *mandator* against the third party (at least, in the case of a *special* mandate, though, when *general*, only as an extraordinary aid); and hence the third party was exposed to the *direct* action of the *mandatarius*, and to the *utilis* action of the *mandator*; but the former action could be repelled by an *exceptio*, when brought by the *mandatarius* against the wish of the mandator.

1557. In respect of the objects embraced, the *mandatum* might be either general (*generale*), *i.e.*, include all the mandator's affairs, or special (*speciale*), *i.e.*, restricted to a particular matter; and, in respect of the interest involved, the text, following *Gaius* (Dig. 17, 1, 2) has six divisions, viz.:—

(1) *Mandantis tantum gratia*. This was the most usual, and included such cases as the mandator asking you to manage his affairs, buy him an estate, or act as sponsor (*ante*, par. 1384).

(2) *Sua et tua; e.g.*, A, owing B 100 aurei, tells B to stipulate that sum from C, who owes it to A. This stipulation extinguishes by novation C's debt to A, and A's debt to B; but, if C does not pay, A remains liable as mandator, and B has an action *ex stipulatu* against C, and an action *mandati* against A. The example given by Justinian, of the *fidejussor* authorising the creditor to sue the principal debtor at the risk of the surety, had lost its interest at that time, as the law, in respect of the surety being released as a fidejussor, but liable on the mandate (see

ante, par. 1401), was altered A.D. 531, *i.e.*, two years before the date of the Institutes.

(3) *Aliena tantum;* *e.g.*, A, in B's absence, tells C to manage B's affairs, in which case A has no interest at first, and therefore reciprocal obligations do not arise until C has actually commenced to perform the mandate.

(4) *Sua et aliena;* *e.g.*, when property common to the mandator and a third party.

(5) *Tua et aliena;* *e.g.*, A tells B to lend money *at interest* to a third party, though, if without interest, the contract would be (3) only.

(6) *Tua tantum gratia.* This was useless *(supervacuum)*, as being mere counsel, *e.g.*, A tells B to put his money out in the purchase of an estate, instead of at interest; but the opinion of *Sabinus* prevailed that A would be liable if he told B to lend money to a particular person, because this would no longer be non-obligatory as mere counsel, for B would not have done it unless it appeared to be the intention of A, in giving the mandate, to render himself personally responsible, and not simply to give an opinion as to the solvency of the borrower, and the same reasoning applies if A told B to give time to B's debtor at A's risk.

The position of the mandator in (2) and (5), and in (6) when liable, bears a great analogy to that of the *fidejussor*, as he becomes a surety *(cautio)* towards the creditor for the debt. Hence these are particular kinds of *intercessio* (*ante*, par. 1411); and in the Digest Code and Novels are treated together under the title *De fidejussoribus et mandatoribus;* and hence also equity applied the rules relating to *accessory* contracts to both mandataries and fidejussors, so as to bring the former under, *e.g.*, the prohibitions of the *s. c. Velleianum* in respect of *women*, as well as the *beneficia discussionis, divisionis,* and *cedendarum actionum;* but a difference existed in that the counsel and influence of the *mandator* brought about the contract, so that he would find it less easy to obtain the *extra-ordinem* aid of the prætor to defend himself than a *fidejussor* would under similar circumstances, and as the mandate was an independent contract, not an accessory to the principal, it followed that (1) the action brought by the *mandatarius* against the *mandator* would not release the debtor, nor *vice versâ*, as *formerly* was the case (*ante*, par. 1264) with *sponsores, fidepromissores* or *fidejussores;* (2) the mandator, by paying, did not release the debtor for whom he was responsible; (3) the mandator, even after having paid the mandatarius, could get a cession of the latter's action against the debtor, the debt not being extinguished as it would be in the case of a fidejussor (*ante*, par. 1401, γ).

1569. (§ viii) A mandatum, to do an illegal or immoral act, was void, and the *mandatarius* must not exceed the limits of the mandate; for, if he did, no action lay against the *mandator*, though the latter had an action to the extent of the interest he had, that the mandate should be executed *(quatenus mea interest implesse eum mandatum si modo implere potuerit,* Gai. Inst., iii, § 161); but the opinion of the *Proculians* prevailed against Sabinus, and it was held that if the mandatarius, in carrying out the mandate, exceeded the limit, he could avoid greater loss, and, perhaps, the infamy resulting from the *mandati* action, by losing the difference; for example, if he was directed to bind himself at a term, and he did it purely and simply, he would only have the *mandati* action at the expiration of the term; and so, if he sold an estate for less than ordered, he must make up the difference to the mandator, otherwise the latter would still remain owner.

1571. The mandatum might be *extinguished* by :—
  (1) *Consent* of both.
  (2) The *will* of one, *i.e.*, either by the *revocatio* of the *mandator*, or the *renunciatio* of the *mandatarius*. In the first case, *after the mandatarius knows* of the revocation (α) the commission is extinguished altogether, before execution *(si adhuc integra res sit)*, but (β) for the future only, if the carrying out of the *mandatum* had commenced (Dig. 17, 1, 15, Paul). In the second case, as a mandate, when once accepted, must be either executed or immediately renounced, the *renuntiatio* must be made so as to give the *mandator* an opportunity of doing the work himself, or through another, otherwise an action lies *nisi justa causa intercessit, e.g.*, sudden illness, or capital enmity, or insolvency of the mandator.
  (3) *Death* of either; but if the mandatarius has executed the *mandatum* in bonâ fide ignorance of the death of the *mandator*, he will still have the *mandati* action against the representatives to indemnify him, just as debtors are released from their debts when they have paid the steward *(dispensator)* of Titius, in ignorance of his having been freed or deprived of his functions, or alienated, but if the heirs of the *mandatarius* execute the mandate, they will have no claim, as they cannot plead ignorance of his death.

1575. (§ xiii) Although the *mandatum* must be gratuitous, so that, if a price was paid, it thereby changed its character, and fell under *locatio-conductio*, or other class of contract *(originem ex officio atque amicitia trahit: contrarium ergo est officio merces,* Dig. 17, 1, 1, 4 Paul), yet payments by way of remuneration *(remunerandi gratia honor)*, rather than as price, came to be held binding, and did not prevent the transaction being a mandate. Hence, payment to the liberal professions *(liberalia studia)* came, from the very nature of the service performed, under this head, and the rule was extended to every sort of mandate about a matter not customarily made the subject of hire, but for which a certain fixed salary had been specially agreed upon, though in *all cases* of such *paid* mandates the suit to enforce them could only be *extra-ordinem* before the Prætor, or Præsides of the provinces, who, after *causa cognita*, had power to award the *honorarium*, and even to reduce it below the amount fixed by agreement.

1577. *Actions relating to the mandatum.* The *Actio-mandati* was *directa* when in favour of the *mandator*, but *contraria* for the *mandatarius*, because the latter sprang from *ex post facto* obligations. Both were *bonæ fidei*, and the *infamy* entailed by condemnation in the *direct* action might also, in particular cases, result from the *contraria* actio; see *post*, par. 2336.

In addition to the regular actions between third parties and the *mandatarius*, the former had against the *mandator* the *utilis quasi institoria*, and the *mandator* had also *utiles* actions against them (see *ante*, par. 1552).

1579. *Pacts.* In strictness, any agreement *(pactum, pactio, conventio, pactum conventum, ante,* par. 1200) outside the above *civil law contracts* produced no legal bond, but practically the number of contracts was tacitly extended by their gradual recognition under civil, prætorian, and imperial law.

1580. *Pacts provided with actions by the civil law.*

Pacta adjecta. All *bonæ fidei* contracts admitted of accessory agreements, modifying or explaining them, and forming one whole with them, but it was essential that they should be made at the same time as the contract itself, *i.e., ex continenti,* so as to form an integral part.

According to Ulpian (Dig. 18, 3, 4) the opinion of *Sabinus* prevailed, and the execution of these *pacta adjecta* was sued for by the *contract action*, though *Proculus* was in favour of the *actio in factum præscriptis verbis (post,* par. 1598) when the *pactum adjectum* had for its object (1) to consider the contract as null in a certain event (see *ante*, par. 1481), or (2) when some *datio* or *traditio* had been already executed, so as to bring the contract within those *do ut des, do ut facias (post,* par. 1590), and opinion subsequently inclined to the view that in these particular cases *either* action could be brought. If the *pactum adjectum* to a contract *bonæ fidei* occurred after an interval (*ex intervallo*) it, like all other pacts, could only give rise to an *exception*, hence it was only available for the defence (*ex parte rei*), not *ex parte actoris*, though the plaintiff could make use of it as a *replication*, as this was equivalent to an exception, and it was of service to *diminish*, but not to augment, the obligation. These *equity exceptions* to *bonæ-fidei* contracts were, however, implied, and did not require to be inserted in the formula by the Prætor, and if such a pact occurred in a purely consensual contract, where nothing had as yet been done, it would be held to revoke the first, and to found a new contract.

In a contract *stricti juris*, the *pactum adjectum*, whether *ex continenti* or *ex intervallo*, formed no part of the contract, and could only produce an *exception*, which had to be demanded of the Prætor, and inserted by him in the formula, but in the course of time the strict boundaries of the civil law contracts were effaced, and in respect of *pacta adjecta ex continenti* distinctions were recognised, viz. :—

(α) In the *mutuum* all clauses added in respect of the time, place, or mode of reimbursement, etc., formed part of the contract, and could be sued to execution by the *condictio certi*, but if, *e.g.*, ten aurei were delivered, with the clause that eleven were owed, only ten could be claimed by the *condictio*, for the obligation in the *mutuum* is formed *re*, and cannot exceed the sum actually delivered, and for the same reason *interest* could not be included. Hence the *mutuum* does not fall within the general rule derived from the Twelve Tables (see Table vi, § i), and applying to *innominati* contracts (*post*, par. 1590) that *in traditionibus rerum quodcumque pactum sit, id valere manifestissimum est* (Dig. 2, 14, 48 *Gaius*).

(β) In the *verbis*, the whole contract being comprised in the words of the interrogation and answer, the pact necessarily fell outside, but the facilities afforded as to the words used, and the favourable interpretation given them, tended to relax the rule (see *ante*, par. 1235, 1359, 1392), so that Paul's opinion (Dig. 2, 14, 4, 3) was confirmed, and a pact made immediately after a stipulation was looked upon as forming part of it, *e.g.*, that the capital should not be demanded whilst the interest was paid, but (Dig. 45, 1, 1, 3, *Ulpian*) if the promissor promised differently to the stipulators' interrogation, and the stipulator agreed immediately to the promise as made, a *new* stipulation was held to be contracted.

(γ) In the *litteris* the distinction was well marked, and the pact would be *outside* the contract.

1590. *Innominati contractus.* The doctrine of consideration was not clearly defined, and the ideas on this subject were of very gradual growth. The expression *civilis causa* denoted the civil law cause, *e.g.*, in contracts *re* the giving or delivering the thing, in *verbis* the words, in *litteris* the writing in the consecrated form, but as a simple non-obligatory *pact*, if *executed* on one side, might give rise to an obligation (*sub-est causa*), the contracts formed *re* (*ante*, par. 1205) were indefinitely extended, though only the true conventions of the *civil law* were called contracts, whilst others, even with particular names (*e.g.*, *permutatio*, *post*, par. 1604) were only *conventiones* springing from part execution, whether *do* or *facio*, and were included under the formulæ (1) *do tibi ut des*, (2) *aut do ut facias*, (3) *aut facio ut des*, (4) *aut facio ut facias*. In the result, under the term *nominati* contracts, jurists referred to the true contracts of the civil law, having special names, and falling under the heads of *re*, *verbis*, *litteris*, *consensu*, whilst *innominati* contracts were pacts changed into contracts by part execution, but the subject is much embarrassed by contradictory views, even in the collections of Justinian.

1595. A common point in all these pacts was that the *civil law* did not allow one person (α) to be unjustly enriched with the property of another, or (β) to have occasioned prejudice to another by his fault, or want of faith, and when the execution on one side consisted of the *datio* of some thing, or the extinction of some right capable of re-establishment, as, *e.g.*, a debt cancelled by acceptilation, and the other side did not perform his part (*re non secuta*) the return of what had been received was enforced by an action called *condictio causa data causa non secuta*, or *condictio ob causam datorum*.

1598. In cases outside these the Sabinians tried to meet the difficulty of repairing the damage done by tracing an analogy to one of the existing civil law contracts, and giving that action; but this was often impossible, in which case, in the time of *Cicero*, the *actio doli* was employed. Subsequently this latter action was retained for agreements falling under the head of *facio ut des*, because the infamy involved was suited to the gravity of the bad faith which refused the agreed return for an irrevocable act or service already done, but in other cases the plan was adopted of giving the party who had *executed* the pact an *incerta civilis actio*, in which the claim of the plaintiff was undetermined (*qua incertum petimus*), and this action, in use in the time of *Labeo*, and common to all *innominati* contracts, was called the *actio in factum præscriptis verbis* (or *in factum*, or *præscriptis verbis*), because the Prætor (besides making the action *bonæ fidei*, by adding the words *ex bona fide* to the formula) set out the *facts* in the *demonstratio*, whilst the *intentio* put a question of civil law (*in jus concepta*), but *incerta, i.e.*, without any fixed limitation *(quidquid ob eam rem* . . . . *dare, facere oportet*), and the condemnation was held to be the amount of interest which the plaintiff, who had executed the pact, had that the other side should have done so too (*ut damneris mihi, quanti interest mea, illud de quo convenit accipere*, Dig. 19, 5, i, Paul), hence, where the *condictio causa data causa non secuta* applied, the plaintiff had the choice of this, or of the *actio in factum*, but in other cases only the latter, *i.e.*, he could only get *damages*, not restitution.

1600. The establishment of these actions led to the idea that so long as the other side had done nothing, the party who had performed should have the power of *revocation* (called by the commentators the *jus pœnitendi*) and that this right should only expire when the other side had executed also *(causa secuta, repetitio cessat*, Dig. 12, 4, 1, *Ulpian*), but after the action *præscriptis verbis* received its fullest extension, and in order to ensure the carrying out of the agreement *(ut fides placiti servetur)* it came to be part of the duty of the judge to see that the other side was not prejudiced by any attempt at withdrawal *(pœnitentia non facit injuriam)*, and this duty would be implied from the terms of the formula, *e.g., si paret Aulum Agerium Numerio Negidio centum dedisse, causa data causa non secuta, quanti ea res erit*, N.N., A.A., *condemnato*.

1604. Amongst *innominati* contracts the following may be mentioned—

De æstimato. By this contract, a person agreed to receive a thing for sale at a certain estimated value, and pay that price for it, whatever the actual proceeds of the sale might be, and to return the thing if the sale did not take place. After much discussion, it was held that the obligation was originated *re*, and that the suitable action was *præscriptis verbis*, which, however, in this case, acquired the name *æstimatoria* or *de æstimato (post,* par. 2135).

Permutatio, i.e., the contract *do ut des* or *exchange.* This also resulted from the *datio* of a thing, and differs from a *sale* in that it is based on a *reciprocal* transfer of property *(utriusque rem fieri oportet),* so that there is no contract if one of the contracting parties delivers a thing not belonging to him, and if he does so the other can immediately sue for the *return* of his property by the *condictio causa data,* etc., or for damages by the action *præscriptis verbis.*

Precarium, i.e., a contract under which an object was gratuitously lent for use on the entreaty of the borrower, so long as the person granting the favour pleased. (*Precarium est, quod precibus petenti utendum conceditur tamdiu, quandiu is, qui concessit, patitur.* Dig. 43, 26, 1, Ulpian). This convention was analogous to the *commodatum,* and was derived from the *jus gentium.* The essential feature in it was the right to restitution at any time (whether the loan was for a term or not), and for this purpose the Prætor gave the interdict *de precario (post,* par. 2310); but, as this could not be used until after *traditio,* it followed that the obligation was formed *re;* and, therefore, finally, the agreement was held to bind civilly, so that, according to *Ulpian* (Dig. 43, 26, 2, 2), the *actio præscriptis verbis* could be used to enforce restitution. The right passed to the *heirs* of the *grantor,* but not to the heirs of the grantee, as it was *personal* to the latter; but a peculiarity of this occupancy at will was, that whilst the grantee held the property, he had the real rights appertaining to *possession,* unless he expressly asked only to detain the thing (*non ut possideret sed ut in possessione esset.* Dig. 41, 2, 10, 1, Ulpian).

Transactio. This contract of compromise, when not made by way of stipulation, but by a simple pact, did not become obligatory until after execution, or part execution, on one side, and it then gave rise to the *præscriptis verbis* action.

1611. *Pacts provided with actions by Prætorian law.*

Pacta prætoria were particular agreements rendered obligatory by consent alone, and provided with a special Prætorian action. An example of those pacts is afforded by the—

Constitutum. If the debtor, or another person, promised by a simple pact to pay on a given day a *pre-existing* debt (*constituere* = to appoint a day for the payment of a pre-existing debt), whether the debt was *civil, Prætorian,* or *natural,* the Prætor enforced it by the Prætorian action *de constituta pecuniâ,* and if no term had been actually fixed, ten days at least was assumed. The obligatory force of this *pact for payment* was only a generalization for all of the liability recognised by the *civil law* in the special case of a banker (*argentarius*), who could be sued by the *actio receptitia* on a *simple promise* to pay on a certain day a debt due by his customer to a creditor (*recipere* = receive a day for payment). As the second obligation resulting from the pact did not extinguish that arising from the debt itself (though *payment* did both at once, *solutio ad utramque obligationem proficit*, Dig. 13, 5, 18, 3, Ulpian), the *constitutum* was an easy method of (1) modifying, by simple pact, the performance of a *civil* obligation, or (2) rendering compulsory the execution of a purely *natural* obligation, or (3) obtaining security (*cautio*) for the debt of another.

At first, the pact only applied to obligations in respect of *pecunia*, *i.e.*, to things *quæ numero, pondere, mensurave consistunt;* but *Justinian* extended it to every thing, and merged the civil *receptitia* action against the banker in the Prætorian action *de constituta pecunia* (see *post*, par. 2104).

As to the Prætorian pact, in respect of an *extra-judicial oath*, see *post*, par. 2109.

1618. *Pacts provided with actions by Imperial law.*
Pacta legitima. This term included certain agreements arising from simple consent, which, though they never received the title of contracts, were, nevertheless, rendered obligatory by Imperial constitutions (*legitima conventio est quæ lege aliqua confirmatur: et ideo interdum ex pacto actio nascitur vel tollitur, quotiens lege vel senatus-consulto adjuvatur.* Dig. 2, 14, 6, Paul, see *post*, par. 1705). Examples are: the pact in respect of a gift (*donatio*), that establishing the dowry (*de dote constituenda*) (see *ante*, par. 571 to 582), and the pact by way of compromise (*compromissum*).

If there was no special action, one common to all was applied, viz.: the *condictio ex lege.*

1619. *Pactum nudum.* These were agreements outside the above classes of pacts, and destitute of any action to enforce them, though they became a fruitful source of *natural* obligations (see part ii, par. 199), the principal effect of which was, that, if the opportunity offered, they could be used as *exceptions.*

1620. *Prohibited agreements.* On motives of public policy certain contracts were prohibited. Any agreement falling within the class was null and void and did not even exist as a *natural* obligation *(post*, par. 1793), so that money paid, or the consequences of part execution, could be recovered by the *condictio indebiti*. Examples are: the pact *ne vendere liceat, i.e.*, that the pledgee in default of payment should not sell the pledge, or the *lex commissoria, i.e.*, that the pledge should be acquired without a sale if the debt was not paid within a certain time, or that interest should exceed the legal limit (see *post*, par. 1658), or the *intercessio* of women under the *s.c. Velleianum* (*ante*, par. 1411), or borrowing money in contravention of the *s.c. Macedonianum* (but see *post*, par. 1807), or dowry contracts contrary to the destination of the dowry *(functio dotis)*, or to the respect due to the husband *(contra receptam reverentiam quæ maritis exhibenda est*, Dig. 24, 3, 14, 1, Ulpian), or agreements relating to games of chance *(alearum lusus)* and wagers relating to them *(sponsiones)*.

Tit. xxvii. De obligationibus quasi ex contractu.

1622. Obligations *quasi ex contractu* were in the nature of contracts, but were based on facts which did not result from any agreement. They were mainly grounded on such considerations as that (α) no one should enrich himself at the expense of another; (β) the liability to repair any damage; (γ) common utility, and duties resulting from family and social relations (see part ii, par. 201, 208).

The text gives five examples; the first two resembling the contract of *mandatum*, the third that of *societas*, and the fifth that of the *mutuum*.

(1) *Negotiorum gestio, i.e.*, the conduct of the business of another person, without any express or even tacit mandate. No contract really existed; but, on account of the obvious utility of remunerating agents of this kind, reciprocal actions were given, viz., the *negotiorum gestorum actio directa*, for the owner of the property against the agent for any loss, as the latter was bound to employ *exactissima diligentia* (see *post*, par. 1633), and the *actio contraria*, for the agent to recover the expenses, etc., he had incurred.

(2) *Tutorship*. In this case, the *tutulæ actio directa* was given to the pupil at the end of tutorship, although no contract actually existed between the pupil and the tutor, whilst the *actio contraria* was open to the tutor. In the case of the *curatorship*, and, by analogy to (1), a *utilis negotiorum gestorum actio directa* was given to the ward against the curator, and the *actio contraria* to the curator (see *ante*, par. 284, 285).

(3) *Rei communis administratio*. Joint ownership might exist between several persons independent of any partnership agreement. In respect of particular things, as in the case of a common legacy or donation, the action *communi dividundo* lay to compel the undivided share being handed over where one of the joint owners had received the whole, or to recover *necessary* (and probably also *useful*) expenses incurred. In respect of *universalities*, the action *familiæ erciscundæ* was available to compel the partition of an inheritance *(post*, par. 2346) belonging to co-heirs. In some cases, also, the action *finium regundorum* would answer the purpose, as involving *adjudication* of reciprocal obligations, though resulting not from co-ownership, but from the liabilities of neighbours. See part ii, par. 229 (6), *ante*, par. 312 (4), and 1544 (2).

(4) *Hereditatis aditio*. As to the obligations of the heir towards the legatees, etc., under the will, see *ante*, par. 988.

(5) *Indebiti solutio*. This applied to all sorts of rights which were transferred, although not legally due. The general rule was

that he who paid by mistake that which he believed he owed, but did not, had the *condictio indebiti* to recover it back again, for the result of the payment (as in the *mutuum*) was to effect a translation of the ownership; but, as this involved the power of alienation, the insane and pupils had a *revindicatio* on the ground that they were not able to alienate ; and the *condictio indebiti* could only be brought against them for the amount by which they had been enriched at the time of the *litis contestatio*. In some cases, however, the property could *not* be *re-demanded ;* as, where the person paid the amount rather than run the risk of having to pay a further amount by way of penalty in the event of condemnation after denying his liability; for example, anciently, denial of liability might involve double the amount in respect of legacies of a fixed sum (*per damnationem certa constituta, e.g.*, I condemn my heir to give Titius 100 aurei), instead of *incertum constitutum*, as "the sum which is in my coffer"; and the rule was extended by *Justinian* to all *legacies*, and *fideicommissa* paid by mistake to *churches* and other places dedicated to religion or charity.

1633. *Culpa.* The damage resulting to a person from (*a*) *casus*, (*β*) *vis major*, or (*γ*) the act or omission of another, would, in the absence of an agreement to the contrary, and in the first two cases, fall upon the owner of the object of the right injured ; whilst, in the third case, if it was done in the exercise of a right, no responsibility would be incurred ; but if it was *unlawful*, or otherwise rendered the person liable, an obligation to repair the damage might follow.

An act contrary to law *(injuria)*, producing damage, and referable to its author as a person *sane* and *free*, fell either under :—

(1) *Dolus*, when the act or omission resulted from the *intention* to produce damage (see part ii, par. 164) ; and it was unlawful to agree beforehand not to be liable for dolus.

(2) *Culpa*, where there was a failure of duty, but *no intention* to injure.

The damage may result from an *act* or an *omission ;* and, as the contract or other particular relation might necessitate *active* care (*diligentia*, called, when applied to the preservation of a corporeal thing, *custodia*), hence, if the person so bound omitted *præstare diligentiam*, the neglect (*negligentia*) would be an *omissio diligentiæ ;* and, therefore, the person would be liable as for *culpa* (*magna negligentia culpa est*. Dig. 50, 16, 226, Paul).

The two degrees of *culpa*, viz. :—(a) *Culpa lata* (or *latior*), which was assimilated to *dolus* (*magna culpa dolus est, culpa dolo proxima*) ; and (β) *culpa levis* (or *levior* or *levissima*) are, together with the expressions *diligens, diligentissimus, exacta, exactissima*, only variations of style, not gradations of *culpa*, until referred to a standard of comparison, of which there are two : the first, absolute, or in the abstract ; the second, relative, or in the concrete, the distinction being based on :—

(1) A comparison of men in general, in which case :—
  (α) *Lata culpa* would be the damaging act or omission that the *least intelligent man* would not have committed.
  (β) *Levis culpa*, the fault of the *most careful paterfamilias*.
(2) *The habitual character of the individual*, in which case :—
  (α) *Culpa lata* would arise if he did not use *more care* than was habitual to him in his own affairs.
  (β) *Culpa levis*, when there was an absence of his usual care.

As a general rule in contracts for the benefit of *one* side only, this side was responsible for (1 β); the other side only for (1 α). Where the benefit was *reciprocal*, both sides were liable to the extent of (1 β), subject to modifications arising out of the particular circumstances. Where he who was charged with the care of a thing had *himself* an interest in a share of it, he was only liable for (2 β), because he had a legal and personal motive for undertaking the responsibility, and for similar reasons the same measure was applied in respect of public functions which could not be refused, as tutorships and curatorships, whilst, in respect of the contracts of *societas* and *depositum*, a similar measure was fixed, based upon the interest which the partner had, and the gratuitous nature of the depositee's duties, as well as upon the idea that it was the fault of the partner or depositor if he selected a negligent partner or depositee.

Practically, however, the absolute and relative standards were combined so as to produce only two kinds of responsibility, viz. :—

(1) Responsibility for faults, according to the care of the most diligent paterfamilias, *i.e.*, involving more care than the person was accustomed to use in his own affairs. This applied to the commoda*tee* (*ante*, par. 1215) and the deposit*or*, because the contract was for their benefit only—the pledgor and pledgee (*ante*, par. 1225), the vendor and purchaser (*ante*, par. 1468, etc.), the locator and conductor (*ante*, par. 1512), because in these cases both sides were concerned—the mandator and mandatee (*ante*, par. 1550), on account of the sacred character of the contract; although, according to an unsupported and doubtful extract from *Modestinus* (Mosaic et Rom. Leg. Coll. tit. 9, c. 2), as the benefit was usually only for the mandator, the mandatary was only liable for *dolus* not *culpa* (*In mandati vero judicio dolus non etiam culpa deducitur*)—the *negotiorum gestor* (*ante*, par. 1622, 1), because he voluntarily and spontaneously undertook the affairs of another; but, if he was constrained to do so by sentiments of affection (*affectione coactus*) in an urgent case, his liability would only fall under the second head.

(2) Responsibility for faults, according to habitual character, *i.e.*, as much care was required as the person was in the habit of using in his own affairs. Under this head, came the commoda*tor* and deposit*ee* (*ante*, par. 1220), because they perform a gratuitous service—*socii* (*ante*, par. 1523), co-owners, co-heirs, and the husband in respect of dowry property, for in all these cases the party undertaking the matter has a personal interest—the tutor and curator, because their duties were imposed upon them.

The above remarks apply to contracts *bonæ-fidei*, for in those *stricti juris* the question could not arise in the action *(condictio)* by which they would be enforced; for example, in the *stipulation*, the promissor was liable to *give*, not to do—*i.e.*, if, *e.g.*, he had promised to deliver a slave who had been killed through any act of his, he, the promissor, would still be liable *ex stipulatu* (*ante*, par. 1328); but, if the death only resulted from negligence or want of care in sickness, he would not be liable in this action because it did not compel him to *do* anything, and the remedy, therefore, if *dolus* existed, must be sought in another form.

1655. *Mora.* This was a technical expression, for which *frustratio*, or *cessatio*, or *dilatio* was sometimes substituted. A debtor was deemed *moram facere* when he delayed, contrary to the rules of law, making restitution or payment, and the same applied to a creditor as to accepting the restitution or payment, as, *e.g.*, if he refused to receive offers validly made, or failed to be at the time and place agreed upon. The consequences in either case being that subsequent prejudicial events, except those arising from the *dolus* or *culpa lata* of the adverse party, were at the risk of the party in *mora* ; and, in respect of a debtor or holder, a liability arose which might not exist in the original contract for interest, or produce, or (more generally) for an indemnity. If the time (*dies*) for the payment of a debt was fixed, or if a person continued to be the holder in consequence of his delict or bad faith, the debtor or holder was said to be in *mora* by the fact itself (*ex re*, or *in rem*, or *in re*); and, therefore, no notice (*interpellatio*) was required, according to the phrase, introduced subsequent to the time of the jurists, *dies interpellat pro homine*, otherwise a demand of performance was necessary before the debtor or holder would be in *mora*, and hence the delay in such cases was said to be *ex persona*, and it would be within the province of the judge to determine whether the summons to pay or deliver had been properly made.

1658. *Usuræ.* The question of *interest* was connected with the principles as to *mora*, and, therefore, was usually treated by the jurists conjointly with it. The engagements contracted under this head related only to obligations involving a sum of money or (rarely) things, *quæ numero, pondere, vel mensura consistunt*. *Sors* or *caput* was the term used to express the amount of the principal obligation, *fœnus (? fœtus)*, or *versura*, or later, *usuræ (? pro usu)* referred to the fraction of this capital due by reason of lapse of time, and *res* (or *pecunia*) *fœnebris* was the capital producing the interest. In consequence of the discord and sedition arising from the exorbitant usury demanded by the patricians from the plebeians, the Twelve Tables fixed the rate, previously *un*limited, at one-twelfth of the capital, *i.e., unciarium fœnus* (see *ante*, Twelve Tables, viii, 18). A subsequent *plebiscitum* in B.C. 345, reduced the rate to one-half this amount, *i. e.*, to one-twenty-fourth per annum, or $4\frac{1}{6}$ per cent. (*semunciarium fœnus*); and another *plebiscitum* in B.C. 340, prohibited loans on interest altogether, but this prohibition was subsequently withdrawn, as, in the time of Cicero, the *maximum legal* interest was that known as *centesima usura* (*legitimæ*, or *maximæ*, or *gravissimæ usuræ*), i.e., 12 per cent. per annum, and this rate lasted down to Justinian. As one-hundredth of the capital became due each month at the *calends*, the term *Calendarium* was applied to the register recording the amount, and *calendarium exercere*, meant lending at interest, whilst the officer employed by a municipality to keep their accounts would be styled *curator calendarii*, and a similar term was used by capitalists to indicate the slave kept by them for the purpose (*Stichum servum calendario præposuerat*).

A person might be liable for interest :—

By *law*, as *e.g.*, when a debtor was in *mora*, or another person's money employed for one's own profit, or on the price due from the purchaser after traditio, or in respect of sums due to a minor of 25.

By *will*, as when so ordered by the testator.

By *agreement*, whether by special stipulation, or by *pacta adjecta ex continenti* to a *bonæ fidei* contract.

Compound interest (*anatocismus*) was prohibited, and *Justinian* (Cod. 4, 32) reduced and varied the rate as follows :—

(1) For *maritime* loans, the previously unlimited rate (*ante*, par. 1213) was fixed at *centesimæ usuræ*, or 12 per cent.

(2) For *commercial* loans, two-thirds (*usque ad bessem centesimæ*), or 8 per cent.

(3) For *ordinary* persons, one-half (*dimidiam centesimæ*), or 6 per cent.

(4) For *illustrious* persons, one-third (*tertiam partem*), or 4 per cent.

Tit. xxviii. Per quas personas nobis obligatio adquiritur.

1665. In respect of the acquisition by us of obligations resulting from contracts, and analogous relations, entered into by—

(1) A *slave*, see *ante*, par. 1280.

(2) A *filius familias*, see *ante*, par. 1298, noting that in those cases where the son retained the ownership, and the father only acquired the usufruct (*ante*, par. 611), the exercise of the action relating to the property nevertheless devolved on the father.

(3) A *freeman* or the *slave* of another possessed by us in good faith, or by a slave of which we have the *usufruct* or *use* in the two cases in which it is possible, viz., (α) when it arises from their labour, or (β) out of our own property, see *ante*, par. 616 (2), (3), (4).

In the case of a slave of whom we have the *use*, the obligation could only result from his labour applied to our *own* property, and therefore the text of Justinian (§ ii, *per eum quoque servum in quo ...usum habemus similiter ex duabus istis causis nobis adquiritur*) is to be restricted to mean that we acquire obligations resulting from (α) the *use* of him, or (β) his labour bestowed on our *own* property.

The text of Justinian (§ iii, *licet antea dubitatur*, etc.) refers to that Emperor's constitution (*Cod.* 4, 27, 3) confirming the opinion of the *Sabinians* against the *Proculians* (Gai. Inst., iii, § 167), that a slave stipulating, by order of one of several masters, acquires for him only who ordered him; and so, if the slave stipulated for, or received by tradition for one only of his masters, whom he mentioned by name (*e.g.*, *Titio domino meo dare spondes?*), he acquired only for him.

1669. *Transference of obligations.* Strictly (except in the case where, as in universal successions, there was a continuance of the *persona*), no transference of obligations by a creditor to another was possible; see part ii, par. 210, and *ante*, par. 312 (3); but the introduction of the practice of suing and pleading by procuration led to the indirect method of effecting the transfer by giving the procurator a right to the benefit of the obligation by a *mandate* (*mandare actiones*, or *actiones persequendas præstare*, or *præstare, cedere actiones*), and the cessionee of the right of action was said to be a *procurator in rem suam*, to indicate that the resulting profit would remain in his hands (*si in rem suam datus sit procurator loco domini habetur*, Dig. 2, 14, 13, Paul). The mandate (*ante*, par. 1550, etc.) in this case was peculiar in that, (α) no account need be rendered, (β) it could not be revoked, and (γ) it was not terminated by the death of either the creditor (*mandator*) or the *mandatarius*. As the cession resulted from the mandate, the consent of the *debtor* was not necessary, and, as the obligation was not changed, the *creditor* could still sue, but if he did, he would be bound to hand over the result to the cessionee, and an *exceptio doli* could be opposed to the creditor by the debtor if the latter had notice of the cession, or if the debtor had been already sued by the cessionee. The Prætor *Rutilius* introduced the *Rutilian* form of suing as procurator, *i.e.*, he ingeniously introduced a modification in the formula to suit the case of a cession (see *post*, par. 2233), but subsequently the actions themselves were given to the cessionee in the *utilis* form, the result of which was to remove the invalidity of a cession to an *infamous* person, as the inability of such persons to postulate for another (*ante*, par. 1161) did not now come in question.

Tit. xxix. Quibus modis obligatio tollitur.

1672. Strictly, the *vinculum juris*, formed *secundum nostræ civitatis jura*, could only be dissolved according to the rules of the same civil law (*ipso jure*), see part ii, par. 211; but after (α) civil, (β) Prætorian, and (γ) *natural* obligations were recognised, there came to be also (α) *civil*, (β) *Prætorian*, and (γ) *natural* modes of release, in the sense that, in respect of (β) and (γ), though the debtor *obligatus manet*, the claim of the creditor for performance could be resisted *exceptionis ope* (*post*, par. 1714), *i.e.*, the two latter served as means of defence, whilst the first only could dissolve a civil obligation.

The Institutes only treat here of the civil methods of dissolving an obligation.

1675. *Performance.* In the time of Justinian, nothing more was required than the delivery of what was due; and the opinion of the *Sabinians* (Gai. Inst., iii, § 168) against the Proculians was confirmed, that the delivery of one thing for another (*aliud pro alio*), called a *datio in solutum*, was a valid payment, if made with the *consent* of the *creditor*. If the payment was made in order to release the debtor by a person who might render his own position worse to a person capable of receiving it (*ante*, par. 602), such payment, though made without the knowledge and against the will of the debtor, extinguished the debt, together with all its accessories, in the shape of sureties, pledges, mortgages, etc.

If after *oblatio, i.e.,* a *bonâ fide* tender validly made of the whole of the debt at the prescribed place and time, the creditor was absent or in *mora* in any way (*ante*, par. 1655), the debtor could obtain his release by placing the sum or object in a public repository *(in publico deponere, obsignare, consignare), e.g.,* in one of the churches *(sacratissimæ ædes)* or other place indicated by the judge.

1687. (§ i) *Release.* On the principle that *Nihil tam naturale est, quam eo genere quidquid dissolvere quo colligatum est* (Dig. 50, 17, 35, *Ulpian*), it was held that contracts formed *re* (as the *mutuum, commodatum, depositum,* and *pignus*), should be dissolved *re, i.e.,* by performance, whilst that for obligations formed *per æs et libram,* an imaginary performance *(species imaginariæ solutionis)* would result if the same operation were repeated in the contrary sense, and, as the testament itself was made *per æs et libram*, this method was appropriate for a legatee to release to the heir a legacy *per damnationem*, as well as (probably on account of the peculiar solemnity and publicity attaching thereto) to absolve a person from complying with a *judicial sentence (quod ex judicati causa debetur)*, and generally to liberate a debtor in respect of *certa pecunia, i.e.,* things *quæ pondere numero mensurave constant (...deinde asse percutit libram, eumque dat ei a quo liberatur, veluti solvendi causa* (Gai. Inst., iii, § 174).

In the same way contracts *verbis* would be dissolved by a stipulation of payment (*acceptilatio*), and probably (though the authorities are silent) an entry in the debtor's ledger with the consent of the creditor cancelled a debt contracted *litteris*. So also simple dissent might dissolve *consensual* contracts (*post*, par. 1705).

Justinian, in the Institutes, does not refer to any other mode of *imaginaria solutio* than the *acceptilatio*. It was the only form in his time, and could be used for all kinds of contracts; for, though strictly, the *solutio verbis* would be incompetent to dissolve an obligation contracted in any other way than *verbis*, and, at the most, could only have the force of a pact, and serve as an exception (*si acceptilatio inutilis fuit tacita pactione id acturus videtur ne peteretur*, Dig. 2, 14, 27, 9, Paul); yet as *novatio* (*post*, par. 1691) of any obligation could be effected by putting it in the form of a *stipulatio*, and as this stipulation, so substituted for the original contract, could be dissolved in whole or in part by the *solutio verbis* (*i.e.*, by *acceptilatio*), it became possible to apply this as a mode of release *ipso jure* to *all* contracts, and for this purpose *Aquilius* Gallus (a disciple of *Mucius* and master of *Servius Sulpicius*, and the friend and colleague of Cicero in the prætorship, B.C. 65), introduced, amongst other formulæ of practical utility (*e.g.*, *ante*, par. 697, 3), the—

(§ ii) *Aquiliana stipulatio*, which was so framed as to reduce all the pre-existing liabilities to one verbal obligation, and then by the acceptilation to release the debtor absolutely from all he owed up to that day. The form which served as a model for the *writing* used as evidence of stipulations (*ante*, par. 1359), promises, and acceptilations, and which might be modified to suit the particular case, or only partially employed, as where it was desired actually to effect a *novatio*, ran as follows:—*Quidquid te mihi ex quacunque causa* (generic expression) *dare, facere oportet oportebit* (present and future), *præsens in diemve* (referring to conditions involved), *quarumque rerum mihi tecum actio* (action *in personam*), *quæque adversus te petitio* (action *in rem*), *vel adversus te persecutio* (extraordinary aid of magistrate), *est eritve, quodve tu meum habes* (refers to vindication), *tenes* (physical detention), *possidesve* (civil possession), *dolove malo fecisti quominus possideas* (this clause was added *after* the time of Aquilius Gallus, and refers to the liability of him who has fraudulently put property out of his own possession, in order to defeat the person who had the right to claim it), *quanti quæque earum rerum res erit, tantam pecuniam dari stipulatus est Aulus Agerius, spopondit Numerius Negidius. Item ex diverso Numerius Negidius interrogavit Aulum Agerium: Quidquid tibi hodierno die per Aquilianam stipulationem spopondi, id omne habesne acceptum? respondit Aulus Agerius: Habeo, acceptum que tuli.*.

1691. (§ iii) *Novatio.* The *civil* law recognised as a means of dissolving an obligation the substitution of a *new contract* in its place, whether the obligation had resulted from one of the contracts *re, verbis, litteris, consensu*, or from a *quasi* contract, delict or *quasi* delict (*Novatio est prioris debiti in aliam obligationem...transfusio atque translatio...omnes res transire in novationem possunt*, Dig. 46, 2, *Ulpian*), and the original contract might have been only *natural* (*post*, par. 1793); but (although *forced* novations occurred in the course of a lawsuit, *post*, par. 1704) the *new* contract must be formed *verbis* or *litteris*, for, in respect of the latter, Theophilus lays down, in his paraphrase, that *novatio* was effected by the inscription of the *nomen* (*ante*, par. 1414), though Gaius makes no mention of it.

Novation might extinguish the former liability, although the substituted stipulation was void, as in the case of a debt owing to Titius by a third party being stipulated for by Titius from a *pupil* without the authorisation of his tutor; but it was finally settled that the original debtor would not be released in the case of a subsequent stipulation made by a slave (Gai. Inst., iii, § 179); for though in either case a *natural* obligation results, yet novation arises only from an obligation contracted *verbis*, and the *slave*, unlike the *pupil*, could not promise at all, and only stipulate as the agent of his master. It was also finally settled that, if the stipulation constituting the novation was *conditional*, no novation would take place, and the original obligation would remain in force unless the condition was fulfilled; for if the condition failed, the obligation depending upon it, and which was to effect the novation, would not have come into existence (*non statim fit novatio, sed tunc demum cum conditio extiterit*: Dig. 46, 2, 8, 1, and 14 Ulpian).

Just as a third party could pay a debt (*ante*, par. 1675), so he could extinguish the debtor's obligation by *novation* with the creditor (whose consent was always required, but not that of the debtor); and if this were done without the assistance of the original debtor, this kind of suretyship was called *expromissio;* but if the *expromissor* was procured by the debtor, it was called *delegatio* (*delegare est vice sua alium reum dare creditori, vel cui jusserit.* Dig. 46, 2, 11, and 17, Ulpian). So, by order of the original creditor, a *new creditor*, or a *new debtor and creditor*, may be substituted by means of *novatio (opus est ut jubente me tu ab eo stipuleris: quæ res effecit ut a me liberetur et incipiat tibi teneri: quæ dicitur, novatio obligationis.* Gai. Inst., ii, § 38). If, though the same debtor and creditor remained, the original contract resulted from any other form than the *stipulation*, there would be *novatio;* for, otherwise, *acceptilatio*, as a means of dissolving obligations, would not be possible (the case of stipulations following on the delivery of the money in loans, *ante*, par. 1435, being quite exceptional), but a stipulation to produce *novatio* of a stipulation must have something new in it *(si quid novi sit)*, *e.g.*, adding or suppressing a condition, a term or a *fidejussor* (which name is substituted in the text of Justinian for the word *sponsor* used by Gaius (Inst. iii, § 178), in respect of whom the opinion of the Sabinians prevailed that *novatio* would result). Hence *novatio* may result from changing the debtor or creditor, or both, or simply the debt—and whether the two obligations both existed, the second as an accessory to the first, or whether *novatio* had been effected, depended formerly on the *intention* of the parties, but *Justinian* (Cod. 8, 4, 28) decided that *novatio* only took place when the parties had expressly and formally declared that that was the object of the new contract.

1704. A sort of involuntary *novatio* occurred at two of the stages of actions *in personam*, called *judicia legitima*, and conceived *in jus*, viz.:—(1) At the joinder of issue (*litis contestatione*), and (2) at the sentence *(ex causa judicati)*. *Ante litem contestatam dare debitorem oportere; post litem contestatam condemnari oportere, post condemnationem judicatum facere oportere* (Gai. Inst. iii, § 180), but the

BOOK III—TIT. XXIX. 305

effects of these *in*voluntary judicial novations differed from the voluntary, *e.g.*, the former did not extinguish mortgages existing on the original debt.

1705. (§ iv) The dissolution of *consensual* contracts by *consent* only occurred if no alteration had taken place, *i.e.*, if nothing had been done *(omnibus integris manentibus,* Dig. 2, 14, 58, Neratius), for if there had been execution in any way, or if the thing had perished, a revocation of accomplished facts would be impossible, and the subsequent pact would not act *ipso jure*, but only by way of an *exceptio*, which, however, need not necessarily be inserted in the formula, since the action was *bonæ fidei (ante*, par. 1580), *e.g.*, a pact *(in factum) de non petendo*, waiving a portion of the purchase money, and made after delivery of the thing, or its destruction, without the fault of the vendor, would act as an *exceptio*, and a subsequent pact (restoring the original contract) could be used by the plaintiff as an *exceptio* on his side and be taken account of by the judge. If, however, the pact *de non petendo* related to an obligation *stricti juris*, the *exceptio* would have to be inserted in the formula, and to this the plaintiff would have to insert a *replication* of the subsequent contrary pact, if such existed; though this would not be necessary if, instead of the exception in *factum*, the general exception *de dolo malo* had been inserted, as it would then be within the province of the judge to take account of subsequent pacts, but whether the pact *de non petendo* was *personal*, or to include the *fideijussores*, so as to release them also, was a question of *intention*.

A simple pact might, in some cases, extinguish *ipso jure* the liability, as, *e. g.*, in the actions *injuriarum* and *furti*. *Quædam actiones per pactum ipso jure tolluntur : ut injuriarum item furti... nam et de furto pacisci lex permittit* (Twelve Tables, ii, 4, and viii, 2; Dig. 2, 14, 17, 1, Paul; and 7, 14, Ulpian); and hence such pacts were included by *Paul* amongst *pacta legitima.*

Papinian lays down that an agreement to dissolve a *natural* obligation would of itself dissolve it *(Quod vinculum æquitatis, quo solo sustinebatur, conventionis æquitate dissolvitur*, Dig. 46, 3, 95, 4); and he further holds that the fidejussor was liberated by the pact as well as the pupil, if, *e.g.*, a fidejussor had been given by a pupil who had bound himself without the authorization of his tutor (*post*, par. 1793).

An extinction *ipso jure* of obligations also resulted, anciently, from the disappearance of the *debtor* in the case of *minima capitis deminutio (ante*, par. 1152), and of the *creditor* in the case of an *in jure cessio* of the inheritance by the heir to another, after the heir had made *aditio*, for then the debtors of the inheritance would be released.

1711. In addition to the causes of dissolution discussed in this title, viz. :—(1) Performance, (2) *Acceptilatio*, (3) *Novatio*, (4) Mutual dissent, civil law obligations might also be extinguished by—

(5) *Confusio*, *i.e.*, when the creditor and the debtor became

x

united in the same person as, *e.g.*, by the effect of an inheritance. In this case the debt was not really extinguished, except in so far as it was impossible to bring an action against oneself, and hence in complicated cases the obligation might continue to exist, so that if the obstacle resulted from the *querela inofficiosi*, the action would revive, or in the case of a *restitutio*, the action would be restored.

(6) *Loss of the thing due, i.e.*, a debtor was released when the thing certain (*species*) had perished without his fault *(civiliter...resolvitur... cum in eamdem personam jus stipulantis promittentisque devenit...aut cum res in stipulationem deducta sine culpa promissoris in rebus humanis esse desiit,* Dig. 46, 3, 107, Pomponius), unless he was responsible for risks resulting from his being in *mora* or otherwise (see *ante*, par. 1328, 1468, 1633); but this is really an example of a material obstacle intervening and not of an extinction of the obligation.

The question of the *revival* of the obligation, if the thing destroyed was restored, led to divergences of opinion, *Celsus* (Dig. 32, 73, 3) holding that it did, as in the case of a legacy of a slave, who, after becoming free, refell into slavery; but *Paul* (who lived more than a century later) probably represents the better opinion when he lays down that the obligation does *not revive* (Dig. 46, 3, 98, 8), at least if the thing might be regarded as *new*, and the slave in the above example, after refalling into slavery, would be held to be like another man, and therefore a new thing.

1714. *Exceptions.* For the cases in which, though according to the civil law, the obligation subsisted, yet the debtor could defeat it *exceptionis ope*, based upon a pact of release, or oath, or compromise, or compensation, see *post*, par. 2248.

ABSTRACT OF BOOK III.

Inheritances ab intestato.

These only arise when it is certain that there will be no testamentary inheritance, and hence it is at this moment and not at the death of the deceased, that the capacity, quality, and degree of the heirs are determined, though they must have been born, or at least conceived, in the lifetime of the deceased.

The *Twelve Tables* established two orders of heirs, viz.—(a) the *heredes sui*, and (β) the *agnates*. In certain cases, and for certain persons, came in (γ) the *Gentiles*.

Heredes sui, by the Twelve Tables, were those who, at the death of the deceased, were in his power, without any intermediate person, and took *per capita*, but *Prætorian* law included *emancipated* children and children *given in adoption*, when they had been sent out of the adoptive family in the lifetime of the *natural* father. Subsequently, an Imperial Constitution included *descendants* of *daughters*, giving them the share of their deceased mother, less one-third, if there were *heredes sui* besides them, but only one-fourth deducted if only agnates. *Justinian* confirmed the Prætorian law as to *emancipated* children, and children given in *adoption* did not lose any rights of succession in the *natural* family, unless the adoption was made by an ascendant, and *descendants* of *daughters* could take the *whole* if only agnates remained.

Agnates, by the *Twelve Tables*, included only the members of the *civil* family actually in it. They took *per stirpes*, and succeeded *ad infinitum*. An *intermediate jurisprudence* incapacitated *women* in the sense that, unless they were consanguineous sisters, their agnates could succeed them, but not *vice versâ*. A constitution of Anastasius called the *emancipated* brothers and sisters with the agnate brothers and sister, but with a certain diminution; and *Justinian*, in respect of *women*, restored the law of the Twelve Tables, allowing them to succeed to their agnates; in respect of *emancipated* children, he struck out the diminution imposed by Anastasius, and allowed their children of the first degree to succeed; in respect of children given in *adoption*, there was no longer any loss of the rights of family; in respect of the relations through *women*, he called to the fraternal succession, as if they were agnates, *uterine* brothers and sisters, and, in default, their children of the first degree.

For *heredes sui* and *agnates* there was no devolution, *i.e.*, if the first degree refused (in cases where a refusal could occur) the entire order was passed over, and the next order was called, but *Justinian* established devolution from degree to degree, so that the next order was not called until the preceding was exhausted.

Gentiles. This succession, in respect of races of pure ingenuous origin, over the property of other races descended from them whose origin could be traced through clientship or freedom, disappeared in the latter years of the republic.

Ascendants (male and female), children in succession of mother and of ancestress.

Under the *Twelve Tables* there could never be any question as to the legal succession of *paternal* ascendants, for either their children could have no inheritance, as being in their power, or no civil bond existed between them, and this latter reason always applied to *maternal* ascendants and *female ascendants*.

The testamentary succession of the *filius familias*, in respect of his *castrense* or *quasi castrense peculium*, did not apply to the inheritance *ab intestato;* hence, in the latter case, the paterfamilias retook the property by right of peculium.

Imperial constitutions established an altogether exceptional sort of succession as to property coming to *filii* (or *filiæ*) *familias*, from their mother or the maternal line,—the order being (α) their descendants (male and female); (β) their brothers and sisters, whether of the same bed or not; (γ) their father or other ascendant, according to degree.

Justinian extended the order of succession to the *peculium castrense* or *quasi castrense*, left *ab intestato*, and gave it (1) to the children of the deceased, (2) to the brothers and sisters, and, in default, the paterfamilias ascendant took it *jure communi*, *i.e.*, by right of peculium. In the case of an *emancipated* son, the *fiducia* contract was always assumed, and the above order was followed instead of the ascendant emancipator, as formerly, coming in on the footing of a *patron* in the first rank of agnates.

By the *s.c. Tertullianum*, the mother only (not the ancestress) succeeded to her offspring if, being *ingenua*, she had had three children, or, if *freed*, four. Justinian gave them the right, although they had only had one child, and in the succession she came after the children of the male or female deceased for a *pars virilis* with brothers and sisters; but if only *sisters*, the mother took half, the sisters dividing the remaining half. Reciprocally, children succeeded to their *mother* by the *s.c. Orphitianum* in the first rank, as if *heredes sui*, and subsequently the succession to their *ancestress* was accorded also.

Cognates were brought in by the Prætor as a third order, and these included all relations according to proximity, but only to the sixth degree, or the seventh in the case of children of second cousins, and the Prætor did not make them *heirs* proper, but only *possessores bonorum*.

The *succession to freed persons*, by the Twelve Tables, was (1) the *heredes sui*, (2) the *patron and his children*, but the freed person could, by testament, otherwise dispose of the inheritance. The Prætor gave the patron, when his turn arrived, a right to half the succession, of which he could not be deprived, either by the adoption of a child or by testament, and the *Lex Papia*, called the *patron*, with the *heredes sui*, for a *pars virilis*, when the inheritance exceeded 100,000 sesterces, and there were less than three children.

Justinian returned to the *ab intestato* succession of the *Twelve Tables:* the patron only coming in in default of all *heredes sui*, or children ranked with them, and *cognates*, *i.e.*, collaterals of the patron to the *fifth* degree, coming in the third order. In respect of *testamentary* succession, the freedman, if he had less than 100 aurei, could freely dispose of his property, leaving nothing to his patron, but above that sum the patron, in his order of succession, had an irrevocable right to one-third, free from any legacy or fidei-commissum. In the time of *Claudius* the patron might assign his freedman to one or more of his children in power, and the right of succession then belonged exclusively to him or them and their posterity.

The *Possessio bonorum* was a sort of hereditary right, introduced by the *Prætor*, to aid, supplement, or correct the civil law, and might be:—

(1) *Testamentary*, when of two kinds, (α) *contra tabulas*, to get possession of the inheritance in spite of the dispositions made by testament; (β) *secundum tabulas*, to get possession conformably to the testament.

(2) *Ab intestato*, viz.—(α) *unde liberi*, for children; (β) *unde legitimi*, for all those whom a *lex*, a *senatus consultum*, a *constitution*, or other *legal* disposition, called to the succession; (γ) *unde cognati*, for *cognates*; (δ) *unde vir et uxor*, for husband or wife.

But *heredes sui*, if they had let pass the possession *unde liberi* which was proper to them, were not prevented from coming in *unde legitimi*, or even under *unde cognati*, and the same rule applied to agnates, and other legal heirs.

Justinian regulated the succession of *freedmen*, like that of *ingenui*, but formerly the order for them was besides that (α) *unde liberi* for descendants, and (β) *unde legitimi* for the patron and his children in power, also (γ) *unde decem personæ* for the particular case of an *ingenuus* emancipated to a stranger who had freed him, when the ten persons of his natural cognation were called in preference to the manumittor, who in strict law would have the hereditary rights of patronage, (δ) *tum quem ex familia* for the nearest member of the civil family of the patron, (ε) *unde liberi patroni patronæ-que et parentes eorum*, for the children of the patron or patroness, whether in power or not, and for their ascendants, (ζ) *unde cognati manumissoris*, for cognates of the patron, but the patron and his children could in default of taking possession under (β), obtain it through (δ), (ε), or (ζ).

Finally, a *possessio bonorum, ut ex legibus senatus-ve consultis* was promised to those on whom it was conferred by special legislative disposition.

Under Justinian, the *possessio bonorum* might be accepted within *one year* for descendants and ascendants, and *one hundred days* for others in any way sufficient to manifest intention, after which there was devolution to the next degree, and, in default, to the next possessio bonorum. It might also be repudiated, and distinctions formerly existed as to whether it was *cum re* or *sine re*, in the one case being secured from eviction under the civil law, in the other not.

These *edictales* possessions were also distinguished from those *decretales*, of which latter examples are that *ventris nomine*, and that *ex Carboniano*.

Hotchpot. Under the *Collatio bonorum*, introduced by the Prætors, and successively extended by imperial constitutions, and by *Justinian*, descendants, in certain cases, when coming to the succession of their ascendants, had to throw in advances made to them before the re-distribution of the whole.

Accrual between co-heirs took place by *law*, without their knowledge and against their will, in both testamentary and *ab intestato* successions, as well as in the *possessio bonorum*.

The *transmission of the inheritance*, as a general rule, did not take place if the heir or the *possessor bonorum* died before accepting, but the right of transmission was introduced in certain cases by imperial constitutions, and *Justinian* decided in favour of it when the heir died within the year of the opening of his rights, and before the expiration of the interval for deliberation.

Ereptorium. In certain cases the legacy, fidei-commissum, or inheritance was taken away on the ground of indignity, and, as a general rule, it then went to the *fiscus*, but in some cases, instead of being confiscated, it passed to the next in degree.

Actions relating to ab intestato successions, and to the possessio bonorum.

In addition to *utiles* forms of the *hereditatis petitio* and *familiæ erciscundæ* action, which applied to both *ab intestato* and testamentary successions, the *possessor bonorum* could also claim the *quorum bonorum interdict*.

Other universal successions than by inheritance.
Amongst these were:—

(1) The acquisition, which took place when a paterfamilias received a person *sui juris* into his paternal or marital power, thereby acquiring all the property of that person, except that which was destroyed by the change of status. Under *Justinian* this could only apply to the case of *arrogation*, and owing to the modifications introduced into the law by that emperor, the arrogator acquired only the usufruct, not the ownership, of the property of the person arrogated.

(2) *Addictio* was introduced by *Marcus Aurelius*, in order to support the freedom of the slaves in the case of a *testamentary* inheritance abandoned by the instituted persons, and subsequently it was extended to inheritances *ab intestato*, in which freedoms were given by codicils. *Justinian* further extended it to include freedom *inter vivos* or *mortis causa*.

(3) *Bonorum emptio.* This sort of universal prætorian succession, for the benefit of the purchaser, took place when the creditors applied for the sale of the universality of the property and rights of their debtor. It fell into disuse with the ordinary procedure.

(4) Justinian repealed the *s.c. Claudianum*, by which an *ingenua* who had united herself to a slave, and persisted in the union, was handed over to the master of the slave.

Obligations.

Two persons are indispensable as *subjects* of these *personal* rights, viz., (1) the creditor, or *active* subject, and (2) the debtor, or *passive* subject, and the *object* is always, ultimately, a thing to be furnished *(alicujus solvendæ rei)*, *i.e.*, a thing which in the juridical sense can be included under the words *dare, facere, præstare.*

Kinds of obligations.

The definition in the text only refers to the obligation under the *civil* law, but a threefold classification existed, viz.:—

(1) *Civiles*, *i.e.*, those obligations existing and producing their full effects, according to the civil law.

(2) *Prætoriæ (honorariæ)*, *i.e.*, those introduced by the prætor, and provided by him either with special actions, or with *utiles* forms of the corresponding civil actions.

(3) *Naturales*, *i.e.*, those recognised by the rules of the *jus gentium* and the maxims of natural reason, but producing *no* action, though they could be used by way of *exception* or discharge, or as the basis of an accessory contract.

Sources of obligations.

The facts generating obligations arise from (1) mutual consent, (2) voluntary or involuntary injury of another, (3) voluntary or involuntary benefit at the expense of another, (4) family and social relations. In respect of obligations arising from consent, the civil law only recognised the *vinculum juris* in the few cases rigorously prescribed by it, but the sphere of obligations was gradually extended by the Prætor's edict, jurisprudence, imperial constitutions, and the rules of the *jus gentium*, so that four modes of contracting were recognised, viz.: (1) *re*, (2) *verbis*, (3) *litteris*, (4) *consensu.*

In the case of damage caused wrongfully, the civil law, under the head of *noxa* (later *maleficium, delictum*) defined a certain number of cases, and *prætorian* law made some additions. Hence *two* sources existed, viz., *contract* and *delict*, and when jurisprudence recognised other facts generating obligations, but not falling under either of these two classes, though resembling one or other, four kinds were distinguished, viz.: (1) *ex contractu*, (2) *quasi ex contractu*, 3) *ex maleficio*, (4) *quasi ex maleficio.*

Obligationes ex contractu.

Contracts formed *re*. These four were engendered by simple *traditio*, *i.e.*, by the essential element in the original *nexum* deprived of the material symbolism and sacramental formula, which accompanied that mode of contracting, for the terms *mutuum, commodatum, depositum, pignus*, in their origin, indicated not the kind of contract, which was always *per æs et libram*, but the thing of which it was the object.

Mutuum. Here one of the contracting parties, who must be the *owner*, transferred to the other in ownership things *in genere*, and the obligation was that they should be *returned* at a given time in the same quality and quantity.

Commodatum. The *commodans* gratuitously allowed another to have the use of a thing *in specie* for a given time, but, as the contract did not transfer either ownership or possession, it might apply to the property of a third party. Two obligations resulted, viz., (1) that the borrower should preserve and *return* the thing, (2) that the commodans should indemnify the borrower if *ex post facto* events connected with the property entailed expenses or damage. The *borrower* was usually responsible for *dolus*, as well as for the *culpa*, that a very diligent paterfamilias would not commit; the *commodans* for *dolus* and *culpa gravis*.

Depositum. Here the *deponens* retains the ownership and possession of the thing *in specie*, which the *depositarius* gratuitously takes charge of. Two obligations result: (1) on the part of the *depositarius*, to keep with such care as he would employ in managing his own affairs, and return when demanded, (2) for the *deponens* to indemnify for *ex post facto* expenses incurred about the thing, and his responsibility includes all kinds of *culpa*.

Pignus appears under two aspects, viz.:—

(1) In respect of the *real* right conferred on the creditor by the agreement itself, without the necessity of *traditio*. The debtor (pawnor) retained the ownership (if he had it), but the legal effects of possession were shared between him and the creditor; so that the *debtor* preserved the benefit as regards *usucapion*, but the *creditor* acquired the right to all actions, and possessory interdicts which tended to maintain the thing in his power.

(2) In respect of the *contract*. This only existed in consequence of the delivery of the thing *(re)*. Two obligations resulted, (1) that the *creditor* should take care of the thing, and restore it after complete satisfaction of his debt, (2) that the debtor should indemnify for *ex post facto* expenses incurred in the preservation of the thing, and both contracting parties were reciprocally bound for every kind of *culpa*.

As to *actions*. The *mutuum* gave rise to the unilateral *condictio a stricti juris actio*, derived from the ancient law, and common to the various strict civil law contracts. The *commodatum depositum* and *pignus* were each provided with special *bonæ fidei* actions *(commodati, depositi, pigneratitia)*, deriving their names from the contract, and there were *directa* or *contraria*, according to the position of the contracting party.

Contracts formed *verbis*. These were the first derivation of the *nexum*, and arose from the use of the sacramental formula without the material symbolism. Of the three forms (α) *dotis dictio*, (β) *jurata operarum promissio liberti*, and (γ) *stipulatio et promissio*, the last was the most general and important.

Stipulatio was the technical name for the interrogation put by the future creditor, and *promissio* referred to the affirmative reply of the future debtor; the two together constituted the verbal contract called *stipulatio*, and in its origin was reserved to *Roman citizens*.

It might apply to any kind of lawful obligation, but it only produced a bond on the part of the *promissor*, and (like the *mutuum*) gave rise to the *condictio certi* when the object was a sum of money, otherwise to the *condictio incerti*, called in this case *actio ex stipulatu*.

There might be several *stipulators*, or several *promissors*, and all the *interrogations* might come first, and then all the answers, in which case one single contract resulted, and the two or more co-stipulators, or two or more co-promissors, were called *con-rei (correi)*, and each was a creditor or debtor *in solidum*, or one *stipulatio* and *promissio* might form a complete and principal obligation, to which, by way of guarantee, and as an *accessory*, a new and distinct verbal contract could be added, in which the same object was stipulated for from the same debtor by a second *stipulator*, or promised to the same creditor by a second *promissor*. The person so joining himself to the principal creditor was called an *adstipulator*, whilst the surety of the principal debtor was an *adpromissor*. Only one kind of *adstipulator* existed, and the use of such persons fell into disuse when the facilities for pleading by procuration were increased, but the advantages resulting from the use of *adpromissores* led to three classes, according to the formula used, viz. : (1) the *sponsor* (from *sponsio*) reserved to Roman citizens, (2) the *fidepromissor*, derived from the extension of the *sponsio* to strangers, under the formula *idem fidepromittis?* (3) the *fidejussor*, so called from the formula *fidejubes* (or other equivalent expression), and employed to evade the narrow rules confining the use and liabilities of the two first, for the *sponsio* and *fidepromissio* could only be joined to a verbal contract at the time it was made, but the *fidejussio* could be used as a security for any obligation, either before or after it had arisen.

Stipulations were divided into (1) *conventionales, i.e.*, derived from the agreement of the parties, (2) *prætoriæ, i.e.*, arising only *in jure*, and by order of the *prætor*, (3) *judiciales, i.e.*, ordered by the *judge in judicio*, (4) *communes, i.e.*, those made by order of the *prætor* or of the *judge*.

Contracts formed *litteris*. This second derivation of the *per æs et libram* form of contract was based on the obligatory character attached to an entry in a special register. The sum, the object of the obligation, inscribed in consecrated formula in the domestic ledger, was held to be weighed and delivered on one side *(pecunia expensa lata)*, and as received on the other *(accepta relata)*, hence the name of *expensilatio* for the contract. The benefits of this kind of obligation were extended to strangers in the form of *syngraphæ* and *chirographæ*, and then fell into disuse, for the introduction of the exception *non numeratæ pecuniæ* caused the merger of the *chirographum* with the *cautio*, or simple proof by writing, at least where the *cautio* referred to a *mutuum*, and in this state the contract *litteris* passed into the legislation of Justinian.

Contracts formed *consensu*. These four were derived from the *jus gentium*. They produced *ultro citroque* obligations, and their effects were determined *ex æquo et bono*.

Emptio venditio. The principal obligation here was for the *venditor* to procure for the *emptor* the power of having a thing, as if he were owner of it, and for the *emptor* to pay the *venditor* a certain *pretium* in money. Although formed by simple consent, *Justinian* prevented its completion until reduced to writing, if the parties had so agreed, and the *arrhæ* (formerly only a sign of the conclusion of the contract) were made by *Justinian* a means of withdrawal. The contract only produced obligations, so that the *venditor* was not obliged to render the *emptor* owner of the property sold, though the *emptor* must transfer the ownership in the price paid, but the obligation of the *venditor* included the transference of the possession of the thing, and the guarantee against *eviction*, as well as against secret faults; the extent of the liability under the last head being regulated by custom, and by the edict of the *Curule Ædiles*. Both *venditor* and *emptor* were liable, not only for *dolus*, but for every kind of *culpa*.

After completion of the contract, and before *traditio*, the risk of the thing passed to the *emptor*, both as to profit and loss, including total destruction, if without any fault or *mora* of the *vendor*, unless by pact or stipulation the liability was otherwise extended or restrained. The *direct* and *bonæ fidei* actions *empti (ex empto)* for the *emptor*, and *venditi (ex vendito)* for the *venditor*, included all obligations derived, *ex æquo et bono*, from the contract and its accessory pacts. The *actio æstimatoria (quanto minoris)* lay for a diminution of the price, and the *actio redhibitoria*, introduced by the edict of the *Ædiles*, related to vices entitling the purchaser to return the thing.

Locatio-conductio. Here the *locator* bound himself to procure for the *conductor* the power of using or taking the produce of a thing, and the other agreed in return to pay a certain price in money, and, as the contract might also take the form of work or services, to be paid for proportionally to duration *(operæ)*, or in respect of a given piece of work to be done at a fixed price *(opus)*, there were three kinds of letting, viz.: (1) *rerum*, (2) *operarum*, (3) *operis*. Under Justinian, if the parties had agreed to reduce the contract to *writing*, this must be done before it would be binding, and both parties were responsible, not only for *dolus*, but also for all kinds of *fault*. The delivery of the thing let conferred no *real* right on the *conductor*, but the death of the *locator*, or of the *conductor*, did not terminate the contract, which continued until the expiration of the time agreed upon, unless the nature of the work made it *personal* to the individual who had undertaken it.

The *directa* and *bonæ fidei* actions, *locati* for the *locator* and *con-*

ducti for the *conductor*, included all obligations equitably resulting from the contract or accessory pacts. Some particular actions and interdicts served to enforce certain real rights given as security for these obligations, as the *Serviana actio* and the *interdictum Salvianum* open to the *locator*, in respect of *rural estates*, and the *quasi Serviana (hypothecaria) actio* for houses, whilst the interdict *de migrando* could be used against the *locator* who attempted to hinder the departure of the tenant.

Emphyteusis. The *contract* based upon the payment of a periodical rent by the tenant to the owner, and the *real right* arising on the *traditio* of the estate in execution of the contract, are to be distinguished, and it was not until the time of *Zeno* that this form of tenancy acquired a name, a separate existence, and an exclusive action. The contract produced no other effect than to bind the contracting parties in respect of the *emphyteusis* to be established, and was enforced by the *emphyteuticaria* action given to either party; but through the real right the *emphyteuta* acquired *utiles* forms of the actions which would be given to an owner; and provided he did not deteriorate the property, the tenant could make any modifications he pleased, or even transfer his rights to another. The duration of the tenancy was indefinite, and it passed to successors by will or *ab intestato*.

Societas. This contract, by which two or more persons agreed that there should be between them a certain community of property, was formed by simple consent, and produced *ultro citroque* obligations determined *ex æquo et bono*. It might be (1) *Universorum bonorum*, (2) *Universorum quæ ex quæstu veniunt*, (3) *Negociationis alicujus*, (4) *Vectigalis*, (5) *Unius rei*. The contributions of the partners might be unequal, and consist of property or labour. The principal obligation involved was for each *socius* to bring the contribution, work, or industry promised, and to share, in the proportion agreed, the gain or loss which, in the absence of agreement, was presumed equal, though it might be unequal, and one or more might participate in the *gain* only. The partners were mutually liable for *dolus*, but *culpa* would not be attributed to them, unless they had not used the personal diligence which they would have employed about their own affairs.

In respect of *third* parties, the obligations of the *socii* were regulated by the principle (1) that the *societas* is a complex contract, involving between the partners an express or tacit *mandate*, (2) that, even in the case of a mandate, obligations generally only existed between those who were parties to the transaction. The contract was terminated (1) *ex personis, i.e.,* by *death, max.* or *med. c.d.* (formerly also by *minima*), by confiscation (*publicatio*) or *bonorum cessio* of one of the partners, (2) *ex rebus, i.e.,* by the loss of the thing, or the completion of the object for which the partnership was formed, (3) *ex voluntate, i.e.,* by the *renuntiatio* of one of the partners, but subject to responsibility in the case of fraudulent or unseasonable retirement, (4) *ex tempore, i.e.,* by the expiration of the time agreed upon, (5) *ex actione, i.e.*, by a suit to dissolve the partnership.

Condemnation in the *direct* and *bonæ fidei* action *pro socio* only extended *in quantum facere potest*, but imported *infamy*, and was for the purpose of getting execution of the contract, whilst by the *communi dividundo* action a partner could get a cessation of the community of interest in a common thing. These two actions did not destroy one another, but were cumulative, except that, in points common to them, what was recovered by the one could not be again obtained by the other. The same remark applied to the actions *furti, vi bonorum raptorum, legis Aquiliæ*, or any others which might be open to one of the parties in respect of the common property.

Mandatum. Under this contract, formed by simple, even tacit, consent, the *procurator (mandatarius)* agreed gratuitously to act in his own name for the benefit of the *mandans (mandator)* either generally or in one or more determined matters. The result of the agreement was to produce an *obligation* on the side of the *mandatarius* to fulfil the mission with which he was charged, to render an account, and to restore to the *mandans* all objects and rights acquired, but *ex post facto* the *mandans* might be liable to reimburse the *mandatarius* for all expenses incurred, as well as to release him from all obligations contracted in execution of the *mandatum*. Both parties were responsible for every kind of *culpa*, but as regards third parties, strictly the *mandatarius* only was bound, though ultimately, by *utiles* actions and other indirect means, even ownership could be acquired or alienated by the effect of the *traditio* made in the name of the *mandans to* or *by* the *procurator.*

The benefit of the contract may be for (1) the *mandans* only, (2) the *mandans* and the *mandatarius*, (3) a third party only, (4) the *mandans* and a third party, (5) the *mandatarius* and a third party; but the mandate given in the interest of the *mandatarius* only was useless. In some cases the *mandatum* bore a strong analogy to the *fideijussio*, and therefore fell under the head of *intercessio*, as when the *mandator* became responsible for the debt of another. The mandatum expired by (1) the consent of both, (2) the will of one, *i.e.*, by the revocation of the *mandans* or the renunciation of the *mandatarius*, and (3) the death of either. The *mandati* actions, *directa* for the *mandans* and *contraria* for the *mandatarius*, were *bonæ fidei*, and the first entailed infamy. Ultimately third parties acquired *utiles quasi institoriæ* actions against the *mandans*, and in most cases the *mandans* had *utiles* actions against third parties.

Pacts.
Agreements not falling within the civil law *contracts* in strictness produced no bond, but various legal effects were gradually given to them by—

(1) *Civil law,* as where execution was allowed to be enforced by the same action as the contract in the case of (α) pacts joined to a *bonæ fidei* contract at the time of its formation *(pacta adjecta ex continenti).* So an obligation was recognised where (β) the pact had been followed by execution on the part of one of the parties, *i.e.,* a contract was held to have arisen *re.* This originated the class of *innominati* agreements summed up in one of the four operations, "*do ut des, do ut facias, facio ut des, facio ut facias*", and which produced in general for the benefit of him who had executed the contract an *incerta civilis* action, called the *actio in factum præscriptis verbis,* because the fact creating the obligation was set out as a preamble in the first part of the formula, but, if the contract had been formed by the giving of a thing or the extinction of some right susceptible of re-establishment, the restitution of the thing, or the re-establishment of the right, might be obtained by the *condictio causa data, causa non secuta;* whilst for pacts executed on one side, involving *facio ut des,* the *actio doli* lay.

(2) *Prætorian law.* Particular agreements came to be recognised as *Pacta prætoria,* and were enforced by a prætorian action, *e.g.,* the *actio de pecunia constituta* was given to compel the execution of the *constitutum, i.e.,* the promise made by simple pact to pay on a given day a pre-existing civil, prætorian, or natural debt; and this became a means of modifying, by simple pact, the performance of a *civil* obligation, or of rendering obligatory a purely *natural* obligation, or of becoming security for the debt due from another person.

(3) *Imperial law.* Under the Emperors, certain pacts *(pacta legitima)* were enforced by the *condictio ex lege,* when no special action was given, *e.g.,* the pacts *donatio, de dote constituenda,* and *compromissum.*

Pacts not included under the above heads fell into the class of *nuda pactio,* and produced only *natural* obligations, whilst other agreements, *prohibited* on the ground of morality, or justice, or public order, or the necessity of affording special protection to certain persons, produced no action or exception, and that which had been paid in pursuance of them could be recovered back by the *condictio indebiti.*

Obligationes quasi ex contractu.

The greater number of these are analogous to some civil law contract, *e.g.,* the *negotiorum gestio, tutela,* and *curatela,* resemble the *mandatum;* the accidental community of undivided ownership, and the position of co-heirs in an inheritance, resemble the *societas;* and payment made by mistake, when not due, bears a strong resemblance to the position of the parties to a *mutuum.*

Culpa.

An unlawful act *(injuria),* causing damage and done by a *sane* and *free* agent, fell under the head of *dolus* when committed with the design to injure, and under *culpa* when there was no such intention.

In all cases, responsibility for *dolus* is implied, and no agreement to the contrary would be good; but *culpa* admits of different degrees; for although men are bound to abstain from all acts hurtful to others, they are not, in general, also bound to use such activity or watchfulness *(diligentia, custodia)*, as that its omission *(negligentia)* would result in damage to another; but if in the particular case this *diligentia* is necessary, its absence would be *culpa*, of which the jurists distinguish two degrees, viz., (α) *culpa lata*, (β) *culpa levis*, the standard of comparison being either *absolute, i.e.*, in respect of men in general; or *relative, i.e.*, in respect of the habitual character of the particular individual; in the first case, his care being compared for *culpa lata* to that which the first comer would have used, and for *culpa levis* to that which would be expected from the most diligent paterfamilias; whilst, in the second case, his care is compared to that which he habitually uses in his own affairs.

Mora.

This is the delay, contrary to law, attributable to him who ought to make, or of him who ought to receive, restitution or payment. If it occurred *ex re, i.e.*, by the fact itself, there was no necessity for any demand, otherwise it was *ex persona*, and did not arise until after a demand of performance. The risk of the property fell upon him who was in *mora*, as well as a liability for interest or produce, or an indemnity.

Usuræ.

This term refers to the fraction of the capital due to the creditor over and above the principal sum, on account of the time during which the creditor is deprived of his property. The maximum rate remained fixed from the time of Cicero down to Justinian at *centesimæ usuræ, i.e.*, one per cent. per month, or twelve per cent. per year. Justinian lowered it, and varied it according to the quality of the person or the nature of the loan, but compound interest was forbidden.

Acquisition of obligations.

As a general rule, obligations are acquired by those who have been the actors in the events productive of the obligation; but as the *slave* and the *filius familias* had no other *persona* than that of the *paterfamilias* in whose power they were at the time, obligations resulting from events to which they were parties were acquired by him, subject to the rules respecting the *peculia* of the *filius familias*, and to the principles governing the position of slaves or of free persons possessed in good faith, of whom the paterfamilias had only the usufruct or the use. In strictness, strangers could not be the means of acquiring for others; but prætorian law and jurisprudence rectified this by indirect means.

Transference of obligations.

According to the civil law, *personal* rights could not be transferred from the creditor to another person; but, indirectly, this cession was effected by giving the cessionee a mandate to make use of the actions resulting from the obligation for his own benefit, *i.e.*, making him a *procurator in rem suam;* and although in principle this procurator could only act as a *mandatarius*, yet jurisprudence and imperial constitutions finally gave him *utiles* actions, of which he could avail himself directly.

Dissolution of obligations.

A civil obligation could only be dissolved conformably to the civil law (*ipso jure*); but in many cases, where in strictness the obligation continued to subsist, prætorian law and jurisprudence gave the debtor *exceptions* by which he could defend himself against the claim of the creditor, and hence the rule of the commentators, *obligatio aut ipso jure, aut per exceptionem tollitur.*

Solutio (performance) is the primary mode of extinguishing obligations. This may be made by a third party, with or without the knowledge and against the will of the debtor; and (if the creditor was willing) it was finally held that the delivery of *aliud pro alio*, called a *datio in solutum*, released the debtor *ipso jure;* and on the refusal of the creditor to receive, or in his absence at time and place appointed, a valid tender *(oblatio)*, followed by payment into court *(obsignatio)*, also freed the debtor from liability.

Novatio also dissolved an obligation by replacing it with a new one; but though all obligations could be so dealt with, only the *stipulatio* and the contract *litteris* could be employed to effect the novation, except in the case of novations resulting from the different phases of a trial. The original obligation might be civil, prætorian, or purely natural; but the stipulation substituting a new debt for the first must be in form, a valid civil law verbal contract, and the new obligation intended to be produced must exist and be efficacious—at least naturally. The new verbal obligation replacing the first may be contracted, (α) either by a new debtor *(ex promissor)* towards the same creditor, with or without the knowledge, or even against the will, of the first debtor; (β) by the same debtor towards a new creditor, on the order of the former one; (γ) by a new debtor towards a new creditor, on the order of the former creditor; (δ) by the same debtor towards the same creditor, in which case, if the first obligation resulted from a stipulation, the subsequent stipulation, in order to effect novation, must contain something new in it; and *Justinian* decided that novation should in any case only take place when the contracting parties expressly declared that such was their intention.

Release was anciently effected by the same means that served to form the obligation, and therefore an *imaginaria solutio* was gone through by the *per æs et libram* method in respect of obligations so contracted; and subsequently the release *verbis* (*i.e.*, the interrogation of the creditor as to his having received the subject of the contract, and his affirmative reply) was generalised, and under the name of *acceptilatio* applied to all obligations whatever. For this purpose, it sufficed to transform by novation the obligation to be extinguished into a verbal contract, and then dissolve it by acceptilation.

The *four consensual* contracts could be *dissolved* by consent alone if there had not been any execution or loss on either side.

Confusio and the *loss* of the thing due, without the fault or *mora* of the debtor in obligations of things certain, were really obstacles in the way of performance resulting from the persons or the things, rather than cases of extinction of obligations.

BOOK IV.

Tit. i. De obligationibus quæ ex delicto nascuntur.

1715. These obligations all spring from the fact itself *(omnes ex re nascuntur, id est, ex ipso maleficio)*, and are only *delicts* when so characterised and provided with an action by the civil law. The text only treats of them in respect of the obligations and private actions to which they give rise.

1717. *Theft (furtum)* is defined as *contrectatio rei fraudulosa, lucri faciendi gratia, vel ipsius rei, vel etiam usus possessionisve*. Hence, to constitute theft, there must be :—

(1) A *dealing* with the *thing itself;* that is, some displacement of it, the *intention* not being sufficient, and, therefore, by the better opinion, *immoveables* could not be the subjects of theft (Gai. Inst. ii, § 51, and *ante*, par. 519).

(2) *Fraud—Fur est qui dolo malo rem alienam contrectat* (Paul, Sent., 2, 31, 1).

(3) The *intention* of appropriating it for self or others; and *Theophilus*, in his paraphrase, correctly adds that there must further be :—

(4) Some *damage* sustained by another person *(lædens aliquem)*.

1718. (§ iii) *Justinian* adopts the opinion of *Gaius* (Inst. iii, § 183), derived from *Labeo*, that there were only two kinds of theft, viz. :—

(1) *Furtum manifestum*. This, according to *Justinian*, was

committed when the thief was caught with the stolen property in his possession before reaching his destination; though, according to other opinions, it was either *restricted* to the case of (1) the thief being taken in the act or (2) on the spot, or *extended* to (3) any time, any where, if the goods were in the possession of the thief.

According to the Twelve Tables (viii, § 14), the thief, if a *slave*, was scourged and put to death; but, if *free*, he was, after the scourging, *addictus* to the person aggrieved, though it was a disputed question whether he thereby became a slave, or, like a free man *in mancipio*, was merely assimilated to one (Gai. Inst. iii, § 189). This vindictive penalty was altered by the prætor for both *free* persons and *slaves* to *four* times the value.

(2) *Nec manifestum.* This included the cases not coming under *manifestum.* The penalty fixed by the Twelve Tables was *double*, and remained the same under the prætor's jurisdiction.

Paul (Sent. 2, 31, 2), following Sulpicius and Sabinus, speaks of two other kinds of theft, viz., (3) *conceptum* and (4) *oblatum*; but as, according to a constitution of Diocletian and Maximinian (Cod. vi, 2, 14), the *actio furti nec manifesti* lay for knowingly receiving and concealing stolen goods, the distinctions resulting from accidental peculiarities connected with the discovery of the property were unnecessary. On this ground, the four following actions, existing in the time of *Gaius*, (the two first established by the Twelve Tables, and the other two by the Prætor) are represented by Justinian as having fallen into disuse, viz. :—

(1) *Actio furti concepti*, with a penalty of *three* times the value (falling upon the person in whose possession it was found, whether the actual thief or not) where the stolen property was accidentally discovered or found after an informal search by consent and in the presence of witnesses, as opposed to the *actio furti lancelicioque concepti* (abolished by the *Lex Æbutia*) given on the discovery of the property after a solemn search, wearing a girdle only, and holding a plate, and for which the *penalty* was assimilated to the *furtum manifestum* (Twelve Tables, viii, § 15).

(2) *Actio furti oblati*, given to B against A, with a penalty of *three* times the value (Twelve Tables, viii, § 15), when stolen property was intentionally deposited by A with B, in order that it might be seized at B's rather than at A's.

(3) *Actio furti prohibiti*, given against the person who opposed a search in the presence of witnesses, and introduced by the prætor with a penalty of *quadruple*, as the Twelve Tables had only ordered in such a case the *lancelicioque* search to be made (Gai. Inst. iii, § 192).

(4) *Actio furti non exhibiti*, given by the prætor with a penalty of *quadruple* against the person who did not produce stolen property searched for and found in his possession.

1722. Although *intention* was a necessary ingredient, yet the taking of a thing might constitute theft if it was done with the *knowledge* that it was against the will, or contrary to the intention, or not really with the consent, of the owner. Hence, a liability to the *actio furti* might arise where a creditor or depositee *used* the thing that had been pledged or entrusted to him, or if he who had the *usus* for one purpose employed it for another (*e.g.*, in the case of silver plate to be used at a feast taken on a voyage, or a horse to be used for a ride taken for longer, or into battle).

Justinian also decided, contrary to the rules of strict law, that the owner of a slave would have the *actio servi corrupti (post*, par. 1779, γ), as well as the *actio furti*, against the person who persuaded the slave to steal any object from his master, and bring it to him, though the slave disclosed the proposal to his master, and took the thing to the intended thief on his master's order, for the acts of the thief had been consummated as far as they depended on him, though the slave was not really corrupted and the object was delivered by the master's order, the difficulty as to calculating the penalty under the *actio servi corrupti* being met by estimating the depreciation in the value of the slave if he had been actually corrupted.

So, if a *free* person, *e.g.*, a child in power (or a wife *in manu*, or person in *mancipio*, Gai. Inst. iii, § 199), was taken away (as in the example given by *Theophilus* of a child to be *heir*, if in such a town at the death of the testator and the thief took him to another town), the *actio furti* would lie, and the value would be calculated according to the interest the *paterfamilias* had in the possession of the child. So also a person may be liable to the action in respect of his own property, as where a debtor deprives his creditor of the property pledged to him.

Accomplices were only liable to the *actio in factum*, and not to the *actio furti*, unless they had co-operated in the theft by actually *giving assistance (ope) intentionally (et consilio)*, as if, *e.g.*, they knocked money out of a person's hand for the thief to pick up, or, with the same object, dispersed cattle by means of a piece of red cloth, or planted a ladder for the thief, or broke the windows, or the door, or lent ladders, or tools, for the purpose, or succeeded in persuading a slave to fly in order that he might be stolen; and the *actio furti* would lie against the *accomplices* of a person in power, although no such action could arise between the *paterfamilias* and the person *in power* if the latter stole anything from the former.

On the ground that *intention* was a necessary ingredient, an *impubes* was only liable *si proximus pubertati sit*, see part ii, par. 86.

1726. *Actions relating to theft*.

(1) *Actio furti*. This was a penal action for the purpose of getting the *thieves* separately, or any of their *accomplices*, condemned each for the whole amount in a *pecuniary* penalty of *quadruple* in the case of *furtum manifestum*, and of *double* for *nec manifestum*. It was independent of any other actions used for the purpose of *recovering* the property.

The action could be brought concurrently by any one or more

persons who were concerned in the preservation of the property, and who had it in his or their possession by some title or other at the time, as in the case of the *nudus* owner, the user, and the usufructuary in respect of their several interests. The right passed to their *heirs* and *successors*; but, on the other hand, the *owner* might not be able to bring it, if the property was out of his possession, and if the person who had it was responsible for it, hence it was open to the creditor in the case of a *pledge* stolen, even if the debtor (*i.e.*, the real owner) was the thief; and so also a *fuller* in respect of clothes sent him to clean, or a tailor employed to mend them, could, if a price had been agreed upon for their work, avail themselves of the *actio furti*, for the owner had the *actio locati* against them, unless the fuller or the tailor was insolvent, in which case the owner would have the *actio furti* so as to prevent his being a loser. In the case of a *deposit* (*ante*, par. 1220), as the depositee was not liable for *custodia*, he could not bring the *actio furti*, which was accordingly only open to the depositor, though, in the case of a *loan*, after Justinian's amendments of the law, the owner *(commodator)* had the choice between the *actio commodati* against the borrower (in which case the latter had the *actio furti* against the thief), or the *actio furti* against the thief, when the commodatee was released; but, if the commodator brought his action against the commodatee in ignorance of the theft, and the borrower did not satisfy the claim, he could abandon it for the *actio furti* against the thief, after which the commodatee would be released from liability, whatever might be the result of the action against the thief. A *bona fide* purchaser, whether really owner or not, could also bring the *actio furti;* but a purchaser before *traditio* had no title to the possession of the property, and, therefore, could not avail himself of the action, though he had a right to claim the cession of the action from the vendor.

The amount of the *penalty* was estimated by ascertaining the highest value of the property since the theft, *i.e.*, not of the thing itself, but of the damage sustained by the owner in consequence of being deprived of the thing *(quod actoris interfuit)*, as in the case of receipts *(tabulæ, cautiones, chirographa)* being stolen.

(2) *Actio vindicandi*, or the *actio ad exhibendum*, open to the *owner* of the property to recover it from any possessor or person who had ceased to possess in consequence of bad faith.

(3) *Condictio furtiva*. A *personal* action given (exceptionally and *odio furum*, in addition to the *vindicatio*) against the *thief* or his *heirs* to enable the *owner* to recover the property back, or in the event of its destruction, to get damages for the loss (calculated as in the *furti actio*), together with interest; but (except the *actio furti*), if the owner recovered the property back with its accessories, or its value, by one of these actions, the others would not lie (see *ante*, par. 384).

Tit. ii. De vi bonorum raptorum.

1738. When a *moveable* thing, however small, had been carried off *dolo malo* and *vi*, the injured party had the option between a public criminal accusation under the *lex Julia, de vi privata (post*, par. 2360), against the robber *(improbus fur)*, or the special private action *vi bonorum raptorum* introduced by the *Prætor*.

The rules of the *actio furti (ante*, par. 1726) applied as *to whom* it would be given, but they were not quite so strict, as it was sufficient if the thing was taken from amongst the property of the injured person (*res ablata ex bonis meis*), so that a deposit*ee*, if he had some interest in the preservation of the thing, was included. The plaintiff recovered the *quadruple;* but, as this amount included the value of the thing, the penalty was only *triple*, and, as this quadruple was calculated on the value of the *thing itself*, and was reduced after *one year* to the *simple value*, it was better to bring the *actio furti manifesti* if the thief was caught in the act, or *nec manifesti* if the year had elapsed. The action would lie in addition to the *actio furti*, but *not vice versâ*, and the *vindicatio* and *ad exhibendum* actions were also open, except that, as the penalty *included* the value of the thing, these could not be brought after this action had terminated successfully. As the action was partly *penal*, it would *not* lie against the *heirs* of the robber; though, if they had benefited, the *condictio* was available against them. As *wrongful intention* was a necessary ingredient, the action *vi bonorum raptorum* would not lie against a person who seized the property believing himself to be rightly entitled; but, to prevent forcible entry on *immoveables*, or the abstraction by force of *moveables*, such acts were punished under a constitution of Valentinian Theodosius and Arcadius (Cod. 8, 4, 7) by the loss of the thing if the person was actually owner; and, if not, he had to pay the value of it, in addition to restoring it.

Tit. iii. De lege Aquilia.

1746. This *plebiscitum*, passed on the proposition of the tribune *Aquilius*, dates (according to the paraphrase of *Theophilus*) from the third secession of the plebs to the Janiculum, B.C. 286. It repealed all former laws (including the Twelve Tables) relating to unlawful damage (Dig. 9, 2, 1, *Ulpian*), and consisted of three heads, viz. :—

(1) *Qui servum servamve, alienum alienamve quadrupedem vel pecudem* (*i.e.*, domesticated animals in flocks or herds, as horses, mules, sheep, etc., not wild animals or dogs), *injuria* (*i.e., nullo jure* unlawfully, the question of *intent* being immaterial) *occiderit quanti id in eo anno plurimi fuerit* (*i.e.*, the highest market value for which the slave could have been sold during *the year previous*), *tantum æs dare domino damnatus esto* (Dig. 9, 2, 2, *Gaius*). This head, therefore, related to the total *destruction* of certain *corporeal* things; viz., *slaves* or *cattle*, and if these were *unlawfully killed* the owner could recover by means of the *damni injuriæ ex lege Aquilia actio* their highest value during that year. From the defi-

nition it follows that such cases would be *e*xcluded from the operation of the law, as killing a robber, if there was no other means of escape, or repelling force by force (*vim enim vi defendere omnes leges, omnia que jura permittunt,* Dig. 9, 2, 45, 4, *Paul*). Hence also, a soldier would not be liable who whilst practising the lance exercise killed a passing slave (unless the place was not destined for such a purpose), nor a workman, lopping the branches of a tree, if he had shouted to give warning before the log fell (if not in a public road, not necessary to cry out), but the player would be liable who struck a tennis ball so violently as to cause it to bound against the hand of a barber, and thereby cut the throat of the slave he was shaving, unless the place was one ordinarily used for the game, or otherwise much frequented, in which case the barber would be liable, though not if the slave had himself selected the dangerous spot (Dig. 9, 2, 11, *Ulpian*). Negligence, heedlessness, and want of skill are *i*ncluded, as in the case of a physician who abandoned the care of a slave after an operation, and who would be liable if the patient died, or if the operation was improperly performed, or if wrong medicine was administered, and in the same way a mule driver or rider would be liable if from unskilfulness or weakness an accident happened.

The *heir* was not liable, except to the extent enriched, because the action was *penal* in so far as the slave or animal might have been of less value at the time of death than during the year previous, and because the amount recovered was *doubled* if the liability was denied. The condemnation of one of several defendants did not release the others, and (as in the case of *theft*) the *interpretatio* of the jurisprudents (not the terms of the *law* itself), led to the value being estimated according to the damage sustained, including accessories, as in the case of a slave who was instituted heir, and killed before *aditio* (*ante*, par. 616) or one of a pair of mules, or one of a set of four chariot horses, or one of a company of slave actors being killed. In addition to this private civil action for a pecuniary indemnity, the person killing a *slave* was also liable to a criminal accusation under the *Lex Cornelia* (*post*, par. 2357).

(2) This head related to the destruction of certain *i*ncorporeal rights, for the discovery of the *MS.* of *Gaius* (Inst. iii, § 215, 216) shewed that an action (which *Justinian* states had fallen into disuse) lay against the *adstipulator* (*ante*, par. 1377) to recover the damage (*quanti ea res esset*) sustained by the *fraudulent release* of the *debtor* by *acceptilation* (*ante*, par. 1687), for though the original *stipulator* could sue the adstipulator by the *mandati actio*, the action under the *lex Aquilia* gave the additional advantage of entailing *double* the penalty if the liability for the extinction of the debt was denied.

(3) *Cæterarum rerum, præter hominem et pecudem occisos, si quis alteri damnum facit quod usserit* (burnt), *fregerit* (broken), *ruperit* (fractured), *injuria, quanti ea res erit in diebus triginta proximis tantum æs domino dare damnatus esto* (Dig. 9, 2, 27, 5,

Ulpian). This head therefore related to the loss of any *other* objects than those enumerated under the first head, or the *deterioration* of any, and if the injury was occasioned *ex dolo aut culpa*, the owner could recover the highest value during the thirty preceding days. From the definition it follows that if there was no other means of escape, and a person tore down the walls of a neighbouring house to stop a fire, or cut the cables of another vessel when his own vessel was being driven against them by a storm, he would *not* be liable for the damage, because the act would not be unlawful.

1757. The mode of occasioning the damage led to the following distinctions, viz.:—

(1) The *actio legis Aquiliæ directa* was restricted to the *owner*, and only lay if the damage was done *corpore corpori*, *i.e.*, *by* the person liable *to* the person or thing injured, as where a person threw the slave of another over a bridge, and he was thereby drowned in the river below, though if the damage was *consequential* only, as where the slave of another was persuaded to climb a tree, or descend a well, and was thereby killed or injured, the remedy must be sought by the—

(2) *actio utilis Aquiliæ* (also called the *actio utilis in factum ex lege Aquilia*), given to the owner, *bona fide* possessor, usufructuary, or creditor pledgee, by the Prætor, as an extension of the above, and entailing similar consequences. If the damage was only indirect, as where a person moved by compassion released the slave of another from his chains to enable him to flee; the—

(3) *actio in factum* would have to be used in the absence of any special action covering the particular case.

If the owner selected the appropriate civil action, *e.g.*, *depositi, commodati, locati,* etc., he was not prohibited from bringing the *actio legis Aquiliæ* to obtain any surplus recoverable under that action.

Tit. iv. De injuriis.

1764. The term *injuria* properly includes *omne quod non jure fit*, but it was also specially used in the senses of—

(α) the fault productive of damage to another, as in the *lex Aquilia*,

(β) the injustice or iniquity of a judge pronouncing contrary to law,

(γ) outrage or affront *(contumelia)*.

The last is the meaning of the word under the *actio injuriarum*, which was a *private civil action* brought by the party injured, or his procurator, tutor, or other representative, for the purpose of obtaining a *pecuniary penalty*, the amount of which was, under *prætorian* law, fixed by the *plaintiff*, though the judge might award a lesser sum. The *injured party* could also commence a *criminal accusation*, under which the judge inflicted *extra-ordinem* severe punishments for certain injuries (*e.g.*, death for violent attempts at chastity, see *post*, par. 2360), and *Zeno* (Cod. 9, 35, 11) allowed persons not below the rank of *illustris* to bring or defend this criminal accusation by procuration.

BOOK IV—TIT. IV.   327

The *intention* to commit the outrage or insult must exist, hence neither a lunatic nor an *impubes* (not yet *doli capax*) could be guilty of *injuria*, although they might be the objects of it. The offence may be committed *aut re aut verbis*, as (α) by striking a person, or (β) causing a crowd to assemble round him or his dwelling, or (γ) pretending to be a creditor, and taking possession of his goods, or (δ) writing, composing, and publishing a libel, or (ε) following a respectable woman (*materfamilias*), or children of either sex, or attempting the chastity of a woman, or (ζ) insulting a person by treating him as a slave, or (η) affecting his intellect by the administration of drugs, or (θ) by having attempted, or been instrumental, in causing any of these things to be done.

1767. (§ ii) The injury may be direct or consequential, *i.e.*, done to oneself, or *through* others, as to a wife or child *in power*, and several persons might be separately injured through one, and therefore have distinct actions, according to their several interests (the damages varying according to their personal dignity), as (α) the wife herself, (β) her father, and (γ) her husband, in the case of an injury to a wife not *in manu viri, i.e.*, still under the power of her father, or even in the case of an intended wife, and if the husband was in *power* a fourth person would be injured, viz., the father-in-law, through the son, but the father would bring both the action for the indirect injury to himself, and the direct action open to his son in power, unless the father was absent or without a procurator, in which case the son could himself sue.

1771. (§ iii) In strictness, no *personal* injury could be done to a slave, and therefore only one action in the master's own name could be brought, and that only in respect of any damage intentionally done to the slave for the purpose of injuring the master, but the prætor gave the *master* also a *prætorian actio injuriarum*, for injuries to the slave not directed against the master, as when his slave had been struck without any order of the master, or (after *causa cognita*) for other lesser indignities to the person of the slave, according to his value (see *ante*, par. 47).

If there were several owners, the injury done to them was estimated according to the rank of each, but the value recoverable under the *utilis* action for the injury to the slave would be determined proportionally to their shares in him. The *utilis* action was restricted to the *owner*, but the original action would be given to the *usufructuary* or the *bona fide possessor* if the injury was directed against them.

1775. According to *Paul* (Sent. 5, 4, § 6) the *actio injuriarum* was introduced *aut lege (i.e.*, by the Twelve Tables, see viii, §§ 1, 2, 3), *aut more (i.e.*, by the Prætorian law), *aut mixto jure*, by this probably referring to the *lex Cornelia de Sicariis*, which, though directed principally to the subject of murder (see *post*, par. 2357), also gave a *private* action where violent injury resulted from a person being (1) struck, (2) scourged, or (3) his domicile entered by force. *Lex itaque Cornelia ex tribus causis dedit actionem ; quod quis pul-*

satus verberatus-ve domus-ve ejus vi introita sit. (Dig. 47, 10, 5, *Ulpian*).

1776. (§ ix) *Atrox injuria.* This meant an injury *aggravated* by reason of its nature, as from the

(α) *fact, e.g.,* wounded or struck with rods.

(β) *place, e.g.,* in the theatre or the forum.

(γ) *person, e.g.,* a magistrate, senator, or patron.

(δ) *part* injured, *e.g.,* the eye.

The *condemnation* in these cases was greater, the *maximum taxatio* being fixed by the prætor himself in the formula (Gai., Inst. iii, § 224), and the fact that the injury was *atrox* enabled a freedman to bring the *actio injuriarum* against his patron, or a son not in power against his father, though otherwise it would not lie.

1778. The *actio injuriarum* was *extinguished* by:—

(1) not having shown any resentment at the time *(dissimulatione)*.

(2) although resented at the time, yet the action not brought within the year.

(3) death, for, the action being *personal*, it did not pass to the *heirs*, unless the joinder of issue *(litis contestatio)* had already taken place.

1779. Besides the delicts mentioned in these four titles of the Institutes, the following may be added, because specially characterised as such, and provided with a particular action by civil or prætorian legislation, *e.g.*—

(α) The delicts indemnified by means of the *actio de tigno juncto*, and the *actio arborum furtim cæsarum*, both of which were derived from the Twelve Tables (see Table vi, §§ 7, 8, 9, and *post*, par. 2346), and involved a penalty of *double*, the *actio legis Aquiliæ* being also available in the second case.

(β) The cases covered by the *actio rerum amotarum* which was given against a *wife* who had made away with any property in anticipation of divorce, or against a *husband* who similarly dealt with the wife's *parapherna*. This action, although arising from a delict, and instituted after divorce, was only for the pursuit of the property, because, during marriage, or in respect of delicts which had been committed during marriage, no action involving disgrace could be brought between husband and wife *(nam in honorem matrimonii turpis actio adversus uxorem negatur,* Dig. 25, 2, 1, Paul), though, for abstractions made after the dissolution of the marriage, the *actio furti* would lie.

(γ) A number of *Prætorian* actions were also introduced to punish certain classes of delicts, as, *e.g.*—

The *actio servi corrupti* involving a penalty of *double*, and lying against a person concealing the flight of a slave, or persuading him to do an unlawful act.

The *actio vi bonorum raptorum et de turba,* for damage caused in a crowd *(in turba)* wrongfully *(dolo malo)*, and entailing a penalty of *double* within the year, or the simple penalty after the expiration of that time.

The *actio de incendio, ruina, naufragio, rate, nave expugnata*, which involved a penalty of *quadruple* within the year, or the simple penalty afterwards on those who profited by the confusion attending disasters, such as a house taking fire or falling down, or a shipwreck, or an attack on a vessel or boat, to plunder, remove, or conceal property.

(δ) A plaint falling under the head of *crimen expilatæ hereditatis* could be heard *extra-ordinem* before the city prefect or president of the province when there had been an abstraction of property belonging to an inheritance before the heir had made *aditio* or was in possession, for, as the act did not fall within the definition of theft, the *actio furti* would not lie.

Where several delicts had been committed simultaneously, the private penal actions belonging to each could be exercised concurrently (see *ante*, par. 1722).

Tit. v. De obligationibus quæ quasi ex delicto nascuntur.

1781. Obligations resulting from unlawful and damaging acts, with or without a guilty intention, and not specially characterised as delicts, nor included under the class of contracts, were said to arise *quasi ex delicto* (see *ante*, par. 1622). The mischief occasioned by the injurious act was remedied by means of an *actio in factum* based upon the circumstances of the case.

The text of the Institutes, by way of example, cites the cases of :—

Si judex litem suam fecerit, i.e., a judge became responsible for the consequences of a suit if, with wrongful intent, he gave an unjust sentence (*cum dolo malo in fraudem legis sententiam dixerit*) through favour, enmity, or corruption, even if the result was brought about by *ignorance (licet per imprudentiam*, Dig. 50, 13, 6, *Gaius*), though no other reason can be assigned for the distinction between this *quasi*-delict of a judge and the unskilfulness of a physician (*ante*, par. 1746, 1), except that the latter, being done *corpori*, was classed as a *delict*, and fell under the *lex Aquilia*. Gaius (Inst. iv, § 52) states that the judge would also be responsible in damages if he altered the amount of the sum fixed in the *condemnatio* or exceeded the *maximum taxatio* inserted by the prætor (*post*, par. 1935). The measure of damages recovered by the *actio in factum* was left to the discretion of the judge to settle according to the loss sustained by the injured party in consequence of the non-success of his suit (*In quantum de ea re æquum religioni judicantis videbitur*), and the action lay against the judge *himself*, whether he was in the power of a *paterfamilias* or not, and was independent of the *right of appeal*, because a new trial might be impossible under some circumstances or worthless in others, as where the adversary was insolvent.

Injuries resulting from things being *poured out* or *thrown down* (*dejectum effusumve*) from a house, gave rise to an *actio in factum* which was *popularis*, *i.e.*, open to anyone, and, if there were several, then to the persons most interested (*e.g.*, the heirs of the deceased); and as the *actio legis Aquiliæ* was available against the *individual* who had caused the damage, this action lay against the *paterfamilias* inhabiting the house, or against the *owner* of that part of it, or against a son himself, though under power, if he lived apart. The damages were fixed at *double* the value of the injury caused, and a penalty of fifty *aurei* if a free man was killed, but if only injured the amount of damages was settled by the judge, after taking into account expenses incurred for medical attendance, together with the value of the work lost through resulting bad health. So the placing or hanging *(positum aut suspensum)* over a public way anything likely to cause damage *by falling* was punished by means of the same action with a penalty of ten *solidi*.

The commander of a *ship* and the manager of an *inn* or *stable* (*exercitor navis aut cauponæ aut stabuli*), in which damage or theft had occurred through the act of some one employed by them, were also liable, under *Prætorian* law, to an action *in factum* for *double* the amount, at the suit of the injured party or his heir. Against the actual wrong-doer himself the civil *actio furti* or *legis Aquiliæ* could be brought, and the *actio in factum* for the *quasi*-delict was independent of any other action for restitution of the property arising out of any contract or *quasi*-contract with the captain or inn-keeper.

1793. *Natural obligations.*
These usually sprang from :—
(1) *Simple pacts*, *i.e.*, from agreements not specially recognised as binding, but which had been made between competent parties in good faith, and without any immoral or unlawful tendency *(Pacta conventa, quæ neque dolo malo neque adversus leges, plebiscita, senatus-consulta, edicta principum, neque quo fraus cui eorum fiat, facta erunt, servabo*, Dig. 2, 14, 7, 7 Ulpian), though, if such agreements had not been invested with an action, they could only be enforced by indirect means (*ante*, par. 1619).

(2) The *incapacity* of certain classes to contract *civil* or *prætorian* obligations, *e.g.*:—

(a) *Slaves* had strictly no *persona* (part ii, par. 21); but in the case of their *delicts*, if the master for the time being refused to make compensation, he must abandon them, and, if freed, the action became personal against the slave himself, for *natural* equity recognised the liability. So also, as the representative of the master, the slave might bind third parties towards him and under *prætorian* law, and within certain limits, bind the master himself (*ante*, par. 1280); but for acts beyond this, whether *ex persona domini* or *ex persona sua*, no civil or Prætorian liability arose out of his contracts or pacts, though under natural law (*ante*, par. 19) a *natural* obligation might be entailed, and therefore the proposition *in personam servilem nulla cadit obligatio* (Dig. 50, 17, 22 Ulpian) is to be understood with this reservation, as expressed in the text: *Servi ex delictis quidem obligantur; et si manumittantur, obligati remanent. Ex contractibus autem civiliter quidem non-obligantur, sed naturaliter et obligantur et obligant* (Dig. 44, 7, 14 Ulpian).

(β) *Freedmen* were liable under *natural* law (independently of any civil engagement) to render the services styled *operæ officiales (ministerium)*, *i.e.*, domestic duties *(natura enim operas patrono libertus debet*, Dig. 12, 6, 26, 12 Ulpian), but not any other kind (*ante*, par. 67).

(γ) *Sons* in power, or other members of the same civil family, could not contract between themselves; but the *natural* obligation thereby resulting might be sufficient to give such contracts validity in the event of the death of the *paterfamilias* or their emancipation; and though the son *ex persona patris* was in the position of a slave, still *ex persona sua*, and in respect of strangers (except so far as the *s.c. Maced.* applied, *post*, par. 1807) he could bind himself *civilly*, as if a *paterfamilias* (*ante*, par. 1298), and after *minima c.d.*, resulting from change of *family*, a *natural* liability, in respect of *obligations* incurred prior to the adoption, existed, upon which a *prætorian* action was based (*ante*, par. 1152).

(δ) *Wives* were considered to be bound *pietatis causa, i.e.,* out of affection for the husband and children, and without any *civil* engagement, to bring something by way of *dowry* to add to the family store, and they therefore could not reclaim any such property, even though delivered over by mistake.

(3) The *extinction* of the civil or prætorian obligation as in the case of—

(α) Prescription or a judicial sentence.

(β) The heir *ex testamento* or *ab intestato* carrying out the wishes of the deceased expressed in an informal will, or abstaining from the retention of the *quarta Falcidia* or other property to which he was in strictness entitled.

(γ) The *pupil* binding himself without the *authorisation* of his tutor, and therefore *civilly* liable only to the extent he was enriched (*ante*, par. 244); but a *natural* obligation existed (in spite of the contradictory texts of *Neratius* and *Licinius Rufinus*, Dig. 12, 6, 41, and 44, 7, 59), which could be guaranteed by a *fidejussor* (*ante*, par. 1392), and admitted of valid ratification or novation after majority.

(δ) The *insane* and the *prodigus* are presumably placed by *Ulpian* (Dig. 46, 1, 25) on the same footing as the pupil; but, in respect of the suretyship of a third person, other texts (Dig. 45, 1, 6, *Ulpian*, 46, 70, 4, Gaius) state positively that no *natural* obligation existed which could form a basis for the collateral security.

1806. The *effects* of natural obligations may be classed under five heads, viz.:—
(1) *Performance;* for if once intentionally executed, the natural obligation was sufficient to prevent the amount being reclaimed as not due and paid by mistake.
(2) *Exceptions* could be founded upon them, and they might be the subject matter of *set-off* if the opportunity offered.
(3) *Novation* could be based upon them.
(4) *Accessory contracts* of the civil law, such as the *fidejussio*, *pignus*, or *hypotheca*, could be added to them.
(5) Power of *ratification.*

These effects might all be united in natural obligations resulting from *pacts*, or from agreements made by a *slave*, or from contracts between *persons in power*; but as a general rule (2) and, in some cases, (4) could not come in question.

1807. *Unlawful* agreements could not be the basis of a natural obligation (*ante*, par. 1620), but an exception existed (*naturalis obligatio manet*, Dig. 14, 6, 10, Paul) in the case of money borrowed in contravention of the *s.c. Macedonianum* (*post*, par. 2217); for a son could not reclaim the amount if, after the death of the father and after becoming *sui juris*, he had paid the amount in whole or in part. This exception, however, did not exist in respect of the *s.c. Velleianum* (*ante*, par. 1411); for the former enactment was intended to protect the father against the son and the lender, whereas the latter was for the protection of the woman herself.

1808. The *extinction* of *natural* obligations might be effected in the ordinary way, or by simple *natural* modes, as, *e.g.*, a pact to dissolve it or a compromise, in which cases the *civil* obligations, *e.g.*, *fidejussiones*, which had been based upon them, would be thereby also dissolved; see *ante*, par. 1705.

1809. *Alternative obligations and joint and several liabilities.*

The *three* elements of an obligation, viz., (1) the *creditor*, (2) the *debtor*, and (3) the *thing* due, may be variously complicated; for the *object* may be in the *alternative* (*illud aut illud*), and the liability will then vary according as the choice rests with the debtor or the creditor. So the *creditor* or the *debtor* may be one or several; and the question then arises whether each creditor or debtor is bound *in solidum*, or whether the more common rule is followed by which the benefit or liability is *pro parte;* and, if the latter, whether the shares are *equal* (*virilis*) for each person, or *proportional* to the individual interest.

1817. The *in solidum* cases are numerous, *i.e.*, those in which *one* creditor had the right to demand, and *one* debtor was liable to pay the whole amount, but *one* payment extinguished the whole liability for all, *e.g.*:—
(1) Obligations *stricti juris.* Here the contract *verbis*, in the case of several co-stipulators, or co-promissors, exhibits this liability in its strictest form (*ante*, par. 1264). So in the case of

co-sponsors and co-fideipromissors (up to the *Lex Furia*), as well as fidejussores (*ante*, par. 1384, 1392). The contract *litteris* probably also involved liability *in solidum* (though there is no text in support of this, except as to *bankers*), and a bequest by *legacy* could be so worded as to involve either alternative *legatees*, entitled *in solidum* (*Si Titio aut Seio, utri heres vellet legatum relictum est*, Dig. 31, 16, Paul) or alternative *heirs* liable *in solidum* (*Lucius Titius heres meus aut Mævius heres meus decem Seio dato*, Dig. 30, 8, 1, Pomponius).

(2) *Bonæ fidei* contracts. Independent of special agreement, a liability *in solidum* was assumed in the case of several common *commodatees*, *locatees*, *depositees*, and *mandataries*, as well as in the case of several *mandators pecuniæ credendæ*, *i.e.*, in respect of their position as joint guarantors; and the same rule held in respect of several *argentarii* associated together, or several tutors or curators.

(3) In the special *Prætorian* obligations enforced under the actions *de peculio*, *institoria*, or *exercitoria*, the liability on the owners was *in solidum* in respect of the acts of their agent (*institor*) or captain (*magister navis*).

(4) In respect of *dolus, vi, delicta*, and *quasi-delicta*, the liability, when joint, was *in solidum*, *i.e.*, in so far as the civil reparation due from the joint tort-feasors was concerned; but the condemnation of one (*e.g.*) thief did not release or modify the personal liability of the others in respect of the *penalty* imposed.

1822. The liability *in solidum* was subject to marked differences in respect of details, as, *e.g.*, whether, in consequence of the *electio* resulting from applying to *one (in jus vocatio)* or joining issue with him *(litis contestatione)*, the co-debtors were released, or whether they remained liable until actual payment of the debt, as was always the case in respect of co-debtors under *Justinian* (Cod. 8, 41, 28). Whether, also, on the receipt of the amount by one creditor, or its payment by one debtor, the remaining creditors or debtors could compel a partition of the profit or the loss; as also whether the right to the *beneficium divisionis* or *cedendarum actionum* (*ante*, par. 1401) existed in favour of a debtor sued *in solidum*, though the effect of the innovations of Justinian (Nov. 99, c. 1) seems to be that the *divisionis beneficium* could be claimed as a matter of right by all co-debtors except those liable for delicts.

The effects of *culpa*, of *mora*, of *novatio*, of the pact *de non petendo*, of *confusio*, *minima c.d.*, or interruption of prescription, also caused variations in respect of the liability *in solidum*.

An attempt has been made by modern writers to classify *in solidum* obligations thus:—

(α) *Correales*, *i.e.*, those *in solidum* obligations resulting from the contract *verbis*, or from the testament.

(β) *In solidum*, *i.e.*, those arising from other causes; but this division is unsatisfactory, and foreign to Roman jurisprudence.

1825. In respect of the *joint heirs* of an inheritance, the Twelve Tables (v, § 9) laid down the rule that the property divided itself in the eye of the law proportionally to the respective shares ; and if a division was impossible (as in the case of prædial servitudes and some obligations *facere*), one or more of the heirs took the debt or credit *in solidum*, and the rest obtained an indemnity by means of the action *familiæ erciscundæ* (*post*, par. 2346). If the object to be received or delivered was certain (*e.g.*, such a house or such an estate), each heir was held to be creditor or debtor in respect of his *share;* but if the thing was *in genere* (as a horse) or *alternative* (as Stichus or Pamphila), or if there was a *penal* clause to the obligation, the liability was *in solidum*. So, also, the heirs detaining a thing lent or deposited with the deceased would be liable *in solidum;* but special rules regulated the rights of several heirs of a depositor as to the restitution of an indivisible thing deposited with the deceased.

Tit. vi. De Actionibus.

1829. The term *actio* may mean (1) the *act* itself of applying to the competent authority for the recognition of a right, or (2) the *right* itself of so applying, or (3) the *means* provided for exercising the right, *i.e.*, in the first case the word refers to a *fact*, in the second to a *right*, and in the third to a *form*.

Other meanings of a technical character also attached to the word, and these were more or less narrow according to the epoch, and varied with the growth of the *three* successive systems of procedure, which are sketched out below by way of introduction to the text of this title ; see also part i, par. 140, 250, 334, 427, and part ii, par. 241, 269.

First system. Legis actiones.

1833. *Origin and general character.* The *five* actions constituting the mode of procedure under this system are indicative of an infant civilisation ; and, after existing upwards of five centuries, were gradually absorbed in the system founded by the *prætor peregrinus*, though only completely effaced by *Justinian* ; see part ii, par. 256, 257.

In strictness, the term *legis actio* included only the consecrated rite performed *in jure*, and hence the doubt in reference to the classification of the *pignoris capio* action mentioned by *Gaius* (see *post*, par. 1893).

The system was particularly characterised by the following peculiarities, viz.—(α) It was exclusively reserved to citizens ; (β) no one could sue by a representative, except in a limited number of special cases (see *post*, par. 2228) ; (γ) the misuse of a technical word was fatal to the further prosecution of the suit ; (δ) after rejection, the action could not be recommenced, but the condemnation (as in the third system, and unlike the formulary system) need not necessarily be *pecuniary*.

1845. *Organisation of the judicial authority.* The distinction between the authority of the *magistrate* and the *judge, i.e.,* between *jus* and *judicium* existed from the earliest times (part ii, par. 247, 256), for the king could refer a cause to a judge instead of deciding it himself, and the two actions *per judicis postulationem* and *per condictionem* were expressly for the purpose of obtaining the appointment of a judge (see part i, par. 140, 242); so, also, though the analysis of the kinds of authority belongs to a more mature period of Roman jurisprudence, the germs existed of the distinctions, as to *do, dico, addico* (part i, par. 290), as well as in respect of the *jurisdictio* and *imperium mixtum, i.e.,* the *civil* authority to declare and enforce the law, and *cognitio* and *imperium merum, i.e.,* the authority to investigate and punish in *criminal* matters.

The *College of Pontiffs* prepared the ritual of the *Legis actiones*, and through it the king, as the first Pontiff chosen by the patrician caste, acquired his powers as a *magistrate* in *private* affairs. From him this *jurisdictio* and *imperium* subsequently devolved successively on the consuls, prætors, ædiles, prætor peregrinus, and the superior officers of the *municipia (Duumviri Jure Dicundo, Præfectus J. D.)* See part i, par. 36, 41, 93, 140, 160, 161, 176, 191, 222, 225.

The *judges*, in respect of matters of *obligation* or *possession*, appear from the earliest period to have consisted of two kinds, viz., the *judex* and the *arbiter*, whilst other matters were referred to the *College of Centumviri* (or to the *Decemviri*), whose creation probably indicates the political enfranchisement of the *plebeians*, whilst the *transition* period, leading to the recognition of *strangers*, is probably marked by the establishment of the *Recuperatores* (see part i, par. 162, 166, 206, 283).

1856. *Procedure—Actions for the decision of the case.*
(1) The *actio sacramenti* was originally the only form (see part i, par. 140, 1), and therefore remained applicable to every case not specially provided with another *legis actio* (Gai. Inst. iv, § 13). It was, in fact, a reciprocal challenge to deposit in the hands of the Pontiff a sum of money called the *sacramentum;* and on the sentence of the judge being delivered to the effect that the *sacramentum* of the successful party was *justum*, and therefore the other *injustum*, the object of litigation was lost by the latter, and his share of the *sacramentum* forfeited to the *ærarium* (see Twelve Tables, ii, § i; and *post*, par. 1916, 1). Hence there was no middle course, as the sentence decided absolutely for or against the assertion of one of the parties, in respect of the matter in dispute.

The action probably commenced by an informal preliminary statement, and then a simulated combat (*manuum consertio*) took place between the claimants in the presence of the object of litigation, which must therefore be brought before the tribunal.

1864. If the thing could not be brought *in jure*, the magistrate went to the place; but, for *immoveables* (as buildings and estates), the practice grew up of one expelling the other, and taking him before the magistrate with a tile or a clod to represent the object. This method was called *deductio*, and when done by order of the Prætor and in the presence of witnesses, after having challenged one another to it before the tribunal, it was called *deductio quæ moribus fit;* but, in the time of *Cicero* (who turns the whole procedure into ridicule, *Pro Murœna*, c. 12), the parties brought a clod or other thing to represent the object, so that the forcible *deductio* was assumed.

One of the claimants then seized the object (*e.g.*, a slave), and placing over him a rod (*vindicta, festuca,* see part, ii, par. 150), pronounced the *vindicatio,* "*Hunc ego hominem ex jure Quiritium meum esse aio secundum suam causam, sicut dixi, ecce tibi vindictam imposui*".

The adversary went through the same pantomime, and then the Prætor interfered with the words "*Mittite ambo hominem*"; upon which both litigants let go.

The first vindicator then questioned his adversary as to the grounds of his claim, "*Postulo, anne dicas, qua ex causa vindicaveris?*" The adversary replied, that he had acted in accordance with his rights, "*Jus peregi sicut vindictam imposui*". The first speaker then, asserting that his adversary had no title, challenged him to stake a sum (500 or 50 asses, according to the value of the property) upon the issue of a trial. "*Quando tu injuria* (without right) *vindicavisti,* D. (or L.), *æris sacramento te provoco*". The adversary replied by a similar challenge, in the words, "*Similiter ego te*".

The Prætor then gave *interim possession (vindicia)* to the *possessor* or to the claimant *(petitor),* as seemed most just, pending the settlement of the case by the judge, who would now be appointed, and before whom the *non*-possessor would appear as plaintiff, the possessor giving his adversary guarantors *(prædes litis et vindiciarum)* for the restitution of the thing and the produce, if the issue of the trial required it; but where *liberty* was involved, this interim possession had always to be given, so as to favour it (Twelve Tables, vi, § 6).

The most important application of this action was in respect of claims of *quiritarian ownership* and of *real* rights, including questions of *status,* whether as to liberty, citizenship, or family; whilst, for the *pursuit of obligations,* the MS. of Gaius is illegible, but the formula probably varied according to the circumstances, and the action was early replaced by (2) and (3), *post,* par. 1870, 1876.

1868. Whether the *Lex Pinaria,* mentioned by *Gaius* (Inst., iv, § 15), only fixed the *delay* of *thirty* days, within which the judge was to be given to the parties, or whether this law actually introduced the *appointment* of the judge, is uncertain.

The expression *manuum consertio,* indicating the placing of the hand on the subject of litigation (*manu asserere*), gave rise to the term *assertor,* used especially in reference to the vindicator of a person's liberty *(assertor libertatis),* and the *vindicta* used in the action led to the term (1) *vindicatio* for all real actions, and (2) *vindiciæ*, which at first signified the thing in dispute, then the interim possession of this thing, and finally the produce received during this possession.

1870. (2) The *actio per judicis postulationem*.

As in many cases the *sacramentum* action was found unsuitable or impossible, necessity compelled a recourse to the simpler form of merely demanding a judge, and this action probably existed before the Twelve Tables, for the demand of a judge is there sanctioned in the cases of the—(1) *arbiter finium regundorum*, Table 7, § 5; (2) *arbiter familiæ erciscundæ*, Table 5, § 10; (3) *arbiter aquæ pluviæ arcendæ*, Table 7, § 8; (4) *arbitri vindiciæ falsæ*, Table 12, § 3; (5) *Arbitrium ad exhibendum*, for the production of a thing to be vindicated, Table 6, § 9; and subsequently it was applied to tutorships, fiduciary agreements, purchases and sales, lettings, mandates, partnerships, obligations *facere* or *præstare*, as well as those involving *dare* of uncertain things and cases of the loss of property through *dolus*.

The portion of the MS. of *Gaius* treating of this action is lost, but probably, after the alternate interrogations of the parties, came the formula in which the plaintiff asked the prætor for a judge (see part i, par. 140, 2), and the defendant probably made the same demand "*similiter ego judicem arbitrum-ve postulo uti des*". The suit was, therefore, no longer to decide whether the *sacramentum* was *justum* or *injustum*, but became tantamount to an *arbitration*, and originated the class of actions afterwards called *bonæ-fidei* in the formulary system.

1876 (3). *Actio per condictionem.* This action was commenced by the plaintiff appearing *in jure* to claim the appointment of a judge within thirty days when the demand consisted of some certain thing (see part i, par. 242), that is, this action withdrew from the *sacramenti actio* the only remaining kind of *obligation*, except that *damni infecti* (part i, par. 244) to which it could still be applied.

As the object was fixed, a *judex* was always employed, and probably, if the defendant failed to appear in thirty days, he was held *confessus* or *judicatus*, and, therefore, liable to the action *per manus injectionem*.

At the date of the *Lex Æbutia*, these three *Leges actiones*, therefore, probably stood thus :—

(1) *Actio sacramenti* for questions of *status*, quiritarian ownership and successions, *i.e.*, all *real* rights and heard before the *centumviri*.

(2) *Actio per judicis postulationem*, for *obligations* not involving the giving *(dare)* of things certain and generally heard by an *arbiter*.

(3) *Actio per condictionem* for obligations to give *(dare)* quantities or things certain and always decided by a *judex*.

1883. *Actions for execution.* These consisted of the :—

(1) *Actio per manus injectionem*. In the case of *real* rights, decided by a *legis actio*, the sentence affected the thing itself; and, if

necessary, the power of the state could be used for the purpose of putting the person, recognised as owner by the result of the suit, in possession; but, in the case of *obligations*, unless the property of the debtor had been specially pledged by the *nexum* (see part ii, par. 46, 3), or fell under the exceptional cases covered by the *per pignoris capionem* action, the successful party would be only a creditor, and, therefore, the old law gave this action against the *person* of the debtor to compel the execution of the sentence, and, as the seizure took place *in jure*, it is distinguishable from other extrajudicial seizures of the person (see *post*, par. 1896), to which the term *manus injectio* was also applied.

According to the Twelve Tables (see part i, table iii), after judgment or confession of liability, an interval of thirty days *(dies justi)* was allowed for payment; and, in default, the creditor appeared before the *magistrate* and went through the form of seizing the debtor, saying at the same time "*quod tu mihi judicatus sive damnatus es (e.g., sestertium x millia) quæ dolo malo non solvisti ab eam rem ego tibi sestertium x millium judicati manus injicio*" (Gai. Inst.,iv, § 21). The debtor was compelled to submit, and, in consequence of being thus sentenced, he was from that moment treated as a *slave*, so that any subsequent defence must be raised through a solvent surety *(vindex)*. If the latter's interference to reclaim him and free him was unsuccessful, the debtor became *addictus* by order of the Prætor (without a judge), and the creditor then took him to his house as his prisoner. At this stage, the debtor was a slave in *fact*, though not yet in law; and, therefore (as opposed to the position of *nexi*, see part ii, par. 46, 3), neither his children nor his property fell into the power of the creditor; but, after sixty days (see as to food and chains, Table iii, §§ 3, 4), during which, on three market days, he was brought before the magistrate in the *comitium* and proclamation made of the sum owing, he became a slave in *law*, thereby suffering *capitis deminutio*, entailing the termination of his life as a citizen and as a *free*-man, and at the same time his creditor's rights were extinguished, and he might be sold over the Tiber or put to death.

Besides the use of this action strictly as a mode of obtaining *execution* it was also, subsequently to the Twelve Tables, adapted to meet the case of the denial of the debt by the defendant or his surety, *i.e.*, the effect of the laws cited by *Gaius* (Inst. iv, §§ 22, 23, 24), viz., the *leges Furia (de Sponsu), Publilia* (see *ante*, par. 1384, 2, 4), *Furia testamentaria* (as to legacies), and *Marcia* (as to interest), was to make this a regular action to try the creditor's right. For this purpose, instead of the words *quod tu mihi judicatus sive damnatus es*, the plaintiff stated the circumstances of the case, and added "*ob eam rem ego tibi pro judicato manum injicio*", and the magistrate then heard the case without sending the parties before a judge, or the words *pro judicato* were omitted, and the action was then called *pura*, and was tried without any assumption of judgment having been previously pronounced.

Hence the action existed under three forms, viz. :—
(1) *Manus injectio judicati.*
(2) *Manus injectio pro judicato.*
(3) *Manus injectio pura.*

Subsequently by a law (illegible in Gaius), the first two were assimilated to the third, so that the debtor could always defend himself *(manum sibi depellere et pro se lege agere licebat)*, except in the case of a judicial condemnation, or when called upon to reimburse the sum a *sponsor* had paid for him *(excepto judicato et eo pro quo depensum est.* Gai. Inst., iv, § 25).

1893. (2) *Actio per pignoris capionem.* Under this so-called action, the creditor himself took, whilst pronouncing sacramental words, a thing, as a pledge, belonging to the debtor, and the latter could only redeem it by paying the amount due (Gai. Inst., iv, § 32). This form of proceeding was altogether exceptional in the system, for (a) it was not done in the presence of the prætor, but *extra jus;* (β) it might be done in the absence of the debtor; and (γ) it might take place even on *nefasti* days, and hence it was not classed by some as a *legis actio*, see part i, par. 140.

Its introduction was due partly to *custom* and partly to *law*, for, prior to the Twelve Tables, this means of execution against the property of the debtor was open to soldiers against those who had been assigned to them by the tribune of the *ærarium* to provide their pay *(stipendium)* or the cost of the purchase and equipment of a horse (*æs equestre*) or of forage (*æs hordearium*), see part i, par. 70. The *Twelve Tables* (see part i, table xii, § 1) gave it to the creditor for the price of a viction or for the hire of a beast of burden when the sum to be received was intended to be employed in sacrifices, and a law *(? Lex Censoria*, but illegible in Gaius Inst., iv, § 28) gave it to *publicani* as a means of enforcing the payment of the public taxes.

1896. *Review of the system.*

All the *Legis actiones* (except the *pignoris capio*) took place *in jure*, and the mode of proceeding may be summed up thus :—

In jus vocatio. The summons to the defendant was delivered in all simplicity by the plaintiff calling upon him to appear; and, on his refusal, the process called

Antestatio was gone through, *i.e.*, witnesses were called upon to take notice of his refusal, and their ears touched, whilst certain sacramental words were pronounced (?) "*licet te antestari*", after which an extrajudicial

Manus injectio could be used to compel the defendant to go, unless he tendered a surety (*vindex*) to undertake his cause, though custom early introduced the principle that a citizen's house was inviolable, and that no force could be used against an ascendant or a patron (without the special authorisation of a magistrate), or persons of dignity, such as prætors, or consuls, or a pontiff proceeding to sacrifice, or a man or woman going through the ceremony of marriage.

After a preliminary statement had been made to the magistrate, the particular *actio legis* applicable to the case was gone through, and, if it was *per manus injectionem*, the sentence was given by the magistrate himself.

After an interval of thirty days, the parties appeared again before the magistrate, and

Addictio took place, or a

Datio judicis, i.e., a *judex* or an *arbiter* was appointed, or the case sent to the *centumviri*. The parties then mutually agreed as to the

Comperendinatio, or undertaking to appear before the judge on the third day *(perendinus dies)*, and the suit so far was, therefore, called *res comperendinata*. This reappearance before the *judge* was guaranteed by

Vadimonium, i.e., the reciprocal giving of sureties (*vades*), and the same process had to be gone through when the suit before the *magistrate* could not be terminated in one day. Hence, there were three kinds of sureties, viz.: (1) the *vindex*, who took the cause on himself and released the defendant; (2) the *præs*—(a) *sacramenti*, or surety for costs to the magistrate, and (β) *litis et vindiciarum* or surety for interim possession to the opposite party; (3) the *vas*, or the guarantor for reappearance.

After this came the last act *in jure*, viz., the

Litis contestatio, i.e., as all the above proceedings were *oral*, the litigants now appealed to the witnesses to attest what had passed before the magistrate "*testes estote*", and hence the process was called *contestari litem*.

When the parties appeared before the *judge*, the

Causæ collectio (or *conjectio*) took place, *i e.,* brief statements by the litigants of their case, after which proof was tendered by witnesses, followed by an examination of the place. The pleadings were then gone through in detail, after which came the

Sententia, which terminated the duties of the judge.

For *execution*, the successful party must, if there was any difficulty, return to the *magistrate*, and, through his *imperium*, *real rights* would be given him *manu militari* and *obligations* (except in the case of the *pignoris capio*, or the *per æs et libram* surety engagements) enforced by seizing *per manus injectionem* the *person* of the debtor.

Justice was administered publicly, in the *forum*, in daylight, the setting of the sun terminating the procedure for that day (Twelve Tables, i, § 6), and the *jurisdictio* of the magistrate was only exercisable on *dies fasti* (see part i, par. 41, 176), though this did not affect the *pignoris capio*; and, in B.C. 68, a *Lex Hortensia (de nundinis)* made the market days *(nundinæ)*, which took place every ninth day, *dies fasti*, for the convenience of country people.

Second system. Formula procedure.

1909. *Origin and development.* This system resulted from the creation of the office of the *Prætor Peregrinus* in the sixth century of Rome, shortly before the *Leges Silia* and *Calpurnia* introduced the last action of the law, viz., the *condictio*.

For the probable causes tending to the substitution of *formulæ* for the procedure under the first system, see part i, par. 252.

1911. *Ordinaria judicia.* Owing to the system being intended for *aliens*, two peculiarities resulted, viz. :—

(1) The *formula* was originally always *in factum concepta* (for the *prætor peregrinus* could not propose a question of *civil* law), and (prior to the extension of the system to citizens) it consisted of two parts only, viz. (a), the facts stated by the parties, and to be verified by the *recuperatores* (part i, par. 162), *e.g.*, *Recuperatores sunto. Si paret Aulum Agerium apud Numerium Negidium mensam argenteam deposuisse eamque dolo malo Numerii Negidii Aulo Agerio redditam non esse;* (β) the condemnation or absolution to be pronounced according to the facts proved, *e.g., Quanti ea res erit, tantam pecuniam recuperatores Numerium Negidium Aulo Agerio condemnate: si non paret, absolvite.*

(2) The condemnation was necessarily *pecuniary*, because the prætor could not award ownership (or any fragments of it) *ex jure quiritium*, nor could he directly compel the execution of any obligation according to the rules of the civil law (see *post*, par. 1935).

1916. The attempt to adapt the system to the wants of *citizens* by fusing it with the existing procedure, may be observed in the—

(1) obligatory system of *sponsiones* existing in the early formula procedure both for actions and interdicts, the origin of which may be traced as follows. After the *lex Silia* created the *condictio*, the actual deposit of the *sacramentum* (*ante*, par. 1856) was dispensed with, and the parties only bound themselves to make the payment by means of a quiritarian verbal promise *(per sponsionem)* with guarantors *(prædes sacramenti)*, the prætor himself interrogating the parties and the sureties, *(spondes ne? spondeo)*, so that they were directly answerable to him. Subsequently this was reduced to a promise made by the litigants to each other, without sureties, for the payment of a sum which should go, not to the public treasury, but to the successful party. By this *sponsio* of the plaintiff and *re-stipulatio* of the defendant, therefore, a *personal* liability *to one another* was incurred in the *condictio in jure* in respect of a penal sum which should be gained by the successful party in matters of obligation in addition to the object in litigation. This was compulsory in some actions and interdicts (*post*, par. 2336), but voluntary or permissive in others, and the scale was fixed in some cases, not in others (see *post*, par. 1924); and hence the term *agere per sponsionem,, i.e., cum periculo*, as opposed to *agere per formulam, i.e., sine periculo.*

(2) use of actions by formula founded *fictitiously* on a *legis*

actio and producing the same result, *Quæ ad legis actionem exprimuntur* (as opposed to *Quæ sua vi ac potestate constant*), e.g., the fiction of the *pignoris capio* given to *publicani* (Gai. Inst., iv, § 32).

(3) the close imitation in the *formula*, or statement addressed by the *magistrate* to the judge, of the statements made to one another by the litigants in the *legis actio* (see part i, par. 252). This is especially to be noted when *citizens* came to use the formula so that true questions of *civil* law, and quiritarian ownership had to be dealt with. To meet this the *formula* would be *in jus concepta (de jure quæritur)*, e.g., (a) *si paret Numerium Negidium Aulo Agerio sestertium x millia dare opertere;* or (β) *quiquid paret Numerium Negidium Aulo Agerio dare facere oportere;* or (γ) *si paret hominem ex jure Quiritium Auli Agerii esse.* This form involved a preliminary part to indicate the subject matter *(res de qua agitur)*, and, therefore, the formula would have three parts, viz., (1) *demonstratio*, to indicate the facts to the judge. " *Judex esto. Quod Aulus Agerius apud Numerium Negidium mensam argenteam deposuit qua de re agitur;*" (2) *intentio*, stating the question of law on the plaintiff's facts. "*Quidquid ob eam rem Numerium Negidium Aulo Agerio dare facere oportet ex fide bona:*" (3) *condemnatio*, or power given to the judge to condemn or absolve. "*Ejus judex Numerium Negidium Aulo Agerio condemnato, nisi restituat: si non paret absolvito.*"

1924. When the *Lex Æbutia* legalised this system, the jurisdiction of the college of *centumviri* in respect of *damnum infectum* (part i, par. 244) was practically superseded by a more summary procedure (*ante*, par. 1313, 2), and the method of *sponsiones* (*ante*, par. 1916) was employed to bring under the *formula* system those claims of ownership and other *real* rights still contested by means of the *legis actio*. This was effected by making the plaintiff challenge his adversary by a *sponsio* "*si homo, quo de agitur, ex jure quiritium meus est sestertios xxv nummos dare spondes?*" and, on an affirmative response by the defendant, the *real* right was indirectly decided in determining the question of the conditional obligation, *i.e.*, whether the money was due or not. As the amount of the *sponsio* was for this purpose immaterial, it was fixed at the will of the parties, and hence *Gaius* (Inst., iv, § 94) says, this *sponsio* was not *penal* but *prejudicial, i.e.*, merely used to get jurisdiction. The possessor, however, had to give guarantors *(cum satisdatione)* that if he failed he would restore the thing and the produce, and therefore the stipulation was called *pro præde litis et vindiciarum*, hence imitating the *prædes litis et vindiciarum* of the old *sacramentum* action; but, in the *legis actiones*, there was an equality at first between the parties as *vindicator*, and *counter-vindicator*, whereas here there was necessarily a plaintiff and a defendant (possessor), for the plaintiff vindicated and had to prove his ownership; whilst the defendant, after having answered to the stipulation *pro præde litis et vindiciarum*, and to the *sponsio*, remained on the defensive. Subsequently, the parties could proceed either by this *per sponsionem* method, or directly *per formulam petitoriam*, i.e., on a formula framed directly as to the thing itself *(si paret hominem ex jure Quiritium Auli Agerii esse)* without interpolating a nominal obligation in order to get jurisdiction, and therefore *Gaius* (Inst., iv, § 91) lays down that two sorts of actions were open for matters *in rem*. *(In rem actio duplex...aut enim per formulam petitoriam agitur, aut per sponsionem).*

1926. The word *actio* now denotes more particularly the right conferred by the magistrate to recover before a judge that which is due, and there are as many actions as rights to pursue, but the word is also technically restricted to *personal* actions only (including *condictiones, post,* par. 1965), for the reason that *formulæ* were originally only employed in matters of *obligation*. The proper word for claims of *ownership* or other *real* rights is *petitio* (or *vindicatio, post,* par. 1963), whilst the term *persecutio* indicated the *cognitio* of the cause *extra-ordinem* by the magistrate himself without reference to a judge, see part i, par. 427, and part ii, par. 275, 288.

1927. *Organization of the judicial authority.* The constitution of the provinces, the rise of the imperial power, and the creation of new magistracies, together with the struggles between the classes of citizens and the consequent changes in the lists of judges, indirectly led to alterations in procedure; but two direct changes resulted from the adoption of the formulary system, viz.:—

(1) The gradual decadence of the college of *centumviri*, and—

(2) The use at Rome by citizens as well as aliens of the *recuperatores* in addition to the *unus judex* or *arbiter*, see part i, par. 162; part ii, par. 266.

1929. *Partes formularum.* The formula might consist of—

(α) *one* part, viz., the *intentio* as in the *præjudicium* (*post*, par. 2112), where only a decision in respect of a *fact* was wanted for subsequent use, *e.g.*, whether such an one was free, or as to the amount of a dowry (*Præjudicium vero est formula ex sola intentione constans. Neque enim condemnationem in se habet:* Theophilus paraphrase); and the *præjudicialis formula* would probably run, *Judex esto. Præjudicio quærito an...* etc.; or, simply, *Judex esto...an.*

(β) *two* parts, viz., the *intentio* and the *condemnatio*, as where used for *peregrini* (*ante*, par. 1911).

(γ) *three* parts, when the *demonstratio* was placed at the head of it (*ante*, par. 1916).

(δ) *four* parts, i.e. when the *adjudicatio* was added, which occurred in three actions only (part i, par. 249).

1935. The *condemnatio* might be:—

(1) *Certæ pecuniæ, e.g., Judex Numerium Negidium Aulo Agerio sestertium x millia condemna: si non paret absolve.*

(2) *Incertæ pecuniæ cum taxatione,* by which a maximum was fixed which the judge must not exceed *(taxatio certæ pecuniæ),* but he may give less, *e.g., Ejus judex, duntaxat x millia condemna : si non paret absolve.*

(3) *Taxationis incertæ,* as *e.g.,* where the sum to be recovered was to be limited to the actual amount received as the result of the transaction and the extent of the peculium. "*Aulo Agerio Numerium Negidium duntaxat de eo quod in rem versum est et de peculio*", or, as far as his means allowed *(A. A. N. N. duntaxat in id quod facere potest condemna).*

(4) *Infinita, i.e., sine taxatione,* as in the *ad exhibendum* action or in claims of ownership, etc., *e.g., Quanti ea res erit, tantam pecuniam judex N. N. A. A. condemna ; si non paret absolvito,* or, *(intentio) quidquid ob eam rem dare facere oportet ex bonafide, (condemnatio) ejus judex N. N. A. A. condemnato,* etc., or *quidquid paret,* etc.

1937. The inconvenience of a *pecuniary* condemnation, where the claim involved a *real* right or a question of ownership, was got over by including in the *condemnatio* the words "*nisi restituat*", or (less frequently) adding to the *intentio* (*e.g.,* in the case of an estate), the words "*neque is fundus Aulo Agerio restituatur*", or, in the case of obligations where restitution was impossible, "*neque eo nomine Aulo Agerio a Numerio Negidio satisfactum erit*".

The power thus conferred on the judge to order restitution was called *arbitrium,* and the order itself *jussus ;* but the jurists did not recognise this clause as a distinct part of the formula, though the effect of it was, that the *pecuniary* condemnation only followed if the defendant did not (willingly or *manu militari*) restore the property or make compensation. Probably at first the property would be restored from fear of the *pecuniary* condemnation in default ; but, prior to the time of Cicero, the *imperium* of the magistrate was called into play when the restitution of a *corporeal thing* was required, see *post,* par. 1983 (3).

1939. *Adjectiones.*

The necessity of palliating the rigour of the civil law led to the insertion of accessory clauses in the formula, *e.g.,* the—

1940. *Præscriptio.* This addition to the formula was introduced by custom, and was so called from the place it occupied at the head of the formula (*præ-scribere*). It sometimes formed part of or answered the purpose of the *demonstratio,* and always preceded the *intentio.*

The plaintiff *(actor)* used this clause usually for the purpose of limiting his claim, as *e. g.,* if he wished to bring an action to recover only the part of the debt already due, he would insert the præ-scription "*ea res agatur, cujus rei dies fuit*", for if he used the general formula he would only get by the *condemnatio* the amount actually proved due, but it would cover the whole debt, and, therefore, exclude any further relief. So if he only wished to obtain the promised mancipation of an estate sold to him he would use the præscription, *ea res agatur de fundo mancipando,* to prevent the general formula excluding him from subsequently suing for the *traditio,* or other essential to the acquisition of the property.

The defendant *(reus)* used the clause as a negative condition for the purpose of preventing the further prosecution of the suit. Hence, he would insert the *præscriptio:*—

Quod præjudicium non fiat, if the plaintiff's claim was merely accessory to the principal matter to be contested, as, for example, where the plaintiff applied for a partition of the inheritance by the *actio familiæ erciscundæ,* and the defendant denied his title of *heir; ea res agatur, si in ea re præjudicium hereditati* (or *prædio,* or *fundo partive,* etc.), *non fiat.* This was distinct from the *præjudicial action* (*ante,* par. 1929), for it often happened that the setting up the *præjudicia præscriptio* compelled recourse to a præjudicial *action* to decide the principal fact.

Fori, if he denied that the *forum* (*i.e.,* the magistrate) had jurisdiction to inquire into the matter.

Temporis, or *annalis,* or *longi temporis,* where he insisted that the limited time within which the action must be brought had expired, or where he had been ejected by the owner of the property, though he was the *bona fide* possessor of the provincial estate for ten (or twenty) years. This class of præscription endured after the formula system had been forgotten, and the term has descended to modern times with a different meaning, see *ante,* par. 514.

The use of *præscriptiones* by the *plaintiff* continued during the existence of the formulary system ; but, prior to the time of *Gaius* (Inst., iv, § 133), and without influencing their effects, these clauses, when inserted by the *defendant,* were transformed into *exceptiones* and placed at the end of the *intentio,* so that, instead of the preliminary heading, *ea res agatur si...non,* etc., the words *si non* came after the *intentio* (see *post,* par. 1945), and then the terms *præscriptio* and *exceptio* became synonymous, and the *præjudicia* became a species of the latter.

1945. *Exceptio.* If an action was sustainable by the civil law, but inequitable or contrary to any senatus consultum, or special law, the Prætor was obliged to allow the action to proceed (especially if the facts relied on by the defendant required verification), but after the *intentio (e.g.), si paret Numerium Negidium Aulo Agerio sestertium x millia dare oportere,* an accessory clause, always negative in form, was inserted, called the *exceptio,* because it exceptionally excluded in the given case, the affirmative condition *si paret,* etc., stated in the *intentio,* and acted as a *negative condition* on the *condemnatio, e.g., (exceptio parti conventi) si inter Aulum Agerium et Numerium Negidium non convenit-ne ea pecunia peteretur,* or (*exceptio doli mali,* see *post,* par. 2167, 4), *si in ea re nihil dolo malo Auli Agerii factum, sit neque fiat...condemna,* etc., so that the judge only condemned if (1) the statement of the plaintiff in the *intentio* was proved, and if (2) the statement of the defendant in the *exceptio* was not proved.

1946. If the exception was inserted in the *condemnatio* (as in the case of the limitation of the *taxatio* by the *exceptio quod facere potest*, see *ante*, par. 1935, 3), it did not have the effect of defeating the action, but only of limiting the amount to be recovered, and therefore this class of exception is tacitly excluded when it is said that all exceptions are inserted by the defendant for the purpose of rendering the condemnation conditional. (*Omnis exceptio objicitur quidem a reo, sed ita formulæ inseritur, ut conditionalem faciat condemnationem*, Gai. Inst., iv, § 119).

Replicatio, duplicatio, triplicatio, etc. These were equivalent to exceptions, and were inserted alternately by the *plaintiff* and *defendant* for the purpose of defeating the previous plea, see *post*, par. 2283.

1947. The clause *nisi restituat*, whether occurring in the *intentio* or in the *condemnatio* (see *ante*, par. 1937), was also clearly an *adjectio*, although not separately described as such.

1950. *Preparation of the formula.* Practically, the *plaintiff* decided upon the kind of action, and selected his own *præscriptiones* (if any), *demonstratio, intentio, condemnatio*, and (if required) *taxatio*. The *defendant* then stated the *præscriptiones* and *exceptiones* upon which he relied, after which the plaintiff put in his *replicationes*, etc. (see part i, par. 251); and, at the same time, the *prætor* inserted any *præscriptiones* or *exceptiones* he thought equitable. After the formula had been drawn up, both the plaintiff and the defendant had liberty to a limited extent to alter its terms, but on the termination of these discussions *in jure* (*pro tribunali*), the magistrate settled the formula in his own name, and the litigants then had to run the risk of the effect of the statements inserted.

1951. *Different kinds of actions.* The most important classifications were:—

1952. *Actions in rem and in personam.* For the origin of this universal and fundamental division, see part ii, par. 187, 275; and, as the examples cited in the latter paragraph are *in jus conceptæ*, *i.e.*, involving questions of *law*, it follows that, strictly speaking, the original formulæ, which were only *in factum conceptæ*, belonged to neither class, though they were always referred to one or other, according to the subject matter, and in all actions the *condemnatio* is necessarily always *in personam*, for, though the right is *in rem*, yet a particular defendant exists in each particular case.

1960. *Personales actiones in rem scriptæ.* These actions, exemplified by the *actio quod metus causa* (*post*, par. 2129), are really *in personam*, but the division originated with modern interpreters from the fact that, though given by the Prætor only *in factum*, they were (unlike the action *de dolo*, *post*, par. 2145) expressed generally, *i.e.*, without any designation of a particular defendant, it being sufficient that there had been *metus* to enable them to be brought against anyone who had profited by it even in good faith, whereas the action *de dolo* was said to be *in personam*, because only given against the author of the fraud or his heirs.

1962. *Actiones mixtæ.*
A defendant might be liable to a plaintiff in respect of a *real* as well as a *personal* right, as in the case of *e.g.* the *depositum*, where a *real* right exists in respect of the thing and a *personal* right against the particular depositee, but the plaintiff must sue by separate actions of *depositi* or *rei vindicatio*, as the defendant could not be both absent and present in the *intentio*.

Similarly, the three actions: (1) *familiæ erciscundæ;* (2) *communi dividendo;* and (3) *finium regundorum*, although involving *real* rights, are *in personam* and *quasi ex contractu*, for they presuppose the co-heirship, co-ownership, or neighbouring ownership; and, if otherwise, the dispute of this point would be a *præjudicium*, which would have to be first determined, unless in the case of the first *two* the plaintiff was in possession, when a sufficient presumption would exist in his favour to enable the judge to decide the question of the *real* right of co-heirship or co-ownership whilst settling the *personal* right; and in the third case, as the plaintiff usually charged the defendant with encroachment, and the defendant retaliated with a similar complaint, the judge had to decide (adjudicate) which part of the land belonged to each; but, although the judge, therefore, generally in (3), and often in (1) and (2), in deciding the question of the *obligation*, decided also the *real* right involved, no third division of actions into those *mixtæ* was ever invented until, after the formula procedure was no longer in use, something like it was introduced, see part ii, par. 275, and *post*, par. 2119.

1963. *Vindicatio* (or *rei vindicatio*). This term was restricted to those actions *in rem*, in which the *ownership* of the thing was claimed, *i.e.*, sinking the *right* in the thing itself, and *vindicationes rerum incorporalium* referred to claims of fractions of this ownership as usufruct, servitude, etc.

1965. *Condictio.* This action for the purpose of enforcing the execution of a civil obligation retained its name after the notification to the defendant had ceased to exist, see part i, par. 242. It was peculiar in that it always remained *unilateral* and *stricti juris*, although extended from *certa pecunia* (*i.e.*, in respect of a fixed sum of money only) to *certa res* (part i, par. 242), and then to obligations in respect of indeterminate things under the title of *condictio triticaria*, wheat (*triticum*) being the most usual object of a *mutuum* or *stipulatio*. Finally, the term came to include any action *in personam* as opposed to an action *in rem*, though it was never applied to an *actio in factum*.

1971. *Actions in jus or in factum.*
This distinction was due to the historical origin of the formula, see *ante*, par. 1911, 1916. The *actio in factum concepta* drawn up for the use of *peregrini* put no question of law, and, therefore, had no *demonstratio* or *intentio* properly so-called; but, in cases where the person, though a *citizen*, had strictly no separate *persona* (*e.g.*,

a person *alieni juris* as a *filius-familias*) so that he could not have a civil law action *(in jus concepta)* in his own name, the prætor would draw one up *in factum*, and hence the *album* contained on civil law points formulæ prepared both *in jus* and *in factum*, *e.g.*:—

Formula *in jus* for *depositum*, *(demonstratio)* "*judex esto. Quod Aulus Agerius apud Numerium Negidium mensam argenteam deposuit qua de re agitur*" (*intentio juris civilis* with characteristic expressions, *dare facere oportet*). "*Quidquid ob eam rem N. N. A. A. dare facere oportet ex fide bona.*" (*Condemnatio*) *ejus judex N. N. A. A. condemnato, nisi restituat ; si non paret absolvito*".

Formula *in factum*. (First part, corresponding to *demonstratio* and *intentio* united and putting question of *fact.*) "*Judex esto. Si paret Aulum Agerium apud Numerium Negidium mensam argenteam deposuisse, eam que dolo malo Numerii Negidii Aulo Agerio redditam non esse.*" "*Quanti ea res erit tantam pecuniam judex Numerium Negidium Aulo Agerio condemnato ; si non paret, absolvito*" (Gai. Inst. iv, § 47).

1979. *Utiles actiones*. The prætor had *two* methods of constructing these, viz., either by a formula—

(1) *In factum*, in which the *condemnatio* contained the same consequences as in the action intended to be imitated, *e.g.*, the *actio in factum utilis ex lege Aquilia* (*ante*, par. 1757). These actions were usually extensions of the *directæ actiones* of the civil law to *cases* not altogether within its sphere, or to *persons* to whom it could not strictly be given (see *ante*, par. 1971).

(2) *Fictitia*. This occurred in the *fictitiæ actiones*, which differed from the class of actions mentioned at par. 1916 (2), and were included under the general head of *utiles actiones*. Here the prætor presumed the existence of a civil law quality which did not exist, *i.e.*, he drew up *in jus* part of the *intentio* on the fictitious hypothesis of the action to be imitated, and extended, as in the examples given by *Gaius* (Inst. iv, §§ 34 to 38), viz.—

(a) the *bonorum possessor, loco heredis* (*ante*, par. 1099), who, *ficto herede*, had a *rei vindicatio* (*Judex esto : si Aulus Agerius Lucio Titio heres esset, tum si fundum de quo agitur, ex jure quiritium ejus esse oporteret*, etc.), or an action *in personam* (*Tum si paret Numerium Negidium Aulo Agerio sestertium X millia dare oportere*).

(β) Similar actions would lie in favour of the *bonorum emptor* (*ante*, par. 1161), and in the same way

(γ) the person in process of acquiring by *usucapion*, and who had lost possession, would be allowed a formula based on the assumption that the usucapion was complete *(fingitur rem usucepisse)*, as in the case of the *publiciana in rem actio* (*post*, par. 2073), where the formula was *in factum fictitia*, the *intentio* putting a question *in factum*, followed by a fictitious *conceptio in jus*, *e.g.*, *Judex esto : (infactum concepta) si quem hominem Aulus Agerius emit, et is ei traditus est anno possidisset (in jus concepta) tum si eum homi-*

nem, de quo agitur, ejus ex jure Quiritium esse oporteret, etc. So also—

(δ) *peregrini* were feigned to be *citizens* in order to apply the civil formula *in jus* for or against them,

(ε) the *capitis deminutio* of a debtor (as of a woman after *coemptio*, or of a man after *adrogation*) was also assumed not to have taken place, in order that the action against her or him might not be lost to the creditors *(ante,* par. 1152).

1981. *Actio in factum præscriptis verbis.* This is to be distinguished from the *actio in factum*, as it was *in jus concepta, i.e.,* with a *civil law intentio (civilis intentio), "Quidquid ob eam rem . . . dare facere oportet"*, and the only part involving the *factum* was the *demonstratio*, for here, as this was the appropriate action for contracts without any peculiar name, the Prætor was compelled to set out a preliminary statement of the facts, instead of referring simply to the contract by name (see *ante,* par. 1598).

1982. *Actio de dolo malo in factum composita* (or *temperata).* The ordinary *actio de dolo malo (post,* par. 2145) was a prætorian *in factum* action, but from the form in which it was drawn up, "if there has been *dolus* in the matter on the part of the defendant," it necessarily left the judge a certain latitude in respect of the legal or moral consideration attaching to the act done. If, therefore, it was undesirable to use it, on account of the *infamy* attaching to the action, the formula would be so modified as to instruct the judge simply to determine whether the particular fact had been done without considering whether it came under the head of *dolus* or not, and the action, *quod metus causa*, could be similarly dealt with (see *post,* par. 2261).

1983. *Actiones stricti juris, bonæ fidei, arbitrariæ.*

In the *actio sacramenti* the judge decided simply whether the *sacramentum* was *justum* or *injustum (ante,* par. 1856), and the same remark applies to the *per condictionem*, whether it was *dare certam pecuniam* or *rem certam*, but in the *per judicis postulationem* the judge (frequently an *arbiter*) was allowed a certain latitude *(ante,* par. 1870), and as this distinction passed into the *formula* system, it led to the present division, which is based on the extent of the powers conferred on the judge by the formula.

(1) *Stricti juris judicia.* These actions were *in jus concepta*, and left the judge *(judex)* nothing but the decision *(judicium)* of a question of civil law respecting a *unilateral* obligation, *dolus* and *set off* had to be the subject of separate actions, or of *exceptions inserted* in the formula, and any claim in respect of produce or interest would usually only be allowed from the time of the *litis contestatio*, except in the case of the *condictio indebiti*, and other actions of the restitution class.

(2) *Bonæ fidei judicia.* In these actions special words were added to the bare question of law, *e.g.*, in the *fiducia* action *"ut inter bonos bene agiter oportet"*, or in the *rei uxoriæ* action *(post,* par. 2136), *" quod æquius melius"*, by which the judge was authorised

to take equitable considerations *(ex bona fide)* into account in making his award *(arbitrium)*. Hence the judge could include (α) every act of *dolus* on the part of the plaintiff or the defendant, without the *plaintiff* having to rely upon a special stipulation *(clausula doli, cautio de dolo)*, or bringing the Prætorian action, *de dolo malo*, and the *defendant* was relieved from the necessity of inserting any exception *de dolo;* (β) ordinary *usage*, and see as to pacts *in continenti, ante,* par. 1580; (γ) *set off*, see *post*, par. 2167; (δ) produce or interest when the debtor was *in mora* (*ante*, par. 1655).

(3) *Arbitrariæ judicia*. These absorbed the *real rights* still protected by the *sacramentum* action, after the *stricti juris* and *bonæ fidei* actions had replaced, in respect of *obligations*, the *per condictionem* and *per judicis postulationem*. The class derived its name from the *jussus* (or *arbitrium*), inserted in the *formula petitoria*, for the purpose of obtaining *restitution* (see *ante*, par. 1937), but in other respects the action was not *bonæ fidei*, for the judge could not decide *ex æquo et bono* as to the existence of the right involved, though the *arbitrium* itself was made *ex æquo et bono*, *i. e.,* taking all considerations into account. Probably one or more *arbiters* were employed, and if the defendant complied fully with the terms of the *jussus* he was discharged from further liability, but if only the principal thing was restored, the *produce* and the *accessories* would form the subject of the *condemnatio*. If the *jussus* was *not* obeyed, the *condemnatio* served as a mode of punishment, for it was *incerta* (*quanti ea res erit*), and, though the judge was not bound to adopt the sum so stated, the amount was usually fixed by the plaintiff taking an *oath* (*jusjurandum in litem*, see *post*, par. 2049) as to the indemnity due to him.

1996. Hence formulæ *stricti juris* and *bonæ fidei* were proper for actions *in personam*, whilst the formula *arbitraria* was specially designed for actions *in rem*, whether (α) *civil* (as the *rei vindicatio*, the *confessoria*, and *negatoria* actions), or (β) *Prætorian* (as the *Publiciana, Serviana, quasi Serviana* actions), and it also exceptionally included (γ) two *civil* actions *in personam*, (the *ad exhibendum* and *finium regundorum* actions), (δ) two *Prætorian* personal actions *(Quod metus causa,* and *de dolo malo)*, for these four actions all have a restitutory or exhibitory character, besides (ε) the *utilis* action, *de eo quod certo loco*, and (ζ) the actions *depositi* and *commodati*, when the words *nisi restituat (N.R.)*, or *eumque dolo malo redditam non esse* were added.

The above remarks as to the three classes of actions (*stricti juris, bonæ fidei, arbitrariæ)* apply exclusively to *civil* actions *in jus conceptæ, i.e.*, putting a question of civil law, for actions *in factum* were apart, and could not be said properly to come under the head of *stricti juris* or *bonæ fidei*, though many were *arbitrariæ* (in so far as the order to *restore*, or to *make compensation*, preceded the condemnation), but then the extent of the powers conferred on the *judge* depended entirely on the nature of the *fact* stated in the *intentio*, and the amount and quality of the *condemnatio*, as in the actions cited *ante*, par. 1982.

2001. The opinion of the *Sabinians* against the *Proculians* (Gai. Inst., iv, § 114) was adopted by *Justinian*, that execution by the defendant before sentence absolved him in all actions (*omnia judicia esse absolutoria*, Justinian Inst., iv, 12, § 2), though previously in actions *stricti juris*, owing to the *novation* effected by the original obligation, the defendant was condemned in respect of the new obligation arising from the action if the *intentio* was proved true, whether he had voluntarily executed or not.

2002. *Penal* actions arising from delicts or quasi delicts must be classed apart, as they were not *stricti juris*, or *bonæ fidei*, or *arbitrariæ*, though as a *judex* (not an *arbiter*) was employed, the decision would be a *judicium*.

2003. *Judicia legitima* or *imperio continentia*.

In spite of the fusion of the law applicable to *citizens* and strangers effected by the introduction of the *formulary* system, a remnant of the exclusiveness characteristic of the *legis actiones* lingered in a *territorial* and *city* distinction, according to which actions were classed as :—

(1) *Legitima judicia (judicia quæ legitimo jure consistunt)*, in which the trial by formula took place,—(α) in Rome or within one mile of it,—(β) by a Roman citizen *unus judex*,—(γ) litigants all *citizens*,—(δ) after being once commenced they continued in force, like the *legis actiones*, until sentence was given, but see *post*, par. 2242,—(ε) after being once exercised they were exhausted for that object,—(ζ) these were the only actions in which the *adjudicatio* could really establish *rights* of servitude or (?) *dominium ex jure quiritium*.

(2) *Judicia imperio continentia*, *i.e.*, actions based on the *imperium* of the magistrate, and—(α) used when any of the first three essentials to a *legitimum judicium* were wanting, as where the judge or one of the parties was a *peregrinus*, or when the cause was heard (as in the case of all trials in the provinces) before *recuperatores*, whether the litigants were both citizens or not,—(β) lasted only during the power of the particular magistrate from whom they emanated (*tamdiu valent, quamdiu is qui ea præcipit imperium habebit*, Gai. Inst., iv, § 105), so that the death of the magistrate, or his resignation, or in the provinces the change of the governor, destroyed all the actions organised by him, and hence litigants crowded at the commencement of each annual magistracy to get formulæ assigned to them in their turn,— (γ) never extinguished the right for the pursuit of which the action was brought, except in so far as they could be used by way of *exception* (see *post*, par. 2046).

2011. *Extraordinariæ cognitiones* (see part ii, par. 288). This summary procedure, involving neither judge nor formula, existed in the *legis actiones* in the case of the *manus injectio* (*ante*, par. 1883), but was largely developed, and acquired a special name under the *formulary* system.

2015. The *civil* matters which came within its cognizance may be classed under the heads of—

(1) Cases in which the *jurisdictio* of the magistrate sufficed, as where the *in jure cessio* applied, or where the facts were admitted, or the action or interdict was refused.

(2) Cases in which the *extraordinaria cognitio* was given by special enactments, as in respect of *fidei-commissa* (*ante*, par. 950) or suits against *publicani* (Tacit. Ann. xii, 51).

(3) Cases where it was used as a means of filling up the gaps or obviating the rigours of the civil law, as in the case of (α) *persons*, when it took into account complaints of a slave against his master (*ante*, par. 89, 1), or of a son against the paterfamilias; (β) *matter*, as in claims of support between ascendants, descendants, patrons, and freedmen, or in respect of the fees of barristers, and other members of the liberal professions, etc.

(4) Cases where the *imperium* was required for execution, *manu militari*, whether independently of any trial, or before, during, or after sentence of a judge. It was chiefly under this last head that fell—

(α) *Prætorian stipulations* (see *ante*, par. 1313, 2).

(β) *Restitutiones in integrum*. When no simpler means existed, and sufficient equitable motives justified it, the prætor, *extra ordinem*, and after *causa cognita*, made a decree by which a person prejudiced by the rigour of the strict civil law, in respect of a contract, suit, or other proceeding, involving the loss of a right or entailing some obligation, was replaced in the position he occupied before the loss occurred. The claim must have been made within *one (utilis)* year (extended by Justinian to four years *continui*) after the person prejudiced was in a position to demand the interference of the prætor. *Under* 25, the fact of *minority* alone might be good ground for the restitution if prejudiced, but *over* that age the principal causes were, violence, *dolus*, *mimina c. d.* (in which case the interval was not limited, and allowed as of course without *causa cognita*, see *ante*, par. 1152), lawful error, necessary absence, the infirmities of age (Paul. Sent. I, 7, § 2), or other just cause (see *post*, par. 2077), as the loss of a peremptory *exceptio* that had been omitted, or the injustice of the terms of a formula (Gai. Inst. iv, § 57, and 125); but these *extra-ordinem restitutiones in integrum* are distinguishable from the same result attained by the permission to bring the actions (or insert the exceptions) *quod metus causa*, or *de dolo*, or other suit of a rescissory character involving application to a judge.

(γ) *In possessionem missiones*. These were granted either as a mode of securing the preservation of the eventual right (see *ante*, par. 990, 1124, 1161) or to crush resistance opposed to the prætor's decrees. They were generally, in respect of a *universality* (*post*, par. 2024); but they might be *in singulas res*. The effect of this *missio* was only to make the property a sort of *pignus prætorium*, in respect of the fact of possession; but involved the power of keeping it and watching it *(custodia et observatio)*, and the possession for the time being was protected by a special interdict or actio *in factum*, though subsequent measures were necessary in order either to acquire the true civil possession or to have the power of selling the property, as in the case of *damnum infectum*, see *ante*, par. 1313 (2).

2024. *Methods of forced execution.*

Under the formulary system these were necessarily always for the purpose of compelling the payment of a sum of money ascertained by the *condemnatio* (except in the case of the *jussus* of the *arbitrariæ* actions, *ante*, par. 1983, 3), and they fall under the heads of—

(α) *Duci jubere.* This order obtained from the prætor *extra ordinem*, authorised the creditor to take a debtor and detain him in his house, until he had worked off the amount. The debtor did not thereby cease to be *ingenuus*, nor did he become a slave in fact or in law, and his children were not obliged to serve for the debt of their father. The establishment of these private prisons *(privata carcera)* was forbidden by *Zeno*, but the system of working for the profit of the creditor continued, at least as a mode of compelling execution, down to the time of *Justinian*, and this was in fact in a less rigorous form the same right of the creditor against the *person* of the debtor, which was carried out probably down to the time of the *leges Juliæ* in the *addictio* of the *legis actio per manus injectionem* (*ante*, par. 1883), and the delay of thirty days after being *judicatus* or *confessus* remained, though the judge might abridge or extend the time to twice that period. The *missio in possessionem* (*ante*, par. 2015, γ) of the creditor of the *universitas rerum* of the debtor was, however, the true *Prætorian* law substitute for the *manus injectio*. Here the *property* (*i.e.*, the *juridical persona*) was substituted for the *physical persona*, and after the thirty days the prætor gave *extra ordinem* the decree *duci jubere*, as well as that authorising the universality of the goods being sold by the creditors after the formalities detailed *ante*, par. 1161. This

(β) *Emptio bonorum* for the benefit of the private creditors of an insolvent debtor was probably deduced from the

(γ) *Sectio bonorum* of the *civil* law, or public sale *sub hasta* (see part ii, par. 229, 7) for the benefit of the state, made by the Quæstors of the treasure, of the universality of the goods of a person criminally condemned after a public accusation involving confiscation (*ante*, par. 1539, 1). The sale was authorised by the *interdictum sectorium* (*post*, par. 2303), or order made by the prætor *extra ordinem*, and those who acquired this property were called *sectores* (Gai. Inst. iv, § 146), because they usually intended to re-sell the goods in detail; and, as they were *universal* successors by the *civil* law, this method is included by *Varro* in the means of acquiring *dominium ex jure Quiritium*.

A A

(δ) *Bonorum cessio*. A *lex Julia* (? one of the *leges Juliæ Judiciariæ*, part i, par. 244), towards the end of the Republic, allowed a debtor (? unfortunate and *bona fide*) to make a *voluntary assignment* of his property for the benefit of his creditors, and thereby avoid *imprisonment* and *infamy*; but in opposition to the *prætorian* discharge of the debtor after the *bonorum emptio* (*ante*, par. 1161), in this case the creditors retained the right of suing him *quantum facere potest* in respect of any unpaid balance if he subsequently acquired property.

(ε) *Distractio bonorum*. This term refers to the exception introduced by a *senatus consultum* prior to the time of Marcus Aurelius and *Gaius*, in favour of the debtor who was a *clara persona* (*e.g.*, a senator or his wife), viz., that the sale should be in detail by a *curator*, in which case no infamy attached, and no universal succession resulted, though the debtor was still liable for any balance remaining due to the creditors. After the decline of the formula procedure, this privilege became the common right.

(ζ) *Prætorian pignoris capio*. This mode of execution on the *property* of the debtor was sanctioned by imperial constitutions at least as far back as Antoninus Pius. It bore an analogy to the *legis actio per pignoris capionem* (*ante*, par. 1893), except that the seizure was made by the *magistrate* instead of by the creditor. After *confession* of the debt, or *condemnation*, and on the expiration of the delay permitted for voluntary performance, the magistrate (*extra ordinem*) seized, by means of the officers of his court (*officiales, viatores, apparitores, executores*), some property of the debtor sufficient to cover the debt. The order observed was, (1) *res mobiles*, and if insufficient, (2) *res soli*, and then (3) *jura*.

This *pignus prætorium* could be redeemed within two months by payment of the debt, otherwise it was sold by the court, and the debt paid out of the proceeds; or, if there was no purchaser, the property was *addictus* to the creditor at a fixed price.

2033. The mode of procedure seems to have been—After the *legal delay* the creditor summoned his debtor *in jus*, when, if the Prætor acted *extra ordinem*, and ordered any one of the above methods of execution, no action took place, but if the fact of the sentence, or the obligation resulting from it, was disputed, the Prætor gave the formula of the *judicati actio* (*post*, par. 2274), by which the matter was sent before a *judge* for his decision, the debtor giving the *cautio judicatum solvi* (*post*, par. 2237).

2034. *Review of the formula system.*
The procedure observed *in jure* involved the following:—

(1) *In jus vocatio*. This in principle remained the same as under the *legis actiones*, but the magistrate can interpose his authority so as to put additional pressure on the defendant, as by taking pledges, or by giving an action for the recovery of a pecuniary

penalty (*mulcta*) against the defendant, as well as those abetting him in refusing to appear.

(2) *Fidejussor judicio sistendi causa*. This surety was under a pecuniary penalty, fixed in the *stipulatio*, for the appearance of the defendant *in jure*, in obedience to the *vocatio in jus* (and replaced the *vindex*, i.e., the third party undertaking the defence in his own name), but, if the defendant did not appear in the first instance, and no one undertook his defence, the only method of getting over his absence was to put the plaintiff in possession of the property, by way of security (*missio in possessionem custodiæ causa*), see *ante*, par. 2015 (γ).

(3) *Actionis denuntiatio*. It was customary, but not obligatory, at the same time as the *vocatio in jus*, to inform the defendant of the nature of the claim, and the kind of action about to be brought against him (see *post*, par. 2060).

(4) *Actionis editio* (or *postulatio*). The plaintiff orally, or in writing, or by pointing it out on the album, indicated the action he intended to bring, and the formula he wished to use, but previous to the *litis contestatio* he might modify his demand, or change the form of the action.

(5) *Vadimonium*. If the defendant claimed a delay before the remainder of the proceedings *in jure* were completed, or if the case could not be terminated the same day, he must give security for his reappearance *in jure* on the day fixed. This was done, according to the nature of the case, by a simple verbal stipulation (*purum*), or by oath (*jurejurando*), or by fidejussors (*cum satisdatione*), or recuperators might be at once named (*recuperatoribus suppositis*) to condemn him in the pecuniary penalty fixed if he did not appear.

2041. If the subject matter fell within the *jurisdictio* of the magistrate, or if the plaintiff failed to make out his case, or if the defendant admitted (*confessio in jure*) the claim as stated by the plaintiff (for otherwise a judge would be required to assess the damages), or if one of the litigants put the other on oath as to the existence of the disputed right (*jusjurandum in jure*), the cause was decided *extra-ordinem*, otherwise the next step was—

(6) *Accommodare actionem*, i.e., on the demand of the plaintiff (*actionis impetratio*) to appoint a judge, and prepare the formula. For this purpose either party, or the magistrate, might put questions (*interrogatio in jure*), which the interrogated party was bound to answer if they related to facts personal to himself, *e.g.*, whether the defendant was the *heir* or the original debtor, or whether (in a noxal action) he was the owner of the slave, or to ascertain the age of either of the parties when this affected the right involved.

(7) *Litis contestatio*. This now only indicated the joinder of issue resulting from the close of the proceedings *in jure* by the settlement of the formula, and its delivery to the parties, but it

opened an important phase in the suit, as the parties were now under an obligation *quasi ex contractu* (perpetual and transmissible for or against heirs, *post*, par. 2242), to proceed with the trial and incur the effects of the sentence, *i.e.*, the action had commenced (*res in judicio deducta, lis inchoata, lis contestata*), and would go on in spite of the default of the plaintiff or defendant, for if the defendant now failed to appear, the plaintiff could get the Prætor to publish an *edictum*, renewed once or twice at intervals of about ten days, the last of which was *peremptorium*, and made the defendant *contumax*, and the suit was then decided in his absence. The property in litigation also became *inalienable*, and the judge, litigants, and property in dispute, having all been ascertained, nothing could now be altered except by a *restitutio in integrum*, but the death of the judge, or of one of the litigants, or the appointment of a procurator, might cause a change of *person* (*judicii*, or *litis translatio*), which would be effected by the required alteration of the name being made by the Prætor in the part of the formula appointing the judge, or in the *condemnatio*.

2046. If the action was (1) *in personam*, as well as a (2) *legitimum judicium*, and the formula was (3) *in jus concepta*, the new *obligation* resulting from the *litis contestatio* was *civil*, and hence *ipso jure* by *novatio* extinguished the old obligation (see *ante*, par. 1264, 1704, and 2003), but if wanting any of these three conditions, no novation was effected, and the defendant was bound both by the original *right* and by the new obligation resulting from the *litis contestatio*: for if the action was (α) *in rem*, an obligation could not effect novation of a *real* right, if (β) *in factum*, a fact is incapable of novation, and if (γ) a *judicium imperio continens*, a permanent right could not be destroyed by a mere temporary authority, but an exception *rei in judicium deductæ* would rebut a renewal of the claim in another action at the same time if the pending action was actually proceeding (*in judicium deducta*), and was competent to cover the subject matter in dispute, otherwise a *replicatio* would defeat the exception.

2047. The case now came before the judge (*in judicio*), and the parties produced their proofs by witnesses (*testes*) and documents (*instrumenta, tabellæ, cautiones*), the cause was pleaded (*causæ peroratio*), and, if not clear, adjourned (*litem ampliare*), and new pleadings prepared (*prima, secunda, tertia, actio*).

2049. The judge might, to supplement the proof, require an oath from either of the litigants, and this *jusjurandum in judicio* was distinct from the oath taken by the plaintiff (*jusjurandum in litem*) to fix the amount of the damages (see *ante*, par. 1983, 3).

2050. The judge may declare on oath that the case is not clear to him (*non liquet*), and so abstain from any decision. Then if there are *several*, the judgment may be limited to the opinion of the rest of the judges, or the Prætor may replace him by ordering another *judicium*. In *præjudicia* actions only a fact or a right is decided, and others require only an *adjudicatio*, but the *condemnatio* is always in respect of a precise sum of money (*certæ pecuniæ*), and the sentence is to be delivered publicly and orally *(pronuntiare)*, though it may be read from a paper (*ex tabella recitare*).

2051. The *sentence* terminated the judge's powers, and caused the obligation for the case to be judged resulting from the *litis contestatio*, to be, as it were, *soluta*; and if the defendant was condemned, a new obligation arose, viz., that of executing the sentence (see *ante*, par. 1704), but the original right, whether extinguished by the *litis contestatio* (*ante*, par. 2046), or still existing, was not touched by the sentence, except that in the latter case the defendant had now, besides the exception *rei in judicium deductæ*, the exception *rei judicatæ*, to rebut a renewal of the claim (Gai. Inst. iv, § 106).

2053. The sentence may be—

(1) *Cancelled* by the plaintiff demanding of the magistrate a new trial, or by the defendant opposing the execution of the sentence on the ground that the judgment was *null*, as being in violation of some law, senatus consultum, or constitution, or defective in form, or of no value from the want of jurisdiction of the magistrate or judge, or from the incapacity of one of the parties.

(2) *Revoked* by a *restitutio in integrum*, granted in consideration of particular or extraordinary causes, or on the ground of minority (see *ante*, par. 2015, β).

(3) *Revised* on appeal (*appellatio*), see part i, par. 208. From the time of Augustus (? in virtue of the *lex Julia judiciaria*) the *right of appeal* was claimed immediately, orally (*inter acta voce appellare*), or in writing within a limited interval (*libelli appellatorii*), and the magistrate or judge appealed against then gave the requisite authority in writing to the appellant (*litteræ dimissoriæ*, or *apostoli*). Execution was suspended pending the appeal to the superior magistrate, and the action might finally come before the Emperor, in which case a detailed statement (*relatio, consultatio*) was transmitted by the judge to the imperial tribunal.

Third System. Extraordinaria judicia.

2055. *Origin and development.* The gradual substitution of the *cognitio extraordinaria* for the *judicium ordinarium* of the formula procedure, took place concurrently with the development of the imperial rule into absolute power (see part i, par. 427).

2057. *Organisation of the judicial authority* (see part ii., par. 291).

2060. *Review of the system.* The *in jus vocatio* ceased to be a private act, and acquired a public character, as, though it might be oral, it was usually made by a citation (*libellus citationis*), delivered to the defendant by an officer of the court (*executor* or *viator litium*), to whom the defendant gave the security for his appearance called the *cautio judicio sistendi,* which replaced the *vadimonium,* but the *actionis editio* (see part i, par. 579), as well as, after Theodosius (A.D. 428), the *actionis impetratio* have disappeared, and the mode of communicating the *in jus vocatio* led also to the disuse of the *actionis denuntiatio* (see *ante*, par. 2034, 3), though Constantine had made the delivery of this by an officer of the court compulsory.

2064. As the parties when *in jus* were also *in judicio*, the *litis contestatio* had no longer the same effect (*ante*, par. 2041), so that, though it put the parties under an obligation to have the suit tried, it did not in any case by *novatio* extinguish the original right.

2066. The *sentence* had also undergone modification. After the time of the Emperors Valentinian, Valens, and Gratian, it must be *written*, on pain of nullity, publicly read from the minute (*periculum*) made on the record, which, after being signed by the judge, was inserted in a register, and from this copies might be had if required.

2067. The means of *forced execution*, and the methods of opposing the execution of the sentence, by asserting its nullity, or obtaining restitution, or appealing to a superior court, remain nearly as before (see *ante*, par. 2024).

2068. The *text of the Institutes* does not treat of actions in respect of their *form*, but only as to the *right* they confer of suing, and the definition given by *Justinian*, viz. :

Actio nihil aliud est quam jus persequendi in judicio quod sibi debetur is borrowed from the formulary system, and inaccurate under his system, for the word *judicio* applied to the right given by the *magistrate* to go before a *judge* (see part i, par. 250), and the word *debetur* covers obligations only with which at first formulæ were alone concerned (*ante*, par. 1926), whereas the word *actio* now had the extended meaning given in part i, par. 427.

Actions in rem and *in personam*.

2069. (§ i) For the origin and nature of these actions see *ante*, par. 1952. The action *in rem* claiming ownership, *i.e.*, the *rei corporalis vindicatio*, could only be brought if the parties were in one particular situation, viz. : when the thing of which A claimed the ownership was in the possession of B ; for to maintain A in possession *interdicts* were used, whilst in respect of the vindication of *in*corporeal things, for which no true possession could exist, as, *e.g.*, in the case of

(§ ii) *rights of servitude* there were two positions in which an *in rem* action might occur, viz., when the action was (1) *confessoria*, *i.e.*, when B claimed a right over a thing which A, as owner or possessor, declared to be free from any servitude of the kind insisted on (*si paret jus utendi fruendi*, or *jus eundi, agendi*, etc., *mihi esse*), and when the action was (2) *negatoria* (or *negativa*), *i.e.*, when A, the owner of the property and in possession, denied the right of, and attacked him who exercised and claimed the servitude (*si paret jus utendi fruendi fundo meo adversario non esse*) ; and this is probably the one case referred to by *Justinian*, in which he who possesses acts the part of plaintiff (*sane uno casu qui possidet nihilominus actoris partes obtinet*). Both these actions in fact claim a right, for the second is only *negative* in form, as it amounts to an affirmation of full ownership, the separate existence of a fraction of it existing in favour of somebody else being denied, and both these actions could also be brought where the enjoyment was only threatened or disturbed, *i.e.*, although quasi possession already existed, as in the first case, if B was actually using the servitude he wished to vindicate, and in the second case if A was in the free enjoyment of his property, though, by analogy, *quasi possessory interdicts* were subsequently given, and became the more usual mode of procedure (see *ante*, par. 507).

2072. (§ iii) *Prætorian actions.* Actions *in rem* and *in personam* were also divided into *civil* and *prætorian*, the latter being either (1) *fictitiæ*, or (2) *in factum conceptæ.* See *ante*, par. 1979 (1) (2).

Examples of *prætorian* actions *in rem* are given in the four following sections, the first three examples being *fictitiæ* actions.

2073. (§ iv) *Actio Publiciana* (see *ante*, par. 1979, γ), probably named after the *Q. Publicius*, who was prætor in the time of Cicero. This was in fact a *utilis vindicatio*, entailing similar results as the *vindicatio* in respect of produce, accessories, expenses, *culpa*, etc., and though for the protection of the *possessor* who had not yet acquired the property by usucapion, it was fictitiously based on *ownership* not possession.

It could be applied in four ways, viz. :—

(1) When after a thing *mancipi* had been delivered by the *dominus*, but not by a *jus Quiritium* method, it was lost before *usucapion* could give the possession necessary to sustain a *civil rei vindicatio*.

(2) When the thing (*mancipi* or *nec*) had been received *ex justa causa* and *bona fide*, but not from the owner (*a non domino*), and possession was lost before the time of *usucapion* had expired ; but if the action was brought against the *real* owner, the latter could insert the *exceptio justi dominii* (*si ea res possessoris non sit*, or *si dominus ejus rei possessor non sit*), to which, if circumstances allowed it, the plaintiff could reply with, *e.g.*, the *replicatio rei venditæ et traditæ* as in the case of No. 1, where the owner had become again possessed of a thing *mancipi*, sold and delivered by him to the purchaser without mancipation, or the *replicatio doli mali* would lie, though only against the author of the fraud or his heirs. When the action was brought against the possessor himself, in the way of acquiring by *usucapion* or *prescription*, *Ulpian* held (with the *Sabinians*) that if both the plaintiff and the possessor had received the property from one and the same person, other than the owner (*ab eodem non domino*), the

first who was put in possession, *i.e.*, the first who was *in causa usucapiendi* was to be preferred (and this was the opinion of *Neratius* and the *Proculians* for all cases); but when the property had been bought of different persons, neither of whom was the owner *(a diversis non dominis)* actual possession gave the preference *(melior causa sit possidentis quam petentis).* See Dig. 6, 2, 9, § 4, *Ulpian*, and 19, 1, 31, § 2, *Neratius.*

(3) When there could be no question of *usucapion*, as *e.g.*, in the case of provincial lands of which the possessor could not become owner, and, therefore, could not bring the civil *rei vindicatio*; but the property was lost before or after the *prescriptive* time had elapsed.

(4) When, though the plaintiff had really become owner, yet having lost the possession, he preferred this action to the civil *rei vindicatio*, because it did not compel him to prove the ownership in those from whom he derived title. See *ante*, par. 540 (1).

As the difference between *mancipi* and *nec mancipi* was suppressed, and *usucapion* and *prescription* had been merged, only (2) and (4) existed under Justinian. The action could not apply to things incapable from any cause of *usucapion* (see *ante*, par. 519); but as custom rendered *usufruct* and *rural* and *urban servitudes* capable of acquisition by long use, this action became available for their protection. See *ante*, par. 461 (4).

2077. (§ v) *Actio Publiciana rescissoria.* Inversely for the protection of the *owner*, whose property had been acquired by *usucapion*, a *rei vindicatio (utilis) rescissoria*, or this action (which possessed the advantage of not involving proof of title), lay, after *causa cognita* by the prætor, to *rescind* the *usucapion (rescissa usucapione)* acquired by a possessor, *i.e.*, to obtain a *restitutio in integrum*, and on this account both actions are called *rescissoria*, though there was no special *actio Publiciana rescissoria* as the commentators assert, this being merely an *utilis* application of the former. These actions, based upon the *fictitious* assumption that *usucapion* had not taken place, could be brought within the *four* continuous years which represented the *utilis annum* of the edict (*ante*, par. 2015, β), and the cases in which they could be applied were :—

(1) When the usucapion had been running in favour of the possessor through the *absence* of the *owner* caused by some lawful reason *(justa causa)* as *metu, reipublicæ causa, vinculis, servitute, hostium-que potestate.*

(2) When, though the *owner* was present, the acquisition by usucapion had been accomplished in consequence of the *possessor* being absent from any cause at the time when the *in jus vocatio*, and the *litis contestatio* could not take place against an absent person (see *ante*, par. 2034, 2); but the necessity for the action was removed when, under *Justinian*, the owner need not wait for the return of the possessor, but could stop the usucapion of the absent possessor by a notice (*libellus*) signed by three witnesses, or presented to the Præses, Bishop, or defensor of the city (*ante*,

par. 538, 3). So if the owner had recovered the possession, and the person who had acquired the property by usucapion vindicated it, the owner could repel him by an *exception*, which he would be allowed to insert in the defence after *causa cognita* by the prætor.

The fictitious *rescissoria* action might also be used to meet other cases requiring *restitutio in integrum*, as where an alienation had been made by a *minor* to his prejudice, or by a person over twenty-five years under the constraint of fear. See *ante*, par. 2015 (*B*).

2083. (§ vi) *Actio Pauliana*. Similarly for the protection of *creditors* this action *in rem* could be brought by them for the recission of *alienations* fraudulently made by an insolvent debtor.

The creditors first obtained the *missio in possessionem* in respect of the debtor's property, and then brought this *rei vindicatio* against any holder of the property with the formula *fictitiously* constructed on the hypothesis that the delivery had never been made *(rescissa traditione)*, and that, therefore, the goods in question still remained amongst the other property of the debtor (for the case of fraudulent *enfranchisements* provided against by the *Lex Ælia Sentia*, see *ante*, par. 70) ; but this *actio fictitia* and *rescissoria* was distinct from the *actio Pauliana in personam* (*in factum concepta* and *arbitraria*) given for the revocation, not only of alienations, but in respect of any act of the debtor in fraud of his creditors, provided it tended to diminish the value of the estate. It lay against the *debtor* and the *accomplices* of his fraud, even though no longer in possession, as well as against those who had gratuitously profited, but only to the amount benefitted.

2087. (§ vii) *Actio Serviana*. In the same way for the protection of *mortgagees* this *prætorian* action *in rem* was given against third holders. It was at first restricted to the landlord of a rural estate to whom, according to an ancient practice, the property of the tenant (*colonus*) had been pledged as security for the rent ; but the *Quasi Serviana* (or *hypothecaria*) *actio* (with the formula, not fictitiously drawn up, but simply *in factum*) was introduced by a subsequent prætor to cover all other cases of pledge (see *ante*, par. 1520, 2 and 4) ; and, finally, before the time of Cicero the *hypotheca* or real right, entailing this action for its enforcement against third holders, could be conferred on a creditor by a simple verbal agreement without traditio, and there was no difference between *pignus* and *hypotheca*, except that the former usually referred to moveables, and implied *traditio*.

The action was also called a *vindicatio pignoris* or *persecutio hypothecaria* or *pigneratitia*, though the last term was generally reserved for the action in *personam* brought in respect of the obligation arising out of the contract of pledge (*ante*, par. 1230).

The ancient practice, still existing, concurrently with other modes, in the time of *Gaius* (Inst. ii, § 59, 70) and *Paul* (Sent. ii, 13), was actually to transfer by *mancipation* the property pledged, subject to an accessory contract of *re*-mancipation (*sub-fiducia, sub-lege re-*

mancipationis) on re-payment of the money advanced, and of this nature were the *per æs et libram* (or *nexum*) obligations entered into by a debtor in respect of his person and property.

The creditor thus became temporary *dominus ex jure Quiritium*, and had a *rei-vindicatio*, but in practice the possession, or the rents and profits might be reserved to the debtor by means of the *precarium*, or by keeping an account of the produce, and, finally, the contract of *pignus* (*ante*, par. 1225) was originated when the creditor was satisfied with the simple detention of the thing as security, but this involved the introduction of a *fictitious real* action to meet the difficulty, if possession was lost, of the simple detention of the property, not entitling the pledgee to bring an action *in rem* against third holders.

2095. The rights of the creditor (pledgee or mortgagee) as finally developed were :—

(1) To *sell* the thing *(jus vendendi seu distrahendi)*. Originally the creditor only had the power of detaining the property, but this special right, though not extended to all classes of creditors, was subsequently conferred upon him, and became such an essential element, that the pact *ne vendere liceat* would not affect the power of sale if the debt was due, if the sale was made on account of the sum secured, and according to the terms of agreement, or in default of those fixed by law, but the *lex commissoria* clause was prohibited (see *ante*, par. 595, and 1620).

(2) To be *paid* out of the *price* in *preference* to other creditors. If there were several mortgagees, the rule was (in respect of both the pignus and hypotheca) *Potior tempore, portior jure* (Cod. 8, 18, 4, Const. Ant.), so that a *mortgagee* with an earlier title of *hypotheca*, though *not* in possession, might be preferred to a *pledgee* holding the pignus, but certain mortgagees took precedence by law, *e.g.*, those who had expended sums for the utility or preservation of the thing itself pledged, and for other examples, see *post*, par. 2101. This class of mortgage has been called by the commentators *privileged*, and only differed from an ordinary *mortgage* in respect of the right of preference not being according to *date*, but according to the rank which had been assigned to it by the particular law (*privata lex*) specially conferring the favour.

(3) To avail himself of the *Quasi Serviana actio* against third holders, or any subsequent mortgagee detaining the property, to compel a recognition of those *real* rights of the mortgagee, included under (1) and (2).

Although translations of *ownership* could only be effected by the ostensible fact of *tradition*, or certain *civil* means, a *mortgage* could be *secret*, as proof of the date and existence of the mere verbal agreement sufficed. Hence, no means existed of knowing whether the property was already mortgaged or not, until an indirect method was introduced by the Emperor Leo (Cod. 8, 18, 11), viz., that of giving *priority* to mortgages made by an *instrumentum publice confectum*, *i.e.*, by deed prepared by the magistrate, or a public notary, or at least subscribed by three men of good reputation, but this regulation was not imperative.

2101. *Tacit mortgages.* These existed, independent of agreement—

(1) By law or jurisprudence in favour of, *e.g.*, (α) the landlord of an *urban* estate, as security for rent over the things brought by the tenant into the building; (β) the landlord of a *rural* estate, but only on the products of the immoveable, as an agreement was required to pledge the things brought for cultivating the estate; (γ) the legatee over the share of the inheritance belonging to each heir, see *ante*, par. 988; (δ) the fiscus, in respect of arrears of taxes, etc.; (ε) pupils, minors, and lunatics (by constitutions of Constantine the Great, and subsequent Emperors) over all the property of their tutors and curators, see *ante*, par. 277; (ζ) the lawful wife over the property of her husband, for the restitution of the dowry, see *post*, par. 2136.

(2) By the authority of the magistrate, *e.g.*, (α) the *pignus prætorium* resulting from the *missio in possessionem bonorum*, or, (β) the Prætorian *pignoris capio*, see *ante*, par. 2015 (γ) and 2024 (ζ).

Everything capable of being bought or sold could be the object of a mortgage, without any distinction as to moveables and immoveables, or whether the property was corporeal or incorporeal (as a usufruct or a debt, though some distinction existed as to prædial servitudes), particular (*singularis*), or universal (*rerum universitatis*), and the agreement might also include not only all the existing property of the mortgagor, but also all that would be acquired in the future.

The mortgage was *indivisible*, in the sense that the right existed in respect of the entire debt and its accessories, not only on the whole of a thing mortgaged, but on each of its parts and their accessories, so that if partial payment were made, the whole of the property still remained pledged for the balance, and inversely, if part of the property perished, the remainder was liable for the whole debt.

2103. *Beneficium separationis.* This Prætorian institution is connected with the subject of mortgage, and occurred under various circumstances, as, *e.g.*, when the creditors and legatees of an inheritance obtained an order from the Prætor separating the patrimony of the deceased from that of the heir, so that they might be preferred to the personal creditors of the heir in respect of the first-named property, and similar provisions existed as to the *peculium castrense.*

2104. Examples of *prætorian* actions in *personam* are :—

(§ viii) *Actio de constituta pecunia*, introduced by the Prætor, in analogy to the *actio receptitia*, which latter was a perpetual *civil* law action peculiar to *argentarii*, applying to any kind of object, and based, independently of the pre-existing cause, and by an exception to the ordinary rules of the civil law, upon a simple agreement on his part to pay.

The *prætorian* action was given against anyone (including *argentarii*), but it was based upon a presumed antecedent debt. It only lasted a year, and was confined to things "*quæ pondere numero mensurave constant.*"

Justinian (Cod. 4, 18, 2) merged the two actions by suppressing the name *receptitia*, and making the action *de constituta pecunia* perpetual, and allowing it to be given against any person, for any object, but only when the agreement to pay referred to an antecedent debt, see *ante*, par. 1611.

(§ x) *Actio de peculio*. For the variety of actions falling under this head, see *post*, par. 2212.

2109. (§ xi) *Actio de jurejurando* (or *an juraverit*). If the parties, in order to avoid a trial, agreed that one of them should put the other on his oath as to a certain transaction, *e.g.*, if the *plaintiff* who asserted himself to be a creditor had sworn, by the desire of the supposed debtor, that the sum was due to him, then, if payment was refused, the prætor (who recognised the transaction by his edict) gave the creditor this *Prætorian* action *(in factum)*, in which the judge had only to ascertain the fact of the oath. On the other hand, as the oath had more weight than the debt, the action would be refused altogether, if, *e.g.*, it had been put to the *defendant* and he had sworn that he owed nothing, or if, being possessor of the property, he swore it belonged to him, *i.e.*, if the oath had been taken before the prætor, or was not denied; but if the fact itself of the oath was disputed, the defendant would insert it in the formula in the form of an exception *de jurejurando*.

This *extra-judicial* oath was distinct from those given *in jure*, or *in judicio*, see *ante*, par. 2034 (5), 2041, 2049, and *post*, par. 2265.

2111. (§ xii) *Actio de albo corrupto*. This was a *popularis* prætorian *penal* action to punish anyone damaging or altering the *album*, and (as in the case of any alteration of the edicts of the emperors) entailed the penalties attaching to falsifications. Other examples of this numerous class of penal actions are afforded by the *actio in factum* given against the son or freedman summoning his father or patron *in jus* without permission (see *post*, par. 2339, 5), and that given against a person preventing another, by force or fraud, from appearing *in jus* (*ante*, par. 2034).

2112. (§ xiii) *Præjudiciales actiones*. These resemble *real* actions in that they are not for an obligation, and the fact or the right is stated in a general (*in rem*) manner; but, on the other hand, actions *in rem* always tend to a condemnation or discharge which these do not, and though these usually refer to questions of *status* (*i.e.*, real rights, as free birth, liberty, patronage, paternity, filiation, etc., see *ante*, par. 1929, *a*), yet they were not necessarily limited to this head, for the action might relate, *e.g.*, to *quanta dos sit*, or whether the *sponsores* or *fidepromissores* had been informed of the extent of the obligation (see *ante*, par. 1384, 1), or *an res de qua agitur major sit centum sestertiis* (Paul, Sent., 5, 9, § 1) or *an bona jure venierint* (Dig. 42, 5, 30, Papirius Justus.)

The real rights could also be asserted by ordinary actions entailing the *condemnatio* of the defendant, and they were then equivalent to the *vindicationes* from which the *in jure cessio* method sprang, see *ante*, par. 82, and for an example of such a *vindicatio* with *adjecta causa*, see *ante*, par. 175. The *liberalis causa* existed before the Twelve Tables (vi, 6), and was inserted in those laws by Appius Claudius (Dig. 1, 2, 2, 24, Pomponius). It gave rise to either a *vindicatio* or a *præjudicium*, and might occur in two ways:—

(1) To declare a person a *slave* and open to anyone claiming to be owner or usufructuary of the assumed slave.

(2) To get a supposed slave declared a *free man*. This was formerly done by a *lictor* or *assertor libertatis*, the man being treated as a thing, the subject of the *vindicatio* (see *ante*, par. 57, 2), and the trial only decided the matter as between the *assertor* and the pretended *master*, so that *three* fresh trials could be brought by three more *assertores*, but subsequently the action was open to the man himself, his relations, or wife, and *Justinian* made the judgment final against all.

The *status* of a person could be contested even after his death; but, according to the Emperors Claudius and Nerva (Dig. 40, 15, 4), the action must be brought within five years if it was desired to attribute a less advantageous position than that possessed at the time of death.

Actions in pursuit of the thing, or of a penalty, or both (mixtæ).

2116. (§ xvii) All *real* actions are brought for the recovery of the thing, and so are nearly all *personal* actions arising from contract, though in the case of *necessary* deposit the action is *mixed*, as it may entail a penalty of *double* if the defendant denies the deposit (see *ante*, par. 1220). The expression *penal* only referred to private actions giving the plaintiff a pecuniary penalty independent of the reparation to be made for the damage sustained, as in the *actio furti*, which was brought for the penalty only, the thing itself being recovered by a separate action (*vindicatio*), but when the penalty and the thing were *both* sued for in the *same* action it was called *mixed*. Examples of such actions are those *vi bonorum raptorum, legis Aquiliæ (post*, par. 2127), and *ex legato quod venerabilibus locis relictum est*, the last of which lay in respect of legacies or fideicommissa left to places dedicated to religion, if the bequest was denied or if the property was not handed over until claimed at law (see *ante*, par. 1622, 5).

Actions which seem mixed as being both in rem and in personam.

2119. (§ xx) Ulpian (Dig. 44, 7, 37, i) applies to the three actions (1) *familiæ erciscundæ*, (2) *communi dividundo*, (3) *finium regundorum*, the term *mixed* (or *duplicia*, see *post*, par. 2318), because each litigant being both plaintiff and defendant, judgment might be pronounced against either or both, whereas in ordinary actions based on the formula, only the *defendant* could be condemned.

The compilers of the Institutes, however, in penning the lines "*mixtam causam obtinere videntur tam in rem quam in personam*", were guided solely by the apparently dual nature of the rights claimed by the plaintiff, for in the time of *Justinian* the formula system had disappeared, and therefore there was no impossibility for the *intentio* being at once *in rem* and *in personam* (see *ante*, par. 1962).

Actions for the simple, double, triple, or quadruple.

2125. (§ xxi) This distinction related to the amount of the *condemnatio* as opposed to the *intentio*, and had no necessary connection with the actual value of the object in dispute, for the *intentio* might include more than this value. Hence an action was—

2126. (§ xxii) *in simplum* when the *intentio* ran *quanti ea res erit*, or *quidquid ob eam rem dare aut facere oportet*, and the *condemnatio* was *tanti condemna*; for though the *quantum* of the *intentio* might be proved to be the quadruple of the value, yet if the *condemnatio* was only for this *quantum*, the action would be simple; hence an action *ex stipulatione* for a *stipulatio duplæ*, as security in a contract of sale (*ante*, par. 1465) would only be *in simplum*, although the *intentio* would be double or triple.

2127. (§ xxiii) *in duplum*. Examples are, the actions *furti nec manifesti*, and *servi corrupti*, which were always for the *double*, whilst others were not necessarily so, as the *damni injuriæ ex lege Aquilia* (*ante*, par. 1746), and that in respect of necessary deposit (*ante*, par. 1220), which were only for the *double* when the claim was denied, whilst simple delay in the delivery might involve *double* damages, as in the case of the action *sacrosanctis locis* (*ante*, par. 2116).

2128. (§ xxiv) *in triplum*. Examples are, the actions *furti concepti*, and *furti oblati* (both abolished, see *ante*, par. 1718). The penalty of triple the damage sustained (obtained by a *condictio ex lege*) was also inflicted by *Justinian* instead of the loss of the *action* in the case of *plus petitio* (*post*, par. 2154), *i.e.*, when the claim was too great in the *libellus conventionis* (*ante*, par. 2060), on the delivery of which the defendant had to pay the viator's fees *(sportulæ)*, which were regulated by the amount of the claim. These fees were payable by both plaintiff and defendant, but if the officers of the court demanded more than the amount fixed by tariff, *Justinian* rendered them liable to a *condictio ex lege* for the quadruple.

2129. (§ xxv) *in quadruplum*. Examples are the action *furti manifesti*, and the action in respect of money given for setting on foot or desisting from a vexatious suit. In the case of the—

Actio quod metus causa, the *quadruple* could be obtained if the action was brought within the year, but only the simple penalty if used as a perpetual action. It was given to him who had consented by reason of grave and actual violence to do an act resulting in the loss or diminution of rights, for which also the exception *quod metus causa* (*post*, par. 2259), or the *restitutio in integrum* (*ante*, par. 2015) could be used, the latter being given by the judge if the most likely to ensure justice, even though the other two would lie in the particular case, and both the *action* and the *exception quod metus causa* might be directed against any person who had profited by the right even in good faith, but the action being *arbitraria* (*ante*, par. 1983), the penalty could be avoided by re-transferring the ownership or the real right alienated (with all accessories), or releasing the executory or re-constituting the executed obligation.

Bonæ fidei, stricti juris, and arbitrariæ actions.
2135. (§ xxviii) Although this division resulted from the procedure by formula (*ante*, par. 1983), it was retained in the subsequent system, the judgment being *ex æquo et bono* in all actions *bonæ fidei*, whilst *civil* lawsuits were dealt with strictly.

To indicate the *bonæ fidei* class is to enumerate the actions which had been, at any given period, exceptionally made so. *Justinian* refers to the following:—

(1) The actions of the three *real* contracts—(α) *commodati*, (β) *depositi*, (γ) *pigneratitia*.

(2) Those of the four *consensual* contracts—(α) *ex empto-vendito*, (β) *locato-conducto*, (γ) *pro socio*, (δ) *mandati*.

(3) Those of four *quasi*-contracts, of which two are analogous to the *mandatum*, viz.—(α) *negotiorum-gestorum*, (β) *tutelæ*, and two analogous to the *societas*, viz. (γ) *familia-erciscundæ*, (δ) *communi-dividundo*.

(4) The action *in factum præscriptis verbis*, which, originally applying only to the contracts *permutatio* and *de æstimato*, was subsequently generalised for all *innominati* contracts (*ante*, par. 1598).

(5) The *real* action *hereditatis petitio* which *Justinian*, to settle the doubts on the subject, decided to range under the *bonæ fidei* class (*post*, par. 2167, α).

(6) The action *ex stipulatu*, in respect of the restitution of a *dowry*, which had the *bonæ fidei* character impressed upon it from the *rei uxoriæ* action merged in it by *Justinian* (*post*, par. 2136).

(7) The actions which, resulting from stipulations, were assimilated to *bonæ fidei* actions, in consequence of the express addition of the *doli clausula* to the stipulation (*post*, par. 2149).

This list differs from that given by *Gaius* (Inst., iv, § 62), in the substitution of (1, γ) for the action *fiduciæ* which had ceased to exist (*ante*, par. 2087), and in adding Nos. (3, γ and δ), (4), (5), (6), (7).

2136. (§ xxix) *Actio rei uxoriæ*. The *dos* (*ante*, par. 582) could be constituted in three ways, viz. :—

(1) *dos data*, *i.e.*, when the property composing the dowry was absolutely transferred at the time to the husband.

(2) *dos dicta*, *i.e.*, when a solemn promise was made without any previous interrogation.

(3) *dos stipulata*, *i.e.*, when the ordinary forms of interrogation and promise were gone through.

To *enable the husband* in the case of (2), and (3) to enforce payment a *condictio* lay, which when brought in respect of (3) was called *ex stipulatu*.

To *compel the husband to restore* the *dos* after the dissolution of the marriage, the *rei uxoriæ* action could be brought by anyone entitled to the return of the dowry. This action was *bonæ-fidei*, including in the formula the words *quod æquius melius* (*ante*, par. 1983), and the husband—

(a) Could make certain customary retentions, the number of which (see Ulp. Reg., vi, § 9) was cut down by *Justinian*, though he allowed *necessary* expenses to be deducted unless the dowry consisted of other things than money, in which case the husband had only a right of detention until the amount was reimbursed to him. In respect of *useful* expenses, *Justinian* substituted the *actio mandati* or *negotiorum gestorum*, according to circumstances, in lieu of the deduction formerly allowed, and the husband could only indemnify himself for expenses falling under the head of *luxury* by removing any part of the property (*jus tollendi*) capable of being so dealt with (Cod. 5, 13, 5).

(β) had an interval of *three* years, within which to restore by thirds (*annua, bima, trima die*) things *quæ pondere, numero, mensurave constant*.

(γ) had the *beneficium competentiæ* (see *post*, par. 2163).

(δ) could not be sued by the wife's heirs unless he (the husband) was in *mora*.

(ε) if he (the husband) was deceased and had left the wife any property, whether as heir, or by way of legacy, or *fidei-commissum*, the edict *de alterutro* compelled her to *elect* between one or the other of her rights.

If a special stipulation had been made with the husband as to the return of the *dos* the *actio ex stipulatu* was the proper form for enforcing the claim. This being a *stricti juris* action the husband was bound by the exact terms of the stipulation, and could not avail himself of (a) (β) or (γ), the action passed to the heirs of the parties concerned, and the doctrine of election did not apply.

Justinian merged the two actions under the name of the latter (*ex stipulatu*), making it *bonæ-fidei* (*i.e.*, when applied to the *dos*), the husband to have the *beneficium competentiæ*, and one year to restore other than immovables, but by way of security a tacit *privileged* mortgage over the property of her husband was held to exist in favour of the wife, *i.e.*, *personal* to her and her descendants, whilst her other heirs had only the ordinary mortgage.

2143 (§ xxxi) *Arbitrariæ actiones*. As under the formula procedure (*ante*, par. 1983) so under the *extraordinaria* system, the judge after having fixed the amount of satisfaction due *ex æquo et bono* made an order *(jussus* or *arbitrium)*, which if not obeyed within a certain interval entailed condemnation *quanti ea res erit*. Amongst these arbitrariæ actions was the—

2145. *Actio de dolo malo.* This entailed infamy on the author of the fraud, or those who had profited by it, but not on the heirs. The condemnation was in *simplum*, and it lasted for one year, after which only the *actio in factum* lay to the extent enriched. On account of the *infamy* involved, it could only be brought when no other means existed by which the interests of the injured party could be equally well protected, *i.e.*, if the damage could not be met by the two other Prætorian remedies for *dolus*, viz., the *exceptio doli mali* (which did *not* entail infamy) or the *restitutio in integrum*, but this rule was not imperative and only served to guide the discretion of the magistrate, as in the case of the action *quod metus causa* (see *ante*, par. 2129).

2149. *Doli clausula.* If this express guarantee against *dolus (de dolo malo cautio)*, e.g., "*Eaque sic recte dari fieri fide*," or "*dolum malum abesse abfuturumque esse*," was included in a contract *verbis* it would be taken into account in the *stipulatio* action. The effect of this would be that the action would lose its *stricti juris* character (see *post*, par. 2260), and become *incerta*. For example, in the case of a claim for a *stipulatio damni infecti* (*ante*, par. 1313, 2), which the party who ought to make it had refused to give, the formula would be drawn up *fictitiously*, as if the stipulation had been made (... *Quidquid eum Q. Licinium ex ea stipulatione L. Seio dare facere oporteret ex fide bona*, lex Gall. cisalp., 1, 20). The insertion of this clause was customary in some contracts as in the *compromissum*, and obligatory in a large number of prætorian stipulations.

2150. *Actio de eo quod certo loco.* If there was a condition in a contract to the effect that the money should be paid in a *certain place* the creditor could only claim to be paid there, but the debtor might never appear at the *place*, so that there could be no *in jus vocatio*; for though the *forum* at Rome, or at the domicile of the debtor, would always be competent to deal with the question, still the judge in those places could not order the payment to be made except within the limits of his jurisdiction. This in a *bonæ-fidei* action, or in a *stricti-juris* action with an *intentio incerta*, would be of no consequence, because the judge could take into account the difference of the place, but in a *stricti juris* action in respect of a *res certa*, as a fixed sum of money or a determined quantity of things, as so much wine or oil, or such a slave, the judge could not order them to be paid at that place, nor could he take into account the difference of the place named in the contract, so that the creditor might be guilty of *plus petitio* (*post*, par. 2154), and risk the loss of his action because *loco plus petitur*.

In such a case the prætor met the difficulty by modifying the condictio in such a way that the *intentio* remained *certa*, but the action became *arbitraria* and the *condemnatio incerta ex æquo et bono*, so that the judge could estimate the amount of payment to be

B B

made, taking into consideration the difference of place, or require proper security that the payment would be made at the place indicated. The formula in this action for a sum of money would probably run, "*Index esto: si paret Numerium Negidium Aulo Agerio centum Ephesæ dare oportere, neque eo nomine Aulo Agerio a Numerio Negidio satisfactum erit, quanti ea res erit condemna.*"

Errors in the damages claimed and causes diminishing the amount.
2154. (§ xxxiii) *Plus petitio.* This might occur in four ways, viz. :—

(1) *re*, as if 10 aurei were due and 20 claimed.

(2) *tempore*, as if the claim was made before the time or condition was fulfilled.

(3) *loco*, see *ante*, par. 2150, for the action specially introduced to avoid this difficulty.

(4) *causa*, as if the plaintiff claimed *one* of two things when the option rested with the defendant, or the slave Stichus was claimed when only *a* slave was due.

If this *plus petitio* occurred in the *intentio* it was formerly fatal, for the claim of the plaintiff not being justified, the judge had no alternative but to absolve the defendant *(si paret ... condemna ; si non paret ... absolve)*, the result being that the right brought *in judicio* was extinguished either *ipso jure* (by *novatio*) or *exceptionis ope* (*ante*, par. 2046), and the right of action was at the same time destroyed *(causa cadebat)*, but this was impossible in a *bonæ-fidei* or *stricti juris* action with a formula *incerta* (*ante*, par. 1260), *i.e.*, where the *intentio* ran, *quidquid paret dare facere oportere*, because the plaintiff only claimed what should be deemed right, though, in the *stricti juris* action, *plus petitio* would hold where the *intentio* was *certa* even if the *condemnatio* was *quanti ea res erit*, for the judge had only to ascertain the *value* of the *object* claimed in the *intentio*.

If the *plus petitio* existed in the *demonstratio* it would not have the same injurious effect unless the *demonstratio* was combined with the *intentio* (*ante*, par. 1971), for it is the *intentio* which determines the claim, and *plus petitio* in the *condemnatio* would damage the defendant, not the plaintiff, but the former could obtain rectification of the formula by means of a *restitutio in integrum* (*ante*, par. 2015).

2157. As under the *extraordinaria* procedure, the judge was no longer bound by the terms of the formula, these rules (which are detailed with care by *Gaius*, Inst. iv, §§ 53 to 60) lost their rigour, and by a constitution of *Zeno*, Emperor of the East, A.D. 474 (Cod. iii, 10, 1), the penalty for bringing an action before the time was to be *double* the first delay, no interest in the interval, and all the defendant's costs to be paid before the action was renewed.

The result of the controversy as to the effect of bringing an action before the accomplishment of a *condition precedent* appears to have been that the plaintiff would be nonsuited, but permitted to renew the action at the proper time, and *Justinian* (Cod. iii, 10,

2, 2) made any other kind of *plus petitio* involve *triple* the damages, including triple the excess of the fees charged the defendant by the *executores* (*ante*, par. 2128).

2161. (§ xxxiv) If the plaintiff claimed *less* than was due, he could only recover the balance by waiting, and bringing another action under *another* Prætor, otherwise he would be defeated by the *exceptio litis dividuæ* (*post*, par. 2276); but after the time of *Zeno* the judge could take account of the surplus in the same action and also correct a *mistake*, as if one thing was claimed for another (*e.g.*, Stichus for Erotes), or a right claimed by testament when it should have been by stipulation, though formerly in these cases the first suit would have been lost, and a second action necessary.

2163. (§ xxxvi) The effect of the *beneficium competentiæ* was to prevent the plaintiff obtaining the full amount of his claim, for by means of the *exceptio quod facere potest* (*ante*, par. 1946), the defendant could restrict it to the value of his property, and this was extended so as to mean that the debtor must not be left absolutely without means *(ne egeat)*. This privilege was *personal*, and did not pass to the heirs, but it could be claimed amongst others by—

(α) ascendants sued by their descendants;

(β) brothers as between themselves;

(γ) patrons, or a patroness, or their children, or ascendants, sued by a freedman;

(δ) married persons as between themselves, and extended by Antoninus Pius to all claims, except those resulting from *delicts*, see *ante*, par. 2136 (γ);

(ε) partners suing each other in the action *pro socio*;

(ζ) donors sued by donees, but the valuation of the donor's property was not made until his *debts* had been *deducted*, so that the donee might not profit by the liberality as against creditors for value;

(η) insolvent debtors making a *cessio bonorum* as against creditors and fide jussors;

(θ) masters or fathers in respect of the *peculium* of a slave or a son.

2167. (§ xxxix) *Compensatio.* The plaintiff's claim might also be diminished on the ground of *set off*, though, as this never *extinguished* obligations, set off is not reckoned amongst the civil law methods of *solutio* (*ante*, par. 1672).

Modestinus defines *compensatio* as *debiti et crediti inter se contributio*, and *Pomponius* explains the use of it thus, "*Ideo compensatio necessaria est, quia interest nostra potius non solvere, quam solutum repetere* (Dig. 16, 2, 1, and 3).

Gaius (Inst. iv, § 61 to 68) mentions *three* classes of cases in which, under the formula system, as existing in his time, the inconvenience of confining the judge simply to a sentence of condemnation or absolution in respect of the matter stated in the *intentio*, was got over by admitting a claim of set off, viz.—

(1) *Bonæ fidei* actions. These generally involved obligations *ultro-citroque*, and the judge had the power, *ex officio judicis*, to condemn only for what was equitably due *(ex æquo et bono)*, and he therefore took into account what the plaintiff owed the defendant, whether the objects were of the same class or not, provided they were appreciable in money, and arose *ex eadem causa*, but not otherwise, for the judge could not inquire into matters outside the *intentio*.

(2) *Argentarii* cases. Bankers were required to restrict the *intentio* of *stricti juris* actions to a claim of the *balance* due on the running account with their client "*si paret Titium sibi* (i.e., to the *argentarius*), *x millia dare oportere amplius quam ipse Titius debet*", so that if the banker claimed the smallest amount more than the exact balance due, he lost his action, for the *intentio* stated a fixed sum, and he had failed to prove it (see *post*, par. 2190), but the set off to be allowed the defendant need only be in respect of the *same kind* of thing and must be susceptible of being balanced, *e.g.*, money with money, wine with wine.

(3) *Deductio* cases, of which the *bonorum emptor* is an example, for this purchaser of the debtor's estate (*ante*, par. 1161), *debet cum deductione agere*, i.e., he could only sue those who were both debtors and *creditors* of the estate for the *balance* due to the estate after deducting the amount due to them by him as representing the bankrupt. This *deduction* was made in the *condemnatio* *(Numerium Negidium Aulo Agerio condemna quod superest deducto eo quod invicem sibi defraudatoris nomine debetur)*, and therefore rendered it *incerta*, so that the plaintiff did not run the risk of *plus petitio* (as in the case of the banker), and it was immaterial that the *deductio* was in respect of a different *kind* of thing or that it included sums not yet due, for the judge probably had the power of making an allowance in favour of the plaintiff for the time still to run.

The doctrine of compensation is also stated by Justinian (§ xxx) to have been admitted (or more probably the previous practice was regulated) by a rescript of the Emperor *Marcus Aurelius*, in respect of—

(4) *Stricti juris* actions, to which the *exceptio doli* was opposed by the defendant. In these cases the fear of the consequences of the exception led to the *set off* being introduced, for if the *exceptio doli* was opposed negatively to the *intentio* (*ante*, par. 1945) it would, if proved, necessarily *release* the defendant and *destroy* any further right of action on the part of the plaintiff.

It may be presumed that the insertion of the *exceptio doli* was allowed as a mode of punishing the bad faith of the plaintiff when he had refused, during the course of the procedure *in jure* up to the *litis contestatio*, to allow the formula to be so modified as to offer by *compensatio* in the *intentio*, or *deductio* in the *condemnatio*, an equitable question for decision. Examples of the use of the *exceptio doli* in this way are to be found in—

(α) Actions *in rem* of the *arbitraria* class (*ante*, par. 2143), and therefore *ex æquo et bono*, in which *retention*, rather than compensation, was involved, and the object was to reach the *plaintiff* by means of the defence, as *e.g.*, in the *rei vindicatio* brought against a possessor in *good faith*, when, if deductions were not allowed him *ex eadem causa* by the plaintiff for expenses incurred, or for repairs, or for the produce consumed, etc., the loss of the action might be entailed by the insertion of the *exceptio de dolo malo* (see *ante*, par. 394, 398, 400). So, in respect of an indivisible thing, as the legacy of a right of way, an *exceptio doli* could be opposed if the legatee, when vindicating it, did not offer to deduct the fourth part of its value in those cases where the heir was entitled to retain the *quarta Falcidia* (Dig., 44, 4, 5, 1, Paul).

In the case of the *petitio hereditatis* the opinion prevailed that the judge could take into account and deduct the expenses incurred by the possessor in good faith who was compelled to restore the inheritance to the heir without the necessity of inserting the *exceptio doli*, though, by way of precaution, it might be relied upon by the defendant, until Justinian made the action *bonæ fidei* (*ante*, par. 2135).

(β) Actions *in personam*. In these the deductions *ex eadem causa* more nearly resemble compensation, as where the plaintiff lost his whole claim in a *stricti juris* action, if being a pupil, a lunatic, or other person incapable of receiving payment without certain formalities, he re-demanded the debt already paid, without deducting the profit made by the first payment (see *ante*, par. 602, 2). So in the case quoted (Dig., 44, 4, 2, 7) by *Ulpian* (who lived after the rescript of Marcus Aurelius), as having been cited by *Julianus* (who lived anterior to that date), of a *statu liber* being bought as a slave, under the guarantee *(stipulatio duplæ)* against eviction, and giving the purchaser the sum (10 aurei) which was the condition of liberty. Upon the latter being evicted and suing the vendor under the *stricti juris* action in respect of the *stipulatio duplæ*, the *exceptio doli mali* would defeat the action if the purchaser did not deduct the 10 aurei.

2190. In these cases of *set off* to *stricti juris* actions, if the plaintiff did not wish to run the risk of the *exceptio doli* by persisting in his whole claim, he could—

(α) admit the deduction out of court and reduce the claim accordingly;

(β) insert a *præscriptio* (*ante*, par. 1940), by which, if he was in doubt as to the existence of the set off, he left it an open question for the decision of the judge, in an *arbitraria* action, how much was due to him;

(γ) allow the reduction by way of *compensatio* in the *intentio*, for it appears from Cod. 4, 31, 5, that this mode of drawing up the formula was extended to other persons than *argentarii* (*ante*, par. 2167, 2), and the *intentio* might be rendered *incerta* by not putting in a fixed sum, but using the words *quidquid paret amplius*, etc.;

(δ) allow the insertion of the defendant's counter-claim as a *deductio* in the *condemnatio*, *ante*, par. 2167 (3);

(ε) give the *stricti juris intentio* a *bonæ fidei* character by drawing it up in the form *quidquid paret dare facere oportere ex fide bona amplius quam*, etc. (see *ante*, par. 2149).

If, however, the case came before the judge by means of a formula containing the *exceptio doli*, and this exception was proved; that is, if it was shewn that the assertion as to compensation advanced by the defendant was well founded, and that the refusal of the plaintiff to take notice of it had the character of *dolus*, the defendant was released from all obligation in respect of the matters at issue, though probably in all actions in which the question of compensation could enter, if, before sentence was passed, the plaintiff consented to give the defendant satisfaction, he would avoid the effects of the exception, but whether *in jure* or *in judicio*, the *exceptio doli* was the means of coercion by which the plaintiff was induced (from the fear of the consequences of its insertion) to take notice, in some way or other, of any just claim of set off advanced by the defendant.

2197. It is probable that the compulsory compensation in actions *stricti juris*, resulting from the plaintiff submitting, after the time of Marcus Aurelius, to a modification of the formula under pain of the loss of the action by the *exceptio doli*, related to things of the same nature *(ex pari specie)*, though voluntary compensations introduced with the consent of the plaintiff might be *ex dispari specie*, otherwise matters of the latter class claimed by the defendant could only be taken into account by the judge when included in the *demonstratio*, as then the words *qua de re agitur* would cover them, and the terms of the *intentio* "*quidquid paret ex fide bona*" sufficed to meet the case.

2198. The *extraordinaria* procedure gave increased facilities for the introduction of the principle of compensation, as, when the formula, together with its accessories, including the *exceptio doli*, was no longer demanded *in jure*, the judge ceased to be confined within the precise limits of his written instructions as to taking the set off into account and condemning the defendant only for the balance. Hence (α) the effect of the *exceptio doli* in entailing the loss of the action, if the bad faith of the plaintiff was proved, though existing in principle, became merely nominal, (β) the condition that the set off should be *ex pari specie* and *ex eadem causa* disappeared, and (γ) the question of compensation was further affected by the fact that the plaintiff could now also be condemned.

Finally, *Justinian* (Cod. 4, 31, 14) gave the judge power in all actions (except as below) to take the defendant's set off into account, provided it was ascertained *(liquida)*, so as to be capable of easy verification.

2200. The *actio depositi* was, however, specially excepted from the above rules, so that, *e.g.*, if a like sum was owed by the *depositor* it could not be set off against the sum of money *deposited* with the depositee, for the *thing itself* is the object, the return of which is sought to be enforced.

Tit. vii. Quod cum eo contractum est qui in aliena potestate est.

2201. The rigour of the civil law principle of the non-liability of the *paterfamilias* for the acts of those in his power, whether slaves or free, was modified by the rules introduced in respect of—

(1) *Contracts* and *quasi-contracts*, for which, under *Prætorian* law, the *paterfamilias* was liable when he had (α) given an order, *express* (action *quod jussu*) or *implied* (actions *institoria, exercitoria, tributoria,* and *de peculio*), or when he had (β) profited by the act of the slave or the son (action *de in rem verso*).

(2) *Noxal* actions *(post,* par. 2219). The *civil* law, by creating these actions, recognised the obligations resulting from the *delicts* and *quasi-delicts* of persons *alieni juris*, on the ground that the *paterfamilias* should be liable at least to the extent of his rights of ownership over persons in his power.

2204. The actions given under these heads were in reality only the ordinary direct actions modified to suit their *indirect* use, and hence they are called by the commentators *actiones adjectitiæ qualitatis*. In the actions *quod jussu, institoria,* and *exercitoria,* the change would only affect the first part of the formula, whilst the *condemnatio* would remain *in solidum* (as if the master had himself contracted), but the latter also would require to be modified in the actions *de peculio et de in rem verso,* and in *noxal* actions, so as in the one case to *limit* the amount, and in the other to permit of abandonment (see *post,* par. 2212 and 2221).

2206. (§ i) *Jussus domini* meant an order anterior to the slave's contract, but ratification was equivalent to a mandate, and therefore sufficed to render the master liable in the action *quod jussu,* and if the slave was only the instrument of the master, as where the latter directed that money borrowed by him should be paid to the slave for him, a *condictio* pure and simple would lie.

2207. (§ ii) The *actio exercitoria* lay against a shipowner in respect of the contracts, etc., entered into by others with his slave or other person, as a freeman or the slave of another, or their *substitute* (even against the will of the shipowner), whilst acting by the owner's orders, as the commander *(exercitor)* of his ship, and was grounded on the principle that such engagements were looked upon as if made with the shipowner himself.

2208. The *actio institoria* lay, for similar reasons, against the principal, in respect of engagements entered into with his slave, or a freeman, or the slave of another (but not their substitute), acting as manager *(institor)* of some business (see *ante,* par. 1552).

2211. (§ iii) The *actio tributoria* was given against the master on the complaint of a creditor that the former had been guilty of *dolus* in the division of the *peculium*, and any resulting profit, employed in commerce by a slave with the *knowledge* of the master, for it devolved upon the master to make the distribution, but he was only entitled to retain an equal and proportionate share with all the other creditors who had claims against the peculium.

2212. (§ iv) The *actio de peculio et de in rem verso* was usually combined so as to form *one* action, *i.e.*, the *demonstratio* and *intentio* stated the nature of the obligation contracted by the slave, together with the legal claim resulting, whilst the *condemnatio* was *double*, for it directed the judge to condemn the *master* for the profit realised by him out of the *peculium* employed by the slave without the will of the master, and for the surplus to the extent of the *peculium* (see *ante*, par. 1935).

The *actio de peculio* alone would recover the amount from the master to the extent of the *peculium*, where no profit had been realised by him, or the *actio de in rem verso* would enable the creditor to get the amount from the master to the extent he had profited where the slave had never had, or had not then, any *peculium*, or had died or been freed or alienated upwards of a *(utilis)* year.

The judge did not examine into the value of the *peculium*, unless the master had not profited, and if the value was ascertained, any debts due by the slave to the master or to anyone in his power were deducted, though not debts due by the slave to his subordinates *(vicarii)*, because, when paid they would still form part of the same slave's *peculium*. Necessary expenses incurred for the benefit of the master were held equivalent to profit realised by him, *e.g.*, if his slave borrowed 10 aurei and paid 5 aurei to a creditor of the master, the latter would be liable for this amount in the action *de in rem verso*, but if the slave spent the other five the master would only be liable in the *actio de peculio* to the extent of the slave's *peculium*.

2215. The creditor would be guided by the particular circumstances of the case as to using the *actio de peculio et de in rem verso*, and thereby foregoing his right to any other available action. The *actio de peculio* had the advantage that in it the rule applied *melior est conditio possidentis*, so that the master was always preferred to any other creditor, and a creditor, after being paid, was not liable to the other creditors having claims on the *peculium*. The *actio de in rem verso* involved proof that profit had been realised by the master, yet if this could be done the creditor might get the whole amount due; whereas in the *tributoria*, the creditors could only come upon that *part* of the *peculium* employed in the business, and a creditor on receiving payment by its means had to give security that he would meet the claims of the other creditors on their applying for their distributive shares; though, on the other hand, this action had the advantage that all the creditors were placed upon an equal footing with the master and with each other.

2216. (§ vi) The above remarks apply equally to *children in power*, with the addition that the *paterfamilias* was liable also out of his son's *peculium*, in respect of an obligation contracted by the son for another person, though the master was never liable for the slave's mandate or fidejussory contract for another person than him (Dig., 15, 1, 3, 9, Ulpian), but a limitation of the father's liability existed under the—

2217. (§ vii) *Senatus consultum Macedonianum*. This enactment, the text of which is given by *Ulpian* (Dig., 14, 6, 1), was passed, according to Tacitus (Ann., 11, 13), in the reign of *Claudius*; or, according to Suetonius (Vesp., 11), in that of *Vespasian*, and it derived its title either from *Macedo*, a famous money-lender, or from the name of a young spendthrift. It applied to the *mutuum* contract, and under it, if money was borrowed by a descendant, the loan was not annulled (*ante*, par. 1411 and 1807); but the action brought in respect of it against a son or grandson, daughter or granddaughter (in or out of power), or against the father or ancestor, was either refused (when the *s.c. Maced.* directly applied), or, if the facts were doubtful, an *exception* was allowed the defendant, as when, *e.g.*, the lender *bona fide* thought the borrower a *paterfamilias*, but whether referring to the denial of the action, or the allowance of the exception, the expression used was always the *exception of the s.c. Maced.*

2218. (§ viii) In lieu of any of the above actions the direct civil *condictio* could be brought against the paterfamilias when the contract or quasi-contract made with the slave, or other person in power, was of such a nature as to be capable of reduction into the pursuit of a *stricti juris unilateral obligation*, for the jurisprudents finally admitted that a *condictio* would lie against a person who had acquired, without just cause, the property of another, or had profited by it, whether voluntarily or involuntarily, by himself or another. In this case the action was based, not on contract, but on the fact of the defendant having been enriched by the property of another, though owing to the peculiar character (*ante*, par. 1965) of the *condictio*, it was unsuitable in cases where the actions *empti* or *venditi, locati*, or *conducti, pro socio, præscriptis verbis*, etc., etc., applied, and therefore those actions would have to be used with the modification necessary to make them indirect Prætorian actions, *quod jussu, institoria, exercitoria*, or *de peculio et de in rem verso*.

Tit. viii. De Noxalibus actionibus.

2219. The term *noxal* indicates, not a peculiar kind of action, but the quality attached to an ordinary action when given against the master or *paterfamilias* on account of the obligation resulting from the delicts of slaves or *filii-familias, i.e.*, it denotes the modification *(e.g., nisi ex noxali causa servum dedat)* by way of alternative condemnation accompanying the various actions for delicts, such as *furti, vi bonorum raptorum, injuriæ, ex lege Aquilia*, etc.

2220. (§ i) *Noxa* is defined as *corpus quod nocuit (id est servus)*, and *noxia* (or also *noxa*) as *ipsum maleficium, veluti furtum*, *damnum, rapina, injuria* (see part i, Twelve Tables, viii; part ii, par. 208, and *ante*, par. 2204).

2221. (§ iii) The master could avoid the action by abandoning his slave whilst the proceedings were *in jure*, and so, when *in judicio*, he could claim his discharge from liability if the abandonment was made (or, without any fault on his part, it became impossible to make it) after the action was brought, or sentence had been passed, as the right of abandonment was the means placed in the hands of the master to avoid the penalty *(in facultate solutionis)* according to the terms of the condemnation, e.g., "*Publium Mævium Lucio-Titio in decem aureos condemnd, aut noxam dedere*", still the *noxal* action was not *arbitraria* (except by analogy), for there was no previous order *(jussus)* of the judge.

2222. A *single* mancipation served to abandon a son (see *ante*, par. 166) because it was held, according to *Gaius* (Inst., iv, § 79) and the Sabinians (in opposition to the Proculians), that the clause in the Twelve Tables, in respect of the *three* mancipations, only related to voluntary agreements.

When the son had satisfied the creditor, into whose power he had fallen as the result of a *noxal* action, he became *sui juris*; and so, if a slave could find the means of satisfying the master to whom he had been abandoned, he became free by the aid of the Prætor, in spite of his former master, as the abandonment was equivalent to a transference of the ownership in perpetuity.

2224. (§ v) All *noxal* actions followed the delinquent *(omnis autem noxalis actio caput sequitur)*, hence from *noxal* they might become *direct*, and *vice versâ* (*ante*, par. 1793, 2, a), and *noxal* actions were given against the master rather as the *possessor* than as the *owner* of the slave, and therefore if the slave had taken flight, or was possessed by another, so that abandonment was impossible, the action would not be allowed.

2225. (§ vi) As *natural* bonds (*ante*, par. 1280) do not seem to have been extended to the case of *delicts*, there could be no obligation existing between the master and the slave, and therefore no *noxal* action would arise, even if after the delict had been committed by the slave against the master, the slave passed into the power of another or was freed. The same rule applied if the slave was freed or alienated after the *master* had committed a delict towards him, and *Justinian* adopted the opinion of the Sabinians, that if the slave came into your power after having, whilst in the power of another, committed a delict against you, the right of action was extinguished, although the Proculians held the action to be only dormant (Gai. Inst., iv, § 78).

2226. (§ vii) The use of *noxal* actions, in respect of *children*, fell into disuse, as being inconsistent with the feelings of the age, and direct actions were allowed against the children themselves (see *ante*, par. 153 and 1298).

Tit. ix. Si quadrupes pauperiem fecisse dicatur.

2227. *Pauperies* was defined as *damnum sine injuria facientis datum*, and therefore denoted the damage caused, without wrongful intent, by an animal devoid of reason.

The *actio de pauperie,* under which the owner of the animal causing the damage was compelled either to abandon it or repair the damage, was a peculiar action of a *noxal* character and existed by itself. It was derived from the Twelve Tables (viii, § 6), though only *quadrupeds* are there referred to, but jurisprudence extended this to include all kinds of animals, whether quadruped or biped, provided they were under the power of man, whilst a *utilis* action was available in the case of wild animals, whose ferocity was by nature untamable, unless the animal, after doing the damage, had recovered its liberty, in which case no action lay, for the owner had ceased to have property in it and could not abandon it.

(§ i) Independently of the above action, and concurrently with it, another action lay under the Ædilitian Edict when, contrary to its provisions, a dog, boar pig, wild boar, bear, or lion, had been kept near a public highway, the penalty being in the discretion of the judge if a free man was injured, otherwise the damages were assessed at *double* the amount of the injury sustained.

Tit. x. De iis per quos agere possumus.

2228. The power of *representation* was gradually developed as follows:—

(1) Under the *legis actiones* the principle of *non-representation* was in full force unless the person was acting (α) *pro populo,* (β) *pro libertate,* (γ) *pro tutela,* (δ) *ex lege Hostilia* for prisoners in the power of the enemy, or persons absent on business of the republic, or on behalf of minors in the tutorship of such persons, (ε) for a *peregrinus,* as when a citizen brought the *actio repetundarum* for him, (ζ) as a *vindex, i.e.,* undertaking the cause of, and becoming surety for, a defendant.

(2) Under the *formula* system the inconveniences of non-representation were at first remedied by allowing a *cognitor* to be appointed in the presence of the magistrate and the adversary, either *specially, e.g.,* in the *vindicatio* of an estate, (Plaintiff) "*Quod ego a te fundum peto, in eam rem Lucium Titium tibi cognitorem do*"; (Defendant) "*Quando tu a me fundum petis in eam rem Publium Mævium cognitorem do*"; or *generally, e.g. (Plaintiff)* "*Quod ego tecum agere volo in eam rem L.T. cognitorem do*"; (Defendant) "*Quando tu mecum agere vis, in eam rem P.M. cognitorem do*". If the person so appointed were absent, he was not a cognitor until he knew of and accepted the office (Gai. Inst., iv, § 83).

In later times a *procurator* could be appointed by a simple mandate, but he then acted according to the mandate rules (*ante,* par. 1550 and 1669), *i.e.,* in his own name, at his own risk, and took upon himself the result of the trial. Hence, he was called the *dominus litis*, and was required to find security that his acts would be ratified. In the same way the *negotiorum gestor*, the *tutor* (in the cases where the *Legis actio pro tutela* did not apply), and the *curator*, were admitted to sue in their own name, though the last two were not generally required to find security unless they were *defendants* (see *post*, par. 2237).

2233. *Formula Rutiliana.* The modified *formula* introduced by the Prætor *Publius Rutilius* (? B.C. 100), containing the name of the principal in the *intentio*, whilst the name of the representative appeared in the *condemnatio*, ran thus: (*e. g.*, Lucius Titius acting for Publius Mævius), *Si paret Numerium Negidium Publio Mævio sestertium X millia dare oportere, judex Numerium Negidium Lucio Titio sestertium X millia condemna, si non paret absolve* (Gai. Inst., iv, § 86); but in the *actio judicati*, where a *cognitor* was employed, the result was for or against the principal, and by the time of Alexander Severus this was allowed also in the case of a *procurator præsentis, i.e.*, appointed by the principal in person, *apud acta*.

(3) Under the *extra-ordinem* procedure the power of representation was further developed by assimilating the *procurator* to the *cognitor*, and under *Justinian* the latter did not exist. The *procurator* was appointed by mandate without any formalities, and he might be absent or the appointment made without the knowledge of the adversary. Only the procurator who, as a *negotiorum gestor*, was acting without a mandate (and then called a *defensor*), was liable to give the security *ratam rem dominum habiturum* or *judicatum solvi*, and on the subsequent ratification of his acts the *actio* or *exceptio judicati* was given against the *principal*, just as in the case of a procurator acting by mandate.

2236. The *actio judicati* (*post*, par. 2274) was given for or against the *pupil* if the tutor had fulfilled a compulsory duty, but it would lie for or against the tutor himself if he had acted as a representative when he need only have completed the *persona* of the pupil by giving his *auctoritas*, and the same rule applied to the *curator* of a minor of twenty-five years, though the action was always necessarily given for or against the curator of a lunatic.

Tit. xi. De satisdationibus.

2237. The kind and extent of *security* required before an action could proceed, varied with the nature of the action, and the *period* in the history of Roman law.

(1) In actions *in rem* formerly the *interim possessor (i.e.,* the *defendant)* gave the security called—

Cautio judicatum solvi, by which the defendant and his sureties guaranteed (a) that the *litis æstimatio, i.e.*, the estimated value of the property should be paid by the defendant if he was unsuccessful and did not restore the property, (β) that the defendant would appear to defend the action. If the defendant refused to give this security an interdict *(post*, par. 2316) transferred the possession to the *plaintiff*, on the latter giving the security. When a *procurator* was employed he had to give similar security, though this was not the case with a *cognitor*, as, when acting as defendant, his principal was bound to give it for him. Hence, if the *party* in possession failed in the suit, and did not restore the property, or pay its estimated value, the other side could sue both him and his *fidejussors*, either in an action *ex stipulatu* based upon the *cautio*, or *ex judicato* based upon the judgment.

The *plaintiff* did not give security, but a *procurator* acting for him had to find sureties that his principal would ratify his acts (*ratam rem dominum habiturum*, Gai. Inst., iv, § 98, and *ante*, par. 2228, 2), otherwise there would be no protection against the principal himself subsequently bringing another action, for though in the case of a *cognitor* the right of the person represented was *ipso jure* extinguished, this was not so in the case of a *procurator*, even after the time when (if acting under an express mandate) he was put on the same level as a cognitor, and the right of the principal to bring an action could only be defeated by the *exceptio doli* or that *rei judicatæ*.

(2) In actions *in personam* the rules as to the *plaintiff* were as above, and the defendant was only obliged to give the *cautio judicatum solvi* if he was acting for another, when in all cases it must be given, either by the representative or the real defendant for him, according to the rule *nemo defensor in aliena re sine satisdatione idoneus esse creditur*.

2239. (§ ii) After *Justinian*, whether in *real* or *personal* actions, the defendant was only called upon to give the security which represented the *vadimonium* of the formula system (*ante*, par. 2034, 5), and called—

Cautio judicio sistendi, i.e., an undertaking that he would appear to defend the suit. This might be done by a surety (*fidejussor judicio sistendi*), or by a promise on oath (*juratoria cautio*), or a simple promise (*nuda promissio*), according to the rank of the individual, but if a *procurator* was employed, whether as plaintiff or defendant, without an express registered mandate, or confirmation of the appointment by his principal *in judicio*, security had to be given by the procurator that the real plaintiff would ratify the action, and the same rule applied to tutors and curators if another person was employed by them to defend the action.

2241. (§ iv) If the defendant was present he could at once enable the procurator to act for him either by appearing before the judge and confirming the appointment by binding himself in a stipulation *judicatum solvi*, or by becoming extra-judicially the *fidejussor* of his own *procurator*, but in either case the defendant's property was pledged, and the obligation descended to his heirs. In addition, the defendant must give an undertaking that he will present himself to hear sentence pronounced, and in default his *fidejussor* would be liable to pay the amount of the judgment.

If the defendant was not present any person could undertake his defence on giving the security *judicatum solvi.*

Tit. xii. De perpetuis et temporalibus actionibus et quæ ad heredes et in heredes transeunt.

2242. Under the formulary system an important distinction existed between—

(α) The length of time which might elapse before the action was barred *after* it had been commenced by the delivery of the formula to the parties. In respect of this the effect of the *litis contestatio (ante,* par. 2034, 7) was to render the right acquired under it perpetual and transmissible for and against heirs until the *lex Julia Judiciaria* (Gai. Inst., iv, § 104) limited the time to eighteen months.

(β) The *time* within which the *right of action* was barred. As the period differed in different cases a division of actions into two classes resulted, viz. :—

(1) *perpetual,* consisting of *civil* actions, *i.e.,* those founded on a law, a senatus consultum, or a constitution, with some exceptions, *e.g.,* the action against *sponsores* and *fidepromissores* was barred after *two* years by the *Lex Furia (ante,* par. 1384), and the action *de lege Julia repetundarum (post,* par. 2362) after *one* year when brought against heirs.

In the lower Empire Imperial constitutions barred all actions (real or personal) if they were not brought within *thirty* years after the event which had given rise to them, though in some exceptional cases the time was extended to *forty* years, *e.g.,* in the case of the *actio hypothecaria,* when the property remained in the hands of the debtor (so that this action lasted longer than the action for the debt itself, an anomaly explained by the fact that the *natural* obligation which subsisted after the extinction of the debt sufficed to keep alive the claim in respect of the mortgage); but the term *perpetual* continued to be used as a mode of distinguishing the *thirty* years action from those becoming barred at a shorter period.

(2) *temporary, i.e.,* barred after *one* year, and consisting of *prætorian* actions, with some exceptions, *e.g.,* the *actio furti manifesti,* the actions given to the *bonorum possessor* and to the *emptor bonorum,* as well as the *actio Publiciana,* and generally actions *in pursuit* of the *thing,* which were *perpetual* probably because they were derived by analogy from the civil law, but not actions of the *rescissoria* class (*ante,* par. 2077), because they were created in opposition to the rules of the civil law.

2246. (§ i) The *transmissibility, or not, of actions for or against heirs* made another division, *e.g.*—

Penal actions, such as the *actio furti, vi bonorum raptorum, injuriarum,* or *damni injuriæ,* did not lie *against* the *heirs* of the delinquent, and the rule applied to *mixed* actions, *i.e.,* those *pœnæ et rei persequendæ*, but not to *rei persecutoriæ* penal actions, for these were given against heirs (see *ante*, par. 1726, 3), and in any case the heirs were liable to the extent benefited, though not to the punishment. They could be brought *by the heirs* of the plaintiff except the *actio injuriarum*, the *actio de inofficioso testamento*, and other actions founded on a *personal* offence. After the *litis contestatio*, however, penal actions pass both *to and against heirs* (*ante*, par. 2034, 7).

In actions founded on *contract* the *heirs* of the deceased were *not* liable in the cases cited by *Gaius* (Inst. iv, § 113) of the *adstipulator, sponsor*, and *fide promissor*, but these classes of sureties had disappeared prior to *Justinian*, and the passage *(aliquando ex contractu actio contra heredem non competit)* copied by him from Gaius is, therefore, inaccurate, for the *heirs* were responsible even for the *dolus* committed by the deceased whether they had profited or not, except in the case of necessary *deposit* (see *ante*, par. 1220), though in the case of actions *stricti juris*, as a charge of *dolus* could not be included, recourse would have to be had to the actio *de dolo*, which would not lie against heirs unless they had profited by the fraud.

Tit. xiii. De Exceptionibus.

2248. The use of exceptions resulted from—

(α) *Prætorian* equity, which, when creating the formula system, introduced them for the purpose of correcting the rigour of the civil law, but subsequently additions were made to them by—

(β) laws, *e.g.*, *lex Cincia* (see *ante*, par. 566) ; *lex Julia* (see as to the exception, "*nisi bonis cesserit*", *post*, par. 2284) ; *lex Falcidia* (as in the case cited, *ante*, par. 2167, α), though usually the effect of this last law was to involve *plus petitio* if the legatee claimed more than his due.

(γ) *senatus-consulta, e.g.*, *s. c. Velleianum, Macedonianum, Trebellianum* (*ante*, par. 959, 1411, 2217).

(δ) *constitutions, e.g.*—the rescript of *Hadrian* as to the exception, "*si non et illi solvendo sint*", which could be opposed to the claim of the *beneficium divisionis*, when the insolvency of some of the *fidejussores* was disputed (*ante*, par. 1392)—the rescript of *Marcus Aurelius* as to *dolus*, and set off in *stricti juris* actions *(ante*, par. 2167).

(ε) *civil* law, as where an exception was allowed to be opposed to a *prætorian* action, *e.g.*, the exception *justi dominii* against the *Publiciana actio* (*ante*, par. 2073, 2), the *s. c. Velleianum* against the prætorian actions *constitutum* or *hypotheca* (*ante*, par. 1411.)

The insertion of an exception by the defendant was not equivalent to an admission of the plaintiff's *intentio*, and the plaintiff must therefore prove his claim, after which the defendant had to prove his exception *(reus in exceptione actor est*, Dig. 44, 1, 1, Ulpian).

The object of the *exceptio* was to give the judge an opportunity of examining into the facts connected with it which he could not otherwise do, and it would therefore be required in *stricti juris* actions as well as in those *arbitrariæ* (including *real* actions) and in *factum* and *penal* actions, but it would be unnecessary in *bonæ-fidei* actions, which from their nature gave the judge this power (see part ii, par. 280, and *ante*, par. 1945, 1983).

2258. If the facts were sufficient to justify the Prætor in refusing an action altogether, but some doubt arose as to their existence, he would not take upon himself the verification of the facts, but, putting the doubt into the form of an exception, send the case before a *judge*, as, *e.g.*, in the case of a disputed oath *(post,* par. 2265).

The examples given by Justinian of exceptions include the—

2259. (§ i) *Exceptio metus causa.* This plea was drawn up in a general form *(si in ea re nihil metus causa factum est)*, and, therefore, it was said to be *in rem scripta (ante,* par. 1960), for, as the violence was often done by unknown and disguised persons, the exception was grounded on the fact of the consent or other act of the injured person having been *metu coactus,* and was directed against the violence itself whoever might be the author.

2260. *Exceptio doli mali.* This could only be used against the *person* who had committed the *dolus* (including his heirs and successors *causa lucrativa*), for the exception was not inserted for the purpose of obtaining a penalty, but was in respect of the subject matter of the action in which fraud was involved *(dolo inductus)*, as in the example given, *ante,* par. 1945. As *dolus* comprised everything contrary to good faith, it necessarily included *violence* and *error,* and these pleas *(ante,* par. 2259; *post,* par. 2261) were, therefore, only special forms of the *exceptio doli,* so that the latter would cover them, except that if the adversary himself (or his heirs, etc.) had not been guilty of the violence this exception would not lie, though as the terms of the *exceptio doli* included past and present acts it included the fact of claiming the thing if this was contrary to good faith, and, therefore, could be used in the case of *set off,* etc. (see *ante,* par. 2167).

This exception, when inserted in a formula *stricti juris (ante,* par. 2167, 4), did not transform the action into a *bonæ fidei* suit, though the *clausula doli* did so *(ante,* par. 2149); but this latter was a special clause inserted in the *intentio* and was distinct from an *exceptio* or *replicatio doli.* The two texts *(replicatio doli opposita bonæ fidei judicium facit,* Cod. 8, 36, Const. Antoninus; *Doli non inutiliter opponetur exceptio; bonæ fidei autem judicio constituto,* etc., Dig. 39, 6, 42, Papinian) relied upon for the opposite view only indicate that by the insertion of the *exceptio* or the *replicatio doli,* the judge had the power, as far as these exceptions permitted, to inquire into the good faith of both the plaintiff and the defendant, and to this extent the action became *ultro citroque* and *bonæ fidei.*

2261. *Exceptio in factum composita.* This was merely a form into which other exceptions could be thrown for the purpose of limiting the judge to a *fact* only, without any question of law being involved (like actions of the same character, *ante,* par. 1971, 1979, 1982, as, for example, the *exceptio doli "si nihil in ea re dolo actoris factum sit*", would be reduced to the statement of a fact by wording it, *e.g.*, "if the plaintiff did not cause it to be believed that the object for which he stipulated the sum of ten thousand sesterces was made of gold, whereas the material was brass". It was used in cases of *error* because the facts often required to be set out in a narrative form, as in the case given above, where a *stipulatio, i.e.*, a contract *stricti juris*, had resulted from grave error *(errore lapsus)*, rendering the enforcement of the promise inequitable, and making the act of the adversary in taking advantage of it equivalent to *dolus* (see *ante*, par. 1370). All questions of *dolus* or violence could be stated in this form and *vice versâ*, and the exception would have to be drawn up in this way where a patron or ascendant was involved, as in that case an exception attacking his character could not be employed.

2263. (§ ii) *Exceptio non numeratæ pecuniæ*. This was *in factum composita*, and might be included under the general head of the *exceptio doli*. It met the case of, *e.g.*, the lender having for additional security first stipulated for the return of money lent, and then bringing an action on the stipulation, although the money had never been delivered. As to the special peculiarity in respect of the burden of proof in the case of this *exceptio* see *ante*, par. 1435.

2264. (§ iii) *Exceptio pacti conventi*. This was also *in factum composita* and could equally be included under the *exceptio doli* if preferred. It was unnecessary in such actions as *furti* or *injuriarum*, because by the Twelve Tables the agreement itself extinguished the action (see *ante*, par. 1705 and 1945).

2265. (§ iv) *Exceptio juris-jurandi*. This was also *in factum composita*, and as the oath was a special kind of pact, it might be replaced by the *exceptio pacti conventi* or *doli* (see *ante*, par. 2109).

2267. (§ v) *Exceptio rei judicatæ vel in judicium deductæ*. This was based upon the maxim *res judicata pro veritate accipitur*, and at the time of the *Legis actiones*, if a suit was once tried, the right of action was exhausted.

Under the *formula system*, in the case of a *personal* action, drawn up *in jus*, and of the *legitimum judicium* class, the *novatio* effected by the *litis contestatio* extinguished the *personal obligation* of the debtor sued, and the *novatio* resulting from the *condemnatio* extinguished this last *novatio*; hence as the original obligation had disappeared, the action could not be renewed, but in other cases a fresh action could put the same question in dispute, and as the judge when simply verifying the *intentio* in the second action would have no power to consider anterior judgments, it would be necessary to insert the *exceptio rei judicatæ (si ea res judicata non sit)*, or, if the sentence in the first action had not yet been given, the *exceptio rei in judicium deductæ (si ea res in judicium deducta non sit)* (see *ante*, par. 2046, 2051).

It is probable that the exception had to be formally inserted in *bonæ fidei* actions also, as it would not be included under the expression *ex fide bona*, for the exception protected both bad and good

C C

prior judgments until set aside by appeal or otherwise, and under *Justinian* there being no *novatio* resulting from either the action or the sentence, the suit could in all cases be renewed, and therefore this mode of defeating the claim would be required, though, as the system was *extra-ordinem*, there was no actual insertion of the exception in a formula, and the judge could at once consider both the claim and the defence.

In order that the exception might apply, it was necessary that the new action should raise—

(1) the same question, *i.e.*, involve the same *thing* and the same *claim* about the thing, and be

(2) between the same *persons*, though the form of the action might be different.

But if the new action was founded on *another right*, the exception would not hold, as for example if the plaintiff having lost a *vindicatio* sued by *condictio*, for he would now be claiming as a *creditor*, whereas at first his title was based on *ownership*.

2274. *Actio judicati*. If the *fact* of *judgment* having been given was disputed (*si quæratur judicatum sit necne*) this action could be brought to determine the point (see *ante*, par. 2033), and if the defendant lost the suit the *condemnatio* was *double*.

2276. (§ viii) After an action had commenced, the character of an exception was always the same, but, whilst still in the hands of the *defendant*, *i.e.*, *before* action, and in respect of their use as a means of defence should an action be brought, exceptions may be divided into—

(1) *perpetuæ et peremptoriæ*, *i.e.*, those which may be used at any distance of *time* (perpetual) and always with decisive *effect* (peremptory), (*quæ semper agentibus obstant et semper rem de qua agitur perimunt*) so that the plaintiff could not avoid them by postponing his action. Such are the exceptions *doli mali, quod metus causa, pacti conventi* (*Cum ita convenerit ne omnino pecunia peteretur*) though the *actions* corresponding to the first two were *temporary* in that they had to be brought within a certain time after the discovery of the *dolus*, &c. (see *ante*, par. 2129 and 2145) and hence the adage, *Temporalia ad agendum, perpetua ad excipiendum*.

(2) *temporales et dilatoriæ*, *i.e.*, those which prevented the defendant being attacked within a certain *time*, and therefore had the *effect* of compelling the plaintiff to postpone his action (*Quæ ad tempus nocent et temporis dilationem tribuunt*). Such are—the exception *pacti conventi cum ita convenerit ne intra certum tempus ageretur*—the exception against the *division* of actions (*litis dividuæ*) which could be opposed to a plaintiff who, after suing for part of a debt, sued for the balance during the same prætorship (*ante*, par. 2161)—the exception against the *separation* of actions (*rei residuæ*) which could be inserted by the defendant if a plaintiff who, having several claims against him, after having brought some actions, attempted, during the same prætorship, to bring

the remainder, which he had postponed in order that they might come before another set of *judices* (Gai. Inst., iv, §§ 56, 122). Formerly, if the action was brought within the time, and defeated by the dilatory plea, it could not be recommenced (*neque post tempus olim agere poterant*), for the Prætor, on the ground that the right of action was gone by its having been already before the court, would (a) refuse the action altogether, or (β) if there was any dispute about the sentence, he would allow the insertion of the exception *rei judicatæ*, or (γ) if the action was pending, so that no judgment had been pronounced, then the *exceptio rei in judicium deductæ*. Justinian, however, placed the case under the constitution of *Zeno* (*ante*, par. 2157) with regard to claims made before they were due, *i.e.*, a penalty of *double* the delay fell on the plaintiff, together with all the costs incurred by the defendant in consequence of the action to which he had been subjected before the time.

(3) *dilatoriæ ex persona, i.e.*, exceptions grounded on the *incapacity* of the person appointed to sue, and therefore dilatory in the sense that they involved the time lost before the plaintiff could avoid them, by substituting another person, as in the case of the *Procuratoriæ* and *cognitoriæ* exceptions, which were allowed to be inserted when a *procurator* or *cognitor* was appointed who had not the power to act in such a capacity, *e.g.*, a soldier or a woman, but the incapacity arising from the *infamy* of the person appoint*ing* or appoint*ed* fell into disuse, and was abolished by *Justinian* (see *ante*, par. 1669).

Tit. xiv. De Replicationibus.

2283. The rules relating to *exceptions* apply equally to *replications*, for the latter are exceptions to exceptions (see part ii, par. 280) as *e.g.* if to the defendant's *exceptio pacti conventi* not to sue, a *replicatio* was inserted by the plaintiff of a pact agreeing to set aside the former pact, but the plaintiff was not allowed to meet an *exceptio doli* by a *replicatio doli*, for otherwise he might gain the action in spite of his own fraud, and hence when *dolus* existed on both sides, that of the plaintiff was punished (Dig. 44, 4, 4, 13, Ulpian).

The defendant could reply by the *duplicatio*, the plaintiff by the *triplicatio*, and so on.

2284. Exceptions were called—

(1) *rei cohærentes* when they resulted from the thing itself so as to affect the right to claim it, and were therefore open, not only to the debtor, but to all those liable as fidejussors for him. Such was the case with exceptions based upon pacts *in rem, i.e.*, made in respect of the thing, as *e.g.*, a general pact not to sue, and so as to the exceptions *rei judicatæ, doli, jurisjurandi*, or *vi*; and the debtor was interested that his sureties should be able to use them, for if the fidejussors were compelled to pay, they would come upon him by the *actio mandati* for reimbursement, though, if the fidejussors had acted in that capacity from motives of liberality

and with a view to make him a gift (*donandi animo*) they could not avail themselves of the exception, for they would not in so doing be indirectly compelling the debtor to pay.

(2) *personæ cohærentes* when they resulted from some *personal* circumstance which was exclusive to the debtor, so that they only protected him, his heirs and successors, and were not available for fidejussors, as in the case of pacts made *in personam*, *i.e.*, in respect of the particular individual as, *e.g.*, that the debt shall not be demanded from such a person, in which case not even the heirs are included, and therefore the fidejussors would be liable, even though they could come upon the debtor, for this must have been foreseen, similarly the exception "*nisi bonis cesserit*" was only open to the debtor who had assigned all his property for the benefit of creditors (*ante*, par. 2024), and could be opposed to the fidejussors themselves, and so of the exception *quod facere potest* (*ante*, par. 2163).

2287. *Præscriptiones* in the original sense (*ante*, par. 1940) did not exist under *Justinian*, and the term, after becoming synonymous with *exceptiones*, subsequently denoted specially the exception resulting from possession *longi temporis*.

Tit. xv. De Interdictis.

2288. For the origin and nature of *interdicts* see part i, par. 290, part ii, par. 285.

Under *Justinian*, as the system of a prætor appointing a judge by means of a formula had been suppressed, and as the party who would formerly have applied to the prætor for an interdict, would now go direct to the judge for the protection of his interests, the interdict lost its character, and only gave rise to an action in the sense that the suit would be conducted before the judge as if it was an action of the *utilis* character based upon an interdict.

2297. (§ i) *Prohibitory, restitutory, exhibitory interdicts*.

The classification of interdicts as (1) *prohibitoria*, (2) *restitutoria*, (3) *exhibitoria*, arose from the final formula of the first being *Vim fieri veto* (or *veto*), of the second *Restituas*, of the third *Exhibeas*, and the difference appears to have exercised some influence on the subsequent trial (see *post*, par. 2325).

2298. Examples of the *formulæ* used by the prætor will be found in the fragments from the works of *Ulpian*, inserted principally in the forty-third book of the Digest of Justinian. Amongst these are the text of the interdicts relating to—

Sacred objects, *e.g.*, the interdict forbidding any damage being done in a sacred place, "*In loco sacro facere inve eum immittere quid veto*" (Dig. 43, 6, 1).

Religious objects. In respect of these, the right of *interment* was protected as well as the right of raising a sepulchre.

Public matters. Under this head a great number of interdicts existed, *e.g.*, those of the *prohibitory* class preventing damage being done in public *places*, or in public *roads* and *ways;* of the *restitutory* class, as to restore, *i.e.*, to repair the damage done, or to protect the right of *user* of the public way, or to compel the dedication of the way to the public, the prætor being guided in these matters by the maxim, *Viam publicam populus non utendo amittere non potest* (Dig. 43, 11, 2, Javolenus). So *prohibitory* interdicts forbade anything being done tending to impede the navigation of public *rivers*, or to changing the course of running *water*, and others, of the *restitutory* class, compelled the re-establishment of things in the way the public had hitherto enjoyed them, and so other interdicts protected the *right* to navigate rivers and public lakes, as well as to load and unload ships on their shores.

2301. *Personal exhibitory* interdicts. Recourse was had to these in cases where the absence of any pecuniary interest prevented the use of the *ad exhibendum* action (Dig. 10, 4, 13, *Gaius)*. Amongst these interdicts were included the following, viz. :—

De libero homine exhibendo, i.e., an interdict designed to secure individual liberty, like the English writ of *habeas corpus*. Under it the prætor ordered the immediate production of a freeman by whomsoever detained, "*Quem liberum dolo malo retines, exhibeas*" (Dig. 43, 29, 1). The order was granted to any person, but in case of more than one claimant to the person most interested. It was perpetual, and the man so detained must be at once produced in public.

De liberis exhibendis. This was for the purpose of obtaining for the *paterfamilias* the production of a son in power who was being detained, or hidden by some other person *(ante,* par. 175), and as a result of it the interdict *de liberis ducendis* would be given to guarantee the father's right to take away his son.

De liberto exhibendo. By this the patron obtained the production of the *freed*man for the purpose of compelling him to perform certain services which he had contracted to do (Gai. Inst., iv, § 162).

According to *Paul* (Dig. 10, 4, 12) the action *ad exhibendum* would lie, as well as an *interdict*, where the production of a person was required by any one previous to *vindicating* him as a *free*man or as a *slave*.

2302. (§ ii) *Interdicts to acquire, or to retain, or to recover possession, and those (double) to acquire and to recover possession.*

Possessory interdicts *(ante,* par. 431) were those given for the protection of *private* interests *(rei familiaris causa)*, and were of four kinds, viz. :—

2303. (§ iii) (*a*) *Adipiscendæ possessionis causa comparata, i.e.*, interdicts for the purpose of obtaining the possession of that which the claimant did *not* previously possess. This class included the—

Quorum bonorum or *restitutory* interdict specially applying to the prætorian institution of *possessio bonorum* in respect of the universality of the hereditary property, and it was given to the *possessor bonorum* against any person holding any of the property in question by the title of *heir* or *possessor*. The effect was to place the claimant in an analogous position to that he would have occupied as the result of the *petitio hereditatis*, which he, as a *possessor* simply, could not use, and inversely the *heir* could only use the interdict when he was also the *possessor bonorum* and relied upon that title, in which case the interdict had the advantage of only involving the necessity of proving that he was a *possessor (ante,* par. 830, 1099, and 1141). So, also, the *possessor bonorum sine re (ante,* par. 1123) would have this interdict to assist him, and enable him to stand on the defensive, should a person under the title of *heir* attempt to evict him.

Quod legatorum. This was given to the *heir* or to the *possessor bonorum* to enable them to obtain the restitution of property which had been taken possession of without leave by a person under the title of legatee *(legatorum nomine).*

Salvianum. This interdict was distinct from the *actio Serviana (ante,* par. 1520), but, like it, was given to the *owner* of a *rural* estate, in default of payment of rent, to enable him to get possession of that property of the tenant which specially secured the rent. This interdict does not seem to have been open to any other mortga*gee*, but it was probably extended so as to be used against third holders, for *Julianus* lays down (Dig. 43, 33, 1) that the *interdictum Salvianum utile* would be given to obtain possession of the child born in the house of the purchaser of a female slave, when the latter after being pledged as security for the rent had been sold off the estate by the tenant.

Possessorium. *Gaius* (Inst. iv, § 145) alludes to this interdict which was given in favour of him who had bought the universality of the goods of a debtor, and he remarks that it was similar to the—

Sectorium interdict, which authorised the sale of the confiscated property of a condemned criminal. See *ante*, par. 2024, (β) and (γ).

2306. (§ iv) (β) *Retinendæ.* This class included the—

Uti possidetis. A prohibitory interdict forbidding any interference with, or violence to, him who was in possession *at the time* of the *litis contestatio (Uti eas ædes quibus de agitur, nec vi, nec clam, nec precario, alter ab altero possidetis, quominus ita possideatis vim fieri veto.* Dig. 43, 17, 1 ; *Ulpian).* It applied to all *immoveables*, and had to be used within *one* year of the cause arising. The person who claimed the interdict must be in possession *nec vi, i.e.,* not by force ; *nec clam, i.e.,* not clandestinely ; *nec precario, i.e.,* not in virtue of a concession lasting only so long as the donor of it pleased *(ante,* par. 1604); but to enable the possession *vi, clam,* or *precario,* to be *opposed* to the demand of the interdict these modes must have been used against the *adversary himself,* in order to obtain the disputed possession, as it was immaterial whether these vices existed in respect of third parties.

Utrubi (Utrubi hic homo quo de agitur, majore parte hujusce anni fuit, quominus is eum ducat, vim fieri veto. Dig. 43, 31, Ulpian). This applied to all *moveables*, and maintained him in possession who had had it longest *nec vi, nec clam, nec precario* (as regarded his adversary) *during the previous year*, but under *Justinian* a preference was given (as in the *uti possidetis*) to him who was in possession *at the time* of the *litis contestatio, nec vi*, etc., as to his adversary.

The principal object of both the above interdicts was to decide who was to be the *possessor* (and therefore the defendant), and who the *plaintiff* in the subsequent trial as to the right of ownership, the possessor having the advantage that if the *plaintiff* could not prove that the property belonged to him, the possession remained with the defendant, although the property might belong to somebody else, and it was customary in doubt to decide against the *plaintiff* (see *ante*, par. 346).

These interdicts were also used to guarantee the *possession* against interference or violence, although there was no actual deprivation of possession.

2310. (§ vi) (γ) *Recuperandæ*. These interdicts are exemplified by the—

Unde vi (Unde tu illum vi dejecisti, aut familia tua dejecit, de eo quæque ille tunc habuit, tantummodo intra annum, post annum de eo quod ad eum pervenit, judicium dabo. Dig. 43, 16, 3, 9, Ulpian). This applied to *immoveables* only (as for *moveables* the interdict *utrubi*, or the actions *vi bonorum raptorum, furti*, or *ad exhibendum*, could be used). It was *annual*, and it was immaterial whether the expulsion by violence had been effected *armed (vis armata)* or *not armed (vis quotidiana)*, whether the dispossessed person possessed *vi, clam*, or *precario*, as regarded the adversary, though formerly a distinction existed, viz. : if armed (whether with sticks and stones, or with breastplates, swords, and helmets) the interdict was given in any case, however the dispossessed person had acquired possession ; but if *unarmed* the interdict was not available, unless the dispossessed person had been in possession *vi, clam*, or *precario*, as regarded his adversary. The person using the violence was liable under the *Lex Julia de vi privata* (unarmed) *aut de vi publica* (armed) *(post*, par. 2360), and the violent occupation of *moveables* or *immoveables* was also punished under a constitution of Valentinian, Theodosius, and Arcadius (see *ante*, par. 1738).

De precario (Quod precario ab illo habes, aut dolo malo fecisti, ut desineres habere, qua de re agitur, id illi restituas. Dig. 43, 26, 2, Ulpian). This enabled the owner to recover the possession of an *immoveable* from the concessionee *precario (ante*, par. 1604) who refused to restore it.

For the *utiles* interdicts for the protection of *quasi possession*, and for the special interdicts relating to certain *servitudes*, see *ante*, par. 507.

2316. (δ) *Adipiscendæ et recuperandæ*. This fourth division included those for *acquiring* or *recovering* possession, *e.g.*—

Quem fundum (? terms—*quem fundum Autus Agerius a te petit, si litem non defendas, ita eum illi restituas*). This interdict would be given in order to transfer the interim possession of the disputed property to the plaintiff when the *defendant* (possessor) in an action *in rem* refused to defend, *i.e.*, refused to give security for the restoration of the property and its accessories in case he lost the suit *(ante,* par. 2237). A¹ter this, the position of the defendant and the plaintiff was reversed, and if the *defendant* wished to assert his right he must now act as *plaintiff*.

Quam hereditatem. This interdict applied in the same way to a *petitio hereditatis*.

Quem usum-fructum. This applied in the same way to rights of *usufruct*, and propably other interdicts existed in respect of other servitudes.

In these cases the claimant either acquired the possession he had never previously had or recovered his former possession, and in this sense they are called *double* interdicts, and the examples given above are taken from a fragment of the *institutes of Ulpian*, for this class of interdict had ceased to exist prior to Justinian, and the reference to them in the Digest results only from the inadvertent insertion by the editors of a passage from *Paul*, " *Sunt interdicta, ut diximus, duplicia, tam recuperandæ quam adipiscendæ possessionis* (Dig. 43, 1, 2, § 3).

2318. (§ vii) *Simple and double* (or *mixed*) *interdicts in the sense of each litigant being both plaintiff and defendant*.

Interdicts are said to be :—

(1) *Simplicia*, when one of the suitors is plaintiff and the other defendant *(alter actor alter reus est)*, as in the case of *restitutory* or *exhibitory* interdicts, whilst of *prohibitory* interdicts *some* were simple, as where the prætor forbad something to be done in a sacred place, or in the bed of a river, for here the plaintiff wished to prevent the act being done, and the defendant wished to do it, but in other cases the interdicts were—

(2) *duplicia*, *i.e.*, the position of the parties was equal, both being plaintiffs and defendants, as in the case of the interdicts *uti possidetis* and *utrubi*, and therefore in these two the *sponsio* and *restipulatio* were also *double*, *i.e.*, the unsuccessful party lost double the sum staked (see *post*, par. 2330).

The *duplicia* interdicts were also called *mixed*, like the three actions mentioned *ante*, par. 2119, and this special nature of these interdicts had an important bearing on the action, which resulted from it, as the condemnation or absolution would apply as much to one of the parties as to the other, and *Gaius* remarks (Inst., iv, § 160) that the prætor in the terms of his edict equally alludes to both litigants in the words *uti possidetis*, and *utrubi hic homo ... fuit*.

2319. (§ viii) *Procedure in respect of interdicts.* The substitution of the *extraordinaria* for the *ordinaria judicia* did away with all the special institutions of the formula system in respect of the issue of interdicts, but *Gaius* (Inst. iv, § 161 to 170) treats of the procedure at length.

In jus vocatio. This for an interdict was the same as for an action, and if the defendant was hiding or absent, and no one offered to take up the defence, the possession of goods could be given by means of the *missio in possessionem.*

In jure. The prætor did not enquire whether the asserted facts were true or false, but whether, assuming the facts to be true, they were good ground for the issue of an interdict, *i.e.*, for an imperative order commanding or prohibiting the particular thing in question, and if the facts were evident, or if the right of the plaintiff was admitted by the defendant, the prætor put an end to the matter by virtue of his *jurisdictio* and *imperium*, and if necessary enforced execution, but otherwise, and if the parties persisted in going on, a trial was organised in which the interdict served as the basis or law of the parties, and therefore it served also as the point of departure for the examination of the rights of the parties and for the calculation of the produce, and as the interdict related exclusively to the cause, and was personal to the parties, *Ulpian* (Dig. 43, 1, 1, 3) calls all interdicts *personal*, "*Interdicta omnia licet in rem videantur concepta, vi tamen ipsa personalia sunt.*"

2322. Probably in the origin of the formula system the procedure for all interdicts was *per sponsionem et restipulationem*, for by this means the *prætorian* interdict resulted in a true Quiritarian *civil* law obligation *(ante,* par. 1924), and, in order to give a stronger sanction to the order of the prætor, the *sponsio* in the case of an interdict was *penal*, *i.e.*, the amount was such as to make it a form of punishment for persisting in an act injurious to the public interest or tending to a breach of the peace.

The *sponsio* put by the plaintiff to the defendant probably ran, "Do you promise to give so much if something has been done by you contrary to the edict of the prætor who has delivered this interdict to us," and the *restipulatio* put by the defendant to the plaintiff would be to the effect, "Do you promise to give so much if nothing has been done by me contrary to the edict of the prætor who delivered the interdict to us," and on the affirmative response to these questions the liability was incurred.

2324. The effect of the delivery of the formula by the prætor would be to bring the parties before a judge, or before *recuperatores*, in order to settle the question whether an order of the prætor, based upon his edict, had been contravened or not. If the judges selected were *recuperatores* the matter could be disposed of at once, for they might be taken from the bystanders (see part i, par. 162), and therefore one of the objects contemplated by the parties in using the interdict, viz., the shortening of the delay incident to an ordinary action would be attained, and Valentinian, Valens, and Gratian (Cod. Theod. 11, 36, 22), dispensed with the *in jus vocatio* in the interdict *quorum bonorum*, in order that this method of procedure, introduced for the purpose of celerity, might not lose its efficacy.

2325. In the case of *restitutory* or *exhibitory* interdicts the pecuniary condemnation was found insufficient, and therefore to meet such cases the method previously adopted in *real* actions was introduced, *i.e.*, the *formula* was made *arbitraria (ante*, par. 1983, 3) by means of the addition to the formula of the words "*nisi restituat*" or *nisi exhibeat*. This enabled the judge, if he thought the claimant in the right, to make an order *(jussus)*, on the execution of which, whether voluntary or *manu militari*, by the defendant, the latter was absolved; otherwise he was condemned in damages *(Quanti ea res est condemnatur*, Gai. Inst. iv, § 163). Hence, in these cases, there was no *sponsio*, and therefore the procedure was *sine periculo* (unless the defendant replied to the claim by commencing the *judicium calumniæ, post*, par. 2337), but this expeditious method was only allowed when either of the parties claimed it from the prætor immediately after the delivery of the interdict and before leaving the court, so that the suit might be organised at once, otherwise the procedure by *sponsio* (*e.g.*, on the part of the claimant "*si contra edictum prætoris non exhibueris,*" or *non restitueris*, etc.), and *restipulatio* must be followed, as was always the case in prohibitory interdicts, for the *pecuniary* condemnation here sufficed. *Et modo cum pœna agitur, modo sine pœna: cum pœna, velut cum per sponsionem agetur: sine pœna, velut cum arbiter petitur. Et quidem ex prohibitoriis interdictis semper per sponsionem agi solet; ex restitutoriis vero vel exhibitoriis modo per sponsionem, modo per formulam agitur quæ arbitraria vocatur* (Gai. Inst. iv, § 141).

2330. The two litigants in an interdict of the *duplicia* class (*ante*, par. 2318, 2), as in the case of the *uti possidetis*, and probably in that of the *utrubi* also were perfectly equal, each claiming to be the *possessor*, just as they were in the old *legis actiones*, where ownership was involved (see *ante*, par. 1924).

In the case of the *interdict*, the question as to who was to have *interim possession* of the property and its produce during the trial, was decided by giving it to that one of the two litigants who made the highest bidding for it, and the *contentio fructus licitationis* therefore corresponded to the arrangement made as to the *vindiciæ* of the *actio sacramenti* (*ante*, par. 1864).

The person to whom the interim possession was awarded then guaranteed the restitution of the property and produce, if he failed in the action, by a special stipulation called the (?) *fructuaria stipulatio* which corresponded to that made *pro præde litis et vindiciarum* (*ante*, par. 1924).

After this came the *double sponsio et restipulatio, i.e.*, one of the claimants challenged the other by a *sponsio* running, *e.g.*, "If I have a right to the possession do you promise to give me so much," and on the affirmative reply by the other claimant, the latter put the *re-stipulatio* to the first claimant : " If on the contrary you have no right to the possession, do you promise to give me so much ?" The latter claimant would then go through the same *sponsio* and *re-stipulatio* on his side, so that both sides incurred a liability of *double* the amount of the challenge.

The *formula* was then delivered to the parties, and on the case coming before the judge, he decided which *sponsio* and which *re-stipulatio* was *justa* by examining, on the basis of the interdict, to whom the possession really belonged.

If the *interim possessor*, *i.e.*, the highest bidder, was found to be in the wrong, he was condemned

(1) to pay the amount of the *sponsio* and *restipulatio* made by him, whilst his adversary would be released from the *sponsio* and *restipulatio* he had made.

(2) to pay the sum bid for the *interim* fruits as a penalty for having retained by this means a possession and an enjoyment not belonging to him.

(3) to *restore* the property and the *interim* produce by virtue of the promise made in the *fructuaria stipulatio*, but if he refused to make this restitution, only a *pecuniary* condemnation would result, though in the case of the *formula arbitraria* restitution could be enforced *manu militari*.

If the *non*-possessor lost the suit he was condemned to pay the amount of the *sponsio* and *restipulatio* made with his adversary, and the interim possessor was absolved from all his promises and in addition kept the property and the interim produce, for the possession had been adjudged to him as the result of the trial.

Subsequently the *fructuaria stipulatio* was not absolutely necessary, and if it was omitted and the non-possessor gained the cause, he could, according to *Gaius* (Inst. iv, § 169) call to his aid two special actions, viz. : the—

(α) *judicium Cascellianum* to recover possession of the property.

(β) *judicium fructuarium* to recover the interim produce.

These actions fell under the head of *judicium secutorium*, because they were consequent on the victory in respect of the *sponsio*, and they were probably both *arbitrariæ*, so that by their means *restitution* could be obtained, although the two interdicts *uti possidetis* and *utrubi*, out of which they arose, were simply *prohibitory*.

Tit. xvi. De pœna temere litigantium.

2335. Various methods were adopted to prevent actions being commenced or sustained by parties guilty of *calumnia*. This term was used in respect of malicious prosecutions in general, *i.e.*, it included not only criminal accusations brought against an innocent person, but applied also to *civil* suits which were undertaken by the plaintiff, or sustained by the defendant, in bad faith. The essence of *calumnia*, like the crime of *theft*, consisted in the *intention*, and he was guilty of it who knew that he was acting without right, but brought his action for the purpose of oppressing his adversary, founding his hope of success rather on the error or iniquity of the judge than on the justice of his cause.

The mode of restraining groundless litigation in the time of *Gaius* (Inst. iv, § 171 to 184) was—

2336. In respect of the *defendant* by—

Sponsio, or the challenge which, under the formula system, could be put to the defendant by the plaintiff, so that he who was condemned had to pay to the other the amount so risked (*ante*, par. 1916), *e.g.*, in the *compulsory sponsio* of one-third in the action *de pecunia certa credita*, of one-half in the action *de pecunia constituta*, and for that in *prohibitory* interdicts see *ante*, par. 2330.

Pecuniary penalty of *double*, in some cases if the defendant had denied and contested the right (*adversus infitiantem in duplum agimus*, Gai. Inst. iv, § 9), as in the actions *judicati, depensi, damni injuriæ ex lege Aquilia* and that *legatorum per damnationem relictorum*. In other cases the condemnation was for the *double, triple,* or *quadruple,* according to the *nature* of the action, whether the claim was denied or not (see *ante*, par. 2127).

Oath (jusjurandum). If none of the other methods of repression were available, the plaintiff was allowed to require the defendant to swear that he was not sustaining the suit in a spirit of bad faith, and in the case of heirs, women and pupils, the *oath* appears to have been usually substituted for the *sponsio* or the penalty of *double*.

Ignominia, *i.e.*, the infamy entailed by the loss of the *pro socio* action or by being condemned in the *direct* actions *tutelæ, mandati, depositi,* etc. (see part ii, par. 74), though not in respect of the *contraria* actions against the *pupil, mandator, depositor,* etc., as these latter were only for the purpose of getting the statement of account made and settled, except in the case of the *mandator* condemned by the *contraria mandati* after refusing to refund to his *fidejussor* the debt the latter had paid (Dig. 3, 2, 6, 5, Ulpian). Infamy resulted in the case of the actions *furti, vi bonorum raptorum, injuriarum,* and *de dolo,* even if the matter was compromised and settled out of court, for this implied an avowal of the delict and the infamy attached to the act itself, not merely to the condemnation.

2337. In respect of the *plaintiff* by—

Calumniæ judicium. This action could be brought by the *defendant* in opposition to the claim set up in bad faith by the plaintiff, either whilst the action brought by the latter was pending or after the plaintiff had lost the suit, and on proof of *calumnia* the plaintiff in the principal cause was condemned in one-tenth of the value involved in that suit. The same action could be opposed to an *interdict* (*ante*, par. 2325) applied for under similar circumstances, but the measure of damages in the *condemnation* in this case was increased to one-fourth (or ? one-fifth) of the value involved.

Contrarium judicium. This was a *cross* action which the defendant was allowed to bring, without any enquiry as to whether *calumnia* was involved or not, but simply on the ground that the plaintiff had *failed* (α) in such an action as that *injuriarum*, or (β) in proceedings against a woman taken on the ground that she had fraudulently transferred property of which, on the death of her husband, and in the name of her unborn child, she had been put in interim possession, or (γ) in an action brought against a person on the ground that after the plaintiff had received a grant of possession by the prætor his entry had been opposed. The condemnation in the case of (α) being one-tenth, but in (β) and (γ) one-fifth of the value involved (Gai. Inst. iv, § 177).

Restipulatio. This was equivalent to the *sponsio* in respect of the defendant (*ante,* par. 2336) and was a penalty resulting from the mere fact of losing the action

Jusjurandum, or the oath *non calumniæ causa agere,* which the defendant could elect to require of the plaintiff in *lieu* of, but not in addition to any of the above.

2339. (§ 1) Prior to *Justinian* the *sponsio,* the *calumniæ judicium,* the *contrarium judicium* and the *re-stipulatio* had fallen into disuse, and the methods employed to repress vexatious suits were—

(1) *jusjurandum. Justinian* considerably extended the use of the oath, and by constitutions (Cod. ii, 59, 2, and iii, 1, 14, 1) he compelled both plaintiff and defendant *pro calumnia jurare,* and the advocates (*patroni causarum*) had to make oath that there was a good cause of action or defence. These oaths were taken on the Evangelists before commencing the action.

(2) liability to *damages* and *costs* if the action was commenced or defended in bad faith.

(3) liability to *double* (the insertion of the words *vel tripli* is an *erratum* in the text of *Justinian*) damages if the *defendant* was defeated after denying the right of the plaintiff, or a *penalty* of double, quadruple, etc., arising from the nature of the action itself (see *ante,* par. 2336).

(4) *infamy* resulting from certain actions (see *ante,* par. 2336).

(5) *penalty* for suing ascendants, patrons, etc., without permission having been first obtained of the magistrate. The edict of the prætor fixed a fine of fifty solidi in these cases (see *ante,* par. 1896 and 2111).

Tit. xvii. De officio judicis.

2342. This title deals with the duty of the judge in respect of the sentence to be pronounced in actions brought before him.

A judge was bound to take care that he gave no sentence contrary to the constitutions, customs, or laws, the latter term, under Justinian, including the whole law, though under the formulary system the obligation of the judge, strictly, only related to the *civil* law.

A sentence contrary to law was void in itself, so that without appealing (*ante,* par. 1781) the suit could be re-commenced, and the penalty of *deportation* was incurred by the *judge* if he had acted intentionally.

2343. (§ i) In *noxal* actions the sentence must be drawn up in the alternative (see *ante*, par. 2221), and the part of the condemnation which could be enforced consisted in the *pecuniary* penalty, so that if the *actio judicati* was brought on the sentence, it could only relate to this part, the power of abandonment being voluntary.

2344. (§ ii) In *real* actions, if the plaintiff was unsuccessful, the defendant possessor must be absolved, but if the decision went against the latter, restitution of the property and the produce must be ordered, though, in the absence of fraud, a reasonable demand for time would be granted, provided fidejussors were forthcoming to guarantee the estimated value of the subject matter in litigation, and a distinction must be drawn in respect of the produce gathered by a possessor, according as he was acting in good or bad faith, though after the suit had commenced the produce not gathered, or not consumed after gathering, was to be, in any case, taken into account.

2345. (§ iii) In the *ad exhibendum* action the defendant is to be liable for the thing and its produce as it existed at the time the demand was made, including the interim fruits before the thing is actually produced under the *jussus*, which in this *arbitraria* action preceded the condemnation. Security must be given if time is allowed for the production, otherwise, in case of delay, the condemnation is to be for damages measured by the importance to the plaintiff that the thing was produced immediately (see *ante*, par. 384, 1983, (3), 2143).

2346. (§ iv) In the *familiæ erciscundæ* action the objects contained in the inheritance must be separately adjudicated to each heir, the ownership being thereby immediately vested in him (see part i, par. 249, and *ante*, par. 1622, (3), 1825, and 2119). If one of the heirs received less than his share, the *condemnatio* must fix a sum by way of indemnity, to be paid him by the others, and the same rule applied in respect of produce gathered or property deteriorated or consumed by one or more of the heirs, but if the action was brought for condemnation in respect of these personal claims only, no adjudication would be involved.

In the *communi dividundo* action the rules are the same where several objects are to be distributed, or where one object (as an estate) can be conveniently divided, in which case the ownership of the parts is to be given to the several claimants subject to compensation in the event of inequality, but where the thing is indivisible (as a slave, or a mule) the ownership must be vested in one claimant, subject to the payment to the other of a fixed sum by way of equivalent.

In the *finium regundorum* action *adjudication* is only required if the boundaries required alteration, *i.e.*, in early times (see part i, Twelve Tables, vii, § 4), if the *fines* or interval of five feet between fields needed some alteration in direction or otherwise, in which case the person benefiting by the land so vested in him must be condemned towards the loser in a fixed sum. The condemnation should also include a pecuniary penalty if an impediment was offered to the measurement of the fields by order of the judge, or if the limits had been fraudulently altered by removing the landmarks or cutting the boundary trees (see *ante*, par. 1779 *a*), and for these offences public penalties to the extent of relegation might also be inflicted.

Tit. xviii. De Publicis Judiciis.

2348. For the mode in which *criminal* law was introduced and enforced see part i, par. 81, 272, 281, 441, 578.

The institutes of *Gaius* make no mention of this subject, and the text of Justinian merely refers to it by way of introduction to the enumeration of a few of the laws passed for the punishment of particular crimes, for, in his time, the *publica judicia* procedure, as opposed to the *cognitio extraordinaria*, had completely disappeared, and of the laws which organised it only the penalty remained.

2353. (§ i) *Publica judicia* were not conducted by *action*, but by way of accusation, and were called *publica* because the right of bringing a *public prosecution* devolved, generally, on all citizens, even if they were personally strangers in the matter, but *women* (on account of their sex), *pupils* (on account of their age), *infamous* persons (on account of their crimes), and persons having less than fifty aurei (on account of their poverty), were not allowed to bring these accusations unless the crime affected them personally or their near relations. The accuser was bound over to prosecute, and was responsible, *calumniæ causa*, in respect of the *libellus* of accusation, which, after signing, he presented to the prætor or the pro-consul, and which ran, *e.g.*, Consul et dies (*i.e.* date) *Apud illum prætorem vel proconsulem Lucius Titius professus est se Mæviam lege Julia de adulteriis ream deferre: quod dicat eam cum Gaio Seio in civitate (illius) mense (illo), consulibus (illis) adulterium commisisse* (Dig. 48, 2, 3, *Paul*).

2354. (§ ii) These *Publica judicia* were divided into—

(1) *capitalia, i.e.*, those accusations entailing the loss of the *caput* of a citizen (*ante*, par. 205), as where conviction resulted in death, or interdiction from fire and water, or deportation, or condemnation to the mines.

(2) *non capitalia, i.e.*, the remainder.

All *publica judicia* entailed *infamy*, though the *judicia extraordinaria* only drew this penalty after them when the *private* civil condemnation by action for the same crime or delict also entailed infamy.

Amongst *publica judicia* were those resulting from the—

2355. (§ iii) *Lex Julia majestatis*, which was introduced by (?) *Julius Cæsar* against persons conspiring against the state. The penalty was death, and the memory could be condemned even after death (*ante*, par. 999).

2356. (iv) *Lex Julia de Adulteriis*, passed under *Augustus*, B.C. 17 (or 16), against adulterers and also against the seducer without violence (see *post*, par. 2360) of a virgin or widow of good character. The penalty for adultery was originally only partial confiscation of the property of the woman and her accomplice, but Constantine increased the punishment to death, which was, however, reduced by Justinian to confiscation of half the property, if the guilty persons were of honorable condition, but if of low estate, then corporal punishment with relegation.

2357. (§ v) *Lex Cornelia de sicariis (et veneficis)*, passed under the dictatorship of *Cornelius Sylla*, B.C. 81. This law punished with death those guilty of *homicide*, by murdering a person with a weapon of some sort in their hand (assassins being called *sicarii* from *sica* a short sword), and it included *poisoners*, who by odious artifices, poisons and magic charms, caused the death of a man, or who publicly sold injurious drugs. For other provisions of this law see *ante*, par. 1775.

2358. (§ vi) *Lex Pompeia de parricidiis*, passed in the Consulship of *Cn. Pompey*, B.C. 52. This law was especially directed to the punishment of the murderers of near relations, and the word *parricide* (see part i, par. 94, 2) was held to include not only the murder of an ascendant, but also that of a collateral to the degree of cousin, as well as the first degree of persons in direct line allied by marriage, and also the patron and patroness. It also included the murder of children by their mother or ancestor, but not by their father. The penalty was derived from the ancient law, and existed at the time of the Twelve Tables (viii). It consisted in sewing up the murderer or his accomplice (whether a stranger to the murdered man or not) in a sack, with a dog, a cock, a viper, and an ape, and throwing him into the river or the sea.

2359. (§ vii) *Lex Cornelia de falsis*, or *testamentaria* (or *testamentaria nummaria*, because falsifying money was included in the penalties). This law was also passed under Sylla *(ante, par. 2357)*, and was directed against those who had falsely written, sealed, read, or substituted a testament, or other deed, or made, engraved, or impressed a false seal, knowingly and with wrongful intent. The *penalty* for *slaves* was *death*, for a *free* man, *deportation*.

2360. (§ viii) *Lex Julia de vi publica seu privata*, passed (?) under *Cæsar* or *Augustus*. The penalty for violence effected with arms was *deportation*, and without arms *confiscation* of one-third property (see *ante*, par. 1764 and 2310), but the *forcible* abduction (see *ante*, par. 2356) of a girl, a widow, a person devoted to religion, or other women, was punished by the *death* of the ravisher and his accomplices.

(§ ix) *Lex Julia peculatus*, passed (?) by *Cæsar* or *Augustus* against those who made away with public money, or sacred or religious objects. The penalty for *magistrates* (including their accomplices and those who knowingly acted as receivers) guilty of embezzling the public money during their term of office was *deat'*, for others *deportation*.

2361. (§ x) *Lex Fabia de plagiariis.* This law existed in the time of *Cicero*, and was directed against those who wrongfully concealed, put, or kept in irons, sold, gave, or bought a Roman citizen, whether *ingenuus* or freed, or even the slave of another, without the consent of his master. The penalty in some cases was *death*, in others of a less rigorous character.

2362. (§ xi) *Lex Julia de Ambitu*, passed under *Augustus* against bribing or unlawfully intriguing to buy, force, or induce the giving of votes in elections to public functions. This and the subsequent laws passed to check the same practice became of little use when the powers and honors of the State were conferred by the Emperor.

Lex Julia repetundarum, passed under *Julius Cæsar* to punish the judge, or public functionary, who received money or other bribe, for not doing his duty, or doing less or more, or even conforming to it (see *ante*, par. 2242, 1).

Lex Julia de annona passed under (?) *Cæsar* or *Augustus* against coalitions, to prevent the arrival, or raise the price, of corn or other provisions.

Lex Julia de residuis, passed under *Cæsar* or *Augustus* for the punishment of those who improperly retained public monies which had been paid over to them, or confided to them, for a purpose to which it had not been applied.

ABSTRACT OF BOOK IV.

Obligationes ex delicto.

The term *delict* only referred to those unlawful acts characterised as such by the legislature, and provided with a particular remedy.

Furtum is defined as the fraudulent abstraction of a thing itself, or of its use or possession. It can only occur in the case of moveables, and is distinguished into *manifestum* and *nec manifestum*. The action for the former entailing a penalty of *quadruple* the value, and for the latter *double*. The *owner* had also the *condictio furtiva* against the thief based on his personal liability to return the property, as well as the *vindicatio*, or *ad exhibendum* actions against all possessors, but though the *actio furti* was independer ' any action for the recovery of the thing, these latter only lay until any one of them had been satisfied.

Vi bonorum raptorum. This action resulted from the prætor's edict, and only lay in respect of *moveables*. It was at the same time *penal* and in pursuit of the thing, as the value of it was comprised in the condemnation of *quadruple*, *i.e.*, the penalty was limited to the *triple*, and only the simple value could be obtained after *one* year had elapsed, but the injured party could chose the action most advantageous to him, whether *furti* or *vi bonorum raptorum*.

The *Lex Aquilia* related to damage done wrongfully, *i.e.*, contrary to law, and contained *three* heads.

The *first* avenged the killing of slaves or quadrupeds, of the class of animals feeding in flocks, by awarding the owner their highest value during the *year* preceding.

The *second*, which had fallen into disuse, related to the *ad-stipulator* who had released the debtor by acceptilation, and thus extinguished the debt in fraud of the stipulator.

The *third* covered the case of the wrongful *destruction* of any other thing than slaves and flocks, or the *deterioration* of any kind of property, and gave an action against the delinquent for the highest value of the thing during the *thirty* days preceding the delict.

The *direct* Aquilian action only lay when the damage was *corpore et corpori*, for if the first condition was wanting recourse must be had to the *utilis Aquiliæ*, and when the second was wanting, *i.e.*, when the injury did not consist in the damage of any body, the action would have to be *in factum*.

Injuria. This term in the *actio injuriarum* was restricted to cover only cases of affront or outrage, which might arise by acts or words, provided the *intention* to injure was involved. It might affect the injured party directly, or through persons placed under his power or protection, in which latter case there were as many actions and distinct condemnations as persons injured. The penalties were originally established by the *Twelve Tables*, but they were modified by *prætorian* law, and by the *lex Cornelia*. The injury might be more or less grave, according to the act, the place, or the person, and the measure of damages would be thereby affected.

The action was extinguished by (1) *dissimulatio*, *i.e.*, tacit abandonment, as where no resentment was shewn at the time ; (2) *prescriptio*, *i.e.*, when *one* year was allowed to elapse before the action was brought ; (3) *death* before the commencement of the action.

As in the case of other delicts, if a criminal suit existed to cover the particular facts, it could be used if preferred.

Obligationes quasi ex delicto.

Unlawful and injurious acts not characterised as delicts by the legislature were said to be analogous to them, and damages could be recovered in respect of them by an action *in factum*. Examples are, (a) the case of the judge *qui litem suam fecit*, (β) the responsibility of the *paterfamilias* for damage caused by that which has been thrown or cast from his dwelling, (γ) the liability of the person who suspends or places objects in a perilous manner on the public way, (δ) the position of the captain of a ship, or an innkeeper, for thefts or other damage committed by their servants in the ship or in the inn.

Natural obligations.

Some of these arise from the peculiar character of Roman Law, as those resulting (1) from the exclusion of pacts in the rules governing contracts, or (2) from the maxims affecting the status of individuals, as in the case of slaves, or persons who contract together whilst forming part of the same family.

Others are based on more general considerations, as where the *natural* bond continues to subsist in spite of (α) prescription, or (β) a judicial sentence, or (γ) the informality of a will, or (δ) the absence of the tutor's authority for the acts of the pupil.

The *effects* of the natural obligation usually include the possibility of using it by way of an exception, as well as of making it serve as a valid ground of compensation, suretyship, payment, novation, or ratification.

Alternative and joint and several obligations.

The essential elements of an obligation may so vary as to involve either (1) plurality of *objects* of the obligation, as where they are *alternative (illud aut illud)*, in which the effects differ according as the choice belongs to the debtor or the creditor, or (2) for one same thing due, there may be a plurality of *creditors*, or of *debtors*, or of both, and it is then necessary to determine whether the benefit or the liability divides *pro parte*, or remains *in solidum*, and an obligation which should in principle be divided amongst the creditors or debtors may nevertheless continue *in solidum*, because its nature or the circumstances of the case render it indivisible.

Actions.

The word *action*, besides technical meanings, signified (1) the *fact* of the application to the competent authority, or (2) the *right* of so doing, or (3) the *form* provided for exercising the right.

Systems of Procedure.

(1) *Legis actiones.* This sacerdotal and patrician system abounding in symbolic pantomimic acts and sacramental words, was exclusively reserved to citizens. In the sixth century of Rome, it was partially suppressed in favour of forms previously observed in the case of *peregrini*, but the merger of the first in the second system was nevertheless a gradual process, and the primitive system continued to exist in some exceptional cases, either actually or fictitiously, until the last traces were effaced by Justinian.

The word *action* here denotes the procedure in its entirety, and includes the *five legis actiones*, which were so many different sacramental methods of suing in different cases.

(2) *Formula procedure.* The essential character of the *ordinaria judicia* consisted in the *formula*, or sort of conditional sentence prepared *in jure*, by which a judge was nominated and empowered to verify the statement of matters of fact or points of law there set out, and further directed as to the sentence to be pronounced and returned to the prætor. After the system was applied to *citizens*, the formula was developed into four principal parts, viz., the *demonstratio, intentio, condemnatio*, and (in three cases only) *adjudicatio*. Other parts were accessories *(adjectiones)* to these, viz., the *præscriptio, exceptio, replicatio, duplicatio*, etc.

This system legislatively installed by the *Lex Æbutia*, and definitely organised by the two *Leges Juliæ judiciariæ*, remained in vigour from the sixth to the eleventh century of Rome, and then gradually merged into the third system.

The word *actio* here denoted more particularly the right conferred by the magistrate to go before a judge, but it was also technically restricted to *personal* actions, because *formulæ* were originally only employed in respect of obligations.

(3) *Extraordinaria judicia.* This was the only system existing under Justinian, and it was characterised by the absence of any distinction between the *magistrate* and the *judge*. As it was exceptionally employed under the formula procedure, it was called on that account *extra-ordinem cognitio*, but a constitution of *Diocletian*, in A.D. 294, established the system as the rule in the provinces, and it became subsequently generalised for the whole empire. Traces of the system for which it was substituted were, however, nominally retained, and Justinian characterises the change effected by saying that, "Now all trials are extra-ordinary" *(Extra-ordinem sunt hodie omnia judicia).*

The Institutes only refer to actions in respect of the right itself of suing, and at this epoch the action considered as a right was nothing else than the power of directly appearing before the judicial authority and claiming, without any special concession, what was due.

Different divisions of actions. At the time of the *extra-ordinary* procedure the principal divisions were nine in number, viz. :—

(1) *Actions in rem and in personam— præjudicial actions—actions which seem mixed (in rem and in personam).*

The division of actions into *real* and *personal* is deduced from the nature of the right claimed, for in a *real* action the plaintiff maintains that he has a right of greater or less extent in some corporeal or incorporeal thing, whereas in the *personal* action the plaintiff sues for the execution of an obligation binding on the defendant.

The expressions *in rem* and *in personam* were derived from the *formula* system, for the *intentio* of an action *in rem* was drawn up generally, whilst the *intentio* in the action *in personam* contained the name of the person who had incurred the obligation. Hence, whilst the *division* of actions into those *in rem* and *in personam*, is derived from the nature itself of the right, their *designation* was drawn from the preparation of the formula.

The action *in rem* was applied to all varieties of real rights, *i.e.*, to *ownership* and its various dismemberments, such as rights of usufruct, servitude, emphyteusis, superficies, rights of pledge or mortgage, as also to claims of liberty, free birth, paternity, and others of that nature relating to status.

For claims of the *ownership* of a corporeal thing the action bore the special name of *rei vindicatio*, derived from the *legis actiones* system.

For *servitudes* it is distinguished into *two* kinds, viz., *actio confessoria*, when the plaintiff maintained that he had a right of servitude over property belonging to another, and *actio negatoria*, where the owner of the property maintained that a right of servitude claimed by his adversary did not exist.

For *status* the action was called *præjudicialis*, and the *formula* was peculiar in not containing any *condemnatio*, the existence of the fact or right in dispute being the only question for the judge, and, although under Justinian there was no preparation of the formula, the character of the action remained the same.

The actions *familiæ erciscundæ, communi dividundo*, and *finium regundorum*, were said to be *mixed* in the sense that they were both *in rem* and *in personam*, but under the formula system it was impossible that the *intentio* could be drawn up both generally *(in rem)* and against a person individually *(in personam)*, and therefore the division must have arisen subsequently. In respect of the right, as pursuing the execution of an obligation created *quasi ex contractu*, between co-heirs or co-owners, or between neighbours, these actions were *in personam*, though from the nature of the case nearly always in the action *finium regundorum*, and often also in the actions *familiæ erciscundæ*, or *communi dividundo*, the judge had (in addition to the *condemnatio*, in respect of the obligation) collaterally by his *adjudicatio* to award ownership, *i.e.*, a *real* right, and in the time of Justinian, when the formality of the reduction of the formula had ceased, this twofold duty necessarily still existed.

(2) *Civil and Prætorian actions.*
This division is based on the authority establishing the action.

A *civil* action was founded on a law, a senatus-consultum, a constitution, or any other source of civil law.

A *prætorian* action derived its force from the edict of the prætor.

Under the *formula* system, the two principal methods employed by the prætor to invest with actions cases not sanctioned by the civil law, was to construct the formula on a fictitious hypothesis *(fictitiæ actiones)*, or, more frequently, to draw it up *in factum, i.e.*, with an *intentio* stating the question for the judge, not as a proposition of law but as a matter of fact *(actiones in factum conceptæ)*.

Amongst *prætorian* actions *in rem* were (1) the *Publiciana actio*, constructed on the fictitious hypothesis that *usucapion had been* accomplished, (2) the *rei vindicatio rescissoria*, and (3) the *Publiciana rescissoria*, both drawn up on the inverse hypothesis that *usucapion had not* been accomplished, and (4) the *Pauliana in rem rescissoria*, which assumed that the alienation made by a debtor in fraud of his creditors had *not* taken place. Actions prepared *in factum* are illustrated by the *actio Serviana* given to the landlord of a rural estate, against any third holder of things expressly pledged by the farmer as security for rent, and the *actio quasi-Serviana* (or *hypothecaria*) for the pursuit of any other right of pledge or mortgage. Amongst *prætorian* actions *in personam* were the *actio de pecunia constituta* (in which Justinian merged the ancient *civil* action *receptitia*), the actions *de peculio, de jurejurando*, the penal actions against any alteration of the album *(de albo corrupto)*, against the *vocatio in jus* of an ascendant or of a patron without previous authorization, and against violence or other obstacle to the exercise of a *vocatio in jus*.

(3) *Actions rei, or pœnæ, or tam pœnæ quam rei, persequendæ causa.*

This division is deduced from the nature of the advantage which the plaintiff derived from the action.

Actions in pursuit of the thing include all actions *in rem*, and nearly all those derived from contracts, though in the case of necessary *deposit* the action had not always this character.

The *penal* actions were only actions of private law containing a pecuniary condemnation for the benefit of the plaintiff, as in the case of the actions *furti manifesti* and *nec manifesti*.

The *mixed* actions involved a pecuniary penalty, for the benefit of the plaintiff, over and above what was due by way of restitution or reparation of the injury sustained, as in the case of such actions resulting from delicts as the *vi bonorum raptorum*, and that *ex lege Aquilia*—as well as the action of necessary deposit (for *double*) when directed against him who received the deposit, or against his heir personally guilty of *dolus*—and so as to the action (in *double*) against those who waited to be summoned *in judicio* before they delivered to churches or other sacred places the property bequeathed by legacy or fideicommissum.

(4) *Actions for simple, double, triple, or quadruple.*

This division resulted from an arithmetical computation of the difference between the amount of the damages and the estimated value of the property, that is, under the formula system, between the amount inserted in the *intentio* and that fixed by the *condemnatio*.

(5) *Actions bonæ-fidei, stricti juris, arbitrariæ.*

This division was deduced from the nature and extent of the powers conferred on the judge by the formula.

The *stricti juris* action confined the judge to a question of *civil* law, and disregarded any considerations of equity or good faith which were not included in the principles of that law. This class included as a general rule all *civil* actions.

The *bonæ-fidei* action, by means of expressions equivalent to *ex fide bona*, directed the judge to condemn or absolve according to good faith, so that (α) *dolus*, (β) usage, (γ) set-off, (δ) produce and interest, would be taken into account by the judge. *Justinian* cites as *bonæ-fidei* actions in his time (1) the actions of three *real* contracts, (2) those of the four *consensual* contracts, (3) those of four *quasi* contracts, (4) the action *præscriptis verbis*, (5) the *hereditatis petitio*, (6) the action *ex stipulatu* in restitution of dowry, (7) stipulation actions involving the *doli clausula*.

The *arbitraria* action was introduced to avoid the inconvenience of all condemnations being *pecuniary*. The clause *nisi restituat*, or other equivalent expression, enabled the judge before his sentence to issue a *jussus* (or *arbitrium*) for restitution or satisfaction to be made to the plaintiff, and, if this order was obeyed by the defendant he was released from liability, otherwise he was condemned in a sum usually fixed by the oath of the plaintiff. Although under *Justinian* no formula was prepared, the principles governing this division remained the same.

All *real* actions under the formula system were *arbitrariæ*, whether *civil* or *prætorian*, besides two *civil* and two *prætorian* personal actions which were of a restitutory or exhibitory character, together with the peculiar action *de eo quod certo loco*.

It is a question whether all *noxal* actions became *arbitrariæ* by the mere fact of taking the *noxal* character.

(6) *Direct and indirect actions.*

The first are given against a person for obligations resulting from his own acts or from the acts of those to whom he has succeeded.

The second lay against a person in respect of the acts of those in his power, for though according to the *civil* law the paterfamilias was not bound by contracts or *quasi* contracts entered into by his sons or slaves, *prætorian* law met these cases by modifing the ordinary direct action so as to produce the *indirect* actions, *quod jussu*, *institoria*, *exercitoria*, *tributoria*, *de peculio et de in rem verso*, whilst for obligations resulting from the *delicts* or *quasi* delicts of persons *alieni juris* the *civil* law itself created the class of *noxal* actions lying against the paterfamilias.

(7) *Noxal and pauperies actions.*

Noxal actions were derived from the *civil* law, and were based on the principle that the paterfamilias ought to be liable at least to the extent of his right of ownership over the individual or animal causing damage, and the term noxal implied that the actions arising out of delicts or quasi delicts were so modified by the insertion of the words *aut noxæ dedere* as to be rendered *arbitrariæ*, so that the party against whom the action was directed had the power of releasing himself from the obligation by abandoning the person or the animal who had committed the act causing damage.

The action *de pauperie* was an altogether peculiar noxal action derived from the Twelve Tables, and lay against the owner of an animal to recover any damage sustained.

(8) Perpetual and temporary actions.

This division is based on the length of time before the right of bringing an action is barred. Originally the expression *perpetual* meant literally an indefinite duration, and included in general all *civil* actions, whilst *temporary* actions were commonly limited to *one* year, and included the majority of *prætorian* actions, but whilst the Prætor limited to *one* year's duration *penal* actions of his own invention or those actions in pursuit of the thing which were in opposition to the *civil* law (as in the case of *rescissoria* actions), he nevertheless made *perpetual* the *penal* actions, such as *furti manifesti* (and generally actions in pursuit of the thing), which were given in imitation of the *civil* law.

After the constitutions of the lower empire, every action, whether *real* or *personal*, was barred after *thirty years*, though extended to forty years in a small number of exceptional cases.

(9). Actions transmissible, or not, for or against heirs.

As a general rule the heir, continuing the legal persona of the deceased, was liable to, or could avail himself of, all the actions lying for or against the deceased, except where the right or the obligation attached to the *physical* persona, so that actions for the protection of rights, such as usufruct, use, habitatio, etc., did not pass *to* the heirs, nor the *actio injuriarum, inofficiosi testamenti*, and others depending on personal matters. In actions *against* the deceased, penal actions in which the criminality was exclusively personal to the author of the delict did not lie *against* the heirs, except to the extent the delict of the deceased had enriched them, but if the *litis contestatio* had taken place in the lifetime of the deceased, every action, whether for, or against him, became transmissible for or against his heirs.

Condemnatio.

The sentence either *condemned* or *absolved* the defendant, but in the three actions *familiæ erciscundæ, communi dividundo* and *finium regundorum*, it could contain, in addition, an *adjudicatio*, and was peculiar in that the sentence might be pronounced against either of the parties, whilst in *præjudicial* actions the decision only asserted the existence or not of a right or of a fact.

The *condemnatio* under the *legis actiones* system could reach directly the object of the litigation, but under the *formula* system it was always pecuniary, whilst in the *extraordinary* procedure, and particularly under Justinian, the early practice was revived, so that the sentence could be either in respect of a fixed sum of money (*certæ pecuniæ*), or in respect of the thing (*rei*) in litigation, and the judge could even condemn the plaintiff.

Plus petitio.

Under the *formula* procedure, if the *intentio* claimed more than was actually due, the plaintiff would either *ipso juro*, or *exceptionis ope*, be defeated, and the defendant released, but under *Justinian* the effects of an excess in the demand were of a less dangerous character.

Plus petitio might arise in four ways, viz., in respect of the *thing*, the *time*, the *place*, or the *mode*. Under *Zeno*, if the plaintiff brought his action before the time, he was subjected to *double* the original delay, without being able to claim the interest accruing in the interval, and he could not renew the action without first reimbursing the defendant all the costs already incurred. *Justinian* repressed every other kind of *plus petitio* by compelling the plaintiff to pay the defendant *triple* the damage that the exaggeration of his claim had caused him, and particularly triple the excess of fees charged by the *executores*, but mistakes, such as claiming *less*, or one thing for another, could be remedied by amendment at the trial.

Compensatio.

Set-off was never a recognized mode for the *extinction* of debts, but under the formula system set-off might be admitted in three different cases, viz. :—

(α) In *bonæ fidei* actions it would be taken into account by the judge in respect of matters *ex eadem causa* even though *ex dispari specie*, so that the defendant was only liable for the balance.

(β) In *argentarii* actions, in which the banker, in order to avoid *plus petitio*, was obliged to allow a set-off in respect of obligations (*ex dispari causa*) if the objects were *ex pari specie*.

(γ) In *stricti juris* actions the fear of the *exceptio doli* had the same result, for if the plaintiff persisted up to the *litis contestatio* in refusing to modify the formula, so as to allow the judge to take account of the defendant's set-off, he would sanction the insertion of the *exceptio doli*, involving, if proved, the loss of the action, but though the set-off might be *ex dispari causa*, it probably had to be *ex pari specie*.

In *arbitrariæ* actions the plaintiff could, from the nature of these suits and up to the sentence of the judge, make the payments or reimbursements for which he was liable, and so avoid the effects of the *exceptio doli*.

If the set-off was admitted, it had a retrospective effect, so that the balance was calculated at the moment of the co-existence of the reciprocal claims.

The substitution of the *extraordinary* for the ordinary procedure greatly affected the rules of set-off, for (1) the judge had a general jurisdiction to adjust the claim in default of the *plaintiff* doing so, besides being able to condemn the *plaintiff* if necessary; and (2) the exceptions, or other modifications formerly used, did not need to be inserted in a formula to enable the judge to exercise the powers which formerly resulted from them.

Justinian allowed set-off in all actions (except the *depositi*), whether it was *ex pari* or *ex dispari causa*, provided it was *liquida*, *i.e.*, a claim capable of being ascertained in law, and probably it was not necessary that the set-off should be *ex pari specie*.

Beneficium competentiæ.

Where family or other ties existed between the debtor and the creditor, as in the case of ascendants sued by descendants, patrons by freedmen, etc., the debtor could not be condemned beyond the extent of his means, and this was extended to imply that he must not be reduced to absolute want.

For this purpose, under the formula system, the *condemnatio* was restricted by means of the *exceptio quod facere potest (duntaxat in id quod facere potest condemna)*.

Exceptions.

The greater number of exceptions were introduced by the prætor, though some resulted from laws, senatus-consulta, or imperial constitutions, or even arose from the *civil* law.

Under the *formula* system they were used as restrictions either to the claim stated in the *intentio* or to the amount fixed by the *condemnatio*, and they were employed when the judge could not, as a matter of law, entertain some particular circumstance alleged by the defendant, but which, if true, would either release the defendant from liability or restrict the amount of damages.

In *bonæ fidei* actions all exceptions founded on good faith were implied by law, and therefore need not be inserted.

The *exceptio doli mali* lay for *dolus* in general, and therefore included those based on *metus causa* or error.

The *exceptio in factum composita* was not a peculiar kind, but a form into which any exception might be thrown in order to restrict the judge to the determination of a particular fact only, as in the case of the exceptions *pecuniæ non numeratæ, pacti conventi, jurisjurandi, rei judicatæ*, etc.

The division of exceptions into (1) *perpetual* and *peremptory*, and (2) *temporary* and *dilatory*, referred to their duration and effect whilst in the hands of the defendant, and in this sense the duration of the first was unlimited, *i.e.*, they might be opposed to the plaintiff at any time, and prevented his ever exercising the right of action. The second class were only available for a time, and therefore only procured for the defendant a delay in respect of the plaintiff's right to bring the action.

Originally, any exception, if successfully opposed to the action, prevented the plaintiff suing again, because the subject-matter having been once brought into court, the action in respect of it was consumed; but *Justinian* modified this point in respect of *dilatory* exceptions by only *doubling* the previous delay, and throwing all the costs upon the plaintiff.

Certain exceptions were *dilatory* on account of the *person:* as in the case of those called *procuratoriæ*, which set up the incapacity of the procurator employed by the opposite litigant.

The *replicatio* could be opposed by the plaintiff to the defendant's exception, and so with the *duplicatio, triplicatio,* etc.

Certain exceptions could be used not only by the debtor, but by all those liable for him, including his successors; whilst others were exclusively personal to him, as in the case of those based on a *cessio bonorum*, a personal pact, or the *beneficium competentiæ*.

Interdicts.

These were decrees or private edicts granted by a magistrate, and imperatively ordered or forbad something.

They were at the outset probably exclusively employed to supplement the general law in respect of such matters coming directly under public authority, as the preservation of things devoted to divine or religious or public uses. They were then extended to cover cases of urgency in *private* matters where summary interference was necessary to avoid a breach of the peace, as in disputes about the *possession* of property.

If the person against whom the interdict was directed did not submit, a trial was the result, and the interdict served as the basis of the formula under which the judge received his instructions.

Interdicts are divided into (1) *prohibitory*, (2) *restitutory*, or (3) *exhibitory*, according as they forbad something, or contained an order to restore or produce something.

Possessory interdicts consisted of those—

(1) *adipiscendæ*, as the *quorum bonorum* and *Salvianum*..
(2) *retinendæ*, as the *uti possidetis* and *utrubi*.
(3) *recuperandæ*, as the *unde vi*.
(4) *tam adipiscendæ quam recuperandæ*, or *double* interdicts in the sense that they were given both to acquire and to recover, as in the case of the *quam fundum, quam hereditatem* and *quam usufructum*.

The distinction of interdicts into *simple* or *double* depended upon the first involving a plaintiff and a defendant, whilst the second made both disputants at the same time plaintiff and defendant.

The suppression of the formula system and of the *ordinaria judicia* led to direct recourse being had to the appropriate action, without any preliminary demand for an interdict.

Penalties on groundless litigation.

The methods in use in the time of *Justinian* for preventing the conduct of suits *calumniæ causa* were (1) the *oath* taken by plaintiff, defendant, and their advocates; (2) the liability of the defendant in certain actions to *pecuniary* penalties, as where the condemnation was *doubled* on denial of the plaintiff's right, or where *double, triple,* or *quadruple* damages resulted from the nature of the action itself; and (3) the *infamy* resulting from conviction or even admission of delicts such as theft, violence, *dolus*, or *injuria*; (4) the necessity for permission to sue an ascendant or a patron.

Duties of the judge.

A judge must pronounce according to law, otherwise he incurred the risk of public penalties, and the sentence given by him would be null and void. The text applies this principle to the case of *noxal* actions which involve an alternative condemnation, to *arbitrariæ* actions, which admit of a *jussus* preceding the condemnation, and to the three actions *familiæ erciscundæ, communi dividundo*, and *finium regundorum*, which may involve an *adjudicatio* in addition to the condemnation.

Publica judicia.

Public prosecutions were either (1) *capitalia* or *non capitalia*, but always involved *infamy*. They were based on special laws, defining the crime, the penalty, and the procedure. The right of commencing such prosecutions devolved with few exceptions on all citizens, but the accuser was responsible that there was no malicious intent in presenting the *libellus* containing the accusation.

The Institutes only give a few summary ideas on the subject, for this special procedure had merged in the *judicia extraordinaria*, and as the matter of *criminal* law was held to be outside an elementary treatise on private law, *Justinian*, after enumerating some of the laws passed for the punishment of particular crimes, refers students to the Digest for more ample details. *Sed de publicis judiciis hæc exposuimus, ut vobis possibile sit summo digito et quasi per indicem ea tetigisse: alioquin diligentior eorum scientia vobis ex latioribus Digestorum seu Pandectarum libris, Deo propitio, adventura est.*

INDEX.

Abduction, 400
Absence, effect of, 360, 379
— legal, 80
Absolutorium, 351
Abusus, 92
Accensi, 6
Acceptilatio, 92, 205, 263, 302, 320, 325, 402
Accessio, 85, 147, 221
— possessionum, 168
Accessories, 206
— to a stipulation, 263, 313
— exceptions to rule of, 206
— to a theft, 322
Accommodare actionem, 355
Accomplice, 322
Accrual, 206
— between co-heirs, 188, 253, 310
— — co-legatees, 201, 239
Accursius, 67, 70
Accusatio capitalis, 123, 399
Achaia, 46
Acquisitio ex lege, 203
— modes of, 93, 140, 146, 221
— per adrogationem, 254
— per universitatem, 94, 177
Acquisition through others, 175, 300, 318
Act, 85
— of the civil law, 126
— — — jus gentium, 87, 126, 177
Actio, 16, 28, 38, 48, 90, 94, 95, 98, 334, 343
— ad exhibendum, 149, 218, 323, 344, 350, 389, 391, 398, 401
— adjectitiæ qualitatis, 375
— ædilitia, 379
— æstimatoria, 279, 281, 294, 314
— an juraverit, 364
— arbitraria, 350, 361, 367, 369, 373, 378, 383, 395, 398, 406, 412
— arborum furtim cæsarum, 328
— bonæ fidei, 349, 367, 384, 385, 406
— calumniæ, 396
— cedere, 301
— certæ creditæ pecuniæ, 266
— civilis, 350, 359, 405
— incerta, 293, 317, 369
— commodati, 258, 260, 312, 323, 350, 367
— communi dividundo, 28, 93, 287, 296, 316, 347, 365, 367, 398, 405, 408, 412
— condicticia, 258
— conducti, 284, 314, 367, 377
— confessoria, 218, 227, 284, 350, 358, 405

Actio contraria, 133, 260, 312
— damni injuriæ, 273, 276, 366, 382, 396
— de æstimato, 294
— de albo corrupto, 364, 406
— — constituta pecunia, 363, 383
— — dolo, 293, 317, 346, 350, 352, 369, 383, 386, 396
— — — in factum, 349
— — dote, 367
— — distrahendis rationibus, 132, 139
— — eo quod certo loco, 350, 369, 407
— — incendio, etc., 329
— — in rem verso, 375, 376, 377, 407
— — inoff. test., 193, 233, 383, 408
— — jure-jurando, 364, 406
— — lege Julia repet., 382
— — partu agnos., 120
— — Pauperie, 379, 407
— — peculio, 333, 364, 375, 376, 377, 406
— — pecunia certa credita, 396
— — Pecunia const., 294, 307, 396, 406
— depensi, 272, 273, 396
— depositi, 260, 312, 347, 350, 366, 367, 374, 396, 466, 410
— de tigno juncto, 151, 328
— directa, 133, 260, 312, 348
— duplicia, 365
— emphyteuticaria, 284, 315
— empti, 276, 280, 281, 288, 314, 367, 377
— exercitoria, 333, 375, 377, 407
— ex legato quod venerabilibus locis, etc., 365, 366, 406
— ex stipulatu, 133, 139, 262, 273, 281, 288, 299, 313, 366, 367, 368, 369, 381, 407
— ex testamento, 218, 241, 262
— famil. ercisc., 12, 28, 93, 197, 198, 218, 219, 235, 241, 253, 296, 334, 345, 347, 365, 367, 398, 405, 408, 412
— fictitia, 88, 257, 348, 359, 361, 405
— — utilis, 255
— fiduciæ, 349, 367
— finium regundorum, 28, 93, 296, 347, 350, 365, 398, 405, 408, 412
— furti, 147, 149, 305, 322, 324, 328, 365, 377, 382, 385, 391, 396, 401
— — concepti, 321, 366
— — lance licioque concepti, 321
— — manifesti, 324, 366, 382, 401, 406, 408
— — nec manifesti, 321, 366, 401, 406
— — non exhibiti, 321

INDEX.

Actio furti oblati, 321, 366
— — prohibiti, 321
— hereditaria, 196
— honoraria, 38
— hypothecaria, 173, 219, 241, 284, 315, 361, 382, 383, 406
— in duplum, 366, 406
— in factum, 144, 293, 322, 326, 329, 330, 346, 347, 350, 356, 359, 361, 364, 369, 384, 402, 405
— — — præscriptis verbis, 281, 291, 293, 294, 317, 349, 367, 377, 407
— injuriarum, 144, 146, 305, 326, 327, 377, 382, 383, 385, 397, 402, 408
— in jus, 347, 350
— — personam, 89, 96, 198, 346, 348, 350, 356, 358, 373, 381, 404
— — quadruplum, 366
— — rem, 89, 96, 155, 346, 350, 356, 358, 361, 365, 373, 380, 392, 404
— — — confessoria, 164
— — — negatoria, 164
— — simplum, 366, 406
— — sup. legit., 192, 197, 235
— — triplum, 366
— institoria, 288, 291, 316, 333, 375, 377, 407
— judicati, 354, 380, 381, 386, 396, 398
— legati, 218, 241
— legat. per damnat. relict., 396
— legis, 16, 19, 23, 24, 27, 28, 29, 36, 38, 47, 48, 95, 98, 266, 334, 379, 385, 394, 403, 404
— — Aquiliæ, 324, 326, 328, 330, 348, 365, 366, 367, 396, 402, 406
— legitima, 263
— locati, 276, 284, 314, 323, 367, 377
— mandati, 268, 271, 273, 288, 367, 368, 387
— — contraria, 291, 315, 396
— — directa, 291, 316, 396
— mixta, 96, 347, 365, 382, 404, 406
— mutui, 258
— negativa, 358
— negatoria, 227, 284, 350, 358, 405
— negot. gest., 133, 139, 296. 367, 368
— noxalis, 264, 375, 377, 398, 407, 412
— Pauliana, 361, 406
— per condictionem, 335, 337, 349
— per jud. post., 13, 16, 27, 29, 335, 337, 349
— perpetua, 366, 382, 408
— per manus inject., 11, 16, 337, 353
— — pignoris cap., 15, 16, 334, 339, 342, 354
— personalis, 173, 343
— — in rem scripta, 346
— pigneratitia, 260, 312, 367
— pœnæ et rei persequendæ, 383
— pœnalis, 324, 325, 351, 364, 365, 382, 384, 401, 406, 408
— popularis, 144, 330, 364

Actio præ-judicialis, 108, 120, 345, 356, 364, 404, 405, 408
— prætoria, 90, 350, 405
— — in personam, 359, 406
— — in rem, 363, 406
— prima, 356
— pro socio, 272. 273, 276, 284, 287. 316, 367, 371, 377, 396
— — tutela, 380
— Publiciana, 168, 223, 350, 359, 382, 383, 406
— rescissoria, 360, 406
— — utilis, 284, 348
— quanto minoris, 279, 281, 314
— quod jussu, 375, 377, 407
— — metus causa, 366, 369, 386
— receptitia, 294, 363, 406
— redhibitoria, 267, 279, 281, 314
— rei persequendæ causa, 406
— — uxoriæ, 173, 206, 349, 367
— repetundarum, 379
— rerum amotarum, 328
— rescissoria, 171, 382, 408
— Rutiliana, 257
— sacramenti, 16, 19, 27, 30, 84, 95, 266, 335, 337, 349, 394
— sacrosanctis locis, 356
— secunda, 356
— sepulchri violati, 144
— Serviana, 284, 315, 350, 361, 362, 390, 406
— servi corrupti, 322, 328, 366
— stricti juris, 349, 367, 369, 372, 373, 383, 406
— subsidiaria, 131, 133, 139
— suspecti tutoris, 15, 133, 139
— temporalis, 261, 382, 386, 408
— tertia, 356
— tributoria, 375, 407
— tutelæ contraria, 132, 133, 139, 296, 367, 396
— utilis, 90, 133, 301, 348, 402
— venditi, 279, 281, 288, 314, 367, 377
— vindicandi, 323
— vi bonor. rapt., 328, 365, 377, 382, 391, 396, 401, 406
— — — — et de turba, 328
Action, 24, 31
— definition of, 358, 403, 404
— divisions of, 404
— against fathers and masters, 375
— — heirs, 382, 408
— civil and prætorian, 405
— direct and indirect, 407
— effect of failing in, 397
— for things or penalties, or both, 406
— form of, 358
— noxal, 407
— perpetual and temporary, 408
— real and personal, 404
— right of, 358
— time within which can be brought, 382
— vexatious, 366
Actor, 103, 130, 544

INDEX. 415

Actor, children of, 79
— municipis, 268
Actress, marriage with, 57, 79
Actus, 157
Adcrescendi jus v. jus
Addicere, 33
Addicti, 8
Addictio, 13, 24, 78, 93, 340, 353
— bonorum v. Bonorum
— in diem, 280
Addictus, 77, 115, 338, 354
Aditio hereditatis v. hereditatis
— — by slave, 176
Ademptio legatorum, 211
Adjectiones, 96, 344, 404
Adjudicatio, 13, 24, 28, 93, 142, 296, 343, 356, 398, 404, 405, 408, 412
— establishing servitudes, 381
Adjudicatus, 77
Adjunctio, 149
Adlecti, 4
Adopted children, 37, 243, 307
— disinheriting of, 230
Adoptio, 77, 114, 115, 116, 123, 137
Adoptor extraneus, 116, 185
Adpromissor, 263, 313
Adrogatio, 77, 94, 115, 123, 136, 254
Adscriptitii, 53
Adstipulator, 263, 270, 313, 325, 402
— heir of, 383
Adulterini, 78
Adulterium, 77, 400
— with slave, 186
Advances to children, 252, 310
Adversaria, 274
Advocati, 49
Ædes, 84
Ædiles, 23
— cereales, 35
— curules, 17, 39, 279
— majores, 17, 22
— plebeii, 10, 17, 23
Ædilitiæ stip. v. stipulatio
Ædilitium edictum, v. edictum
Ælius, 71
Æquum, 134
Ærarii, 36
Ærarium, 39, 43, 81, 143, 335
— prefect of, 43
Æs equestre, 7, 339
— hordiarium, 7, 339
Æstimatio, 293, 367
Affinitas, 78, 112, 136
Africa, 56, 57, 62
Africanus, 44
Age, 6, 80
Ager privatus, 83, 84
— publicus, 9, 30, 83, 281
— Romanus, 3, 9, 20, 34, 82
— vectigalis, 281
Agere, 26
— cum periculo, 341
— per formulam, 341

Agere per formulam petitoriam, 343
— sponsionem, 341, 343
— sine periculo, 341
Agnati, 122
Agnatio, 24, 63, 78
Agreements prohibited, 295
— unlawful, 332
Agri assignati, 84
— limitati, 148
— quæstorii, 84
— occupatorii, 84
— subcisivi, 84
— vectigales, 84
Agricolæ, 53, 75
Agro romano, 9
Aire, 56
Alaric, 56
Album, 8, 36, 348
— protection of, 364
Alciat, 70
Alearum lusus, 296
Alexander, 64, 65
Alexandria, 98, 125
Alibi, 269
Alienatio by others than owner, 174
— fraudulent, 361
— not allowed to owner, 174
— per æs et libram, 13, 77
Alieni juris, 24, 76, 108
Allies, 7
Alluvio, 147, 148
Amalfi, 68
Ambassadors, 144
Ambitus, 401
Anastasian emancipation, 120
Anastasius, 64, 114
Anatocismus, 300
Anatolius, 61, 64
Ancus Martius, 5
Anianus, 56
Animus dominii, 145, 155
Annæus Seneca, 214
Annales Maximi, 24
Anniculus, 113
Annus continuus, 352, 360
— utilis, 352, 360, 376
Anselm of Aosta, 68
Antapocha, 88
Antecessor, 61
Antestatio, 339
Antiochus, 54
Antiqui, 64
Antiquo, 35
Antinomy, 59
Antoninus Pius, 41, 44, 60, 172, 212, 354
Antony, 35
Apocha, 88
Apostates, 54, 79
Apparatus, 69
Apparitores, 354
Appeal, origin of, 23
— right of, 15, 49, 96, 357
Appearance in an action, 364, 380

416 INDEX.

Appellatio, 44, 357
Appius Claudius, 13, 19, 26, 71, 365
Aquæductus, 157
Aquæhaustus, 157
Aquilius Gallus, 184, 303
Arbiter, 15, 18, 23, 29, 51, 335, 343, 349
— aquæ pluv. arcend., 14
— familiæ ercisc., 337
— finium reg., 337
— vindiciæ falsæ, 337
Arb tration, 51, 337
Arbitrium, 344, 350, 369, 407
— ad exhibendum, 337
Arbores, 16
Arca, 275
Arcadius, 54
Arcifinales, 148
Argentarius, 276, 294
— action against, 363
— liability of, 333
— set off against, 372, 409
Argument of Justinian's Institutes, 99
Arians, 57
Aristocracy of money, 5
— of race, 5
Arius, 51
Arms, loss of, 118
Army, power of, 48
Arrha, 110, 277, 314
Ars boni et æqui, 134
Arson, 14
Aruspices, 54
As, divisions of, 187, 232
Assem dare, 6
Assertor libertatis, 104, 336, 365
Assessor, 40
Assignatio libert., 249
Assignment to creditors, 354, 388
Assidui, 6
Astrologers, 54
Athanasius, 64
Athenians, customs of, 102
Athens, civil law of, 101
Atrium, 26
Atrox, 328
Attic legislation, 10
Attila, 56
Auctor, 127
Auctoritas, 37, 127
— of senate, 4, 7, 19, 22
— tutoris, 127, 129, 138
Auctoritatem præstare, 127, 278
Audientia episcopalis, 51
Auditorium, 41, 44, 49
Augurs, 8, 19, 37
Augustus, 32, 38, 40, 41, 42, 48, 50, 75, 86, 107, 115, 213, 216, 357, 400, 401
Aulus Ofilius, 44
Authenticæ, 61
Auxilium, 23
— extraordinarium, 251
Avignon, 70
Azo, 70

Bailee, 15
Ballot, 35
Balsamon, 66
Bandsmen, 6
Bankruptcy, 79, 372
— of partner, 286
Barbarians, eruption of, 47, 48
— transfer of, 53
Barbarus, 21, 46, 75
Bartolus, 70
Basil, 64
Basilica Julia, 19
Basilicæ, 64, 65
Beaufort, de, 1
Bec, Abbey of, 68
Bederina, 57
Bees, 221
Bekk, 67
Belisarius, 57, 99
Beneficium abstinendi, 194
— cedend. act., 274, 289, 333
— competentiæ, 354, 368, 371, 410, 411
— deliberandi, 195
— discussionis, 289
— divisionis, 272, 273, 289, 333, 383
— excussionis, 273
— inventarii, 195, 235
— legis Corneliæ, 183
— — Falcidiæ, 214
— ordinis, 273
— separationis, 193, 234, 363
Berytus, 60, 61
Biener, 67
Bigamy, 112
Bigleniza, 57
Bishops, 51, 62, 98, 105, 360
Blastares, 66
Blondeau, 71
Blume, 59
Bœtius, 57
Bologna, 67, 68, 70
Bona, 83
Bona fide emptor, 323
— fide possessor, 177
— vacantia, 166, 222
Bonæ fidei actions, v. actio
— — list of, 367, 407
— — origin of, 337
— — set off in, 372, 409
— — contracts v. contract
Bonorum addictio, 255, 256, 310
— cessio, 257, 265, 286, 315, 354, 371, 411
— collatio, 252, 309
— distractio, 354
— emptio, 286, 310, 353
— emptor, 256, 348, 372, 382
— possessio, 37, 94, 179, 249, 309, 382, 389
— — ab intest., 250, 309
— — contra tab., 185, 189, 230, 243, 250
— — cum re et sine re, 252, 390
— — decret., 252, 309
— — edic., 252, 309

INDEX. 417

Bonorum possessio ex test., 250, 309
— — claiming, 251
— — repudiation of, 251
— — secund. tab., 191, 233, 250, 309
— — tum quem ex fam., 250, 309
— — — quibus ex leg., 251, 309
— — vent. nom., 252, 309, 397
— — unde cog., 250, 309
— — — manumis, 251, 309
— — — decem pers., 250, 309
— — — legit., 250, 309
— — — liberi, 243, 250, 309
— — — patroni, 251, 309
— — — vir et uxor, 251, 309
— possessor, 37, 308, 390
— — loco heredis, 348
— — sine re, 390
— proscriptio, 256
— publicatio, 286
— sectio, 286, 353
— venditio, 256
Boundaries, v. Fines
Bourges, 70
Brachylogus, 69, 89
Breviarium Alaricianum, 56, 57, 68
— Aniani, 56
Brocarda, 69
Budé, 70
Bulgarians, 62
Bulgarus, 69
Burglary, 40
Burgundians, 56, 57
Byzantine law, v. Law
Byzantium, 51

Caduca, 43, 44, 45, 142, 188, 201, 202, 239, 253
Cæcus, 183
Cæsar, Julius, 27, 31, 35, 40, 44, 116, 181, 399, 401
Cahors, 70
Calendar, 5
Calendarium, 300
Caligula, 32
Callide, 286
Callistratus, 47, 60
Calocyrus Sextus, 65
Calumnia, 215, 395
Campania, land of, 31
Canon, 53, 281
— law, 60
Canuleium plebiscitum, 17
Capitation tax, 36
Capite censi, 6
Capitis dem., 78, 122, 136, 162, 338, 348
— — max., 78, 122
— — med., 78, 123
— — min., 78, 123, 305
Capito, 41
Capitol, 22
Captain of ship's liability, 330
Captives, care of, 51
— position of, 119

Caput, 5, 75, 78, 124, 299
Caracalla, 43, 45, 46, 50, 76, 80, 82, 104
Carcera privata, 353
Cariolanus, 10
Carthage, 25
Cassians, 42
Cassiodorus, 57
Cassius, 42, 44, 46
Caste, 79
Castrati, 81, 111, 116
Castrense pec., v. Peculium
Castrensiani, 52
Casus, 69, 297
Catholici, 79
Cattle, 324
Cato, 26, 71, 200
Catoniana reg., 170, 199, 205, 236
Causa, 270, 276, 292
— cadere, 370
— calumniæ, 399, 411
— civilis, 292
— falsa, 238
— justa, 167, 360
— liberalis, 104, 365
— lib. quærend., 113
— lucrativa, 200, 384
— pietatis, 331
— rei familiaris, 389
— reipublicæ, 360
— solutionis, 268
Causæ conjectio, 340
— collectio, 340
— erroris prob., 114
— peroratio, 356
— probatio, 113
Cautio, 88, 91, 270, 271, 276, 289, 313, 356
— damni infecti, 266
— de dolo, 266, 350, 369
— judicat. solvi, 266, 354, 380, 398
— judicio, sist., 357, 381
— juratoria, 381
— legat., 219, 267
— Muciana, 209, 238
— ratam rem dom. hab., 380, 381
Cavalry, 6
Cavere, 26
Celeres, 6, 39
Celsus, 41, 42, 44
— on the validity of legacies, 200, 205
— on the revival of obligations, 306
Celtic race, 1
Censiti, 53
Censor, 17, 22, 79
Census, 5, 104, 123
Centumviri, 18, 23, 28, 29, 36, 49, 191, 335, 337, 342, 343
Centuriæ, 6
Ceræ, 88
Ceres, 14, 17, 21
Ceritum tabulæ, 17
Cervottus, 70
Cessatio, 299
Cessio bonorum, v. Bonorum

E E

Cessio in jure, v. In jure
Ceteri, 184
Chance, games of, 296
Charisius, 58
Charles the Bald, 68
Charta, 88, 276
Chartres, Bishop of, 68
Chartula, 276
Child, abandonment of, 378
— care of, 51
— emancipated, 137
— exposure of, 57, 109, 120
— natural, 77, 113
— property of, 109
— prostitution of, 126
— rules as to condition of, 103
— sale of, 52, 109, 136
— status of, 135
Chirographum, 88, 205, 276, 313
Christianity, influence of, 43, 49, 52, 75, 79
— introduction of, 47, 54
— religion of empire, 51
Christians, 47, 51, 57, 79
— heterodox, 57, 62
Church of domicile, 186
— — legacy to, 297
— property, 144
Cicero, 3, 10, 26, 27, 32, 33, 34, 35, 40, 41, 61, 71, 74, 86
— on adoption, 114
— on the bonorum vend., 256
— on the contract litteris, 274
— — — deductio, 336
— — — gentiles, 245
— — inofficious wills, 191
— — soldiers' wills, 179
— — substitutions, 189
Circus charioteers, 57
Cisalpine Gaul, 35
Citation law, 54
Cives, latini, peregrini, 46
Civil law, 8, 23, 36, 49, 62, 101
Civis, 20, 35, 48, 50, 75, 79
— illegal detention of, 401
Civitas, 45, 75, 78
— absq. suff., 20
Civitates fund., 21
— fœd., 20
— lib., 20
Claim, excess of, 370
— mistake in, 371, 387
— surplus over, 371
Clam, 390
Clarissimi, 52
Classes, 6
Claudian family, 246
— Marcellian family, 246
Clausula codicill., 217, 241
— doli, 350, 367, 369, 384, 407
Clemens, 45
Clergy, 68
Clientage, 3

Clientes, 3, 15, 25
Clotare, 68
Code Athenian, 13
— meaning of word, 58
Codes of Byzantine Emp., 64
Codex, 216, 274
— Greg., 50, 54, 55, 56, 58, 59
— Hermog., 50, 54, 55, 56, 58, 59
— Just., 58, 64
— legis Visigoth., 56
— Repet. Prælec., 60
— Theod., 51, 54, 56, 57, 58, 59, 75
— vetus, 58
Codices, 88
Codicil, 41, 43, 50, 86, 88, 216, 240
Coelibes, 42, 52, 63, 111, 186, 202
Coemptio, 8, 37, 77, 117, 129, 349
Coemptionator, 117
Cognatio, 24, 37, 38, 50, 63, 78, 245, 247
— servilis, 247
Cognitio, 335, 343
— extraordinaria, 30, 32, 47, 62, 351, 357, 399, 404
— suspecti, 133, 139
Cognitor, 266, 379, 381, 387
Co-heir, liability of, 298
Cohorts, 40
Coinage, falsification of, 400
Colientes, 3
Collatio bonor., v. Bonorum
— Mosaic. et Rom. leg., 55.
Collegam appellare, 23
Collegatarius, 201, 239
— re, 201, 203, 204, 239
— re et verbis, 201, 203, 204, 239
— verbis, 201, 203, 204, 239
Coloni, 53, 75
— censiti, 103
— liberi, 53
Coloniæ, 7, 25, 35, 45
— militariæ, 35
— Romanæ, 20, 35, 76
— togatæ, 20
Colonus, 281
— property of, 361
— rights of, 153
Comites consist., 51
Comitia calata, 104, 178, 179, 229
— centuriata, 6, 9, 10, 15, 17, 22, 23, 31, 34, 35, 77
— curiata, 3, 4, 7, 22, 23, 245
— tributa, 10, 17, 18, 19, 22, 23, 31, 34, 35
Comitium, 3, 338
Commentaries, 47
Commercium, 8, 20, 75, 82, 92, 180
Commixtio, 147, 150
Commodans, 258, 312
Commodatum, 38, 93, 258, 302, 312
Commodum, 279, 314
Comœdus, 103
Compeditus, 103
Compensatio, 332, 371, 384, 403, 407, 409
— compulsory, 374

INDEX. 419

Compensatio liquida, 410
— voluntary, 374
Comperendinatio, 340
Compromissum, 294, 295, 317, 369, 396
Conception, 103
Concubinatus, 77, 112, 113, 136
Condemnatio, 28, 96, 262, 341, 342, 343, 344, 346, 348, 350, 356, 366, 369, 370, 374, 375, 376, 386, 394, 396, 397, 404, 408, 409, 410
Condem. absolv. non liq., 32
Condictio, 29, 95, 96, 299, 312, 343, 347, 375, 377
— causa data, &c., 293, 294, 316
— certi, 174, 225, 260, 262, 273, 281, 313
— de omni certa re, 27, 347
— ex lege, 174, 225, 295, 317, 366
— ex stipulatu, 368
— ex testamento, 218
— furtiva, 149, 323, 401
— incerti, 262, 313
— indebiti, 171, 208, 219, 261, 274, 295, 297, 317, 349
— in jure, 341
— ob causam dat. 293
— title to support, 386
— triticaria, 347
— utilis, 288
— quasi re non sec., 174, 225
Conditio, cancellation of, 261
— illegal, 188, 210
— impossible, 188, 210
— joint, 188
— mixed, 261
— negative, 261
— pœnæ nom., 210
— potest., 261
— precedent, 370
— separate, 188
— suspensory, 280
Conductor, 281, 282
— ejectment of, 283
— obligation of, 283, 298, 314
Confarreatio, 8, 37, 77, 117
Confessio, 88, 354
— in jure, 355
Confessus, 353
Confusio, 147, 150, 221, 305, 320
Connubium, 8, 17, 20, 46, 75, 77, 111, 136
Consanguinity, 247
Conscripti, 4
Consensual contracts, v. Obligatio
Consensus, 87, 90, 110
— of curator, 129, 139
Conservus, 264
Consideration, v. Causa
Consilia, 70
— semestria, 41
Consilium, 18, 41, 145
Consistorium, 41, 44, 49, 52, 61
Consobrinus, 51, 98
Consolidatio, 163
Constans, 86

Constantine, 43, 50, 51, 52, 105, 358
— Copronymus, 64
— Harmenopulus, 66
— jurist, 60
— Lascaris, 66
— of Nicæa, 65
— Palæologus, 66
— Porphyrogenitus, 65
— son of Basil, 64
— the Second, 53, 86
Constantinople founded, 51
— judges at, 48
— school of, 54, 61, 64
Constantius, 53, 54, 62, 86
Constitutiones imp., 40, 44, 50, 64, 65, 101, 383
Consolidatio, 163
Constitution, political, 15
Constituere, 294
Constitutum, 294, 317, 383
Constructio, 150
Consul, 38, 39, 44, 51
Consultatio, 357
— veteris cujus juris, 55
Contentio fructus licit, 394
— juris, 28
Contracta fiducia, 119, 124, 245, 251, 308
Contract (v. also Obligatio), 24, 38, 50, 63
— accessory, 332, 361
— actions in respect of, 365
— bilateral, 90, 277
— bonæ fidei, 279, 299, 333
— do ut des, 291, 292, 294
— — — facias, 291, 292, 317
— facio ut des, 292, 293, 217
— — — facias, 292, 317
— imperfectly sunallagmatic, 288
— innominate, 260, 292, 317, 367
— liability of heirs on, 383
— — — paterfamilias, 375
— nominate, 292
— produces obligations only, 280
— prohibited, 295, 317
— quasi, 367
— real, 258, 367
— responsibility in, 298
— stricti juris, 299
— unilateral, 277
— validity of, 267
Contractus, 89, 90
Contrectatio, 320
Contubernium, 78, 112, 136, 257
Contumax, 356
Contumelia, 326
Conventio, 90, 258, 291, 292
— in manum, 251
— legitima, 295
Convents, 62
Conventus, 96
Co-owner, liability of, 298
Corporations, 15, 81
Corpus, 326

420   INDEX.

Corpus authenticum, 61
— juris canonici, 58, 67
— — civilis, 58
— Theodosianum, 56
Coruncanius, 71
Correctores, 44
Correales, 333
Correi, 313
— promittendi, 262
— stipulandi, 262
Council nominating tutors and curators, 51
Counter-claim, 374
Crassus, 35
Cratinus, 61
Credere, 258
Creditor in mora, 299
— in solidum, 263, 313, 332
— joint, 333
— mortgagee, 362
— pledgee, 362
— of peculium, 376
— pro parte, 332
— protection of, 361
Creditum, 89
Cretio, 106, 186, 195, 234
— continua, 195
— vulgaris, 195
Crimen, expilatæ hered., 329
Criminal accusation, 7, 62
— property of condemned, 390
— law, 14, 23, 31, 36, 49, 62, 399, 412
— jurisdiction, 39
Crimina extraordinaria, 32, 49
Cubicularii, 52
Cubidius, 64
Cujas, 42, 55, 57, 70, 265
Culpa, 279, 285, 297, 317
— definition of, 297
— gravis, 312
— lata, 297, 318
— levis, 297, 318
— magna, 297
— standards of comparison, 297, 318
Cura, 81, 139
— as a quasi contract, 296, 317
— dispensation from, 52, 131
— legitima, 139
— measure of liability in, 298
— termination of, 130
Curatela, v. Cura
Curator, 81, 127, 129
— calendarii, 300
— honorarius, 129
— legitimus, 129
— nomination of, 51, 130
— suspectus, 133
— tacit mortgage of property of, 363
— bringing an action, 380
Cures, 1
Curia, 3, 4, 5, 20, 23, 49, 86, 114, 118
Curiales, 3, 49, 114
— flamines, 3

Curiæ subjecti, 49
Curionia sacra, 3
Curule chairs, 1
Curialis, origo, 49
Curis, 1
Custodia, 297, 318, 343, 353, 355
Custodes mittere, 120
Custom, 8
Cyrill, 64

Damian, 68
Damage, v. Damnum
— accidental, 14, 297
— corpore corpori, 326, 402
— consequential, 326
— unlawful, 297, 325, 402
Damages, 278, 329, 330, 394, 397
— assessment of, 355, 379
— causes diminishing amount of, 370
— error in claim of, 370
Damnum, 14
— infectum, 28, 266, 342, 353
Dare, facere, præstare, 89, 311
Datio, 279, 291, 292, 294
— in solutum, 302, 319
— judicis, 340
Daughters, disinheritance of, 184
Deaf, 81, 269
— and dumb, 81
Debitor, 89, 305
— accomplices of fraud of, 361
— capitis dem. of, 349
— exceptions limited to, 388
— fraudulent, 361
— in mora, 299
— in solidum, 263, 313, 332
— joint, 333
— nexum of, 362
— release of, 305, 306
Debt, deduction of, 371
— legacy of, 205
— transference of, 142
Decemviri, 10, 19, 36, 335
Decision of the case, actions for, 335
— — fact, 343
Decisions, the fifty, 59
Decrees, imperial, 40
Decretum, 68, 97
— Gratiani, 67
— principis, 40, 49
Decuries, 32
Decuriones, 49, 62
Dediticii, 7, 50, 75, 76, 106, 186
Deductio, 84, 336, 372
Defamation, 14
Defendant possessor, 342
Defensor, 380
Defensores civitatum, 54, 62, 98, 125, 360
De jure civili in art. redig., 27
Delatores, 44
Delegatio, 304
Delictum, 14, 91, 311, 320, 401
    between married persons, 371

INDEX. 421

Delictum, effect of avowal of, 396, 412
— joint, 333
— liability of paterfamilias for, 375, 377
Dementes, 81
Deminutio, 124
Demonstratio, 28, 342, 343, 404
— certa, 208
— combined with intentio, 348, 370
— falsa, 206, 208, 238
— plus petitio in, 370
Denunciatio actionis, 355, 358
Deponens, 259
— liability of, 298, 312
— rights of heirs of, 334
Deportatio, 118, 123, 398, 400, 401
Depositarius, 239
— liability of, 298, 312
Depositum, 38
— contract of, 38, 90, 259, 312, 347
— formula for, 348
— necessarium, 259, 365, 366, 383, 406
— no set off, in, 375
Derelictum, 155
Desidia, 285
Detentio nuda, 92
Detestatio sacrorum, 179
Devolution, 244, 307
De usurpationibus, 26
Dictator, 9, 34
Dies, 87, 299
— cedit, 162, 199, 236, 237
— certus, 210
— continui, 87
— incertus, 188, 210, 238
— intercisi, 5
— interpellat., 299
— justi, 338
— fasti, 5, 16, 19, 26, 87, 340
— nefasti, 5, 87
— perendinus, 340
— utiles, 87, 252
— venit, 162, 199, 236
Digest of Justinian, 41, 42, 59, 64, 73, 99
Digesta, 47, 59
Digestum novum, 69
— vetus, 69
Dilatio, 299
Diligentia, 297, 318
— exacta, 297
— exactissima, 296, 297
— quanta suis rebus, 298
Diocese, 52
Diocletian, 45, 47, 50, 51, 62, 96
— constitution of, 48, 404
Disinheriting of children, 37, 183, 230
Dispensator, 103, 290
Disputatio fori, 22
Dissimulatio, 328, 402
Divini, 49
Divortium, 42, 77, 111, 113, 269
Do, dico, addico, 33, 335
Doli capax, 128

Dolus, 38, 280, 297, 317, 348, 383, 407, 410, 412
— bonus, 87
— definition of, 87, 297
— exception based on, 384
— guarantee against, 369
— in dividing peculium, 376
— in respect of set off, 374
— liability of heirs for, 383
— malus, 87
— modes of punishing, 369
— responsibility for, 297, 318, 333, 369
Dolum malum abesse præstare, 279, 369
Domicilium, 79, 367
Dominica potestas, 141
Dominium (v. also Ownership), 12, 37, 50, 92, 140, 220, 221
— bonitarium, 37, 93, 140, 145, 220
— ex jure Quiritium, 12, 19, 23, 83, 92, 140, 144, 220, 336, 353
— ex lege, 43, 253
— kinds of, 92, 140
— loss of, 154, 225
Dominus, 282
— ex jure Quiritium, 362
— legitimus, 140
— litis, 380
— order of, 375
Domitian, 47
Domus, 92
Donatio, 169, 223, 317, 371
— ante nuptias, 173, 224
— inter virum et uxorem, 172
— inter vivos, 171, 223, 225
— mortis causa, 169, 212, 223, 224
— non mortis causa, 169
— propter nuptias, 112, 173, 223, 224
Dorotheus, 60, 61, 64, 99
Dos, 55, 85, 110, 112, 172, 223, 224, 270
— action to ascertain amount, 364
— adventitia, 173
— alienation of, 224
— conditional on marriage, 170, 173
— data, 367
— dicta, 368
— husband's rights in respect of, 368
— immovables of, 173, 175
— legacy of, 205
— mode of settling, 367
— prælegata, 206
— profectitia, 173
— protection of, 363
— receptitia, 173
— restitution of, 367
— stipulata, 368
Dotale instrumentum, 110
— prædium, 84
Dotis datio, 172
— dictio, 173, 224, 260, 312
— legatum, 20
Doubt, 88
Dowry, v. Dos
Doxapater, 66

Draco, law of, 100
Droit, 100
Drugs (injurious), sale of, 400
Duæ hastæ, 18
Ducas, 66
Duci, jubere, 353
Dumb, 81, 269
Dumoulin, 69
Duo rei, stipul. et prom., 262
Duplicia judicia, 18
Duplicatio, 97, 346, 387, 404, 411
Dupondii, 61
Dupondius, 187
Duumviri, 20, 49
— jure dicundo, 335
Dux, 52

Ecclesia, 105
Ecloga ad Proc. mut., 66
— legum, 64
— privata, 64
Edicere, 33
Edit sur la paix du royaume, 68
Edicta, v. Edictum
Edictales, 61
Edictum, 36, 97
— ædilitium, 33, 267, 279, 281, 314, 379
— de alterutro, 368
— de rebus cred., 258
— divi Hadriani, 44
— inter duos, 34
— magistratus, 101
— Mediolanense, 51
— novum, 34
— of Julianus, 44
— peremptorium, 356
— perpetuum, 34, 44
— prætoris, 33, 73
— principis, 40
— provinciale, 33, 59
— repentinum, 34
— successorium, 252
— Theodorici, 57, 67
— tralatitium, 34
— urbanum, 59
Editio, 62
— actionis, 355, 358
Educator, 103
Education under Justinian, 61
Egregii, 52
Ejectment, 283
Electio, 207, 333
— by wife, 368
Electoral power, 7, 23, 36, 48
Emancipated children, v. Child
— succession of, 307, 308
Emancipatio, 119, 123
— Anastasian, 120
— compulsory, 120
Embezzlement of trust-money, 400, 401
Emphyteusis, 84, 91, 93, 165, 228, 282, 283, 315
Emphyteuta, 282, 315

Emphyteuticarius, 282
Empire, Byzantine, 63
— council of, 52
— division of, 47, 54
Emperor, council of, 52
— of the East, 54, 66
— of the West, 54, 56
— power of, 48
Emptio rei speratæ, 278
— spei, 278
— sub corona, 93
— sub hasta, 93, 353
— venditio, 38, 91, 277, 278, 314
Emptor, 278
— familiæ, 179, 229
— obligations of, 279, 298, 314
Enchiridium, 64
Enemy's field, 5
Enfranchisement, 75, 104
— effects of, 75
— fraudulent, 361
Epanagoge, 64
— aucta, 66
Epicureans, 30
Episcopalis audientia, 51
Episcopi, 51
Epistola principis, 40
— fideicommissaria, 217
— freedom by, 105
Epitome ad Proch. mut., 65
— legum, 65
— novellarum, 60, 64, 68
Epochs of Roman Law, 71
Equality, dogma of, 75
Equites, 6, 7
Ereptorium, 142, 253, 310
Erciscundi, 42
Error, 87, 270, 384, 385
— in damages claimed, 370
Etruscans, 1, 4
Eustathius Romanus, 66
Event, 74, 85
Evictio, 278, 373
Exarchate of Ravenna, 58, 62, 67
Exceptio, 38, 48, 96, 306, 332, 345, 370, 383, 404, 410
— cognitoria, 387
— de jurejurando, 364
— dilatoria, 387, 411
— divisions of, 386, 387, 410
— doli, 151, 152, 175, 205, 219, 261, 276, 301, 305, 345, 350, 352, 369, 372, 381, 384, 385, 386, 387, 410
— effect of, 383, 409
— equity, 291
— in factum, 384, 385, 410
— in rem scripta, 384
— judicati, 380
— juris jurandi, 385, 387, 410
— justi dominii, 359, 383
— legis Cinciæ, 171
— litis dividuæ, 371, 386
— longi temporis, 388

INDEX. 423

Exceptio nisi bonis cesserit, 383, 388
— object of, 383
— origin of, 383, 410
— pacti conventi, 261, 345, 385, 386, 387, 410
— pecuniæ non numeratæ, 88, 276, 313, 385, 410
— peremptoria, 352, 386, 410
— perpetua, 171, 277, 386, 410
— personæ cohærens, 388
— procuratoria, 387, 411
— pro minore Viginti., etc., 130
— quod facere potest, 346, 371, 388, 410
— — metus causa, 352, 367, 384, 386
— rei cohærens, 387
— — in judicium deductæ, 263, 356, 357, 385, 387
— — judicatæ, 263, 357, 381, 385, 387, 410
— — residuæ, 386
— — venditæ et traditæ, 141
— restitutæ hereditatis, 214
— s.c. Macedonianum, 377, 383
— s.c. Trebellianum, 383
— s.c. Velleianum, 274, 383
— si non et illi solvendo sint, 383
— temporalis, 386, 410
— vi, 387
Exchange, 277, 281, 294
Excusatio, 131
Execution, actions for, 337
— before sentence, 351
— effects of, 290, 292, 293, 294, 305, 316
— modes of enforcing, 340, 353, 358
— suspension of, 357
Executor litium, 357, 371
Executores, 354, 409
Exercitor, 285
— navis, 330, 375, 403
Exheredatio, 230
Existimatio, 78
Expenditure, public, 36
Expenses, claims in respect of, 362, 368, 373
Expensilatio, 91, 275, 313
Experentia Romani, 66
Expromissio, 304
Expromissor, 304, 319
Extraneus, 1·7

Factio testamenti, v. Testamenti factio
Factum, 85, 95
— decision of, 343, 384
— juridical, 86
— statement of, 349
Falcidian portion, 212, 240
Familia, 75
— change of, 123, 245
— idea of, 76, 178, 228
— different acceptations of word, 76, 135
— gradual extinction, 78
— loss of, 78, 123
  pecuniaque, 83, 178

Familiæ erciscundæ, v. Actio
— mancipatio, 229
Fainosi, 79
Farreum, 77, 117
Fasces, 1
Feciales, college, 5, 8
Ferrara, 70
Ferruminatio, 150, 221
Festuca, 86, 104, 336
Feudal system, 3
Fiction of the lex Cornelia, 119
Fictions, 88
Fidei commissaria epistola, 217
— hereditas, v. Heredetas
— commissarius, 214, 240
— — prætor, 98, 213
— committens, 213
— — oath of, 215, 219
Fideicommissum, 43, 98, 223, 240, 352
— ab intestato, 215
— contrasted with legacies, 198, 216
— liberty granted by, 104, 216
— of debt, 205
— of inheritance, 213, 219
— origin of, 40, 86, 213, 216
— rer. sing., 213, 215, 219, 240
Fidejussio, 313
Fidejussor, 263, 271, 272, 305, 313, 396 398
— donandi animo, 388
— exceptions available to, 387
— insolvency of, 383
— judicio sistendi causa, 355, 381
— security given by, 380
Fide-promissio, 271, 313
Fide-promissor, 263, 271, 313, 364
— heir of, 383
Fiducia, 142
Fiduciarius, 213, 240
Filii perduellium, 186
Filius familias, adoption of, 16
— acquisition through, 300, 318
— emancipation of, 16
— natural liability of, 331
— peculium of, 52, 307
— property of, 52, 63, 78
— stipulation of, 265
— will of, 63
Fines, 398
Fiscus, 38, 39, 43, 45, 81, 98, 143, 168, 253
— mortgage in favour of, 363
Flaccus, L., 41
Flamens, 51, 117
Flamines Diales, 123
Flavianum jus, 19
Flavius, Cnæus, 19, 26
Flock, legacy of, 206, 238
Florence, 68
Fœnus, v. Usuræ
— nauticum, 258
— semunciarium, 300
— unciarium, 15, 299
Fontainebleau, library at, 66

424   INDEX.

Forcible entry, 324
Foreign policy, 7, 20, 35
Foreigners at Rome, 20, 25
Formula, 21, 36, 38, 404
— adaptation to citizens, 342
— arbitraria, 350, 394, 395
— bonæ fidei, 350
— decay of, 47, 48, 50
— division of actions according to, 367
— employed for obligations, 343
— fictitia, 341, 348, 369
— incerta, 370
— in factum, 341, 346, 348, 361
— — jus, 342, 346, 348, 356
— in respect of dowry, 368
— introduced for aliens, 341, 343
— mode of preparing, 346
— of interdicts, 388, 393
— of testaments, 53
— origin of, 340
— parts of, 341, 342, 343
— per siglas expressæ, 27
— petitoria, 266, 343, 350
— præjudicialis, 343
— procedure, 28, 96, 340, 354, 404
— Rutiliana, 380
— stricti juris, 350, 384
— suppression of, 53, 62, 86
Forum, 19, 22, 95, 218, 340, 345, 369
Fragmenta Vaticana, 55, 161, 170
France, law in, 68, 69, 70
Francis the First, 66
Franks, 56, 57
Fratres, Divi, 45
Fraud, v. Dolus
Freedman, 75, 103
— classes of, 50, 105
— definition of, 104, 135
— descendants of, 245
— duties of, 106
— natural liability of, 331
— oath of, 254
— production of, 389
— succession to, 41, 107, 247, 308
— suing patron, 364
— will of, 248, 308
Freedom in fraud of creditors, 107, 186
Freedwomen, succession to property of, 247
Freeman possessed in good faith, 300
— reclaimed from slavery, 365, 389
— reduced to slavery, 53, 103
French law, 70
Fructuaria stip., v. Stipulatio
Fructuarius, 177
Fructus, 92
— legacy of, 162
Frustratio, 299
Functio dotis, 295
Fundus, 84
— cum instrumento, 206
— fiscalis, 282
— instructus, 53, 85, 206

Fundus patrimonialis, 282
— rei privatæ, 282
Funerals, 15
Fur, 320
Furiosus, 81, 129, 242, 269
— natural liability of, 331
Furtum, 11, 14, 15, 40, 54, 401, 412
— acts included under, 84, 166
— conceptum, 14, 321
— definition of, 320, 401
— essence of, 395
— lance licioque conceptum, 14, 321
— liability of impubes for, 322
— manif., 14, 77, 320, 401
— nec manif., 14, 77, 321, 401
— non exhibitum, 321
— oblatum, 14, 321
— prohibitum, 321
— release from liability to, 305
Fuscianus, 42

Gaius, 45, 54, 72, 354
— classification of persons by, 108
— division of law by, 101
— epitome of, 56
— Institutes of, 43, 45, 60, 61, 73, 99
— on actions in rem, 343
— — bonæfidei actions, 367
— — caduca, 43
— — compensatio, 371
— — disinheritance, 148
— — edicts, 44
— — fictitious actions, 348
— — impossible conditions, 188
— — interdicts, 389, 390, 392, 393, 394, 395
— — legacies, 197
— — legitimation, 113
— — mandates, 117
— — mortgages, 361
— — noxal abandonment, 378
— — ownership, 83, 140
— — partnership, 284
— — perpetual leases, 282
— — postliminium, 119
— — postumi, 121
— — plus petitio, 370
— — puberty, 128
— — senatus-consulta, 32
— — servitudes, 158
— — set off, 371
— — Solon's code, 13
— res quotidianæ of, 99
— — the arrha, 277
— — — bonorum venditio, 256
— — — condition of children, 103, 119
— — — contract litteris, 275
— — — division of things, 140
— — — exceptio litis dividuæ, 386
— — — — rei judicatæ, 357
— — — — residuæ, 386
— — — fraudulent release of debtors, 325

INDEX. 425

Gaius on the lex imperii, 41
— — — liability of a judge, 329
— — — — heirs of sureties, 383
— — — mancipium, 77
— — — manus, 117
— — — — injectio action, 329
— — — modes of restraining groundless litigation, 396
— — — ownership of pictures, 152
— — — pignoris capio action, 334
— — — possessio bonorum, 252
— — — schools of law, 42
— — — senate, 40
— — — sponsio, 342
— — — succession to freedmen, 249
— — — suppression of the legis actiones, 27, 86
— — — tutelage of women, 128
— — — twelve tables, 10
— — theft, 320
— — trusts, 216
— — wills, 180
Galatæ, 109
Galerius, 50
Gallus, 47
Gascony, 56
Gaul, 53, 56, 57
Gauls, 17, 19, 46
Gener, 112
Generalisation of Roman Law, 73
Genseric, 56
Gens, 3, 4, 5, 9, 78, 103, 245
— togata, 46
Gentiles, 54, 139, 307
— succession of, 245
Gentilitas, 24, 37, 50
Gentis enuptio, 246
Genus, 85
Geometricians, 54
German school of law, 73
Germanic laws, 56
Germanicus, 115
Gestation, 12, 88, 104, 112, 135
Geta, 45
Gibbon, 71
Giraud, 71
Gleba, 86
Glossa, 69
Glossators, 69
Gobidas, 64
Gods, multiplication of, 37
Gojaric, 56
Gondobald, 57
Gosia, 69
Goths, 56, 57
Gracchus, Caius, 31, 32
— Tiberius Sempronius, 30
Gradus agnationis, 243
— cognationis, 247
— in bon. poss., 249
Græco-Roman law, 66
Grammatici, 132
Great gloss, 70

Grecian poetry, influence of, 1
Greek church, 63
— edit. Justinian's works, 63
Gregorian code, v. Codex
Gregorianus, 50, 72
Gregory Doxapater,
Grex, 85
Guardianship, 12
— dispensation from, 52
Guards, night, 40
— prætorian, 52

Habeas corpus, writ of, 389
Habere in bonis, 37
Habitatio, 164, 227
Hadrian, 40, 44, 60, 383
— council of, 41
Hæretici, 54, 57, 79
Hagiotheodoritus, 65
Hasta, 19, 86
Hastæ duæ, 19
— Sabinæ, 2
Hanbold, 67
Heedlessness, 325
Heimbach, 67
Heredis institutio, 185
Hereditas, 12, 85, 178
— ab intestato, 94, 178, 242, 306
— acceptance of, 195
— conditions respecting, 188
— damnosa, 195, 214
— definition of, 228
— division of, 187
— ex testamento, 94, 178, 179, 228
— fideicommissaria, 94, 213, 237, 239, 240
— jacens, 81
— partition of, 296
— pers. vicem sustinet, 178, 188
— repudiation, 196
— slave of, 264
Hereditatis aditio, 127, 194, 195, 234, 296
— expilatæ crimen, 329
— petitio, 196, 235, 253, 367, 373, 390, 392, 407
— repudiatio, 196, 235
Heres, 178, 231, 306
— action for and against, 382, 408
— alternative, 333
— entitled to quarta Falcidia, 373
— ex asse, 218
— extraneus, 194, 234
— fiduciarius, 240
— joint, 333
— necessarius, 193, 234, 257
— solus et necessarius, 108, 186, 188
— suus, 190, 242, 306
— — ab intestato, 183
— — et necessarius, 194, 234, 244
— three classes of, 93, 234
— voluntary, 194
Heretics, v. Hæretici

F F

INDEX.

Hermaphroditus, 80
Hermogenianus, 50, 58, 72
Herus, 178
Hexabiblus, 66
Hispala Fecenia, 246
History of Roman law, 1
Homicide, 15, 400
Honorarium, 290
Honorius, 43, 53, 54
Horatii, family of, 76
Horatius, 17
Hortensius, 19
Hostis, 21, 75
Hotchpot, 309
House, 83
— inviolability of, 339
Hugo, 71
Humanistes, 70
Huns, 56, 58
Husband, action for dowry by, 368
— liability as to dowry, 298, 368
Hypatius, 57
Hypotheca, 93, 165, 228, 259, 361, 383
— privileged, 362

Iberians, 1
Idolators, 57
Ignominia, 396
Ignorantia, 87
Illustres, 52, 247, 326
Imagines majorum, 22
Immixtio, 194, 234
Immovables, v. Res immobiles
Imprudentia, 329
Impetratio, v. Postulatio
Imperator, 39
Imperitia, 325
Imperium, 4, 15, 22, 23, 40, 47, 62, 344, 352, 393
— meaning of, 94
— merum, 335
— mixtum, 335
Impotent, 116
Improbus, 229
— fur, 324
Impubes, 81
In causa caduci, 43, 202, 239
Incestuosi, 78
Incestus, 77, 112, 120, 186
Incola, 79
Incurables, 81
Indebiti solutio, v. Solutio
Indignus, 229
Infamia, 79, 133, 288, 291, 316, 349, 369, 411, 412
— effects of, 257, 301, 387, 399
Infans, 80, 138
Infantiæ proximus, 80, 138
Infantry, 6
Infirmitas, 80
Infitiatio, 396
Infortiatum, 69

Ingenuus, 3, 63, 75, 103, 135, 245, 250, 309, 353, 401
Inheritance, v. Hereditas
In judicio, 94
In jure, 94
— — cedens, 142
— — cessio, 13, 16, 24, 93, 95, 104, 142, 351, 365
— — — of usufruct, 163
Injuria, 14, 297, 317, 324, 402, 412
— atrox, 325
— kinds of, 326
— release from liability for, 305
In jus vocatio, v. Vocatio
In libertatem proclamare, 103, 104
Innkeeper, liability of, 330, 403
Innominati contractus, v. Contract
Inquilinus, 53, 103, 281
Insane, v. Furiosus
Insolidum liability, 332
— obligations, 333
Institor, 285, 333, 375
Institutes, 59
— of Callistratus, 60
— — Florentinus, 60, 102
— — Gaius, 45
— — Justinian, 59, 64, 68, 73, 99
— — Marcian, 60
— — Paul, 60
— — Ulpian, 60
Institutio, 185
— ad cert. temp., 188
— ex re certa, 187
— heredis, 185, 231
— pura, 188
— sub conditione, 188
Institutions, civil and political, 2
Institutiones, 47, 59
Instrumenta, 83, 88, 356
— domestica, 88
— privata, 88
— publica, 88
Instrumentum, 206
— ad probat. matrim., 110
— dotale, 110
— publice confect., 362
Insulæ, 83
Intellectus possidendi, 145
Intellectum, 80
Intentio, 28, 96, 342, 343, 366, 404
— bonæ fidei, 374
— certa, 262, 369, 370
— civilis, 349
— effect of clausula doli in, 384
— — exceptio doli on, 372
— incerta, 293, 369, 370, 373
— in factum, 348, 405
— in jus, 293, 348
— interpretation of, 205, 385
— of action in rem, 404
— — — personam, 404
— plus petitio in, 370
— quantum of, 366

INDEX.   427

Intentio, set off in, 373
— stricti juris, 374
Intention, 145, 321, 324, 327, 329, 395, 402
Intercedere, 274
Intercessio, 10, 23, 36, 274, 289, 316
Intercessor, 274
Interdicere, 33
Interdictio aquæ et ig., 118, 123
Interdictum, 34, 48, 97, 388, 411
— acquirendæ poss., 221, 389
— adipiscendæ poss., 155, 394, 411
— classification of, 388, 411
— conservandæ poss., 221
— de aqua quotid., 164
— — cloacis, 164
— — fonte, 164
— — itinere act. pri., 164
— — liberis duc., 389
— — — exhib., 389
— — libero exhib., 389
— — liberto exhib., 389
— — migrando, 315
— — precario, 294, 391
— — ripis, 164, 389
— — tabulis exhib., 218
— duplex, 155, 392, 394, 411
— effect of, 393
— exhibitorium, 388, 392, 394
— mixed, 392
— origin of, 97, 388, 411
— personale, 393
— possessorium, 223, 358, 389, 390, 411
— — quasi, 359
— procedure in time of Gaius, 393
— — — — — Justinian, 388, 393
— prohibitorium, 97, 388, 392, 395, 396
— quam heredit., 392, 411
— quem fundum, 392, 411
— — usumfruct., 392, 411
— quod legat., 219, 241, 390
— quorum bonor., 250, 253, 310, 389, 394, 411
— recuperandæ poss., 155, 221, 389, 392, 411
— restipulatio of, 393
— restitutorium, 388, 389, 392, 394
— retinendæ poss., 155, 389, 390, 411
— Salvianum, 284, 315, 390, 411
— — utile, 390
— sectorium, 353, 390
— simplex, 392, 411
— sponsio of, 393
— unde vi, 164, 227, 391, 411
— uti possidetis, 84, 164, 229, 390, 392, 394, 395, 411
— utile, 164, 391
— utrubi, 84, 164, 171, 227, 391, 392, 394, 395, 411
— veluti possessorium, 164
Interest, v. Usuræ
Interment, right of, 388
International law, 5, 100, 134

International treaties, 18
Interpellatio, 299
Interpretatio, 22
— juris, 27
Interrex, 41
Interrogatio in jure, 355
Intestacy, partial, 122
Intestabiles, 183, 230
Intestate succession, 63, 242, et seq.
Inventory of tutor, 126
Ionian race, 1
Irnerius, 68
Isodorus, 64
Islands, 148, 221
Issue, joinder of, 355
Italian cities, free, 21
Italy, division of, 44
— subjugation of, 19, 35, 46, 56, 57, 58, 62, 67, 140
Iter, 157
Ives of Beauvais, 68

Jacobus, 69
Javolenus, 42, 44
Jettison, 155
Jews, 54, 57, 79, 112
John, 57, 59, 60
— Lascaris, 66, 70
— Nomophylax, 65
— of Antioch, 60, 66
Jovianus, 54
Judex (v. also Judices), 15, 18, 23, 29, 32, 48, 51, 335, 337, 340
— appointment of, 336
— choice of, 94
— duties of, 411
— kinds of, 95, 96, 335
— office of, 94, 404
— punishment of, 398, 401
— qui litem suam facit, 329, 402
Judicatum solvi, v. Cautio
Judicatus, 77, 353
Judicem ejerare, 94
— sumere, 94
Judices, v. Judex
— in albo relati, 32
— judgment of several, 356
— lists of, 32, 40
— majores, 48, 49
— pedanei, 48, 49, 98
— selecti, 32, 48
Judicia absolutoria, 350
— arbitraria, 350
— bonæ fidei, 349
— capitalia, 399, 412
— duplicia, 18
— extraordinaria, 30, 47, 49, 50, 96, 98, 266, 357, 399, 404, 412
— imperio continentia, 351
— legitima, 304, 351
— ordinaria, 30, 47, 96, 341, 357, 404
— publica, 399, 412

Judicia stricti juris, 349
Judicial authority, organisation of, 357
— power, 7, 23, 36, 49, 62
Judicium, 15, 28, 36, 47, 62, 94, 96, 98, 335, 349, 351, 358
— animi, 80, 127
— calumniæ, 394, 396
— Cascellianum, 395
— contrarium, 397
— fructuarium, 395
— imperio continens, 356
— legit., v. Legitimum
— quadruplex, 19
— secutorium, 395
Judgment, ex æquo et bono, 367
— mode of denying, 386
— — — reviewing, 357
Julian, Emp., 54
Juliani novell. epit., 60
Julianus, 41, 42, 44, 54, 60, 64, 72, 373, 390
Jumenta, 279
Jura, 56, 58, 100, 225, 354
— in bonis, 107
Juris contentio, 28
— interpretatio, 27
— præcepta, 100, 134
— prudentia, 27, 38, 48, 100, 134
— vinculum, 89, 301, 311
Juris-consults, 22, 26, 27, 36, 39, 41
— classification of works of, 47
Jurisdictio, 15, 19, 23, 47, 62, 97, 335, 340, 352, 355, 369, 393
— meaning of, 94
Jurisperiti, 27
Jurisprudents, 27, 41
Jurists, 58, 63, 65
Jury, 29, 32, 36, 95
Jus (v. also Law), 15, 47, 73, 94, 96, 98, 134
— abutendi, 145, 156, 161
— accessionis, 147
— adcrescendi, 184, 189, 225
— ad rem, 89
— Ædilium, 34
— Ælianum, 27
— and judicium, 335
— antiquum, 43, 203
— aureorum annul., 104
— caduca vind., 43, 201, 239
— capiendi ex. test., 42, 106, 182, 186, 202, 231
— civile, 20, 22, 62, 100, 134
— — Flavianum, 19
— — Papirianum, 7
— civitatis, 20, 75
— commune, 245, 308
— constituere, 40, 158
— definition of, 100
— deliberandi, 195
— dicere, 18, 33
— distrahendi, 362
— fruendi, 145, 161

Jus gentium, 24, 25, 33, 38, 76, 86, 90, 91, 93, 103, 221
— — definition of, 101
— honorarium, 33
— honorum, 20, 257
— imperfectum, 171
— in personam, 89
— in re, 89
— in rem, 89
— Italicum, 21, 46, 82, 92, 140, 165
— Latii, 21, 46
— latinitatis, 21, 35
— liberorum, 42, 46, 50. 52, 246
— luminum, 158
— moribus constit., 102
— naturale, 100, 102
— non scriptum, 27, 36, 102, 134
— operarum servi, 227
— optimum, 20
— — legati, 198
— pascendi, 157
— personarum, 102
— poenitendi, 293
— postliminii, 82, 103, 118, 168, 183, 242
— potestatis, 118
— prætorium, 34, 44, 134
— principale, 53
— privatum, 2, 4, 8, 20, 24, 33, 37, 40, 49, 52, 55, 57, 62, 100, 101, 102, 123, 134
— projiciendi, 158
— prospectus, 158
— protegendi, 158
— publice respondendi, 41
— publicum, 2, 7, 15, 22, 35, 47, 48, 62, 100, 123, 134
— Quiritium, 8, 20, 30, 36, 38, 101
— regenerationis, 104
— respondendi, 102
— sacrum, 2, 8, 15, 23, 37, 49, 51, 62, 100, 123
— scriptum, 8, 22, 30, 44, 101, 134
— suffragii, 20, 21, 257
— superficiarium, 228, 283
— tollendi, 368
— tripertitum, 179
— trium liberorum, 246
— utendi, 145, 161
— vendendi, 362
— veteris Latii, 46
— vindicandi, 145
Jusjurandum, (v. also Oath), 88, 396; 397, 411
— in judicio, 356, 364
— injure, 355, 364
— — litem, 350, 356
— pro calumnia, 397
Jussum, 73, 100, 134
Jussus, 344, 350, 369, 378, 394, 398, 407, 412
— domini, 375
Justa causa, v. Causa
Justæ nuptiæ, v. Marriage

INDEX. 429

Justice, public administration of, 95, 340
Justin, 57
Justinian, 40, 41, 43, 54, 57, 72, 76
— buildings of, 58
— definition of action by, 358
— laws of, 58, 63, 67
— life of, 57
— titles of, 99
— wars of, 57
Justitia, 100, 134
Justum initium, 167
— matrimonium, 77, 109, 136
Justus titulus, 166

King, v. Rex
Knights, 5, 22, 26, 32, 34
— ring of, 104
Koran, 66

Labeo, 4, 41, 72, 90, 119, 216, 320
Laboulaye, 23
Lacedemonians, 102
Læsio, 280
Laferrière, 68, 69
Lance, 2, 8, 16, 86, 104
Land of colonies, 20
Landlord, rights of, 363, 390
Lanfranc, 18
Lares, 5, 114
Lascaris, 66, 70
Latifundia, 282
Latin race, 1
Latinæ coloniæ, 21
Latini, 7, 21
— coloni, 21, 50, 76
— juniani, 46, 50, 75, 76, 106, 135, 186
— nominis coloniæ, 21
— veteres, 20
Latium, cities of, 20
— vetus, 7, 20
Laudemium, 282
Law, v. Jus.
— basis of, 73
— Byzantine, 63, 64, 65, 66
— civil and prætorian, conflict of, 38
— consequences of, 74
— definition of, 74, 134
— division of, 73, 134
— ecclesiastical, 63, 66
— elements producing, 173
— epitome by Hermogenian, 51
— Georgian, 64
— history of, by Pomponius, 45
— idea of, 73
— Isaurian, 64
— Lombardian, 68
— modern German school of, 73
— Rhodian, 64
— schools of, 39, 41, 42, 54, 60, 61, 64, 67, 68, 69, 70
— state of under Justinian, 58

Lawyers, education of, 27, 59, 61
Legacy, v. Legatum
Legal forms, object of, 86
— studies, 59
Legatarius, 236
— alternative, 333
— demonstratio of, 238
— mortgage in favour of, 363
— partiarius, 208, 214, 237, 240
Legatee, v. Legatarius
Legati, Cæsaris, 39
— proconsulis, 26
Legatum, 43, 197, 218, 223
— additions to, or losses of, 206, 212, 237
— ademptum, 211, 238
— as a mode of succession, 94
— by whom may be made, 236
— certum constit., 297
— changes by Justinian, 198
— charitable, 365
— conditional, 200, 209, 219, 238
— conjunctim, 201, 239
— contrasted with fideicommissum, 199, 235, 240
— debiti, 205
— definition of, 197, 235
— denial of liability to pay, 297, 365
— destitutum, 201
— determination of, 208
— dies cedit of, 199
— — venit of, 199
— disjunctim, 201, 239
— dotis, 205
— ereptitium, 201, 211
— extinction of, 211
— generis, 207, 237
— illegal, 209
— impossibile, 209
— in causa caduci, 43
— incertum constit., 297
— informalities in, 208
— in singulos annos, 162
— invalidity of, 238
— inutile, 205
— interdict in respect of, 390
— irritum, 201
— joint and separate, 201
— lapsed, 43
— liberationis, 205, 237
— limitation of, 208
— mode of leaving, 236
— nominis, 207, 237
— of house, 206
— — immovables, 84
— — liberty, 216
— — movables, 84
— — peculium, 206
— — right of way, 373
— — usufruct, 162
— operarum servi, 164
— optionis, 207, 237
— paid by mistake, 297

Legatum per damnationem, 198, 202, 207, 218, 235, 297
— per præceptionem, 198, 202, 218, 235
— per vindicationem, 142, 197, 202, 218, 235
— persons capable of receiving, 207, 209
— pœnæ nomine, 210, 238
— pro non scripto, 201, 202, 208
— release of to heir, 302
— revocation of, 205, 238
— sinendi modo, 198, 202, 218, 235
— subject to negative condition, 209
— — — term, 210
— things which may be left as a, 200, 204, 207, 237
— to posthumous extranei, 208
— — slave, 199
— — — of heir, 176, 209
— — uncertain persons, 208
— who may be charged with, 209, 236
Leges (v. also Lex), 22, 42, 56, 58
— agrariæ, 30
— barbarorum, 56
— conductionis, 283
— curiatæ, 7
— emptionis, vendit., 280
— frumentariæ, 31
— judiciariæ, 32
— Julia et Papia, 42, 45, 112, 113, 170, 199, 200, 201, 213
— Juliæ, 27, 353
— — judiciariæ, 354, 404
— novæ, 42
— publiliæ, 19
— regiæ, 7
— sacræ, 10
— tabellariæ, 35
— Valeriæ, 9
— XII Tabularum, 10
Legions, service in, 46
Legis actiones, v. Actio legis
— characteristics of, 334
— decline of, 95
— equality of litigants in, 342
— organisation of, 335
— procedure under the, 335
— replaced by formulæ, 95
— system of, 95, 334
Legislative power, 7, 22, 35, 48, 62
Legitima, 234
— conventio, 295
— portio, v. Portio
Legitimatio, 77, 113, 114, 136
Legitimum judicium, 263, 356, 385
— tempus, 277
Lentulus, 216
Leo, on mortgages, 362
— the Isaurian or Iconoclast, 64
— — philosopher, 64, 65, 113
Levis nota, 79
Lex (v. also Leges), 10, 13, 22, 24, 36, 93, 101, 142

Lex Æbutia, 27, 29, 47, 86, 95, 321, 337, 342, 404
— Ælia Sentia, 43, 103, 105, 106, 107, 113, 135, 213, 361
— annua, 33, 36, 44
— Apuleia de sponsu, 272, 273
— — majestatis, 31
— Aquilia, 260, 271, 273, 324, 329, 366, 402
— Atilia, 125, 128, 138
— Atinia, 36, 166
— Aurelia, 32
— bonorum ven., 256
— Calpurnia, 27, 341
— — de repet., 31
— Canuleia, 19, 77
— Cassia tabell., 35
— Censoria, 339
— Cincia, 55, 170, 171, 203, 383
— Claudia, 129, 139
— commissoria, 280, 295, 362
— Cornelia de edictis, 33
— — — falsis, 31, 183, 400
— — — sicariis, 31, 325, 327, 400, 402
— — — sponsu, 272, 273
— — judiciaria, 32
— — testamentaria, 31, 118, 183, 220, 400
— curiata, 3, 7, 8, 23, 26, 36, 40, 115
— decemviralis, 10
— Dei, 55
— de imperio, 41
— de responsis prudent., 45, 54
— Fabia de plag., 31, 401
— Falcidia, 170, 171, 192, 211, 214, 234, 239, 383
— Furia, 171, 251
— — Caninia, 43, 107, 108, 135
— — de sponsu, 272, 273, 333, 338, 382
— — test., 27, 211, 338
— Fusia camina, 108
— Gabinia tab., 35
— Gondoboda, 57
— Hortensia, 19, 32, 101
— — de nund., 340
— Hostilia, 379
— imperii, 41
— Julia, 86, 111, 166, 224, 354, 383
— — agraria, 31
— — caducaria, 251
— — de adult., 173, 400
— — — ambitu, 401
— — — annona, 401
— — — bonis cedend., 256
— — — civitate, 34
— — — marit. ordin., 42
— — — residuis, 401
— — — vi, 324, 391, 400
— — et Papia Poppæa, 42, 213
— — — Titia, 125, 138
— — judiciaria, 27, 357, 382
— — majestatis, 399

INDEX. 431

Lex Julia peculatus, 400
— — repetundarum, 401
— — testamentaria, 201
— — Velleia, 184
— Junia Norbana, 44, 46, 101, 105, 106, 113, 135, 201, 213
— — Velleia, 184, 230
— Lætoria, 129
— Lectoria, 129
— Licinia de modo ag., 30
— — Mucia de civ., 31
— Livia, 32
— Luctatia de vi., 31
— Mensia, 103
— mancipii, 24
— Marcia, 338
— Maria de ambitu, 31
— Papia Poppæa, 42, 52, 77, 129, 131, 139, 142, 186, 202, 203, 213, 218, 236, 248, 253, 308
— Papiria, 7
— Petillia Papiria, 19
— Petronia, 109
— Pinaria, 336
— Plætoria, 129
— Plautia, 166
— — de civit., 34
— Pompeia de parricid., 400
— — jud., 32
— prima Servilia, 32
— privata, 362
— Publilia, 7, 272, 273, 338
— Quinavicennaria, 129
— Regia, 3, 7, 40
— Romana, 56, 68, 71
— — Burgund., 56
— — Visigoth., 56
— Scribonia, 159, 160, 226
— Sempronia agra., 30
— — frum., 31
— — jud., 32
— Servilia jud., 32
— — repetund., 31
— Silia, 27, 341
— Theodosiana, 56
— Thoria agraria, 31
— Tribunicia, 7
— Valeria Horatia, 17
— Visellia, 101
— Voconia, 171, 185, 212, 213, 231, 244
Libel, 14
Libellus, 168, 276, 360, 399, 412
— appel., 357
— citat., 357
—· convent., 366
— repud., 113
Liberalia studia, 79, 290
Liber legum, 56
Liberatio, 205
Liberi, 75, 103
Libertas, 75, 78, 336
— definition of, 102, 135
— directa, 104

Libertas fideicommissaria, 104, 107
— imperfect, 105
— tacit revocation of, 187
Libertinus, v. Freedman
Libertus, v. Freedman
— orcinus, 104, 255
Liberty, v. Libertas
Libripens, 90, 117, 179
Licinius, 50, 51
— Rufinus, 331
Lictor, 1, 2, 3, 41, 86
— libertatis, 365
Lignum, 216
Linea recta, 78
— transversa, 78
Lis contestata, 356
— inchoata, 356
Litem ampliare, 356
— contestari, 340
— denuntiare, 278
— suam facere, 329
Litigation, restraints on groundless, 395, 411
Litis æstimatio, 380
— contestatio, 304, 328, 333, 340, 354, 355, 357, 358, 360, 372, 382, 383, 385, 390, 391, 408
— translatio, 356
Littera Bononiensis, 68
Litteræ apostoli, 357
— dimissoriæ, 357
Litteris contract, v. Obligatio
Livy, 7, 40, 246
Locatio conductio, 38, 91, 93, 281, 314
— — extinction of, 283
— — operarum, 281, 284, 314
— — operis, 281, 284, 314
— — pacts modifying, 283
— — rerum, 281, 283, 314
— — tacit renewal of, 283
Locator, 281
— obligations of, 283, 298, 314
Loire, 56
Lombards, 67
Lothaire, 67
Luceres, 2, 3
Lucumo, 2, 3
Lunar year, 5
Lunatic, protection of, 363
— set off against, 373
Lustrum, 5
Lyons, 45

Macedo, 377
Macedon, conquest of, 36
Macer, 47
Mackeldey, 71
Macrinus, 43
Magic arts, 14, 15
Magister, 256
— equitum, 9, 118
— militum, 52, 118
— navis, 333

INDEX

Magistracies, imperial, 39, 48, 51
Magistracy, dual system of, 23
Magistrate, kinds of, 95, 96, 98
— position of, 94, 404
— provincial, 52
— selection of, 3
— tenure of office of, 22
Magistratum appellare, 23
— edicta, 48, 101
Magistratus pedarii, 22
— pop. Rom., 101
Majestas, 399
Majority, 81
Malaga, tables of, 45
Maleficium, 91, 311, 320
Mancipatio, 8, 12, 13, 20, 24, 50, 63, 77, 82, 84, 93, 115, 117, 141
— imag. famil., 179
— noxali causa, 77, 378
Mancipia, 2, 53
Mancipium, 8, 24, 37, 50, 77, 78, 82, 92, 93, 103, 117, 123
Mandans, 287, 316
— liability of, 316
Mandare actiones, 301
Mandatarius, 270, 287, 316, 319
— liability of, 298, 316
— payment to, 290
Mandator pecuniæ cred., 333
Mandatum, 38, 91, 287, 316, 379
— analogy to the fidejussio, 289, 316
— extinction of, 290, 316
— generale, 288
— illegal, 289
— immoral, 289
— kinds of, 288, 316
— of slave, 377
— principis, 40
— quasi contracts resembling, 296, 317, 367
— rules involved in societas, 285, 315
— speciale, 288
Manes, 144
Manners and customs, 8, 24, 38
Manual of civil law, 27
Manuals of Byzantine emperors, 64
Manu asserere, 336
— capere, 8
Manumissor extraneus, 117, 119, 250
Manumissio, 16, 75, 104, 105, 108, 142, 171
Manus, 8, 13, 24, 37, 50, 77, 78
— dissolution of, 117
— injectio, 11, 256, 338, 339, 351, 353
— modes of acquiring, 117
Manuum consertio, 13, 16, 86, 335, 336
Marcianus, 47, 50, 53, 54, 59, 60
Marcellus, 41, 54, 104
Marcus Aurelius, 40, 41, 42, 45, 50, 55, 130, 189, 277, 354, 372, 373, 383
Marinus, 64
Marital power, 13, 117
Marius, 6, 34

Marriage, 15, 76, 77, 109, 136
— dissolution of, 112, 136, 368
— effects of, 112
— impediments to, 111
— law of, 109
— nullity of, 112
— requisites to, 110, 136
— second, 113
— subsequent, 114
Mars, field of, 6
Martinus Gosia, 69
Master, power of, 50
Mater (v. also Mother), 42
— familias, 76, 80, 113, 136
Mathematicians, 54
Matrimonium, v. Marriage
Matrona, 113
Matthew Blastares, 66
Maxentius, 50
Maximin, 50
Maximinian, 50, 51
Membranæ, 88
Memoria damnata, 399
Menas, 60
Mensularii, 276
Mente captus, 81
Merces, 281
Merx, 277
Metallum, 143
Metus, 346, 360, 361
— action in respect of, 366
— exception based on, 384
Michael Attaliota, 65
Micron, 65
Military administration, 98
— service, 6
Ministeriani, 52
Ministerium, 331
Minors, immovables of, 130
— protection of interests of, 129, 361, 363, 379
Miscelliones, 42
Missio in possessionem, 97, 256, 352, 353, 361, 363, 393
— — custodiæ causa, 355
Mistake, correction of, 371
Modestinus, 41, 47, 54, 72
— on set off, 371
— — the mandatum, 298
Mœcianus, 41, 45
Money, 8, 277
Mons Cœlius, 2
— Quirinalis, 2
— Sacer, 10
Montpellier, 69, 70
Monumenta, 87
Mora, 299, 318, 368, 398
— ex persona, 299, 318
— ex re, 299, 318
Mores majorum, 22
Mortgage, 361
— indivisibility of, 363
— mutual obligation in, 382

Mortgage, natural obligation in, 382
— privileged, 362
— property capable of, 363
— secret, 362
— tacit, 131, 363, 368
Mortgagee, protection of, 361, 390
— rights of, 362
Mortis causa capio, 171, 223
Moses, law of, 55
Mosaic et Rom., &c., collatio, 55
Mother, succession of, 246
— succession to, 52, 247, 307
Movables, v. Res mobiles
Mutiana cautio, 209, 238
Mucius, Quintus, 27, 45
Mulcta, 355
Municeps, 21, 79
Municipia, 21, 25, 45
Mutual consent, 90
Mutus, v. Dumb
Mutuum, 38, 90, 162, 258, 260, 275, 276, 311, 377
— accessory clauses to, 292
— dissolution of, 302

Narses, 58, 61
Nasica, Caius Scipio, 26
Natural law, v. Jus
— state, 75
Naturales liberi, 113
Nautica pecunia, 258
Neapolis, 46
Negligentia, 285, 297, 318, 324
Negotiorum gestio, 296, 317
— gestor, 298, 380
Neratius, 41, 92, 331, 360
— Priscus, 42, 44
Nero, 46, 47
Nerva, 40, 42, 44, 365
Nexi, 8, 19, 24, 338
Nexum, 8, 13, 24, 38, 77, 78, 90, 93, 260, 311, 312, 362
Nexu vinctus, 77
Nexus, 77
Nicæa, council of, 51
Nicetas, 64
Niebuhr, 1, 2, 3, 4, 45, 97, 124, 245
Niger, 46
Nisi restituat clause, 344, 346, 350, 394, 407
Nobilissimi, 52
Nobility, new, 52
Nomen, 89, 91, 275
— novation of, 303
— transcriptitium, 91, 275, 276
Nomina arcaria, 275
Nominati contractus, 292
Nomocanon, 60, 66
Non liquet, 356
Nonsuit, 370
Notati, 79
Novæ leges, 42

Novatio, 91, 263, 275, 276, 287, 303, 319, 332, 356, 358
— by conditional stipulation, 304
— effect of, 370, 385
— involuntary, 304, 351
Novellæ, 55, 56, 58, 59
Noverca, 112
Noxa, 13, 14, 91, 117, 311
— definition of, 377
Noxal action, 15, 377
Noxia, 377
Nuda detentio, 92, 220
— pactio, 317
— proprietas, 162
— — of slave, 186
— repromissio, 266
— traditio, 222
Nudum pactum, 295
Numa Pompilius, 5
Nummarii, 276
Nuncupatio, 13, 24, 90, 179
Nundinæ, 340
Nunneries, 62
Nuntius, 288
Nuptiæ, v. Marriage
Nurus, 112

Oath, v. Jusjurandum
— action in respect of, 364, 384
— by way of security, 381
— exception in respect of, 385
— extrajudicial, 295, 364
— of freedmen, 254
— of fidei-commissarius, 215
— of heir, 217
— of trustee, 213
— sanctity of, 5
Oblatio, 302, 319
— curiæ, 114
Obligatio (v. also Contract), 89, 257, 311
— acquired through others, 264, 300
— acquisition of, 318
— action for enforcing, 336
— alternative, 332, 403
— civilis, 38, 90, 301, 311, 319, 356
— condition attaching to, 188
— consensu, 38, 50, 91, 277, 288, 305, 311, 314, 330, 367
— damni infecti, 337
— definition of by Justinian, 89, 311
— — — Paul, 89
— dissolution of, 301, 319
— elements of, 332
— enforcement of, 338
— evictionis nomine, 278
— ex contractu, 91, 311
— ex delicto (maleficio), 91, 311, 401
— extinction of, 91
— facere, 333
— honoraria, 90, 311
— in solidum, 263, 332
— joint, 403
— kinds of, 311

G G

Obligatio, litteris, 38, 91, 274, 292, 302, 303, 311, 313, 319, 333
— naturalis, 38, 90, 94, 264, 295, 301, 304, 305, 311, 317, 330, 332, 378, 382, 403
— nature of, 257
— novatio of, 303
— prætoria, 38, 90, 301, 311
— pro rata, 263
— quasi ex contractu, 90, 91, 296, 311, 317, 356, 405
— — — delicto, 91, 311, 320, 329, 402
— re, 38, 90 110, 258, 292, 311
— revival of, 306
— several, 332, 403
— soluta, 357
— source of, 90, 257, 311
— stricti juris, 332, 377
— transference of, 91, 200, 301, 319
— ultro citroque, 91, 314, 372
— unilateral, 377
— verbis, 24, 90, 260, 266, 270, 292, 302, 311, 312, 332, 369
Obsequia, 106
Observatio, 353
Obsignatio, 302, 319
Occupancy at will, 294
Occupatio, 93, 140, 146, 221
Octavius Cæsar, 19, 35, 115
Odilo, 69
Odofredus, 67
Officiales, 354
Officium, 259
— judicis, 372, 397
— pietatis, 191
Olympic games, 46
Omissio diligentiæ, 297
Omission of children in will, 230
Onus probandi, v. Proof
Operæ, 107
— officiales, 331
Operarum jurata prom. lib., 260, 312
Opiniones, 102
Optimum jus, v. Jus
Optio, 207
— tutoris, 128
Orbi, 42, 52, 63, 186, 202
Orcinus, v. Libertus
Ordo judiciorum, 48
Ordinaria judicia, v. Judicia
Origin of Rome, 1
Orleans, 70
Orthodoxi, 79
Ostrogoths, 56, 57, 131
Outrage, 402
Ovilia, 35
Ownership, v. Dominium
— at time of Twelve Tables, 140, 220
— — — — Gaius and Ulpian, 140
— — — — Justinian, 144
— definition of, 220
— vesting of, 398
Oxford, 69

Pact (v. also Pactum), 38, 50, 291, 316, 403
— accessory, 280, 283
— oath, a kind of, 385
— personal, 411
— prætorian, 38
— servitudes created by, 158
— simple, 330
Pactio, 258, 291
— nuda, 317
Pactum (v. also Pact), 258, 291
— adjectum, 291
— — ex continenti, 291, 300, 317
— — — intervallo, 290
— conventum, 90, 291, 330
— de dote constituenda, 295, 317
— — non petendo, 305, 387
— in personam, 388
— — rem, 387
— legitimum, 295, 305, 317
— ne vendere liceat, 175, 295, 362
— nudum, 295
— prætorium, 294, 317
Padua, 46
Pagan rites, abolition of, 54, 118
Pagani, 47, 51, 62
Palatine hill, 2
Palatini, 52
Pandectæ, 47
— of Justinian, 59
— Florentinæ, 68
Pannormia, 68
Papiani responsa, 56
Papinian, 42, 45, 46, 50, 54, 55, 59, 61, 72, 210, 215, 217, 305, 384
— responses of, 56
Papinianistes, 45, 61
Papirius, 45, 71
— Carbo, 35
— Cœlius Caldus, 35
— Justus, 50
— Sextus, 7, 26
Parapherna, 173, 328
Paris, library, 64
— University of, 69
Paris-cidium, 9
Parricidium, 400
Pars virilis, 248, 263, 308, 332
Partes secanto, 11
Partitio, 207, 237
Partnership, v. Societas
Pasquier, 70
Pater, 2, 42
— familias, 2, 8, 76, 136, 178, 402
— — bonus, 161
— — diligentiss., 283, 298
— — liability for acts of others, 330, 402
— — non-liability of, 375
— — permission to sue, 364
Paternal power, v. Potestas
Patres, 2
— conscripti, 4
— maj. and min. gent., 4
Patria potestas, v. Potestas

INDEX. 435

Patriæ pater, 39
Patricians, v. Patricii
Patrician consuls, 9
Patricii, 2, 3, 51
— privilege of, 118
Patron, 3, 15, 25
— form of exception against, 385
— guardianship of, 248
— succession to freedmen, 248, 308
— power of assigning freedmen, 249, 308
— permission to sue, 364, 397, 406, 412
Patronage, rights of, 106, 135, 245, 251
Patronus, v. Patron
— causæ, 397
Paulus Emilius, 36
— Julius, 46, 50, 53, 54, 55, 62, 72, 87, 121
— — Institutes of, 60
— — notes on Papinian, 50, 59
— — on interdicts, 389, 392
— — — injuria, 327
— — — mortgages, 361
— — — pacts, 292
— — — the revival of obligations, 306
— — — theft, 321
— — — wills, 217
— — sentences of, 46, 50, 55, 56, 73
Pauperies, 14, 379
Pauperistes, 69
Pavia, 68, 70
Pawnor, rights of, 312
Pays de coutume, 71
— — droit écrit, 71
— — loi Romaine, 71
Peculatus, 400
Peculium, 53, 81, 85, 176, 228, 371
— adventitium, 52, 179, 183, 228
— castrense, 40, 50, 176, 180, 181, 183, 228, 230, 363
— fraudulent division of, 376
— legacy of, 206, 238
— profectitium, 176, 228
— profit resulting from, 376
— quasi-castrense, 52, 176, 183, 228, 230
— of slave, 109, 206
— succession to, 245, 308
Pecunia, 8, 83, 295
— accepta relata, 275, 313
— certa, 275, 276
— data, 275
— expensa lata, 275, 313
— fœnebris, 299
— nautica, 258
— stipulata, 275
Pegasians, 42
Pegasus, 42
Pelasgians, 1
Penalty, actions in respect of, 365, 383, 398
— double, 396, 411
— for crimes, 400
Pensio, 281, 283
People, the, 22
Pepo, 68

Per æs et libram, 8, 12, 13, 362
Peregrinus, 21, 29, 46, 75, 349, 379
— formula for, 343
Perfectissimi, 52
Performance, 91, 302, 319, 332
— demand of, 299
Periculum, 279, 314, 358
Perizonius, 1
Permutatio, 277, 292, 294, 367
— status, 122
Persians, 58, 62
Persecutio, 47, 303, 343
— hypothecaria, 361
— pigneratitia, 361
Persona, 8, 24, 37, 50, 63, 74, 76, 102, 134, 175
— alieni juris, 136
— capable of alienating, 228
— clara, 354
— divisions of, 102, 135
— excepta, 43, 203
— extinction of, 81
— fictitious, 74, 81
— incerta, 121, 184, 185, 230
— in respect of capacity, 135
— — — family, 135
— — — society, 135
— kinds of, 134
— loss of, 123
— natural, 74
— non-representation of, 175, 177
— of pupil, 126
— physical, 254
— privata, 254
— publica, 254
— sale of juridical, 256
— servilis, 75
— singularis, 74
— turpis, 79, 192
— vilis, 79
Personality of law, 56, 67, 68
— — rights, 89
Persons, v. Persona
Perugia, 70
Petitio, 303, 343
— hereditatis, v. Hereditatis
— — fideicommissaria, 219, 241
— — prætorian, 253
Petitions, 40
Petitor, 336
Petri excep. leg. Rom., 69
Philo, Q. Publilius, 7
Philosophy, Greek, 47
— schools of, 44
Philoxenes, 64
Physician, liability of, 325, 329
Phocas, 64
Photius, 66
Pictures, 152, 221
Pigeons, 148, 221
Pignoris capio, v. Actio
— — origin of, 339
— — prætorian, 354, 363

436 INDEX.

Pignus, 38, 90, 93, 165, 228, 259, 312, 362
— implies traditio, 361
— obligations involved in, 302
— protection of, 361
— prætorium, 353, 354, 363
— sale of, 84, 362
Pisa, 68, 70
Place as an element in a contract, 369
Placentinus, 69
Plaintiff, non-possessor, 342
Plantatio, 151
Plautus, 129
Pleading, 38, 62, 171
Plebeians, v. Plebs
— political enfranchisement of, 335
Plebiscitum, 10, 17, 19, 21, 22, 32, 36, 42
— definition of, 101
Plebs, 3, 4, 5, 10, 22, 34
— secession of the, 9, 19, 324
Pliny, 18, 46
Pledgor and pledgee, liability of, 298, 362
Plus petitio, 205, 261, 366, 369, 383, 409
— — kinds of, 370, 409
Pœna, 395
Poiema, 65
Poison, administering, 15, 400
Police, 22
Poll tax, 36
Political law, 48, 51
Pollicitatio, 258
Polytheism, 49, 54
Pompey, 34, 35, 400
Pomponius, 7, 25, 26, 32, 41, 42, 44, 45, 85, 266
— on set off, 371
Pontifex Maximus, 8, 23, 24, 26, 39
Pontiffs, 5, 16, 37, 51, 54
— college of, 8, 19, 115, 335
Poor, guardians of, 51, 54
Popilius Rufus, 255
Popularis actio, 330
Populi fundi, 21
Populi-scitum, 101
Populum lustrare, 5
Populus Rom., 3, 81
— — Quirit., 2
Portio legitima, 192, 194, 212, 233, 240
Possessio, 12, 92, 145, 220, 228
— advantage of, 376, 391
— bonorum, v. Bonorum
— civilis, 92, 145
— corporalis, 145
— fact of, 92
— interdict to obtain, 389
— interim, 15, 336, 380, 392, 394, 395
— legal, 145, 153, 154, 220
— longi temporis, 388
— loss of, 154, 225
— lucrativa, 152
— naturalis, 145
— vi, clam, precario, 390
— physical, 145, 153, 220
— protection of, 353, 358, 359, 397

Possessio, prætorian, 145
— pro herede, 196
— quasi, 146, 164, 221, 227, 359, 391
— right of, 92, 145
— tacking of, 167
— vacua, 278
Possessor, 145, 394
— absence of, 360
— in good faith, 373, 398
— of freeman, 177
— of slave, 177
— plaintiff, 359
Postliminium, 118, 183, 230, 264
Postulatio, 257, 301
— actionis, 29, 48, 355, 358
— formulæ, 29
— judicii, 29
Postumus, 121
— alienus, 184, 208
— disinheriting of, 121, 184, 230
— suus, 184
— tutor of, 121
— Velleianus, quasi, 184, 230
Potestas, 8, 24, 37, 76
— abstinendi, v. Beneficium
— dissolution of, 137
— dominica, 108, 118, 136
— dominorum, 77
— marital, v. Manus
— meaning of, 136
— patria, 8, 11, 37, 52, 63, 77, 109, 118, 136, 255
— tribunicia, 23
Poverty, effect of, 399
Præceptores, 41
Præceptum commune, 134
Prædium, 84
— emphyteuticarium, 282
— italicum, 21, 34, 46, 63, 82, 140, 219
— provinciale, 21, 25, 46, 63, 82, 140, 165, 219, 360
— stipendiarium, 84
— tributorium, 84
Præfecti prætorio, 39, 52
Præfecturæ, 21, 25, 52, 58
Præfectus, 21
— ærarii, 43
— annonarum, 40
— at Constantinople, 54
— jure dicundo, 335
— prætorius, 39, 44, 49, 52, 58, 62, 98, 118
— urbi, 39, 49, 62
— vigilum, 40
Præjudicium, 343, 347, 356, 365
Præs, 340
— litis et vind., 266, 336, 340, 342
— sacramenti, 266, 340, 341
Præscriptio, 14, 53, 96, 160, 165, 222, 223, 331, 344, 359, 388, 402, 404
— annalis, 345
— as to set off, 373
— fori, 345

INDEX. 437

Præscriptio, in formula, 344
— interruption of 168
— longi temporis, 165, 345, 388
— longissimi temporis, 168, 223
— præjudicia, 345
— temporis, 345
— use of by plaintiff, 345
— — — — defendant, 345
Præmia patrum, 43
Præses provinciæ, 39, 49, 360
Præsides, 44
Præsumptio, 88
— juris, 88
— — et de jure, 88, 269
Præstare actiones, 301
Prætor, 17, 39, 49, 51, 62
— fideicommissarius, 44, 98, 213, 219
— peregrinus, 18, 25, 29, 33, 75, 101, 334, 341
— provincial, 25
— urbanus, 17, 22, 23, 25, 32, 33
Prætoria, 95
Prætorian conventions, 63
— succession, 242, 249, 306
Prætorium jus, v. Jus
Precarium, 294, 362, 390, 391
Preference, rights of, 362
Prescription, v. Prescriptio
Prerogativa, 6
Pretium, 277, 281
— justum, 281
— minus, 281
Priestly offices, election to, 3
Priests, 51
— Colleges, 5
— of Jupiter, 118
Principum placita, 101
Priority in respect of mortgages, 362
Prisoners, acting on behalf of, 379
Private law, v. Jus
— — Constantine's innovations in, 52
— — division of, 101, 134
— — objects of, 102
Privigna, 112
Probatio, v. Proof
Procedure, 335, 354, 370, 374
— systems of, 95
Prochiron, 64
— auctum, 66
Pro-consular power, 39
Pro-consuls, 26, 39
Proculeians, school of, 41
Proculus, 42, 44
Procuration, 268, 270, 301, 326
Procurator, 266, 268, 287, 316, 379
— iucapacity of, 387
— in rem suam, 274, 301, 319
— security by, 381
Procuratores Cæsaris, 39
Prodigus, 81, 129
— interdictus, 269
— natural liability of, 331
Produce, 152, 177, 221, 337, 407

Produce, civil, 161, 164, 226
— interim, 395, 398
— natural, 161, 226
— of animals, 148
Profanation, 144
Prohibited agreements, 295, 317
Proletarii, 6, 36
Prolytæ, 62
Promissio, 91, 260, 312
— nuda, 381
Promissor, liability of, 271, 299, 313
Promptuarium, 66
Prooemium of Institutes, 99
Proof, 87
— burden of, 88, 276, 277, 385
Property, acquisition of, 93, 141, 146, 165, 221, 222
— in litigation, 356
Proprætor, 26
Proprietas, v. Dominium
Proscriptio bonorum, v. Bonorum
Provinces, African, 56
— establishment of, 25, 35, 52
Provinciæ populi, 39, 84, 140
— Cæsaris, 39, 84, 140
Provincial governor, 26, 52
Provocatio, 23, 44
— ad pop., 9, 23, 31
Psellus, 66
Pubertas, 80, 81, 110, 128
Pubertati proximi, 80, 128, 138
Pubes, 81
Public law, v. Jus
— revenue, sources of, 36
— roads, 389
Publicani, 26, 339, 352
Publicatio, 286, 315
Publice profiteri, 26
— respondere, 26
Publicius, Quintus, 359
Publicola, Valerius, 9
Publilius Philo, 7
Publius Mucius Scævola, 27
Puhl, 67
Punic wars, 25
Pupillus, 127
— direct action against, 380
— incapacity of, 399
— infans, 126, 138, 265
— mortgage in favour of, 363
— natural obligation of, 331
— power of contracting, 127, 175, 269
— set off against, 373
Pydna, battle of, 36
Pyrenees, 56

Quæstio, 31
— de cland. conj., 31
— de homicid., 31
— de venef., 31, 400
— peculatus, 31
— perpetua, 31, 36

INDEX.

Quæstionum, Resp. et Def. of Papinian, 45
Quæstores, 31, 39
— ærarii, 9, 22, 26, 93, 353
— candidati, 39, 52
— parricidii, 9, 15, 23
— plebeii, 22
— sacri palatii, 52, 118
Quæstus, 285
Quarta Antonina, 116
— Falcidia, 191, 211, 213, 214, 219, 373
— legitima, 193
— Trebelliana, 214
Quasi agnatio, 184
— ex contractu, 296, 367, 375
— ex delicto, 329, 375, 402
— possessio, 146, 164, 221, 227, 391
— postumus, 184
— publica, 133
— pupillaris substitutio, 189
— traditio, 154, 222, 282
— usufruct, 160, 162, 227
Querela inoff. donat., 197, 235
— inoff. test., 185, 197, 235, 240, 252, 306
Questiones, 70
Quinquaginta decisiones, 59
Quinqueviri, 20, 25, 40
Quirinus, 2
Quirinal hill, 2
Quirites, 1, 46

Ramnenses, 3
Rank, 79
Ratification, 332, 375, 380
Ravenna, 56, 58, 67, 68
Re contract, v. Obligatio
— frui licere, 281, 283
— uti præstare, 281, 283
Real action, 362, 365, 367, 384, 398, 404, 407
— contract, v. Contract
— property, law of, 13
— rights, 89, 92, 93, 220, 336, 361, 364
Reciperatores, v. Recuperatores
Recipere, 294
Rector provinciæ, 49, 52, 98
Recuperatores, 18, 23, 26, 29, 335, 341, 343, 351, 393
Redemption clause, 280
Redhibitio, 279
Reditus, 53, 281
Registration, 86, 172, 224
Règle, 100
Regulæ, 47
— of Gaius, 45
— of Ulpian, 46, 55, 73
Rei com. admin., 296
Relatio, 357
Release, 92, 301, 302, 319
Relegatio, 118, 400
Religion, 57, 79, 81
Religious objects, protection of, 388

Religious rites, commentary of Labeo on, 4
— — Pagan, 54
Rem licere habere, 278, 281
— præstare, 278
— tradere, 278
Remancipatio, 361
Rent, 53, 281, 282
Renuntiatio, 287, 290, 315, 316
Repetita prælec. leg., 64
Repetitio, 293
Replicatio, 97, 346, 356, 387, 404, 411
— doli, 359, 384, 387
— pacti conventi, 387
— rei vend. et trad., 359
Representation in actions, 379
Republic, the, 9
— of Cicero, 10
Repudium, 77, 111, 113, 117
Repurgatio vet. leg., 65
Rerum quotid. of Gaius, 45
Res, 74, 81, 140, 142
— accessiones, 85
— alicujus, 83
— capable of division, 84, 219
— certa, 369
— communes, 83, 140, 142, 219
— comperendinata, 340
— corporales, 82, 140, 156, 220
— credita, 258
— definition of, 82, 140, 219
— divini juris, 82, 83, 140, 143, 219, 220
— division of, 24, 37, 50, 62, 82, 140
— extra nost. pat., 83, 142, 219
— fixa, 84
— fœnebris, 299
— fungibiles, 85, 224
— humani juris, 82, 219
— immobiles, 50, 82, 84, 140, 390, 391
— incapable of division, 84
— incorporales, 82, 83, 140, 156, 220
— in genere, 85
— — judicio deducta, 356
— in nost. pat., 83, 142, 220
— judicata, 385
— loss of, 306, 320
— mancipi, 12, 24, 37, 50, 63, 82, 117, 140, 157, 179, 219, 359
— mobiles, 84, 140, 146, 354, 391, 401
— moventes, 84
— nec mancipi, 12, 24, 37, 50, 63, 82, 140, 219, 359
— non fungibiles, 85
— nullius, 83, 143, 146, 147, 155, 220
— principales, 85
— privatæ, 83, 142, 220
— publicæ, 83, 140, 142, 219
— quæ pond., etc., 85, 295
— — usu consum., 85
— religiosæ, 82, 140, 144, 220
— sacra familiæ, 82, 114
— sacræ, 82, 140, 143, 220
— sanctæ, 82, 140, 144, 220

INDEX. 439

Res singulares, 85
— singulorum, 83, 85, 142, 220
— soli, 84, 354
— universitatis, 83, 143, 220
— uxoria, 61, 172
— vincta, 84
Rescriptum principis, 40, 49, 51, 114, 383
Respondere, 26
Responsa papiani, 56
— prudent., 26, 36, 101
— — sig., 41
Responsio, 91
Respublica, 81
Restipulatio, 266, 341, 393, 397
— double, 392, 395
— justa, 395
— of interdict, 393
Restitutio, 118, 306
— in integrum, 97, 130, 133, 139, 175, 191, 195, 235, 256, 352, 356, 357, 360, 367, 369, 370
— mode of obtaining, 344, 350, 395, 398
Revenue, 36
Revindicatio, 297
Revocatio, 290, 293, 319
Reus, 345
— in exceptione actor est, 383
— promittendi, 260
— stipulandi, 260
Rex, 4, 7, 31, 40
— as a magistrate, 335
Rhone, 56
Right of way, v. Via
Rights, 89
— political, 20
— real, v. Real
— transmissibility of, 199, 382
Rivers, 143
— banks of, 143, 220
— bed of, 148
— interdicts in respect of, 389
Road, 13, 157
— dedication of, 389
Rogatio, 22
Roman law, 38
— — periods in history of, 71
— — study of forbidden, 69
— laws published by Germans, 56
Rome, 20, 80, 98, 131
— burning of, 17
— origin of, 1, 2
— public schools at, 54, 61, 67
— sacking of, 56
Romani coloni, 76
Romulus, 2, 3, 4, 6, 7, 39
Rufinus, 55
Rural estate, landlord of, 362, 390
Rutilius Publius, 256, 301, 380

Sabatius, 57
Sabines, 1, 2, 3
Sabinians, school of, 41

Sabinus, 41, 54, 72, 289, 291
— Cælius, 42
— commentaries on, 59
— Masurius, 41, 42, 44
Sacer esto, 3
Sacerdotal functions, 4
Sacra familiæ, 82
— gentis, 82
— privata, 4, 76, 123
— publica, 4
— res, v. Res
— — protection of, 388
Sacramenti actio, v. Actio
Sacramentum, 16, 335, 341
— justum, 335
— injustum, 335
Sacred law, v. Jus
Sacrifices, family, 76
Sacrilege, 144, 388
St. Jerome, letters of, 45
— Louis, 71
Sailor, will of, 182
Sale, v. Emptio venditio
— accessory pacts to, 280, 366
— ad pretium particip., 103, 123
— alternative, 279
— conditional, 279, 280
— difference from exchange, 294
— form of contract, 277
— in genere, 279
— in specie, 279
— of property of another, 280
— per æs et lib., 86, 90, 179
— per avers., 279
— rescission of, 280
Salpensa, tables of, 45
Salvian, 53
Saone, 56
Satis accipere, 273
— dare, 273
Satisdatio (v. also Cautio), 266, 273, 342, 380, 398
— curat., 131, 139
— tutorum, 131, 139
Saturninus, 47
Savigny, 46, 97, 124, 145, 257
Scævola, 45, 53, 54, 71
Scale-bearer, 15
Scapula, 249
Scholæ, 41
Scholia, 65
Scholiasts, 65
Schools of law, v. Law
Scribentes, 70
Scribere, 26
Scripta, 88
Scriptura, 88, 276
Seashore, 142
Seal, falsification of, 400
Secretum, 95
Sectio bonorum, v. Bonorum
Sectores, 353
Securitas pleniss., 175

Seditious meetings, 15
Seduction, 400
Seine, 56
Sella curulis, 22
Semel heres, semper heres, 188
Senate, v. Senatus
Senators, plebeian, 4
— restrictions on marriage, 57
Senatus, 4, 7, 22, 31, 39, 40, 44, 48, 52
— auctoritas, 22
— consultum, 22, 32, 36, 40, 101
— — Claudianum, 101, 257, 310
— — Largianum, 249
— — Macedonianum, 32, 101, 265, 295, 331, 332, 377, 383
— — Neronianum, 198, 236
— — Orphitianum, 247, 250
— — Pegasianum, 191, 212, 213, 214, 240
— — Sabinianum, 243
— — Tertullianum, 52, 246, 250, 308
— — Trebellianum, 101, 214, 240, 383
— — Velleianum, 33, 274, 289, 295, 332, 383
Senatus habendi, 36
Senectus, 81
Seniorum, 6
Sentences of Paul, v. Paulus
Sentence, alternative, 398
— cancellation of, 357
— capital, 123
— effect of, 337, 357
— mode of delivering, 356, 358
— revision of, 357, 358
— revocation of, 357
— unjust, 329, 397
Sententia, 29, 340
— ex tabella recitare, 357
Sententiæ, 47, 102
— et opin. juris-con., 44
Septa, 35
Sepulchre, ownership of, 15, 144, 388
Sequester, 259
Sequestratio, 259
Serfdom, 63
Serfs, 75
Servants, domestic, 75
Servitus (servitude), 13, 84, 136, 225
— altius non toll., 158
— continuous, 157
— discontinuous, 159
— establishment of, 158, 351
— extinction of, 159, 226
— indivisibility of, 156, 160, 163, 226, 334
— in solo, 157
— mortgage of, 363
— navigandi, 157
— oneris ferendi, 157
— personal, 156, 160, 225, 226
— prædial, 156, 225
— protection of, 358, 360, 391, 405
— quasi, 158
— real, 84
— rural, 83, 157, 226

Servitus, superficial, 157
— tigni immittendi, 158
— urban, 83, 157, 226
Servitus (slavery), 8, 75
— causes leading to, 103, 135
— definition of, 102, 135
— recognition of, 101
Servitudes, v. Servitus
Servius Tullius, 4, 9, 30, 36
Servus, 2, 75, 103
— abandonment of, 378
— acquisition through, 176, 300, 318
— appointed heir, 186, 231
— — tutor, 121
— as a creditor, 264
— — debtor, 264
— censitus, 53
— contracts of, 376
— definition of, 102
— delict of, 330, 377
— fidejussory contract of, 377
— freeing of, 43, 51, 75, 104, 135, 174
— hereditarius, 187
— injury to, 327
— mandatum of, 377
— mode of claiming, 365
— of another person, 300
— of several masters, 174, 187, 264, 301
— ordinarius, 206
— peculium of, 176, 376
— persona of, 264, 330
— pœnæ, 103, 118
— pop. Rom., 103, 143
— publicus, 264, 268
— relationship between, 267
— right to labour of, 164, 227, 301
— sine domino, 265
— status of, 75
— stipulation of, 264, 301
— substituted heir, 190, 231
— unlawful killing of, 304, 324
— vicarius, 376
Set off, v. Compensatio
Severus, Alexander, 41, 43, 47, 58, 60, 71, 122, 380
— Septimius, 40, 45, 46, 51, 130
Sex, 80
Sextus Ælius, 26, 27
Shipowner, liability of, 375
Sica, 400
Sicarii, 400
Sicily, 58, 62
Silentiarii, 52
Slave, v. Servus
Slavery, v. Servitus
Societas, 38, 91, 284, 315
— conditional, 286
— dissolution of, 286, 315
— in fact, 338
— in law, 338
— kinds of, 284, 315
— Leonina, 285
— measure of liability in, 298, 315

INDEX.

Societas, obligations involved, 285
— quasi contracts resembling, 317, 367
— totorum bonorum, 284, 286
— vectigalis, 285, 286, 315
Socii Latini, 21, 76
Socius, 284
— liability of, 298, 315
Socrus, 112
Solarium, 283
Soldiers, immunities of 79, 235
— incapacities of, 121, 387
— wills of, 40, 50, 181, 229
Solidarity, 263
Solidi capacitas, 43, 204
Solon, laws of, 13, 101
Solum, v. Prædium
Solutio, 89, 263, 319, 357
— civil modes of, 301, 371
— imaginaria, 92, 302, 319
— indebiti, 296, 317
— litteris, 92, 303
— per æs et libram, 92, 302
— per errorem, 297
— verbis, 92, 302, 320
Solutus, 77
Son, disinheritance of, 184
— suing father, 364
Sors, 299
Spadones, 81, 203
Spain, 46, 56, 57
Spartacus, 34
Species, 85, 149
Specificatio, 147, 149
Spectabiles, 52
Spondeo, 261
Sponsalia, 77, 110
Sponsio, 24, 91, 266, 271, 296, 313, 393
— compulsory, 341, 396
— double, 392, 394, 396
— justa, 395
— of interdict, 393
— penal, 342, 393
— prejudicial, 342
Sponsor, 263, 271, 304, 313, 364
— heir of, 383
— reimbursement of, 339
Sportulæ, 366, 371
Spurii, 77, 112, 247
States of the church, 67
Statu liber, 107, 135, 373
Status, 19, 23, 336
— action in respect of, 364, 405
— change of, 78, 122
— elements of, 75, 138
— loss of, 78
— of deceased person, 365
— not affected by loss of rank, 124
Stephanus of Berytus, 64
Stillicidium, 158
Stipendium, 17, 39, 339
Stips, 260
Stipula, 260

Stipulatio, 24, 38, 63, 91, 260, 303, 312, 355
— accessories to, 271
— Ædilitia, 267
— analogy to mutuum, 275
— Aquiliana, 303
— communis, 131, 267, 313
— conventionalis, 267, 313
— damni infecti, 369
— de dolo, 266, 367, 369
— de persequendo servo, 266
— de rato, 267
— divisions of, 266
— dotis, 224
— duplæ, 279, 281, 366, 373
— emptæ et vend. hered., 214, 240
— error in, 270, 385
— ex bonis moribus, 269
— ex turpi causa, 269
— extinction of, 267, 402
— fructuaria, 394
— illegal, 269
— immoral, 269
— impossible, 269
— in diem, 261
— induced by violence, 269
— inelegans, 269
— inter absentes, 269
— inutilis, 267
— invalid, 270
— in writing, 269
— joint, 262
— judicialis, 266, 313
— judicatum solvi, 266
— liability in, 299
— motive inducing, 270
— nominatim of public slave, 265
— nullius momenti, 267
— of a fact, 262, 265
— of filii-familias, 265
— of pupil, 269
— of representative, 266
— partis et pro parte, 208, 214, 237, 240
— per sponsionem, 341
— pœnalis, 268
— post mortem suam, 271
— præpostera, 270
— prætoria, 266, 268, 313, 352
— pro præde litis et vind., 266, 342, 394
— pura, 261
— rem pupilli salvam fore, 267, 268
— servorum, 263
— sub conditione, 261, 268, 269
— to effect novatio, 302, 304, 319
Stirps, 245
Stoicism, 30, 75
Stolo C. Licinius, 30
Stranger, acquisition by, 177
Studiosi, 41, 61
Stuprum, 77, 112, 113, 136
Subjecti, 35
Subscriptio, 180, 229
Subsellium, 95

H H

INDEX.

Substitutio, 232, 375
— by soldiers, 190
— pupillaris, 188, 189, 232
— quasi pupillaris, 188, 189, 233
— vulgaris, 188, 189, 232
Successio, law of, 12, 23, 24, 37, 50, 63, 94, 242, 243, 248, 253, 254, 307, 310
— ab intestato, 63, 242
— adgnatorum, 242, 243, 307
— cognatorum, 247, 308
— ex s.c. Claudiano, 257
— libertorum, 247
— per addict. bonor., 255
— — bonorum vend., 256
— — capita, 242
— — stirpes, 242
— — universitatem, 177, 228, 284, 310
— to ascendants, 244, 307
— — dediticii, 106
Suetonius, 30, 377
Suicide, 38
Sui juris, 24, 76, 108
Sulpicius Servius, 71, 209, 285, 303
Summæ, 69
Superficiarius, 283, 284
Superficies, 93, 165, 283
Superscriptio, 180
Surdus, v. Deaf
Surety, kinds of, 340
Sulla, 31, 32, 34, 36, 37, 41, 272, 400
Suspecti cognitio, 133
Symbatius, 64, 65
Syngraphæ, 88, 276, 313
Synopsis Basil., 65
— legum, 66
— minor, 65

Tabellæ, 356
— voting, 35
Tabellarius, 183
Tabellio, 195, 277
Taberna, 85
Tables, the ten, 10
— — twelve, 10
Tabulæ, 88, 216, 274
Tabularius, 115
Tacitus, 377
Tacking, 167, 222
Tarentum, 19
Tarpeian rock, 14, 15
Tarquinius Priscus, 5
— Superbus, 7
Tatienses, 3
Tatius, 3
Taxatio, 26, 328, 329, 344, 346
Taxation, 25, 35, 36, 45, 46, 49
Taxes, enforcement of, 339
Taurisium, 57
Tegula, 86
Temere litigantes, 395
Temple of Jupiter, 5
— of Bellona, 5

Temples, 185
— closing of, 54
Tempus continuum, 87
— incertum, 188
— legitimum, 277
— utile, 87
Tenant, tacit mortgage of property, 363, 390
Territorial law, 68, 351
Testamentaria tutela, 121
Testamenti factio, 20, 42, 76, 180, 182, 185, 194, 229, 231
— nuncupatio, 179, 229
Testamentum, 12, 24, 37, 50, 63
— apud hostes, 183
— calat. com., 24, 179, 229
— codicils attached to, 217
— definition of, 179
— desertum, 191
— destitutum, 191, 211
— ex lege Cornelia, 183
— falsification of, 400
— forms of, 229
— freedom given by, 104
— historical order, 179
— imperfectum, 233
— injustum, 233
— inofficiosim, 37, 191, 233
— invalidation of, 190, 233
— inutile, 191
— irritum, 191, 211, 233
— legitimation by, 114
— means to obtain possession of, 218
— militare, 40, 181, 229
— mystique, 180
— non jure fact., 233
— nuncupatum, 181
— of blind, 183, 230
— — captives, 119, 183
— — diseased persons, 182
— — freedmen, 248, 308
— — murdered paterfamilias, 196
— — pubes son by father, 189
— — sailors, 182
— — slaves, 182
— — women, 83
— opening of, 42, 217, 218, 241
— per æs et lib., 24, 179, 229, 302
— per mancip., 24, 63, 178
— prætorianum, 179
— preservation of, 217
— procinctum, 179, 229
— ruptum, 190, 211, 233
— tripertitum, 179, 229
— tutor given by, 121
— uno contextu, 178, 180, 229
— valid as codicil, 217
— who could not make, 20, 119, 182
— witness to, 179, 229
Testator, insolvent, 108, 188
Testis, 15, 87, 180, 229, 356
Thalleleo, 64
Theft, v. Furtum

INDEX. 443

Theobald, 69
Theodora, 57, 112
Theodoric, 57
Theodorus, 64
Theodosius, 358
Theophilus, 32, 59, 60, 61, 72, 99, 102, 242, 322
— paraphrase of Institutes, 61, 64, 66, 93, 256, 320, 324, 343
Thesaurus, 153
Things, v. Res
Theodosius, 43, 48, 54, 62
— code of, 50
— projected code, 55
Thracians, 62
Tiberius, 40, 41, 44, 75, 101, 115
— Coruncanius, 26
Time and place, 87
Titus, 44, 45
Tombs, 5, 82
Tort, 14
Tort-feasor, joint, 333
Toulouse, 70
Towns, government of, 49
Traditio, 12, 24, 93, 153, 222, 278
— necessity of, 362
— nuda, 153, 222
— quasi, 154, 222
— rescission of, 361
Trajan, 40, 44, 46
Trajectitia, 258
Transactio, 294
Translatio judicii, 356
— legatorum, 211
— litis, 356
Tractatus, 70
Treason, 44, 49, 242
Treasure trove, 153, 222
Treasury, Imperial, 39
— public, 39
Trebatius, 216
Trebellius, 214
Trespass, 146
Tribes, 3, 7
Tribonian, 57, 58, 59, 60, 72, 99
— life of, 61
Tribonianism, 59, 115
Tribules, 3
Tribunal, 95
— annual, 32
— perpetual, 32
— ponere, 95
Tribuni, 40
— ærarii, 25, 32
— militum, 17
— plebis, 10, 22, 23, 34, 36
Tribunician power, 39
Tribunum appellare, 23
Tribus, 3
Tributarius, 53
Tributum, 39.
Tripertita, 27

Triplicatio, 97, 346, 387, 411
Tripondius, 187
Triticum, 347
Triumvirate, 35
Triumviri, 20, 25
Trust, particular, 213
— subject-matter of, 216
— universal, 213
Trustee, 213
— oath of, 213, 241
Tryphoninus, 119
Tullius, 6
Turba, 328
Turpitudo, 79
Tutela, 12, 81
— a magistratibus data, 125, 138
— adgnatorum, 122
— as a quasi contract, 296, 317
— definition of, 120
— derived from natural law, 125
— fiduciaria, 124, 138
— how terminated, 52, 128, 139
— kinds of, 125
— legitima, 125, 138, 254
— of women, 12, 24, 37, 50, 80, 83, 128, 139
— parentium, 124
— patronorum, 124, 138
— testamentaria, 121, 137
Tutor, 12, 80
— administration of, 125, 138
— agnate, 122, 138
— appointed by magistrate, 51, 125, 131
— Atilianus, 125
— auctoritas of, 127, 175
— authority when required, 80
— bringing an action, 380
— cessicius, 128
— dativus, 121
— duties of, 126
— excuses of, 131, 139
— female, 121, 125
— fiduciarius, 124, 129
— honorarius, 126
— inventory by, 126
— juliotitianus, 125
— legitimus, 122, 124, 128, 138
— measure of liability, 298
— onerarius, 128
— optivus, 128
— punishment of, 134
— prætorianus, 127
— security by, 126, 138, 267
— suspectus, 133
— tacit mortgage of property of, 131, 363
Tutorem dare, 131
— nominare, 131
— potiorem nominare, 132
Tutoris optio, 128
Tyre, 46

444 INDEX.

Twelve Tables, 10, 73, 76, 82, 140, 150, 211, 327
— — as to compromising theft and injuries, 385
— — division of inheritance resulting from, 333
— — fragments of, 11
— — law of succession of, 242, 306
— — on noxal abandonments, 378
— — — the actio de pauperie, 379, 408
— — — — liberalis causa, 365
— — — — precarium, 294
— — — — pignoris capio, 339
— — rate of interest by, 299
— — rule favouring liberty, 336

Ugo, 69
Ulpian, 43, 46, 53, 54, 55, 72, 83, 87
— division of law by, 101
— — — things by, 140
— Institutes of, 60, 392
— notes on Papinian, 50, 59
— on caduca, 43
— — gifts, 169, 210
— — interdicts, 388, 393
— — manus, 117
— — mixed actions, 365
— — modes of acquiring ownership, 141
— — pacts, 291
— — partnership, 284
— — postliminium, 119
— — public slaves, 265
— — set off, 373
— — usucapion, 359
— — user, 163
— — wills, 179
Universitas, 85, 143, 237
— facti, 85
— juris, 85
— rerum, 85, 353
Unde liberi, 185
Unwritten law, v. Jus
Uprauda, 57
Urban estate, landlord of, 363
User, rights of, 389
Usucapio, 12, 13, 14, 24, 83, 84, 93, 141, 222, 278, 348, 359, 406
— definition of, 141
— effects of, 165
— of servitudes, 226
— — slave, 177
— rescission of, 360
— things incapable of, 222
Usufructuary of slave, 177, 300
— rights of, 153, 161, 226
Usufructus, 55, 160, 226
— divisibility of, 226
— establishment of, 162, 227
— extinction of, 162, 227
— in singulos annos, 227
— legacy of, 199
— of son's property, 52, 176, 254
— protection of, 360, 392

Usufructus, quasi, 162
Usuræ, 15, 258, 299, 300, 309, 318, 407
Usureceptio, 142
Usurpatio, 168, 223
Usurpatum ire trinoctio, 117
Usus, 92, 93, 163, 227
— as to wives, 37, 77, 117
— auctoritas, 13, 141, 278
— fructus, 93
— improper, 322
— nudus, 163
— of slave, 177, 300
Uterini, 244, 307
Uti rogas, 35
Uxor, v. Wife
— injusta, 111

Vacarius, 69, 376
Vacatio of women, 42, 203
Vadimonium, 266, 340, 355, 357, 381
Valence, 69
Valens, 42, 44, 51, 54
Valentinian, 48, 51, 54, 55, 62, 394
Valerius, 17
Vandals, 56, 57
Varro, 353
Vas, 340
Vatican library, 55
Vectigal, 20, 25, 30, 35, 46, 285
Veii, 17
Velati, 6
Velum, 95
Venditor, 278
— obligations of, 278, 296, 314
Venefici, 400
Venia ætatis, 130
Verba civilia, 199, 236
Verbis contract, v. Obligatio
Verna, 103
Verona, 45
Verres, 33
Versio vulg. Novell., 61
Verus Lucius, 41, 45, 47
Versura, 299
Vespasian, 46
Vestal Virgins, 12, 51, 118, 123, 129
Veto, 10, 22, 23
Vi, 333, 390
Via, 157
Viator litium, 354, 357, 366
Vi bonorum raptorum, 324
Vibennus Cælius, 2
Vicarii of dioceses, 52
— (slaves), 103, 206
Vicarius, 49, 98
Vico, 1
Villici, 53
Vinculum juris, 89, 301, 311
Vindex, 338, 339, 340, 355, 379
Vindicans, 142
Vindicatio, 16, 95, 96, 155, 343, 347, 365, 389, 401
— origin of term, 336

INDEX. 445

Vindicatio pignoris, 361
— rei, 155, 347, 359, 361, 362, 372, 405
— — corporalis, 358
— — rescissoria, 360, 406
— rerum incorporal., 347, 358
— title to support, 386
— utilis, 184, 348, 350, 359
— with adjecta causa, 120, 365
— words of, 336
Vindicator, 342
Vindicia, 336
Vindiciæ, 337, 394
Vindicta, 16, 29, 336
— freedom by, 104
Violence, v. Vis.
Vir, 112
Virginia, 13
Virginius Valens, 255
Viritim, 36
Vis, 87, 102, 280, 412
— action in respect of, 367
— armata, 391
— exception based on, 384
— major, 283, 297
— tribunicia, 23
— quotidiana, 391
Visigoths, 56, 57
Vites, 16
Vitium, 166
Vocatio in jus, 62, 333, 339, 354, 357, 360, 369, 393, 394, 406
Voluntas, 87
Voting, 6, 22, 401
Vulgate, 68
Vulgo concepti, 120
— quæsiti, 78

Wagers, 296
Walls, protection of, 144
War, ceremony observed in declaring, 5

War, civil, Marius and Sulla, 34
— servile, 34
— social, 34
Warnkœnig, 71
Werner, 68
Western Empire, fall of, 55
Wife, 77, 109
— natural obligation of, 331
— liability for debt of husband, 40, 274
— position of, 117
— tacit mortgage over husband's property, 363
Will, v. Testamentum
Witte, 67
Witness, v. Testis
Women, 80
— abduction of, 400
— cessio bonorum by, 265
— fictitious sale of, 129
— free, 42, 246
— freed, 42, 246
— incapacity of, 185, 387, 399
— intercessio of, 274, 295
— institution of as heirs, 186, 244
— power to contract, 265, 274
— seduction of, 400
— succession of, 246
— — to, 308
— tutelage of, v. Tutela
— vacatio of, 42
Writing as a mode of proof, 86, 269, 303, 313, 314
Written law, v. Jus
— definition of, 102

Zacharia, 67
Zazius, 70
Zen , 91, 282, 315, 326, 353, 370, 371, 387, 409
Zonoras, 66

www.ingramcontent.com/pod-product-compliance
Lightning Source LLC
Chambersburg PA
CBHW030212170426
43201CB00006B/62